American History told by Contemporaries

EACH VOLUME INDEXED AND SOLD SEPARATELY.

BY THE SAME EDITOR

A Source-Book of American History

The *Source-Book* is independent of the four volumes of *Contemporaries*, and contains no articles which appear in the larger series.

THE MACMILLAN COMPANY

60 FIFTH AVENUE, NEW YORK

American History told by
Contemporaries

VOLUME II

BUILDING OF THE REPUBLIC

1689–1783

THE MACMILLAN COMPANY
NEW YORK · BOSTON · CHICAGO · DALLAS
ATLANTA · SAN FRANCISCO

MACMILLAN AND CO., Limited
LONDON · BOMBAY · CALCUTTA · MADRAS
MELBOURNE

THE MACMILLAN COMPANY
OF CANADA, Limited
TORONTO

American History told by Contemporaries

VOLUME II

BUILDING OF THE REPUBLIC

1689–1783

EDITED BY

ALBERT BUSHNELL HART

PROFESSOR OF HISTORY IN HARVARD UNIVERSITY
MEMBER OF THE MASSACHUSETTS HISTORICAL SOCIETY
AUTHOR OF "FORMATION OF THE UNION," "EPOCH MAPS,"
"PRACTICAL ESSAYS," ETC.

NEW YORK

THE MACMILLAN COMPANY

LONDON : MACMILLAN & CO., LTD.

· PRINTED IN THE UNITED STATES OF AMERICA ·

Preface

THE work of which this is the second volume is an attempt to bring before the minds of Americans a picture of the life of their forefathers as the latter saw it themselves. It is the conviction of the editor that there is need of a series which in reasonable compass may accomplish two objects : first, to open up for the use of schools, of libraries, of readers, and of investigators, texts of rare or quaint writings which shall be authoritative, so far as they go ; secondly, to make the contemporary writers tell their own story of the events of American history and the aspirations of Americans, from the foundation of the colonies to the present day. The editor believes that such material makes the past vivid to pupil, student, and reader ; and that from a succession of such episodes as are here set forth, so fitted together as to make a kind of continuous narrative, a more permanent impression is made on the mind than from the reading of an equal amount of secondary writings.

In selecting material the same principles have been followed as in Volume I : the first authoritative edition has been sought — in a few cases manuscript sources have been used ; all pieces in foreign languages appear in translation ; the copy is meant to be an absolute transcript of the original in paragraphing, wording, spelling, and capitalization ; nothing appears not found in the original, and all omissions are indicated ; at the end of each extract is a statement of the place whence the extract is taken. Of course some of the printed originals are not faithful transcripts of the manuscripts, but I have aimed in all cases to reproduce the best text available.

In making up the volume I have drawn less on documents, — charters, messages, resolutions, declarations, instructions, statutes, and treaties, — than on those kinds of material in which the personality of the writer plays a greater part, — journals, letters, reports, discussions, and reminiscences. Whenever a piece could be found which is both character-istic and well written, it has been chosen over a piece which is equally accurate but has less literary merit. By references to Tyler's admirable *History of American Literature,* and *Literary History of the Revolution,* and other like works, I have tried to make it easy to learn the place of writers in the literature of the country.

The aim of the first half of this volume is to show the interest and the continuance of colonial history from the end of the seventeenth century to the outbreak of the Revolution. The lessons of this " forgotten half-century " are not to be found in the petty events of each colony, but in the growth of principles of government and of a social and economic system. Hitherto it has been hard to study this important formative period, because the illustrative material was so scattered : perhaps this volume will help to bring out the significance of the growth of an American spirit which made union and independence possible.

The history of the American Revolution, which is the subject of the second part of the volume, has usually been written as annals of military campaigns. In this volume I have sought to bring out, from the writings of the time, the real spirit of the Revolution : the ill-judged restric-tive system of the home government ; the passionate arguments for and against taxation ; the fervor of the irregular opposition in the colonies. I have tried to let patriots, Englishmen, and loyalists speak for them-selves, and thus to make clear that increasing and unappeasable discon-tent which preceded and explains the Revolution.

It is the editor's hope that both sections of this book may serve as an adjunct to school and college text-books, as material for topical study, and as a resource for those who like to know what manner of men their fathers were.

The courtesy of the Harvard College Library has opened to me all the stores of that vast collection ; and to Miss Addie F. Rowe is due special credit for skilful verification and vigilant proof-reading.

ALBERT BUSHNELL HART.

CAMBRIDGE, January 1, 1898.

Contents

PART I

PRACTICAL INTRODUCTION
FOR TEACHERS, PUPILS, STUDENTS, AND LIBRARIES

CHAPTER I — THE SOURCES AND HOW TO FIND THEM

CHAPTER II — USE OF SOURCES

PART II

THE SEPARATE COLONIES

CHAPTER III — NEW ENGLAND

Contents

CHAPTER VI — GEORGIA

PART III

COLONIAL GOVERNMENT

CHAPTER VII — PRINCIPLES OF ENGLISH CONTROL

CHAPTER VIII — THE COLONIAL GOVERNOR

Contents

CHAPTER IX — COLONIAL ASSEMBLIES

CHAPTER X — COLONIAL COURTS

Contents

CHAPTER XI — COLONIAL LOCAL GOVERNMENT

PART IV

COLONIAL LIFE

CHAPTER XII — THE LIFE OF THE PEOPLE

CHAPTER XIII — COMMERCE AND CURRENCY

CHAPTER XIV — INTELLECTUAL LIFE

CHAPTER XV — RELIGIOUS LIFE

CHAPTER XVI — SLAVERY AND SERVITUDE

PART V

INTERCOLONIAL, 1689-1764

CHAPTER XVII — THE FRENCH COLONIES

CHAPTER XVIII — THE INDIANS

CHAPTER XIX — INTERCOLONIAL WARS

CHAPTER XX — THE FRENCH AND INDIAN WAR

PART VI

CAUSES OF THE REVOLUTION

CHAPTER XXI — NEW CONDITIONS OF ENGLISH CONTROL

CHAPTER XXII — THE WEST

CHAPTER XXIII — THE STAMP ACT CONTROVERSY

Contents

CHAPTER XXIV — THE REVENUE CONTROVERSY

CHAPTER XXV — THE ISSUE OF COERCION

PART VII

CONDITIONS OF THE REVOLUTION

CHAPTER XXVI — THE PATRIOTS

CHAPTER XXVII — THE LOYALISTS

CHAPTER XXVIII — THE AMERICAN FORCES

Contents

CHAPTER XXXI — FIRST STAGE OF THE WAR, 1775–1778

CHAPTER XXXII — FRENCH ALLIANCE, 1778–1779

CHAPTER XXXIII — CRISIS IN DOMESTIC AFFAIRS, 1779–1782

American History told by Contemporaries

PART I

PRACTICAL INTRODUCTION
FOR TEACHERS, PUPILS, STUDENTS, AND LIBRARIES

CHAPTER I — THE SOURCES AND HOW TO FIND THEM

1. What are Sources?

IN the current discussions on the teaching and study of history, one of the most frequent expressions is "the sources," or "original material." What do these words mean? As history is an account of the past actions of men, every historical statement must go back to the memory of those who saw the events, or to some record made at the time. Tradition is the handing down of memories from one person to another; indeed, one of the most famous of American sources, — the Norse Sagas on the discovery of America, — was thus transmitted for three centuries before it was finally put into writing. Such transmissions are likely to get away from the first form as years go on, and may change into legends, such as have already formed around Washington's life. A more trustworthy form of transmitting earlier memories is by auto-biography, or by reminiscence written out in later life; but narratives set down long after the events are apt to become twisted by the lapse of the years between the event and the making of the record, and thus their chief value is to reproduce the spirit of the times. In preparing this volume such works have been sparingly used. Graydon's *Memoirs*

(No. 170) and Heath's *Memoirs* (No. 218) are examples of such books.

Much more important are the records and memoranda made at or very near the time of the event. Sometimes silent monuments may be all that is left : the British earthworks at Saratoga are still a memorial of Burgoyne's campaign; and the house of General Gage at Danvers, Massachusetts, still stands to tell us that its occupant was a man of taste and substance.

Laws, proclamations, and other public documents are sources of great value, because they not only describe, but constitute the event : they bear the signatures, the affixing of which gives them validity ; they are drawn up even before the event takes place. Examples are the royal order creating the Board of Trade (No. 46), and the veto message of Governor Morris (No. 65).

Of greater literary interest are the narratives of explorers, travellers, and visitors, in which American history is rich : an instance is Peter Kalm's travels (No. 112). As travellers have, however, often too lively a sense of the importance of their own impressions, a more valuable kind of source is the contemporary journal, written from day to day during the events described. When made by men who were the helmsmen of a commonwealth, like John Adams (Nos. 24, 79, 153, 189), they have the highest historical credit ; for they are forged fresh from the mint, and reveal what even the official records may conceal. Even when written without any expectation of publication, they furnish valuable evidence : no better example can be found than the diary of Stephen Williams (No. 160) or that of William Pynchon (No. 208).

The letters of public men, or even of private men, have the same double value of a tale unvarnished and written at the moment ; and they also reveal the writer's character. Such are the familiar letters of King George III (Nos. 158, 215). More elaborate are the arguments or controversial pamphlets intended for circulation at the time, such as John Dickinson's *Farmer's Letters* (No. 149) and Tom Paine's *Common Sense* (No. 186) ; but such sources are often warped by party feeling. Narratives composed immediately after events have passed, like Madison's review of the southern campaign (No. 211), have the value of careful, considerate composition while the facts are fresh.

Historical sources, then, are nothing less or more than records made at or near the time of the events, by men who took part in them, and who are therefore qualified to speak.

2. Educative Value of Sources

LIKE other literature, the office of history is to record, to instruct, and to please. History has natural claims on the interest of a student or reader, for it deals with stirring events, with human character, and with the welfare of the race; hence, if well narrated, there is in this subject something to arouse the minds of young and old, and to develop them when aroused. The training element of history as a school subject has been discussed in many places : a list of references to such discussions appears in Channing and Hart's *Guide to the Study of American History*, § 15. The value of sources, as a part of that study, has long been in the minds of the scholars and antiquarians who have painfully preserved and reprinted the old narratives, and it begins to be appreciated by the reading and teaching public. The most authoritative suggestions on the study of history in schools lay stress on the use of such material.

Sources are indeed the basis of history; but not mere raw material, like the herbaria of the botanist or the chemicals of a laboratory, — stuffs to be destroyed in discovering their nature. As utterances of men living when they were made, sources have in them the breath of human life : history is the biology of human conduct. No historical question can be settled without an appeal to the sources, or without taking into account the character of the actors in history.

Nobody remembers all the history he reads; the bold and striking events seize hold of the mind, and around them we associate the less notable incidents. A source, however, fixes such a bold and striking event in its most durable form. Volumes about the Indians will not tell us so much that we shall remember as Adair's or Carver's personal experiences (Nos. 113, 116).

Hence the instructing power of history depends in considerable part on the sources. They do not tell all their own story; they need to be arranged and set in order by the historian, who on the solid piers of their assurances spans his continuous bridge of narrative. But there are two sides to history : the outward events in their succession, with which secondary historians alone can deal; and the inner spirit, which is revealed only by the sources. If we could not know both things, it would be better to know how Zenger was tried for criticising government (No. 72), than what had been the history of freedom of the press in the

colonies up to that time. The sources, therefore, throw an inner light
on events : secondary writers may go over them, collate them, compare
them, sometimes supplement them, but can never supersede them.

As for entertainment, the narratives of American discovery are the
Arabian Nights of history for their marvels and adventures. The tale
of the founding of Louisiana (No. 109) is a classic of romantic literature. Other pieces please by their quaintness, such as Gabriel Thomas's
glowing description of Pennsylvania (No. 25), or Bolzius's simple account
of the Salzburgers in Georgia (No. 40). Others of these selections are
mile-stones in the growth of a national literature, stretching all the way
from Cotton Mather's verbose style (No. 92) or Dummer's rugged
Defence of the New-England Charters (No. 48), through Franklin's
Autobiography (No. 81), to Francis Hopkinson's humor (No. 96) and
jefferson's full pipe-organ of splendid sentences (No. 188). As an
account of the planting of a civilization in the wilderness, of the growth
of free government, of a power to discuss great political questions with
force, the sources of American history are a contribution to the world's
literature.

---

3. Classification of Sources on the Colonies and the Revolution

ASSUMING that the use of sources needs no further argument, the
next important question is, What sort of material is available on
the colonial and revolutionary periods ? For convenience of reference
the pieces in this volume may be classified into a few general categories,
as follows : —

The most important unwritten records stand along the sea-coast.
These consist of old forts, such as the battery at Cambridge, Massachusetts, or the earthworks at Yorktown ; of public buildings, of which many
date from the seventeenth century, as the State House at Newport,
Pennsylvania Hall in Philadelphia, and the Court House at Hillsboro ; of
churches, as the Old South in Boston, St. Michael's in Charleston, and the
old Swedes' Church (1700) in Philadelphia ; and of dwelling-houses, such
as the Wayside Inn at Sudbury, Massachusetts, the Bond house at Edenton, North Carolina, the Byrd mansion at Westover, near Richmond, the
Chew house at Germantown, and Mount Vernon. Such remains may be
used by visiting them, or by showing photographs of them. In several

parts of the country, as in the National Museum at Washington, the Field Museum at Chicago, and the Peabody Museum at Cambridge, there are collections of the implements and arts of the aborigines of North and South America.

Manuscript records ordinarily appeal only to the investigator, for whose benefit are the suggestions in Winsor's *Narrative and Critical History*, VIII, 413 *et seq.*, and in Channing and Hart, *Guide to American History*, § 35. Two classes of written records may, however, sometimes be used by beginners, — family papers and local records. From the unpublished town records of Brookline, Massachusetts, for example, pupils in the high schools have drawn some interesting material. It is worth while to make pupils acquainted with the handwriting of the seventeenth and eighteenth centuries, many facsimiles of which are found in Winsor's *Narrative and Critical History*, and in many other places. The letter of Alexander Scammell (No. 162) is a striking example of valuable unpublished materials which are still to be found among family papers. The Historical Manuscripts Commission, created in 1895 by the American Historical Association, is bringing to light unsuspected treasures of this kind, which will be found in the *Reports* of that Commission, beginning with that for 1897.

In this volume much use has been made of the official public records of various kinds, because they contain the most apt illustrations of the workings of colonial government, and because in the time of the Revolution public bodies became the spokesmen of the communities in their new relations. The votes and proceedings of the revolutionary period are livelier and more characteristic than is usually the case in such material, as may be seen in the town-meeting vote of 1765 (No. 140).

Public records have been printed in elaborate collections for all the thirteen colonies. Sets of the charters are printed in Ben. Perley Poore, *Federal and State Constitutions;* in H. W. Preston, *Documents illustrative of American History;* in many numbers of the *American History Leaflets* and *Old South Leaflets;* and in other collections. Lists of these collections and of the printed colonial laws, with exact titles, may be found below (No. 6) and in Channing and Hart, *Guide to American History*, § 29.

Hardly any state has made up a full set of its own statutes; the best collections are Hening's *Statutes* for Virginia and various editions of Massachusetts laws. In many of the histories of separate colonies or states are appendices of select statutes.

The printed records of the colonial councils and assemblies are also enumerated in Channing and Hart, *Guide*, § 29.   Parts of several of these records, — Rhode Island, 1723, Maryland, 1775, — are reprinted below (Nos. 62, 184).   The best printed records are those of New Hampshire, Massachusetts, Connecticut, Pennsylvania, Maryland, and North Carolina.

The proceedings of various official and unofficial assemblies and meetings are set forth in the following extracts : a colonial council (No. 30) ; a colonial assembly (No. 62) ; a meeting of freeholders (No. 42); an electorate (No. 61) ; courts of various degrees (Nos. 17, 37, 71, 72, 73, 75) ; a city government (No. 76) ; a town-meeting (Nos. 78, 140) ; a vestry meeting (No. 77) ; a Quaker meeting (No. 102) ; colonial Congresses (Nos. 184, 187, 205) ; continental Congresses (Nos. 141, 153, 155, 185, 188, 189, 190) ; committees of Congress (No. 207).

The proceedings of assemblies constitute only a small part of the material available and suggestive for such a collection as this.   Below will be found portions of reports of colonial governors (Nos. 19, 21, 36, 54, 57, 85, 88, 110, 135, 154), and of governors' letters and messages (Nos. 63, 65, 70, 125).   Other colonial officials are also represented : colonial secretaries (Nos. 60, 124) ; a collector of customs (No. 87) ; colonial agents (Nos. 68, 146) ; a surveyor-general (No. 111) ; a comptroller-general (No. 117) ; an envoy to the Indians (No. 115) ; a judge (No. 150), and several chief justices (Nos. 18, 148, 157) ; boundary commissioners (No. 38).

The British administration of colonial affairs is represented by letters and mandates of the Lords of Trade (Nos. 26, 55, 58, 67, 89, 104) ; communications from the secretaries for the colonies (Nos. 27, 43, 56, 128, 144), and from the trustees of a colony (No. 42) ; a letter of the Archbishop of Canterbury (No. 101) ; proceedings before a committee of the House of Commons (No. 143) ; a speech in Parliament (No. 142) ; an Act of Parliament (No. 45) ; a royal mandate (No. 46) ; and letters of the king (Nos. 158, 215).

Among the colonial dignitaries who are cited in this volume as witnesses to the history of their times are the following governors : Cranston (No. 19) ; Wentworth (No. 21); Sharpe (No. 36) ; Dummer (No. 48) ; Keith (No. 49) ; Pownall (Nos. 53, 59, 66, 74) ; Cosby (No. 54); Clinton (No. 57) ; Johnston (No. 63) ; Lewis Morris (No. 65) ; Dinwiddie (No. 70) ; Bellomont (No. 85); Burnet (No. 88) ; Belcher (No. 100) ; Spotswood (No. 110) ; Hopkins (No. 125) ; Dunmore

(Nos. 135, 154) ; Patrick Henry (No. 203). Many of these men were highly educated, all had unrivalled opportunities of knowing the actual forces of colonial history, and some became the advisers of the English government, among them Pownall and Hutchinson.

Other colonial worthies who appear below are Samuel Sewall (Nos. 18, 103) ; Roger Wolcott (No. 22) ; John Conrad Wyser (No. 29) ; Samuel Quincy (No. 41) ; President Clap (No. 90); Increase Mather (No. 93) ; Nathaniel Ames (No. 95) ; Lewis Morris (No. 97) ; Colonel Brewton (No. 118).

The following English and foreign statesmen and publicists have also been used : Edward Randolph (No. 34) ; Oglethorpe (No. 39) ; Edmund Burke (Nos. 44, 52) ; John Wise (No. 47) ; Montesquieu (No. 51) ; William Pitt, Lord Chatham (Nos. 128, 142) ; Earl of Waldegrave (No. 130) ; John Wilkes (No. 132) ; Horace Walpole (No. 145) ; Samuel Johnson (No. 156) ; Lafayette (No. 172) ; Mirabeau (No. 178) Vergennes (No. 216).

Besides the governors and other colonial officials mentioned above, large use has been made of the writings of the great statesmen of the revolutionary epoch. The works of Benjamin Franklin (Nos. 68, 81, 94, 133, 143, 199, 217), of John Adams (Nos. 24, 79, 153, 189, 217), and of George Washington (Nos. 108, 174, 195, 206) are the foundation of an accurate knowledge of the actual workings of the revolutionary spirit. To these may be added the writings of Josiah Quincy (No. 139); Alexander Hamilton (No. 173) ; Thomas Jefferson (No. 188) ; Robert Morris (Nos. 194, 210) ; James Madison (No. 211) ; John Jay (No 217) ; and Henry Laurens (No. 217).

The pamphleteers and controversial writers include several of the above, and also Edward Randolph (No. 34) ; Jeremiah Dummer (No. 48) ; Keith (No. 49) ; Pownall (Nos. 53, 59, 66, 74) ; Zenger (No. 72) ; Francis Hopkinson (Nos. 96, 196) ; Thomas Story (No. 98) ; Judge Sewall (No. 103) ; Stephen Hopkins (No. 125) ; James Otis (No. 131) ; John Wilkes (No. 132) ; Martin Howard (No. 138); Dennis de Berdt (No. 146) ; Charles Chauncy (No. 147) ; John Dickinson (No. 149) ; Samuel Johnson (No. 156) ; Drayton (No. 157) ; Timothy Dwight (No. 164) ; Jonathan Odell (No. 167); Mirabeau (No. 178) ; Stansbury (No. 182) ; Thomas Paine (No. 186).

On the Revolution, and to a less degree on the earlier period, valuable extracts have been taken from the journals, private letters, and reminiscences of those who had knowledge of public affairs. While less formal

than the public records, or the careful state papers and official correspondence and arguments of the statesmen mentioned above, they have
the value of unstudied testimony, and they cause an impression of the
human side of the history.   The principal authors of this kind cited in
this volume are Sewall (No. 18) ; Eliza Lucas (Nos. 35, 83) ; Stephens
(No. 43) ; Pettit (No. 61) ; John Adams (Nos. 79, 153, 189) ; Franklin (No. 81) ; Nathaniel Ames (No. 95) ; Thomas Story (No. 98) ;
Wesley (No. 99) ; John Woolman (No. 106) ; Eddis (No. 107) ;
Washington (No. 108) ; Daniel Boon (No. 134) ; Josiah Quincy (No.
139) ; Thomas Hutchinson (No. 148); John Tudor (No. 151) ; John
Andrews. (No. 152) ; Stephen Williams (No. 160) ; Alexander Scam-
mell (No. 162) ; Huntington (No. 163) ; Odell (No. 167) ; Curwen
(No. 169) ; Richard Smith (No. 185) ; Mrs. Abigail Adams (No. 192) ;
William Pynchon (No. 208).

Other journals and letters more directly concerned with military
affairs are those of Curwen (No. 120) ; Colonel Winslow (No. 126) ;
anonymous account of Braddock's defeat (No. 127) ; Captain John
Knox (No. 129) ; Chastellux (Nos. 137, 176) ; Graydon (No. 170) ;
Lafayette (No. 172) ; Thacher (No. 175) ; Drowne (No. 177) ; Pausch
(No. 179) ; Boudinot (No. 180) ; Simcoe (No. 181) ; André (No. 183) ;
Clinton (No. 193) ; Baroness Riedesel (No. 197) ; Dr. Waldo (No.
198) ; John Trumbull (No. 200) ; George Rogers Clark (No. 201) ;
Steuben (No. 202) ; John Paul Jones (No. 204) ; General Greene
(No. 212) ; Lord Cornwallis (No. 214) ; General Heath (No. 218).

Travellers in the eighteenth century, until the Revolution was impending, were fewer and less quaint than in the period before 1689.   The
principal foreign visitors and observers were Andrew Burnaby (No. 32)
and Peter Kalm (Nos. 112, 114, 122), both authors who wrote interesting and intelligent accounts.   Lesser foreigners were Bolzius (No.
40) ; "A Swiss Gentleman" (No. 69) ; De la Harpe (No. 109) ;
Captain Carver (No. 116).   The revolutionary visitors were Chastellux
(Nos. 137, 176) ; Lafayette (No. 172) ; Pausch (No. 179) ; Baroness
Riedesel (No. 197) ; Steuben (No. 202) ; the anonymous writer on
De Grasse (No. 213) ; Cornwallis (No. 214).

Native or resident observers were the following : Captain Goelet (Nos.
23, 84) ; Gabriel Thomas (No. 25) ; "Richard Castelman" (No. 28) ;
Keith (No. 49) ; Douglass (No. 50) ; Pownall (Nos. 53, 59, 66, 74) ;
Madam Knight (No. 80) ; Benjamin Franklin (No. 81) ; Colonel Byrd
(No. 82) ; Cotton Mather (No. 92) ; John Woolman (No. 106) ;

William Eddis (No. 107) ; Adair (No. 113) ; John Filson (No. 134) ; Joseph Doddridge (No. 136).

The newspapers have furnished several pieces for this volume. Though the colonial newspaper was usually dull, and there was no system of circulating accurate news, yet nothing better reflects the spirit of the age than such extracts as are found on the runaway advertisements (No. 105) ; on privateers (No. 121) ; on mobs (No. 161) ; on the Tories (No. 168) ; on Lexington and Concord (No. 191) ; on the Confederation (No. 209).

In the eighteenth century there was already a school of formal historians (see list below, No. 7). Out of these, extracts have been made from the following : Daniel Neal (No. 20) ; Robert Proud (No. 31) ; Robert Beverly (No. 33) ; Edmund Burke (Nos. 44, 52) ; Sir William Keith (No. 49) ; William Douglass (No. 50) ; William Gordon (No. 219) ; David Ramsay (No. 220).

Among colonial authors many were ministers of the gospel, of various denominations. Such were Lawson (No. 16) ; Burnaby (No. 32) ; Maury (No. 37) ; Bolzius (No. 40) ; Clap (No. 90) ; Byles (No. 91) ; Cotton and Increase Mather (Nos. 92, 93) ; John Wesley (No. 99) ; Doddridge (No. 136) ; Chauncy (No. 147) ; Williams (No. 160) : Dwight (No. 164) ; Odell (No. 167) ; and Gordon (No. 219). Physicians wrote much less ; yet several important pieces are taken from the writings of Dr. Douglass (No. 50) ; Dr. Thacher (No. 175) ; Dr. Waldo (No. 198) ; and Dr. Ramsay (No. 220).

Some of the most highly educated, brilliant, and witty writers of the eighteenth century were women ; and quotations appear from Eliza Lucas (Nos. 35, 83) ; Sarah Kemble Knight, one of the best observers of her time (No. 80) ; Mrs. Reed (No. 165) ; Mrs. Adams, perhaps the most distinguished woman in the Revolution (No. 192) ; and the courageous Baroness Riedesel (No. 197).

Verse writers were few, and only a few pieces have proved to be so illustrative of historical incident as to come into this volume. These are Byles's eulogy of George I (No. 91) ; verses in an almanac (No. 94); " Ballad of Pigwacket " (No. 119) ; Paine's " Liberty Tree " (No. 159) ; Dwight's " Columbia " (No. 164) ; " Nathan Hale " (No. 171) ; Stansbury's " Lords of the Main " (No. 182) ; Francis Hopkinson's " Battle of the Kegs " (No. 196).

4. Libraries of Sources in American History

NO library has anything approaching a complete set either of originals or of reprints of the historical writings of colonial and revolutionary times. Nevertheless, one who examines the books in a special library of Americana is amazed at the number, variety, and interest of the material. Six great libraries deserve special mention, all growing collections, and several of them purchasers of rarities at great prices : 1. The John Carter Brown Library at Providence, kept up as a private collection, but under the direction of a trained specialist librarian. 2. The Lenox Library at New York, also brought together by a private man, but now a part of the great New York Public Library. 3. The Boston Public Library, containing the Prince Collection and other valuable accumulations of many private gifts, supplemented by purchases. 4. The Harvard College Library, which contains a well classified collection, abounding in rarities. 5. The Library of Congress, containing great treasures of early books and manuscripts, as yet uncatalogued and almost unexplored. 6. The library of the American Antiquarian Society at Worcester, especially rich in colonial and later newspapers.

Of many early prints there are but half a dozen copies extant, and it is almost impossible for later libraries to secure sets equally complete with the older collections. Nevertheless, there are numerous and valuable Americana in the libraries of Cornell University, Columbia University, the University of Pennsylvania, and the Wisconsin Historical Society. In each state a special historical society is likely to collect early printed works, newspapers, and reprints on the history of that state. Some libraries will lend rare books directly, or through a local librarian who makes himself responsible.

Abroad, the largest collection of Americana is that of the British Museum, containing some unique pamphlets not to be found in America ; and there are also rare pamphlets in the Bodleian Library of Oxford. In England is also a great reservoir of colonial manuscript material, chiefly in the Public Record Office. Transcripts of many of these documents have been made and transferred to America, as, for example, the Minutes of the Lords of Trade, which are in the Pennsylvania Historical Society. Continental archives have also material on discovery and colonization, especially those of Simancas in Spain, and those of France, Genoa, and Venice.

5. Reprints of Collected Sources on the Colonies and the Revolution

NEARLY all the important early works have been reprinted, sometimes verbatim, oftener with corrections of spelling and grammar.
Many such reprints are made by historical societies ; others are gathered
in series, as Rider's *Rhode Island Historical Tracts*, and Munsell's
Historical Series. Others appear in special reprint editions, with introduction and notes by a special editor. A few have been facsimiled,
notably the Declaration of Independence (Force, *American Archives*,
Fifth Series, I, 1597, and elsewhere). For making transcripts or for
verifying a passage, the original edition is always preferable even to a
careful reprint.

For many of the separate colonies there are collections of documents,
which may be found through Winsor, *Narrative and Critical History*,
II–V, and Channing and Hart, *Guide to American History*, §§ 23, 29.
There are also several valuable collections of related documents, some of
which are enumerated below. The colonial collections specially mentioned contain many documents concerning all the colonies. The titles
in this list do not include collections of sources bearing exclusively on
the history of a single colony, nor do they contain colonial archives, or
the many valuable collections of state and local historical societies. Such
material may be found through Channing and Hart, *Guide*, §§ 23, 29, 31,
34, 77–130, and through A. P. C. Griffin, *Bibliography of American Historical Societies* (in American Historical Association, *Report* for 1895).
Tyler, in his *American Literature* and *Literary History of the Revolution*
(No. 15), gives lists of sources.

John Almon, *A Collection of Interesting Authentic Papers, relative to the Dispute between Great Britain and America, shewing the Causes and Progress
of that Misunderstanding, from 1764 to 1775*. London, 1777. — Always
cited as the *Prior Documents*.

John Almon, *The Remembrancer, or Impartial Repository of Public Events*.
17 vols. London, 1775–1784. — Vols. XII–XVII edited by John De-
brett.

*The Annual Register, or a View of the History, Politicks, and Literature, for
the Year 1758*. London, 1759–. — This series has been continued annually, to the present time. It includes a narrative history of the year, and
republications of contemporary letters and other material.

Alden Bradford, *Speeches of the Governors of Massachusetts from* 1765 *to* 1775; *and the Answers of the House of Representatives to the same.* Boston, 1818. — These documents describe many of the controversies leading up to the Revolution.

Congress of the United States, *Journals of Congress. Containing the Proceedings* [1774–1788] (contemporaneous edition). 13 vols. Philadelphia, 1777–1788. — Also a reprint in 13 vols. (Philadelphia, 1800–1801), and another in 4 vols., under the title *Journals of the American Congress: From* 1774 *to* 1788 (Washington, 1823).

Congress of the United States, *Secret Journals of the Acts and Proceedings of Congress.* 4 vols. Boston, 1821. — Extracts omitted in making up the public journals, especially on the history of the Confederation and on foreign affairs.

Evert Augustus Duyckinck and George Long, *Cyclopædia of American Literature; embracing Personal and Critical Notices of Authors, and Selections from their Writings. From the Earliest Period to the Present Day.* 2 vols. New York, 1856.

Peter Force, compiler, *American Archives: Fourth Series. Containing a Documentary History of the English Colonies in North America* [1774–1776]. 6 vols. Washington, 1837–1846. — *Fifth Series. Containing a Documentary History of the United States* [1776–1783]. 3 vols. Washington, 1848–1853.

Albert Bushnell Hart and Edward Channing, editors, *American History Leaflets.* 30 numbers (to be had separately). New York, 1892–1896. — Includes many colonial documents.

George P. Humphrey, *American Colonial Tracts.* Rochester, May, 1897–. — Published monthly; to be had separately.

Thomas Hutchinson, *A Collection of Original Papers relative to the History of the Colony of Massachusetts-Bay* [1628–1750]. Boston, 1769. — A useful set.

Edwin Doak Mead, editor, *Old South Leaflets.* 75 numbers (to be had separately or bound in 3 vols.). Boston, 1883–1896. — Many historical pieces; texts not carefully collated. Valuable for schools.

Frank Moore, *Diary of the American Revolution. From Newspapers and Original Documents.* 2 vols. New York, etc., 1859–1860. — A well-chosen series of extracts arranged chronologically, covering the years 1775–1781.

Frank Moore, editor, *Songs and Ballads of the American Revolution.* New York, 1856.

Hezekiah Niles, *Principles and Acts of the Revolution in America.* Baltimore, 1822; also a reprint, New York, 1876. — This is a very useful volume, though many of the selections are very dull. It covers the period 1765–1783.

Edmund Bailey O'Callaghan and Berthold Fernow, editors, *Documents relative to the Colonial History of the State of New-York.* 15 vols. Albany,
1856–1887. — Much matter not relating exclusively to New York ; includes
a useful index volume.   Vols. IV–VIII, X, XI on the period after 1689.

William Stevens Perry, editor, *Historical Collections relating to the American
Colonial Church.* 5 vols. Hartford, 1870–1878. — A very small edition,
and therefore rare.

Ben. Perley Poore, compiler, *The Federal and State Constitutions, Colonial
Charters, and other Organic Laws of the United States.* 2 parts. Washington, 1877. — A much-needed reprint is in preparation (1897).

Winthrop Sargent, editor, *The Loyalist Poetry of the Revolution.* Philadelphia,
1857.

William L. Saunders, editor, *The Colonial Records of North Carolina* (10 vols.),
and Walter Clark, editor, *The State Records of North Carolina* (4 vols.).
14 vols. Raleigh and Winston, 1886–1896. — Very inconveniently arranged, without contents or index, but abounding in general material.
Covers the period 1662–1780 ; still in progress.

Jared Sparks, editor, *Correspondence of the American Revolution.* 4 vols.
Boston, 1853. — Interesting and valuable letters, addressed chiefly to
Washington. May be picked up at second hand for a small sum.

Jared Sparks, editor, *The Diplomatic Correspondence of the American Revolution.* 12 vols. Boston, 1829–1830. — Arranged rather clumsily ; much of
the same matter appears in better form in Wharton's edition.

Edmund Clarence Stedman and Ellen Mackay Hutchinson, editors, *A Library
of American Literature, from the Earliest Settlement to the Present Time.*
11 vols. New York, 1888–1890. — Part of Vol. II and Vol. III on the period
1689–1783 ; very well chosen, though not with immediate reference to the
historical value of the pieces. An excellent set for a school library, and
often found at second hand.

Anthony Stokes, *A View of the Constitution of the British Colonies, in North-
America and the West Indies, at the time the Civil War broke out on the
Continent of America.* London, 1783. — Contains many writs and forms
from colonial procedure.

John Wingate Thornton, *The Pulpit of the American Revolution : or, the
Political Sermons of the Period of 1776. With a Historical Introduction,
Notes, and Illustrations.* Boston, 1860.

Francis Wharton, editor, *The Revolutionary Diplomatic Correspondence of the
United States.* 6 vols. Washington, 1889. — Official edition, arranged
chronologically, with a valuable introduction.

William A. Whitehead, Frederick W. Ricord, and William Nelson, editors,
Documents relating to the Colonial History of the State of New Jersey.
19 vols. Newark, 1880–1897. — One of the most valuable collections of
colonial sources ; it includes several volumes of reprints from rare newspapers ; still in progress.

6. Select Library of Sources on Colonization

THIS volume contains examples of many colonial writers, but only a short extract from most of them, and many important writers do not appear here at all. For careful study of colonial history, and for extensive topical work, the student or pupil needs a greater range of material; hence every library and high school ought to have at least a few of the sources in complete editions.

The purchase of such books, many of them long out of print, is a work of time. Any library or school may on application receive the catalogues of second-hand dealers, or put a list of desiderata in the hands of a book-seller. The *Publishers' Weekly* inserts (gratis) lists of books sought for by dealers. Often people will give old books of value to a permanent collection, if requested.

First in importance are the general printed collections mentioned in the preceding section (No. 5), or so many of them as the library can afford. Next may come selections from the records of one colony and state out of each of the three groups of southern, New England, and middle colonies. Virginia, Massachusetts, and New York or Pennsylvania were the most important in each group, and have the completest literature. Next to them in general historical interest come the Carolinas, Maryland, and Connecticut. Rhode Island and New Hampshire also have important records.

Below will be found a list of some of the most useful sources. Most of the volumes may be readily purchased new or at second hand, though the large sets are expensive. To these should be added such other colonial records, laws, collections, and histories containing documents as the most available library may be willing to buy (see lists in Channing and Hart, *Guide*, §§ 23, 29, 95–130), especially those of that colony which has the closest relation with the state or the place in which the library is situated. The local records (if printed) should of course be included; and a few of the typical town records, as those of Boston, Worcester, Lancaster, Watertown, Providence, East Hampton (L.I.).

CONTEMPORARY HISTORIANS

Throughout the colonial period, and especially from 1740 to the end of the Revolution, there were writers who set out to make formal histories of one colony or of a group of colonies; and though — with some exceptions, as Hutchinson — they had the use only of limited material, they relate the result of many of their own observations, and reflect the impressions made on the public mind at the time. In some cases they used and have reprinted rare accounts. The principal titles are the following : —

Amos Adams, *A Concise, Historical View of the Perils, Hardships, Difficulties, and Discouragements which have attended the Planting and Progressive Improvement of New England.* Boston, 1769. — A clear and valuable work.

Isaac Backus, *A History of New England, with particular Reference to the Denomination of Christians called Baptists.* 3 vols. Boston, 1777–1796. — Volume II extends from 1690 to 1784. Backus was an historian of the modern type, who searched far and wide for manuscript material.

Jeremy Belknap, *The History of New Hampshire.* 3 vols. Boston, 1742.

[Robert Beverly], *The History of Virginia, in Four Parts* [1584–1720]. London, 1705 (and later editions).

John (Daly) Burk, *The History of Virginia, from its First Settlement to the Present Day.* 3 vols. Petersburg, Va., 1804–1805. — With appendices of documents.

George Chalmers, *An Introduction to the History of the Revolt of the American Colonies.* 2 vols. Boston, 1845. — Also Vol. I, London, 1782.

John Drayton, *Memoirs of the American Revolution, from its Commencement, to the Year 1776 inclusive.* 2 vols. Charleston, 1821. — Really the work of William Henry Drayton (No. 157), written between 1776 and 1779.

William Gordon, *The History of the Rise, Progress, and Establishment, of the Independence of the United States of America.* 4 vols. London, 1788 (or 3 vols. New York, 1789). — See below, No. 219.

Alexander Hewatt, *An Historical Account of the Rise and Progress of the Colonies of South Carolina and Georgia.* 2 vols. London, 1779.

Stephen Hopkins, *An Historical Account of the Planting and Growth of Providence.* (In Rhode Island Historical Society, *Collections*, VII, 13–65.) — One of the earliest attempts at local history.

Thomas Hutchinson, *The History of the Colony of Massachusets Bay* [Vol. I, 1764]. *The History of the Province of Massachusetts Bay . . . until the Year 1750* [Vol. II, 1767]. *The History of the Province of Massachusetts Bay, from the Year 1750, until June, 1774* [Vol. III, 1828]. — Volume III of this work is an account of the causes of the Revolution. Hutchinson was the most careful and scientific writer of his time, though prejudiced by his own position as governor of a contumelious colony.

Cotton Mather, *Magnalia Christi Americana: or, The Ecclesiastical History of New-England.* London, 1702. (Three reprints, 2 vols., Hartford, 1820, 1853, 1855.) — Hardly historical in spirit. — See *Contemporaries*, I, No. 148.

Daniel Neal, *The History of New-England containing an Impartial Account of the Civil and Ecclesiastical Affairs of the Country to the Year of our Lord,* 1700. *To which is added The Present State of New-England.* 2 vols.   London, 1720. — Also a later edition. — See below, No. 20.

Samuel Penhallow, *History of the Wars of New-England with the Eastern Indians* [1703–1725].   Boston, 1726. — Reprinted, 1859.

Robert Proud, *The History of Pennsylvania, in North America* [1681–1742]. 2 vols.   Philadelphia, 1797–1798. — Proud was a Quaker who came to Pennsylvania in 1759.   The book was written from 1778 to 1780. — See below, No. 31.

David Ramsay, *The History of the American Revolution.* 2 vols.   Philadelphia, 1789. — Ramsay was a member of Congress in 1782, 1783, 1785–1786, and used the documentary material of that body.   His work has many merits. — See below, No. 220.

David Ramsay, *The History of South-Carolina, from its First Settlement in* 1670, *to the Year* 1808.   2 vols.   Charleston, 1809.

Samuel Smith, *The History of the Colony of Nova-Cæsaria, or New-Jersey.* Burlington, N. J., 1765.

William Smith, *The History of the late Province of New-York, from its Discovery, to* . . . 1762.   2 vols.   (New York Historical Society, *Collections,* IV–V.)   New York, 1829–1830. — With documents.   Smith lived in New York from his birth in 1728 to his departure as a loyalist exile in 1783. Volume II (1736–1762) is therefore contemporary.

C. Stedman, *The History of the Origin, Progress, and Termination of the American War.* 2 vols.   London, 1794. — Really by William Thomson. A British view.

Mercy Warren, *History of the Rise, Progress, and Termination of the American Revolution.   Interspersed with Biographical, Political and Moral Reflections.* 3 vols.   Boston, 1805. — Mrs. Warren was the sister of James Otis.   Her work shows spirit and intelligence, though it is expressed in ʾ pedantic fashion.

PUBLIC RECORDS AND SPECIAL COLLECTIONS

Upon the varieties and uses of public records a discussion appears above (No. 3).   Here is a brief list of some of the most important collections.   Most of them may be had, either from the state or society publishing them, or at second hand.   Single volumes or partial sets are often available.   A long list of such works may be found in Channing and Hart, *Guide,* § 29.   In many cases, parts of records are printed in the collections or proceedings of state historical societies (see No. 5 above).

Boston, *Reports of the Record Commissioners of the City of Boston.* (Edited by William Henry Whitmore and William S. Appleton.) 27 vols. 1876–1896. — Contains records of Boston, Dorchester, Roxbury, the Boston Selectmen's Minutes, etc. The most important single set of town records.

Canada, *Reports on Canadian Archives.* (By Douglas Brymner, archivist.) 15 vols. Ottawa, 1881–1896. — Very valuable, and still in progress.

Concord, N. H., *Concord Town Records* [1732–1820]. Concord, 1894.

Connecticut, *The Public Records of the Colony of Connecticut* [1636–1776]. (Compiled by James Hammond Trumbull and Charles J. Hoadly.) 15 vols. Hartford, 1850–1890.

East Hampton, *Records of the Town of East-Hampton, Long Island.* 4 vols. Sag-Harbor, 1887–1889.

Louisiana, *Historical Collections of Louisiana.* (Edited by Benjamin Franklin French.) 5 vols. New York, 1846–1853. Second Series, 2 vols., New York, 1869–1875. — Covers the French relations in the southwest.

Maryland, *Archives of Maryland* [1636–1777]. (Edited by William Hand Browne.) 16 vols. Baltimore, 1883–1897.

New Hampshire, *Records* [1623–1800]. (Compiled by Nathaniel Bouton, Isaac W. Hammond, and Albert S. Batchellor.) 27 vols. Concord, etc., 1867–1896.

New York, *Documents relative to the Colonial History of the State of New-York.* (Edited by Edmund Bailey O'Callaghan and Berthold Fernow.) 15 vols. Albany, 1856–1887. — One of the best sets ever published on colonial history; includes documents of all kinds, conveniently arranged, printed, and indexed; valuable on all the colonies. It may readily be bought at from $10 to $20 a set.

Pennsylvania, *Colonial Records* [1683–1790]. 16 vols. Philadelphia, 1852–1853. — *Pennsylvania Archives* [1664–1790]. (Compiled by Samuel Hazard.) 12 vols. Philadelphia, 1852–1856. — *Pennsylvania Archives*, Second Series. (Edited by John B. Linn and William H. Egle.) 19 vols. Harrisburg, 1874–1890.

Rhode Island, *Records of the Colony of Rhode Island and Providence Plantations in New England.* (Compiled by John Russell Bartlett.) 10 vols. Providence, 1856–1865.

South Carolina, *Historical Collections of South Carolina* [1492–1776]. (Compiled by B. R. Carroll.) 2 vols. New York, 1836. — Many interesting papers on the south.

Virginia, *The Statutes-at-Large, being a Collection of all the Laws of Virginia* [1619–1792]. (Compiled by William Waller Hening.) 13 vols. Philadelphia and New York, 1823. — Perhaps the most important set of colonial statutes printed.

Worcester, Mass., *The Records of Worcester.* (Edited by Franklin Pierce Rice.) (Worcester Society of Antiquity, *Collections*, Vols. I–XIV.)

c

JOURNALS, MEMOIRS, AND REMINISCENCES

In addition to the works from which extracts are taken for this volume, and the titles of which appear at the ends of the pieces (for an enumeration, see No. 3 above), the following may be mentioned : —

Thomas Anburey, *Travels through the Interior Parts of America* [1776–1781]. 2 vols. London, 1789.

William Bartram, *Travels through North and South Carolina, Georgia, East and West Florida* . . . [1773–1778]. Philadelphia, 1791.

Anne Grant, *Memoirs of an American Lady : with Sketches of Manners and Scenes in America, as they Existed previous to the Revolution.* (Edited by James Grant Wilson.) Albany, 1876. — Also earlier editions.

Thomas Hutchinson, *The Diary and Letters of His Excellency, Captain-General and Governor-in-Chief of His Late Majesty's Province of Massachusetts Bay, in North America.* (Compiled by Peter Orlando Hutchinson.) 2 vols. Boston, 1884–1886.

Charles Lee, *Memoirs.* . . . *To which are added his Political and Military Essays also, Letters to, and from many distinguished Characters, both in Europe and America.* (Edited by Edward Langworthy.) London, 1792.

Christopher Marshall, *Extracts from the Diary . . . kept in Philadelphia and Lancaster, during the American Revolution* [1774–1781]. (Edited by William Duane.) Albany, 1877.

Return Jonathan Meigs, *A Journal of Occurrences which happened . . . in the Detachment commanded by Colonel Benedictine Arnold.* . . . (No place, no date.)

Gouverneur Morris, *The Diary and Letters of Gouverneur Morris, Minister of the United States to France ; Member of the Constitutional Convention, etc.* (Edited by Anne C. Morris.) 2 vols. New York, 1888.

Count de Rochambeau, *Memoirs . . . relative to the War of Independence of the United States.* (Translated by M. W. E. Wright.) Paris, 1838.

Robert Rogers, *Journals . . . containing an Account of the several Excursions he made under the Generals who commanded upon the Continent of North America during the late War.* London, 1765.

Tench Tilghman, *Memoir . . . together with an Appendix, containing Revolutionary Journals and Letters, hitherto unpublished.* Albany, 1876.

Elkanah Watson, *Men and Times of the Revolution ; or, Memoirs . . . including Journals of Travels in Europe and America, from* 1777 *to* 1842. New York, 1856.

George Whitefield, *Journal of a Voyage from London to Savannah* [Dec. 28th, 1737–May 7th, 1738.] London, 1739. — Also other editions.

Eliza Wilkinson, *Letters . . . during the Invasion and Possession of Charlestown, S. C. by the British in the Revolutionary War.* (Edited by Caroline Gilman.) New York, 1839.

COLLECTED WORKS OF PUBLIC MEN

Besides the authors from whom extracts are taken for this work (see No. 3 above), the following are important : —

George Chalmers, *Opinions of Eminent Lawyers on various points of English Jurisprudence, chiefly concerning the Colonies, Fisheries, and Commerce, of Great Britain.* 2 vols. London, 1814. — Reprinted, 1 vol., Burlington, 1858.

Charles, Marquis Cornwallis, *Correspondence.* (Edited by Charles Ross.) 3 vols. London, 1859.

Silas Deane, *Papers* (New York Historical Society, *Collections* for the years 1886–1890). 5 vols. New York, 1887–1891. — Includes much previously unpublished matter.

Charles James Fox, *Memorials and Correspondence.* (Edited by Lord John Russell.) 3 vols. London, 1853–1854.

Philip Freneau, *Poems written and published during the American Revolutionary War.* 2 vols. Philadelphia, 1809. — Also other editions.

John Jay, *Correspondence and Public Papers.* (Edited by Henry P. Johnston.) 4 vols. New York, 1890–1893.

William Pitt, Earl of Chatham, *Correspondence.* (Edited by William Stanhope Taylor, and Captain John Henry Pringle.) 4 vols. London, 1838–1840.

John Witherspoon, *Works.* 4 vols. New York, 1800–1801. — Also 9 vols., Edinburgh, 1804–1805.

BIOGRAPHIES CONTAINING SOURCES

[John Almon], *Anecdotes of the Life of the Right Hon. William Pitt, Earl of Chatham.* Sixth edition. 3 vols. London, 1797.

James Trecothick Austin, *The Life of Elbridge Gerry. With Contemporary Letters.* 2 parts. Boston, 1828–1829. — Part I extends to the close of the American Revolution.

Eben Edwards Beardsley, *Life and Correspondence of the Right Reverend Samuel Seabury, D.D.* Boston, 1881.

Edward Barrington de Fonblanque, *Political and Military Episodes derived from the Life and Correspondence of John Burgoyne.* London, 1876.

George Washington Greene, *The Life of Nathanael Greene.* 3 vols. New York, 1867–1871.

James Kendall Hosmer, *The Life of Thomas Hutchinson, Royal Governor of the Province of Massachusetts Bay.* Boston, 1896.

Robert Henry Lee, *Memoir of the Life of Richard Henry Lee.* 2 vols. Philadelphia, 1825.

Alexander Slidell Mackenzie, *Life of Paul Jones.* 2 vols. Boston, 1841.

John Marshall, *The Life of George Washington*. 5 vols. Philadelphia, 1804–1807.— Also an abridged edition in 2 vols., 1832.

Josiah Quincy, *Memoir of the Life of Josiah Quincy, Junior, of Massachusetts Bay* [1744–1775]. (Edited by Eliza Susan Quincy.) Boston, 1875. — Also other editions.

Kate Mason Rowland, *The Life of George Mason* [1725–1792]. 2 vols. New York, 1892.

Charles Janeway Stillé, *The Life and Times of John Dickinson* [1732–1808]. (Pennsylvania Historical Society, *Memoirs*, Vol. XIII.) Philadelphia, 1891. — Also printed separately.

Charles Janeway Stillé, *Major-General Anthony Wayne and the Pennsylvania Line in the Continental Army*. Philadelphia, 1893.

Charlemagne Tower, Jr., *The Marquis de La Fayette in the American Revolution*. 2 vols. Philadelphia, 1895.

George Tucker, *The Life of Thomas Jefferson . . . with Parts of his Correspondence never before published*. 2 vols. Philadelphia, 1837.

William Tudor, *The Life of James Otis*. Boston, 1823.

Henry Cruger Van Schaack, *The Life of Peter Van Schaack*. New York, 1842.

William Vincent Wells, *The Life and Public Services of Samuel Adams. . . . With Extracts from his Correspondence, State Papers, and Political Essays*. 3 vols. Boston, 1865.

Barrett Wendell, *Life of Cotton Mather the Puritan Priest*. (Makers of America Series.) New York, 1891.

A GOOD COLLECTION OF SOURCES ON THE PERIOD 1689–1783

Out of the books enumerated above, and other works, a few may be selected. Most of the exact titles appear in the above lists, or in the foot-notes to the pieces below, if not otherwise indicated. The books out of print may be found through a dealer in second-hand books. An asterisk (*) indicates the most useful books for a small library.

John Adams, *Works*. (10 vols.)

*John Adams and Abigail Adams, *Familiar Letters*.

American History Leaflets. (30 nos.)

Thomas Anburey, *Travels*. (2 vols.)

William Bradford, *Life and Correspondence of Joseph Reed*. (2 vols.)

Edmund Burke, *Account of the European Settlements*. (2 vols.)

*Andrew Burnaby, *Travels*.

B. R. Carroll, *Historical Collections of South Carolina.* (2 vols.)
*Correspondence of the American Revolution. (Sparks, 4 vols.)
Samuel Curwen, *Journal and Letters.*
John Dickinson, *Writings.* (2 vols.)
Documents relating to the Colonial History of New Jersey. (19 vols.)
*Documents relative to the Colonial History of New-York. (Vols. IV–VIII, X, XI.)
William Douglass, *Summary.* (2 vols.)
**Benjamin Franklin, *Works.* (Sparks and Bigelow, 10 vols.)
Alexander Graydon, *Memoirs.*
William Heath, *Memoirs.*
Francis Hopkinson, *Miscellaneous Essays.* (3 vols.)
Gilbert Imlay, *Topographical Description.*
Peter Kalm, *Travels.* (2 editions.)
Maryland *Archives.* (16 vols.)
Cotton Mather, *Magnalia.*
**Frank Moore, *Diary of the Revolution.* (2 vols.)
New Hampshire *Records.* (27 vols.)
**Hezekiah Niles, *Principles and Acts of the Revolution.*
Old South Leaflets. (75 nos., or 3 vols.)
Thomas Paine, *Writings.* (Several editions.)
Thomas Pownall, *Administration of the Colonies.*
William Pynchon, *Diary.*
Madame Riedesel, *Letters and Memoirs.* (2 editions.)
Samuel Sewall, *Diary.* (3 vols.)
Stedman and Hutchinson, *Library of American Literature.* (Vols. II–III.)
W. L. Stone, *Letters of Brunswick and Hessian Officers.*
James Thacher, *Military Journal.*
*Town records of Boston or Providence or Worcester.
John Trumbull, *Autobiography.*
**George Washington, *Writings.* (Sparks, 12 vols.)
Barrett Wendell, *Cotton Mather.*
Francis Wharton, *Revolutionary Diplomatic Correspondence.* (6 vols.)
John Woolman, *Journal.*

CHAPTER II — USE OF SOURCES

7. How to find Sources on the Colonies and the Revolution

TO the accumulating mass of original material there was till a few years ago no general guide. The historians writing in the eighteenth century used what they could find. The second group of American historians, headed by George Bancroft, Jared Sparks, and Francis Parkman, made elaborate collections of transcripts of documents. Winsor, Lecky, Tyler, Weeden, Fiske, and others of the present school of historians have liberally used the printed records and may be tracked through their foot-notes.

There are three methods of reaching the sources which bear on colonial and revolutionary history. First, and most convenient for a quick search to verify a particular point, are the elaborate foot-notes in general or local histories. A list of serviceable secondary works will be found below (No. 15). Most important for this purpose are R. Frothingham, *Rise of the Republic;* J. G. Palfrey, *History of New England;* George Bancroft, *History of the United States* (original edition) ; W. B. Weeden, *Economic and Social History;* M. C. Tyler, *History of American Literature* and *Literary History of the Revolution.* Most of such books contain a bibliography of the books cited. In the monographs on colonial history and institutions, especially in the *Johns Hopkins University Studies,* will also be found reliable foot-notes.

The second method is through the catalogues of libraries containing valuable collections. The most important are those of the Boston Public Library (*Bates Hall*) and *Supplement;* Boston Athenæum ; Peabody Institute (Baltimore) ; and the card catalogue of the Harvard College Library. The catalogues of the state libraries and state historical societies are also sometimes valuable.

The third method is through special bibliographies of the subject. Most elaborate is Joseph Sabin's *Dictionary of Books relating to America* (19 vols., New York, 1868–1891), which is an attempt to give the titles (alphabetically by authors) of all the books printed on America up to 1867, with many references to the libraries in which particular rarities are found. When completed, the work is to have an index by subjects; it includes no estimate of the value of books mentioned. The most remarkable contributions to the knowledge of sources are Justin Winsor's *Memorial History of Boston* (4 vols., Boston, 1880–1881), *Reader's Handbook of the American Revolution* (Boston, 1880), and *Narrative and Critical History of America* (8 vols., Boston, 1886–1889). This last work, a monument of learning and well-directed industry, devotes eight large volumes to narrative accounts and to critical statements as to the bearing and value of authorities, both original and secondary; and it makes frequent mention of libraries in which the books are to be found. It is invaluable to the student of sources, for it searches out and discriminates between editions, it mentions reprints, and it is arranged in a convenient method, and is indexed.

The most recent book (in which the authors acknowledge the help they have gained from Winsor) is Channing and Hart, *Guide to the Study of American History* (New York, 1896). This is a brief work, covering in 500 small pages the field of Winsor's volumes, and extending on down to 1865; the sources mentioned are selected out of the confused mass of available material and are arranged in successive paragraphs. In Part I are various classified lists, chiefly of sources; and under each of the topical headings is a special selection of sources.

With these and similar aids, students who have the use of a large library may go directly to the sources most important for their purpose. There is also a special guide to the voluminous collections of the state historical societies, viz., A. P. C. Griffin, *Bibliography of American Historical Societies*, republished from the *Annual Report of the American Historical Association*, 1895; also a selected list in Channing and Hart, *Guide*, § 31. Colonial records are enumerated in the *Guide*, § 29; some of them are enumerated above (No. 6).

To locate a particular book in a library is often a matter of patience and dexterity. The first thing is to get the exact title from the catalogue or from some other printed list, and to be sure that there is no confusion of editions. A critical reprint is a help in understanding the bearing of the source, and Winsor is an unfailing aid on critical points. The first authoritative edition of a source is usually to be preferred.

In making notes and citing references, the rule is absolute that every extract which is in the words of the author should be set off by quota-

tion marks ; and that all omissions within such a quoted extract should
be shown by points or stars (. . . * * *).   Exact dates should be
noted, with especial observance of the fact that dates between January 1
and March 25 fall in one year in " Old Style " reckoning, and in the
following year in " New Style."   In 1752 England accepted the new
calendar ; hence all later dates are in " New Style."   In old documents,
since March is the first month, September is the seventh (as the name
suggests), and December is the tenth.   A common precaution (sometimes found in the original) is to give both years : as February 1, $17\frac{31}{32}$
(see No. 21 below).

---

8. Use of Sources by Teachers

O F the three offices of sources in teaching, — supplying material,
furnishing illustration, and giving insight into the spirit of the
times, — all are important.   It is not to be expected that any but the
most highly-trained specialist will found all or his chief knowledge of
history on sources ; but parts of the field may thus be underlaid by
actual contact with the material.   For example, such topics as the
witchcraft delusion (Nos. 16–18), the founding of Georgia (ch. vi), the
expulsion of the French from North America (ch. xx), or the naval
warfare of the Revolution (Nos. 177, 194, 204), may be readily worked
up from the narratives of the time ; indeed, even such a limited collection
as this volume contains throws light upon them.

For illustrations and additions to the text-book in class work, teachers
will find some use of the sources enlivening and interesting to the pupil.
For example, Washington's quest of Palatines (No. 108) shows how the
labor system of the colonies troubled practical men.   Chastellux and
Steuben (Nos. 176, 202) bring out the merits of the American army.
Story and Wesley (Nos. 98, 99) show how other churches began to rise
side by side with the Episcopal and Congregational.   Brief extracts from
such originals, or paraphrases of the narrative recounted to the class,
will serve to rivet the more general events in the minds of the pupils.

Perhaps the most important service which sources perform for the
teacher is to fill his mind, — and through him the pupil's mind, — with
the real spirit of the age described.   Franklin (No. 81) was a man
writing to fellow-men, and while reading we cannot help sharing his
experiences.   The records of the Providence town-meeting (No. 78)

bring out the multifariousness of Rhode Island interests. The gossip of William Pynchon (No. 208) is a sample of the daily table-talk of his generation. Pettit (No. 61) lets us into the details of local politics in 1764 ; Madame Knight (No. 80) infuses into her readers her own cheerful and indomitable nature ; Doddridge (No. 136) shows us the hardship and grimness of the frontier life, which was the lot of many Americans ; and the fate of the loyalists may be read in the plaints of Samuel Curwen in England (No. 169). Contact with the sources has some of the effects of visiting the scenes, in the way of leaving in the mind a clear-cut impression.

Sources will therefore bear reading several or many times, so that the mind may be permeated with them. The teacher cannot be too familiar with the controversies over the settlement of Georgia (Nos. 39–44) ; with the character of colonial assemblies (Nos. 61–68) ; with the arguments pro and con in regard to the Revolution (Nos. 131, 138, 141, 142, 146, 147, 155, 156, 157) ; with the favorable views of the American army held by foreign observers (Nos. 172, 176, 202, 214) ; with the argument for independence (No. 186). Of course the teacher will also use connecting secondary matter, so as to show how one event follows another, and what is the relation between events (see No. 14 below).

Some very successful teachers deliberately choose what may be called the episodic method, especially with young classes : they present a series of intellectual pictures of successive stirring events, without trying to make a complete narrative. Such a method has much to commend it, and is aided by the use of brief selected sources.

---

9. Use of Sources by Pupils

ONE of the main objects of this work is to bring together in convenient form a body of material suitable for use by pupils, even though immature. Hence, pieces have been selected which have an interest in themselves, though taken out of their connection ; and there has been care to exclude numerous passages which are suitable enough for older students, but which are too strong and plain-spoken for children. Pupils cannot be expected to found their knowledge of history on sources, because they have not the judgment to distinguish between the different kinds of material ; but it is believed that the use of such a collection as this, — or of such parts of it as there may be time to read, — will fix many of the most important events and tendencies mentioned in the text-book. For example, no second-hand account of the Indians can compare in " holding power " with the narratives of Adair and Carver (Nos. 113, 116).

Perhaps the principal value of the educational side of sources for pupils lies in the aid which such material gives to intelligent topical work and to the preparation of "special reports." Of course, many of the advantages of topical study (which is discussed at large in Channing and Hart, *Guide to American History*, §§ 67, 68) may be had from the use of good secondary books, new to the user ; but such work does not teach the most important lesson of all, — that history is the search for truth, and that truth must depend on the ultimate sources. No pupil, by the use of this volume or of any other collection, can overset a conclusion of Parkman's ; but he may learn that Parkman's greatness lies in his graphic and effective grouping of what he learned from sources.

A topic prepared with access to sources is therefore to the pupil's mind a creation, or rather a building up from materials known to be sound ; it is an exercise in the kind of work which every historian must do, but which, in an elementary form, may be done by any young beginner in the subject. It often may stimulate the pupil to learn more about the picturesque men whose narratives he reads, — about the witches, who acted so like poor, tormented, innocent people (Nos. 16, 17), and the jaunty travellers, Thomas and Castelman and Byrd (Nos. 25, 28, 82). It is therefore natural that the requirements in history for entrance to college, drawn up by a conference at Columbia University in February, 1896, suggest sources as a part of the pupil's material ; and that the American Historical Association also favors that method for "vitalization" of the study.

As extracts for reading, many of the pieces in this volume have unique value. The language of the eighteenth century differs little from that of our own time ; but there is a delightful freshness and vigor in such writers as Neal (No. 20), Goelet (No. 23), Beverly (No. 33), Wise (No. 47), Eliza Lucas (No. 83), Wesley (No. 99), Adair (No. 113), Knox (No. 129), Pausch (No. 179), and Greene (No. 212).

To sum up briefly : the pupil may get a foot-hold in the world of colonial thought by reading properly-chosen and related extracts from sources ; he may get a peculiar and valuable training by working out some particular point. For instance, a very good exercise might be to work up, from the material in this volume, the condition of slaves, or ot colonial schools ; or the dealings of the colonists with Indians ; or the methods of raising troops for the Revolution ; or the early American navy.

———————◆———————

10. Use of Sources by Students and Investigators

TWO theories of historical teaching contest for the field of education through history : the first, or English method, aims to ground students in well-chosen secondary books, which they are to read, assimilate, and compare, and the divergences between which they must note, though they have not the means to reconcile them. Even in English universities only the most highly-specialized historical students use sources as an essential part of their study and training.

The opposing method expects some knowledge of the original material. The student's work is based upon some rather brief text-book or combination of books, but from all students collateral use of sources is required. The English method may be compared to an orderly ship canal, going straight to the end, with an ascertained depth of water, but always shallow and confined : the other method, to a natural river, abounding in deep pools, and joined by a multitude of branches which one cannot explore, with many unfordable places, but winding among human habitations, and giving glimpses of human life.

To facilitate study through sources, a variety of written exercises have been devised, for which students gather and compare original evidence on important points. The merits of this system have been set forth above (Nos. 8, 9). Though applicable at all ages, the use of sources becomes more and more valuable, however, as the student advances ; and when he reaches the highest stage of the student's work, — the preparation of materials for a thorough-going account of some episode or period, — sources are the reservoirs from which he must draw most of his knowledge.

Such a collection as this book contains may serve as a beginning to the ambitious student ; but it will have accomplished less than its design if it do not lead him to wish for the full texts from which these extracts are taken, for additional information on some one question which interests him, and for that acquaintance with original material and the methods of using it which gives a student at once an insight into past times and a power to reproduce them before the minds of his readers.

Former historians have had to collect and organize their material in painful and expensive fashion. Jared Sparks and Francis Parkman each accumulated a costly set of transcripts of manuscripts. For future historians, much of the most valuable material is now in print; and though no one will ever again set himself to George Bancroft's task of writing a general history of the United States entirely from sources, the special works which are to be the foundation of new views must rest wholly on such materials. Although large collections of printed sources are now available, many of them have not yet been examined by competent writers, and discoveries of great importance are still to be made by the investigator. For example, the manuscript of Boudinot's valuable reminiscences (No. 180) had not been printed till 1896.

---

11. Use of Sources by Readers

FOR the numerous class of persons who have not the opportunity to be students, or the inclination to investigate, sources are useful by way of arousing the imagination and filling up the sketch made by the secondary writer. All that has been said about the usefulness of materials for the teacher and pupil applies equally to the self-taught. Sources alone are one-sided, because they lack perspective and comparison of views, and because they leave great gaps. Secondary works alone are also one-sided, because they tell us about people, instead of letting the people tell us about themselves. The ideal method is to read a brief sketch of colonial history, such as Professor Fisher's *Colonial Era;* then some illustrative extracts from sources; then a fuller work like that of Parkman or like John Fiske's books, with a larger collateral use of sources. Upon the general subject of home study of American history, Channing and Hart have a discussion in the *Guide to American History*, § 13.

Among the reprints in this book likely to be most interesting to readers are the witches' testimony (No. 17); Goelet on Boston (Nos. 23, 84); Gabriel Thomas on Pennsylvania (No. 25); Burnaby on New York (No. 32); Eliza Lucas on Carolina (Nos. 35, 83); the slavery question in Georgia (No. 42); Douglass on colonial government (No. 50); Clinton on a governor's perquisites (No. 57); Morris's veto (No. 65); Zenger on his prosecution (No. 72); Providence town-meeting (No. 78); extracts from Franklin's autobiography (No. 81); a plea for protective duties

(No. 86) ; Ames's college diary (No. 95) ; Wesley's journal (No. 99) ; Woolman's journal (No. 106) ; Colden on the fur trade (No. 111) ; Adair on the Indians (No. 113) ; Knox on Quebec (No. 129) ; Doddridge on the West (No. 136) ; Franklin's examination (No. 143) ; Andrews's account of the Tea-Party (No. 152) ; Sam Johnson's tory argument (No. 156) ; Scammell's love-letter (No. 162) ; Graydon on recruiting (No. 170) ; Chastellux's visit to Washington's camp (No. 176) ; Pausch's army life (No. 179) ; Richard Smith on the Continental Congress (No. 185) ; Abigail Adams on the siege of Boston (No. 192) ; Dr. Waldo on Valley Forge (No. 198) ; John Paul Jones's capture of the Serapis (No. 204) ; Pynchon's diary (No. 208) ; Gordon's retirement of Washington (No. 219).

———◆———

12. Use of Sources by Libraries

THE triple object of most libraries is to entertain, to inform, and to instruct. Sources may fulfil all these objects. Boys who like Robinson Crusoe will certainly like Thomas (No. 25), Franklin (No. 81), Goelet (No. 84), Ames (No. 95), Adair (No. 113), Clark (No. 201), and Jones (No. 204). Girls who enjoy Strickland's *Queens of England* will like lively Eliza Lucas (Nos. 35, 83), and the steadfast Abigail Adams (No. 192). The student of German history will be glad to follow the Germans into the new world (Nos. 29, 40, 179). The colonial writers ooze with rugged, genuine human nature, interesting to those who are interested in their kind. Who can read of Oglethorpe in Georgia (No. 39), or of Daniel Boone (No. 134), or of Major André (No. 183), without wishing to know more of these men and their writings?

The other functions of the library — to inform and to instruct — are equally provided for by proper use of sources, which are the adjunct of the teacher, the reservoir of the pupil, and the nutritious intellectual food of the general reader. Of the extracts in this volume, those from works like Sewall's, John Adams's, and Franklin's are available in many libraries in the full text ; but many of the pieces are hard to come at, and for a person whose time is limited such a selection as this may be more useful. As regular standard reading matter, the libraries may well provide some sources.

In those larger libraries which aim at general completeness, or at special historical collections, it is an obvious duty to put abundant sources on their shelves, for the benefit of the students and investigators who must have a large range. The sources are scientific material comparable with the fossils of the palæontologists, by the use of which the popular books are to be written, as well as the general scientific treatises. Not to have them is to ignore one of the principal objects of libraries, — the preservation of accumulated knowledge from age to age.

For libraries especially is intended the list of most valuable sources printed above (Nos. 5, 6), which may suggest purchases in this field.

---

13. Caution in using Sources

VALUABLE as are original records, they must be used intelligently or they will mislead. First of all, they are not all of equal authority or of equal value. To turn an inexperienced student unguided among sources is to invite errors, for sometimes even sources are untruthful. How is the tyro to know, for example, that letters purporting to be written by George Washington were forged and set afloat during the Revolution? Sometimes a writer bears internal evidence of malice or of untruthfulness, as Simcoe in his account of his loyalist corps (No. 181), in which his animus against the patriots is plain enough. But, without warning, how is one to know that Edward Randolph (No. 34), shrewd observer as he was, was sent to the colonies with the mission of finding something wrong, and was bound to justify his employment? The value of many sources depends on the writer's truthfulness, which cannot be attacked without training and the sifting of later evidence. Most reprints of old pieces, especially those in the proceedings of historical societies, include a critical account of the writer. Other criticisms may be found in Moses Coit Tyler, *History of American Literature during the Colonial Time* (2 vols.), and *Literary History of the American Revolution* (2 vols., New York, 1897) ; in Justin Winsor, *Narrative and Critical History of America* (8 vols., Boston, 1886–1889) ; in Henry T. Tuckerman, *America and her Commentators* (New York, 1864) ; in S. Austin Allibone, *Critical Dictionary of English Literature, and British and American Authors* (3 vols., Philadelphia, 1858–1871). Extracts from records and formal documents (as in Nos. 21, 38, 78, 187), may usually be relied upon ; but even such a document as Vergennes's despatch (No. 216) is a special plea, and does not state the whole truth.

In the next place, even contemporaries had not all the same opportunities for seeing things. Maury (No. 37) knew that Patrick Henry had made a tremendous speech against him, but he probably understood the law of his case very imperfectly. Dr. Douglass's views of his countrymen (No. 50) are tinged by his conviction that other doctors did not understand how to treat small-pox ; Edmund Burke (No. 44) was at a long distance from the colonies ; Colonel Winslow (No. 126) did not take seriously to heart the misery of the transported Acadians ; Captain Pausch (No. 179) felt a natural hostility toward the rival British troops. Nearly all the pieces in this volume are the statements of eye-witnesses, recorded at or near the time ; but even they must have taken flying rumors, as did Dunmore (No. 154), Williams (No. 160), and Pynchon (No. 208). Violent prejudices and prepossessions make it necessary to supplement such narratives as Lawson's (No. 16), Sam Johnson's (No. 156), and Drayton's (No. 157) by calmer testimony and by statements from the other side ; and this is especially necessary in the intensity of feeling attending such a period as the Revolution. We cannot understand the real causes and force of that mighty movement unless we realize how strong was the opposition ; inasmuch as even good and honest writers may not have the gift of lucid description, and may flounder about like Dr. Douglass (No. 50) or Thomas Story (No. 98).

But while secondary writers may correct the errors of the original writers, and show the relation of one event with another, they have also their prejudices and make their mistakes. One of the first lessons to be learned by a child beginning the study of history is that it is difficult and often impossible to get at the exact truth, just as it is hard to get at the facts of every-day current events. To the secondary book one must look for a survey of the whole field, — an indispensable service ; to sources we must still turn for that reality, that flavor of real human life and thought, which may be had only by reading the words written while history was making.

14.　Use of Secondary Works

FOR the indispensable background of narrative history there is a large literature. The best way of teaching a young class is by a text-book ; but the ground as fast as traversed must be extended by the use of sources for reading, — perhaps for reading aloud, — and for simple topical work (see No. 9 above). The pupil should go beyond the material in this volume, if libraries be available. For older classes there should be a fuller text-book, preferably one which has brief specific bibliographies ; and pupils may be encouraged to make little studies of the biography of writers in this volume, and of the events of which parts are related, using additional sources so far as available. For college classes a more extended narrative may be used as the basis ; and the reading of all the selections in this volume may be required, and enforced by proper examinations ; in addition there should be written work. For the most advanced students of American history this collection is only a nucleus around which to group their studies from sources.

The secondary book has then two functions : to cover the whole field, bridging over the gaps between sources ; and to furnish a starting-point from which the pupil, reader, or student may reach the sources, so as to extend the text-book, to check its statements, and to enliven them.

———◆———

15.　Select List of Secondary Works on the Eighteenth Century and the Revolution

THE secondary material on the period covered by this volume is scanty on the first half century, and over-abundant on the revolutionary period. There is still much need of a critical account of the development of the colonies from the revolution of 1688 to the French war of 1750. Almost the only properly-trained writer on colonial government is Herbert L. Osgood (*American Historical Review*, II, 644, III, 31, 244). The historians of the period are characterized in Winsor, *Narrative and Critical History*, and in Charles Kendall Adams, *Manual of Historical Literature* (New York, 1882). Some of the books most useful to the pupil, student, or reader are enumerated below.

SCHOOL HISTORIES

Not less than forty school histories of the United States have been put upon the market. Of these the older ones are now quite useless for proper study, because they were usually prepared by writers who knew little of American history; because they are dull; because they give too much space to obscure Indian wars; and because they are not adapted to use in connection with other books. A new literature of text-books has sprung up, written by some of the foremost scholars in American history, interesting, beautifully illustrated, provided with maps, and aiming to lead those who use them to consult and read other books. Some of these useful text-books are the following: —

Mary Sheldon Barnes and Earl Barnes, *Studies in American History.* Boston, 1896 (pp. x, 433). — Made up in great part of extracts from sources.

Edward Channing, *A Student's History of the United States.* New York, 1898 (pp. xxxix, 603). — Especially arranged for work on secondary writers and in sources; abounds in practical suggestions, lists of books, references to sources, etc. Excellent for the home reader.

Edward Eggleston, *A History of the United States and its People for the Use of Schools.* New York, 1888 (pp. x, 416). — Very strong on colonial life; excellent pictures.

John Fiske, *A History of the United States for Schools.* Boston, 1894 (pp. xxi, 553). — Delightfully written, but brief; excellent questions, involving topical study.

Thomas Wentworth Higginson, *Young Folks' History of the United States.* New York, revised to 1886 (pp. vi, 460, 33). — A very popular and successful book; of especial interest on the colonial period.

Alexander Johnston, *A History of the United States for Schools.* New York, revised, 1895 (pp. xx, 489). — Stronger on the period after 1787; many maps, and a list of secondary books.

Harry Pratt Judson, *The Growth of the American Nation.* (College edition.) Meadville, 1895 (pp. 359). — Continuous text; convenient form.

John Bach McMaster, *A School History of the United States.* New York, 1897 (pp. 476, 31). — More relative space to the period after 1783; many references to secondary material.

D. H. Montgomery, *The Student's American History.* Boston, 1897 (pp. 523, lv). — Many sketch maps; lists of books, including sources.

William A. Mowry and Arthur May Mowry, *A History of the United States for Schools.* Boston, 1896 (pp. xii, 437). — Very attractive make-up; convenient for class use.

Allen C. Thomas, *A History of the United States.* Boston, 1894 (pp. xiii, 415, lxxiii). — A good, plain, sensible book, with abundant references for parallel reading.

BRIEF GENERAL HISTORIES

For class use or for reading, the most convenient short accounts of colonial conditions and of the Revolution are as follows : —

Edward Channing, *The United States of America* [1765–1865]. New York, 1896. — A hundred pages on the causes and conditions of the Revolution.

George Park Fisher, *The Colonial Era* (American History Series, I). New York, 1892. — Comes down to 1756, with an intelligent account of the condition of the colonies.

George Washington Greene, *Historical View of the American Revolution*, Boston, 1865. — One of the best brief expositions of the Revolution.

Albert Bushnell Hart, *Formation of the Union* [1750–1829] (Epochs of American History, II). New York, revised, 1897. — Four chapters on the revolutionary period.

Thomas Wentworth Higginson, *A Larger History of the United States*. New York, 1886. — A charming study of American life, and especially of the conditions of frontier warfare.

Henry Cabot Lodge, *A Short History of the English Colonies in America*. New York, 1881. — Deals particularly with social conditions in the eighteenth century.

Henry Cabot Lodge, *George Washington* (American Statesmen Series). 2 vols. Boston, 1889. — Vol. I is an excellent account of the political and military progress of the Revolution.

John T. Morse, Jr., *Benjamin Franklin* (American Statesmen Series). Boston, 1889. — A good life of the American most representative of his time.

William Milligan Sloane, *The French War and the Revolution* (American History Series, II). New York, 1893. — A good survey of the revolutionary period.

Reuben Gold Thwaites, *The Colonies* (Epochs of American History, I). New York, revised, 1897. — Four chapters on the colonies after 1700.

PART II

THE SEPARATE COLONIES

CHAPTER III — NEW ENGLAND

16. Salem Witches (1692)

BY REVEREND DEODAT LAWSON (1704)

Lawson was minister at Salem Village (now Danvers), where the witchcraft excitement first broke out. His account is paralleled by those of Calef and Increase Mather. — Bibliography: Charles W. Upham, *Salem Witchcraft*, I, 268–284, II, 76–92, 525–537; Winsor, *Memorial History of Boston*, II, ch. vi, notes; Channing and Hart, *Guide*, § 129.

IT pleased God in the Year of our Lord 1692. to visit the People at a place called *Salem Village* in NEW–ENGLAND, with a very Sore and Grievous Affliction, in which they had reason to believe, that the Soveraign and Holy GOD was pleased to permit Satan and his Instruments, to Affright and Afflict, those poor Mortals in such an Astonishing and Unusual manner.

Now, I having for some time before, attended the work of the Ministry in that Village, the Report of those *Great Afflictions*, came quickly to my notice ; and the more readily, because the first Person Afflicted, was in the Minister's Family, who succeeded me, after I was removed from them ; in pitty therefore to my Christian Friends, and former Acquaintance there, I was much concerned about them, frequently consulted with them, and fervently (by Divine Assistance) prayed for them ; but especially my Concern was augmented, when it was Reported, at an Examination of a Person suspected for Witchcraft, that my Wife and Daughter, who Dyed Three Years before, were sent out of the World under the Malicious Operations of the Infernal Powers ; as is more fully represented in the following Remarks.   I did then *Desire*, and was also *Desired*, by some concerned in the Court, to be there present, that I might hear what was alledged in that respect; observing therefore, when I was amongst them, that the Case of the Afflicted was very amazing, and deplorable; and the Charges brought against the Accused, such as were Ground of Suspicions yet very intricate, and difficult to draw up right Conclusions about them. . . .

1. One or two of the first that were Afflicted, Complaining of unusual Illness, their Relations used *Physick* for their *Cure*, but it was altogether in vain.

2. They were oftentimes, very *stupid* in their Fits, and could neither hear nor understand, in the apprehension of the Standers by, so that when *Prayer* hath been made, with some of them, in such a manner as might be audible in a great Congregation; yet when their Fit was off, they declared they did not hear so much as one Word thereof.

3. It was several times Observed, that when they were discoursed with, about GOD or CHRIST, or the Things of *Salvation*, they were presently afflicted at a dreadful Rate, and hence were oftentimes *Outragious*, if they were permitted to be in the Congregation, in the Time of the Publick Worship. . . .

5. They affirm'd, That they saw the *Ghosts* of several departed Persons, who at their appearing, did instigate them, to discover such as (they said) were Instruments to hasten their Deaths; threatning sorely to afflict them, if they did not make it known to the Magistrates; they did affirm at the Examination, and again at the Tryal of an accused Person, that they saw the Ghosts of his two Wives (to whom he had carryed very ill in their Lives, as was proved by several Testimonies) and also that they saw the Ghosts of *My Wife* and *Daughter*, (who dyed above three Years before) and they did affirm, that when the very Ghosts looked on the Prisoner at the Bar, they looked red, as if the Blood would fly out of their Faces, with Indignation at him: The Manner of it was thus; Several Afflicted being before the Prisoner at the Bar, on a sudden they fixed all their Eyes together, on a certain Place of the Floor before the Prisoner; neither moving their Eyes nor Bodies, for some few Minutes, nor answering to any Question which was asked them; so soon as that Trance was over, some being removed out of Sight and Hearing, they were all one after another asked what they saw, and they did all agree, that they saw those *Ghosts* above mentioned; I was present, and heard and saw the whole of what passed upon that Account, during the Tryal of that Person who was accused to be the Instrument of Satan's Malice therein.

6. In this (*worse than Gallick*) Persecution by the *Dragoons* of Hell, the Persons afflicted were harrassed at such a dreadful rate, to write their Names in a Devil-Book, presented by a Spectre unto them ; and One in my hearing said, *I will not, I will not Write, it is none of God's Book, it is none of God's Book* ; *it is the Devil's Book for ought I know :* And when they stedfastly refused to sign, they were told if they would but touch or take hold of the Book it should do : And *Lastly*, The Diabolical Propositions were so low and easy, that if they would but let their Clothes, or any thing about them, touch the Book, they should be at ease from their Torments, it being their Consent that is aimed at by the Devil in those Representations and Operations.

7. One who had been long afflicted at a stupendious rate, by two or three Spectres, when they were (to speak after the manner of Men) *tyred out* with tormenting of her, to *Force* or *Fright* her to sign a Covenant with the Prince of Darkness, they said to her, as in a Diabolical and Accursed Passion, *Go your ways and the Devil go with you, for we will be no more pestred and plagued about you.* And ever after that she was well, and no more afflicted that ever I heard of.

8. Sundry Pins have been taken out of the Wrists and Arms of the Afflicted ; and one in time of Examination of a suspected Person, had a Pin run through both her *Vpper* and her *Lower* Lip, when she was called to speak ; yet no apparent festering followed thereupon, after it was taken out.

9. Some of the Afflicted, as they were striving in their Fits, in open Court, have (by invisible means) had their Wrists bound fast together with a real Cord, so as it could hardly be taken off without cutting. Some Afflicted have been found with their Arms tyed, and hanged upon an Hook, from whence others have been forced to take them down that they might not expire in that Posture.

10. Some Afflicted have been drawn under Tables and Beds, by undiscerned Force, so as they could hardly be pull[ed] out : And one was drawn half way over the Side of a Well, and was with much difficulty recovered back again.

11. When they were most grievously afflicted, if they were brought to the Accused, and the suspected Persons Hand but laid upon them, they were immediately relieved out of their Tortures ; but if the Accused did but look on them, they were instantly struck down again : Wherefore, they use to cover the Face of the Accused, while they laid their Hands on the Afflicted, and then it obtained the desired Issue ; for it

hath been experienced (both in Examinations and Tryals) that so soon as the Afflicted, came in sight of the Accused, they were immediately cast into their Fits; yea, though the Accused were among the Crowd of People unknow to the Sufferers, yet on the first view were they struck down; which was observed in a Child of four or five Years of Age, when it was apprehended, that so many as she could look upon, either directly or by turning her Head, were immediately struck into their Fits.

12. An iron Spindle of a woollen Wheel, being taken very strangely out of an House at *Salem* Village, was used by a Spectre, as an Instrument of Torture to a Sufferer, not being discernable to the Standers by; until it was by the said Sufferer snatched out of the Spectres Hand, and then it did immediately appear to the Persons present to be really the same iron Spindle.

13. Sometimes in their Fits, they have had their Tongues drawn out of their Mouths to a fearful length, their Heads turned very much over their Shoulders; and while they have been so strained in their Fits, and had their Arms and Legs, *&c.* wrested, as if they were quite dislocated, the Blood hath gushed plentifully out of their Mouths, for a considerable time together; which some, that they might be satisfied that it was real Blood, took upon their Finger and rubbed on their other Hand. I saw several together thus violently strained and bleeding in their Fits, to my very great astonishment, that my fellow-Mortals should be so grievously distressed by the invisible Powers of Darkness. For certainly, all considerate Persons, who beheld these things, must needs be convinced, that their Motions in their Fits were Præternatural and Involuntary, both as to the *Manner* which was so strange, as a well Person could not (at least without great Pain) screw their Bodies into; and as to the *violence* also, they were Præternatural Motions, being much beyond the ordinary Force of the same Persons when they were in their right Minds. So that being such grievous Sufferers, it would seem very hard and unjust to censure them of consenting *To*, or holding any voluntary Converse or Familiarity *with* the 𝔇𝔢𝔳𝔦𝔩.

14. Their Eyes were for the most part fast closed in their Trance-Fits, and when they were asked a Question, they could give no Answer; and I do verily believe, they did not hear at that time, yet did they discourse with the Spectres as with real Persons; asserting Things, and receiving Answers, affirmative or negative, as the Matter was. For Instance, One in my hearing thus argued *with*, and railed *at* a Spectre, *Goodn——* be gone! be gone! be gone! Are you not ashamed, a

Woman of your Profession, to afflict a poor Creature so? What hurt did I ever do you in my Life? You have but two Years to live, and then the 𝔇𝔢𝔳𝔦𝔩 will torment your Soul for this : Your Name is blotted out of God's Book, and it shall never be put into God's Book again. Be gone for shame, are you not afraid of what is coming upon you? I know, I know, what will make you afraid, the Wrath of an angry God : I am sure that will make you afraid.   Be gone, do not torment me ; I know what you would have, (*we judged she meant her Soul:*) but it is out of your reach, it is clothed with the white Robes of Christ's Right-eousness.   This Sufferer I was well acquainted with, and knew her to be a very sober and pious Woman, so far as I could judge ; and it appears that she had not in that Fit, voluntary Converse with the 𝔇𝔢𝔳𝔦𝔩 ; for then she might have been helped to a better Guess about that Woman above-said, as to her living but two Years, for she lived not many Months after that time. . . .

16. Some of them were asked how it came to pass that they were not affrighted when they saw the *Black-man,* they said they were at first, but not so much afterwards.

17, Some of them affirmed, they saw the *Black-man* sit on the Gal-lows, and that he whispered in the Ears of some of the *Condemned Per-sons* when they were just ready to be turn'd off; even while they were making their last Speech. . . .

19. Some of them, have sundry times seen a *White-man* appearing amongst the Spectres, and as soon as he appeared, the *Black-Witches* vanished : They said : This *White-man* had often foretold them, what respite they should have from their Fits ; as sometimes a day or two, or more, which fell out accordingly.   One of the Afflicted said she saw him in her Fit, and was with him in a *Glorious Place,* which had no *Candle* nor *Sun,* yet was full of Light and Brightness ; where there was a multi-tude in *white Glittering Robes,* and they sang the Song in *Rev.* 5. 9. *Psal.* 110. *Psal.* 149. she was loth to leave that Place, and said *how long shall I stay here, let me be along with you?*   She was grieved, she could stay no longer in that Place and Company.

20. A young Woman that was afflicted at a fearful rate, had a Spectre appeared to her, with a white Sheet wrapped about it, not visible to the Standers by, until this Sufferer (*violently striving in her Fit*) snatch'd at, took hold, and tore off a Corner of that Sheet ; her Father being by her, endeavoured to lay hold upon it with her, that she might retain what she had gotten ; but at the passing away of the Spectre, he had such a vio-

lent Twitch of his Hand, as if it would have been torn off; immediately thereupon appeared in the Sufferers hand, the Corner of a Sheet, *a real cloth, visible* to the Spectators, which (*as it is said*) remains still to be seen.

Deodat Lawson, *Christ's Fidelity the only Shield against Satan's Malignity* (Boston, 1704), Appendix, 93–109 *passim*.

---

17. Witches' Testimony (1692)

BY CLERK EZEKIEL CHEEVER

The original minutes of the witch trials at Salem, still well preserved, afford the most striking proof of the inadequacy of the evidence and of the terror of the prosecutors. — Bibliography: Winsor, *Memorial History of Boston*, II, ch. vi, notes; Channing and Hart, *Guide*, § 129.

Salem ffeb[y] the 29th 169½

WHEREAS M[rs] Joseph Hutcheson, Thomas Putnam, Edward Putnam, and Thomas Preston, Yeomen of Salem Village in ye County of Essex, personally appeared before vs and made Complaint on Behalfe of their Majes[ts] against Sarah Good the wife of William Good of Salem Village aboves[d] for suspition of Witchcraft by her Committed, and thereby much Injury donne by Eliz. Paris, Abigail Williams, Anne Putnam and Elizabeth Hubert all of Salem Village afores[d] Sundry times within this two moneths and Lately also don, at Salem Village Contrary to y[e] peace of our Souer[n] L[d] and Lady W[m] & Mary, King & Queen of Engld &c — You are therefore in theire Majesties names hereby required to apprehe[d] & bring before vs, the said Sarah Good to morrow aboute ten of y[e] clock in y[e] forenoon at y[e] house cf Lt Nathaniele Ingersalls in Salem Village or as soon as may be then and there to be Examined Relating to y[e] aboves[d] premises and hereof you are not to faile at your perile.

Dated. Salem, feb[r] 29th 169½

JOHN HATHORNE ⎱ Assis[ts].
JONATHAN CORWIN ⎰

To Constable George Locker.

I brought the person of Saragh Good the wife of William Good according to the tenor of the within warrant, as is Attest by me

1 March 169½   GEORGE LOCKER — Constable

Anno : Regis et Reginee Willm et Mariae
nunc Anglice &c. Quarto

Essex ss.

The Juro^{rs} for our Sovereigne Lord and Lady the King and Queen, pr^esent, That Sarah Good the wife of William Good of Salem Village in the County of Essex, Husbandman, the Second Day of May in the forth year of the Reigne of our Sovereigne Lord and Lady William and Mary by the Grace of God of England, Scotland ffrance & Ireland King and Queen Defenders of the ffaith &c and Divers other Days and times as well before as after, certaine Detestable arts called Witchcrafts and Sorceries, Wickedly and ffeloniously hath vsed, Practised and Exorcised, at and within the Township of Salem in the County of Essex aforesaid, in, upon and against one Sarah Vibber wife of John Vibber of Salem aforesaid, Husbandman, by which said wicked Arts, she the said Sarah Vibber the said Second Day of May in the fourth year abovsaid and divers other Days and times as well before as after was and is Tortuered Afflicted, Pined, Consumed, wasted and Tormented, and also for Sundry other Acts of witchcraft by said Sarah Good committed and done before and since that time ag^t the Peace of our Sovereigne Lord & Lady the King & Queen theire Crowne and Dignity and ag^t the forme of the Statute in that case made and Provided.

Witnesses
Sarah Vibber Jurat
Abigail Williams Jurat
Elizabeth Hubbard "
Ann Putnam Jurat
Jno Vibber Sworne . . .

The examination of Sarah Good before the worshipfull Assts John Har
thorn Jonathan Curran

(H.) Sarah Good what evil Spirit have you familiarity with

(S. G.) None.

(H.) Have you made no contracte with the devil
Good answered no.

(H.) Why doe you hurt these children

(g) I doe not hurt them. I scorn it.

(H) Who doe you imploy then to doe it.

(g) I imploy no body

(H) What creature do you imploy then.

(g) no creature but I am falsely accused.

(H) why did you go away muttering from Mr Parris his house.

(g) I did not mutter but I thanked him for what he gave my child.

(H) have you made no contract with the devil.

(g) no.

(H) desired the children all of them to look upon her and see if this were the person that had hurt them and so they all did looke upon her, and said this was one of the persons that did torment them — presently they were all tormented.

(H) Sarah Good do you not see now what you have done, why doe you not tell us the truth, why doe you thus torment these poor children

(g) I doe not torment them.

(H) who do you imploy then.

(g) I imploy nobody I scorn it.

(H) how came they thus tormented

(g) what doe I know you bring others here and now you charge me with it.

(H) why who was it.

(g) I doe not know but it was some you brought into the meeting house with you.

(H) wee brought you into the meeting house.

(g) but you brought in two more.

(H) who was it then that tormented the children.

(g) it was osburn.

(H) what is it you say when you go muttering away from persons houses

(g) if I must tell I will tell.

(H) doe tell us then

(g) if I must tell, I will tell, it is the commandments. I may say my commandments I hope.

(H.) what commandment is it.

(g) if I must tell I will tell, it is a psalm.

(H) what psalm.

(*g*) after a long time shee muttered over some part of a psalm.

(H) who doe you serve

(g) I serve God

(H) what God doe you serve.

(g) the God that made heaven and earth. though shee was not willing to mention the word God. her answers were in a very wicked spitfull manner. reflecting and retorting against the authority with base and abussive words and many lies shee was taken in it was here said that her husband had said that he was afraid that she either was a witch or would be one very quickly. the worsh. Mr. Harthon asked him his reason why he said so of her, whether he had ever seen any thing by her, he answered no, not in this nature, but it was her bad carriage to him, and indeed said he I may say with tears that shee is an enemy to all good.

Salem Village March the 1st 169½
    Written by Ezekiell Chevers
                                    Salem Village March th 1st 169½ . . .

                    Salem Village March the 1st 169½

Sarah Osburne the wife of Alexander Osburne of Salem Village brought before vs by Joseph Herrick constable in Salem, to answer Joseph Hutcheson and Thomas putnam &c yeomen in s^d Salem Village Complainants on behalfe of theire Majes^{ts} against s^d Sarah Osburne for Suspition of Witchcraft by her Committed and thereby much Injury don to the bodys of Elizabeth Parris, Abigail Williams Anna Putnam and Elizabeth Hubert, all of Salem Village aforesaid, according to theire Complaint, according to a Warrant, Dated Salem ffebu^y 29th 169½

Sarah Osburne vpon Examination denyed ye matter of fact (viz) y^t she ever vnderstood or vsed any Witchcraft, or hurt any of ye aboue s^d children.

The children aboue named being all personally present accused her face to face which being don, thay ware all hurt, afflicted and tortured very much ; which being ouer and thay out of theire fitts thay sayd y^t said Sarah Osburne, did then come to them and hurt them, Sarah Osburn being then keept at a distance personally from them.   S. Osburne was asked why she then hurt them, she denyed it, it being asked of her how she could soe pinch and hurt them and yet she be at that distance personally from y^m, she Answered she did not then hurt them, nor never did, she was asked who then did it, or who she Imploy to doe it, she Answered she did not know y^t ye Divell goes aboute in her likeness to doe any hurt.   Sarah Osburn being told y^t Sarah Good one of her Companions had vpon Examination accused her, she nottwithstanding denyed ye same, according to her Examination, wch is mor at Large giuen in as therein will appeare.

            p. vs.   JOHN HATHORNE ⎱ Assits.
                           JONATHAN CORWIN ⎰

(H) what evil spirit have you familiarity with.

(O) none.

(H) have you made no contract with the devill.

(O) no I never saw the devill in my life.

(H) why doe you hurt these children.

(O) I doe not hurt them.

(H) who do you imploy then to hurt them.

(O) I imploy no body.

(H) what familiarity have you with Sarah Good.

(O) none. I have not seen her these 2 years.

(H) where did you see her then.

(O) one day a going to town.

(H) what communications had you with her.

(O) I had none, only, how doe you doe or so, I did not know her by name.

(H) what did you call her then.

Osburn made a stand at that, at last said, shee called her Sarah.

(H) Sarah Good saith that it was you that hurt the children.

(O) I doe not know that the devil goes about in my likeness to doe any hurt.

Mr Hathorn desired all the children to stand up and look upon her and see if they did know her, which they all did and every one of them said that this was one of the women that did afflict them, and that they had constantly seen her in the very habit, that shee was now in, theire evidence do stand that shee said this morning that shee was more like to be bewitched, than that shee was a witch. Mr Hathorn asked her what made her say so, shee answered that shee was frighted one time in her sleep and either saw or dreamed that shee saw a thing like an indian all black which did prick her in her neck and pulled her by the back part of her head to the dore of the house

(H) did you never see anything else.

(O) no.

it was said by some in the meeting house that shee had said that shee would never be tied to that lying spirit any more.

(H) what lying spirit is this, hath the devil ever deceived you and been false to you.

(O) I doe not know the devil I never did see him.

(H) what lying spirit was it then.

(O) it was a voice that I thought I heard.

(H) what did it propound to you.

(O) that I should goe no more to meeting, but I said I would and did goe the next Sabbath day.

(H) were you never tempted furder.

(O) no.

(H) why did you yield thus far to the devil as never to goe to meeting since

(O) Alas. I have been sike and not able to goe. her husband and others said that shee had not been at meeting this yeare and two months. . . .

Salem Village March 1ˢᵗ 1691.

Titiba an Indian woman brought before vs by Consᵗ Joseph Herrick of Salem vpon Suspition of witchcraft by her committed according to yᵉ complaint of Jos. Hutcheson and Thomas Putnam &c of Salem Village as appears p warrant granted Salem 29 ffebrʸ 169½ Titiba vpon examination and after some deny all acknowledged yᵉ matter of fact according to her examination giuen in more fully will appeare, and who also charged Sarah Good and Sarah Osburne with yᵉ same . . .

(H) Titibe whan evil spirit have you familiarity with.

(T) none.

(H) why do you hurt these children.

(T) I do not hurt them,

(H) who is it then.

(T) the devil for ought I know.

(H) Did you never see the devil.

(T) The devil came to me and bid me serve him.

(H) Who have you seen.

(T) Four women sometimes hurt the children.

(H) Who were they.

(T) Goode Osburn and Sarah Good and I doe not know who the other were. Sarah Good and Osburne would have me hurt the children but I would not she further saith there was a tale man of Boston that she did see.

(H) when did you see them.

(T) Last night at Boston.

(H) what did they say to you.

they said hurt the children

(H) and did you hurt them

(T) no there is 4 women and one man they hurt the children and

they lay all upon me and they tell me if I will not hurt the children they
will hurt me.

(H) but did you not hurt them

(T) yes, but I will hurt them no more.

(H) are you not sorry you did hurt them.

(T) yes.

(H) and why then doe you hurt them.

(T) they say hurt children or wee will doe worse to you.

(H) what have you seen.

an man come to me and say serve me.

(H) what service.

(T) hurt the children and last night there was an appearance that
said kill the children and if I would no go on hurting the children they
would do worse to me.

(H) what is this appearance you see.

(T) Sometimes it is like a hog and sometimes like a great dog, this
appearance shee saith shee did see 4 times.

(H) what did it say to you

(T) it s the black dog said serve me but I said I am afraid he said
if I did not he would doe worse to me.

(H) what did you say to it.

(T) I will serve you no longer. then he said he would hurt me and
then he looked like a man and threatens to hurt me, shee said that this
man had a yellow bird that kept with him and he told me he had more
pretty things that he would give me if I would serve him.

(H) what were these pretty things.

(T) he did not show me them.

(H) what also have you seen

(T) two rats, a red rat and a black rat.

(H) what did they say to you.

(T) they said serve me.

(H) when did you see them.

(T) last night and they said serve me, but I said I would not

(H) what service.

(T) shee said hurt the children.

(H) did you not pinch Elizabeth Hubbard this morning

(T) the man brought her to me and made me pinch her

(H) why did you goe to Thomas Putnams last night and hurt his
child.

(T) they pull and hall me and make me goe
(H) and what would have you doe.
        Kill her with a knif.
Left. Fuller and others said at this time when the child saw these per-
sons and was tormented by them that she did complayn of a knife, that
they would have her cut her head off with a knife.
(H) how did you go
(T) we ride upon stickes and are there presently.
(H) doe you goe through the trees or over them.
(T) we see nothing but are there presently.
[H] why did you not tell your master.
[T] I was afraid they said they would cut of my head if I told.
[H] would you not have hurt others if you cold.
[T] They said they would hurt others but they could not
[H] what attendants hath Sarah Good.
[T] a yellow bird and shee would have given me one
[H] what meate did she give it
[T] it did suck her between her fingers.
[H] did not you hurt Mr Currins child
[T] goode good and goode Osburn told that they did hurt Mr Cur-
rens child and would have had me hurt him two, but I did not.
[H] what hath Sarah Osburn.
[T] yellow dog, shee had a thing with a head like a woman with
2 legges, and wings. Abigail Williams that lives with her Uncle Parris
said that she did see the same creature, and it turned into the shape
of Goode Osburn.
[H] what else have you seen with Osburn.
[T] another thing, hairy it goes upright like a man it hath only
2 leggs.
[H] did you not see Sarah Good upon Elizabeth Hubbard, last
Saterday.
[T] I did see her set a wolfe upon her to afflict her, the persons
with this maid did say that she did complain of a wolfe.
T. shee further saith that shee saw a cat with good at another time.
[H] What cloathes doth the man go in
[T] he goes in black clouthes a tal man with white hair I thinke
[H] How doth the woman go
[T] in a white whood and a black whood with a top knot
[H] doe you see who it is that torments these children now.

[T] yes it is Goode Good, shee hurts them in her own shape
[H] and who is it that hurts them now.
[T] I am blind now.   I cannot see.

Salem Village   Written by Ezekiell Cheevers.
March the 1st 169½   Salem Village March 1st 169½

[William Elliot Woodward, compiler], *Records of Salem Witchcraft* (Rox·
bury, 1864), I, 11–48 *passim.*

———————◆———————

18. Guilt Contracted by the Witch Judges (1697)

BY CHIEF JUSTICE SAMUEL SEWALL

Sewall was a distinguished Massachusetts man; for a time a minister, later a judge.
In the latter capacity he joined in the condemnation of the witches.   His public
humiliation is characteristic of the time. — Bibliography: Tyler, *American Literature,* II, 99–103; Winsor, *Memorial History of Boston,* II, ch. vi, notes; Channing
and Hart, *Guide,* § 129. — See *Contemporaries,* I, No. 149.

COPY of the Bill I put up on the Fast day; giving it to Mr. Willard
as he pass'd by, and standing up at the reading of it, and bowing
when finished; in the Afternoon.

Samuel Sewall, sensible of the reiterated strokes of God upon himself and family; and being sensible, that as to the Guilt contracted
upon the opening of the late Comission of Oyer and Terminer at Salem
(to which the order for this Day relates) he is, upon many accounts,
more concerned than any that he knows of, Desires to take the Blame
and shame of it, Asking pardon of men, And especially desiring prayers
that God, who has an Unlimited Authority, would pardon that sin and
all other his sins; personal and Relative: And according to his infinite
Benignity, and Sovereignty, Not Visit the sin of him, or of any other,
upon himself or any of his, nor upon the Land: But that He would
powerfully defend him against all Temptations to Sin, for the future;
and vouchsafe him the efficacious, saving Conduct of his Word and
Spirit.

Diary of Samuel Sewall (Massachusetts Historical Society, *Collections,* Fifth
Series, V, Boston, 1878), I, 445.

19. An Explanation by Rhode Island (1699)

BY GOVERNOR SAMUEL CRANSTON

Cranston was annually elected governor of Rhode Island for thirty years (1696–1726); a firm, popular, and successful administrator. This letter is addressed to the Lords of Trade. — Bibliography : Arnold, *Rhode Island*, I, 544–548; Winsor, *Narrative and Critical History*, III, 376–380, V, 163; Channing and Hart, *Guide*, § 133. — For previous Rhode Island history, see *Contemporaries*, I, ch. xvii.

RIGHT Honorable : Your letter bearing date Whitehall, October the 25th, 1698, came to our hands the 5th of April last, as likewise the duplicate of the same, we received the same day ; wherein your Lordships do signify your observation of the long interval between the date of your letter, the 9th of February, 1698–9, and our-answer to the same.

May it please your Lordships : We shall not justify ourselves wherein we have been remiss, or negligent in that affair ; and hope your Lordships will not impute any thing of contempt in us for the same ; and we shall for the future endeavor to be more dilligent and observant in returning your Lordships an answer, and giving an account of the affairs of this government.   But we having no shipping that sails directly from this Collony, and many times we are disappointed for want of timely notice from other places, the which has been a great disappointment to us in the performance of our duty to your Lordships.

Your Lordships are also pleased to signify that our letter was principally in vindication of our conduct in relation to piracies and pirates, &c. We hope your Lordships will put that constructions upon our writing, that we do not vindicate ourselves, wherein we have ignorantly erred, or for want of better knowledge and a right method we have gone out of the due form and practice your Lordships have now prescribed for us ; and wherein we did or do vindicate ourselves, it is in our innocency, and it's said sins of ignorance ought to be forgiven.   And we do humbly beg your Lordships' pardon for the same, hoping for the future to be more circumspect.   Your Lordships having been so favorable as to give us directions and instructions, the which we accept as a most bountifull favor from you, and shall with our best endeavors follow the same accordingly.

Your Lordships are also pleased to require a copy of all private commissions which have been granted to any persons from this government, with the bonds, &c.   And in obedience to your Lordships' command,

E

we have herewith sent copies of such commissions (if they may properly
be so called), they being only defensive, and were granted by the
Deputy Governor (contrary to the mind of the then Governor), and he
not knowing the due form and method in such cases, took no bonds,
concluding as he hath solemnly declared, that they were bound upon a
merchandizing voyage ; their design being unknown to the authority.

Your Lordships are further pleased to require copies of the tryall of
George Cutler and Robert Munday, with all proceedings from first to
last, relating to the same ; and of all other persons and things in the like
case.   Likewise a copy of the laws and Acts of this government, all
which we have accordingly done.   Humbly submitting ourselves to your
Lordships' favorable constructions upon any thing that may therein be
found amiss ; we being wholly ruled and governed by the good and
wholesome [laws] of our Mother, the kingdom of England, as far as the
constitution of our place will bear ; and we doubt not, but your Lordships are sensible that in these remote parts, we cannot in every punc-
tillo follow the niceties of the laws of England ; but it will be a great
damage to his Majesty's interest in the settling and peopling the country.

We do also acknowledge the receipt of your Lordships' letter bearing
date Whitehall, February the 3d, 1698-9, with his Majesty's Instructions,
relating to the observation of the Acts of trade, &c. ; all which we
kindly accept, and shall with the best of our endeavors comply with the
same, and we do further acknowledge the receipt of a letter bearing
date Whitehall, January the 24th, 1698-9 (the which came to our hands
the 24th instant), wherein his Majesty gives us to understand, that
severall ships of force have been fitted out of Scotland, with an intent to
settle in some parts of America, contrary to his Majesty's knowledge,
forbidding of us to hold any correspondency with them, whilst they are
engaged in the aforesaid enterprise ; commanding us to send your Lordships an account of our proceeds therein.   In obedience to which, we
forthwith issued out a Proclamation concerning the same, a copy of
which, we herewith send you, and it shall be our further endeavor to see
it duly executed.

And may it please your Lordships to accept this further information :
that on the beginning of April last, arrived a ship upon our coast, which
was by the men that did belong to her, sunk, as they have since confessed. It was a hagboat, of about four hundred tons, belonging to
London, bound for the Island of Borneo, in the East India, whereof one
Capt'n Gullop was Commander. And at the Island of Polonoys, near

the Island of Sumatra, their Commander being on shore with severall others, the boatswain's mate of said ship, one Bradish, with severall others combined, and run away with her, leaving their Commander and severall others, on shore, at said Island of Polonoys.

And for your Lordships' better information, we have herewith sent you the examination of one of the men, now a prisoner in his Majesty's jail in this government, who after the sinking of the said ship, distributed themselves into severall parts of this country, and are all taken and secured in the severall governments, except one, with the greatest part of their money that they brought with them.

We having in our hands to the value of twelve hundred pounds, or thereabouts; all which we shall secure till further orders from your Lordships, we having used all the dilligence we can for discovering what more may be distributed about the country.

We shall always for time to come be very observant in following your Lordships, advice and Instructions, in all cases relating to his Majesty's interest, and once more humbly begging your Lordships' favorable constructions in what of weakness may appear in us. We being a plain and mean sort of people, yet true and loyall subjects to his Most Excellent Majesty, King William, and we hope time will make manifest the same to your Lordships, we being not insensible of the many enemies we have, who hath and do make it their business to render us (to his Majesty and your Lordships), as ridiculous as they can, and to present things to your Lordships quite contrary to what they are or were. For instance, there is one Esquire Randolph, who was employed by the Commissioners of his Majesty's Customs, who did publickly declare he would be a means to eclipse us of our priviledges; and we know he picked up severall false reports against us. But we do not doubt your Lordships will in time have a further insight and knowledge of such men's actions, and we humbly beg of your Lordships, that you will not entertain any reports against us, so as to give any determination on the same, to our ill conveniency till we can have liberty to answer for ourselves; we having commissionated and appointed Jahleel Brenton, Esq'r (his Majesty's late Collector of his Customs in these parts), our Agent to answer to what shall be objected against us, or in any other matter or thing, relating to this his Majesty's Collony, begging your Lordships' favor towards him in what shall appear just and right.

So having not further to offer to your Lordships at present, but humbly submitting ourselves to his Most Excellent Majesty, and your

Lordships' favorable constructions of what herein shall appear amiss; wishing his Majesty a long and peaceable reign, and your Lordships health and prosperity under his government.

Your Lordships' most humble servants,

SAMUEL CRANSTON, Governor.

Newport, on Rhode Island, the 27th of May, 1699.

John Russell Bartlett, editor, *Records of the Colony of Rhode Island, and Providence Plantations, in New England* (Providence, 1858), III, 373–375.

---

20. An Historical Sketch of New England (1720)

BY DANIEL NEAL

Daniel Neal was an intelligent historian, one of the few careful writers of his time. — Bibliography: Winsor, *Narrative and Critical History*, V, 157–158; Channing and Hart, *Guide*, § 130. — For previous New England history, see *Contemporaries*, I, Part V.

The Inhabitants of New-England. THE Inhabitants of *New-England* are the Posterity of the old *English Puritans* or *Nonconformists* to the Church of *England*, who chose to leave their native Country, and retire into a Wilderness, rather than submit to such Rites and Ceremonies in Religion as they apprehended sinful. They did not differ with the Church in any of the Articles of her Faith, but they scrupled the Vestments, kneeling at the Sacrament, some Parts of the Common-Prayer, and the promiscuous Admission of all Persons to the Communion; for these things they were silenced and deprived of their Livings, which put great Numbers of the Ministers under a Necessity of removing with their Followers to *America*.

Their Numbers, and military Strength. THE Number of Planters that went over to *New-England* before the Year 1640, were about 4000; after which for the next 20 Years they had no Increase but what sprung up from among themselves; In the Reigns of King *Charles* II. and King *James* II. great Numbers of *Dissenters*, both Ministers and People went over, to avoid the Hardships they suffer'd from the Church; and it deserves to be taken Notice of, that the Increase of the *English* Plantations abroad depends very much on the Treatment the Dissenters from the Established Church of *England* meet with at home: When they are allowed the free Exercise of their Civil and Religious Liberties, they love their native Country too well to leave it; but when they are oppress'd in so tender a Point as their Consciences, 'tis but reasonable to suppose, that many of them will go where they can make themselves easy; for the Confirmation of this Observation, we need look no further at present than *Ireland*, from whence, if I am rightly inform'd, above 6000 *Scotch Presbyterians* have shipp'd off themselves and their Effects within these few Years for the Plantations of *America*, chiefly on the Account of the Uneasinesses they were under, with Regard to the free Exercise of their Religion: And great Numbers are still going over every Summer, which if the Legislature are not pleas'd to take into Consideration, may in Time very much weaken, if not totally subvert the Protestant Religion in that Kingdom.

To such Causes as these, *New-England* owes the vast Increase of its Inhabitants . . . the whole Number of Inhabitants must now amount to 160 or 165,000, and of them about 30 or 35000 fighting Men, which is the Military Strength of the Country.

FROM this Calculation we may conclude, that the Province of *New-England* is in no great Danger at present from any of its Neighbours, for the *Indians* are an inconsiderable Body of themselves, and if the *French* should joyn them, though they might ravage the Frontiers by their flying Parties, they could make no Impressions upon the Heart of the Country; besides the *Indians* are divided, some being in Alliance with the *French*, and others with the *English*; so that in case of a War they may be play'd one against the other. . . .

As the Government of *New-England* is dependant on the Crown of *England*, so is their Trade; 'tis impossible *Their Trade.* to make an exact Estimate of the Exports and Imports from *New-England*, without examining the Custom-House-Books, but 'tis computed by the most experienced Merchants trading to those Parts, that they receive from hence all Sorts of Woollen-Drapery, Silks, Stuffs, and Hats; all Sorts of Linnen, and printed Callicoes, all Sorts of Iron Manufacture, and *Birmingham* Ware, as Tools for Mechanicks, Knives, Scissars, Buckles, Nails &c. to the Value of 100,000 *l.* annually, and upwards.

IN Return for these Goods, our Merchants export from thence about 100,000 Quintals of dried Cod-fish yearly, which they send to *Portugal*, *Spain*, and the several Ports of *Italy*, the Returns for which are made to *London* out of the Product of those Countries, and may amount to the Value of about 80,000 *l.* annually. . . .

BUT in the Concerns of Civil Life, as in their Dress, Tables, and Conversation, they affect to be as much *English* as possible; there is no

Fashion in *London*, but in three or four Months is to be seen at *Boston*, nay, they are fond of the very Name and Person of an *English* Man, insomuch that some who have had no great Affection for the People on the Account of their Preciseness, have yet been so agreeably entertain'd by them, as to leave the Country with Regret. In short, the only Difference between an *Old* and a *New-English* Man is in his *Religion* ; and here the Disagreement is chiefly about the Liturgy, and Church-Government, the one being for a National Church, govern'd by *Arch-Bishops, Bishops*, and a *Convocation :* The other esteeming all Ministers to be of the same Order, and every Society of Christians meeting together in the same Place, a compleat Christian Church, having all Ecclesiastical Jurisdiction within itself, without being subject to a Classis, Synod, or Convocation any further than for Advice.

Their Political Interests. IT can't be denied but there are two State-Factions in *New-England*, as well as in most Kingdoms of *Europe*, which have arisen partly from a private narrow *Spirit* in some leading Men, who are a Sort of Spies upon the Gover[n]ment they live under, and express their Dislike of the Management of publick Affairs in all Companies, chiefly because themselves have no Share in it ; but I can assure the World, that *Religion* is no Part of the Quarrel, for there being no Sacramental Test for Preferments in the State, all Parties of Christians among them are easy ; Happy People ! as long as Religion and the State continue on a separate Basis ; the Magistrate not medling in Matters of Religion any further than is necessary for the Preservation of the publick Peace ; nor the Churches calling for the Sword of the Magistrate to back their Ecclesiastical Censures with corporal Severities. May they long continue on this Foot a Sanctuary to oppressed *Protestants* in all Parts of the World !

BUT after all, it will be impossible for *New-England* to subsist of itself for some Centuries of Years ; for tho' they might maintain themselves against their Neighbours on the Continent, they must starve without a free Trade with *Europe*, the Manufactures of the Country being very inconsiderable ; so that if we could suppose them to rebel against *England*, they must throw themselves into the Arms of some other *Potentate*, who would protect them no longer than he could sell them to Advantage ; the *French* and *Spaniards* are Enemies to their Religion and Civil Liberties, and the *Dutch* are too cautious a People, to run the Hazard of losing their own Country, for the Alliance of another at so great a Distance ; 'Tis therefore the Grand Interest of *New-England* to remain subject to the Crown of *England*, and by their dutiful Behaviour to merit the Removal of those few Hardships and Inconveniences they complain of; no other *Power* can, or will protect them, and next to their own, 'tis impossible their Religion and Civil Liberties should be in better Hands than in a Parliament of *England*.

AND I must do the People of *New-England* so much Justice as to acquaint the World, that their Inclinations as well as Duty lead them to this; they love the *English* Constitution, and would live and dye in the Defence of it, because when that is gone, they know their own must soon follow; In the Reigns of King *Charles* and King *James* II. all the Men of Reflection throughout the Country seem'd to be dispirited, and in Pain for the *Protestant Religion*, and *English Liberty*, but when the good Providence of God brought about the Happy Revolution, they began a Jubilee of Joy, which has continued almost ever since. When the Protestant Succession in the Illustrious House of *Hannover* was in Danger, no People in the World pray'd more heartily for its taking Place; and when it pleased Almighty God to bring His Majesty to the Throne of his Ancestors, none of his Subjects in any Part of his Dominions celebrated the Auspicious Day with louder Acclamations of Joy and Thankfulness. In a Word, the People of *New-England* are a Dutiful and Loyal People, and *that* which the Protestant-Dissenters of the City of *London*, declared with so much Justice to His Majesty, in their *Address* occasioned by the late Rebellion, is litterally true of their Brethren in this Country, That King GEORGE *is not known to have a single Enemy to His Person, Family, or Government in all* New-England.

Daniel Neal, *The Present State of New-England* (Chapter XIV of his *History of New-England*, II, London, 1720), 600–616 *passim*.

---

21. The Condition of New Hampshire (1730/1)

BY LIEUTENANT-GOVERNOR JOHN WENTWORTH

This piece, very similar in character to those in Nos. 19 above and 22 below, is unsigned, but appears to be by Wentworth, who was at this date the only representative of the home government. — Bibliography: Winsor, *Narrative and Critical History*, V, 163–164; Channing and Hart, *Guide*, § 123. — For previous New Hampshire history, see *Contemporaries*, I, ch. xix.

*A*NSWERS *to the Queries sent from the Right Honorable the Lords of Trade and Plantations.* — *January* 22, 1730.

1. The situation of the province of New-Hampshire, is between the

province of the Massachusetts Bay, and the late province of Maine, bordering about fifteen miles in width upon the Atlantic Sea, or Western Ocean. — The nature of the country, as to the ground, is rough, uneven, and hilly, but for the most part a good soil, being a mixture of clay land and loam, well watered, and suitably adapted for hemp and flax, and having considerable meadows in it. As to the climate, 'tis cold. Portsmouth, the capital of the province, is in forty three degrees and twenty minutes north latitude, and sixty eight degrees west from London, settled by good observations.

2. The province has no other boundaries than what are expressed in the King's commission to the Governor, and they are from three miles to the northward of Merrimack river on the one side, to Pascataqua river on the other, and no other bounds are mentioned in the said commission, and both of them are in dispute with the government of the Massachusetts Bay.

3. As to the Constitution of the government, the supreme power here, is vested in the Governor and Council, (appointed by the King,) and a house of representatives, (chosen by the people,) who make laws, &c.

4. The trade of the province is lumber and fish. The number of shipping belonging to the province, are five, consisting of about five hundred tons ; and there are about three or four hundred tons of other shipping, that trade here (annually) not belonging to the province. The seafaring men, are about forty. The trade is much the same as it hath been, for some years past.

5. The province makes use of all sorts of British manufactures amounting to about five thousand pounds sterling, annually in value, which are had principally from Boston.

6. The trade of this province to other plantations is to the Caribbee Islands, whither we send lumber and fish, and receive for it rum, sugar, molasses and cotton ; and as to the trade from hence to Europe, it is to Spain, or Portugal, from whence our vessels bring home salt.

7. The method to prevent illegal trade is by a collector appointed at home.

8. The natural produce of the province is timber (of various kinds (viz.) (principally) oak, pine, hemlock, ash, beech and birch,) and fish, and they are the only commodity's of the place.

The timber is generally manufactured into beams, plank, knees, boards. clapboards, shingles and staves, and sometimes into house

frames, and the value of those commodity's annually exported from
hence to Europe and the West-India Islands, is about a thousand
pounds sterling. *Mem.* Besides what is above mentioned, the coast-
ing sloops from Boston, carry from hence thither in fish and timber,
about five thousand pounds per annum.

9. No mines are yet discovered, except a small quantity of Iron ore
in two or three places.

10. The number of inhabitants, men, women and children, are about
ten thousand whites, and two hundred blacks.

11. The inhabitants are increased about four thousand within this
few years last past, a thousand of which (at least,) are people from Ireland, lately come into, and settled within the province ; another reason
of the increase of late more than formerly, is a peace with the Indians
the four last years.

12. The militia are about eighteen hundred, consisting of two regiments of foot, with a troop of horse in each.

13. There is one fort or place of defence, called Fort William and
Mary, situate on the great Island in New-Castle which commands the
entrance of Pascataqua river, but is in poor low circumstances, much
out of repair, and greatly wanting of stores of war, there not being
one barrel of gun-powder, at this time in, or belonging to that garrison.

14. There are no Indians in this province now in time of peace, that
we know of.

15. There are no Indians in the neighborhood of this province that
we know of, except in the eastern parts of the province of the Massachusetts Bay, and what their number or strength is, we are not
acquainted.

16. We have no neighboring Spaniards, or other Europeans, except
the French, who, according to the best intelligence we can get, are extremely numerous and strong both at Canada and Cape-Breton.

17. The effect which the French settlements have on this province is,
that the Indians are frequently instigated and influenced by them to
disturb the peace and quiet of this province, we having been often put
to a vast expense both of blood and treasure, to defend ourselves against
their cruel outrages.

18. The revenue arising within this province is three hundred ninety
and six pounds, by excise, which is appropriated towards the Governor's
salary, and about three or four barrels of gun-powder, from the shipping,

which is spent at the fort. There is no other revenue, but by tax on polls and estates.

19. The ordinary expense of the government is about fifteen hundred pounds per annum, now in time of peace; the extraordinary and contingent charges, as repairs of the fort, powder, &c., are about five hundred pounds more.

20. The establishments are six hundred pounds per annum salary on the Governor, eight shillings per diem on each Councillor, and six shillings per diem on each Representative during the session of the general assembly, and a hundred and fifty pounds per annum on the officers, and soldiers at the fort. There is no other establishment civil or military within the government, but the general assembly make allowances from time to time as they see meet, to the Treasurer, Secretary, &c. The Judges, Justices, Sheriffs, Clerks, and all other officers' fees are fixed by a law to be paid by the parties and persons whom they serve, but they have nothing out of the treasury. All the officers, civil and military, hold their places by commission from the Governor, except the Councillors, appointed by the King; the Recorder of deeds, chosen by the general assembly, the Clerks of courts, nominated by the Judges of the said courts respectively, and Selectmen, Assessors, Constables, Tythingmen and other town officers, chosen by the towns, at their respective town meetings.

New-Hampshire Historical Society, *Collections* (Concord, 1824), I, 227–230.

———◆———

22. Affairs in Connecticut (1740–1758)

BY ROGER WOLCOTT (1759)

Wolcott's experience in the military and civil affairs of Connecticut, and his office as governor, make him an admirable source of information. — Bibliography: Tyler, *American Literature*, II, 44–46; Winsor, *Narrative and Critical History*, V, 163; Channing and Hart, *Guide*, § 130. — For previous Connecticut history, see *Contemporaries*, I, ch. xviii.

M R. PRESIDENT: You have several times moved me to write a *History of New England*, especially of *Conecticott*. I have told you I wanted both ability and materials. Since that two of the Councill have moved me to the same, or that at least I would write what hath fallen within my remembrance and observation.

This must needs be a lame thing, but choosing rather to appear weak than disobliging, I enclose you the following minit. . . .

In 1740, his present Majestie ordered an expedition against the Spanish West Indies to be comanded by the Lord Cathcart. Two companys were from Conecticut under Capt. Newberry and Capt. Siliman. They landed at Cartagene and took several forts. It was supposed the Spaniards bought the town of Cartagene. Most of the American forces dyed of sickness in this expedition. A hard winter closed the year.

In 1745, the New England governments made an expedition against Cape Breton under General Pepperill with an army of 3,700 men, which as the generall then told me during the siege of Louisbourg was reduced to 3100 valids. After a siege of forty-nine days, on the 17th of June the city with the islands of Cape Breton, St. Johns &c. was surrendered to the English : the French inhabitants were sent to France.

From the granting of the charter until 1747, the Governor and Deputy Governor were chosen and declared to be chosen, as well as the Assistants, if they had more votes for the office than any other person, but now some active men that were given to change fomented an opinion that the Governor nor Deputy Governor were not chosen unless they had more votes then all that were scattered among other persons. These men were of such activity and influence that in 1749 neither the Governor nor Deputy Governor could be declared chosen because not according to this standard, but since neither of them wanted but a few votes the Assembly elected them. Thus they were not blown down tho much shaken at the root. The freemen being acquainted by this that the greater part did not vote for the present Governor and Deputy Governor were prone to mischief : there was some reason for it tho' unknown to them, and made them attentive to be informed what it was. The opinion was kept up, but when it happened there was no choice according to this standard the Assembly elected those that had most votes, so there was no alteration made and the end of these schemers not answered as yet, nor like to be untill something farther was done.

In the beginning of 1754, emmisarys were very busie in spreading a report that the Governor had extracted vast sums of the supercargo of a Spanish ship put into New London by distress, and so embarassed the affair that the Colony was lyable to pay for the ship and cargo, and that the Governor had pleaded with the Assembly to tax the Colony for it. These reports were so imprest that in most towns they were discoursed of as certain facts. Tho this was a palpable breach of peace there was not a justice found to bear any testimony against it except the court at Litchfield.   Yea those very men that had approved the Governor's conduct in the Assembly now did nothing to assert the truth in his vindication.

At the next election the Governor was thrown down with a vengeance, and when down thought worthy of no more respect than a comon porter.

When he saw himself thus for future despised and hated by all as a betrayer of his trust and enemy to the Colony which had conferred so many honours upon him he found it a burden too heavie to be easie under.   He, therefore, complained to the Assembly that he was condemned unheard, and therefore petitioned that he might be examined upon oath concerning these facts before the Assembly, and submitted himself wholly to their censure, but the doors were shut against him. Yet after this election the aforesaid opinion for the choice of the Governor and Deputy Governor ceased like some other plagues that are periodical, and may it forever cease.

What one Governor suffers and another gains by an intrigue is of no great importance to the public, yet in my opinion it is best to let things proceed in their natural course and that our wise men did wisely to stop this opinion as foolish and dangerous, for according to the proverb What is bad for me may be bad for thee, by turns.

In the year 1755, an expedition was made against the French in North America under Gen^ll Shirly and General Johnson.   General Shirly did nothing but blunder.   Gen^ll Johnson beat the French at Lake George and erected a fort there.   Gen^ll Bradock was defeated and slain.

In 1756, the expedition was renewed, and by the misconduct of Gen^ll Shirly and Gen^ll Web the French took Oswego and our flotta on Ontario. The fort was demolished and the garrison led into captivity.

In 1757, Gen^ll Web lost Fort William Henry and our flotta on Lake George.   The garrison capitulated to before him, but the French suffered the Indians to murther many of them and strip and horribly abuse the rest.   The fort was demolished.

> Great Britain dost thou take delight
> To see America look chearly?
> Suspend us in no spider's *Web*
> And never more send us a *Shirley*.

In 1758, Gen^ll Amherst took Louisbourg, the islands of Cape Breton, St. Johns &c.   The inhabitants were sent to France.   Gen^ll Abercrombie

came off with loss and Carilong.   We took Fort Frontenac and in the
fall of the year Dequesne by Gen[ll] Forbs.

S[r]. Since it is upon your desire I have exposed myself by this mean
performance, I hope you will receive it with candour.   I have nothing
but my memory to depend upon, which in a man advanced to the
eighty-first year of his age is but a poor library.   Yet I am confident
the chronology and the facts are true and will be found so when inquired
into.

I have long wished for a History of New England and hoped Mr. Prince
his *Chronologie* would have laid a good foundation for it, but he has left
it unfinished.

This small mite cast into this treasury is my whole substance, and
if men of ability would out of their abundance cast in proportionally
we might have a good History of the Colony and of New England,
before it is too late to get materials.

I am &c.

R. WOLCOTT.

To Mr. President Clap.

Connecticut Historical Society, *Collections* (Hartford, 1895), III, 325–336
passim.

---

23. " Boston the Metropolis of North America "
(1750)

BY CAPTAIN FRANCIS GOELET

Goelet was a New York merchant, whose diary bears testimony to his lightness of
disposition and to the convivial habits of gentlemen of the time. — Bibliography :
Winsor, *Memorial History of Boston*, II, ch. xvi, notes. — For an earlier estimate
of Boston, see *Contemporaries*, I, No. 146.

BOSTON the Metropolis of North America Is Accounted The Largest
Town upon the Contenant, Haveing about Three Thousand Houses
in it, about two Thirds them Wooden Framed Clap Boarded &c. and
some of them Very Spacious Buildings which togeather with their Gardens
about them Cover a Great deal Ground they are for the most Part Two
and three Stories high mostly Sashd.   Their Brick Buildings are much
better and Stronger Built, more after the Modern Taste all Sashd and
Prety well Ornamented haveing Yards and Gardens Adjoyning Also.

The Streets are very Erregular the Main Streets are Broad and Paved with Stone the Cross Streets are but Narrow mostly Paved Except towards the Outskirts the Towne. The Towne Extends ab^t two Miles in Lenght North and South and is in some places $\frac{1}{2}$ mile and Others $\frac{3}{4}$ mile Broad has One Main Street Run^g the whole Length The Towne from North to South and Tolerable broad the Situation is Vastly Pleasant being on a Neck Land The Tide Flowing on Each Side that Part the Towne may be termed an Island, the water which Parts it from the Main Contenant is about 20 Foot Over with draw Bridges and where the Tide Runs very Strong trough. The Harbour is defended by a Strong Castle of a Hundred Guns Built upon An Island where the Shipping must pass by and within Hale its Situation is Extroardenary as it Commands on Every Side and is Well Built and kept in Exceeding Good Order. The Tyde in the Harbour Flows about 12 or 13 Foot Perpendicular at the Full and Change moon its Very Inconvenient for Loaded Vessells, as they have not more then 12 Foot water at the End the Long wharf, which wharf is noted the Longest in North America being near half an English Mile in Lenght and runs direct out. One side whereof is full of whare Houses from One End to the Other. The Bostoniers Build a Vast Numb^r Vessells for Sale from Small Sloops up to Topsail Vessells from a Hundred Tons to 3, 4 and 5 Hundred Tons, and are noted for Good Sailing Vessels, they Runn mostly upon keene Built and very strong Counted about 15 Saile upon Stocks, which they Launch in Cradills at the full and Change the Moon. This Place has about Twelve Meeting Houses and Three Curches which are all Very Indifferent Buildings of no manner of Architect but Very Plain at the North End they have a Ring of Bells, which are but Very Indifferent. They have but One Markett which is all Built of Brick about Eighty Foot Long and Arch'd on Both Sides being Two Stories heigh the upper part Sashd, which Comprehends Several The Publick Offices the Towne, at the Southermost End is the Naval Office The Middle The Surveyars the Marketts Offices They have Also a Town House Built of Brick, Situated in Kings Street, Its a very Grand Brick Building Arch'd all Round and Two Storie Heigh Sashd above, its Lower Part is always Open Designd as a Change, tho the Merchants in Fair weather make their Change in the Open Street at the Eastermost End, in the upper Story are the Councill and Assembly Chambers &c. it has a Neat Cupulo Sashd all round and which on rejoycing days is Elluminated, As to Government Boston is dependent and Subordinate to Englands for its Laws

&c. being a Kings Government.   The Governour is a Person appointed
from Home who Represents his Majesty.   The Governm^t Laws are
Compyld by the Councill and Great and General Assembly.   the Former Represents the House of Loards and the Latter the Commons, and
the Governour Signs them and then they Pass in a Law.   In Boston
they are very Strict Observers of the Sabath day and in Service times
no Persons are allow'd the Streets but Doctors if you are found upon
the Streets and the Constables meet you they Compell you to go either
to Curch or Meeton as you Chuse, also in Sweareing if you are Catcht
you must Pay a Crown Old Tenor for Every Oath being Convicted
thereof without farther dispute the $\frac{3}{4}$ths of the Inhabitants are Strict
Presbyterians.

Extracts from Capt. Francis Goelet's Journal, in *New-England Historical
and Genealogical Register* (Boston, 1870), XXIV, 62–63.

— ◆ —

24. "Overweening Prejudice in Favor of New England" (1775)

BY JOHN ADAMS

John Adams, schoolmaster, lawyer, public man, member of the Continental Congress,
diplomat, and later vice-president and president of the United States, was one of
the keenest observer of his time. — Bibliography: Channing and Hart, *Guide,* §§ 130,
136.

THERE is in the human breast a social affection which extends to
our whole species, faintly indeed, but in some degree.   The nation,
kingdom, or community to which we belong is embraced by it more
vigorously.   It is stronger still towards the province to which we belong, and in which we had our birth.   It is stronger and stronger as we
descend to the county, town, parish, neighborhood, and family, which
we call our own.   And here we find it often so powerful as to become
partial, to blind our eyes, to darken our understandings, and pervert
our wills.

It is to this infirmity in my own heart that I must perhaps attribute
that local attachment, that partial fondness, that overweening prejudice
in favor of New England, which I feel very often, and which, I fear,
sometimes leads me to expose myself to just ridicule.

New England has, in many respects, the advantage of every other colony in America, and, indeed, of every other part of the world that I know anything of.

1. The people are purer English blood ; less mixed with Scotch, Irish, Dutch, French, Danish, Swedish, etc., than any other ; and descended from Englishmen, too, who left Europe in purer times than the present, and less tainted with corruption than those they left behind them.

2. The institutions in New England for the support of religion, morals, and decency exceed any other ; obliging every parish to have a minister, and every person to go to meeting, etc.

3. The public institutions in New England for the education of youth, supporting colleges at the public expense, and obliging towns to maintain grammar schools, are not equaled, and never were, in any part of the world.

4. The division of our territory, that is, our counties, into townships ; empowering towns to assemble, choose officers, make laws, mend roads, and twenty other things, gives every man an opportunity of showing and improving that education which he received at college or at school, and makes knowledge and dexterity at public business common.

5. Our law for the distribution of intestate estates occasions a frequent division of landed property, and prevents monopolies of land.

But in opposition to these we have labored under many disadvantages. The exorbitant prerogative of our Governors, etc., which would have overborne our liberties if it had not been opposed by the five preceding particulars.

Charles Francis Adams, editor, *Familiar Letters of John Adams and his Wife* (New York, 1876), 120–121.

CHAPTER IV — MIDDLE COLONIES

25. Pennsylvania, the Poor Man's Paradise (1698)

BY GABRIEL THOMAS

Gabriel Thomas, one of the most sprightly and individual of colonial writers, labored for seventeen years to build up the Quaker settlements in America. — Bibliography: Tyler, *American Literature*, II, 228–229; Winsor, *Narrative and Critical History*, V, 242–245; Channing and Hart, *Guide*, § 108. — For previous Pennsylvania history, see *Contemporaries*, I, ch. xxiv.

AND now for their Lots and Lands in City and Countrey, in their great Advancement since they were first laid out, which was within the compass of about Twelve Years, that which might have been bought for Fifteen or Eighteen Shillings, is now sold for Fourscore Pounds in ready Silver; and some other Lots, that might have been then Purchased for Three Pounds, within the space of Two Years, were sold for a Hundred Pounds a piece. . . .

Now the true Reason why this Fruitful Countrey and Florishing City advance so considerably in the Purchase of Lands both in the one and the other, is their great and extended Traffique and Commerce both by Sea and Land, *viz.* to *New-York, New-England, Virginia, Mary-Land, Carolina, Jamaica, Barbadoes, Nevis, Monserat, Antego*, St. *Cristophers, Barmudoes, New-Found-Land, Maderas, Saltetudeous*, and *Old-England*; besides several other places. Their Merchandize chiefly consists in *Horses, Pipe-Staves, Pork* and *Beef* Salted and Barrelled up, *Bread*, and *Flower*, all sorts of Grain, *Pease, Beans, Skins, Furs, Tobacco*, or *Pot-Ashes, Wax*, &c. which are Barter'd for *Rumm, Sugar, Molasses, Silver, Negroes, Salt, Wine, Linen, Houshold-Goods*, &c.

However, there still remain Lots of Land both in the aforesaid City and Country, that any may Purchase almost as cheap as they could at the first Laying out or Parcelling of either City or Country. . . .

. . . the Countrey at the first, laying out, was void of Inhabitants (except the Heathens, or very few Christians not worth naming) and not many People caring to abandon a quiet and easie (at least tolerable) Life in their Native Countrey (usually the most agreeable to all Mankind) to seek out a new hazardous, and careful one in a Foreign Wilderness or Desart Countrey, wholly destitute of Christian Inhabitants, and even to arrive at which, they must pass over a vast Ocean, expos'd to some Dangers, and not a few Inconveniencies : But now all those Cares, Fears and Hazards are vanished, for the Countrey is pretty well Peopled, and very much Improv'd, and will be more every Day, now the Dove is return'd with the Olive-branch of Peace in her Mouth.

I must needs say, even the Present Encouragements are very great and inviting, for Poor People (both Men and Women) of all kinds, can here get three times the Wages for their Labour they can in *England* or *Wales*.

I shall instance in a few, which may serve ; nay, and will hold in all the rest. The first was a *Black-Smith*, (my next Neighbour) who himself and one Negro Man he had, got Fifty Shillings in one Day, by working up a Hundred Pound Weight of Iron, which at Six Pence *per* Pound (and that is the common Price in that Countrey) amounts to that Summ. . . .

. . . *Felt-Makers* will have for their Hats Seven Shillings a piece, such as may be bought in *England* for Two Shillings a piece ; yet they buy their *Wooll* commonly for Twelve or Fifteen Pence *per* Pound. And as to the *Glaziers*, they will have Five Pence a Quarry for their Glass. The Rule for the *Coopers* I have almost forgot ; but this I can affirm of some who went from *Bristol*, (as their Neighbours report) that could hardly get their Livelihoods there, are now reckon'd in *Pensilvania*, by a modest Computation to be worth some Hundreds, (if not Thousands) of Pounds. The *Bakers* make as White Bread as any in *London*, and as for their Rule, it is the same in all Parts of the World that I have been in. . . .

Of *Lawyers* and *Physicians* I shall say nothing, because this Countrey is very Peaceable and Healty ; long may it so continue and never have occasion for the Tongue of the one, nor the Pen of the other, both equally destructive to Mens Estates and Lives ; besides forsooth, they, Hang-Man like, have a License to Murder and make Mischief. *Labouring-Men* have commonly here, between 14 and 15 Pounds a Year, and their Meat, Drink, Washing and Lodging ; and by the Day their Wages is generally between Eighteen Pence and Half a Crown, and Diet also ; But in Harvest they have usually between Three and Four Shilling each Day, and Diet. The *Maid Servants Wages* is commonly betwixt Six and Ten Pounds *per Annum*, with very good Accommodation. And for the *Women* who get their Livelihood by their own Industry, their Labour is very dear, for I can buy in *London* a Cheese-Cake for Two Pence, bigger than theirs at that price when at the same time their Milk is as cheap as we can buy it in *London*, and their Flour cheaper by one half.

Corn and Flesh, and what else serves Man for Drink, Food and Rayment, is much cheaper here than in *England*, or elsewhere ; but the chief reason why Wages of Servants of all sorts is much higher here than there, arises from the great Fertility and Produce of the Place ; besides, if these large Stipends were refused them, they would quickly set up for themselves, for they can have Provision very cheap, and Land for a very small matter, or next to nothing in comparison of the Purchace of Lands in *England* ; and the Farmers there, can better afford to give that great Wages than the Farmers in *England* can, for several Reasons very obvious.

As First, their Land costs them (as I said but just now) little or nothing in comparison, of which the Farmers commonly will get twice the encrease of Corn for every Bushel they sow, that the Farmers in *England* can from the richest Land they have.

In the Second place, they have constantly good price for their Corn, by reason of the great and quick vent into *Barbadoes* and other Islands ; through which means *Silver* is become more plentiful than here in *England*, considering the Number of People, and that causes a quick Trade for both Corn and Cattle ; and that is the reason that Corn differs now from the Price formerly, else it would be at half the Price it was at then ; for a Brother of mine (to my own particular knowledge) sold within the compass of one Week, about One Hundred and Twenty fat Beasts, most of them good handsom large Oxen.

Thirdly, They pay no *Tithes*, and their *Taxes* are inconsiderable ; the Place is free for all Persuasions, in a Sober and Civil way ; for the Church of *England* and the *Quakers* bear equal Share in the Government. They live Friendly and Well together ; there is no Persecution for Religion, nor ever like to be ; 'tis this that knocks all Commerce on the Head, together with high Imposts, strict Laws, and cramping Orders. Before I end this Paragraph, I shall add another Reason why Womens Wages are so exorbitant ; they are not yet very numerous, which makes them stand upon high Terms for their several Services, in *Sempstering, Washing, Spinning, Knitting, Sewing,* and in all the other parts of their Imployments ; for they have for Spinning either Worsted or Linen, Two Shillings a Pound, and commonly for Knitting a very Course pair of Yarn Stockings, they have half a Crown a pair ; moreover they are usually Marry'd before they are Twenty Years of Age, and when once in that Noose, are for the most part a little uneasie, and make their Husbands so too, till they procure them a Maid Servant to bear the burden of the Work, as also in some measure to wait on them too. . . .

Reader, what I have here written, is not a *Fiction, Flam, Whim,* or any sinister *Design,* either to impose upon the Ignorant, or Credulous, or to curry Favour with the Rich and Mighty, but in meer Pity and pure Compassion to the Numbers of Poor Labouring Men, Women, and Children in *England,* half starv'd, visible in their meagre looks, that are continually wandering up and down looking for Employment without finding any, who here need not lie idle a moment, nor want due Encouragement or Reward for their Work, much less Vagabond or Drone it about. Here are no Beggars to be seen (it is a Shame and Disgrace to the State that there are so many in *England*) nor indeed have any here the least Occasion or Temptation to take up that Scandalous Lazy Life. . . .

What I have deliver'd concerning this *Province,* is indisputably true, I was an Eye-Witness to it all, for I went in the first Ship that was bound from *England* for that Countrey, since it received the Name of *Pensilvania,* which was in the Year 1681. The Ship's Name was the *John* and *Sarah* of *London, Henry Smith* Commander. I have declin'd giving any Account of several things which I have only heard others speak of, because I did not see them my self, for I never held that way infallible, to make Reports from *Hear-say.* I saw the first Cellar when it was digging for the use of our Governour *Will. Penn.*

Gabriel Thomas, *An Historical and Geographical Account of the Province and Country of Pensilvania,* etc. (London, 1698), 23-45 *passim.*

———◆———

26. Proposal to Unite the two Jerseys (1701)

BY THE LORDS COMMISSIONERS FOR TRADE AND PLANTATIONS

This piece was prepared by the heads of the Colonial Office in London (commonly called the "Lords of Trade"). Their organization is set forth in *Contemporaries,* I, No. 54, and No. 46 below. — Bibliography: Channing and Hart, *Guide,* § 106. — For previous accounts of New Jersey, see *Contemporaries,* I, ch. xxv.

IN obedience to your excellencies commands, signified to us by Mr. Yard, upon several papers laid before your excellencies, relating to the state of his majesty's provinces of East and West-Jersey, in

America : We have considered all the said papers, together with others of the like nature, that were already in our hands ; and having likewise heard what the proprietors and others had to offer ; we thereupon most humbly report to your excellencies,

That those countries which are now known by the name of East and West New-Jersey, were granted, together with several other territories, by king Charles the second, by letters patents, bearing date the 12th day of March, 1664, to the then duke of York, his heirs and assigns. . . .

That the said duke of York did thereupon grant, convey and assign, the said provinces, (by the names of Nova-Cæsaria or New-Jersey) to John lord Berkeley and sir George Carteret, their heirs and assigns, with all and every the appurtenances thereto belonging, in as full and ample manner as the same was granted to him, by the aforesaid letters patents of king Charles the second.

That his said majesty king Charles the second, by other letters patents, dated the 29th of June, 1674, did again grant and convey to the said duke of York, all the said lands and territories, in the same manner as before expressed ; and that several sub-divisions and sales, having in the mean while been made by the said lord Berkeley, sir George Carteret, and others claiming under them ; he the said duke of York, did, by indenture, dated the 6th day of August, 1680, grant and confirm the province of West New-Jersey, with all the appurtenances thereunto belonging, to Edward Byllinge, of Westminster, gent. in whom the title thereunto then was, and to his heirs and assigns forever ; and did in like manner, by indenture, dated the 14th day of March, 1682, grant and confirm the province of East New-Jersey, with all the appurtenances thereto belonging, to James Earl of Perth, William Penn, esq ; and several other persons, in whom the title to the same then was. . . .

That the present proprietors, who derive their respective titles to their several shares and proportions of the soil of these provinces, by several mean conveyances, from and under the aforementioned grants to Edward Byllinge, and to the Earl of Perth, and other persons to whom the duke of York had immediately conveyed the same ; do in like manner, and by virtue of divers such mean conveyances, claim the same powers and rights of government as were granted by king Charles the second, to the duke of York ; and by him to others, according to the tenor of the aforesaid indentures.

That nevertheless, we do not find, that any sufficient form of government has ever been settled in those provinces, either by the duke of

York, or by those claiming under him, as aforesaid; but that many inconveniencies and disorders having arisen from their pretence of right to govern. The proprietors of East New-Jersey, did surrender their said pretended right to the late king James, in the month of April 1688; which was accordingly accepted by him.

That since his majesty's accession to the crown, the proprietors both of East and West New-Jersey, have continued to challenge the same right as before; and did in the year 1697, apply themselves to us, in order to their obtaining his majesty's approbation of the person whom they desired to have continued governor of the said provinces, but at the same time refused to enter into security to his majesty, pursuant to the address of the right honourable the house of lords, of the 18th of March, 1696, that the person so presented by them the said proprietors, should duly observe and put in execution, the acts of trade; yet nevertheless proceeded, from time to time, to commissionate whom they thought fit, to be governor of those provinces, without his majesty's approbation; according to what is required by the late act, for preventing frauds and regulating abuses in the plantation trade.

That in this manner having formerly commissionated col. Andrew Hamilton, afterwards mr. Jeremiah Basse; then again superceding their commission to mr. Basse, and renewing or confirming that to col. Hamilton; and ever since that also, some of them having sent another commission to one capt. Andrew Bown: The inhabitants sensible of the defect and insufficiency of all those commissions, for want of his majesty's authority, have upon several occasions, some of them opposed one of those governors, some another, according as interest, friendship, or faction had inclined them.

That the inhabitants of East New-Jersey, in a petition to his majesty, the last year, complained of several grievances they lay under, by the neglect or mismanagement of the proprietors of that province or their agents, as particularly, that from the latter end of June 1689, till about the latter end of August 1692 (which was a time of actual war) they had not taken any manner of care about the government thereof. . . .

That it has been represented to us, by several letters, memorials, and other papers, as well from the inhabitants as proprietors of both those provinces, that they are at present in confusion and anarchy; and that it is much to be apprehended, lest by the heats of the parties that are amongst them, they should fall into such violences as may endanger the lives of many persons, and destroy the colony.

That the greatest number of the proprietors of both those provinces residing in this city, being hereby sensible of the necessity of his majesty's authority, for the preserving of peace and good order in those countries, have lately presented a petition to your excellencies; in the preamble whereof, though they still seem to assert their title to the government of the said provinces; yet nevertheless in the end, declare they have agreed, and are ready to surrender the same to his majesty, upon such terms and conditions as are requisite for preservation of their properties and civil interests. . . .

That the proprietors of East New-Jersey, residing there, have signed and sent over hither, to a gentleman whom they have constituted their agent and attorney in that behalf, an absolute and unconditioned surrender of their right to the government of that province, so far as the same is in them, and so far as they are capable of doing it for others concerned with them in that propriety. . . .

Upon all which, we humbly represent unto your excellencies, that not being satisfied, that the aforementioned grants from the duke of York, (the only title upon which the said proprietors claim a right to government) without any direct and immediate authority from the crown, were or could be of any validity to convey that right, (which we have been informed is a power unalienable from the person to whom it is granted, and not to be assigned by him unto any other; much less divided, sub-divided, and conveyed from one to another, as has been done in the present case) We did thereupon humbly represent to his majesty, the 18th of April, 1699, that a tryal might be had in Westminster-Hall, upon a feigned issue, whereby their claim to the right of government, might receive a determination.

That no such determination having yet been made, nor any proceedings (that we know of) had, upon the forementioned surrender; but it being generally acknowledged, both by the inhabitants and proprietors of the aforesaid provinces, that the disorder and confusion they are now fallen into, are so great, that the publick peace and administration of justice is interrupted and violated; and that whilst those disorders continue, there neither is, nor possibly can be, any due provision made, for the guard and defence of that country, against an enemy, we are humbly of opinion, that it is very expedient for the preservation of those territories to the crown of England, and for securing the private interest of all persons concerned, that his majesty would be pleased to constitute a governor over those provinces, by his immediate commission; which together with the instructions, to be also given to the said governor, may contain such powers, authorities and directions, as may be necessary for the establishing there a regular constitution of government, by a governor, council, and general assembly, with other civil and military officers ; and for securing to the proprietors and inhabitants, all their properties and civil rights, in as full and ample manner, as the like are enjoyed by any plantation, under governors appointed by his majesty's immediate commission ; together with such clauses and further provisions, as may be thought reasonable, in order to prevent the interfering of that colony with the interest of his majesty's other plantations; as the proprietary governments in America have generally done.

Samuel Smith, *The History of the Colony of Nova-Cæsaria, or New-Jersey* (Burlington, New Jersey, 1765), Appendix, 566–570 *passim*.

———————◆———————

27. The Separation of Delaware (1703)

BY SECRETARY JAMES LOGAN (1709)

James Logan acted as secretary and agent for William Penn during the many years in which the proprietor was absent from his colony. — Bibliography: Tyler, *American Literature*, II, 233–235; Winsor, *Narrative and Critical History*, V, 208–209; Channing and Hart, *Guide*, § 108. — For previous accounts of Delaware, see *Contemporaries*, I, ch. xxiv.

HENRY GOLDNEY,   Philadelphia, 3d Month the 12th, 1709.
      Esteemed Friend,

I WAS favored last fall with thine and other Friends' answer to mine of 3d month last ; the contents of which were extremely satisfactory, and, on my part, I shall not be wanting to discharge my duty to the utmost of my power. . . .

I now design, through the greatest confidence in thy friendship both to him and me, to be very free with thee in an affair that nearly concerns him and this country in general, in which I shall request thee to exercise thy best thoughts, and, according to the result of these, heartily to employ the necessary endeavours. The case is briefly as follows ;

This government has consisted of two parts ; the Province of Pennsylvania, and the Three Lower Counties on Delaware. To the first the proprietor has a most clear and undoubted right, both for soil and government, by the King's letters patent or royal charter ; for the latter he has much less to show ; for the soil he has deeds of feofment from the Duke of York, but for the government not so much as is necessary. After his first arrival, however, in these parts, he prevailed with the people both of the province and those counties to join in one government under him, according to the powers of the King's charter, which nevertheless extended to the province only, and so they continued, not without many fractions, till after the time of his last departure, when some disaffected persons took advantage of a clause, which he had unhappily inserted in a charter he gave the people, and broke off entirely from those lower counties ; since which time we have had two assemblies, that of the province, acting by a safe and undisputed power, but that of the other counties without sufficient (I doubt) to justify them. Last fall the assembly of those counties took occasion to inquire into their own powers, upon a design to set new measures on foot, and have sent home an address by one of their members, Thomas Coutts's brother, who is to negotiate the matter with the Lords of Trade and the ministry, to obtain powers to some person or other, who the Queen may think fit (though Coutts designs it for himself), to discharge all the necessary duties of government over them.   This, I doubt, will give the proprietary great trouble ; for when the Council of Trade is fully apprized, as by this means they will be, that those counties are entirely disjoined from the province, it is probable they may more strictly inquire into the proprietor's right of government and legislation with the people there ; and it is much to be feared, that they may advise the Queen to dispose of the government of those parts some other way, which would be exceedingly destructive to the interest of the province in general. . . .

Upon the whole, what I have to propose is this, whether it would not be most advisable for the proprietor to consider in time what measures are most fit for him to take for his own and the country's interest, before the blow falls so heavy that it may prove difficult, if at all practicable, for him to ward it off; whether, therefore, it may not be most prudent to part with the government of both province and lower counties together, upon the best terms that can be obtained, before it proves too late for him to procure any.   If he should hold the government of the province, nay even of the whole, during his life, he will never gain any thing by it ; and, after his decease, it will be lost, or at least be put out of the hands of Friends, and perhaps without any previous terms at all, when now he may be capable himself to negotiate a surrender, both to his own particular interest, and greatly to the advantage of the profession ; but, whenever this is done, he should remember our present lieutenant-governor, who will be a sufferer (I fear, at best) by undertaking the charge ; and, if any thing fall of course in the way, I wish he would not quite forget an old trusty servant of his, who has been drudging for him these ten years ; (but that is not the business.) This I thought necessary to advise thee of, considering thee as one of his best and heartiest friends, and desire thee to communicate the matter to such others as may be most serviceable, but by no means expose this letter, for I would have that kept very private.

I have wrote to the same purpose to the proprietary himself very fully ; but finding, by long experience, how little it avails to write to himself alone of matters relating to his own interest, I now choose this method, and give this early notice before the addresses from hence shall come to hand, which, with the address already gone from the lower counties, will certainly do our business, whether the proprietor will agree to it or not, and therefore best take time while it offers. I shall commit this to thy prudence and discretion, and conclude,

Thy real loving friend.
James Logan.

Benjamin Franklin, *Works* (edited by Jared Sparks, Boston, 1836), III, 573–575 *passim*.

---

28.   Philadelphia, "a Noble, Large, and Populous City" (1710)

BY "RICHARD CASTELMAN, GENT."

This account is appended to the early editions of *The Voyages and Adventures of Captain Robert Boyle*, the authorship of which is variously attributed to W. R. Chetwood, Benjamin Victor, and Daniel Defoe. Castelman's account, however, bears marks of authenticity. — Bibliography : Winsor, *Narrative and Critical History*, V, 249. — For previous accounts of Philadelphia, see *Contemporaries*, I, Nos. 161, 163.

THERE are many large, beautiful, well-built Towns in the Province of *Pensylvania*, of which, as I said before, *Philadelphia* is the chief. It is a noble, large, and populous City, standing on as much Ground as our *English* City of *Bristol*, seated upon a Neck of Land form'd by the Rivers *Delaware* and the *Schuylkill*, both navigable many Leagues above the City. It is built square in Form of a Chess-Board, with each Front facing one of the Rivers.

There are several Streets near two Mile long, as wide as *Holborn*, and better built, after the *English* Manner.   The chief are *Broad-street*, *King-street*, and *High-street*, tho' there are several other handsome Streets that take their Names from the Productions of the Country ; as *Mulberry*, *Walnut*, *Beech*, *Sassafras*, *Cedar*, *Vine*, *Ash*, and *Chesnut Streets*.   From these Streets run great Numbers of Courts, Yards, and Allies, with well-built Houses in 'em.   There are several Coves and Docks where large Ships are built ; and by a moderate Computation, there has been launch'd from the Stocks of this City in forty Year, near 300 Sail of Ships, besides Small-Craft, which may in some sort give us an Idea of the Opulency of the Place.   Many of their Merchants keep their Coaches, and the Tradesmens Shops and Streets are well frequented. All Religions are tolerated here, which is one Means to increase the Riches of the Place.   The People of the Church of *England* as by Law establish'd, have a neat, well-built Church, founded in the Year 1695, and I am inform'd the Foundation is laid for another.   The *Quakers* (who are the major Part of the Inhabitants) have several Meetings. There is a *Swedish* reform'd Church, Mr. *Rudman* the Incumbent, a Man of singular Learning and Piety ; who is as much follow'd by the *Quakers*, when he preaches, as the *Protestants*.   I shall beg leave to give one Instance of his Humility and Piety.   When Subscriptions were taking in to build the Church, he subscrib'd a considerable Sum ; but when call'd upon for the Money, he had it not in his Power to pay it ; yet to keep his Word, he contracted with the Master-Builder for so much a-day, to carry the Hod, till he had work'd his Subscription-Money out.   This was an Instance of his Piety and Zeal for Religion ; and I fancy if Churches were to be built after the same Manner in a certain Island, the Work would go but slowly on.   There are single Houses upon the Key that have cost 6000 *l.* the Building.   Mr. *Badcock*'s Brew-house is a noble, large Building, and has in it one single Vessel that will hold eight Ton of Liquor.

In this City is held the Courts of the Province, and the Assembly meet here, which is in the nature of a dependant Parliament, as in those Cities of *France* that are distant from the Capital.   There are three Fairs in the Year, and every Week two Markets.   In time of the Fairs the City is so throng'd, as well as the adjacent Plantations, that it is hard to find a Lodging. . . .

. . . The Number of the Inhabitants is generally suppos'd to be upwards of 15000, besides Slaves.   There is hardly any Trade in *England* but the same may be met with in *Philadelphia* ; and every Mechanick has better Wages ; a Journeyman Taylor has twelve Shillings a Week, besides his Board ; and every other Trade in Proportion has the same Advantage.

There is a Post-Office lately erected, which goes to *Boston* in *New-England, Charles-town* in *Carolina*, and the other neighbouring Places. The uncultivated Ground, which is not grubb'd, sells for ten times the Value it did at first ; though there is none of that sort within ten Miles round the City : And that within the Neighbourhood that was sold for ten Pound at first, will fetch above three hundred now. All Women's Work is very dear there, and that proceeds from the smallness of the Number, and the Scarcity of Workers ; for even the meanest single Women marry well there, and being above Want are above Work. The Proprietor of this fine Country (as I said before) is *William Pen*, Esq ; who has a fine Seat call'd Pensbury, built on three Islets, if I may so call 'em ; for a Branch of the River *Delaware* runs thrice round it. . . .

In the Heat of the Day I sometimes took a Walk with some of the Town to *Fair Mount,* a pleasant Place shaded with Trees on the River *Schuylkill.* . . .

I continu'd at *Philadelphia* near four Months, and was very well entertain'd by the Gentlemen of the Place : I am pleas'd I have it in my Power to pay 'em my publick Acknowledgment of Thanks for all their Favours ; particularly the Reverend Mr. *Brooks,* whom I met with by Chance at *Philadelphia* : His Business there was to raise Subscriptions for a new Church near *New-York* : When he heard of my Misfortunes, he was so generous and charitable as to offer to lend me a Sum of Money he had in his Hands, upon my bare Word only, which I was to return to him from *England* by the Society for Propagating the Gospel in Foreign Parts. As I was not in want of it, I did not accept his intended Favour, but I shall ever gratefully remember his kind Intentions.

I must not forget the many Obligations I had the Honour to receive from his Excellency Governor *Evans,* nor Mr. *Evans* the Commissary, who was particularly civil to me. These Gentlemen, tho' of the same Name, are no otherwise related than by marrying the Daughters of Mr. *Moor,* the Collector of the King's Customs. The Commissary is just gone for *Philadelphia* again, having been in *England* near a Twelvemonth, about an Affair between the present Governor Sir *William Keith* and him, relating to the King's Customs. Among the rest of my Friends, I must not forget the facetious Mr. *Staples,* Dancing-Master, who was the first Stranger of *Philadelphia* that did me the Honour of a Visit, and to his merry Company I owe the passing of many a dull Hour, that probably might have lain heavy upon the Hands of a Man under my Circumstances, depriv'd of Fortune, in a strange Country, having no Friends, in whose Power it was to assist me, nearer than *England*; for Mr. *Jones* was too much involv'd in his own troublesome Affairs at *Bermuda*, to expect any thing from him.   But the Generosity of the *Philadelphians* is rooted in their Natures ; for it is the greatest Crime among them not to show the utmost Civility to Strangers : And if I were oblig'd to live out of my native Country, I should not be long puzzled in finding a Place of Retirement, which should be *Philadelphia*.   There the oppress'd in Fortune or Principles may find a happy *Asylum*, and drop quietly to their Graves without Fear or Want.

The Voyage, Shipwrack, and Miraculous Escape of Richard Castelman, Gent. (appended to *The Voyages and Adventures of Captain Robert Boyle*, London, 1726), 363-369 *passim*.

———◆———

29. The Settlement of the Palatine Germans in New York (1709–1720)

BY JOHN CONRAD WYSER AND OTHER PALATINES

Wyser (or Weiser) was a German, a leader of his countrymen. The Palatines came from the " Pfalz," in the middle Rhine valley, and were forced to emigrate by the miseries of the wars of Louis XIV of France. — Bibliography : Channing and Hart, *Guide*, § 105. — For a previous account of German immigration, see *Contemporaries*, I, No. 163.

THE Case of the Palatines, and others Germans, in the Province of New York in America sheweth.

That, In the year 1709. The Palatines, & other Germans, being invited to come into England about Four Thousand of them were sent into New York in America, of whom about 1700. Died on Board, or at their landing in that Province, by unavoidable sickness

That before they went on Board, they were promised, those remaining alive should have forty acres of Land, & Five pounds Not true vide sterling pr Head, besides Cloths, Tools, Utensils & other contract. necessaries, to Husbandry to be given at their arrival in America

That on their landing their they were quartered in Tents, & divided
No promise but   into six companies, having each a Captain of their own
allowance made.   Nation, with a promise of an allowance of fifteen Pounds
per annum to each commander

That afterwards they were removed on Lands belonging to Mr Living-
stone, where they erected small Houses for shelter during the winter
season

That in the Spring following they were ordered into the woods, to
make Pitch & Tar, where they lived about two years; But the country
not being fit to raise any considerable quantity of Naval Stores, They
were commanded to Build, to clear, & improve the ground, belonging to
a private person

That the Indians hav^g yielded to Her late Ma^ty of pious memory a
small Tract of Land called Schorie for the use of the Palatines, they in
fifteen days cleared a way of fifteen miles through the woods & settled
fifty Families therein

That in the following Spring the remainder of the said Palatines joined
utterlie false   the said fifty families so settled therein Shorie

But that country being too small for their encreasing families, they
Agt Acts not   were constrained to purchase some Neighbouring Land
knowen it   of the Indians for which they were to give Three hund^d
pieces of Eight

And having built small Houses, & Hutts there about one year after
the said purchase some gentelmen of Albani, declared to the Palatines,
that themselves having purchas^d the said country of Schorie of the Govr
of New York they would not permit them to live there, unless an agreement were also made with those of Albany; But that the Palatines having refused to enter into such an agreement, A Sheriff & some officers
were sent from Albany to seize one of their Captains, who being upon
his Guard; The Indians were animated against the Palatines; but these
found means to appease the Savages by giving them what they would of
their own substance.

That in the year 1717 the Governour of New York having summoned
the Palatines to appear at Albani, some of them being deputed went
thither accordingly, where they were told, that unless they did agree
with the Gentlemen of Albany, the Governor expected an order from
England to transport them to another place, And that he would send
twelve men to view their works & improvements to appraise the same &
then to give them the value thereof in money

But this not being done the Palatines to the number of about three Thousand, have continued to manure & to sew the Land   Fictions of that they might not be starved for want of Corn & food   Proprietors.

For which manuring the Gentlemen of Albani have   knows not. put in prison one man and one woman, & will not release them, unless they have suffic^t security of One Hundred Crowns for the former

Now in order that the Palatines may be preserved in the said Land of Schorie, which they have purchased of the Indians, or that they may be so settled in an adjoining Tract of Land, as to raise a necessary subsistance for themselves & their families, they have sent into England Three Persons one of whom is since dead humbly to lay their Case before His Maj^ty, not doubting but that in consideration of the Hardships they have suffered for want of a secure settlement, His Majestys Ministers and Council will compassionate those His faithful Subjects ;

Who, in the first year after their arrival willingly and cheerfully sent Three Hundred men to the expedition against Canada,   true. & afterwards to the Asistance of Albani which was threatened by the French and Indians, for which service they have never received One Penny tho' they were upon the Establishment of New York or New Jersey nor had they received one Penny of the five pounds per   not true head promised at their going on board from England Neither have their commanders received anything of the allowance of fifteen pounds per Annum, and tho' the arms they had given them at the Canada expedition which were by special order from Her late Majesty, to be left in their possession, have been taken from them, yet they are still ready to fight against all the enemies of His Mat^y & those countrys whenever there shall be occasion to shew their hearty endeav^rs for the prosperity of their generous Benefactors in England as well as in America

Therefore they hope from the Justice of the Right Hônble the Lords Commissioners of Trade and Plantations, to whom their Petition to their Excellencies the Lords Justices has been referred That they shall be so supported by their Lordships Report, as to be represented fit objects to be secured in the Land they now do inhabit or in some near adjoining lands remaining in the right of the Crown in the said Province of New York

                    And they shall ever pray as in duty bound &c
2 Aug: 1720.

E. B. O'Callaghan, editor, *Documents relative to the Colonial History of the State of New-York* (Albany, 1855), V, 553–555.

30. "Concerning the Riots & Insurrections in New Jersey" (1744–1748)

BY HIS MAJESTY'S COUNCIL IN NEW JERSEY

The Council was at the same time an executive and a judicial body, and also was one of the two legislative bodies. For the proceedings of a Council, see No. 64 below. — Bibliography: Channing and Hart, *Guide*, § 106.

A BRIEF STATE OF FACTS, concerning the Riots & Insurrections, in New Jersey & the Remedys, attempted, by the Government & the several Branches of the Legislature, to put an End to them, & to restore the Peace of the Province. . . .

By the Affidavits & Papers herein referred to, it will appear, That a Number of Evil minded Men (taking Advantage, of that divided & weak State of the Governm[t] of this Province, & of that Time of War & Rebellion in Gr. Br,) entred into a Combination, & Agreement, to obstruct the Course of legal Proceedings, & to protect themselves from His Maj[tys] known Officers, & from the Process of the Law, in every Case, let their Crimes be ever so high ; And, in Execution of this Scheme, it appears

That, on the 19th *Sept[r]* 1745 100. Men, armed with Clubs, Axes & Crow Bars, came, in a riotous & tumultuous Manner, to the Goal of the County of Essex, &, having broke it open took, from thence, One *Samuel Baldwin*, committed on an Action of Trespass wherein he had refused to give Bail, or enter an Appearance.

That, these riotous People, then, boasted of the great Numbers they could bring together, on any Occasion, & gave out many threatning Expressions ag[t] the Persons that sho[d] endeavour to punish them for this their Crime ; Saying, if any of them were taken, they would come to his Relief with twice the Number they then had, & bring with them 100 Indians.

Two Justices of Essex, with the Undersheriff, according to their Duty, made a Record on their View, ag[t] 27. of the Rioters, known to them, & many other Evil doers & Disturbers of the Kings Peace, to them unknown ; Which was returned into the Supream Court, & Process issued from thence ag[t] the Delinquents.

This Matter being layd before the late Gov[r] he was so justly apprehensive of the dangerous Consequences, of so open & notorious a Contempt of His Maj^{tys} Authority, & the Laws of the Land, that he thought, the Aid of the Legislature necessary to prevent them & therefore recommended, in the strongest Terms, to the then Assembly the granting such Aid, by his Speech to them on the 28. Sepr 1745 ; But, so it hapned, that the then Govr & the Assembly differed in Opinion as to that Matter. . . .

On the 15th of Jan^ry 1745, the Sheriff of Essex, by Vertue of the Gov^rs s^d Warrant, & in Obedience to the Process of the Supreme Court, issued upon the s^d Record, arrested & took *Robt. Young, Thos. Sarjant*, & *Nehemiah Baldwin*, three of the Persons that stood convicted, by the Record of View before ment^d. On the 16th of Jan^ry as he was carrying the s^d Baldwin before One of the Justices of the Supreme Court, agreeable to the Commands of the Gov^rs Warrant, he, & the People whom he had called to his Assistance were assaulted, by a great Number of Men, armed with Clubs & other Weapons, who, in a most violent Manner, rescued & carryed away, the Prisoner, notwithstanding all the Sheriff & his Officers could do to prevent it. The Sheriff then returned to the Goal, in Order to Secure the other two Prisoners, & being Colonel of the Militia, he had posted a Guard, of 30. Men, at the Goal armed with Firelocks for that Purpose.

It appears that, at 2 o'clock in the Afternoon, great Numbers of People came together in a riotous & tumultuous manner in the Town of Newark, that they pay'd no Regard to the Commands of the Magistrates to disperse, or to the Procl^n made to them in the Kings Name, according to the Statute of the 1st of George, but continued together.

It appears that Coll Chetwood sent two Captains, who had the Command of the Newark Companys, with their Drums, to the People, so assembled who, accordingly went, & required those Men that belonged to their Companys, to follow the Drums, but none regarded those Commands.

It appears that one *Amos Roberts*, a principal leading Man among these Common Disturbers, at that Time, mounted his Horse, & called out, *Those who are upon my List follow me*, Which all, or the greatest Part, accordingly did, being then about 300. in Number.

It appears that, the s^d Roberts & his Accomplices, met & armed, as before, came to the Goal in a violent Manner, & having beat & broke thro' the Guard, & *struck the Sheriff* several Blows, they broke open the Goal Doors, & took from thence the two Prisoners above mentioned, & one other, confined for Debt, & then, they gave it out, that if they had stayed till the next Day, they should have had three Times the Numbers.

G

Upon this *second* Riot, the Sheriff & those Justices, then present, made a *Record* thereof, on their own View, ag.ᵗ the s.ᵈ *Roberts & 57. Others* by Name, Inhabitants of the Countys of *Essex* & *Morris*, & Others, to them unknown, to the Number of 300, at the least. . . .

The Gent.ⁿ of the Co.ˡˡ considering that most of the People concerned in the s.ᵈ Riots, are an ignorant People, & greatly imposed on, by a few wicked & designing Men, conceiving that a *Gen.ˡ Pardon*, for the Crimes past, together with the s.ᵈ Riot Act, wo.ᵈ be the easiest & most effectual Method, to restore & secure the Peace of the Province, & knowing that Mercy to Criminals, ought to flow from the Crown, Some of them, therefore, interceded with the then Gov.ʳ to grant a *Gen.ˡ Pardon*, w'ch he seemed inclinable to do. . . .

By Affid.ᵗˢ taken *May* 3.ᵈ & 8.ᵗʰ 1746, It appears that the Infection of the Riots was spreading into West Jersey ; For that the People settled on that Hundred thousand Acre Tract, in the County of Hunterdon, belonging to those Proprietors in & abo.ᵗ London, called the West New Jersey Society, within a fortnight then last past, had two great Meetings, in Order to stand by One Another in Defence of their Poss'ions ag.ᵗ the s.ᵈ Prop.ʳˢ (tho' by the Paper C. N.ᵒ 8, it appears that those People do own the Societys Title to that Tract, & that they themselves had no Pretence of Right to the same ; That they had agreed to a Paper, for that Purpose, & about 70. had signed it, at their Meeting on the 26.ᵗʰ Day of April ; That an Article was, That if any Person, seated on the s.ᵈ Tract, sho.ᵈ refuse to sign that Paper, he sho.ᵈ be dispossesed, by the Rest, & his Improvem.ᵗ sold, by them to the highest Bidder, That sundry People, from Newark, & Eliz.ᵃ Town, were reported to have been present at the last of those Meetings, That, about Ten or a Dozen of them observed to be riding, continually, backwards & forwards, to & from Newark, Elizabeth Town & Cohanzey, where the Society have other Lands, & it was believed in Order to unite all, in One Combination. . . .

By these appear, *Designs formed* by the same Rioters for turning *many other* People out of Poss'ion by Force.   It appears that they had *erected Courts* of Judicature, & *determined Causes*, by hearing One Side, but intended for the future, to hear both Sides ; That they had taken upon them to Choose their *Militia Officers*.   By these appears how they buoy themselves up, with their Numbers, Friends & Strength, not only in New Jersey, but in New York, Long Island, Penilv.ᵃ & New England ; and that they are not afraid of any Thing the Governm.ᵗ can do to them ; And give out that, from their Numbers, Violences & unlawful Actions, its to be inferred that, surely they are wronged & oppressed, or else they would never *rebell ag.ᵗ the Laws*. By these appears Information, That the People on the Societys Tract, had made a firm Agreement, to defend all their Farms there by Mobb, and that *Maidenhead*, & great Numbers of others, had joyned in firm Engagements to stand by one another to Death, tho' they have no Pretence to any Right but Poss'ion & Improvem.ᵗ And that they were resolved sho.ᵈ they be opposed by Fire Arms, to take up Fire Arms to defend theirselves That they would not mind either the Gov.ʳ or the King himself, if of a different Way of thinking from them ; And that the King himself was unable to quell Mobs in England, any other Way than by granting their Desires. . . .

By these it appears, that the Rioters had formed a Design of coming to *Burlington* (where the sev.ˡ Branches of the Legislature are sitting) in a Body on the 16ᵗʰ *Day of December*, & that Advertisements, to give Notice of that Design to the Rioters, had been set up, in sundry Places, requiring their Attendance, for that Purpose.

The Co.ˡˡ & Assembly, on Notice of that Design, in a free Conference, agreed to make Resolves of their sev.ˡ Houses ag.ᵗ it, & to send them to the Sheriffs of the sev.ˡ Countys, from & thro' which, the Rioters were likely to come, to publish, Which was accordingly done, And we have been credibly informed, that many of the Rioters were on their Way, coming, but, on Notice of s.ᵈ Resolves, returned. . . .

On the 18ᵗʰ *of Feb'ry* 1747, His Exc.ʸ gave his Assent to two Acts that had before been past by the Co.ˡˡ & Assembly viz.ᵗ An Act for the *suppressing & preventing of Riots, Tumults & other Disorders*, within this Colony, by w'ch Penaltys or Imprisonm.ᵗˢ are enacted to be inflicted upon Persons that shall be guilty of any of the like Disturbance for the future, & ano.ʳ Act intitled, An Act for avoiding Actions of Slander & for Stay of Proceedings until the 1ˢᵗ Day of Octo.ʳ 1748, in other Civil Actions ag.ᵗ the late Rioters. . . .

The Day before, to witt, the 17ᵗʰ *Day of Feb'ry* 1747, His Ex.ᶜʸ the Gov.ʳ passed His Maj.ᵗʸˢ most gracious Pardon, Entitled, An Act to *pardon* the Persons guilty of the Insurrections, Riots & Disorders raised & committed in this Province. . . .

By the Att.ʸ Gen.ˡˢ Certificate it appears that *no more than Nine Persons* have made any Application to him, for the Benefit of the s.ᵈ Pardon, & as the Fees of Prosecution were payable to him, no more than those 9. Persons who have been prosecuted, have intituled themselves to that Pardon, Yet those who have accepted & complyed with the other Provisoes in the Pardon ment^d its conceiv'd are intitled to more Favour than those who have persisted without any Complyance. . . .

. . . By this Deposⁿ also appears, some of the Means that the Rioters use, to bring & keep People into their Combinations, to witt, Threats to pull down their Houses, if they did not joyn them, & the Fears of Death if they fell from their Engagem^{ts} with them.

By these Depositions appears, more of the Rioters Endeavours, & Ways of drawing innocent People, into their Combin^{ns} & that the Rioters pay Taxes to their Com^{tees} That One Rioter had sayd, he had payd so much from Time to Time, as with a Tax of 13[£] then layd on him, would have been suffic^t to have bought his Plantation — By this Deposⁿ also appears a continual Destruction & Waste of Timber, carryed on by the Rioters for three Years past, upon some Thousands of acres of Land belong^g to P'sons therein named, which before that, were the best timbered Lands in New Jersey, but now, none good left on them, that a Team can easily approach — By this & the other Dispositions it appears that the Rioters of particular Places, have got Captains over them who they call by that Name, & that the said *Amos Roberts seems to be the Chief Captain* of the whole Rioters in this Province.

It appears not to the Council, that any One Poss'ion forcibly entred upon, & detained by, the Rioters, dur^g these Disturbances, has been restored to the Owners, pursuant to the Tenor of the Pardon afs^d & they have good Reason to believe that no One has been restored, but all are Forcibly detained to this Day.

On the 1st *Day of this instant December*, the Co^{ll} of Prop^{rs} of East New Jersey, presented a Mem^l & Representation to the Govr Co^{ll} & Assembly, Setting Forth the miserable State of this Province, for that the Laws have, long ceased to be a Protectⁿ to His Maj^{tys} good Subjects therein, & the Right of the People to that Protection, & to expect that the Legislature of this Province will, at this Time, effectually interpose to enable the Officers of the Gov^rm^t to carry the Laws of the Land into Execution.

William A. Whitehead, editor, *Documents relating to the Colonial History of the State of New Jersey* (Newark, 1883), VII, 207-225 *passim*.

31. Politics in Pennsylvania (1740-1754)

BY ROBERT PROUD (1780)

Robert Proud, one of the few careful and laborious historians who wrote of their own times, was a loyalist. — Bibliography: Winsor, *Narrative and Critical History*, V, 242–246; Channing and Hart, *Guide*, § 108.

DURING the administration of Governor *Thomas*, it is observed that the *enlisting of indented or bought servants*, for *soldiers*, was first permitted to be carried into execution, in the province, before the act of *parliament*, in that case, was made ; which being disagreeable and injurious to many of the inhabitants, and contrary to ancient usage, *John Wright*, one of the people called *Quakers*, a worthy Magistrate of *Lancaster* county, and a Member of Assembly for the same, having spoke his mind freely against it, in the Assembly, was, therefore, with divers others, dismissed from his office, as a Judge, by a new commission which came out for Lancaster without his name ; before which, having got intelligence of the intention, he came to the court, in May, 1741, and took his leave thereof, in a valedictory speech. . . .

Thomas Penn, after this, on the death of his brother *John*, in 1746, became the principal Proprietor, and possessed of three fourths of the province. He lived the longest of the three brothers ; but he appears never to have been very popular, in the province : he is said, in general, to have conducted himself rather too much reserved towards the people, and too nearly attached to certain views, for his private interest, in reference to the province ; which are things opposite to popularity. Besides, the imprudence of some persons in the province, in order to shew their dislike at some part of his conduct, which did not please them, tended to create and increase a similar disposition, where the contrary ought the more to have been cultivated and cherished ; but, in general, he was a person of a worthy character, and of moderate principles.

In the fifth year of Governor *Thomas*'s administration, in October, 1742, at the annual election, for the Members of Assembly, in *Phila-delphia*, happened such an instance of the unwarrantable effect of party spirit, as, at that time, made a lasting impression on the minds of many of the inhabitants. . . .

. . . a large number of sailors, from the shipping in the river *Delaware*, during the time of election (not being any way interested, or, of right, concerned therein) armed with clubs, suddenly and unexpectedly appeared, in a tumultuous manner, and formed a *riot*, at the place

of election, knocking down a great number of the people, both Magistrates, Constables and others, worthy and reputable inhabitants, who
opposed them; and, by violence having cleared the ground, several
of the people were carried off, as dead!

This was repeatedly done, upon the return of the electors; till, at
last, many of the inhabitants, being enraged, took measures to force
them into their ships, and near fifty of them into prison; but they were
soon discharged: for it afterwards appeared, that they had been privately employed, in this work, by some party leaders; it being then in
time of war, when consequently party spirit, which is so nearly allied to
it, and, in the extreme, ends in the same, was encouraged to make
greater efforts, to distract the public proceedings, and under this Governor's administration, by more ways than one, to divert the established
form of the constitution, from its *peaceable order and course*, into that
of its opposite nature; in which an increasing party here, since that
time, though generally under the most specious and plausible pretences,
have ever appeared to take delight: for change is grateful to the human
race; and, probably, no government of mankind is, at all times, entirely
free from factious spirits; and a large number will always be found,
especially where much liberty abounds, which is only proper for the
wise and good, whose interest, as well as pleasure, it will ever be to
favour *revolutional* consequences.

During Governor *Thomas*'s administration, the *Indian* affairs, seem
mostly to have been well managed, and harmony continued with that
people; which has always been a matter of great importance, as well as
expence to this province. But, as before observed, his ardour, in pressing some things of a military nature, appears to have introduced un-
profitable altercation between him and the Assembly, during part of his
administration; which naturally tends to disappointment and dislike,
between parties of such opposite and fixed principles, and so very different views of advancing the public utility, as those of Governor *Thomas*,
and the Assemblies of Pennsylvania were, at that time; but afterwards,
for divers years before his resignation, which was in the summer of
the year 1747, a much better understanding existed between them.

In consequence of Governor *Thomas*'s resignation, the administration,
as usual, devolved on the Council, *Anthony Palmer* being President, till
November, 1748; when *James Hamilton*, of *Pennsylvania*, arrived Governor from *England;* a gentleman of considerable fortune in the province, and well esteemed by the people: he was the son of *Andrew*

Hamilton, before mentioned as a lawyer of note, in *Philadelphia ;* and who likewise had held several eminent public offices, in the government, with reputation.

Governor *Hamilton* continued till his resignation in October, 1754 ; when he was succeeded, in the government, by *Robert Hunter Morris* of *New Jersey*, son of *Lewis Morris* who had been Governor of that province.

Robert Proud, *The History of Pennsylvania* (Philadelphia, 1798), II, 220–231 *passim.*

———◆———

32. " New-York City " (1760)

BY REVEREND ANDREW BURNABY

Burnaby travelled throughout the colonies, and his well-written book is one of the best sources of our knowledge of colonial society. — Bibliography : Winsor, *Narrative and Critical History*, V, 252–258. — For previous accounts of New York, see *Contemporaries*, I, ch. xxiii.

THIS city is situated upon the point of a small island, lying open to the bay on one side, and on the others included between the North and East rivers, and commands a fine prospect of water, the Jerseys, Long Island, Staten Island, and several others, which lie scattered in the bay. It contains between 2 and 3000 houses, and 16 or 17,000 inhabitants, is tolerably well built, and has several good houses. The streets are paved, and very clean, but in general they are narrow ; there are two or three, indeed, which are spacious and airy, particularly the Broad Way. The houses in this street have most of them a row of trees before them ; which form an agreeable shade, and produce a pretty effect. The whole length of the town is something more than a mile ; the breadth of it about half an one. The situation is, I believe, esteemed healthy ; but it is subject to one great inconvenience, which is the want of fresh water ; so that the inhabitants are obliged to have it brought from springs at some distance out of town. There are several public buildings, though but few that deserve attention. The college, when finished, will be exceedingly handsome : it is to be built on three sides of a quadrangle, fronting Hudson's or North river, and will be the most beautifully situated of any college, I believe, in the world. At present only one wing is finished, which is of stone, and consists of twenty-four sets of apartments ; each having a large sitting room, with a study, and bed chamber. They are obliged to make use of some of these apartments for a master's lodge, library, chapel, hall, &c. but as soon as the whole shall be completed, there will be proper apartments for each of these offices. The name of it is King's College.

There are two churches in New York, the old, or Trinity Church, and the new one, or St. George's Chapel; both of them large buildings, the former in the Gothic taste, with a spire, the other upon the model of some of the new churches in London. Besides these, there are several other places of religious worship; namely, two Low Dutch Calvinist churches, one High Dutch ditto, one French ditto, one German Lutheran church, one presbyterian meeting-house, one quakers ditto, one anabaptists do, one Moravian ditto, and a Jews synagogue. There is also a very handsome charity-school for sixty poor boys and girls, a good work-house, barracks for a regiment of soldiers, and one of the finest prisons I have ever seen. The court or stadt-house makes no great figure, but it is to be repaired and beautified. There is a quadrangular fort, capable of mounting sixty cannon, though at present there are, I believe, only thirty-two. Within this is the governor's palace, and underneath it a battery capable of mounting ninety-four guns, and barracks for a company or two of soldiers. Upon one of the islands in the bay is an hospital for sick and wounded seamen; and, upon another, a pest-house. These are the most noted public buildings in and about the city. . . .

Arts and sciences have made no greater progress here than in the other colonies; but as a subscription library has been lately opened, and every one seems zealous to promote learning, it may be hoped that they will hereafter advance faster than they have done hitherto. The college is established upon the same plan as that in the Jerseys, except that this at New York professes the principles of the church of England. At present the state of it is far from being flourishing, or so good as might be wished. Its fund does not exceed 10,000l. currency, and there is a great scarcity of professors. A commencement was held, nevertheless, this summer, and seven gentlemen took degrees. There are in it at this time about twenty-five students. The president, Dr. Johnson, is a very worthy and learned man, but rather too far advanced in life to have the direction of so young an institution. The late Dr. Bristow left to this college a fine library, of which they are in daily expectation.

The inhabitants of New York, in their character, very much resemble the Pensylvanians: more than half of them are Dutch, and almost all traders: they are, therefore, habitually frugal, industrious, and parsimonious. Being however of different nations, different languages, and different

religions, it is almost impossible to give them any precise or determinate
character.   The women are handsome and agreeable ; though rather
more reserved than the Philadelphian ladies.   Their amusements are
much the same as in Pensylvania ; viz. balls, and sleighing expeditions
in the winter ; and, in the summer, going in parties upon the water, and
fishing ; or making excursions into the country.   There are several houses
pleasantly situated upon East river, near New York, where it is common
to have turtle-feasts : these happen once or twice in a week.   Thirty or
forty gentlemen and ladies meet and dine together, drink tea in the
afternoon, fish and amuse themselves till evening, and then return home
in Italian chaises, (the fashionable carriage in this and most parts of
America, Virginia excepted, where they make use only of coaches, and
these commonly drawn by six horses), a gentleman and lady in each
chaise.   In the way there is a bridge, about three miles distant from
New York, which you always pass over as you return, called the Kissing-
Bridge, where it is a part of the etiquette to salute the lady who has put
herself under your protection.

The present state of this province is flourishing : it has an extensive
trade to many parts of the world, particularly to the West Indies ; and
has acquired great riches by the commerce which it has carried on, under
flags of truce, to Cape-François, and Monte-Christo.   The troops, by
having made it the place of their general rendezvous, have also enriched
it very much.   However, it is burthened with taxes, and the present public
debt amounts to more than 300,000l. currency.   The taxes are laid upon
estates real and personal ; and there are duties upon Negroes, and other
importations.   The provincial troops are about 2600 men.   The difference of exchange between currency and bills, is from 70 to 80 per cent.

Before I left New York, I took a ride upon Long Island, the richest
spot, in the opinion of the New-Yorkers, of all America ; and where they
generally have their villas, or country houses.   It is undeniably beautiful,
and some parts of it are remarkably fertile, but not equal, I think, to the
Jerseys.   The length of it is something more than 100 miles, and the
breadth 25.   About 15 or 16 miles from the west end of it, there opens
a large plain between 20 and 30 miles long, and 4 or 5 broad.   There
is not a tree growing upon it, and it is asserted that there never were
any.   Strangers are always carried to see this place, as a great curiosity,
and the only one of the kind in North America.

Andrew Burnaby, *Travels through the Middle Settlements in North-America,
in the Years 1759 and 1760* (London, 1775), 61–67 *passim*.

CHAPTER V — SOUTHERN COLONIES

33. Andros's and Nicholson's Administrations (1690–1705)

BY ROBERT BEVERLY (1705)

Beverly was a Virginian of wealth and high social position. His history of Virginia is of great value, though not impartial. He had a private grudge against Nicholson. — Bibliography: Tyler, *American Literature*, II, 264–267; Winsor, *Narrative and Critical History*, V, 278–284; Channing and Hart, *Guide*, § 99. — For previous history of Virginia, see *Contemporaries*, I, ch. x.

§. 132. *ANNO* 1690. *Francis Nicholson*, Esq ; being appointed Lieutenant-Governor under the Lord *Effingham*, arrived there. This Gentleman discoursed freely of Country Improvements, instituted public Exercises, and gave Prizes to all those, that should excel in the Exercises of Riding, Running, Shooting, Wrestling, and Cudgeling. When the Design of a College was communicated to him, he promised it all imaginable Encouragement. . . .

§. [1]34. *Anno* 1691, an Assembly being called · · ·
The Assembly was so fond of Governor *Nicholson* at that Time, that they presented him with the Sum of three hundred Pounds, as a Testimony of their good Disposition towards him. But he having an Instruction to receive no Present from the Country, they drew up an Address to their Majesties, praying that he might have leave to accept it, which was granted, and he gave one half thereof to the College.

§. 137. Their Majesties were well pleased with that pious Design of the Plantation, and granted a Charter, according to the Desire of Mr. *Blair*, their Agent. . . .

It was a great Satisfaction to the Archbishops and Bishops to see such a Nursery of Religion founded in that new World ; especially for that it was begun in an Episcopal Way, and carried on wholly by zealous Conformists to the Church of *England*.

§. 138. In this first Assembly, Lieutenant-Governor *Nicholson* pass'd Acts for Encouragement of the Linen Manufacture, and to promote the

Leather Trade, by Tanning, Currying, and Shoe-making. He also in that Session pass'd a Law for Cohabitation, and Improvement of Trade.

Before the next Assembly he tack'd about, and was quite the Reverse of what he was in the first as to Cohabitation. Instead of encouraging Ports and Towns, he spread abroad his dislike of them ; and went among the People, finding Fault with those Things, which he and the Assembly had unanimously agreed upon the preceding Session. Such a violent Change there was in him, that it proceeded from some other Cause, than barely the Inconstancy of his Temper. He had receiv'd Directions from those *English* Merchants, who well knew that Cohabitation would lessen their consign'd Trade.

§. 139. In *February*, 1692, Sir *Edmund Andros* arrived Governor. He began his Government with an Assembly, which overthrew the good Design of Ports and Towns : But the Ground-work of this Proceeding, was laid before Sir *Edmund*'s Arrival. However, this Assembly proceeded no farther, than to suspend the Law, till their Majesties Pleasure should be known. But it seems the Merchants in *London* were dissatisfied, and made public Complaints against it, which their Majesties were pleased to hear ; and afterwards refer'd the Law back to the Assembly again, to consider, if it were suitable to the Circumstances of the Country, and to regulate it accordingly. But the Assembly did not then proceed any farther in it ; the People themselves being infected by the Merchants Letters.

§. 140. At this Session Mr. *Neal*'s Project for a Post-Office, and his Patent of Post-Master-General in those Parts of *America*, were presented. The Assembly made an Act to promote that Design ; but by reason of the inconvenient Distance of their Habitations, and want of Towns, this Project fell to nothing. . . .

§. 142. Sir *Edmund Andros* was a great Encourager of Manufactures. In his Time Fulling-Mills were set up by Act of Assembly. He also gave particular Marks of his Favour towards the propagating of Cotton, which since his Time has been much neglected. He was likewise a great Lover of Method, and Dispatch in all Sorts of Business, which made him find Fault with the Management of the Secretaries Office. And, indeed, with very good Reason ; for from the Time of *Bacon*'s Rebellion, till then, there never was any Office in the World more negligently kept. Several Patents of Land were enter'd Blank upon Record ; many original Patents, Records, and Deeds of Land, with other Matters of great Consequence, were thrown loose about the Office, and suffer'd to be dirtied, torn, **and** eaten by the Moths, and other Insects. But upon this Gentleman's Accession to the Government, he immediately gave Directions, to reform all these Irregularities ; he caused the loose and torn Records of Value to be transcribed into new Books ; and order'd Conveniences to be built within the Office, for preserving the Records from being lost and confounded, as before. He prescribed Methods to keep the Papers dry and clean, and to reduce them into such Order, as that any thing might be turn'd to immediately. But all these Conveniences were burnt soon after they were finished, in *October*, 1698, together with the Office itself, and the whole State-house. But his Diligence was so great in that Affair, that tho' his Stay afterward in the Country was very short ; yet he caused all the Records, and Papers, which had been sav'd from the Fire, to be sorted again, and Register'd in Order, and indeed in much better Order, than ever they had been before. In this Condition he left 'em at his quitting the Government.

He made several Offers to rebuild the State-house in the same Place ; and had his Government continued but six Months longer, 'tis probable he would have effected it after such a Manner, as might have been least burthensome to the People, designing the greatest Part at his own Cost. . . .

§. 145. In *November*, 1698. *Francis Nicholson*, Esq ; was removed from *Maryland*, to be Governor of *Virginia*. But he went not then with that Smoothness on his Brow, he had carry'd with him when he was appointed Lieutenant-Governour. He talk'd then no more of improving of Manufactures, Towns, and Trade. But instead of encouraging the Manufactures, he sent over inhuman Memorials against them, opposite to all Reason. In one of these, he remonstrates, *That the Tobacco of that Country often bears so low a Price, that it would not yield Cloaths to the People that make it*; and yet presently after, in the same Memorial, he recommends it to the Parliament, *to pass an Act, forbidding the Plantations to make their own Cloathing*; which, in other Words, *is desiring a charitable Law, that the Planters shall go naked*. In a late Memorial concerted between him and his Creature Col. *Quarrey*, 'tis most humbly proposed, *That all the* English *Colonies on the Continent of North* America, *be reduced under one Government, and under one Vice-Roy ; and that a standing Army be there kept on foot, to subdue the Queen's Enemies* ; surmising that they were intending to set up for themselves. . . .

§. 146. Soon after his Accession to the Government, he procured the Assembly, and Courts of Judicature, to be remov'd from *James* Town, where there were good Accommodations for People, to *Middle Planta-tion*, where there were none.   There he flatter'd himself with the fond Imagination, of being the Founder of a new City.   He mark'd out the Streets in many Places, so as that they might represent the Figure of a *W*, in Memory of his late Majesty King *William*, after whose Name the Town was call'd *Williamsburgh*.   There he procur'd a stately Fabrick to be erected, which he placed opposite to the College, and graced it with the magnificent Name of the *Capitol.*

§. 147.   In the 2^d Year of this Gentleman's Government; there hap-pen'd an Adventure very fortunate for him, which gave him much credit; and that was the taking of a Pyrate within the Capes of that Country. . . .

§. 148.   This Governor likewise gain'd some Reputation by another Instance of his Management, whereby he let the World know, the vio-lent Passion he had to publish his own Fame.

To get Honour in *New-York*, he had zealously recommended to the Court of *England*, the necessity that *Virginia* shou'd contribute a cer-tain *Quota* of Men, or else a Sum of Money, towards the building, and maintaining a Fort at *New-York*.   The Reason he gave for this, was, because *New-York* was their Barrier, and as such it was but Justice, they shou'd help to defend it.   This was by Order of his late Majesty King *William* proposed to the Assembly :   But upon the most solid Reasons, they humbly remonstrated, *That neither the Forts then in be-ing, nor any other that might be built in the Province of* New-York, *cou'd in the least avail to the Defence and Security of* Virginia ; *for that either the* French, *or the Northern* Indians *might invade that Colony, and not come within an hundred Miles of any such Fort.* . . .

§. 149.   Neither was he contented to spread abroad this Untruth there ; but he also foisted it into a Memorial of Col. *Quarry*'s to the Council of Trade. . . .

Certainly his Excellency, and Col. *Quarry*, by whose joint Wisdom and Sincerity this Memorial was composed, must believe that the *Coun-cil of Trade* have very imperfect Intelligence, how Matters pass in that Part of the World, or else they would not presume to impose such a Banter upon them.

But this is nothing, if compar'd to some other Passages of that unjust Representation, wherein they took upon them to describe the People of *Virginia, to be both numerous and rich, of Republican Notions and Principles, such as ought to be corrected, and lower'd in time ; and that then, or never was the Time to maintain the Queen's Prerogative, and put a stop to those wrong pernicious Notions, which were improving daily, not only in Virginia, but in all her Majesty's other Governments. A Frown now from her Majesty, will do more than an Army hereafter,* &c.

With those inhuman false Imputations, did those Gentlemen afterwards introduce the Necessity of a standing Army.

§. 150. Thus did this Gentleman continue to rule till *August* 1705. . . .

[Robert Beverly], *The History of Virginia* (London, 1722), 87–97 *passim.*

---

34. Report of an Investigating Agent in Carolina (1699)

BY EDWARD RANDOLPH

Randolph was sent over by the king as a special agent to investigate the manner in which the colonies carried out the British laws. — Bibliography: Winsor, *Narrative and Critical History*, V, ch. v; Channing and Hart, *Guide*, § 102; *Contemporaries*, I, No. 133. — For previous history of the Carolinas, see *Contemporaries*, I, ch. xii.

AFTER a dangerous voyage at Sea, I landed at Charles Town, in the Province of So. Carolina, & soon after my arrival, I administered the Oath to M^r. Jos. Blake, one of the Proprietors & Governor of this Province. But he is not allowed of by his Ma^{tys}. Order in Council to be Govr., the Act of Parl^t. for preventing frauds being not taken notice of by the Proprietors.

There are but few settled Inhabitants in this Province, the Lords have taken up vast tracts of lands for their own use, as in Colleton County & other places, where the land is most commodious for settlement, which prevents peopling the place, & makes them less capable to preserve themselves. As to their civil Govern^t., 'tis different from what I have met with in the other Proprieties. Their Militia is not above 1500 Soldiers White men, but have thro' the Province generally 4 Negroes to 1 White man, & not above 1100 families, English & French.

Their Chief Town is Charles Town, and the seat of Gov^t. in this Province, where the Governor, Council & Triennial Parliam^t. set, & their Courts are holden, being above a league distance from the entrance to their harbour mouth, wch. is barred, & not above 17 foot water at the highest tide, but very difficult to come in. The Harbour is called by the Spaniards, St. George; it lyes 75 leagues to the Northward of

St. Augustine, belonging to the Spaniards. It is generally laid down
in our English maps to be 2 deg., 45 min., within the southern bounds
of this Province. In the year 1686, one hundred Spaniards, wth Negroes
& Indians, landed at Edistoe, (50 miles to the southward of Charles
Town,) & broak open the house of M^r. Joseph Moreton, then Governor
of the Province, & carried away M^r. Bowell, his Brother-in.law, prisoner,
who was found murdered 2 or 3 days after ; they carried away all his
money & plate, & 13 slaves, to the value of £1500 sterling, & their
plunder to St. Augustine. Two of the Slaves made their escape from
thence, & returned to their master. Some time after, Govr. Moreton
sent to demand his slaves, but the Govr. of St. Augustine answered it
was done without his orders, but to this day keeps them, & says he can't
deliver them up w^thout an ord^r. from the King of Spain. About the
same time they robbed Mr. Grimball's House, the Sec. of the Province,
whilst he attended the Council at Charles Town, & carried away to the
value of above £1500 sterl^g. They also fell upon a settlement of Scotch-
men at Port Royal, where there was not above 25 men in health to oppose them. The Spaniards burnt down their houses, destroyed & carried
away all that they had, because (as the Span^ds. pretended) they were
settled upon their land, and had they at any time a superior force, they
would also destroy this Town built upon Ashley & Cooper Rivers. This
whole Bay was called formerly St. George's, which they likewise lay
claim to. The Inhabitants complained of the wrong done them by the
Spaniards to the Lords Proprietors, & humbly prayed them (as I have
been truly informed) to represent it to His Ma^ty., but they not hearing
from the Lord Prop^rs., fitted out two vessels with 400 stout men, well
armed, & resolved to take St. Augustine. But Jas. Colleton came in
that time from Barbadoes with a Commission to be Govr., & threatn'd
to hang them if they proceeded, whereupon they went on shore very
unwillingly. The Spaniards hearing the English were coming upon
them for the damages, they left their Town & Castle, & fled into the
woods to secure themselves. The truth is, as I have been credibly
informed, there was a design on foot to carry on a Trade with the
Spaniards.

I find the Inhabitants greatly alarmed upon the news that the French
continue their resolution to make a settling at Messasipi River, from
[whence] they may come over land to the head of Ashley River w^thout
opposition, 'tis not yet known what care the Lord's Prop^rs intend to take
for their preservation. Some ingenious gentleman of this Province (not

of the Council) have lately told me the Deputies have talked of mak^g an Address to the Lords Prop^rs for relief, But 'tis apparent that all the time of this French War they never sent them one barrel of powder or a pound of lead to help them.   They conclude they have no reason to depend upon them for assistance, & are resolved to forsake this Country betimes, if they find the French are settled at Meschasipi, or if upon the death of the King of Spain these Countries fall into the hands of the French, as inevitably they will (if not timely prevented), and return with their families to England or some other place where they may find safety & protection.   It was one of the first questions asked me by several of the Chief men at my arrival, whether His Ma^ty. had not sent over some soldiers to preserve them from the French, saying they might all live in this plentiful Country if His Ma^ty. will please to allow them half pay for 2 or 3 years at furthest, that afterwards they will maintain themselves & families (if they have any) in making Pitch and Tar & planting of Indian Corn, His Majesty will thereby have so many men seasoned to the Country ready for service upon all occasions, five such men will do more service by sea or land than 20 new rais^d men from home, they may be brought hither in the Virginia outward bound Ships, 100 or 150 men in a year, till they are made up 1000, it will save the charge of transporting so many another time 2 or 3000 leagues at sea. I heard one of the Council (a great Indian Trader, & has been 600 miles up in the Country west from Charles Town) discourse that the only way to discover the Meschasipi is from this Province by land.   He is willing to undertake it if His Ma^ty. will please to pay the charge wch will not be above £400 or £500 at most; he intends to take with him 50 white men of this Province and 100 Indians, who live 2 days journey east from the Meschasipi, and questions not but in 5 or 6 months time after he has His Ma^ty's commands & instructions to find out ye mouth of it and the true latitude thereof.

The great improvement made in this Province is wholly owing to the industry & labour of the Inhabitants.   They have applied themselves to make such commodities as might increase the revenue of the Crown, as Cotton, Wool, Ginger, Indigo, &^c.   But finding them not to answer the end they are set upon making Pitch, Tar & Turpentine, and planting rice, & can send over great quantityes yearly, if they had encouragement from England to make it, having about 50,000 Slaves to be employed in that service, upon occasion, but they have lost most of their vessels, which were but small, last war by the French, & some lately by the

Spaniards, so that they are not able to send those Commodities to England for a market, neither are sailors here to be had to man their vessels.

I humbly propose that if His Ma^{ty}. will for a time suspend the Duties
upon Commodities, and that upon rice also, it will encourage the Planter
to fall vigilantly upon making Pitch & Tar, &^{c}., wch the Lords Prop^{rs}.
ought to make their principal care to obtain from His Ma^{ty}. being the
only way to draw people to settle in their Province, a place of greatest
encouragement to ye English Navy in these parts of ye world.　Charles
Town Bay is the safest port for all Vessels coming thro' the gulf of Florida in distress, bound from the West Indies to the Northern Plantations ;
if they miss this place they may perish at sea for want of relief, and
having beat upon the coast of New England, New York, or Virginia
by a North West Wind in the Winter, be forced to go to Barbadoes if
they miss this Bay, where no wind will damage them and all things to be
had necessary to refitt them.　My Lords, I did formerly present Your
Lordships with proposals for supplying England with Pitch & Tar, Masts
& all o^r Naval Stores from New England.　I observed when I were at
York in Septr. last, abundance of Tar bro^t. down Hudson's River to be
sold at New York, as also Turpentine & Tar in great quantities from the
Colony of Connecticut, I was told if they had encouragement they could
load several Ships yearly for England.　But since my arrival here I find
I am come into the only place for such commodities upon the Continent
of America ; some persons have offered to deliver in Charlestown Bay
upon their own account 1000 Barrels of Pitch and as much Tar, others
greater quantities provided they were paid for it in Charles Town in
Lyon Dollars passing here at 5^s. p^r. piece, Tar at 8^s. p^r. Barrel, and very
good Pitch at 12^s. p^r. Barrel, & much cheaper if it once became a
Trade.　The season for making those Commodities in this Province
being 6 mo^s. longer than in Virginia and more Northern Plantations ; a
planter can make more tar in any one year here with 50 slaves than they
can do with double the number in those places, their slaves here living
at very easy rates and with few clothes.

The inclosed I received from M. Girard, a French Protestant living
in Carolina.　I find them very industrious & good husbands, but are
discouraged because some of them having been many years Inhabitants
in this Province, are denied the benefit of being Owners & Masters of
Vessels, which other the Subjects of His Majesty's Plantations enjoy,
besides many of them are made Denizons.　If this Place were duly encouraged, it would be the most useful to the Crown of all the Plantations

H

upon the continent of America. I herewith enclose to Your Lordships a Draft of the Town and Castle of St. Augustine, with a short description of it by a Gentleman who has been often there. It's done exactly true, more for service than for show. The Spaniards now, the French, if ever they get it, will prove dangerous neighbours to this Province, a thing not considered nor provided against by the Lords Proprietors. I am going from hence to Bermuda, with His Ma^{ty}. Commissioners, to administer the Oath to the Govr. of that Island, with a Commission for the Judge and other Officers of the Court of Admiralty erected there, from whence I believe it necessary to hasten to the Bahamas Islands, where a Brigantine belonging to New England was carried in as a wreck. The Master & Sailors being pursued by some persons who had commission from Govr. Webb, believing they were chased by Spaniards, forsook their Vessel & went on shore among the Natives to save their lives.

All which is humbly submitted by
Your Lordship's
Most humble Servant,
Ed. Randolph.

The want of a small Vessel to support the loss of the Frigate, which was appointed by the Lords Commiss^{rs}. of the Admiralty to transplant me from one Plantation to another, makes me stay a great while at one place for a passage to another, which is uncertain, difficult & dangerous.

I have by the extreme of cold last Winter in Maryland and Pennsylvania, & by my tedious passage in the Winter time from New York to this place, got a great numbness in my right leg & foot. I am in hopes this warm climate will restore me to my health. I have formerly wrote to your Board & the Commiss^{rs}. of H. M. Customs, the necessity of having a Vessel to transport me from one Plantation to another.

I humbly pray Your Lordships favour to direct that the little residence I am to make in these parts of the World, may be in this Province, & that a Vessel well manned may be sent me hither, which may answer all occasion, my intentions being not to lye idle, for when the Hurricane times come in these parts of the World, I can go securely to Virginia, Maryland & Pensylvania & New England, without fear of being driven from those Plantations by North West Winds, & when they come I can pass from one Plantation to another without difficulty

[William James Rivers], *A Sketch of the History of South Carolina* (Charleston, 1856), 443–447.

35. A South Carolina Settlement (1742)

BY ELIZA LUCAS

Eliza Lucas was an English girl, upon whom was thrown the burden of carrying on a large estate in South Carolina. She later became the wife of Charles Pinckney, chief justice of South Carolina. — Bibliography: Winsor, *Narrative and Critical History*, V, 335–356; Channing and Hart, *Guide*, § 102. — For previous Carolina history, see *Contemporaries*, I, ch. xii.

May 22^d 1742.

I AM now set down my dear Brother to obey your Commands and give you a short description of the part of the World I now inhabit — S^o Carolina then is an Extensive Country near the Sea. Most of the settled part of it is upon a flatt. the Soil near Charles Town sandy but further distant. clay and swamp lands. It abounds with fine navigable rivers and great quan[ti]ties of fine timber — The Country at a great distance that is to say about a hundred and fifty mile from C^{rs} Town very hilly The soil in general very fertile and there are few European or American fruits or grain but what grow here the Country abounds with wild fowl Venison and fish Beef Veal and Mutton are here in much greater perfection than in the Islands tho' not equal to that of England — Fruit extreamly good and in profusion, and the oranges exceed any I ever tasted in the West Indies or from Spain or Portugal. The people in general hospitable and honest and the better sort add to these a polite gentile behaviour. The poorer sort are the most indolent people in the world, or they would never be wretched in so plentiful a country as this. The winters here are fine and pleasant but 4 months in the year are extreamly disagreeable excessive hott much thunder and lightening and musketoes and sand flies in abundance C^{rs} Town the Metropolis, is a neat pretty place the inhabitants polite and live a very gentile manner the streets and houses regularly built. the ladies and gentlemen gay in their dress. upon the whole you will find as many agreeable people of both sexes for the size of the place as almost any where St Phillip's Church in C^{rs} Town is a very Elegant one and much frequented. there are sever^l more places of publick Worship in the town and the generality of people of a religious turn of mind.

I began in haste and have observed no method or I should have told you before I came to Summer, that we have a most charming Spring in this Country especially for those who travel through the Country for the

Scent of the young Myrtle and yellow Jessamine with which the woods abound is delightful. The staple commodity here is rice and the only thing they export to Europe. Beef, Pork and Lumber they send to the West Indies. . . .

Septr 8th 1742.

Wrote to Miss Mary Fayweather in Boston. The same time wrote my Father a full and long acc^t. of 5 thousand Spainyards landing at St Symons. We were greatly alarmed in Carolina ; 80 prisoners now in C^{rs} Town, they had a large fleet, but were scattered by bad weather. Our little fleet from Carolina, commanded by Capt Hardy could not get to ye Gen^{ls} assistance, the Enemy were sailed to St Marks. 'Tis said Capt. Hardy instead of cruising off St Augustine barr where it was probable he would find them returned with all the men to C^{rs} Town, wch has greatly disgusted the Govr and Council as well as the rest of the Inhabitance. There is sent now 3 Men of Warr and 4 provincial vessels under the command of Capt. Frankland. Sent my father his kettle Drums, informed him of Mr Smith seling the rum he sent us, and giving away the preserved sorrel, tho' he assured us it was by mistake put on board a vessel going to Barbadoes and carried there. Sad wretch. Sent for Cowcumber seed — Polly gone to school at Mrs Hicks's at 140 pound per annum.

Eliza Lucas, *Journal and Letters* (edited by Mrs. H. P. Holbrook, Wormsloe, 1850), 17–20 *passim*.

———————◆———————

36. Routine in Maryland (1754)

BY GOVERNOR HORATIO SHARPE

Sharpe was governor of Maryland from 1753 to 1768; his efficiency is well shown by the extract below. — Bibliography : Winsor, *Narrative and Critical History*, III, 553–562, V, 270–272; J. T. Scharf, *Maryland*, I, 442 ff.; Channing and Hart, *Guide*, § 101. — For earlier Maryland history, see *Contemporaries*, I, ch. xi.

IN obedience to your Ldps Instructions I have transmitted Copies of all the Laws made at a Session of Assembly begun & held at Annapolis in this Province the 2^d of Octr 1753 & have fulfilled your Lordsp's pleasure by inclosing therewith a few Observations for the more easy reference to any thing new or of an extraordinary nature by any of them enacted. Such a Bill as your Lordship was pleased to recommend in your Instructions for the Naturalization of German Protestants importing themselves into this Province was brought into the Lower House of Assembly in the Octr Session but did not pass through, however these people suffer no great Inconveniences from the want of such a Law, as there is an Act of Parliament in force in England naturalizing all such Foreigners after a few years Residence in any of His Majesty's Plantations. Advising with your Lordship's Agent & Judge of the Land Office about having parcells of Land surveyed in the several Counties & erected into Mannours I was informed that there is not remaining a Tract of Land (unless one in the Lower part of the Eastern Shore that I have a prospect of Discovering & the Barrens) extensive enough to answer that purpose in any part of the province, except in Frederick County near the Frontiers, & there are two mannours surveyed & reserved in that County already ; if I should by any enquiries get knowledge of Vacancy which will answer that End, or Land contiguous fit to be added to the Mannours already laid out & erected, I will punctually obey your Lordships Instructions. Your Ldp's Expectations of having what Land remains vacant in the more populous parts of the Country sold off at more advanced prices, cannot I am afraid, be answered as much as I wish ; The Method always followed here of locating Land Warrants by selecting the most rich & fertil Land without regarding any regularity of its Area, or making one of its Courses coincide with the Boundary of the adjacent prior patented Tract, has left the Land hitherto remaining Vacant & uncultivated, in such irregular small & incommodious parcells that it is thought scarcely worth any ones While but those on whose possessions it joins, to take it up even at the common Rate. I observed in a Letter to your Ldp's Secretary soon after my Arrival that in some of the Counties there is supposed to be a considerable number of Acres, for which your Ldp receives no Rent. . . .

I have herewith sent for your Ldp's information & satisfaction an exact State of the worth of the respective Ecclesiastical Benefices in the province at this time ; your Ldp will see that the Divisions already made have reduced most of them to a very moderate Value. The misinformation that had been given me made me represent untruly the Income of some of those that are now vacant, which Error your Ldp will be hereby enabled to rectify. . . . Your Ldp's distinguishing marks of Favour to Mr Bacon & Mr Malcolm were delivered them the same Day who expressed a dutiful sense of & thankfulness for the honour your Ldp had been pleased to confer on them which they intend to do themselves the honour of acknowledging by Letter to your Ldp.

The Trustees of the Charity School about to be established in Talbot County gratefully accept your Ldps proposals & are preparing a thankfull Address for the most kind Testimony of your Ldp's Approbation. . . .

I am sorry at being unable to put the Scheme your Ldp : was pleased to intimate for compleating the Governour's House in execution ; for want of being covered the House is now reduced to so bad a State (the Timber work being mostly wasted & demolished) that less than £300 or £400. will not put it in the Condition it was left in by the workmen, & I apprehend to perfect it would require as many Thousand, so large a sum it is impracticable to raise by Lottery in these parts where it is with the greatest Difficulty that £100 or £200 can be raised by that method for executing any work of the most general Utility. . . .

I met the Assembly the 25th of March upon the Business that was mentioned in my Letter dated the 10th of Feby the Contents of which I hope e'er this your Ldp is acquainted with, but neither my utmost Efforts or the Example of the Virginians who had just then granted the Sum of £10,000 for that purpose could induce them to make the least Provision for the Encouragement of the Ohio Expedition. . . . I have taken an Opportunity since my arrival of visiting Baltimore which indeed has the Appearance of the most increasing Town in the Province, tho it scarcely answered the Opinion I had conceived of it : hardly as yet rivaling Annapolis in number of Buildings or Inhabitants ; its Situation as to Pleasantness Air & Prospect is inferior to that of Annapolis, but if one considers it with respect to Trade, The extensive Country beyond it leaves no room for Comparison ; were a Few Gentn of fortune to settle there & encourage the Trade it might soon become a flourishing place but while few beside the Germans (who are in general Masters of small Fortunes) build & inhabit there I apprehend it cannot make any considerable Figure. . . .

Correspondence of Governor Horatio Sharpe (*Maryland Archives*, VI, Baltimore, 1888), I, 52–57 *passim.*

37. The Parson's Opinion of " the Parson's Cause " (1763)

BY REVEREND JAMES MAURY

(TRANSLATED BY ANN MAURY, 1853)

This celebrated case illustrates the relation of church and state in the colonies, and is also the beginning of the public career of Patrick Henry. Maury was an estimable minister of Huguenot ancestry. — Bibliography: Winsor, *Narrative and Critical History*, VI, 24; Maury, *Memoirs of a Huguenot Family;* Channing and Hart, *Guide*, § 134.

December 12th, 1763.

DEAR SIR : — Now that I am somewhat more at leisure, than when I wrote to you by Major Winston, from Hanover, some few days ago, I have sat down to give you the best account I can of the most material passages in the trial of my cause against the Collectors in that Court, both to satisfy your own curiosity, and to enable the lawyer, by whom it is to be managed in the General Court, to form some judgment of its merits. I believe, sir, you were advised from Nov'r Court, that the Bench had adjudged the twopenny act to be no law ; and that, at the next, a jury, on a writ of inquiry, were to examine whether the Plaintiff had sustained any damages, and what. Accordingly, at December Court, a select jury was ordered to be summoned ; but, how far they who gave the order, wished or intended it to be regarded, you may judge from the sequel. The Sheriff went into a public room, full of gentlemen, and told his errand. One excused himself (Peter Robinson of King William) as having already given his opinion in a similar case. On this, as a person then present told me, he immediately left the room, without summoning any one person there. He afterwards met another gentleman (Richard Sq. Taylor) on the green, and, on his saying he was not fit to serve, being a churchwarden, he took upon himself to excuse him, too, and, as far as I can learn, made no further attempts to summon gentlemen. These, you'll say, were but feeble endeavors to comply with the directions of the Court in that particular. Hence, he went among the vulgar herd. After he had selected and set down upon his list about eight or ten of these, I met him with it in his hand, and on looking over it, observed to him that they were not such jurors as the Court had directed him to get, being people of whom I had never heard before, except one, whom, I told him, he knew to be a party in the cause, as one of the Collector's Securities, and, therefore, not fit for a juror on that occasion. Yet this

man's name was not erased.   He was even called in Court, and, had he
not excused himself, would probably have been admitted.   For, I cannot
recollect, that the Court expressed either surprise or dislike that a more
proper jury had not been summoned.   Nay, though I objected against
them, yet, as Patrick Henry (one of the Defendant's lawyers) insisted
they were honest men, and, therefore, unexceptionable, they were immediately called to the book and sworn.   Three of them, as I was afterwards told, nay, some said four, were Dissenters of that denomination
called *New Lights*, which the Sheriff, as they were all his acquaintance,
must have known.   Messrs. Gist and McDowall, the two most considerable purchasers in that county, were now called in to prove the price
of tobacco, and sworn.   The testimony of the former imported, that,
during the months of May and June, 1759, tobacco had currently sold
at 50s. per hundred, and that himself, at or about the latter end of the
last of those months, had sold some hundreds of hhds. at that price,
and, amongst the rest, one hundred to be delivered in the month
of August, which, however, were not delivered till September.   That
of the latter only proved, " That 50s. was the current price of tobacco
that season."   This was the sum of the evidence for the Plaintiff.
Against him, was produced a receipt to the Collector, to the best of
my remembrance in these words : " Received of Thomas Johnson,
Jun'r, at this and some former payments, £144, current money, by
James Maury."   After the lawyers on both sides had displayed the
force and weight of the evidence, pro and con. to their Honors, the
jurors, and one of those who appeared for the Defendants had observed
to them that they must find (or *if they must find*, I am not sure which,
but think the former) for the Plaintiff, but need not find more than one
farthing ; they went out, and, according to instruction (though whether
according to evidence or not, I leave you to judge), in less than five
minutes brought in a verdict for the Plaintiff, one penny damages.   Mr.
Lyons urged, as the verdict was contrary to evidence, the jury ought
to be sent out again.   But no notice was taken of it, and the verdict
admitted without hesitation by the Bench.   He then moved to have
the evidence of Messrs. Gist and McDowell recorded, with as little
effect.   His next motion, which was for a new trial, shared the same
fate.   He then moved it might be admitted to record, " that he had
made a motion for a new trial, because he considered the verdict contrary to evidence, and that the motion had been rejected ; " which, after
much altercation, was agreed to.   He lastly moved for an appeal, which,

too, was granted. This, sir, as well as I can remember, is a just and impartial narrative of the most material occurrences in the trial of that cause. One occurrence more, tho' not essential to the cause, I can't help mentioning, as a striking instance of the loyalty, impartiality and attachment of the Bench to the Church of England in particular, and to religion at large. Mr. Henry, mentioned above (who had been called in by the Defendants, as we suspected, to do what I some time ago told you of), after Mr. Lyons had opened the cause, rose and harangued the jury for near an hour. This harangue turned upon points as much out of his own depth, and that of the jury, as they were foreign from the purpose; which it would be impertinent to mention here. However, after he had discussed those points, he labored to prove " that the act of 1758 had every characteristic of a good law; that it was a law of general utility, and could not, consistently with what he called the original compact between King and people, stipulating protection on the one hand and obedience on the other be annulled." Hence, he inferred, "that a King, by disallowing Acts of this salutary nature, from being the father of his people, degenerated into a Tyrant, and forfeits all right to his subjects' obedience." He further urged, " that the only use of an Established Church and Clergy in society, is to enforce obedience to civil sanctions, and the observance of those which are called duties of imperfect obligation; that, when a Clergy ceases to answer these ends, the community have no further need of their ministry, and may justly strip them of their appointments; that the Clergy of Virginia, in this particular instance of their refusing to acquiesce in the law in question, had been so far from answering, that they had most notoriously counteracted, those great ends of their institution; that, therefore, instead of useful members of the state, they ought to be considered as enemies of the community; and that, in the case now before them, Mr. Maury, instead of countenance, and protection and damages, very justly deserved to be punished with signal severity." And then he perorates to the following purpose, " that excepting they (the jury) were disposed to rivet the chains of bondage on their own necks, he hoped they would not let slip the opportunity which now offered, of making such an example of him as might, hereafter, be a warning to himself and his brethren, not to have the temerity, for the future, to dispute the validity of such laws, authenticated by the only authority, which, in his conception, could give force to laws for the government of this Colony, the authority of a legal representative of a Council, and of a kind and benevolent and patriot Governor." You'll observe I do not pretend to remember his words, but take this to have been the sum and substance of this part of his labored oration. When he came to that part of it where he undertook to assert, " that a King, by annulling or disallowing acts of so salutary a nature, from being the Father of his people degenerated into a Tyrant, and forfeits all right to his subjects' obedience ; " the more sober part of the audience were struck with horror. Mr. Lyons called out aloud, and with an honest warmth, to the Bench, " That the gentleman had spoken treason," and expressed his astonishment " that their worships could hear it without emotion, or any mark of dissatisfaction." At the same instant, too, amongst some gentlemen in the crowd behind me, was a confused murmur of Treason, Treason ! Yet Mr. Henry went on in the same treasonable and licentious strain, without interruption from the Bench, nay, even without receiving the least exterior notice of their disapprobation. One of the jury, too, was so highly pleased with these doctrines, that, as I was afterwards told, he every now and then gave the traitorous declaimer a nod of approbation. After the Court was adjourned, he apologised to me for what he had said, alleging that his sole view in engaging in the cause, and in saying what he had, was to render himself popular. You see, then, it is so clear a point in this person's opinion, that the ready road to popularity here, is, to trample under foot the interests of religion, the rights of the church, and the prerogative of the Crown. If this be not pleading for the " assumption of a power to bind the King's hands," if it be not asserting " such supremacy in provincial Legislatures " as is inconsistent with the dignity of the Church of England, and manifestly tends to draw the people of these plantations from their allegiance to the King, tell me, my dear sir, what is so, if you can. Mr. Cootes, merchant on James River, after Court, said " he would have given a considerable 'sum out of his own pocket, rather than his friend Patrick should have been guilty of a crime, but little, if any thing inferior to that which brought Simon Lord Lovatt to the block ; " and justly observed that he exceeded the most seditious and inflammatory harangues of the Tribunes of old Rome.

My warmest wishes and prayers ever attend you. And besides these there is little else in the power of, my dear Camm,

Your affectionate

J. MAURY.

Ann Maury, *Memoirs of a Huguenot Family* (New York, 1872), 418–424.

38. The Running of Mason and Dixon's Line (1763–1767)

BY THE COMMISSIONERS OF MARYLAND AND PENNSYLVANIA

The commissioners were fourteen in number. The piece is significant as showing the settlement of one of the many boundary controversies, and also as the record of a line which later divided free from slave states. — Bibliography: Winsor, *Narrative and Critical History*, III, 513, V, 273; Channing and Hart, *Guide*, § 107.

1st.   WE have completely run out, settled, fixed and determined a straight line, beginning at the exact middle of the due east and west line mentioned in the articles of the fourth day of July, one thousand seven hundred and sixty, to have been run by other commissioners, formerly appointed by the said Charles, Lord Baltimore, and the said Thomas Penn and Richard Penn, across the peninsula, from Cape Henlopen to Chesapeake Bay, the exact middle of which said east and west line is at the distance of thirty-four miles and three hundred and nine perches from the verge of the main ocean, the eastern end or beginning of the said due east and west line ; and that we have extended the said straight line eighty-one miles seventy-eight chains and thirty links up the peninsula, until it touched and made a tangent to the western part of the periphery of a circle drawn at the horizontal distance of twelve English statute miles from the centre of the town of New Castle, and have marked, described and perpetuated the said straight or tangent line, by setting up and erecting one remarkable stone at the place of beginning thereof, in the exact middle of the aforesaid due east and west line, according to the angle made by the said due west line, and by the said tangent line ; which stone, on the inward sides of the same, facing towards the east and towards the north, hath the arms of the said Thomas Penn and Richard Penn graved thereon, and on the outward sides of the same facing towards the west and towards the south, hath the arms of the said Frederick Lord Baltimore graved thereon ; and have also erected and set up in the said straight or tangent line, from the said place of beginning to the tangent point, remarkable stones at the end of every mile, each stone at the distance or end of every five miles, being particularly distinguished by having the arms of the said Frederick Lord Baltimore graved on the side thereof turning towards the west, and the arms of the said Thomas Penn and Richard Penn graved on the side thereof turning towards the east, and all the other intermediate stones are marked with the letter P on the sides facing towards the east, and with the letter M on the sides facing towards the west, and have fixed in the tangent point a stone with the arms of the said Frederick Lord Baltimore graved on the side facing towards the west, and with the arms of the said Thomas Penn and Richard Penn graved on the side facing towards the east.

2d. That from the end of the said straight line or tangent point, we have run out, settled, fixed and determined, a due north line of the length of five miles one chain and fifty links, to a parallel of latitude fifteen miles due south of the most southern part of the city of Philadelphia, which said due north line intersected the said circle drawn at the distance of twelve English statute miles from the centre of the town of New Castle, one mile thirty-six chains and five links from the said tangent point, and that in order to mark and perpetuate the said due north line, we have erected and set up one unmarked stone at the point where the said line intersects the said circle, three other stones at a mile distance from each other graved with the letter P on the sides facing the east, and the letter M on the sides facing the west, between the said place of intersection of the said circle and the said parallel of latitude, and a third stone at the point of intersection of the said north line and parallel of latitude, which last stone on the sides facing towards the north and east, hath the arms of the said Thomas Penn and Richard Penn graved thereon, and on the sides facing towards the south and west hath the arms of the said Frederick Lord Baltimore graved thereon.

3d. That we have run out, settled, fixed and determined such part of the said circle as lies westward of the said due north line, and have marked and perpetuated the same, by setting up and erecting four stones in the periphery thereof, one of which, at the meridian distance of one mile from the tangent point, is marked with the letter P on the east and the letter M on the west sides thereof.

4th. That we have run out, settled, fixed and determined a due east and west line, beginning at the northern point or end of the said due north line, being the place of intersection of the said north line, with the parallel of latitude, at the distance of fifteen English statute miles due south of the most southern part of the city of Philadelphia, and have extended the said line, two hundred and eighty miles, eighteen chains and twenty-one links due west from the place of beginning; and two hundred and forty-four miles, thirty-eight chains and thirty-six links due west from the river Delaware; and should have continued the same to the end of five degrees of longitude, the western bounds of the Province of Pennsylvania, but the Indians would not permit us. And that we have marked, described, and perpetuated the said west line, by setting up and erecting therein stones at the end of every mile, from the place of beginning to the distance of one hundred and thirty-two miles, near the foot of a hill, called and known by the name of Sideling hill; every five mile stone having on the side facing the north, the arms of the said Thomas Penn and Richard Penn graved thereon, and on the side facing the south, the arms of Frederick Lord Baltimore graved thereon, and the other intermediate stones are graved with the letter P on the north side, and the letter M on the south side ; and that the country to the westward of Sideling hill, being so very mountainous as to render it in most places extremely difficult and expensive, and in some impracticable, to convey stones or boundaries which had been prepared and marked as aforesaid, to their proper stations, we have marked and described the said line from Sideling hill to the top of the Alleghany Ridge, which divides the waters running into the rivers Potowmack and Ohio, by rais-ing and erecting thereon, on the tops of ridges and mountains over which the said line passed, heaps or piles of stones or earth, from about three and a half to four yards in diameter, at bottom, and from six to seven feet in height, and that from the top of the said Alleghany Ridge west-ward, as far as we have continued the said line, we have set up posts at the end of every mile, and raised round each post, heaps or piles of stones, or earth of about the diameter and height before mentioned.

J. Thomas Scharf, *History of Maryland* (Baltimore, 1879), I, 407-409.

CHAPTER VI — GEORGIA

39. "Designs of the Trustees for Establishing the Colony of Georgia" (1733)

BY GENERAL JAMES EDWARD OGLETHORPE

General Oglethorpe was the prime mover in the establishment of the colony as a philanthropic enterprise; a man of the highest character and trustworthiness. — Bibliography: Winsor, *Narrative and Critical History*, V, 392–406; C. C. Jones, *Georgia*, I, chs. iv, v; Channing and Hart, *Guide*, § 103.

IN *America* there are fertile lands sufficient to subsist all the useless Poor in *England*, and distressed Protestants in Europe; yet Thousands starve for want of mere sustenance. The distance makes it difficult to get thither. The same want that renders men useless here, prevents their paying their passage; and if others pay it for 'em, they become servants, or rather slaves for years to those who have defrayed the expense. Therefore, money for passage is necessary, but is not the only want; for if people were set down in America, and the land before them, they must cut down trees, build houses, fortify towns, dig and sow the land before they can get in a harvest; and till then, they must be provided with food, and kept together, that they may be assistant to each other for their natural support and protection.

The Romans esteemed the sending forth of Colonies, among their noblest works; they observed that Rome, as she increased in power and empire, drew together such a conflux of people from all parts that she found herself over-burdened with their number, and the government brought under an incapacity to provide for them, or keep them in order. Necessity, the mother of invention, suggested to them an expedient, which at once gave ease to the capital, and increased the wealth and number of industrious citizens, by lessening the useless and unruly multitude; and by planting them in colonies on the frontiers of their empire, gave a new strength to the whole; and *This* they looked upon to be so considerable a service to the commonwealth, that they created peculiar officers for the establishment of such colonies, and the expence was defrayed out of the public treasury.

FROM THE CHARTER. — His Majesty having taken into his considera·
tion, the miserable circumstances of many of his own poor subjects,
ready to perish for want : as likewise the distresses of many poor foreigners, who would take refuge here from persecution ; and having a Princely
regard to the great danger the southern frontiers of South Carolina are
exposed to, by reason of the small number of white inhabitants there,
hath, out of his Fatherly compassion towards his subjects, been graciously pleased to grant a charter for incorporating a number of gentlemen by the name of *The Trustees for establishing the Colony of Georgia
in America.* They are impowered to collect benefactions ; and lay
them out in cloathing, arming, sending over, and supporting colonies
of the poor, whether subjects or foreigners, in Georgia. And his Majesty farther grants all his lands between the rivers *Savannah and Alatamaha,* which he erects into a Province by the name of GEORGIA, unto
the Trustees, in trust for the poor, and for the better support of the
Colony. At the desire of the Gentlemen, there are clauses in the Charter, restraining them and their successors from receiving any salary, fee,
perquisite, or profit, whatsoever, by or from this undertaking ; and also
from receiving any grant of lands within the said district, to themselves,
or in trust for them. There are farther clauses granting to the Trustees
proper powers for establishing and governing the Colony, and liberty
of conscience to all who shall settle there.

The Trustees intend to relieve such unfortunate persons as cannot
subsist here, and establish them in an orderly manner, so as to form a
well regulated town. As far as their fund goes, they will defray the
charge of their passage to Georgia ; give them necessaries, cattle, land,
and subsistence, till such time as they can build their houses and clear
some of their land. They rely for success, first on the goodness of
Providence, next on the compassionate disposition of the people of
England ; and, they doubt not, that much will be spared from luxury,
and superfluous expenses, by generous tempers, when such an opportunity is offered them by the giving of £20 to provide for a man or
woman, or £10 to a child for ever.

In order to prevent the benefaction given to this purpose, from ever
being misapplied ; and to keep up, as far as human Precaution can, a
spirit of Disinterestedness, the Trustees have established the following
method : That, each Benefactor may know what he has contributed is
safely lodged, and justly accounted for, all money given will be deposited in the Bank of England ; and entries made of every benefaction, in

a book to be kept for that purpose by the Trustees; or, if concealed, the names of those, by whose hands they sent their money. There are to be annual accounts of all the money received, and how the same has been disposed of, laid before the Lord High Chancellor, the Lord Chief Justice of the King's Bench, the Master of the Rolls, the Lord Chief Justice of the Common Pleas, and the Lord Chief Baron of the Exchequer, or two of them, will be transmitted to every considerable Benefactor.

By such a Colony, many families, who would otherwise starve, will be provided for, and made masters of houses and lands; the people in Great Britain to whom these necessitous families were a burthen, will be relieved; numbers of manufacturers will be here employed, for supplying them with clothes, working tools, and other necessaries; and by giving refuge to the distressed Saltzburghers, and other persecuted Protestants, the power of Britain, as a reward for its hospitality, will be encreased by the addition of so many religious and industrious subjects.

The Colony of *Georgia* lying about the same latitude with part of *China, Persia, Palestine,* and the *Madeiras,* it is highly probable that when hereafter it shall be well-peopled and rightly cultivated, ENGLAND may be supplied from thence with raw Silk, Wine, Oil, Dyes, Drugs, and many other materials for manufactures, which she is obliged to purchase from Southern countries. As towns are established and grow populous along the rivers Savannah and Alatamaha, they will make such a barrier as will render the southern frontier of the British Colonies on the Continent of America, safe from Indian and other enemies.

All human affairs are so subject to chance, that there in [is] no answering for events; yet from reason and the nature of things, it may be concluded, that the riches and also the number of the inhabitants in *Great Britain* will be increased, by importing at a cheap rate from this new Colony, the materials requisite for carrying on in Britain several manufactures. For our Manufacturers will be encouraged to marry and multiply, when they find themselves in circumstances to provide for their families, which must necessarily be the happy effect of the increase and cheapness of our materials of those Manufactures, which at present we purchase with our money from foreign countries, at dear rates; and also many people will find employment here, on account [of] such farther demands by the people of this Colony, for those manufactures which are made for the produce of our own country; and, as has been justly observed, the people will always abound where there is full employment for them.

CHRISTIANITY will be extended by the execution of this design; since, the good discipline established by the Society, will reform the manners of those miserable objects, who shall be by them subsisted; and the example of a whole Colony, who shall behave in a just, moral, and religious manner, will contribute greatly towards the conversion of the Indians, and taking off the prejudices received from the profligate lives of such who have scarce any thing of Christianity but the name.

The Trustees in their general meetings, will consider of the most prudent methods for effectually establishing a regular Colony; and that it may be done, is demonstrable. Under what difficulties, was *Virginia* planted? — the coast and climate then unknown; the Indians numerous, and at enmity with the first Planters, who were forced to fetch all provisions from England; yet it is grown a mighty Province, and the Revenue receives £100,000 for duties upon the goods that they send yearly home. Within this 50 years, *Pennsylvania* was as much a forest as *Georgia* in [is] now; and in these few years, by the wise œconomy of William Penn, and those who assisted him, it now gives food to 80,000 inhabitants, and can boast of as fine a City as most in Europe.

This new Colony is more likely to succeed than either of the former were, since Carolina abounds with provisions, the climate is known, and there are men to instruct in the seasons and nature of cultivating the soil. There are but few *Indian* families within 400 miles; and those, in perfect amity with the English: — *Port Royal* (the station of his Majesty's ships) is within 30, and *Charlestown* (a great mart) is within 120 miles. If the Colony is attacked, it may be relieved by sea, from Port Royal, or the Bahamas; and the Militia of South Carolina is ready to support it, by land.

For the continuing the relief which is now given, there will be lands reserved in the Colony; and the benefit arising from them is to go to the carrying on of the trust. So that, at the same time, the money by being laid out preserves the lives of the poor, and makes a comfortable provision for those whose expenses are by it defrayed; their labor in improving their own lands, will make the adjoining reserved lands valuable; and the rents of those reserved lands will be a perpetual fund for the relieving more poor people. So that instead of laying out the money upon lands, with the income thereof to support the poor, this is laying out money upon the poor; and by relieving those who are now unfortunate, raises a fund for the perpetual relief of those who shall be so hereafter.

I

There is an occasion now offered for every one, to help forward this design; the smallest benefaction will be received, and applied with the utmost care: — every little will do something; and a great number of small benefactions will amount to a sum capable of doing a great deal of good.

If any person, moved with the calamities of the unfortunate, shall be inclined to contribute towards their relief, they are desired to pay their benefactions into the Bank of England, on account of the Trustees for establishing the Colony of Georgia in America; or else, to any of the Trustees, who are, &c.

James [Edward] Oglethorpe, *A Brief Account of the Establishment of the Colony of Georgia*, in Force, *Tracts*, etc. (Washington, 1836), I, No. ii, 4–7.

---

40. The Coming of the Salzburg Germans (1733/4)

BY REVEREND JOHANN MARTIN BOLZIUS

(ANONYMOUS TRANSLATION)

Bolzius was a Salzburger minister, who came over with the first emigration of the German Protestants fleeing from the persecution of their prince bishop. — Bibliography: Winsor, *Narrative and Critical History*, V, 395–396; C. C. Jones, *Georgia*, I, ch. xi; Channing and Hart, *Guide*, § 103.

Savannah, Tuesday, *March* 12.

A T the Place of our Landing, almost all the Inhabitants of the Town of *Savannah* were gather'd together; they fired off some Cannons, and cried Huzzah! which was answer'd by our Sailors, and other *English* People in our Ship, in the same manner. Some of us were immediately fetch'd on Shore in a Boat, and carried about the City, into the Woods, and the new Garden belonging to the Trustees. In the mean time, a very good Dinner was prepared for us: And the *Saltzburgers*, who had yet fresh Meat in the Ship, when they came on shore, they got very good and wholesome *English* strong Beer. And besides the Inhabitants shewing them a great deal of Kindness, and the Country pleasing them, they were full of Joy, and praised God for it. We, the Commissary, and Mr. *Zwefler* the Physician, were lodged in the House of the Reverend Mr. *Quincy*, the *English* Minister here.

Wednesday, *March* 13.

OUR *Saltzburgers* were lodged in a Tent, pitch'd on purpose for them, till Mr. *Oglethorpe's* Arrival from *Charlestown*. A *Jew* invited our *Saltzburgers*, and treated them with a good Rice-Soop for Breakfast. And GOD hath also moved the Hearts of several others here, to be very good and hospitable to us. The Country, as the Inhabitants say, is very fruitful; and the Land chose by us, which is about 21 *English* Miles from hence, is still better. All that is sowed, grows in a short Time.

Thursday, *March* 14.

LAST Night we Prayed on shore for the first time, in the *English* Chapel, made of Boards, and used for divine Worship, till a Church can be built; the Use of which is allowed us, during our Stay here. The Inhabitants join with us, and shew much Devotion. The *Jews* likewise, of which there are 12 Families here, come to Church, and seem to be very devout: They understand the *German* Tongue. Though the Chapel is but of Boards, it is very convenient, and pleases the *Saltzburgers*. . . .

Friday, *March* 15.

THIS Day Mr. *Oglethorpe* arrived here, and received our *Saltzburgers* and us in a very friendly manner; and we dined with him. He will speedily give Orders that our People shall go to the Place intended for their Settlement. He being very sollicitous that these poor *Indians* should be brought to the Knowledge of GOD, has desired us to learn their Language; and we, with the Blessing of GOD, will joyfully undertake the Task. . . .

OUR *Saltzburgers* have often been admonished very earnestly to abstain from drinking a certain intoxicating Liquor like Brandy, called *Rum*; which is made of Molosses, in the Islands of the *West-Indies*, &c. because this Liquor hath occasion'd the Death of many People. Some good Persons, who lately visited our *Saltzburgers*, are much pleased with their Devotion, and with the whole of their Behaviour; and on that Account, prophesy much Good to the Country. . .

Tuesday, *March* 19.

MR. *Oglethorpe* went last *Friday* with the Commissary, Mr. *Zwefler*, Mr. *Gronau*, and a *Saltzburger*, to the Place where we are to live with our *Saltzburgers*, in order to shew them the Ground where they are to build their Houses. This Day the Commissary and Mr. *Zwefler* return'd back, and inform'd us much of the Goodness and Fertility of the Ground, as also of the Goodness of the *Indians*. . . .

Wednesday, *March* 20.

. . . THE *Saltzburgers* have (as the other Settlers in *Georgia*) received a Gift from the Trustees, of Arms, Houshold Goods, and working Tools, *viz.* Kettles, Pots, Dishes, Saws, Axes, Shovels, *&c.* . . .

Tuesday, *March* 26.

IT is a great Pleasure to us, that Mr. *Oglethorpe* approved of our calling the River, and the Place where our Houses are to be built, *Ebenezer* ; 1 Sam. vii. 12. *Then Samuel took a Stone, and set it between Mizpeh and Shen, and called the Name of it Ebenezer; saying, Hitherto hath the* LORD *helped us.* Which Denomination is already known among the People that live hereabout. This Word hath at our Arrival here, and when we were yet on board the Ship, made us joyful to the Praise of GOD, and will do it for the future as often as we name the Name of our Town or River, or hear it named. . . .

Saturday, *March* 30.

As, by the Help of GOD, we are now at more Ease, and in better Order, we can take more Care of the Education of the Children ; who come daily several times to our Room, where they are taught proper Texts out of the Holy Scripture, and are Catechized. At Prayers, all is repeated in the Presence of the grown People, whereby they are edified ; as well as by the Catechism, and Texts of the Holy Scripture, that are explained unto them. As soon as we come to our *Ebenezer*, we shall also begin to teach them Reading and Writing.

An Extract of the Journals of Mr. Commissary Von Reck . . . and of the Reverend Mr. Bolzius (London, 1734), 32–50 *passim.*

---

41. A New England Man in Georgia (1735)

BY REVEREND SAMUEL QUINCY

Quincy was a resident minister in Georgia, whose services were not acceptable to the Georgia trustees. He was succeeded by John Wesley. — Bibliography : Winsor, *Narrative and Critical History*, V, 392–406; Channing and Hart, *Guide*, § 103.

Savannah, Oct. 23, 1735.

YOURS by Mr. Foster, together with a kind present, came to hand, for which I return you and my good cousin a great many thanks. We are in daily expectation of the arrival of Mr. Oglethorpe, who comes

over to over-see the building of forts on our frontiers, pursuant to the
king's orders. Affairs here are but in an ill situation, through the discouragements attending the settlement, which have rendered some of
the better sort of people very discontented, and if the trustee, who
comes over, does not remove them, I believe many will leave the place.
The magistrate, to whom the government of the colony was left, proves
a most insolent and tyrannical fellow. Several just complaints have
been sent home against him, which do not meet with a proper regard,
and this has made people very uneasie. Indeed it has a very ill aspect;
for it looks as if they designed to establish arbitrary government, and
reduce the people to a condition little better than that of slavery. There
are some things likewise in their very constitution, which looks this way;
the tenure by which they hold their land subjects them to a kind of
vassalage, not consistent with a free people. In short, Georgia, which
was seemingly intended to be the asylum of the distressed, unless things
are greatly altered, is likely to be itself a mere scene of distress. Some
of the people, to support their extravagance, and others out of real
necessity, have run themselves miserably in debt; the store-keepers
having given them credit in hopes of possessing themselves of their
houses, and even their persons, by obliging them to be their servants;
and if the trustees do not disconcert these designs, great numbers must
be unavoidably ruined; though to do this must needs ruin the store-
keepers, for they are most of them deeply indebted to their merchants
in Carolina: But I think indeed they deserve no pity, because their
designs appear to have been rapacious and dishonest. This is our present condition, and the small improvements that are made on lands, gives
us a very indifferent future prospect. Notwithstanding the place has
been settled nigh three years, I believe I may venture to say there is
not one family, which can subsist without farther assistance, and most
would starve if they had not dependence on the trustees; but the trustees have raised very large assistance to carry it on, and will no doubt
do their utmost to support it, and therefore it is to be hoped that it
may in time come to something, though on the present footing things
are established, it will never be a desirable place, and therefore none
will choose to settle in it who can remove elsewhere, unless it be some
who are particularly favoured by the trustees. . . .

Massachusetts Historical Society, *Collections*, Second Series (Boston, 1814),
II, 188–189.

42. The Question of Slavery in Georgia (1738–1739)

BY FREEHOLDERS AND THE GEORGIA TRUSTEES

The trustees for Georgia had forbidden the use of slaves in the colony, and for years the matter was a bone of contention between the majority of the colonists and the trustees. — Bibliography: Winsor, *Narrative and Critical History*, V, 392–404; C. C. Jones, *Georgia*, I, ch. vi; Channing and Hart, *Guide*, § 103. — On the general question of slavery, see below, ch. xvi.

A. PROTEST OF THE SETTLERS

To the Honourable the Trustees for Establishing the Colony of Georgia *in* America.

May it please Your Honours;

WE whose Names are under-written, being all *Settlers, Free-holders* and *Inhabitants* in the Province of *Georgia*, and being sensible of the great Pains and Care exerted by You in Endeavouring to settle this Colony, since it has been under Your Protection and Management; Do unanimously join to lay before You, with the utmost Regret, the following Particulars. . . . The Land . . . not being capable to maintain the Settlers here, they must unavoidably have recourse to and depend upon Trade: But to our *woful* Experience likewise, the same Causes that prevented the *first*, obstruct the *latter;* for tho' the Situation of this Place is exceeding well adapted for Trade, and if it was encouraged, might be much more improved by the Inhabitants; yet the Difficulties and Restrictions, which we *hitherto have* and *at present do* labour under, debar us of that Advantage: Timber is the only Thing we have here which we might export, and notwithstanding we are obliged to fall it in Planting our Land; yet we cannot manufacture it for a Foreign Market but at double the Expence of other Colonies; as for Instance, the *River of May*, which is but *twenty* Miles from us, with the Allowance of Negroes, load Vessels with that Commodity at one Half of the Price that we can do; and what should induce Persons to bring Ships here, when they can be loaded with one Half of the Expence so near us; therefore the Timber on the Land is only a continual Charge to the Possessors of it, tho' of very great Advantage in all the Northern Colonies, where Negroes are allowed, and consequently Labour cheap. We do not in the least doubt but that in Time *Silk* and *Wine* may be produced here, especially the former; but since the Cultivation of Land with white Servants only, cannot raise Provisions for our Families as before mentioned, *therefore* it is likewise impossible to carry on these Manufactures according to the *present* Constitution. It is very well known, that *Carolina* can raise every thing that this Colony can; and they having their Labour so much cheaper will always ruin our Market, unless we are in some Measure on a Footing with them; and as in *both*, the Land is worn out in *four* or *five* Years, and then fit for Nothing but Pasture; we must be always at a great deal more Expence than they in Clearing new Land for Planting. . . .

But we for our Parts have intirely relied on and confided in Your good Intentions, believing You would redress any Grievances that should appear; and now by our long Experience, from Industry and continual Application to Improvement of Land here, do find it impossible to pursue it, or even to subsist ourselves any longer, according to the *present* Nature of the Constitution; and likewise believing You will agree to those Measures that are found from Experience capable to make this Colony succeed, and to promote which we have consumed our Money, Time and Labour; we do, from a sincere Regard to its Welfare, and in Duty both to You and ourselves, beg Leave to lay before Your immediate Consideration, the *Two* following chief Causes of these our *present* Misfortunes and this *deplorable* State of the Colony, and which, we are certain, if granted, would be an infallible Remedy for *both*.

1*st*, The Want of a free Title or Fee-simple, to our Lands; which if granted, would both induce great Numbers of new Settlers to come amongst us, and likewise encourage those who remain here chearfully to proceed in making further Improvements, as well to retrieve their sunk Fortunes as to make Provisions for their Posterity.

2*d*, The Want of the Use of Negroes, with proper Limitations; which if granted, would both occasion great Numbers of white People to come here, and also render us capable to subsist ourselves, by raising Provisions upon our Lands, until we could make some Produce fit for Export, in some Measure to Ballance our Importation. We are very sensible of the Inconveniencies and Mischiefs that have already, and do daily arise from an unlimited Use of Negroes; but we are as sensible, that these may be prevented by a due Limitation, such as so many to each white Man, or so many to such a Quantity of Land, or in any other Manner which Your Honours shall think most proper.

By granting us, *Gentlemen*, these *Two* Particulars, and such other Privileges as His Majesty's most dutiful Subjects in *America* enjoy, You will not only prevent our impending Ruin, but, we are fully satisfied, also will soon make this the most flourishing Colony possess'd by His Majesty in *America*, and Your Memories will be *perpetuated* to all future Ages, our latest Posterity *sounding* Your Praises, as their *first* Founders, Patrons and Guardians ; but if, by denying us these Privileges, we ourselves and Families are not only ruin'd, but even our Posterity likewise ; You will always be mentioned as the *Cause* and *Authors* of all their Misfortunes and Calamities ; which we hope will never happen.

We are,

with all due Respect,

Savannah,   *Your Honours most dutiful*
9*th* December, 1738.   *and obedient Servants. . .*

B.   ANSWER OF THE TRUSTEES

To the Magistrates of the Town of Savannah, *in the Province of* Georgia.

THE Trustess for establishing the Colony of *Georgia* in *America*, have received by the Hands of Mr. *Benjamin Ball* of *London*, Merchant, an attested Copy of a Representation, signed by You the Magistrates, and many of the Inhabitants of *Savannah*, on the 9*th* of *December* last, for altering the Tenure of the Lands, and introducing Negroes into the Province, transmitted from thence by Mr. *Robert Williams*.

The Trustees are not surprized to find unwary People drawn in by crafty Men, to join in a Design of *extorting by Clamour* from the Trustees an Alteration in the Fundamental Laws, framed for the Preservation of the People, from those very Designs.

But the Trustees cannot but express their Astonishment, that You the Magistrates, appointed by them to be Guardians of the People, by putting those Laws in Execution, should so far forget your Duty, as to put Yourselves at the Head of this Attempt.

However they direct You to give the Complainants this Answer from the Trustees, That they should deem themselves very unfit for the Trust reposed in them by His Majesty on their Behalf, if they could be prevailed upon, by such an irrational Attempt, to give up a Constitution, framed with the greatest Caution for the Preservation of Liberty and Property ; and of which the Laws against the Use of Slaves, and for the Entail of Lands, are the surest Foundations.

And the Trustees are the more confirmed in their opinion of the

Unreasonableness of this Demand, that they have received Petitions from the *Darien*, and other Parts of the Province, representing the Inconvenience and Danger, which must arise to the good People of the Province from the Introduction of Negroes.   And as the Trustees themselves are fully convinced, that besides the Hazard attending that *Introduction*, it would destroy all Industry among the white Inhabitants; and that by giving them a Power to alien their Lands, the Colony would soon be too like its Neighbours, void of white Inhabitants, filled with Blacks, and reduced to be the precarious Property of a Few, equally exposed to Domestick Treachery, and Foreign Invasion; and therefore the Trustees cannot be supposed to be in any Disposition of granting this Request; and if they have not before this signified their Dislike of it, this Delay is to be imputed to no other Motives, but the Hopes they had conceived, that Time and Experience would bring the Complainants to a better Mind: And the Trustees readily join Issue with them in their Appeal to Posterity, who shall judge between them, who were their best Friends; *Those*, who endeavoured to preserve for them a Property in their Lands, by tying up the Hands of their unthrifty Progenitors; or *They*, who wanted a Power to mortgage or alien them: Who were the best Friends to the Colony, *Those* who with great Labour and Cost had endeavoured to form a Colony of His Majesty's Subjects, and persecuted *Protestants* from other Parts of *Europe*, had placed them on a fruitful Soil, and strove to secure them in their Possessions, by those Arts which naturally tend to keep the Colony full of useful and industrious People, capable both to cultivate and defend it; or *Those*, who, to gratify the greedy and ambitious Views of a few Negroe Merchants, would put it into their Power to become sole Owners of the Province, by introducing their baneful Commodity; which, it is well known by sad Experience, has brought our Neighbour Colonies to the Brink of Ruin, by driving out their white Inhabitants, who were their Glory and Strength, to make room for Black, who are now become the Terror of their unadvised Masters.

Signed by Order of the Trustees,
this 20th Day of June, 1739.
Benj. Martyn, *Secretary.*

Pat[rick] Tailfer and others, *A True and Historical Narrative of the Colony of Georgia, in America* (Charles Town, 1741); reprinted in Force, *Tracts*, etc. (Washington, 1836), I, No. iv, 37-53 *passim.*

43. Mr. Whitefield's Orphan-House (1739/40)

BY SECRETARY COLONEL WILLIAM STEPHENS

Stephens was resident secretary in Georgia for the trustees, and later president of the colony. His journal is of great value on account of its accuracy and minuteness. — Bibliography: Winsor, *Narrative and Critical History*, V, 392–406; C. C. Jones, *Georgia*, I, 400–419; Channing and Hart, *Guide*, § 103. — See below, No. 100.

FRIDAY [January 11]. Towards Noon arrived Mr. *Whitfield*, accompanied by three or four in his Travels; and it luckily happening, that Mr. *Norris* arrived Yesterday from the South, it was quickly seen with what Temper they met: When, to the Disappointment of some People, who are pleased best with Contention, upon Mr. *Whitfield*'s shewing the Authority he brought with him, Mr. *Norris*, without the least Emotion, told him, that he should by no Means enter into any Disputes to disturb the Peace of the Church; nor had he ever wrote once to the Trustees concerning it, from the first Notice he had of what was in Agitation; wherefore it was far from his Intention to enter into any Controversy with him; but on the contrary declared, that his Ministry at *Savannah* ceased from that Instant, declining to officiate at Evening Prayer this Night, but left it to Mr. *Whitfield* to take Possession of the Church immediately; who accordingly did so, when a greater Congregation than usual most Days were met, many (I fear) more out of Curiosity than Devotion. He delivered to me in the Afternoon a Letter from Mr. *Martyn*, Secretary to the Trust, dated *June* 1, relating to the Land appointed for his Use, and whereon to set the Orphan-House, &c. which after I had read, he also did; and I told him I would not be wanting in any Thing on my Part to promote what the Trust appointed, and to give him what Assistance I could; but as to the five hundred Acres, Mr. *Habersham*, without conferring with me upon it, when the General was here, applied himself to him, who approved of the Place he had made Choice of, ordered it to be run out, and then signed a Warrant, which he directed me to give the Constable, empowering him to give Possession of it to Mr. *Habersham*; which was done accordingly in some short Time after: And that Mr. *Habersham* had already began fencing and clearing upon it. After his reading the Letter from Mr. *Martyn*, he desired me to let him take a Copy of it; which I would not refuse him.

Saturday. Mr. *Whitfield* lost no Time in setting forward the Work which he professed to have much at Heart, about an Orphan-House;

and rode out to view the Land which Mr. *Habersham* had taken Care to provide against his coming, consisting of five hundred Acres, that he had taken Possession of in his own Name; where Mr. *Whitfield* gave such Orders and Directions as he thought proper. . . .

Sunday. Mr. *Whitfield*'s Name, which of late had made so much Noise in *England*, could not fail drawing all Sorts of People to Church, who professed Christianity, to hear what Doctrine it was that he preached: When both in the Morning and Afternoon, he made our Justification by Faith only, the Subject of his Discourse; taking those Words in St. *Matthew* for his Text, " What think you of Christ? " Which he pressed home with great Energy, denouncing Anathema's on all such as taught otherwise. . . .

Tuesday. What I thought most worth present Observation, arose from the extraordinary Preparations making to build the Orphan-House, &*c*. wherein Mr. *Whitfield* indeed shewed himself much in earnest; and it may be presumed, he expected it would be finished in few Months; in order to which, there was hardly one Sawyer of any Value in Town, but all hired, and engaged by him to go over and work, where he meant to erect that Building: Most of our Carpenters, Bricklayers, &*c*. were likewise engaged by him, and a great Quantity of Scantling Timber, ready sawn, was coming (as I heard) for the more Expedition, from *North-Carolina*. The House that Mr. *Bradley* had lived in, being empty, Mr. *Jones* complimented the first Comers with the Use of, for the present; and Mr. *Whitfield* chose, upon his Arrival, to carry those Friends that came with him thither also, as well as to be with them himself, leaving Mr. *Norris* in Possession of the Parsonage-House (which could not hold more than two or three) till he could conveniently move what he had there, and carry it with him to *Frederica:* But the great House not being finished within, and incommodious on many Accounts, especially by letting the Rain come through the Roof, which was flat; Mr. *Whitfield* agreed with *David Douglass* for the Use of his House (much the largest of any private Lot in Town) at the Rent of 20*l.* Sterling for half a Year only. . . .

Sunday. Mr. *Whitfield* did the Duties of the Day, with more than ordinary Diligence, by reading Prayers at Seven in the Morning; at Ten again, with a Sermon after it; at Three again, the same as at Ten; and a Lecture at Seven in the Evening; besides the Sacrament, which he administred to betwixt thirty and forty People after the second Morning Service: His Sermons both before Noon and after, in the same

Manner as on *Sunday* last, were wholly on the Doctrine of Justification and Regeneration ; which we hoped would ere long be followed by an Exhortation to the Practice of all Christian Duties, that so our Faith might be shewn by our Works ; otherwise a dry and inactive Faith, it is to be feared, might prove a dangerous State. . . .

William Stephens, *A Journal of the Proceedings in Georgia* (London, 1742), II, 243-254 *passim.*

———◆———

44. Need of Relieving Georgia (1749)

BY EDMUND BURKE (1757)

Burke was a well-known English orator and statesman, who later sided with the colonies in their complaints of the home government. He is responsible for the book from which this extract is taken, though it was probably prepared by an unknown hack-writer. — Bibliography : Winsor, *Narrative and Critical History*, V, ch. vi ; Channing and Hart, *Guide*, § 103.

ALL these, and several other inconveniencies in the plan of the settlement, raised a general discontent in the inhabitants ; they quarrelled with one another, and with their magistrates ; they complained ; they remonstrated ; and finding no satisfaction, many of them fled out of Georgia, and dispersed themselves where they deemed the encouragement better, to all the other colonies. So that of above two thousand people, who had transported themselves from Europe, in a little time not above six or seven hundred were to be found in Georgia ; so far were they from increasing. The mischief grew worse and worse every day, until the government revoked the grant to the trustees, took the province into their own hands, and annulled all the particular regulations that were made. It was then left exactly on the same footing with Carolina.

Though this step has probably saved the colony from entire ruin, yet it was not perhaps so well done to neglect entirely the first views upon which it was settled. These were undoubtedly judicious ; and if the methods taken to compass them were not so well directed, it was no argument against the designs themselves, but a reason for some change in the instruments designed to put them in execution. Certainly nothing wants a regulation more, than the dangerous inequality in the number of negroes and whites in such of our provinces where the former are used. South Carolina, in spite of its great wealth, is really in a more defenceless condition, than a knot of poor townships on the frontiers of New England. In Georgia, the first error of absolutely prohibiting the use of negroes, might be turned to very good account ; for they would have received the permission to employ them under what qualifications soever, not as a restriction, but as a favour and indulgence ; and by executing whatever regulations we should make in this point with strictness, by degrees we might see a province fit to answer all the ends of defence and traffic too ; whereas we have let them use such a latitude in that affair, which we were so earnest to prevent, that Georgia instead of being any defence to Carolina, does actually stand in need of a considerable force to defend itself.

As for the scheme of vines and silk, we were extremely eager in this respect in the beginning ; and very supine ever since. At that time such a design was clearly impracticable ; because a few people seated in a wild country must first provide every thing for the support of life, by raising of corn and breeding of cattle, before they can think of manufactures of any kind ; and they must grow numerous enough to spare a number of hands from that most necessary employment, before they can send such things in any degree of cheapness or plenty to a good market. But now there is little said of either of these articles, though the province is longer settled and grown more populous. But the misfortune is, that though no people upon earth originally conceive things better than the English do, they want the unremitting perseverance which is necessary to bring designs of consequence to perfection. We are apt suddenly to change our measures upon any failure ; without sufficiently considering whether the failure has been owing to a fault in the scheme itself ; this does not arise from any defect peculiar to our people, for it is the fault of mankind in general, if left to themselves. What is done by us is generally done by the spirit of the people ; as far as that can go we advance, but no farther. We want political regulations, and a steady plan in government, to remedy the defects that must be in all things, which depend merely on the character and disposition of the people.

At present Georgia is beginning to emerge, though slowly, out of the difficulties that attended its first establishment. It is still but indifferently peopled, though it is now twenty-six years since its first settlement. Not one of our colonies was of so slow a growth, though none had so much of the attention of the government, or of the people in general, or raised so great expectations in the beginning. They export some corn and lumber to the West-Indies ; they raise some rice, and of late are going with success into indigo. It is not to be doubted but in time, when their internal divisions are a little better composed, the remaining errors in the government corrected, and the people begin to multiply, that they will become a useful province.

Georgia has two towns already known in trade ; Savannah the capital, which stands very well for business about ten miles form [from] the sea, upon a noble river of the same name, which is navigable two hundred miles further for large boats, to the second town, called Augusta ; this stands upon a spot of ground of the greatest fertility, and is so commodiously situated for the Indian trade, that from the first establishment of the colony it has been in a very flourishing condition, and maintained very early six hundred whites in that trade alone. The Indian nations on their borders are the upper and lower Creeks, the Chickesaws, and the Cherokees ; who are some of the most numerous and powerful tribes in America. The trade of skins with this people is the largest we have, it takes in that of Georgia, the two Carolinas and Virginia. We deal with them somewhat in furs likewise, but they are of an inferior sort. All species of animals, that bear the fur, by a wise providence have it more thick, and of a softer and finer kind as you go to the northward ; the greater the cold, the better they are clad.

[Edmund Burke], *An Account of the European Settlements in America* (London, 1760), II, 269–273.

PART III

COLONIAL GOVERNMENT

CHAPTER VII — PRINCIPLES OF ENGLISH CONTROL

45. Extracts from a Navigation Act (1695/6)

BY THE PARLIAMENT OF ENGLAND

This is one of a series of statutes regulating colonial trade. See below, Nos. 87, 146. — Bibliography: Winsor, *Narrative and Critical History*, VI, 62–65; Channing and Hart, *Guide*, §§ 133, 147; *Contemporaries*, I, 185, 240, 462.

AN ACT for preventing Frauds and regulating Abuses in the Plantation Trade.

[I.] . . . That after the Five and twentieth Day of March One thousand six hundred ninety eight noe Goods or Merchandizes whatsoever shall bee imported into or exported out of any Colony or Plantation to His Majesty in Asia Africa or America belonging or in his Possession or which may hereafter belong unto or bee in the Possession of His Majesty His Heires or Successors or shall bee laden in or carried from any One Port or Place in the said Colonies or Plantations to any other Port or Place in the same, the Kingdome of England Dominion of Wales or Towne of Berwick upon Tweed in any Shipp or Bottome but what is or shall bee of the Built of England or of the Built of Ireland or the said Colonies or Plantations and wholly owned by the People thereof or any of them and navigated with the Masters and Three Fourths of the Mariners of the said Places onely (except such Shipps onely as are or shall bee taken Prize and Condemnation thereof made in one of the Courts of Admiralty in England Ireland or the said Colonies or Plantations [to bee navigated by the Master and Three Fourths of the

Mariners English or of the said Plantations as aforesaid and whereof the Property doth belong to English Men] And alsoe except for the space of Three Yeares such Foreigne built Shipps as shall bee employed by the Commissioners of His Majesties Navy for the tyme being or upon Contract with them in bringing onely Masts Timber and other Navall Stores for the Kings Service from His Majesties Colonies or Plantations to this Kingdome to bee navigated as aforesaid and whereof the Property doth belong to English Men) under paine of Forfeiture of Shipp and Goods one third part whereof to bee to the use of His Majesty His Heires and Successors one third part to the Governor of the said Colonies or Plantations and the other third part to the Person who shall informe and sue for the same by Bill Plaint or Information in any of His Majesties Courts of Record att Westminster or in any Court in His Majesties Plantations where such Offence shall bee committed. . . .

[VIII.] And itt is further enacted and declared by the Authority aforesaid That all Lawes By-lawes Usages or Customes att this tyme or which hereafter shall bee in practice or endeavoured or pretended to bee in force or practice in any of the said Plantations which are in any wise repugnant to the before mentioned Lawes or any of them soe far as they doe relate to the said Plantations or any of them or which are wayes repugnant to this present Act or to any other Law hereafter to bee made in this Kingdome soe farr as such Law shall relate to and mention the said Plantations are illegall null and void to all Intents and Purposes whatsoever. . . .

[XVI.] [And for a more effectuall prevention of Frauds which may bee used to elude the Intention of this Act by colouring Foreigne Shipps under English Names Bee itt further enacted by the Authority aforesaid That from and after the Five and twentieth day of March which shall bee in the Yeare of our Lord One thousand six hundred ninety eight noe Shipp or Vessell whatsoever shall bee deemed or passe as a Shipp of the Built of England Ireland Wales Berwick Guernsey Jersey or of any of His Majesties Plantations in America soe as to bee qualifyed to trade to from or in any of the said Plantations untill the Person or Persons claymeing Property in such Shipp or Vessell shall register the same as followeth (that is to say) If the Shipp att the tyme of such Register doth belong to any Port in England Ireland Wales or to the Towne of Berwick upon Tweed then Proofe shall bee made upon Oath of One or more of the Owners of such Shipp or Vessell before the Collector and Comptroller of His Majesties Customes in such Port or if att the tyme of such Register the Shipp belong to any of His Majesties Plantations in America or to the Islands of Guernsey or Jersey then the like Proofe to bee made before the Governour together with the Principall Officer of His Majesties Revenue resideing on such Plantation or Island which Oath the said Governours and Officers of the Customes respectively are hereby authorized to administer in the Tenour following (vizt). . . .]

The Statutes of the Realm (London, 1820), VII, 103–107 *passim*.

---

46. Creation of the Board of Trade (1696)

BY KING WILLIAM THIRD

This is a reorganization of the board created in 1660 (*Contemporaries*, I, No. 54), and again changed in 1752. The extract brings out the theory that the details of colonial administration belonged to the crown and not to Parliament. — Bibliography as in No. 45 above.

HIS Majesties Commission for promoting the Trade of this Kingdom and for inspecting and improving His Plantations in America and elsewhere.

WILLIAM the Third by the Grace of God King of England, Scotland, France and Ireland, Defender of the Faith &a. To our Keeper of oure Great Seale of England or Chancellor of England for the time being, Our President of Our Privy Council for the time being, Our first Commissioner of Our Treasury And our Treasurer of England for the time being, Our first Commissioner of our Admiralty and Our Admirall of England for the time being, And our principall Secretarys of State for the time being, And the Chancellor of Our Exchequer for the time being, To Our Right Trusty and Right Well beloved Cousin and Councillor John Earl of Bridgewater, and Ford Earl of Tankerville, To our Trusty and Well beloved Sir Philip Meadows, Kn[t], William Blaithwayte, John Pollexfen, John Locke, Abraham Hill, and John Methwen, Esquires, Greeting. . . .

KNO WYEE therefor that We reposing espetiall Trust and Confidence in your Discretions, Abilityes and Integrities . . . authorize and appoint . . . you, to be Our Commissioners during our Royal Pleasure, for promoting the Trade of our Kingdome, and for Inspecting and Improving our Plantations in America and elsewhere. . . .

K

And We do hereby further Impower and require you Our said Commissioners to take into your care all Records, Grants and Papers remaining in the Plantation Office or thereunto belonging.

And likewise to inform your selves of the present condition of Our respective Plantations, as well with regard to the Administration of the Government and Justice in those places, as in relation to the Commerce thereof; And also to inquire into the Limits of Soyle and Product of Our severall Plantations and how the same may be improved, and of the best means for easing and securing Our Colonies there, and how the same may be rendred most usefull and beneficiall to our said Kingdom of England.

And We do hereby further impower and require you Our said Commissioners, more particularly and in a principal manner to inform yourselves what Navall Stores may be furnished from Our Plantations, and in what Quantities, and by what methods Our Royall purpose of having our Kingdom supplied with Navall Stores from thence may be made practicable and promoted; And also to inquire into and inform your selves of the best and most proper methods of settling and improving in Our Plantations, such other Staples and other Mau[n]ufactures as Our subjects of England are now obliged to fetch and supply themselves withall from other Princes and States ; And also what Staples and Manufactures may be best encouraged there, and what Trades are taken up and exercised there, which are or may prove prejudiciall to England, by furnishing themselves or other Our Colonies with what has been usually supplied from England ; And to finde out proper means of diverting them from such Trades, and whatsoever else may turne to the hurt of Our Kingdom of England.

And to examin and looke into the usuall Instructions given to the Governors of Our Plantations, and to see if any thing may be added, omitted or changed therein to advantage; To take an Account yearly by way oi Journall of the Administration of Our Governors there, and to draw·out what is proper to be observed and represented unto Us ; And as often as occasion shall require to consider of proper persons to be Governors or Deputy Governors, or to be of Our Councill or of Our Councill at Law, or Secretarys, in Our respective Plantations, in order to present their Names to Us in Councill.

And We do hereby further Authorize and impower you Our said Commissioners, to examin into and weigh such Acts of the Assemblies of the Plantations respectively as shall from time to time be sent or transmitted hither for Our Approbation ; And to set down and represent as aforesaid the Usefulness or Mischeif thereof to Our Crown, and to Our said Kingdom of England, or to the Plantations themselves, in case the same should be established for Lawes there ; And also to consider what matters may be recommended as fitt to be passed in the Assemblys there, To heare complaints of Oppressions and maleadministrations, in Our Plantations, in order to represent as aforesaid what you in your Discretions shall thinke proper ; And also to require an Account of all Monies given for Publick uses by the Assemblies in Our Plantations, and how the same are and have been expended or laid out.

E. B. O'Callaghan, editor, *Documents relative to the Colonial History of the State of New-York* (Albany, 1854), IV, 145–148 *passim*.

---

47. "Englishmen Hate an Arbitrary Power" (1710)

BY JOHN WISE

Wise was one of the foremost prose writers of the colonial period, and minister at Ipswich. — Bibliography : Tyler, *American Literature*, II, 104–116; Palfrey, *New England*, III, 525–527; Winsor, *Narrative and Critical History*, VI, ch. i; J. A. Doyle, *English in America, Puritan Colonies*, II, 378; Channing and Hart, *Guide*, § 130.

ENGLISHMEN hate an arbitrary power (politically considered) as they hate the devil.

For that they have through immemorial ages been the owners of very fair infranchizements and liberties, that the sense, favor or high esteem of them are (as it were) *extraduce*, transmitted with the elemental materials of their essence from generation to generation, and so ingenate and mixed with their frame, that no artifice, craft or force used can root it out. *Naturam expellas furca licet usque recurrit.* And though many of their incautelous princes have endeavored to null all their charter rights and immunities, and agrandize themselves in the servile state of the subjects, by setting up their own seperate will, for the great standard of government over the nations, yet they have all along paid dear for their attempts, both in the ruin of the nation, and in interrupting the increase of their own grandeur, and their foreign settlements and conquests.

Had the late reigns, before the accession of the great *William* and *Mary*, to the throne of England, but taken the measures of them, and her present majesty, in depressing vice, and advancing the union and wealth, and encouraging the prowice and bravery of the nation, they might by this time have been capable to have given laws to any monarch on earth ; but spending their time in the pursuit of an absolute monarchy (contrary to the temper of the nation, and the ancient constitution of the government) through all the meanders of state craft : It has apparently kept back the glory, and dampt all the most noble affairs of the nation. And when under the midwifry of *Machiavilan* art, and cunning of a daring prince, this MONSTER, tyranny, and arbitrary government, was at last just born, upon the holding up of a finger ! or upon the least signal given, ON the whole nation goes upon this HYDRA.

The very name of an arbitrary government is ready to put an Englishman's blood into a fermentation ; but when it really comes, and shakes its whip over their ears, and tells them it is their master, it makes them stark mad ; and being of a memical genius, and inclined to follow the court mode, they turn arbitrary too.

That some writers, who have observed the governments and humors of nations, thus distinguish the English :

The emperor (say they) is the king of kings, the king of Spain is the king of men, the king of France the king of asses, and the king of England the king of devils ; for that the English nation can never be bridled, and rid by an arbitrary prince. Neither can any chains put on by dispotic and arbitrary measures hold these legions. . . . to conclude this plea, I find not amongst all the catalogues of heroes or worthy things in the English empire, peers to these undertakers ; therefore we must needs range them with the arbitrary princes of the earth, (such as the great *Czar* or *Ottoman* monarch) who have no other rule to govern by, but their own will. . . .

John Wise, *The Churches Quarrel Espoused* (Boston, 1772), No. ii, 147-148.

48.   " Defence of the New-England Charters " (1721)

BY AGENT JEREMIAH DUMMER

Dummer was a minister in New England, but later entered into English politics. He was agent of Massachusetts in England from 1710 to 1721. This is the most famous statement of the rights of the colonies in this period. — Bibliography : Tyler, *American Literature*, II, 116–120; Palfrey, *New England*, IV, 277–580 *passim;* J. A. Doyle, *English in America, Puritan Colonies*, II, 371–372; Channing and Hart, *Guide*, § 130. — For previous discussions of charters, see *Contemporaries*, I, Nos. 67, 105 109, 114, 116, 135.

THE other Charge in the Bill is, *That they have exercis'd arbitrary Power.*   If this be aim'd at the Proprietary Governments, which however I don't accuse, I have nothing to say, but am sure that the Charter Governments stand clear of it.   The Thing speaks loudly for itself.   For in the Governments, where there are Charters, and those Charters entire, all Officers Civil and Military are elected by the People, and that annually ; than which Constitution nothing under Heaven can be a stronger Barrier against arbitrary Rule. For should it be allow'd, that the People, *corrupted* or *deceiv'd*, might instead of wise Magistrates chuse Tyrants and Oppressors to Lord over them one Year ; yet it can't be imagin'd, that after they have felt the Smart of it, they will do so the next.   Nor can there be a greater Obligation on the Rulers themselves to administer Justice, than that their Election depends on it the next Year.   Hence the frequent Choice of Magistrates has bin ever a main Pillar, upon which all who have aim'd at Freedom in their Schemes of Government, have depended.

The 2d Charge in the Bill against the Charter Governments, that they have exercis'd arbitrary Power, answer'd.

AS the Reason is incontestable, so the Fact is apparent, that these Governments, far from retrenching the Liberty of the Subject, have improv'd it in some important Articles, which the Circumstances of Things in *Great Britain* perhaps don't require, or won't easily admit.

To instance in a few; There has bin from the beginning an Office erected by Law in every County, where all Conveyances of Land are enter'd at large, after the Grantors have first acknowledg'd them before a Justice of Peace ; by which means much Fraud is prevented, no Person being able to sell his Estate twice, or take up more Money upon it than it's worth.   Provision has likewise bin made for the Security of the Life and Property of the Subject in the Matter of Juries, who are

not return'd by the Sherriff of the County, but are chosen by the Inhabitants of the Town a convenient Time before the sitting of the
Courts.   And this Election is under the most exact Regulation, in
Order to prevent Corruption, so far as Humane Prudence can do it.
It must be noted, that Sherriffs in the Plantations are comparatively but
little Officers, and therefore not to be trusted as here, where they are
Men of ample Fortunes.   And yet even here such flagrant Corruptions
have bin found in returning Juries by Sherriffs, that the House of Com-
mons thought it necessary in their last Session to amend the Law in this
Point, and pass'd a Bill for choosing them by Ballot.

REDRESS in their Courts of Law is *easy*, *quick*, and *cheap*.   All Processes are in *English*, and no special Pleadings or Demurrers are admitted, but the general Issue is always given, and special Matters
brought in Evidence ; which saves Time and Expence ; and in this Case
a Man is not liable to lose his Estate for a Defect in Form, nor is the
Merit of the Cause made to depend on the Niceties of Clerkship.   By
a Law of the Country no Writ may be abated for a circumstantial Error,
such as a slight Mis-nomer or any Informality.   And by another Law,
it is enacted, that every Attorney taking out a Writ from the Clerk's
Office, shall indorse his Sirname upon it, and be liable to pay to the
adverse Party his Costs and Charges in Case of Non-Prosecution or
Discontinuance, or that the Plaintiff be Non-suit, or Judgment pass
against him.   And it is provided in the same Act, That if the Plaintiff
shall suffer a Nonsuit by the Attorney's mis-laying the Action, he shall
be oblig'd to draw a new Writ without a Fee, in case the Party shall see
fit to revive the Suit.   I can't but think that every Body, except Gentlemen of the long Robe and the Attornies, will think this a wholesome
Law, and well calculated for the Benefit of the Subject.   For the quicker
Dispatch of Causes, Declarations are made Parts of the Writ, in which
the Case is fully and particularly set forth.   If it be matter of Account,
the Account is annex'd to the Writ, and Copies of both left with the
Defendant ; which being done Fourteen Days before the Sitting of the
Court, he is oblig'd to plead directly, and the Issue is then try'd.
Whereas by the Practice of the Court of *King's Bench*, Three or Four
Months Time is often lost after the Writ is serv'd, before the Cause can
be brought to Issue.

NOR are the People of *New-England* oppress'd with the infinite Delays and Expence that attend the Proceedings in *Chancery*, where both
Parties are often ruin'd by the Charge and Length of the Suit.   But as

in all other Countries, *England* only excepted, *Jus & Æquum* are held the same, and never divided ; so it is there : A Power of *Chancery* being vested in the Judges of the Courts of Common Law as to some particular Cases, and they make equitable Constructions in Others.   I must add, that the Fees of Officers of all sorts are setled by Acts of Assembly at moderate Prices, for the Ease of the Subject.

IT were easy to mention other Articles, but that I persuade my self it is needless.   The Charter Governments are celebrated for their excellent Laws and mild Administration ; for the Security of Liberty and Property ; for the Encouragement of Vertue, and Suppression of Vice ; for the promoting Letters, by erecting Free-Schools and Colleges ; and in one Word, for every Thing that can make a People happy and prosperous.   To these Arts it is owing, that *New-England*, though she has attain'd but little more than the Age of a Man, with all the Disadvantages under which she labours in respect to her Trade and Climate, and almost a perpetual *Indian* War, has hitherto flourish'd far above any other of the Plantations.

THIS being the Case of the Charter Governments, let us turn the Tables, and see how it far'd with them when in an *evil Reign* they lost their Charters.   Then the Governour of *New-England* with Four or Five Strangers of his Council, Men of desperate Fortunes, and bad if any Principles, made what Laws, and levy'd what Taxes they pleas'd on the People.   They, without an Assembly, rais'd a Penny in the Pound on all the Estates in the Country, and another Penny on all imported Goods, besides Twenty Pence *per* Head as Poll Money, and an immoderate Excise on Wine, Rum, and other Liquors. Several worthy Persons, having in an humble Address represented this Proceeding as a Grievance, were committed to the common Jail for a High Misdemanour ; deny'd the Benefit of the *Habeas Corpus* Act ; try'd out of their own County ; fin'd exorbitantly, and oblig'd to pay 160*l*. for Fees, when the Prosecution would hardly have cost them so many Shillings in *Great Britain*.   And to compleat the Oppression, when they upon their Tryal claim'd the Privileges of *Englishmen*, they were scoffingly told, *Those Things would not follow them to the Ends of the Earth*.   Unnatural Insult ! must the brave Adventurer, who with the Hazard of his Life and Fortune, seeks out new Climates to inrich his Mother Country, be deny'd those common Rights, which his Countrymen enjoy at Home in Ease and Indolence?   Is he to be made miserable, and a Slave by his own Acquisitions?   Is the Labourer alone unworthy of his Hire, and shall they *only* reap, who have neither sow'd nor planted? Monstrous Absurdity! Horrid inverted Order!

THESE Proceedings, however Arbitrary and Oppressive, were but the Prelude: The Catastrophe was, if possible, yet more dismal. Having invaded their Liberties, by an easy Transition the next Attack was directly on their Properties. Their Title to their Lands was absolutely deny'd by the Governour and his Creatures upon two Pretences: One, that their Conveyances were not according to the Law of *England*; the Other, that if they might be thought to have had something like a Title formerly, yet it now ceas'd by the Revocation of their Charters. So that they who had fairly purchas'd their Lands, and held them in quiet Possession for above Fifty Years, were now oblig'd to accept new Deeds from the Governour, and pay for them a third Part of their Value, in order to ascertain their Titles, or otherwise they would be seiz'd for the Crown. . . .

A 5th Objection, that the Charter Colonies will grow great and formidable, answer'd.   THERE is one Thing more I have heard often urg'd against the Charter Colonies, and indeed 'tis what one meets with from People of all Conditions and Qualities, tho' with due respect to their better Judgments, I can see neither Reason nor Colour for it. 'Tis said, *that their encreasing Numbers and Wealth join'd to their great Distance from* Britain *will give them an Opportunity in the Course of some Years to throw off their Dependance on the Nation, and declare themselves a free State, if not curb'd in Time by being made entirely subject to the Crown.* Whereas in Truth there's no Body tho' but little acquainted with these or any of the *Northern* Plantations, who does not know and confess, that their Poverty and the declining State of their Trade is so great at present, that there's far more Danger of their sinking, without some extraordinary Support from the Crown, than of their ever revolting from it. So that I may say without being ludicrous, that it would not be more absurd to place two of His Majesty's Beef-Eaters to watch an Infant in the Cradle that it don't rise and cut its Father's Throat, than to guard these weak Infant Colonies to prevent their shaking off the *British* Yoke. Besides, they are so distinct from one another in their Forms of Government, in their Religious Rites, in their Emulation of Trade, and consequently in their Affections, that they can never be suppos'd to unite in so dangerous an Enterprize. It is for this Reason I have often wondered to hear some Great Men profess their Belief of the Feasibleness of it, and the Probability of it's some Time or other actually coming to pass, who yet with the same Breath advise that all the Governments on the Continent be form'd into one, by being brought under one Vice-Roy, and into one Assembly. For surely if we in earnest believ'd that there was or would be hereafter a Disposition in the Provinces to Rebel and declare themselves Independent, it would be good Policy to keep them disunited ; because if it were possible they could contrive so wild and rash an Undertaking, yet they would not be hardy enough to put it in Execution, unless they could first strengthen themselves by a Confederacy of all the Parts. . . .

THE Sum of my Argument is, That the Benefit which *Great-Britain* receives from the Plantations, arises from their Commerce : That Oppression is the most opposite Thing in the World to Commerce, and the most destructive Enemy it can have : That Governours have in all Times, and in all Countries, bin too much inclin'd to oppress : And consequently, it cannot be the Interest of the Nation to increase their Power, and lessen the Liberties of the People. I am so sanguine in this Opinion, that I really think it would be for the Service of the Crown and Nation to incorporate those Governments which have no Charters, rather than Disfranchize those that have.

THE last Thing I propos'd to consider was, how far it may be consistent with Justice, to deprive the Colonies of their Charters, without giving them a fair Tryal or any previous Notice. . . .

The 4th Proposition, That it seems inconsistent with Justice to Disfranchize the Charter Colonies by an Act of Parliament.

. . . It seems therefore a Severity without a Precedent, that a People who have the Misfortune of being a Thousand Leagues distant from their Sovereign, a Misfortune great enough in it self, should UNSUMMON'D, UNHEARD, IN ONE DAY be depriv'd of all their valuable Privileges, which they and their Fathers have enjoy'd for near a Hundred Years. It's true, the Legislative Power is absolute and unaccountable, and King, Lords and Commons may do what they please ; but the Question here is not about *Power*, but *Right:* And shall not the Supream Judicature of all the Nation do right ? One may say, that what the Parliament can't do justly, they can't do at all. *In maximis minima est licentia.* The higher the Power is, the greater Caution is to be us'd in the Execution of it, because the Sufferer is helpless and without Resort.

Jer[emiah] Dummer, *A Defence of the New-England Charters* (London, 1721), 35-76 *passim.*

49. " A Short Discourse on the Present State of the Colonies " (1728)

BY GOVERNOR SIR WILLIAM KEITH

Keith was the last governor of Pennsylvania commissioned by Penn himself. — Bibliography: Winsor, *Narrative and Critical History*, V, 240–258; Channing and Hart, *Guide*, § 133.

WHEN either by Conquest or Encrease of People, Foreign Provinces are possessed, & Colonies planted abroad, it is convenient & often necessary to substitute little Dependant Governments, whose People by being enfranchised, & made Partakers of the Priviledges & Libities belonging to the Original Mother State, are justly bound by its Laws, & become subservient to its Interests as the true End of their Incorporation.

Every Act of Dependant Provincial Governments ought therefore to Terminate in the Advantage of the Mother State, unto whom it ows its being, & Protection in all its valuable Priviledges, Hence it follows that all Advantageous Projects or Commercial Gains in any Colony, which are truly prejudicial to & inconsistent with the Interests of the Mother State, must be understood to be illegal, & the Practice of them unwarrantable, because they Contradict the End for which the Colony had a being, & are incompatible with the Terms on which the People Claim both Priviledges & Protection.

Were these Things rightly understood amongst the Inhabitants of the British Colonies in America, there wou'd be less Occasion for such Instructions & Strict Prohibitions, as are dayly sent from England to regulate their Conduct in many Points ; the very Nature of the King wou'd be sufficient to direct their Choice in cultivating such Parts of Industry & Commerce only as wou'd bring some Advantage to the Interest & Trade of Great Britain, & they wou'd soon find by Experience that this was the solid & true Foundation whereon to build a real Interest in their Mother Country, & the certain Means to acquire Riches without Envy.

On the Other Hand where the Government of a Provincial Colony is well regulated, & all its business & Commerce truly adapted to the proper End, & design of its First Settlement ; Such a Province like a Choice Branch, springing from the Main Root ought to be carefully nourish'd, & its just Interest well guarded ; No little Partial Project or Party Gain, shou'd be Suffered to affect it, but rather it ought to be considered & weigh'd in the General Ballance of the whole State as a usefuh & profitable Member.

For such is the End of all Colonies, & if this Use cannot be made of them, it wou'd be much better for the State to be without them. . . .

From what has been said of the Nature of Colonies & the restriction that ought to be laid on their Trade, is in [it is] plain that none of the English Plantations in America can with any reason or good sence pretend to claim an Absolute Legislative Power within themselves ; so that let their several Constitutions be founded on Ancient Charters, Royal Patent, Custom, Prescription or what other Legal Authority You please, yet still they cannot be possessed of any rightfull Capacity to contradict or evade the force of any Act of Parliament wherewith the Wisdom of Great Britain may think fit to effect them from time to time, & in discoursing of their Legislative Power (improperly so called in a dependant Government) we are to consider them only as so many Corporations at a distance invested with Ability to make Temporary By Laws for themselves agreeable to their Respective Situations & Clymates, but no ways interfering with the Legal Prerogative of the Crown or the true Legislative Power of the Mother State.

If the Governors & General Assemblys of the Several Colonies wou'd be pleas'd to consider themselves in this Light, one wou'd think it was impossible that they wou'd be so weak as to fancy, they represented the King, Lords & Commons of Great Britain within their little Districts ; And indeed the useless or rather hurtfull & inconsistent Constitution of a Negative Council in all the Kings Provincial Governments has it is beleived contributed to lead them into this mistake, For so long as the King [h]as reserved unto himself in his Privy Council the Consideration of, & Negative upon all their Laws, the Method of appointing a few of the Richest & Proudest Men in a small Colony as an upper House, with a Negative on the Proceedings of the King's Lieutenant Governor, & the People's Representations seem not only to Cramp the natural Liberty of the Subject there, but also the Kings Just Power & Prerogative. . . .

It is generally acknowledged in the Plantations that the Subject is entituled by Birth & Right unto the benefit of the Common Law of England, but then as the common Law has been altered from time to time, & restricted by Statutes it is still a Question in many of the American Courts of Judicature wether any of the English Statutes which do not particularly mention the Plantations can be of Force there until they brought it over by some Act of Assembly in that Colony where they are pleaded ; And this creates such Confusion, that according to the Art or influence of the Lawyers. before Judges who by their Education are but indifferently Qualified for that Service, they allow the Force of the particular Statutes, and at other times reject the whole especially if the Bench is inclinable to be partial, which too often happens in those new & unsettled Countries ; & as Mens Liberties & Properties in any Country chiefly depend on an impartial and Equal Administration of Justice, this is one of the most Material Grievances which the Subjects of America have just Cause to complain of ; But while for the want of Schools & other proper Instructions, in the Principles of Moral Vertue, their People are not so well Qualified even to serve upon Juries, & much less to Act on a Bench of Judicature, It seems impracticable to provide a Remedy until a Sufficient Revenue be found out amongst them to support the Charges of sending Judges from England to take their Circuits by turns, on the several Colonies on the Main, which if thought worthy of a Consideration will appear neither to be improper nor unpracticable ; & until that can be done all other Attempts to rectify their Courts of Law will be fruitless, & may therefore be Suspended. . . .

A Militia in an Arbitrary & Tyrannical Government may possibly be of some Service to the Governing Power, but we learn by Experience that in a free Country, 'tis of little Use ; the People in the Plantations are so few in proportion to the Lands, which they possess, that Servants being scarce, & Slaves so excessively dear, the Men are generally under a necessity there to work hard themselves in Order to provide the common necessary's of Life for their Families, so that they cannot Spare a days time without great loss to their Interest. . . .

. . . The Wisdom of the Crown of Britain therefore by keeping its Colonies in that Situation is every [very] much to be applauded while they continue so ; it is morally impossible that any dangerous Union shou'd be form'd among them, because their Interest in Trade & all manner of Business, being entirely seperated by their Independancy, every Advantage that is lost or neglected by one Colony is immediately picked up by another, & the Emulation that continually subsists between them in all manner of Intercourse & Traffick, is ever productive of Envys, Jealousies & Cares how to gain upon each others Conduct in Government or Trade, Every one thereby endeavouring to magnifie their Pretentions to the Favour of the Crown by becoming more usefull than their Neighbours to the Interest of Great Britain. . . .

All that has been said with Respect to the Improvement of the Plantations, will it is supposed signifie but very little unless a Sufficient Revenue can be raised to support the needfull Expences, in Order to which it is humbly submitted whether the Duties of Stamps upon Parchment & Paper in England, may not with good reason be extended by Act of Parliament to all the American Plantations.

William Byrd, *The History of the Dividing Line, between Virginia and North Carolina,* etc. (edited by Thomas H. Wynne, Richmond, 1866), II, 215–227 *passim.*

———◆———

50. Various Kinds of Colonial Government (1747)

BY DOCTOR WILLIAM DOUGLASS

Douglass was a physician and *savant* in Boston; he wrote much, assembling in confused form much of his learning in his *Summary.* His strong prejudices are manifest, but he is a valuable witness. — Bibliography: Tyler, *American Literature,* II, 151–157; H. L. Osgood, in *American Historical Review,* II, 644, III, 31, 244.

General Remarks concerning the British *Colonies in* America.

THE Subject-Matters of this Section according to my first Plan are prolix, being various and copious, and perhaps would be the most curious and informing Piece of the Performance to some Readers ; but as many of our Readers in these Colonies seem impatient for our entring upon the Affairs of their several Settlements, we shall contract the present Section, and shall defer several Articles to the Appendix ; such as, the Rise, Progress, and present State of the pernicious Paper-Currencies ; some Account of the prevailing or Endemial Diseases in our *North-America* Colonies, and many other loose Particulars, the various Sectaries in Religion, which have any Footing in our *American* Colonies shall be enumerated in the Section of *Rhode Island,* where we find all Degrees of Sectaries (some perhaps not known in *Europe*) from NO RELIGION to that of the most wild *Enthusiasts.* Religious Affairs, so far as they may in some Manner appertain to the Constitution of the Colonies, do make an Article in this Section. . . .

Concerning the general Nature and Constitution of British North-American *Colonies.*

ALL our *American* Settlements are properly *Colonies,* not Provinces as they are generally called : *Province* respects a conquered People (the *Spaniards* in *Mexico* and *Peru* may perhaps in Propriety bear this Appellation) under a Jurisdiction imposed upon them by the Conqueror ; *Colonies* are formed of national People *v. g. British* in the *British* Colonies, transported to form a Settlement in a foreign or remote Country.

The first Settlers of our Colonies, were formed from various Sorts of People.   1. Laudably ambitious *Adventurers*.   2. The Malecontents, the Unfortunate, the Necessitous from Home.   3. Transported *Criminals*.   The present Proportion of these Ingredients in the several Plantations varies much, for Reasons which shall be mentioned in the particular Sections of Colonies, and does depend much upon the Condition of the first Settlers : Some were peopled by Rebel *Tories*, some by Rebel *Whigs* (that Principle which at one Time is called *Royalty*, at another Time is called *Rebellion*) some by *Church of England-Men*, some by *Congregationalists* or *Independants*, some by *Quakers*, some by *Papists* (*Maryland* and *Monserrat*) the most unfit People to incorporate with our Constitution.

Colonies have an incidental good Effect, they drain from the Mother-Country the Disaffected and the Vicious (in this same Manner, subsequent Colonies purge the more ancient Colonies) ; *Rhode-Island* and *Providence Plantations*, drained from *Massachusetts-Bay*, the *Antinomians, Quakers*, and other wild *Sectaries*.   Perhaps in after Times (as it is at Times with the Lord Lieutenants and other high Officers in *Ireland*) some *Malecontents* of Figure, capable of being troublesome to the Administration at Home, may be sent in some great Offices to the Plantations.

In our Colonies we have four Sorts of People.   1. *Masters* that is Planters and Merchants.   2. *White Servants*.   3. *Indian Servants*. 4. *Slaves* for Life, mostly *Negroes*.   White Servants are of two Sorts, viz. Poor People from *Great-Britain*, and *Ireland* mostly, these are bound or sold, as some express it, for a certain Number of Years, to reimburse the transporting Charges, with some additional Profit ; the others are Criminals judicially transported, and their Time of Exile and Servitude sold by certain Undertakers and their Agents.

In our *American* Settlements, generally the Designations are, *Province*, where the King appoints a Governor ; *Colony*, where the Freemen elect their own Governor : This customary Acceptation is not universal ; *Virginia* is called a *Colony*, perhaps because formerly a Colony, and the most ancient.

We have some Settlements with a Governor only ; others with Governor and Council, such are *Newfoundland, Nova-Scotia, Hudson's-Bay*, and *Georgia*, without any House or Negative deputed by the Planters, according to the Essence of a *British* Constitution : These, may be said, not colonized.

There are various Sorts of Royal Grants of Colonies.   1. To one or more *personal Proprietors*, their Heirs and Assigns ; such are *Maryland* and *Pennsylvania* ; both Property and Government.   2. The Property to personal Proprietors ; the Government and Jurisdiction in the Crown ; this is the State of *Carolinas* and *Jersies*.   3. Property and Government in the *Crown*, viz. *Virginia, New York*, and *New-Hampshire* commonly called *Piscataqua*.   4. Property in the People and their Representatives ; the Government in the Crown ; as is *Massachusetts-Bay*.   5. Property and Government in the Governor and Company, called the Freemen of the Colony, such are *Connecticut* and *Rhode-Island*.

This last seems to be the most effectual Method of the first *settling* and peopling of a *Colony* ; Mankind are naturally desirous of Parity and Leveling, without any fixed Superiority, but when a Society is come to Maturity, a more distinct fixed Subordination is found to be requisite. *Connecticut, Rhode-Island*, and some of the *Proprietary* Governments, are of Opinion, that they are not obliged to attend to, or follow any Instructions or Orders from their *Mother-Country* or Court of *Great-Britain* ; they do not send their Laws home to the Plantation-Offices to be presented to the King in Council for Approbation or Disallowance : They assume the Command of the *Militia*, which by the *British* Constitution is a *Prerogative* of the Crown : Some Time ago, they refused not only a Preventive Custom-House Office, but likewise a Court of Vice-Admiralty's Officers appointed from Home ; but these Points they have given up, especially considering that the Royal Charter grants them only the Privilege of trying Causes, *Intra corpus Comitatus*, but not a-float or *Super altum mare*.

W[illiam] D[ouglass], *A Summary, Historical and Political, of the first Planting . . . of the British Settlements in North-America* (Boston, 1747), I, 201–208 *passim*.

51. A French Publicist's View of the British Constitution (1748)

BY MONSIEUR CHARLES DE SECONDAT DE MONTESQUIEU

(ANONYMOUS TRANSLATION, 1777)

Montesquieu was a French philosopher and publicist, who had lived in England and who greatly admired the English government as he understood it. His book was much read in the colonies; and he had more influence than any other writer in the development in America of balanced governments of three departments. — Bibliography: Channing and Hart, *Guide*, § 134.

IN every government there are three sorts of power : the legislative ; the executive in respect to things dependent on the law of nations ; and the executive in regard to matters that depend on the civil law.

By virtue of the first, the prince or magistrate enacts temporary or perpetual laws, and amends or abrogates those that have been already enacted. By the second, he makes peace or war, sends or receives embassies, establishes the public security, and provides against invasions. By the third, he punishes criminals, or determines the disputes that arise between individuals. The latter we shall call the judiciary power, and the other, simply, the executive power of the state.

The political liberty of the subject is a tranquillity of mind arising from the opinion each person has of his safety. In order to have this liberty, it is requisite the government be so constituted as one man need not be afraid of another.

When the legislative and executive powers are united in the same person, or in the same body of magistrates, there can be no liberty ; because apprehensions may arise, lest the same monarch or senate should enact tyrannical laws, to execute them in a tyrannical manner.

Again, there is no liberty if the judiciary power be not separated from the legislative and executive. Were it joined with the legislative, the life and liberty of the subject would be exposed to arbitrary controul ; for the judge would be then the legislator. Were it joined to the executive power, the judge might behave with violence and oppression.

There would be an end of every thing, were the same man, or the same body, whether of the nobles or of the people, to exercise those three powers, that of enacting laws, that of executing the public resolutions, and of trying the causes of individuals. . . .

The judiciary power ought not to be given to a standing senate ; it should be exercised by persons taken from the body of the people, at certain times of the year, and consistently with a form and manner prescribed by law, in order to erect a tribunal that should last only so long as necessity requires.

By this method, the judicial power, so terrible to mankind, not being annexed to any particular state or profession, becomes, as it were, invisible. People have not then the judges continually present to their view ; they fear the office, but not the magistrate.

In accusations of a deep and criminal nature, it is proper the person accused should have the privilege of choosing, in some measure, his judges, in concurrence with the law ; or, at least, he should have a right to except against so great a number, that the remaining part may be deemed his own choice.

The other two powers may be given rather to magistrates or permanent bodies, because they are not exercised on any private subject; one being no more than the general will of the state, and the other the execution of that general will.

But, though the tribunals ought not to be fixt, the judgements ought ; and to such a degree, as to be ever conformable to the letter of the law. Were they to be the private opinion of the judge, people would then live in society without exactly knowing the nature of their obligations.

The judges ought likewise to be of the same rank as the accused, or, in other words, his peers ; to the end, that he may not imagine he is fallen into the hands of persons inclined to treat him with rigour. . . .

As, in a country of liberty, every man who is supposed a free agent ought to be his own governor, the legislative power should reside in the whole body of the people. But, since this is impossible in large states, and in small ones is subject to many inconveniences, it is fit the people should transact by their representatives what they cannot transact by themselves.

The inhabitants of a particular town are much better acquainted with its wants and interests than with those of other places ; and are better judges of the capacity of their neighbours than of that of the rest of their countrymen. The members, therefore, of the legislature should not be chosen from the general body of the nation ; but it is proper, that, in every considerable place, a representative should be elected by the inhabitants.

The great advantage of representatives is, their capacity of discussing

L

public affairs. For this, the people collectively are extremely unfit, which is one of the chief inconveniences of a democracy. . . .

Neither ought the representative body to be chosen for the executive part of government, for which it is not so fit ; but for the enacting of laws, or to see whether the laws in being are duly executed ; a thing suited to their abilities, and which none indeed but themselves can properly perform.

In such a state, there are always persons distinguished by their birth, riches, or honours : but, were they to be confounded with the common people, and to have only the weight of a single vote, like the rest, the common liberty would be their slavery, and they would have no interest in supporting it, as most of the popular resolutions would be against them. The share they have, therefore, in the legislature ought to be proportioned to their other advantages in the state ; which happens only when they form a body that has a right to check the licentiousness of the people, as the people have a right to oppose any encroachment of theirs.

The legislative power is, therefore, committed to the body of the nobles, and to that which represents the people ; each having their assemblies and deliberations apart, each their separate views and interests. . . .

But, as an hereditary power might be tempted to pursue its own particular interests, and forget those of the people, it is proper, that, where a singular advantage may be gained by corrupting the nobility, as in the laws relating to the supplies, they should have no other share in the legislation than the power of rejecting, and not that of resolving. . . .

The executive power ought to be in the hands of a monarch, because this branch of government, having need of dispatch, is better administered by one than by many : on the other hand, whatever depends on the legislative power, is oftentimes better regulated by many than by a single person.

But, if there were no monarch, and the executive power should be committed to a certain number of persons, selected from the legislative body, there would be an end of liberty, by reason the two powers would be united ; as the same persons would sometimes possess, and would be always able to possess, a share in both.

Were the legislative body to be a considerable time without meeting, this would likewise put an end to liberty. For, of two things, one would naturally follow : either that there would be no longer any legislative resolutions, and then the state would fall into anarchy; or that these resolutions would be taken by the executive power, which would render it absolute.

It would be need less for the legislative body to continue always assembled. This would be troublesome to the representative, and moreover would cut out too much work for the executive power, so as to take off its attention to its office, and oblige it to think only of defending its own prerogatives and the right it has to execute. . . .

The legislative body should not meet of itself. For a body is supposed to have no will but when it is met: and besides, were it not to meet unanimously, it would be impossible to determine which was really the legislative body, the part assembled, or the other. And if it had a right to prorogue itself, it might happen never to be prorogued; which would be extremely dangerous, in case it should ever attempt to encroach on the executive power. Besides, there are reasons (some more proper than others) for assembling the legislative body: it is fit, therefore, that the executive power should regulate the time of meeting, as well as the duration, of those assemblies, according to the circumstances and exigences of a state, known to itself. . . .

But, if the legislative power, in a free state, has no right to stay the executive, it has a right, and ought to have the means, of examining in what manner its laws have been executed; an advantage which this government has over that of Crete and Sparta, where the Cosmi and the Ephori gave no account of their administration.

But, whatever may be the issue of that examination, the legislative body ought not to have a power of arraigning the person, nor, of course, the conduct, of him who is entrusted with the executive power. His person should be sacred, because, as it is necessary, for the good of the state, to prevent the legislative body from rendering themselves arbitrary, the moment he is accused or tried there is an end of liberty.

In this case, the state would be no longer a monarchy, but a kind of republic, though not a free government. But, as the person, intrusted with the executive power, cannot abuse it without bad counsellors, and such as hate the laws as ministers, though the laws protect them, as subjects these men may be examined and punished. . . .

It might also happen, that a subject, intrusted with the administration of public affairs, may infringe the rights of the people, and be guilty of crimes which the ordinary magistrates either could not, or would not, punish. But, in general, the legislative power cannot try causes; and much less can it try this particular case, where it represents the party aggrieved, which is the people.   It can only, therefore, impeach.   But before what court shall it bring its impeachment?   Must it go and demean itself before the ordinary tribunals, which are its inferiors, and being composed moreover of men who are chosen from the people as well as itself, will naturally be swayed by the authority of so powerful an accuser?   No : in order to preserve the dignity of the people and the security of the subject, the legislative part which represents the people must bring in its charge before the legislative part which represents the nobility, who have neither the same interests nor the same passions. . . .

Here, then, is the fundamental constitution of the government we are treating of.   The legislative body being composed of two parts, they check one another by the mutual privilege of rejecting.   They are both restrained by the executive power, as the executive is by the legislative.

These three powers should naturally form a state of repose or inaction : but, as there is a necessity for movement in the course of human affairs, they are forced to move, but still in concert. . . .

To prevent the executive power from being able to oppress, it is requisite that the armies with which it is intrusted should consist of the people, and have the same spirit as the people, as was the case at Rome till the time of *Marius*.   To obtain this end, there are only two ways ; either that the persons employed in the army should have sufficient property to answer for their conduct to their fellow-subjects, and be enlisted only for a year, as was customary at Rome ; or, if there should be a standing-army composed chiefly of the most despicable part of the nation, the legislative power should have a right to disband them as soon as it pleased ; the soldiers should live in common with the rest of the people ; and no separate camp, barracks, or fortress, should be suffered.

When once an army is established, it ought not to depend immediately on the legislative, but on the executive, power ; and this from the very nature of the thing, its business consisting more in action than deliberation. . . .

In perusing the admirable treatise of Tacitus on the manners of the Germans, we find it is from that nation the English have borrowed the idea of their political government.   This beautiful system was invented first in the woods.

As all human things have an end, the state we are speaking of will lose its liberty, will perish.   Have not Rome, Sparta, and Carthage,

perished? It will perish when the legislative power shall be more corrupt than the executive.

It is not my business to examine whether the English actually enjoy
this liberty, or not. Sufficient it is for my purpose to observe, that it is
established by their laws ; and I inquire no farther.

M. [Charles de Secondat] de Montesquieu, *The Spirit of Laws* (*Complete
Works*, I, Dublin, 1777), Book XI, ch. vi., 198–212 *passim*.

———◆———

52. "The Law in all our Provinces" (1757)

BY EDMUND BURKE

Bibliography as in No. 44 above.

IT has been an old complaint, that it is not easy to bring American
governors to justice for mismanagements in their province, or to
make them refund to the injured people the wealth raised by their
extortions. Against such governors at present there are three kinds of
remedy ; the privy council, the king's bench, and the parliament. The
council on just cause of complaint may remove the governor ; the power
of the council seems to extend no further. The king's bench may
punish the governors for their offences committed in America, as if
done in England. The power of parliament is unlimited in the ways of
enquiry into the crime, or of punishing it. The first of these remedies
can never be sufficient to terrify a governor grown rich by iniquity, and
willing to retire quietly, though dishonourably, to enjoy the fruits of it.
The king's bench, or any other merely law court, seems equally insufficient for this purpose, because offences in government, though very
grievous, can hardly ever be so accurately defined as to be a proper
object of any court of justice, bound up by forms and the rigid letter
of the law. The parliament is equal to every thing ; but whether party,
and other bars to a quick and effectual proceeding may not here leave
the provinces as much unredressed as in the other courts, I shall not
take upon me to determine.

The law in all our provinces, besides those acts which from time to
time they have made for themselves, is the common law of England,
the old statute law, and a great part of the new, which in looking over
their laws I find many of our settlements have adopted, with very little

choice or discretion. And indeed the laws of England, if in the long period of their duration they have had many improvements, so they have grown more tedious, perplexed, and intricate, by the heaping up many abuses in one age, and the attempts to remove them in another. These infant settlements surely demanded a more simple, clear, and determinate legislation, though it were of somewhat an homelier kind ; laws suited to the time, to their country, and the nature of their new way of life. Many things still subsist in the law of England, which are built upon causes and reasons that have long ago ceased ; many things are in those laws suitable to England only. But the whole weight of this ill-agreeing mass, which neither we nor our fathers were well able to bear, is laid upon the shoulders of these colonies, by which a spirit of contention is raised, and arms offensive and defensive are supplied to keep up and exercise this spirit, by the intricacy and unsuitableness of the laws to their object. And thus in many of our settlements the lawyers have gathered to themselves the greatest part of the wealth of the country ; men of less use in such establishments than in more settled countries, where the number of people naturally sets many apart from the occupations of husbandry, arts, or commerce. Certainly our American brethren might well have carried with them the privileges which make the glory and happiness of Englishmen, without taking them encumbered with all that load of matter, perhaps so useless at home, without doubt so extremely prejudicial in the colonies.

[Edmund Burke], *An Account of the European Settlements in America* (London, 1760), II, 302–304.

---

53. The Effect of Royal Instructions (1764)

BY LATE GOVERNOR THOMAS POWNALL

Pownall was the most considerate and liberal of the Massachusetts royal governors (1757–1760), and was later governor of South Carolina. He thought and wrote much on colonial administration. — Bibliography : Palfrey, *New England*, V, 153–176; Channing and Hart, *Guide*, § 134. — For earlier principles of English control, see *Contemporaries*, I, ch. vii.

UPON such review it will appear, under this first general head, in various instances, that the two great points which the Colonists labour to establish, is the exercise of their several rights and privileges, as founded in the rights of an Englishman; and secondly, as what they suppose to be a necessary measure in a subordinate government, the keeping in their own hands the command of the revenue, and the pay of the officers of government, as a security of their conduct towards them.

Under the first head come all the disputes about the King's instructions, and the governor's power, as founded on them.

The King's commission to his governor, which grants the power of government, and directs the calling of a legislature, and the establishing courts, at the same time that it fixes the governor's power, according to the several powers and directions granted and appointed by the commission and instructions, adds, " and by such *further powers, instructions*, and authorities, as shall, at any time hereafter, be granted or appointed you, under our signet or sign manual, or by our order in our privy council." It should here seem, that the same power which framed the commission, with this clause in it, could also issue its *future orders and instructions* in consequence thereof: but the people of the colonies say, that the inhabitants of the colonies are entitled to all the privileges of Englishmen; that they have a right to participate in the legislative power; and that no commands of the crown, by orders in council, instructions, or letters from Secretaries of State, are binding upon them, further than they please to acquiesce under such, and conform *their own actions* thereto; that they hold this right of legislature, not derived from the grace and will of the crown, and depending on the commission which continues at the will of the crown; that this right is inherent and essential to the community, as a community of Englishmen : and that therefore they must have all the rights, privileges, and full and free exercise of their own will and liberty in making laws, which are necessary to that act of legislation, — uncontrouled by any power of the crown, or of the governor, preventing or suspending that act ; and, that the clause in the commission, directing the governor to call together a legislature by his writs, is declarative and not creative; and therefore he is directed to act conformably to a right actually already existing in the people, &c.

When I speak of full uncontrouled independent powers of debate and result, so far as relates to the framing bills and passing them into laws, uncontrouled by any power of the crown or of the governor, as an essential property of a free legislature; I find some persons in the colonies imagine, that I represent the colonies as claiming a power of legislature independent of the King's or governor's negative. — These gentlemen knowing that it is not my intention to do injustice to the colonies, wish me so to explain this matter, that it may not bear even the interpretation of such a charge — I do therefore here desire, that the reader will give his attention to distinguish a full, free, uncontrouled, independent power, in the act of legislation, — from a full, free, uncontrouled, independent power, of carrying the results of that legislation into effect, independent either of the Governor's or King's negative. The first right is that which I represent the Colonists claiming, as a right essential to the very existence of the legislature : The second is what is also essential to the nature of a subordinate legislature, and what the Colonists never call in question. That therefore the point here meant to be stated as in debate, is, Whether a subordinate legislature can be instructed, restricted, and controuled, in the very act of legislation? whether the King's instructions or letters from secretaries of state, and such like significations of his Majesty's will and pleasure, is a due and constitutional application of the governors, or of the royal negative? — The Colonists constantly deny it, — and ministry, otherwise such instructions would not be given, constantly maintain it. After experience of the confusion and obstruction which this dubitable point hath occasioned to business, it is time surely that it were some way or other determined. I do not here enter into the discussion of this point; I only endeavour fairly to state it, as I think it is a matter which ought to be settled some way or other, and ought no longer to remain in contention, that the several matters which stand in instruction, and in dispute in consequence of it, may be finally placed upon their right grounds; in the doing of which it must come under consideration, how far the crown has or has not a right to direct or restrict the legislature of the colonies, — or if the crown has not this power, what department of government has, and how it ought to be exercised ; — or whether in fact or deed, the people of the colonies, having every right to the full powers of government, and *to a whole legislative power*, are under this claim entitled in the powers of legislature and the administration of government, to use and exercise in conformity to the laws of Great Britain, the same, full, free, independent, unrestrained power and legislative will in their several corporations, and under the King's commission and their respective charters, as the government and legislature of Great Britain holds by its constitution, and under the great charter.

Thomas Pownall, *The Administration of the Colonies* (London, 1765), 39–43.

CHAPTER VIII—THE COLONIAL GOVERNOR

54. A Governor's Plea for Patronage (1732)

BY GOVERNOR WILLIAM COSBY

Cosby was governor of New York and New Jersey from 1731 to 1736. His request is such as all the governors were in the habit of making. — Bibliography: Winsor, *Narrative and Critical History*, V, ch. iii. — On Colonial government in general: Channing and Hart, *Guide*, §§ 133, 147; Joseph Story, *Commentaries*, §§ 152–178.

My Lord,

I HAVE y^e honour to aquainte your Grace that Mr Smith Secretary of y^e Jarsys dyed last Tuesday was seven^t this is reckoned one of y^e most considerable places belonging to these Provinces, & yett brings inn noe more then $450 \pounds l$ a year, supposeing that the possesor it was to doe y^e duty himself, which y^e deseasd Gent^{man} never did notwithstanding he had it for above fifteen years, it was executed by two deputies, one for the East division and y^e other for West, the Secretary himself generally living at Philadelfia, so that ye place was to him a sinecure. In this way the Deputys gave him suffitient security, that of ye East paid him 80^{ll} a year, & that of ye West payd him, 180^{ll}. a year, which all in sterling money makes about, 170^{ll}, I have a very good Caracter of the Deputys, therefore have continued them upon ye same footing under my son Billy whom I have named, untill farther orders from your Grace, not doubting but that out of your wanted goodness and indulgent care of us your Grace will further be so kind as to give it to him ; besides it will give me a little more power in that Province then I had which I doe assure your Grace is greatly wanting to Governers in these parts, for ye Secretarys and their Deputys think themselves intirely independent of ye Governers and allmost act accordingly which is a very great hindrance to ye King's affairs, (I doe not spake as to myself for I make ye right use of Mr Clarke he is my first minister) espetially at this time, since I am sorry to inform your Grace, that ye example and spirit of the Boston people begins to spread amongst these Colonys In a most prodigious maner, I had more trouble to manige these people then I could have imagined, however for this time I have done pritty well with them ; I wish I may come off as well with them of ye Jarsys.

My Lord Augustus is with me, he is of all yᵉ young people that I have seen the most agreeable & unaffected with yᵉ finest notions of honesty and honour backed with a most excelant usefull understanding, and if I mistake not will turn out a very clever man.   Grace and the little family joyns in their humble service to your Grace and the Duches, I have sent My Lady Duc[hess] a live beaver, it will eat frute or roots of any kinde, it must be keept near yᵉ round or square ponds

   I am My Lord

      Your Grace most oblidged

        and faithfull servant

           W. Cosby

I beg my service to Miss Betty.

E. B. O'Callaghan, editor, *Documents relative to the Colonial History of the State of New-York* (Albany, 1855), V, 936–937.

---

55. The Commission and Instructions of a Governor (1737/8)

BY THE LORDS COMMISSIONERS FOR TRADE AND PLANTATIONS

The extracts below are in the general form used in sending out all the governors. In the provincial governments the instructions to call assemblies and constitute courts gave privileges similar to those of the charter colonies. — Bibliography: E. B. Greene, *List of Governors' Instructions*, in *American Historical Review*, III, 170.

GEORGE the second by the Grace of God, of Great Britain France and Ireland King, Defender of the Faith &c.   To Our Trusty and Wellbelov'd Lewis Morris Senior Esqʳ *Greeting*. . . . know You that we reposing especial Trust and confidence, in the Prudence Courage and Loyalty of you the said Lewis Morris, of Our especial Grace certain knowledge and meer Motion have thought fit to constitute and appoint & by these presents do constitute & appoint you the said Lewis Morris to be our Captain Genˡ & Governor in chief in and over Our Province of Nova Cæsarea or New Jersey vizᵗ the Division of East & West New Jersey in America, which we have thought fitt to re-unite into One Province and settle under one entire Government.

And we do hereby require and command you to do and execute all things in due manner that shall belong unto your said Command and the Trust We have reposed in you, according to the several powers and

Directions granted or appointed you by this Present Commission and the Instructions and authorities herewith given you, or by such further Powers Instructions and Authorities as shall at any time hereafter be granted or appointed you under our Signet and sign Manual or by Our Order in our Privy Council and according to such reasonable Laws and Statutes as now are in force or hereafter shall be made and agreed upon by you with the Advice and consent of Our Council & the Assembly of Our said Province under your Government in such Manner and Form as is hereafter expressed.

And OUR WILL & PLEASURE is, that you the said Lewis Morris, after the Publication of these Our Letters Patents, do in the first Place take the Oaths appointed to be taken by an Act passed in the First Year of Our late Royall Father's Reign Entil.ᵈ *An Act for the further Security of His Majesty's Person and Government, and the Succession of the Crown in the Heirs of the late Princess Sophia being Protestants, And for Extinguishing the Hopes of the Pretended Prince of Wales & his open and secret Abettors :* As also that you make and subscribe the Declaration mention'd in the Act of Parliament made in the 25.ᵗʰ Year of the Reign of King Charles the Second Entituled *an Act for preventing Dangers which may happen from Popish Recusants* and likewise that you take the usual Oath for the due Execution of the Office and Trust of Our Captain Gen.ˡ & Governor in chief in and over our said Province of Nova Cæsarea or New Jersey as well with regard to the due and impartial Administration of Justice as otherwise, and further that you take the Oath required to be taken by Governors of Plantations to do their utmost that the several Laws relating to Trade and the Plantations be observ'd. . . .

And We do hereby give and grant unto you full Power and Authority to Suspend any of the Members of Our said Council, from sitting voting and Assisting therein if you shall find just cause for so doing.

And if it shall at any time happen that by the Death departure out of Our said Province or Suspension of any of Our said Councillors or otherwise there shall be a Vacancy in Our said Council (any three whereof We do hereby appoint to be a Quorum) OUR WILL & PLEASURE is that you Signify the same unto Us by the first Opportunity that We may under Our Signet and Sign Manual constitute and appoint others in their Stead. . . .

And we do hereby give & grant unto You full Power and Authority with the Advice and Consent of Our said Council from time to time as need shall require to Summon and call General Assemblies of the said Freeholders and Planters within your Government in manner and form as shall be directed in Our Instructions which shall be given You together with this Our Commission. . . .

And You . . . with the Consent of Our said Council and Assembly or a Major Part of them respectively shall have full Power and Authority to make constitute and ordain Laws Statutes and Ordinances for the Publick Peace Welfare and Good Government of Our said Province and of the People and Inhabitants thereof and such others as shall resort thereto and for the Benefit of Us Our Heirs and Successors which said Laws Statutes & Ordinances are not to be repugnant but as near as may be agreable to the Laws and Statutes of this Our Kingdom of Great Britain Provided that all such Laws, Statutes and Ordinances of what Nature or duration soever be within three Months or sooner after the making thereof transmitted unto Us under Our Seal of Nova Cæsaria or New-Jersey for Our Approbation or disallowance of the same, As also Duplicates thereof by the next Conveyance.

And in Case any or all of the said Laws, Statutes and Ordinances (being not before confirm'd by Us) shall at any time be disallowed and not approved and so Signify'd by Us Our Heirs and Successors under Our or their Privy Council unto you . . . or to the Commander in Chief of Our said Province for the time being then such and so many of the said Laws Statutes and Ordinances as shall be so disallowed & not approved shall from thenceforth cease determine and become utterly void and of none Effect anything to the contrary thereof notwithstanding.

And to the end that nothing may be passed or done by Our said Council or Assembly to the Prejudice of Us Our Heirs & Successors We will and Ordain that You . . . shall have and enjoy a Negative Voice in the making and passing of all Laws Statutes & Ordinances as aforesaid.

And you shall and may likewise from time to time as you shall Judge it necessary adjourn prorogue and dissolve all General Assemblys as aforesaid. . . .

And we do further by these Presents give and grant unto you . . . full Power & Authority with the Advice and Consent of Our said Council to erect constitute and establish such and so many Courts of Judicature and Publick Justice within Our said Province under your Government as you and they shall think fit and necessary for the hearing and determining of all Causes as well Criminal as Civil according to Law and Equity and for awarding of Execution thereupon with all reasonable & necessary Powers Authorities, Fees and Privileges belonging thereto As also to appoint and Commissionate fit Persons in the several parts of your Government to Administer the Oaths mentioned. . . .

And We do hereby give and grant unto you full Power and Authority where you shall see Cause or shall Judge any Offender or Offenders in Criminal Matters or for any Fines or Forfeitures due unto Us fit Objects of Our Mercy to pardon all such Offenders and to remit all such Offences Fines and Forfeitures, Treason and Willful Murder alone excepted in which Cases you shall likewise have Power upon extraordinary Occasions to grant Reprieves to the Offenders until and to the Intent Our Royal Pleasure may be known therein.

We do by these Presents Authorize and Impower you to Collate any Person or Persons to any Churches Chappels or other Ecclesiastical Benefices within Our said Province as any of them shall happen to be void.

And We do hereby give and grant unto you . . . by your Self or by your Cap^{ts} & Commanders by you to be Authorized full Power and Authority to Levy Arm Muster Command and Employ all persons whatsoever residing within Our said Province of Nova Cæsaria or New Jersey under your Government and as Occasion shall serve to March from one Place to another or to embark them for the resisting and withstanding of all Enemies Pirates Rebels both at Sea and Land and to Transport such Forces to any of Our Plantations in America (if necessity shall require for the Defence of the same against the Invasion or Attempts of any of Our Enemies and such Enemies Pirates and Rebels, if there shall be Occasion to pursue & prosecute in or out of the Limits of Our said Province and Plantations or any of them and if it shall so please God them to vanquish apprehend and take and being taken either according to Law to put to Death or keep and preserve alive at your Discretion and to Execute Martial Law in time of Invasion or other times when by Law it may be Executed and to do and Execute all and every other thing and things which to Our Capt General and Govr in Chief doth or ought of Right to belong. . . .

Provided Nevertheless that all disorders and Misdeameanours committed on Shore by any Capt Commander Lieu^{t} Master Officer Seaman Soldier or other Person whatsoever belonging to any of Our Ships of War or other Vessels acting by immediate Commission or Warrant from Our said Commiss^{rs} for Executing the Office of Our High Admiral or from Our High Admiral of Great Britain for the time being under the Seal of Our Admiralty may be tryed and punished according to the Laws of the Place where any such Disorders Offences and Misdemeanors shall be committed on Shore. . . .

Instructions to our Trusty and Wellbeloved Lewis Morris Esq.ʳ Our Capt.ⁿ General and Governor in chief in and over Our Province of Nova Cæsarea or New Jersey in America Given at

First With these Our In[s]tructions you will receive Our Commiss.ⁿ under Our Great Seal of Great Britain, constituting you Our Capt.ⁿ General & Governor in chief in & over Our Province of New Jersey, You are therefore with all convenient speed to repair to Our said Province and being there arrived you are to take upon you the Execution of the Place and Trust We have reposed in you and forthwith to call together the following persons, whom We do by these Presents constitute & appoint members of Our Council in and for that Province. . . .

3 You are forthwith to communicate unto Our said Council, such and so many of these Our Instructions, wherein their Advice & Consent are required, as likewise all such others from time to time as you shall find convenient for Our Service to be imparted to them.

4 You are to permit the Members of Our said Council to have and enjoy Freedom of debate and Vote in all Affairs of publick Concern that may be debated in Council. . . .

8 And in the choice & Nomination of the Members of Our said Council, as also of the Chief Officers, Judges, Assistants, Justices and Sheriffs, you are always to take care that they be men of good Life and well affected to Our Government, of good Estates & Abilities & not necessitious People.

9 You are neither to augment nor diminish the Number of Our said Council, as it is already established, nor to suspend any of the members thereof without Good and sufficient Cause, nor without the Consent of the Majority of the said Council. . . .

12. And *Our Will & Pleasure* is that with all convenient speed you call together one Gen.ˡ Assembly for the enacting of Laws for the joint and mutual Good of the whole Province. . . .

14. You are to observe in the passing of Laws that the Stile of Enacting the same be by the Govern.ʳ Council & Assembly and no other ; you are also as much as possible to observe in the passing of all Laws that what ever may be requisite upon each different matter be accordingly

provided for, by a different Law, without intermixing in one & the same Act such things, as have no proper Relation to each other and you are more especially to take Care that no Clause or Clauses be inserted in or annexed to any Act, which shall be foreign to what the Title of such respective Act imports, and that no perpetual Clause be made part of any temporary Law, and that no Act whatsoever be suspended, alter'd, continued, revived or repealed by Genl Words, but that the Title and Date of such Act so suspended alter'd, continued, revived or repeal'd be particularly mention'd and expressed in the enacting part. . . .

17. It is Our express *Will & Pleasure* that no Law for rais^g any Imposition on Wines or other strong Licquors, be made to continue for less than one whole Year, and that all other Laws made for the Supply & Support of the Governm^t shall be indefinite and without Limitation, except the same be for a Temporary Service, and wh^{ch} shall expire and have their full effect within the time therein prefixt.

18. And whereas several Laws have formerly been enacted for so short a time that the Assent or Refusal of Our Royal Predecessors could not be had thereupon before the time for which such Laws were enacted did expire, you shall not for the future give your Assent to any Law that shall be enacted for a less time than two Years (except in the Cases mention'd in the foregoing Article). And you shall not re-enact any Law to which the Assent of Us or Our Royal Predecessors has once been refused without Express Leave for that Purpose first obtained from Us. . . .

20. . . . We do hereby will and require you not to pass or give your Consent hereafter to any Bill or Bills in the Assembly of Our said Province of unusual and extraordinary Nature and importance, wherein Our Prerogative, or the Property of Our Subjects may be prejudiced, or the Trade or Shipping of this Kingdom any ways affected, until you shall have first transmitted to Us the Draught of such a Bill or Bills and shall have receiv'd Our Royal Pleasure thereupon unless you take care in the passing of any Bill of such Nature as before mention'd that there be a Clause inserted therein, suspending & deferring the Execution thereof until Our Pleasure shall be known concerning the same : And it is Our express *Will & Pleasure* that no Duty shall be laid in the Province under Your Government upon British Shipping or upon the Product or Manufacture of Great Britain, And that you do not upon Pain of Our highest Displeasure give your Assent to any Law whatsoever, wherein the Natives or Inhabitants of New Jersey are put on a more Advantageous footing than those of this Kingdom. . . .

22. You are to transmit Authentick Copies of all Laws, Statutes and Ordinances that are now made and in force which have not yet been sent or which at any time hereafter shall be made or enacted within the said Province. . . .

26. Whereas several Inconveniencies have arisen to Our Governments in the Plantations by Gifts and Presents made to Our Governors by the General Assemblies. You are therefor to propose unto the Assembly at their first meeting, after your Arrival, and to use your utmost Endeavours with them that an Act be pass'd for raising and settling a publick Revenue for defraying the necessary Charge of the Government of Our said Province, And that therein Provision be particularly made for a competant Salary, to yourself. . . .

29. Whereas great Prejudice may happen to Our Service and the Security of Our said Province under your Government by your absence from these parts, you are not upon any pretence whatsoever to come to Europe from your Government without having first obtained Leave for so doing, under Our Signet and Sign Manuel or by our Order in Our Privy Council. . . .

36. You shall not displace any of the Judges, Justices, Sheriffs, or other Officers or ministers within Our Said Province without good and sufficient Cause to be signified unto Us and to Our said Comm^{rs} for Trade and Plantations. . . .

42. You are to take care that no Man's life, Member, Freehold or Goods be taken away, or harmed in Our said Province otherwise than by establish'd & known Laws, not repugnant to, but as much as may be agreeable to the Laws of this Kingdom. . . .

44. You shall endeavour to get a Law pass'd (if not already done) for the restraining of any inhuman Severity, which by ill Masters, or Overseers may be used towards their Christian Servants, and their Slaves, and that provision be made therein, that the willfull killing of Indians, & Negroes may be punish'd with Death, and that a fit Penalty be imposed for the maiming of them. . . .

54. And you are also with the Assistance of the Council & Assembly to find out the best means to facilitate & encourage the Conversion of Negroes, & Indians to the Christian Religion.

55. You are to permit a Liberty of Conscience to all Persons (except Papists) so they be contented with a quiet & Peaceable Enjoyment of the same, not giving Offence or Scandal to the Government.

56. You shall take especial care that God Almighty be devoutly and

duely served throughout your Governm.^t the Book of Common Prayer, as by Law establish'd read each Sunday & Holyday, and the Blessed Sacrament administred, According to the Rites of the Church of England. . . .

67. You shall not upon any Occasion whatsoever establish or put in Execution any Articles of War or other Law Martial upon any of Our Subjects, Inhabitants of Our said Province, without the Advice & Consent of Our Council there. . . .

85. And whereas in the late War the Merchants & Planters did Correspond and Trade with Our Enemies and carry Intelligence to them, to the great Prejudice & Hazard of the English Plantations, you are therefore by all possible Methods to endeavour to hinder all such Trade and Correspondence in time of War. . . .

93. And you are upon all Occasions to send unto us by One of Our principal Secretaries of State and to Our Com.^{rs} for Trade and Plant.^s a particular Acc.^t of all your Proceedings & of the Condition of Affairs within your Government.

William A. Whitehead, editor, *Documents relating to the Colonial History of the State of New Jersey* (Newark, 1882), VI, 2–51 *passim.*

———◆———

56. One Thousand Pounds for a Governorship
(1740)

BY SECRETARY GEORGE CLARKE, JR.

Clarke's father came to New York as secretary of the province; later he satisfactorily administered the affairs of New York as lieutenant-governor. The letter is directed to Lord Delaware. — Bibliography: Winsor, *Narrative and Critical History*, V, 200.

My Lord.

MY father since his being appointed His Maj^{tys} Lieut: Govr of New York, has in all his letters to Mr Walpole Auditor Genl and his other friends here, represented that an unruly spirit of independency, and disaffection had at last got to such a hight in that province, that he found the weight and Authority of a Lieut^t Govr, though managed in the best manner, would not be able to subdue it: but that if His Majesty should be pleased to invest him with the Commission of Govr in chief, he had the greatest reason to be assured that as he had naturally the affections of the people, he should be able when they should know what they had to trust to, to carry on His Maj^{tys} affairs with much more success at this important and critical juncture — Mr Walpole seemed lately, so convinced of the truth of these representations, that he was pleased to say, he could wish, Your Lord^p would, to facilitate His Maj^{tys} affairs, move His Grace the Duke of Newcastle in my fathers favour.   Encouraged by this and by Your Lord^{p's} late favours, I most humbly presume to intreat your Lordship, that your Lord^p would in consideration of what is above set forth be pleased to move His Grace the Duke of Newcastle on my Fathers behalf, that he may succeed your Lord^p in that Govern^t. This will greatly facilitate his Maj^{tys} affairs, and as it will be some advantage to my father, and Your Lord^p has been put to great charge in passing Your Commissions ettc.   I shall upon such appointment immediately pay Your Lord^p one thousand Guineas to indemnify Your Lord^p from any loss, or expence occasioned thereby, which is all that the Govern^t there under its present circumstances allows me to offer — I am

> My Lord.
> Your Lordships
> most obedient and most humble servant

London June 20th 1740.   (signed.)   George Clarke Junr

E. B. O'Callaghan, editor, *Documents relative to the Colonial History of the State of New-York* (Albany, 1855), VI, 163-164.

---

57. A Governor's Perquisites (1743–1746)

BY GOVERNOR GEORGE CLINTON

Clinton was governor of New York from 1743 to 1753, at a time when the position had ceased to be financially desirable. — Bibliography: Winsor, *Narrative and Critical History*, V, 200–204.

SHORT heads to show the reasonableness of Governor Clinton's application for an allowance by way of equipage money.   1743.

1st Upon the apointment of Governors the Crown have frequently made an allowance by way of equipage money in order to assist 'em towards defraying the very considerable expence, the equipping and fitting them out for their own Govern^{ts} must necessarily occasion and this without any other reason ;

Whereas in Governor Clinton's case there are many strong reason's, to be offered in support of this application, For :

2nd The Govern^t of New York will not be near so valuable to Govr Clinton as it has been to his predecessors — The Province of New Jersey having always till now been united with New York, and under the same Government, and the salary paid by New Jersey has always been £1000 besides other considerable advantages, so that the making New Jersey a separate and distinct Govern^t makes New York at least £1000 a year less in value to Govr Clinton than it was to his predecessors.

3rd Former Governors had the advantage of one of the four companyes, besides the paying all the four Company's, which were together at least £2000 per annum, but which from the present method of paying those Company's Governor Clinton will be totally deprived of.

4^{rth} Former Governours have always had a mojety of their salary's from the date of their Commission to the time of their arrival in New York, but which from the different method the Assembly's of New York have lately fallen into in raising and paying this salary, Governor Clinton will have no advantage of, but from the time he shall actually arrive at New York, and get an act passed for that purpose.

5th Former Governors have likewise had considerable advantages from granting lands — But Governor Clinton can expect no benefit of this kind, there being now no vacant lands remaining to grant.

This Therefore hoped it will be thought reasonable to make Governor Clinton an allowance, by way of equipage money, towards assisting him, in defraying the expences of fitting himself out for his Government. . . .

My Lord.   [January 26, 1743/4.]

I take the liberty to acquaint your Grace that Lieut^t Govern^r Clark has told me he proposes going from hence in the spring with his family, and has strongly pressed me to trouble Your Grace in behalf of his son Hyde Clark who is a Lieut^t in my company here that you would be pleased to give consent to his being removed from hence into General Oglethorps Regim^t to which the Lieut^t Govern^r has wrott to the General, whereby he hopes with the interest of his Friends he may rise in the service, I shall be highly obliged to your Grace for your concurrance and interest therein, for this reason, that if Lieut^t Clark is removed there will be a vacancy, and as all my predecessors upon the occasion has claimed the nomination of a successor, as an emolument of this Govern^t, so I hope it will be considered by Your Grace to speak to Sr Will^n Young

that I should be indulged with the like privilidge, since so great a part
of my income is curtailed by an appointment of a Governor of the
Jersey, and several large perquisites take off, which before was always
an appendix to this Govern^t and without Your Grace will stand my friend
for me to name the vacancy's here, I shall loose these little douceurs,
which even the Lieut^t Govr has found the advantage off. . . .

New York 10th June 1746.

My Lord.

I must always acknowledge with a great many thanks the many favours
I have received from your Grace and particular the last in obtaining for
me this government, tho' it has fallen far short of what it was represented
in regard to the support of a Governor, and to the climate, which has
been fatal to one of my family, nor have I or any of the rest enjoyed any
share of health since we have been in the Province. I am obliged to
send my son out for change of air, he having had an ague & feaver for
above this ten months, which has wore him to nothing. Therefore I am
become a petitioner in behalf of my self and family, to beg of your Grace
to get me his Majesty's leave to come to England for the recovery of
my health, having very much empaired my hearing and eye sight.

As I offered my service to command the squadron to be appointed to
go against Louisbourg, and took it for granted this present expedition
would follow, and from some hint I had from home, I did not think
I should have failed ; but tho' I did not obtain it, I hope when I have
leave to return to England that the Lords of the admiralty will appoint
me some command to come home with from hence, as I take it for
granted ships will be going home in the fall ; as they appointed Commi-
dore Knowles a command to bring him out to his government. This
I must beg your Graces assistance in, as it may be a chance of making
some little profit going home, which I have had no opportunity of doing
here ; but intirely submitt every thing to Your Grace . . .

E. B. O'Callaghan, editor, *Documents relative to the Colonial History of
the State of New-York* (Albany, 1855), VI, 246–310 *passim.*

58. Recommendation for the Removal of a Governor (1762)

BY THE LORDS COMMISSIONERS FOR TRADE AND PLANTATIONS

This extract illustrates the remedy for persistent disobedience or corruption on the part of a governor.

COPY of Representation from the B: of Trade to the King in Council, for removing M.[r] Hardy from the Government of New Jersey, dated March 27.th 1762 for his having appointed three Judges of that Province during their good behaviour, in Disobedience to his Majesty's Instructions.

To the Kings most Excellent Majesty,

May it please your Majesty . . .

We have already in Our humble Representation to your Majesty of the 11th of November last so fully set forth Our Opinion of the impropriety of the Judges in the Plantations holding their Offices during good behaviour and the operation, w[ch] in the present state of those Plantations such a Constitution would have to lessen their just and proper dependance upon your Majesty's Government that it is unnecessary for Us to add any thing further upon that head, and your Majesty's General Instructions to all your Governors and those Instructions in particular which were grounded upon that Representation are so full and so positive that We cannot offer any thing that may in the least degree extenuate so premeditated and unprecedented an Act of disobedience of your Majesty's Governor of New Jersey, in a matter so essential to your Majesty's interest and Service, not only in that Province but in all other your Majesty's American Dominions.

The appointing M[r] Morris to be Chief Justice after the Contempt he had shown of your Majesty's authority, by procuring a person who had been appointed to that Office in consequence of His late Majesty's Warrant, to be superseded by a Judgment of that Court, in which he claimed to preside by a bare authority of the Governor, is alone such an example of misconduct, as does, in our opinion, render the Governor unworthy of the Trust your Majesty has conferred upon him.

But aggravated as his Guilt is by the mode of the appointment and by the influence which it will necessary have in the neighbouring Provinces of Pensylvania and New York, and particularly in the latter, where the utmost zeal and efforts of the Lieut⁺ Governor has been hardly sufficient to restrain the intemperate zeal and indecent opposition of the Assembly to your Majesty's authority, and Royal Determination upon this point: It becomes, under these Circumstances, our indispensible duty to propose that this Gentleman may be forthwith Recalled from his Government, as a necessary example to deter others in the same situation from like Acts of Disobedience to your Majesty's Orders, and as a measure essentially necessary to support your Majesty's just Rights and authority in the Colonies and to enable Us to do Our duty in the station your Majesty has been graciously pleased to place Us in, and effectually to execute the Trust committed to Us.

Which is most humbly submitted.

SANDYS   E.D ELIOT
SOAME JENYNS   GEO : RICE
E.D BACON   JOHN ROBERTS
                        JOHN YORKE

Whitehall March 27th. 1762

F. W. Ricord and W. Nelson, editors, *Documents relating to the Colonial History of the State of New Jersey* (Newark, 1885), IX, 361–362 *passim.*

---

59. The Ground of Dispute over Salaries (1764)

BY LATE GOVERNOR THOMAS POWNALL

This question was the chief occasion of dispute between governors and their assemblies. Pownall had special opportunities for knowing the difficulties of the situation. — Bibliography as in No. 53 above.

THE next general point yet undetermined, the determination of which very essentially imports the subordination and dependance of the colony governments on the government of the mother country, is, the manner of providing for the support of government, and for all the executive officers of the crown. The freedom and right efficiency of the constitution require, that the executive and judicial officers of government should be independent of the legislative ; and more especially in popular governments, where the legislature itself is so much influenced by the humours and passions of the people ; for if they be not, there will be neither justice nor equity in any of the courts of law, nor any efficient execution of the laws and orders of government in the magistracy : according, therefore, to the constitution of Great Britain, the crown has the appointment and payment of the several executive and judicial officers, and the legislature settles a permanent and fixed appointment for the support of government and civil list in general : The crown therefore has, *à fortiori*, a right to require of the colonies, to whom, by its commission or charter, it gives the power of government, such permanent support, appropriated to the offices, not the officers of government, that they may not depend upon the temporary and arbitrary will of the legislature.

The crown does, by its instructions to its governors, order them to require of the legislature a permanent support.   This order of the crown is generally, if not universally rejected, by the legislatures of the colonies.   The assemblies quote the precedents of the British constitution, and found all the rights and privileges which they claim on the principles thereof.   They allow the truth and fitness of this principle in the British constitution, where the executive power of the crown is immediately administred by the King's Majesty ; yet say, under the circumstances in which they find themselves, that there is no other measure left to them to prevent the misapplications of public money, than by an annual voting and appropriation of the salaries of the governor and other civil officers, issuing from monies lodged in the hands of a provincial treasurer appointed by the assemblies : For in these subordinate governments, remote from his Majesty's immediate influ- ence, administred oftentimes by necessitous and rapacious governors who have no natural, altho' they have a political connection with the country, experience has shewn that such governors have misapplied the monies raised for the support of government, so that the civil officers have been left unpaid, even after having been provided for by the assembly.   The point then of this very important question comes to this issue, whether the inconveniencies arising, and experienced by some instances of misapplications of appropriations (for which however there are in the King's courts of law, due and sufficient remedies against the offender) are a sufficient reason and ground for establishing a measure so directly contrary to the British constitution : and whether the incon- veniencies to be traced in the history of the colonies, through the votes and journals of their legislatures, in which the support of governors, judges, and officers of the crown will be found to have been withheld or reduced on occasions, where the assemblies have supposed that they have had reason to disapprove the nomination, — or the person, or his conduct ; — whether, I say, these inconveniencies have not been more detrimental, and injurious to government ; and whether, instead of these colonies being dependent on, and governed under, the officers of the crown, the scepter is not reversed, and the officers of the crown dependent on and governed by the assemblies, as the Colonists themselves allow, that this measure "renders the governor, and all the other servants of the crown, dependent on the assembly." This is mere matter of experience ; and the fact, when duly enquired into, must speak for itself : — but the operation of this measure does not end here ; it extends to the assuming by the assemblies the actual executive part of the government in the case of the revenue, than which nothing is more clearly and unquestionably settled in the crown. In the colonies the treasurer is solely and entirely a servant of the assembly or general court ; and although the monies granted and appropriated be, or ought to be, granted to the crown on such appropriations, the treasurer is neither named by the crown, nor its governor, nor gives security to the crown or to the Lord High Treasurer, (which seems the most proper) nor in many of the colonies, is to obey the governor's warrant in the issue, nor accounts in the auditor's office, nor in any one colony is it admitted, that he is liable to such account. In consequence of this supposed necessity, for the assembly's taking upon them the administration of the treasury and revenue, the governor and servants of the crown, in the ordinary revenue of government, are not only held dependent on the assembly, but all services, where special appropriations are made for the extraordinaries which such services require, are actually executed and done by commissioners appointed by the assembly, to whose disposition such appropriations are made liable. It would be perhaps invidious, and might tend to prejudging on points which ought very seriously and dispassionately to be examined, if I were here to point out in the several instances of the actual execution of this assumed power, how almost every executive power of the crown lodged in its governor, is, where money is necessary, thus exercised by the assembly and its commissioners. I beg leave here to repeat, that I do not enter into the discussion of these points ; my only aim is, fairly to state them, giving the strongest and clearest explanations I am capable of to both sides, that the discussion may be brought to some deter-

minate issue ; — and from that state of them to suggest, the absolute
necessity there is of their being determined by that part of government,
which shall be found to have the right and power to determine them ;
and to be so determined, that while the rights, liberties, and even privileges of the colonies are preserved, the colonies may be retained in
that true and constitutional dependance to the mother country, and to
the government of the mother country, which shall unite them to it as
parts of one whole.

It is a duty of perfect obligation from government towards the colonies, to preserve the liberty of the subject, the liberty of the constitution : It is a duty also of prudence in government towards itself, as such
conduct is the only permanent and sure ground, whereon to maintain
the dependance of those countries, without destroying their utility as
colonies.

Thomas Pownall, *The Administration of the Colonies* (London, 1765),
49–54.

------◆------

60. A Reprimand to a Colonial Governor (1772)

BY SECRETARY THE EARL OF DARTMOUTH

Dartmouth was one of the English secretaries of state from 1772 to 1775, and in
charge of colonial affairs. This rebuke illustrates the discipline which might be
applied to governors, short of removal (see No. 58 above).

Whitehall. 9. Decr 1772.

Sir,

A S I have mentioned to you in my Dispatch of this day's date N° 4.
that the state of what has passed respecting the lands between the
Rivers Hudson & Connecticut and also respecting grants of Lands in
General, would probably be the subject of a separate letter, I must not
loose this opportunity of telling you that the Reports of the Board of
Trade upon those subjects have not yet been decided upon at the Council Board, and therefore the instructions which I am to give, in consequence of their Lord^pps determination, must be deferred till the next
Packet — It becomes my duty however, in obedience to the King's
commands, to acquaint you, that the deviations from the letter, & spirit
of the Kings instructions in respect to the New Hampshire Townships
to the west of Connecticut River ; to grants of Land to the North of
Crown point, and to Licenses to private persons to purchase lands of the

Indians, are very much disapproved by the King, and that the reasons assigned by you for that deviation in the first of those cases do not appear at present either to excuse or extenuate a disobedience to the King's commands declared in the most clear and positive manner.

I am further to acquaint you that the sentiments expressed in Lord Hillsborough's letter to you of the 4th day of December 1771. concerning the unwarrantable and collusive practice of granting Lands in general are fully adopted by the King's servants, and I was exceedingly surprised to find that such an intimation to you on that subject had not had the effect to restrain that practice, & that the same unjustifiable collusion had been adopted to a still greater extent in the Licenses you have granted to purchase Lands of the Indians.

As all the facts however, are now under examination in the privy Council, I will not anticipate their Lordpps resolutions thereupon; but in the mean time it is the King's pleasure and positive command that you do not, upon any pretence whatever, sign any Grant or Patent for those Lands; that you do not either upon your own judgement, or by the advice of others, presume to depart from the letter of the King's Instructions, or to Act contrary in any respect to such explanations of them as you may have received from those to whom His Majty has intrusted the signification of his commands, which commands ought ever to be held sacred, and which it will be my duty to see obeyed, so long as I continue in the situation in which His Majesty has been graciously pleased to place me —

I am ettc

DARTMOUTH.

E. B. O'Callaghan, editor, *Documents relative to the Colonial History of the State of New-York* (Albany, 1857), VIII, 339.

CHAPTER IX—COLONIAL ASSEMBLIES

61. A Colonial Election (1764)

BY CHARLES PETTIT

Pettit was a relative of Joseph Reed, who was the friend and correspondent of Washington. The incident of the election is typical of such struggles in other colonies. — Bibliography: C. Bishop, *History of Elections in the American Colonies.*

Philadelphia, November 3, 1764.

I DON'T remember that I have told you any thing about our late election, which was really a hard fought one, and managed with more decency and good manners than wou'd have been expected from such irritated partisans as appeared as the champions on each side. The most active or rather at the head of the active on the old side, appeared A. James and T. Wharton; and on the new side, John Lawrence seem'd to lead the van. The Dutch Calvinists and the Presbyterians of both Houses I believe to a man assisted the new ticket. The Church were divided and so were the Dutch Lutherans. The Moravians and most of the Quakers were the grand supporters of the old; the McClenaghanites were divided, tho' chiefly of the old side. The poll was opened about 9 in the morning, the 1st of October, and the steps so crowded, till between 11 and 12 at night, that at no time a person could get up in less than a quarter of an hour from his entrance at the bottom, for they could go no faster than the whole column moved. About 3 in the morning, the advocates for the new ticket moved for a close, but (O! fatal mistake!) the old hands kept it open, as they had a reserve of the aged and lame, which could not come in the crowd, and were called up and brought out in chairs and litters, &c., and some who needed no help, between 3 and 6 o'clock, about 200 voters. As both sides took care to have spies all night, the alarm was given to the new ticket men; horsemen and footmen were immediately dispatched to Germantown, &c., and by 9 or 10 o'clock they began to pour in, so that after the move for a close, 7 or 800 votes were procured; about 500 or near it of which were for the new ticket, and they did not close till 3 in the afternoon, and it took them till 1 next day to count them off.

The new ticket carried all but Harrison and Antis, and Fox and Hughes came in their room ; but it is surprising that from upwards of 3900 votes, they shou'd be so near each other. Mr. Willing and Mr. Bryan were elected Burgesses by a majority of upwards of 100 votes, tho' the whole number was but about 1300. Mr. Franklin died like a philosopher. But Mr. Galloway *agonized in Death*, like a Mortal Deist, who has no Hopes of a Future Existence. The other Counties returned nearly the same members who had served them before, so that the old faction have still considerable majority in the House. Mr. Norris was as usual elected Speaker, but finding the same factious disposition remained, and a resolution to pursue the scheme for a change of the Government, he declined the Chair, and withdrew himself from the House, whereupon Joseph Fox, Esq., was chosen Speaker, but the Governor being absent, (attending his Lower County Assembly,) they dispensed with the form of presenting him for approbation, and went upon business. The first or one of the first resolves they made, was to send Mr. Franklin to London, in the capacity of agent for the Province, to assist Mr. Jackson. The opposition given to this measure, occasioned some debate, in the course of which the new Speaker gave some hints that a debate was needless, as the members had determined the affair without doors. The Gentlemen in the opposition, finding themselves overruled, drew up a protest in form (which you will see in a paper I shall enclose you, directed to be left at the Pennsylvania Coffee House), but could not get it entered on the minutes of the House. Mr. Franklin goes in the Capt. Robinson. Mr. Hamilton I believe will go in the next ship, but in a private capacity. A number of squibs, quarters, and half sheets, were thrown among the populace on the day of election, some so copious as to aim at the general dispute, and others, more confined, to Mr. Dickinson and Mr. Galloway, with now and then a skit at the Doctor, but these had little or no effect.

William B. Reed, *Life and Correspondence of Joseph Reed* (Philadelphia, 1847), I, 36–37.

62. Proceedings of a Colonial Legislature (1723)

BY THE GENERAL ASSEMBLY OF RHODE ISLAND AND PROVIDENCE PLANTATIONS

This brief extract illustrates the variety of colonial business. — Bibliography: Channing and Hart, *Guide*, § 147.   See also *Contemporaries*, I, Nos. 65, 104, 121, 131, 160, and below, Nos. 180, 187.

THE Hon. Samuel Cranston, Governor.
     Richard Ward, recorder.
Col. William Wanton, speaker.
Mr. John Coddington, clerk.

An Act for the better securing the pirates, now in His Majesty's jail, in Newport.

Forasmuch as there are thirty pirates brought into this harbor, by Capt. Solegarr, commander of His Majesty's ship the Grey Hound, and now in His Majesty's jail, in Newport, and it being suspected that they may endeavor to escape from thence, unless they are watched and guarded by night ; —

For the preventing of which, be it enacted by the General Assembly, and by the authority of the same it is enacted, that the field officers of the regiment of the militia on the islands, shall, and they are hereby empowered to order and set a military watch of such and so many men as they shall deem needful and necessary, to secure the said pirates from making their escape if attempted, and to set such penalties on default of not watching, as to them shall seem needful ; and that the charge of the watch be paid out of the general treasury ; any former law, custom or usage to the contrary hereof, in any wise notwithstanding.

Voted, that £100, be remitted out of the general treasury, to our agent in Great Britain, for the service of the colony ; and Col. Wm. Coddington and the general treasurer procure bills of exchange or silver, to that value, and deliver it to the Governor, who is to send it to our agent.

Voted, that the £123, odd money, in the hands of Mr. Robert Gardner, late naval officer, be paid by him to Capt. Simon Ray, to and for the use of New Shoreham, to assist them in rebuilding their pier, they building it in two years' time.

Voted, that the sum of £642 12s. 1d., of torn ragged bills in the treasury, be burnt in the presence of this Assembly ; and it was burnt accordingly.

Voted, that the general treasurer get the colony house repaired, and refitted where needful; and the charges to be paid out of the general treasury.

Voted, that Mr. Daniel Updike, the attorney general, be, and he hereby is ordered, appointed and empowered to gather in the money due to this colony, for the importation of negroes, and to prosecute, sue and implead such person or persons as shall refuse to pay the same; and that he be allowed five shillings per head, for every slave that shall be hereafter imported into this colony, out of the impost money; and that he be also allowed ten per cent. more for all such money as he shall recover of the outstanding debts; and in all respects to have the like power as was given to the naval officer by the former act.

This Assembly is adjourned to the second Tuesday of September next ensuing.

God save the King.

John Russell Bartlett, editor, *Records of the Colony of Rhode Island and Providence Plantations, in New England* (Providence, 1859), IV, 329-330.

---

63. The Dissolution of an Assembly (1736/7)

BY GOVERNOR GABRIEL JOHNSTON

Johnston's experience in North Carolina was repeated in almost all the colonies. — For the refusal of assemblies to separate in 1774-75, see Nos. 184, 187 below.

I WAS obliged to prorogue last Assembly at Edenton which at first promised very fair to settle this Country by enacting some good Laws. But an Emissary from the late Governour who arrived here during their sitting did amuse them with so many representations that it was impossible to do business with them, according to the last prorogation I met them here on the first current and recommended to their consideration the present miserable case of the Province. But instead of mending that the first thing they attempted was to take the Officers who distrained for his Majesty's Quit Rents during the time of Collection into Custody upon which I dissolved them by the enclosed proclamation. I hope Sir you will be so good as to say before their Lordships what I have now wrote to you in a very great hurry, But as the affair is pressing I hope you will excuse any oversight. I am Sir, yours, &c.,

Newbern March 11th 173⁶⁄₇.   GAB: JOHNSTON

NORTH CAROLINA.

By his Excellency Gabriel Johnston Esqre Capt Genl & Govern^r in Chief of the said Province.

A Proclamation.

Whereas the Lower House of Assembly instead of redressing the many Grievances the Country labour under for want of a sufficient maintenance being provided for the Clergy & proper additions to and amendments of the Laws in force which are at present so defective both which have been so often and so earnestly recommended to them, Have taken upon them in a very disorderly and undutiful manner to intimidate his Majesties officers in the execution of their duty by order of them into Custody, thereby to prevent the Collection of the Quit Rents so long due to his Majesty I do therefore by and with the advice and consent of his Majesty's Council, dissolve this Assembly, & this present Assembly is accordingly dissolved.

March 4th 173$\frac{6}{7}$.

William L. Saunders, editor, *The Colonial Records of North Carolina* (Raleigh, 1886), IV, 243–244.

---

64. Minutes of a Colonial Council (1752)

BY SECRETARY CHARLES READ

Read held various positions of trust in New Jersey, and in 1764 was commissioned chief justice of that state. The extract shows the combination of legislative, executive, and judicial functions in the Council. — Bibliography: T. F. Moran, *Bicameral System ;* Channing and Hart, *Guide,* § 147.

THE Minitts of the Council of the Province of New Jersey on the 10th & 11th of August 1752

At a Council held at Elizabeth Town on Monday the Tenth of August 1752

PRESENT

His Excellency the Governour The Hono^ble James Alexander, Andrew Johnston James Hude — Peter Kemble Esq^rs

His Excellency made the following Speech to the Council

Gentlemen of the Council

"This being one of our Stated Quarterly Meetings I shall be glad to hear any thing you have to offer for His Majestys Service as for the good of the Province and I wou'd now more particularly ask your Advice and Opinion whether it may be necessary or Expedient soon to meet the Assembly to see whether the Governour Council and Assembly can fall into any Act or Acts for the Better Suppressing the Riots and disorders which has disturbed the peace of the Province for a great Number of years past (long before my Arrival).

"And also to have your advice whether it may be best to give Orders for an Especial and Speedy prosecution of such as have been or may be Apprehended for Breaking open the Kings Goals of the Province in these things I say I shall be glad of your advice and am always ready Chearfully to join with you in such measure as may be judgd will most of all Contribute to the Establishment of the peace and Tranquility of the Province."

J BELCHER

ELIZABETH TOWN August 10 : 1752

The Council taking the same into Consideration are of Opinion that there is no reason to hope for any Success from any Application to the Assembly in Respect to the Riotts untill His Majesty shall be pleased to send His Especial Commands therein and therefore cannot [advise] His Excellency to call the Assembly on that Account only That as to the prosecutions they are of Opinion that His Majestys Attorney General shou'd proceed according to the known Laws of the Land and that they see no Room to give any particular direction therein.

A Petition from the Mayor Recorder Aldermen and Common Council of the free borough of Elizabeth in behalf of themselves and others the Inhabitants within the said Borough to have their Charters Altered & some further Privligdes &cṭ was read.

A Petition of Joseph Bonney and his Letter of the 20ᵗʰ of July was read.

The Council are of Opinion that Neither His Excellency or the Council can do any thing in Respect to the Petition of Joseph Bonney without aid of the Legislature that for anything that appears there may be relief for him in the Courts of Justice.

The Council taking into Consideration the Petition of the Mayor Recorder &c.ᵃ of the Free Borough of Elizabeth are of Opinion that the same be referred to M.ʳ Alexandr M.ʳ Hude M.ʳ Johnston M.ʳ Kemble M.ʳ Ogden or any three of them and that the Petitioners or some of them have Notice to deliver to the Committee a Draught of the Charter they Petition for.

His Excellency was pleased to Nominate John Roye and Ichabord Tompkins as Justices of the Peace in the County of Somerset to whom the Council agreed.

Orderd they be added to said Commission.

Also Nominated Stephen Crane and Timothy Whitehead to be Justices of the Peace for the County of Essex to which the Council agreed :

Ordered that they be added to the Commission for said Countys in Rank according to their Appointments.

His Excellency by advice of Council signed the following Warrants.

N.ᵒ 200.	To himself for a Quarters Salary due this day . .	250. 0.0
201.	To himself for a Quarters House Rent due this day	15. 0.0
203.	To the Hono.ᵇˡᵉ James Alexander Esq.ʳ for one hundred and Seventy two days Attendance in Council between 29 : of March 1749 to February 14 : 1752	51.18.0
205.	To Samuel Nevill Esq.ʳ Second Justice of the Supreme Court for Attending the Supreme Court at Burlington in May 1752 and for Holding the Court of Nisi Prius and Court of Oyer & Terminer in the County of Hunterdon on the Third Tuesday in May 1752	16. 0.0
206.	To Ditto for his Salary as Second Judge of the Supream Court from the 10 : of May to the 10 : of August 1752	6. 5.0
207.	To Charles Read Esq.ʳ for a Quarters Salary as Clerk of the Council for the Quarter ended this day .	7.10.0
208.	To Ditto for a Quarters Salary as Third Justice of the Supream Court for the Quarter ended this day .	6. 5.0

N

209. To Joseph Warrell Esqr for a Quarters Salary as Attorney General for the Quarter ended this day   7.10.0

210. To Andrew Johnston Esq.ʳ for a Quarters Salary as One of the Treasurers of the Province for the Quarter ended this day 10.00.0

211. To Samuel Smith Esq.ʳ for Quarters Salary as one of the Treasurers of the Province for the Quarter ended this day 10.00.0

212. Samuel Smith Esq.ʳ for Copying the Votes of the General Assembly and the Laws passed in the Sessions at Burlington in September and October 1751   Also for Pens, Ink & Paper   .   .   .   10.18.0

213. To John Smith a Quarters Salary as Clerk of the Circuits for the Quarter ended this day   .   .   5.00.0

214. To William Bradford in full of his Account allowd   141. 1.0

215. To Ditto for One Hundred and Sixty Bound Books of the Laws of the Province as ℔ Act of General Assembly 200.00.0

216. To Anthony Elton for a Quarters Salary as Door keeper to the Council for the Quarter ended this day 2.10.0

M.ʳ Alexander acquainted His Excellency that Lewis Ashfield Esq.ʳ was at the Door attending with his Majestys Mandamus to His Excellency for Swearing and admitting him One of His Majestys Council of this Province with a Certificate of his Acquital by due Course of Law of what he had been Chargd with and allegd as Reason for the Delay of his Qualification and prayd that he might be calld in.

His Excellency adjourned the Council to Meet to morrow morning at Ten O'Clock.

TUESDAY AUGUST 11 : 1752

The Council Met Present His Excellency the Governor The Hon.ᵇˡᵉ James Hude, Andrew Johnston & Peter Kemble Esq.ʳˢ

His Excellency gave the following Answer to the Motion of James Alexander Esq.ʳ of yesterday.

Gentlemen of the Council

"After what I said to you in October last & is on the Council Minits I am Surprized at the Motion made yesterday by M.ʳ Alexander relating to the Kings Mandamus for admitting M.ʳ Ashfield into the Council

wth wch I once more tell you, You have no Business or Concern nor will
I hear anything from you about it this I say to save Yourselves or me
any further trouble and if you are minded to show that Young Gentleman
any Respect I would advise you to teach him his Duty in this matter To
the Kings Governour and when he practices it he shall have my Answer."

J Belcher

Elizabeth Town August 11 : 1752

His Excellency laid before the Board for their Consideration a Charter
proposed for the Incorporation of the Five Dutch reformd Churches in
the Counties of Middlesex, Somersett and Hunterdon wch being Read It
is Orderd that it be Referrd to their next Quarterly meeting and that
in the mean time the Secretary do procure the Statute of Mortmain.

Compared wth Minitts of Council of the Province of New Jersey of
wch this is a true Copy

William A. Whitehead, editor, *Documents relating to the Colonial History of
the State of New Jersey* (Newark, 1885), VIII (i), 103–108 *passim*.

---

65. A Determined Veto Message (1742)

BY GOVERNOR LEWIS MORRIS

Morris was a member of the Council, chief justice, and finally governor of New
Jersey. The extract is selected as an example of the absolute veto of governors.—
Bibliography: E. C. Mason, *Veto Power*, § 7.

THERE are two Acts now before me to which my Assent is desired
. . . but they now come up in two distinct Acts, and if the other
part, with respect to the Enregistring of deeds, had come up in a distinct Act also, then my assent had been desired to three Acts, which had
been formerly repealed, by his Majesty, under one title in one bill ; and
all the three might have been as well ofrid [offered] for my assent as
any two of them as it doth not appear for what particular part the Act
before mentioned was disallow'd of tho' certain it is the whole and all
the parts of it were disallow'd of ; with what View was my Assent desired
to Acts, disallow'd of by his Majesty & that even without a suspending
Clause according to his Instructions, well known to you, unless it was
to Expose me to Just censure for giving such Assent ; and how kind it
was to do so, I leave to be determined by all Indifferent persons ; and

even to the consciences, of those concern'd in the doing of it; & I hope my not Assenting to Laws I am not Impowered to Assent unto will not be call'd a fault; but on the contrary, a Strict adherence to do my Duty which by Gods assistance, nothing shall intimidate me from doing.

There is nothing more common in the mouths of the populace than, Saying give us good laws, and we will Support the Government and what they call good laws, are such only as they like; and Agreeable to this they are made to believe, that if the Governor doth not Assent to such Laws as are Off'red for his Assent, the Assembly are Justifyable in not raising a Support for his Majesty's Government; tho' he is forbid to Assent to those Laws: as in the Cases before mentioned; or tho' the Govern^r himself very much disapproves of them; which (notwithstanding the Attempts of your Honourable House with respect to the bills of Credit made in the year 1724) I hope no body will presume to say, he has not a right to do.

The Assent to Laws we have a power to make ought to be free, and not compell'd in any part of the Legislature, and I believe you would think so your selves, were there any Attempts made to compell your Assent to any Law propos'd by the Council, Yet I may ask with what view those Strong Endeavours were made in your House, to annex a fee bill to the bill for Support of the Government, (a bill to which you would never suffer an Amendment to be made) unless it was to Compell the Governor and Council, to pass that fee bill, in such manner as your Honourable House should pass it without any Amendment?

It is true the attempt did not succeed; and I thank you for what is done but believe most People will think it had been more for the interest of the Publick, if it had been made for a longer time; and it may not be unworthy your Notice to Observe, that this fee bill tho' not Intitled An Act to Inforce Obedience to an Ordinance made for Establishing fees &^c yet whatever title you will please to give it, if it be of the same nature of that which was twice repeal'd, for reasons I need not repeat, it will not be difficult to Say what will be the Success of it or the Sentiments of his Majesty's Ministers concerning it.

Your Bill for making lands Chattels, doth not with any certainty Express what Estate the Purchaser from the Sherriff shall be Vested wth whether in fee or for Life: or years; & for that reason I shall referr it to farther consideration.

Your Bill for paying the Expenses that may arise on Printing Signing &c^a the Sum of £40,000, I am told was intended should be pass'd in a

Secret manner peculiar to itself as usuall; and not sent home, that the Ministry might not know I was to have 500 pounds for passing it, The Offering this, I suppose, you believ'd would be a Sufficient Inducem^t to Obtain my Assent to your £40,000 Act, your making of that offer Shews what your Notions of Virtue and Honour are, & what many of you would do, if in my Case, for a Much less Sum : but you Mistook your Man ; for if I know myself your whole £40,000 would not have Prevail'd upon me to have Acted so mean apart.   If I recommend any bill, it shall be, (what I deem) the intrinsick goodness of it shall induce me to do it, and not any Sum you can give me, If you believ'd money would have influenc'd me to come into your measures, the offer should have been of a different kind, and not of such a nature, that none but a Fool would have been influenced by ; and instead of being an Inducem^t to recommend your bill, or using any Interest to get it pass'd at home would be a Strong motive to the Contrary. . . .

. . . your present bill for making £40,000 being to put so much money into the Loan Offices without any certain Indisputable provision for the Support of the Government, I cannot think it proper for me to Assent unto it ; Had that been done : Had a Sufficient sum of money been by that bill Appropriated to the building of a House and conveniences for the Residence of a Governor, Places and Houses for the Sittings of the Council and Assembly, and for the safe keeping & preserving of the Public records of the Province, whereby many tradesmen and the poor and Labouring part of the Inhabitants of the Province, might have been Imploy'd ; & the money circulated among ourselves ; had there been any Provision made for encouraging and increasing the litle Trade, and the few Manufactures we have, whereby more Trad-men and Labourers might be Imploy'd ; I dont know how far I might have been induced, for these and other good purposes to assent to it : But as none of these things are done, nor I believe intended ; and as without these things, or something of that sort litle of the money will Circulate in this Province, or remain long in it, and consequently will fall in its value, and as the bill is full of Confus'd references, and intricate in its make ; I neither can assent to it myself, nor recommend it to have His Majesty's & by this you will save the £500, Intended for that Purpose.

Thus much for your bills.

F. W. Ricord and W. Nelson, editors, *Documents relating to the Colonial History of the State of New Jersey* (Trenton, 1891), XV, 271–275 *passim*.

66. How to Avoid a Governor's Veto (1764)

BY LATE GOVERNOR THOMAS POWNALL

This suggestion is based on the practice of many assemblies. — Bibliography as in No. 53 above.

THE settling and determining this point is of the most essential import to the liberties on one hand, and the subordination on the other, of the government of the colonies to the government of the mother country. — In the examination of this point, it will come under consideration, first, Whether the full and whole of legislature can be any way, in any special case, suspended ; and next, whether the crown, by its instructions, can suspend the effect of this legislature, which by its commission or charters it has given or declared ; if not, the crown, whether the parliament of Great Britain can do it, and how ; whether it should be by act of Parliament, or whether by addressing the crown upon *a declarative vote*, that it would be pleased to provide by its instructions, for the carrying the effect of such vote into execution, as was done in the case of the paper-money currency.

In the course of examining these matters, will arise to consideration the following very material point. As a principal tie of the subordination of the legislatures of the colonies on the government of the mother country, they are bound by their constitutions and charters, to send all *their acts* of legislature to England, to be confirmed or abrogated by the crown ; but if any of the legislatures should be found to do almost every act of legislature, by votes or orders, even to the repealing the effects of acts, suspending establishments of pay, paying services, doing chancery and other judicatory business : if matters of this sort, done by these votes and orders, never reduced into the form of an act, have their effect without ever being sent home as acts of legislature, or submitted to the allowance or disallowance of the crown : If it should be found that many, or any of the legislatures of the colonies carry the powers of legislature into execution, independent of the crown by this device, — it will be a point to be determined how far, in such cases, the subordination of the legislatures of the colonies to the government of the mother country is maintained or suspended ; — or if, from emergencies arising in these governments, this device is to be admitted, the point, how far such is to be admitted, ought to be determined ; and the validity of these votes and orders, these Senatus Consulta so far declared. For a point of such great importance in the subordination of the colony legislatures, and of so questionable a cast in the valid exercise of this legislative power, ought no longer to remain in question.

Thomas Pownall, *The Administration of the Colonies* (London, 1765), 47–49.

---

67. Disallowance of a Colonial Bill (1770)

BY THE LORDS COMMISSIONERS FOR TRADE AND PLANTATIONS

The ultimate power of disallowance was one way of enforcing instructions, and the chief means of keeping the colonies within bounds. — Bibliography : George Chalmers, *Opinions of Eminent Lawyers* (a collection of recommendations for disallowance).

THE Lords of the Committee of your Majestys most hon[ble] Privy Council for Plantation Affairs having by their Order of the 10th of Nov : last directed us to report to them Our opinion upon a Bill passed in May 1769 by the Council and House of Representatives of your Majesty's Council of New York for emitting £120,000 in paper notes of Credit upon loan, to which Bill your Majesty's late Governor had refused his assent without having first received your Majesty's directions for that purpose.

We did on the 20 of Dec[r] make our report thereupon submitting it to their Lordships to give such advice to your Majesty on this subject as they should think fit, and in the mean time, and until your Majesty's pleasure could be known the Lieut[t] Gov[r] was acquainted with the several steps which had been taken on this occasion & with the difficulties which arose in point of law upon those Clauses of the Bill by which the paper notes to be cancelled were made a legal Tender in the Treasury and loan office of that Colony.

It is Our duty however to observe to your Majesty that notwithstanding their intimation given to the Lieut[t] Gov[r] a new Bill in no material points differing from that now before your Majesty has been proposed in the Assembly of this Colony & having passed that house and been concured in by the Council Your Majestys said Lieut[t] Gov[r] did think fit by their advice to give his assent to it on the 5 day of January last and therefore it becomes necessary for us to lose no time in humbly laying this Act which was received at Our Office yesterday before Your Majesty, to the end that if Your Majesty shall be pleased to signify your disallowance of it, either upon the ground of the doubts in point of law which occurred to the former Bill, or upon a consideration of so irregular a proceeding as that of entering upon a proposition of this nature & passing it into an Act pending the consideration of it before Your Majesty in Council there may be no delay in having Your Majestys Pleasure thereupon signified to the Colony, so as to reach it before that part of the Act which authorizes the emission of the Bills can take effect that is to say on the last Tuesday in June.

How far the Lieut^t Govr is justified in the conduct he has thought fit to pursue on this occasion must be submitted to your Majesty upon the reason assigned by him in his letter to one of your Majestys principal Secretaries of State & to this Board extracts of which are hereunto annexed, but it is Our further duty to observe that the Instruction of July 1766, on the ground of which he says the Council advise him to this step does expressly forbid any law of this nature to be passed without a Clause suspending its execution until your Majestys [pleasure] could be known

E. B. O'Callaghan, editor, *Documents relative to the Colonial History of the State of New-York* (Albany, 1857), VIII, 202–203.

---

68. Dispute over the Agency (1771)

BY AGENT BENJAMIN FRANKLIN

From about 1680 the colonies were in the habit of appointing some person to represent their interests in London; and such agents received salaries. Franklin was agent for several colonies at the same time. — Bibliography: Winsor, *Narrative and Critical History*, V, 216, VI, 53, 89.

Wednesday, 16 January, 1771.

I WENT this morning to wait on Lord Hillsborough. The porter at first denied his Lordship, on which I left my name and drove off. But, before the coach got out of the square, the coachman heard a call, turned, and went back to the door, when the porter came and said, "His Lordship will see you, Sir." I was shown into the levee room, where I found Governor Bernard, who, I understand, attends there constantly. Several other gentlemen were there attending, with whom I sat down a few minutes, when Secretary Pownall came out to us, and said his Lordship desired I would come in.

I was pleased with this ready admission and preference, having sometimes waited three or four hours for my turn ; and, being pleased, I could more easily put on the open, cheerful countenance, that my friends advised me to wear. His Lordship came towards me and said, " I was dressing in order to go to court; but, hearing that you were at the door, who, are a man of business, I determined to see you immediately."   I thanked his Lordship, and said that my business at present was not much ; it was only to pay my respects to his Lordship, and to acquaint him with my appointment by the House of Representatives of Massachusetts Bay to be their agent here, in which station if I could be of any service — (I was going on to say — " to the public, I should be very happy ;" but his Lordship, whose countenance changed at my naming that province, cut me short by saying, with something between a smile and a sneer,)

L. H.   I must set you right there, Mr. Franklin, you are not agent.

B. F.   Why, my Lord?

L. H.   You are not appointed.

B. F.   I do not understand your Lordship ; I have the appointment in my pocket.

L. H.   You are mistaken ; I have later and better advices.   I have a letter from Governor Hutchinson; he would not give his assent to the bill.

B. F.   There was no bill, my Lord ; it was a vote of the House.

L. H.   There was a bill presented to the governor for the purpose of appointing you and another, one Dr. Lee, I think he is called, to which the governor refused his assent.

B. F.   I cannot understand this, my Lord ; I think there must be some mistake in it.   Is your Lordship quite sure that you have such a letter?

L. H.   I will convince you of it directly.   (*Rings the bell.*)   Mr. Pownall will come in and satisfy you.

B. F.   It is not necessary, that I should now detain your Lordship from dressing.   You are going to court.   I will wait on your Lordship another time.

L. H.   No, stay ; he will come immediately.   (*To the servant.*) Tell Mr. Pownall I want him.

(*Mr. Pownall comes in.*)

L. H.   Have not you at hand Governor Hutchinson's letter, mentioning his refusing his assent to the bill for appointing Dr. Franklin agent?

Sec. P.   My Lord?

L. H.   Is there not such a letter?

Sec. P.   No, my Lord; there is a letter relating to some bill for the payment of a salary to Mr. De Berdt, and I think to some other agent, to which the governor had refused his assent.

L. H.   And is there nothing in the letter to the purpose I mention?

Sec. P.   No, my Lord.

B. F.   I thought it could not well be, my Lord; as my letters are by the last ships, and they mention no such thing.   Here is the authentic copy of the vote of the House appointing me, in which there is no mention of any act intended.   Will your Lordship please to look at it? (*With seeming unwillingness he takes it, but does not look into it.*)

L. H.   An information of this kind is not properly brought to me as Secretary of State.   The Board of Trade is the proper place.

B. F.   I will leave the paper then with Mr. Pownall to be ——

L. H.   (*Hastily.*)   To what end would you leave it with him?

B. F.   To be entered on the minutes of that Board, as usual.

L. H.   (*Angrily.*)   It shall not be entered there.   No such paper shall be entered there, while I have any thing to do with the business of that Board.   The House of Representatives has no right to appoint an agent.   We shall take no notice of any agents, but such as are appointed by acts of Assembly, to which the governor gives his assent. We have had confusion enough already.   Here is one agent appointed by the Council, another by the House of Representatives.   Which of these is agent for the province?   Who are we to hear in provincial affairs?   An agent appointed by act of Assembly we can understand. No other will be attended to for the future, I can assure you.

B. F.   I cannot conceive, my Lord, why the consent of the governor should be thought necessary to the appointment of an agent for the people.   It seems to me that ——

L. H.   (*With a mixed look of anger and contempt.*)   I shall not enter into a dispute with you, Sir, upon this subject.

B. F.   I beg your Lordship's pardon; I do not presume to dispute with your Lordship; I would only say, that it seems to me, that every body of men, who cannot appear in person, where business relating to them may be transacted, should have a right to appear by an agent. The concurrence of the governor does not seem to me necessary.   It is the business of the people, that is to be done; he is not one of them; he is himself an agent.

L. H.   (*Hastily.*)   Whose agent is he?

B. F. The King's, my Lord.

L. H. No such matter. He is one of the corporation by the province charter. No agent can be appointed but by an act, nor any act pass without his assent. Besides, this proceeding is directly contrary to express instructions.

B. F. I did not know there had been such instructions. I am not concerned in any offence against them, and ——

L. H. Yes, your offering such a paper to be entered is an offence against them. (*Folding it up again without having read a word of it.*) No such appointment shall be entered. When I came into the administration of American affairs, I found them in great disorder. By *my firmness* they are now something mended ; and, while I have the honor to hold the seals, I shall continue the same conduct, the same *firmness*. I think my duty to the master I serve, and to the government of this nation, requires it of me. If that conduct is not approved, *they* may take my office from me when they please. I shall make them a bow, and thank them ; I shall resign with pleasure. That gentleman knows it, (*pointing to Mr. Pownall,*) but, while I continue in it, I shall resolutely persevere in the same FIRMNESS. (*Spoken with great warmth, and turning pale in his discourse, as if he was angry at something or somebody besides the agent, and of more consequence to himself.*)

B. F. (*Reaching out his hand for the paper, which his Lordship returned to him.*) I beg your Lordship's pardon for taking up so much of your time. It is, I believe, of no great importance whether the appointment is acknowledged or not, for I have not the least conception that an agent can *at present* be of any use to any of the colonies. I shall therefore give your Lordship no further trouble. (*Withdrew.*)

Benjamin Franklin, *Works* (edited by Jared Sparks, Boston, 1838), VII, 508–512.

CHAPTER X—COLONIAL COURTS

69. How Juries were Summoned (1710)

BY " A SWISS GENTLEMAN "

The author of this piece was a Swiss, who went out to America in behalf of a land scheme. Other colonies had substantially the same jury system. — Bibliography: Channing and Hart, *Guide*, §§ 146, 147; B. V. Abbott, *Judge and Jury*.

THO' it is Commendation sufficient for our Laws, to say they are as nigh to those of *England*, as conveniently may be, yet we have in several things refin'd upon the *English* Laws. For instance : The Jurors are not here returned by the Sheriffs, but the Names of all the best qualified Persons in the Country are agreed upon and settled by Act of Assembly, and put together into a Ballot-Box. At the End of every Court this is set upon the Table, before the Judge and Bench, and after it is shaken, a little Child draws out 48 Names, which are read, and a List of them taken by the Sheriff, that he may know whom to summons. These 48 are put in the second Division of the Ballot-Box, out of which, at the opening of the next Court, another Child draws 12, who are to serve as Jurors; and if any just Exception be made, he draws others, untill the Jury be full. The same Method, with little Alteration, is taken in returning Juries for the Sessions of the Peace. The Names of those who have serv'd are put in the third Division of the Box, where they lie till those in the first Division are almost all drawn, and then they are again put into this. The Reason of their lying in the third Division is, because one Set of Persons should not be too much burthen'd, but that all should have an equal Share of the Trouble, as nigh as may be.

The Ballot-Box hath three Locks and Keys, kept by three several Persons appointed by the General Assembly, whereof the Judge of the Court is one ; neither can the Box be opened without the Presence of those three.

The Reason of all this Precaution in returning Jurors is, for the better and more effectual Preservation of the Lives and Estates of the Inhabitants. For the Sheriffs, Marshals, and all other such Officers, being appointed by the Governor, and keeping their Places only during his Pleasure, if the returning of Juries lay in their Power, 'tis more than probable, they might at some time or other, pack such Instruments as would be ready to gratify him, to the Ruin of any Person against whom he had conceiv'd Malice or Displeasure. Considering therefore, how easily frivolous and unjust Prosecutions are set on foot, and Evidences fit for any Turn may be procur'd, nothing can be a greater Security than this noble Law ; for after all the Arts and Management betwixt a bad Governor, Judge, and Attorney-General, to carry on an illegal Prosecution, the whole Contrivance is at last spoiled by the Impossibility of Packing a Jury for the Purpose.

A Letter from South Carolina . . . Written by a Swiss Gentleman (London, 1718), 23–24.

---

70. Charge to a Grand Jury (1753)

BY LIEUTENANT-GOVERNOR ROBERT DINWIDDIE

Dinwiddie was lieutenant-governor of Virginia from 1751 to 1758, and his letters show him to have been vigorous and able. The charge to the grand jury was often made a political harangue. — Bibliography: Winsor, *Narrative and Critical History*, V, 268–270.

Gentlemen of the Grand Jury :

YOU are here assembled and sworn to the Execution of the most Important Trust that can be repos'd in Men. To enact Laws, is indeed the Work of the Supream Legislature, but upon the Execution of those Laws, not only the Happiness, but the very Being of Society more imediately depends. It is therefore from You, Gentlemen, that the Public is to derive whatsoever distinguishes a free and well govern'd Comunity from a Band of migrating Savages, who have no Principal of Action but Appetite, and no rule of Right, but Power. Temptations to Violence, and to Fraud are so various and frequent, that it is no Wonder they are not always resisted. Mankind are perpetually deviating into Disorder and Escaping from the Bond of Society. It is therefore necessary for the Magistrate to watch the Earliest Efforts of Oppression, and the first Sallies of Intemperance with the greatest Circumspection, and imediately to restore the general Order as often as it is interupted. The Crimes by which religion is Prophan'd, Allegiance to the King broken, Property invaded, and reputation sullied, are so multiplied that the List is a Satyre on our Species, and [I] wish I cou'd be excus'd from enumerating the many Ways by w'ch human Nature has been degraded, but I am compell'd to display the Cataloge before you, and some of the Articles I hope you will be able effectually to wipe out.   You are, Gent., to punish all who dare Blaspheam Almighty God, a Crime which seems to include a Capacity for all others, for what may not be dreaded from the Wretch who reviles infinite Goodness, ridicules consumate Wisdom, and defies unbounded Power, as a lower Species of this Offence.   You are to take Notice of the contemptuous Violation of the Sabbath, w'ch is an Outrage on every Christian ; and of the horrid Oaths and Imprecations, w'ch wou'd make a Mahomitan tremble.

Perjury in Judicial Concerns is a dreadful Complicat'n of Guilt, it's a daring Insult on the Deity, and the most scandalous, as well as dangerous Invasion of the Property of Others.

Drunkenness, also, however Venial and trifling in comon Estimation, is to be class[ed] Among the Offences w'ch are more imediately comitted against the Majesty of Heaven, as it debases His Image, and abuses His Bounty.   You are next to present all the Species of Treason and misprison of Treason, w'ch are Offences comitted against His most Sacred Majesty, under w'ch is included : — Counterfeiting the Coin, or bringing false Coin into the Colony, or counterfeiting foreing Coin that are current here, and uttering seditious Words against His Majesty's Person and Gov't.   The Crimes that relate to our Fellow Subjects are — Murder, Burglary, robbing on the High-Way, Stealing, or receiving stolen Goods, riots, routs, or unlawful Assemblies, Assaults, or in general, all Gaming, Bribary, Extortion, keeping disorderly Houses, Cheats, Nuisances and Neglect to repair the High-Ways and Bridges.   Such, Gent, is a List of Crimes you are to present, w'ch, yet, is far from including all possible Methods, by w'ch ingenious Wickedness may deviate from the rules of Society.   For that there is a constant Succession of new Vices, or at least new Modes of Vice, for the Evasion of Legal Punishment, is the constant Experience of every Legislature, as appears from the perpetual enaction of new Laws.   When therefore on Y'r Enquiries, you shall perceive any of these malignant Plants spring up, Y'r Duty to Y'r God, Your King, Y'r Country and Y'r Selves, requires that you exert all Your Power for their imediate Destruction.

Great indeed is this Task, Gent., but the Order of our happy Consti tution directs the Performance thereof, and I Congratulate the Publick and myself, that it is in so able Hands, and I doubt not but that you will acquit Y'r Selves so as to not only to have the Praise of Men, but also the Blessing of God.

My fourth Charge,   Oct'r 16th, 1753.

The Official Records of Robert Dinwiddie (Virginia Historical Society, *Collections*, New Series, III, Richmond, 1883), I, 35–37.

---

71. Records of a Precinct Court (1693/4)

BY THE CLERK OF THE COURT OF PERQUIMANS

This is an interesting example of the records of a court of first instance for petty causes. — Bibliography: Channing and Hart, *Guide*, § 147.

AT A COURT HOLDEN AT THE HOUSE OF DIANA FFOSTERS — THE FFIRST MUNDAY IN FFEBRUARY ANN° DO. 1693–4 . . .

Mrs. Durant enters for her two Grand Children a young sorrell mare with a star in her forhead Called Bonne the same mare & her increase & increases to to Ann and Elizabeth Waller to them and their heires for ever.

Thomas Lepper has proved ten Rights in ye County Court Tho Kent Ann his wife Sarah Kent Rebeccah Kent Ann Kent Junr John Thomas Wm Brown Wm Brickstone Tho Lepper Nicholas Robeson

John Barrow proves three rights by importation Robert Tester Simon Smith and a negroe Jean

Thomas Pierce has proved his rights being Thomas Pierce John Pierce Susanna Ruth Pierce Dorothy Pierce Mary Pierce Mary Bridges John Wilkeson and John Pierce in all nine Rights

Hannah Gosby has entered nine Rights Jno. Gosby Jn° Anderson John Kinsey Richard Waterlow Kathrine Kinsey Jean Anderson & 3 hands from Jno Northcoate Joseph Hepworth Jeremiah White & Henry Clay sen^r in all nine Rights

Peter Gray Proves two Rights for himselfe transporting twice into the Governm^{te} and one given him by John Twegar . . .

Upon a petition exhibited by Jabell Alford praying to have liberty to chuse a Guardian. Ordered that the said Jabell Alford be bound to

Mrs Susanna Hartley Widow untill he be one and twenty yeares of age & that ye said Mrs Hartly be bound and enter into bond to learne him the trade of a Carpenter or Joyner w^thin ye said time. . . .

[November 6.] A Bill of enditem^te was Brought ag^t Wm Shreenes and presented to ye Grand Jury ye Grand Jury finds Billa vera ye Petty Jury was sent out & found ye Priso^r guilty of Petty Larceny & so returned ye Bill whereupon he was ordered by the Court to have 30 lashes upon his naked back stript to his wast & sevearly Whipt and be bound to serve for his Phees one yeare and half from this day 9^brs 9th to his Mr John Hatton besides his former Indenture of ffive yeares . . .

A Bill of enditem^te was brought ag^t Robert White & Vincent White his son & presented to ye Grand Jury The Grand Jury finds Billa vera The petty Jury was sent out and they brought their verdict they found ye prisoners guilty of Grand Larceny & they craved the Benefit of ye clargey wch being granted Ordered that they be branded in ye hand wth the letter T : upon ye Brawn of ye left thumbe wch was executed accordingly on Robt White ; ye other reteined to long^r Time or be delivered by the Palatines Court . . .

Susana Harris enters for her daughter Sarah her proper Marke a crop & two Slitt on ye left ear & an over keele & an under keele on ye Right ear.

William L. Saunders, editor, *The Colonial Records of North Carolina* (Raleigh, 1886), I, 392–402 *passim*.

---

72. A Prosecution for Criticising Government (1734)

BY JOHN PETER ZENGER (1738)

Zenger was the publisher of the *New York Weekly Journal*, and was prosecuted for teaching contempt of His Majesty's government. His acquittal is a landmark in the history of the press and of freedom of speech in America. — Bibliography: Winsor, *Narrative and Critical History*, V, 242; Channing and Hart, *Guide*, § 105.

' *New-York, ss.* BE it remembered, That *Richard Bradley*, Esq ; Attorney General of Our Sovereign Lord the King, for the Province of *New-York*, who for Our said Lord the King in this Parts Prosecutes, in his own proper Person comes here into the Court of Our said Lord the King, and for Our said Lord the King gives the Court here to understand, and be informed, That *John Peter Zenger*, late of the City of *New-York*, Printer, (being a seditious Person, and a frequent Printer and Publisher of false News and seditious Libels, and wickedly and maliciously devising the Government of Our said Lord the King of this His Majesty's Province of *New-York*, under the Administration of His Excellency *William Cosby*, Esq ; Captain General and Governour in Chief of the said Province, to traduce, scandalize and vilify, and His Excellency the said Governour, and the Ministers and Officers of Our said Lord the King of and for the said Province to bring into Suspicion and the ill Opinion of the Subjects of Our said Lord the King residing within the said Province) the Twenty eighth Day of *January*, in the seventh Year of the Reign of Our Sovereign Lord *George* the second, by the Grace of God of *Great Britain, France* and *Ireland*, King, Defender of the Faith, *&c.* at the City of *New-York, did falsly, seditiously and scandalously* print and publish, and cause to be printed and published, a certain *false, malicious, seditious, scandalous* Libel, entituled, *The New-York Weekly Journal, containing the freshest Advices foreign and domestick* ; in which Libel (of and concerning His Excellency the said Governour, and the Ministers and Officers of Our said Lord the King, of and for the said Province) among other Things therein contained are the Words *"Your Appearance in Print at last,* gives a Pleasure to many, tho' most wish you had come fairly into the open Field, and not appeared behind *Retrenchments* made of the supposed Laws against Libelling, and of what other Men have said and done before ; these *Retrenchments*, Gentlemen, may soon be shewn to you and all Men to be weak, and to have neither Law nor Reason for their Foundation, so cannot long stand you in stead : Therefore, you had much better as yet leave them, and come to what *the People of this City and Province* (the City and Province of *New-York* meaning) think are the Points in Question (*to wit*) *They* (the People of the City and Province of *New-York* meaning) *think as Matters now stand, that their* LIBERTIES *and* PROPERTIES *are precarious, and that* SLAVERY *is like to be intailed on them and their Posterity, if some past Things be not amended, and this they collect from many past Proceedings."* (Meaning many the past Proceedings of His Excellency of the said Governour, and of the Ministers and Officers of our said Lord the King, of and for the said Province) . . . among other Things therein contained, are these Words, [*"*] *One of our Neighbours* (one of the Inhabitants of *New-Jersey* meaning) *being in Company, observing the Strangers* (some of the Inhabitants of *New-York* meaning) *full of Complaints, endeavoured to perswade them to remove into* Jersey ; *to which it was replied, that*

o

would be leaping out of the Frying Pan into the Fire; *for, says he, we both are under the same Governour* (His Excellency the said Governour meaning) *and your Assembly have shewn with a Witness what is to be expected from them*; *one that was then moving to* Pensilvania, (meaning one that was then removing from *New-York,* with intent to reside at *Pensilvania*) *to which Place it is reported several considerable Men are removing* (from *New-York* meaning) *expressed in Terms very movong much Concern for the Circumstances of* New-York (the bad Circumstances of the Province and the People of *New-York* meaning) *seemed to think them very much owing to the Influence that some Men* (whom he called *Tools*) *had in the Administration* (meaning the Administration of Government of the said Province of *New-York*) *said he was now going from them, and was not to be hurt by any Measures they should take, but could not help having some Concern for the Welfare of his Country Men, and should be glad to hear that the Assembly* (meaning the General Assembly of the Province of *New-York*) *would exert themselves as became them, by shewing that they have the Interest of their Country more at Heart, than the Gratification of any private View of any of their Members, or being at all affected, by the Smiles or Frowns of a Governour,* (His Excellency the said Governour meaning) *both which ought equally to be despised, when the Interest of their Country is at Stake. You, says he, complain of the Lawyers, but I think the Law it self is at an End,* WE (the People of the Province of *New-York* meaning) SEE MENS DEEDS DESTROYED, JUDGES ARBITRARILY DISPLACED, NEW COURTS ERECTED, WITHOUT CONSENT OF THE LEGISLATURE (within the Province of *New-York* meaning) BY WHICH IT SEEMS TO ME, TRYALS BY JURIES ARE TAKEN AWAY WHEN A GOVERNOR PLEASES, (His Excellency the said Governour meaning) MEN OF KNOWN ESTATES DENYED THEIR VOTES, CONTRARY TO THE RE-CEIVED PRACTICE, THE BEST EXPOSITOR OF ANY LAW: *Who is then in that Province* (meaning the Province of *New-York,*) *that call* (can call meaning) *any Thing his own, or enjoy any Liberty* (Liberty meaning) *longer than those in the Administration* (meaning the Administration of Government of the said Province of *New-York*) *will condescend to let them do it, for which Reason I have left it,* (the Province of *New-York* meaning) *as I believe more will."* To the great Disturbance of the Peace of the said Province of *New-York,* to the Great Scandal of Our said Lord the King, of His Excellency the said

Governor, and of all others concern'd in the Administration of the Government of the said Province, and against the Peace of Our Sovereign Lord the King His Crown and Dignity, &c. Whereupon the said Attorney General of Our said Lord the King, for Our said Lord the King, prays the Advisement of the Court here, in the Premises, and the due Process of the Law, against him the said *John Peter Zenger,* in this Part to be done, to answer to Our said Lord the King of and in the Premises, &c.

R. Bradley, Attorney General.'

To this Information the Defendant has pleaded *Not Guilty,* and we are ready to prove it. . . .

Then Mr. *Hamilton,* who at the Request of some of my Friends, was so kind as to come from *Philadelphia* to assist me on the Tryal, spoke.

Mr. *Hamilton,* May it please your Honour ; I am concerned in this Cause on the Part of Mr. *Zenger* the Defendant. The Information against my Client was sent me, a few Days before I left Home, with some Instructions to let me know how far I might rely upon the Truth of those Parts of the Papers set forth in the Information, and which are said to be libellous. And tho' I am perfectly of the Opinion with the Gentleman who has just now spoke, on the same Side with me, as to the common Course of Proceedings, I mean in putting Mr. Attorney upon proving, that my Client printed and published those Papers mentioned in the Information ; yet I cannot think it proper for me (without doing Violence to my own Principles) to deny the Publication of a Complaint, which I think is the Right of every free-born Subject to make, when the Matters so published can be supported with Truth ; and therefore I'll save Mr. Attorney the Trouble of Examining his Witnesses to that Point ; and I do (for my Client) confess, that he both printed and published the two News Papers set forth in the Information, and I hope in so doing he has committed no Crime. . . .

Mr. Attorney, . . . The Case before the Court is, whether Mr. **Zenger** is guilty of Libelling his Excellency the Governor of **New-York,** and indeed the whole Administration of the Government? Mr. **Hamilton** has confessed the Printing and Publishing, and I think nothing is plainer, than that the Words in the Information are **scandalous, and tend to Sedition, and to disquiet the Minds of the People of this Province.** And if such Papers are not Libels, I think it may be said, there can be no such Thing as a Libel.

Mr. **Hamilton,** May it please your Honour ; I cannot agree with Mr.

Attorney: For tho' I freely acknowledge, that there are such Things as Libels, yet I must insist at the same Time, that what my Client is charged with, is not a Libel; and I observed just now, that Mr. Attorney in defining a Libel, made use of the Words *scandalous, seditious, and tend to disquiet the People*; but (whether with Design or not I will not say) he omitted the Word *false*.

Mr. Attorney, I think I did not omit the Word *false*: But it has been said already, that it may be a Libel, notwithstanding it may be true.

Mr. *Hamilton*, In this I must still differ with Mr. Attorney; for I depend upon it, we are to be tried upon this Information now before the Court and Jury, and to which we have pleaded *Not Guilty*, and by it we are charged with printing and publishing, *a certain false, malicious, seditious and scandalous Libel*. This Word *false* must have some Meaning, or else how came it there? . . .

Mr. Ch. Justice, You cannot be admitted, Mr. *Hamilton*, to give the Truth of a Libel in Evidence. A Libel is not to be justified; for it is nevertheless a Libel that it is *true*.

Mr. *Hamilton*, I am sorry the Court has so soon resolved upon that Piece of Law; I expected first to have been heard to that Point. I have not in all my Reading met with an Authority that says, we cannot be admitted to give the Truth in Evidence, upon an Information for a Libel.

Mr. Ch. Justice, The Law is clear, That you cannot justify a Libel. . . .

Mr. *Hamilton*, I thank your Honour. Then, Gentlemen of the Jury, it is to you we must now appeal, for Witnesses, to the Truth of the Facts we have offered, and are denied the Liberty to prove; and let it not seem strange, that I apply my self to you in this Manner, I am warranted so to do both by Law and Reason. The Last supposes you to be summoned, *out of the Neighbourhood where the Fact is alledged to be committed*; and the Reason of your being taken out of the Neighbourhood is, *because you are supposed to have the best Knowledge of the Fact that is to be tried*. And were you to find a Verdict against my Client, you must take upon you to say, the Papers referred to in the Information, and which we acknowledge we printed and published, are *false, scandalous and seditious*; but of this I can have no Apprehension. You are Citizens of *New-York*; you are really what the Law supposes you to be, *honest and lawful Men*; and, according to my Brief, the Facts which we offer to prove were not committed in a Corner; they are notoriously known to be true; and therefore in your Justice lies our

Safety.   And as we are denied the Liberty of giving Evidence, to prove
the Truth of what we have published, I will beg Leave to lay it down as
a standing Rule in such Cases, *That the suppressing of Evidence ought
always to be taken for the strongest Evidence*; and I hope it will have
that Weight with you. . . .

. . . It is true in Times past it was a Crime to speak Truth, and in
that terrible Court of Star-Chamber, many worthy and brave Men suffered for so doing ; and yet even in that Court, and in those bad Times,
a great and good Man durst say, what I hope will not be taken amiss
of me to say in this Place, *to wit, the Practice of Informations for Libels
is a Sword in the Hands of a wicked King, and an arrand Coward to
cut down and destroy the innocent*; *the one cannot, because of his high
Station, and the other dares not, because of his Want of Courage, revenge
himself in another Manner.*

Mr. Attorney, Pray Mr. *Hamilton*, have a Care what you say, don't
go too far neither, I don't like those Liberties.

Mr. *Hamilton*, Sure, Mr. Attorney, you won't make any Applications ;
all Men agree that we are governed by the best of Kings, and I cannot
see the Meaning of Mr. Attorney's Caution, my well known Principles,
and the Sense I haye [have] of the Blessings we enjoy under his present
Majesty, makes it impossible for me to err, and I hope, even to be suspected, in that Point of Duty to my King.   May it please Your Honour,
I was saying, That notwithstanding all the Duty and Reverence claimed
by Mr. Attorney to Men in Authority, they are not exempt from observing the Rules of common Justice, either in their private or publick
Capacities ; the Laws of our Mother Country know no Exception. . . .

I hope to be pardon'd, Sir, for my Zeal upon this Occasion : It is an
old and wise Caution, *That when our Neighbour's House is on Fire, we
ought to take Care of our own.*   For tho', blessed be God, I live in a
Government where Liberty is well understood, and freely enjoy'd ; yet
Experience has shewn us all (I'm sure it has to me) that a bad Precedent in one Government, is soon set up for an Authority in another ;
and therefore I cannot but think it mine, and every Honest Man's
Duty, that (while we pay all due Obedience to Men in Authority) we
ought at the same Time to be upon our Guard against Power, wherever
we apprehend that it may effect Ourselves or our Fellow-Subjects.

I am truly very unequal to such an Undertaking on many Accounts.
And you see I labour under the Weight of many Years, and am born
down with with great Infirmities of Body ; yet Old and Weak as I am,

I should think it my Duty, if required, to go to the utmost Part of the Land, where my Service cou'd be of any Use in assisting to quench the Flame of Prosecutions upon Informations, set on Foot by the Government, to deprive a People of the Right of Remonstrating, (and complaining too) of the arbitrary Attempts of Men in Power. Men who injure and oppress the People under their Administration provoke them to cry out and complain; and then make that very Complaint the Foundation for new Oppressions and Prosecutions. I wish I could say there were no Instances of this Kind. But to conclude; the Question before the Court and you, Gentlemen of the Jury, is not of small nor private Concern, it is not the Cause of a poor Printer, nor of *New-York* alone, which you are now trying; No! It may in its Consequence, affect every Freeman that lives under a British Government on the Main of *America*. It is the best Cause. It is the Cause of Liberty; and I make no Doubt but your upright Conduct, this Day, will not only entitle you to the Love and Esteem of your Fellow-Citizens; but every Man, who prefers Freedom to a Life of Slavery, will bless and honour You, as Men who have baffled the Attempt of Tyranny; and by an impartial and uncorrupt Verdict, have laid a noble Foundation for securing to ourselves, our Posterity, and our Neighbours, That to which Nature and the Laws of our Country have given us a Right, — The Liberty — both of exposing and opposing arbitrary Power (in these Parts of the World, at least) by speaking and writing Truth. . . .

Mr. Ch. Just. Gentlemen of the Jury. The great Pains Mr. *Hamilton* has taken, to shew how little Regard Juries are to Pay to the Opinion of the Judges; and his insisting so much upon the Conduct of some Judges in Tryals of this kind; is done, no doubt, with a Design that you should take but very little Notice of what I may say upon this Occasion. I shall therefore only observe to you that, as the Facts or Words in the Information are confessed: The only Thing that can come in Question before you is, Whether the Words, as set forth in the Information, make a Libel. And that is a Matter of Law, no doubt, and which you may leave to the Court. But I shall trouble you no further with any Thing more of my own, but read to you the Words of a learned and upright Judge in a Case of the like Nature.

'*To say that corrupt Officers are appointed to administer Affairs, is certainly a Reflection on the Government. If People should not be called to account for possessing the People with an ill Opinion of the Government, no Government can subsist. For it is necessary for all Gov-*

ernments that the People should have a good Opinion of it. And nothing can be worse to any Government, than to endeavour to procure Animosities ; as to the Management of it, this has been always look'd upon as a Crime, and no Government can be safe without it be punished.

'*Now you are to Consider, whether these Words I have read to you, do not tend to beget an Ill Opinion of the Administration of the Government ?   To tell us, that those that are employed know nothing of the Matter, and those that do know are not employed. Men are not adapted to Offices, but Offices to Men, out of a particular Regard to their Interest, and not to their Fitness of the Places ; this is the Purport of these Papers.*'

Mr. *Hamilton*, I humbly beg Your Honour's Pardon ; I am very much mis-apprehended, if you suppose what I said was so designed.

Sir, you know, I made an Apology for the Freedom I found my self under a Necessity of using upon this Occasion. I said, there was Nothing personal designed ; it arose from the Nature of our Defence.

The Jury withdrew, and in a small Time returned, and being asked by the Clerk, Whether they were agreed of their Verdict, and whether *John Peter Zenger* was guilty of Printing and Publishing the Libels in the Information mentioned ?   They answered by *Thomas Hunt*, their Foreman, *Not Guilty.*   Upon which there were three Huzzas in the Hall which was crowded with People, and the next Day I was discharged from my Imprisonment.

[*A Brief Narrative of the Case and Tryal of John Peter Zenger, Printer of the New-York Weekly Journal*], (no title-page, New York, 1738), 10–30 *passim.*

73. An Appeal Case in the Privy Council (1727/8)

BY EDWARD SOUTHWELL

This is the final judgment in one of the few cases actually brought to a decision on appeal to the English government. The practice prepared the way for appeals to our present Supreme Court. — Bibliography : P. L. Ford, *List of some Briefs in Appeal Cases.*

AT THE COURT AT ST. JAMES'S, THE 15TH DAY OF FEBRUARY, 1727.

[L. S.]   *Present:*

The King's Most Excell^t Majesty.

Lord President,	Earl of Scarborough,
Lord Privy Seale,	Earl of Loudoun,
Lord Steward,	Earl of Uxbridge,
Lord Chamberlain,	Earl of Sussex,
Duke of Ancaster,	Visco^t Cobham,
Duke of Newcastle,	Visco^t Torrington,
Earl of Lincoln,	Lord Berkeley of Stratton,
Earl of Westmoreland,	Lieut. General Wills,
Earl of Berkeley,	Sr. Robert Sutton.

Upon reading this day at the Board a Report from the Rt. Honble the Lords of the Committee for hearing Appeals from the Plantations, dated the 20th day of December last . . .

His Majesty, taking the same into his royal consideration, is pleased, with the advice of his Privy Council, to approve of the said report, and confirm the same in every particular part thereof; and pursuant thereunto, to declare, that the aforementioned act, entituled An Act for the settlement of intestate estates, is Null and Void ; and the same is hereby accordingly declared to be null and void, and of no force or effect whatever. And his Majesty is hereby further pleased to order, that all the aforementioned sentences of the 29th June, 1725, of the 28th of Sept^r, 1725, and of the 22d March, 172$\frac{5}{6}$, and every of them, be and they are hereby reversed and set aside ; and that the petitioner, John Winthrop, be, and he is hereby, admitted to exhibit an inventory of the personal estate only of the said intestate, and that the court of probates do not presume to reject such inventory because it does not contain the real estate of the said intestate. And his Majesty doth hereby further order, that the aforementioned sentence of the 22d of March, 172$\frac{5}{6}$, vacating the said letters of administration granted to the petitioner, and granting administration to the said Thomas and Ann Lechmere, be also reversed and set aside ; and that the said letters of administration, so granted to Thomas Lechmere and Anne his wife, be called in and vacated ; and that the said inventory of the said real estate, exhibited by the said Thomas Lechmere and Ann his wife, be vacated ; and that the said order of the 29th of April, 1726, approving of the said inventory and ordering the same to be recorded, be discharged and set aside ; and that the original letters of administration granted to the petitioner be, and they are hereby, established and ordered to stand ; and that all such costs as the petitioner hath paid unto the said Thomas Lechmere by directions of the said sentences, all, every, or any of them, be forthwith repaid to him by the said Thomas Lechmere ; and that the suit brought by the said Thomas Lechmere and Anne his wife, on which the said sentences were made, be and they are hereby dismissed ; and that all acts and proceedings done and had under the said sentences, all, every, or any of them, or by virtue or pretence thereof, be and they are hereby discharged and set aside, and declared null and void. And his Majesty is further pleased to declare, that the aforementioned act of Assembly, passed in May, 1726, empowering the said Thomas Lechmere to sell the said lands, is null and void ; and also that the said order made by the said superior court, bearing date the 27th of Sept^r, 1726, pursuant to the said act of Assembly, allowing the said Lechmere to sell of the said real estate to the value of ninety pounds current money there for his charges, and three hundred and eighteen pounds silver money, is likewise null and void ; and the said act of Assembly and order of the said superior court are accordingly hereby declared null and void, and of no force or effect whatever.

And his Majesty doth hereby likewise further order, that the petitioner be immediately restored and put into the full, peaceable and quiet possession of all such parts of the said real estate as may have been taken from him, under pretence of, or by virtue or colour of the said sentence, orders, acts and proceedings, or any of them ; and that the said Thomas Lechmere do account for and pay to the said petitioner the rents and profits thereof, and of every part thereof, received by him or any one under him, for and during the time of such his unjust detention thereof.

And the Governour and Company of his Majesty's Colony of Connecticut for the time being, and all other officers and persons whatsoever, whom it may concern, are to take notice of his Majesty's royal pleasure hereby signified, and yield due obedience to every particular part thereof, as they will answer the contrary at their peril.

Charles J. Hoadly, editor, *The Public Records of the Colony of Connecticut,* 1726–1735 (Hartford, 1873), VII, 571–579 *passim.*

---

74. Defects of Colonial Judicature (1764)

BY LATE GOVERNOR THOMAS POWNALL

Bibliography as in No. 53 above.

THE crown directs its governor to erect courts and appoint the judges thereto. — The actual appointment of the judges is no where *directly* disputed. —— But the power of erecting courts, according to this instruction, is, I believe, universally disputed; it being a maxim universally maintained by the Colonists, that no court can be erected but by act of legislature. —— Those who reason on the side of the crown, — say, — that the crown does not, by erecting courts in the colonies, claim any right of enacting the jurisdiction of those courts, or the laws whereby they are to act. —— The crown names the judge, establishes the court, but the jurisdiction is settled by the laws of the realm; — and "customs, precedents, and common judicial proceedings of a court are a law to the court, and the determination of courts make points to be law." —— The reasoning of the Colonists would certainly hold good against the erection of any new jurisdiction, established on powers not known to the laws of the realm; but how it can be applied to the opposing the establishment of courts, the laws of whose practice, jurisdiction and powers are already settled by the laws of the realm, *is the point in issue, and to be determined.* It will then be fixed, beyond dispute, whether the crown can, in its colonies, erect, without the concurrence of the legislature, courts of Chancery, Exchequer, King's Bench, Common Pleas, Admiralty, and Probate or Ecclesiastical courts. —— If it should be determined in favour of the reasoning, and the claims of the Colonists, — I should apprehend that the consideration of the points under this head, would become an object of government here, even in its legislative capacity. —— In which view it may be of consequence to consider, how far, and on what grounds, the rights of the crown are to be maintained by courts of King's Bench, &c. and how far the revenues by courts of Exchequer, and how far the crown and subject may have relief by courts of equity. —— If in this view we consider the defects which must be found in Provincial courts, those point out the necessity of the establishment of a remedial general court of Appeal; but if we view the only mode of appeal, which at present exists, we shall see how inapplicable, how inadequate that court is. I cannot, in one view, better describe the defects of the provincial courts in these infant governments, than by that very description which my Lord Chief Justice Hales gives of our county courts, in the infancy of our own government, wherein he mentions,

" *First,* The ignorance of the judges, who were the freeholders of the county.

" *Secondly,* That these various courts bred variety of law, especially in the several counties, for the decisions or judgments being made by divers courts, and several independent judges and judicatories, who had no common interest amongst them in their several judicatories, thereby in process of time, every several county would have several laws, customs, rules, and forms of proceedings. ——

"*Thirdly,* That all the business of any moment was carried by parties and factions, and that those of great power and interest in the county did easily overbear others in their own causes, or in such wherein they were interested, either by relation of kindred, tenure, service, dependence, or application."

Upon the first article of this parallel, it will be no dishonour to many gentlemen sitting on the benches of the courts of law in the colonies, to say, that they are not, and cannot be expected to be lawyers, or learned in the law. And on the second article it is certain, that although it be a fundamental maxim of colony administration, that the colonies shall have no laws contrary to the laws of Great Britain, yet, from the fluctuation of resolutions, and confusion in the construction and practice of the law in the divers and several colonies, it is certain, that the practice of their courts, and their common law, must be not only different from each other, but in the consequence different also from that of Great Britain. In all the colonies the common law is received as the foundation and main body of their law; but each colony being vested with a legislative power, the common law is thereby continually altered; so that (as a great lawyer of the colonies has said) " by reason of the diversity of the resolutions, in their respective superior courts, and of the several new acts or laws made in them severally ; the several systems of the laws of those colonies grow more and more variant, not only from one another, but also from the laws of England."

Under the third article, I fear experience can well say, how powerfully, even in courts, the influence of the leaders of party have been felt in matters between individuals. But in these popular governments, and where every executive officer is under a dependence for a temporary, wretched, and I had almost said, arbitrary support to the deputies of the people, — it will be no injustice to the frame of human nature, either in the person of the judges, of the juries, or even the popular lawyer to suggest, how little the crown, or the rights of government, when opposed to the spirit of democracy, or even to the passions of the populace, has to expect of that support, maintenance, and guardianship, which the courts are even by the constitution supposed to hold for the crown — Nor would it be any injustice to any of the colonies, just to remark in this place, how difficult, if ever practicable it is in any of their courts of common law to convict any person of a violation of the laws of trade, or in any matter of crown revenue. Some of our acts of parliament direct the prosecution and punishment of the breach of the laws of trade, to take its course in the courts of Vice-admiralty : And it has been thought by a very great practitioner, that if the laws of trade were regulated on a practicable application of them to the state of the colony trade, that every breach of them should be prosecuted in the same way. That there should be an advocate appointed to each court from Great Britain, who, having a proper salary independent of the people, should be directed and empowered to prosecute in that court, not only every one who was an offender, but also every officer of the customs, who through neglect, collusion, oppression, or any other breach of his trust became such. — Here I own, was it not for the precedent already established by some of the laws of trade, I should doubt the consistency of this measure with the general principle of liberty, as established in the trials by a jury in the common law courts. If these precedents can reconcile these proceedings to the general principles of liberty, there can be no more effectual measure taken ; yet such precedents should be extended with caution. The defect in most, and actual deficiency in many of the colonies, of a court of equity, does still more forcibly lead to the necessity of the measure of some remedial court of appeal and equity. . . .

Thomas Pownall, *The Administration of the Colonies* (London, 1765), 75–80.

CHAPTER XI — COLONIAL LOCAL GOVERNMENT

75. The Business of a County Court (1681)

BY CLERK EPHRAIM HERMAN

The county court in the southern and middle colonies was rather administrative than judicial, and was the agent of local government. No detailed record of later date than 1681 has been found available. — Bibliography: Armstrong, *Record of the Court at Upland*, Introduction; E. Channing, *Town and County Government;* G. E. Howard, *Local Constitutional History.*

June 14th 1681

ATT a Court held att Kingsesse for Upland County in Delowar River by his may^ties authority June 14th 1681 ;

	MR OTTO ERNEST COCH	
P^rsent	MR ISRAEL HELM	} Justices
	MR LAURENS COCK	

CAPT^N EDM : CANTWELL high Sherrife

Justice LAURENS COCK P^lt } the def^t 2^d default
JUSTA JUSTASSEN Def^t }
The Co^rt Continued this action till next Co^rt day ;

ANDRIES BOEN P^lt } the def^t returned non
MOENS PETER STACKET Def^t } Est Inventus

ARNOLDUS DE LAGRANGE P^lt
Just : OTTO ERNEST COCK Def^t
This action referred till next Court by reason that there's noe Court w^thout Justice otto whoe is a party.

Justice Henry Jones & Justice George Browne were boath fyned for not attending ye Court to suply their places Each 10 pounds according to ye Law booke.

HANNA SALTER P^lt
ANDRIES HOMMAN Def^t
The P^lt not appearing was nonsuited wth Costs ;

William Boyles acquaints ye Co^{rt} that one Robbered michill next heir of Robberd hoskins deceased, is att p^{r}sent alyve in England, and that hee ye s^d will Boyles is by him ye s^d Rob : michill desiered to take Care of ye Estate of ye s^d deceased hoskins wth in this Country ;

Upon Complaint of Christiaen Claassen ; ordered that william Baale Give sattisfact : to Cristiaen for what Land hee had Cleared and all further Improovem^t in Equity

Claes Jansen brings in ye Eare marke for his Cattle & hoggs & desires that ye same may bee recorded ; Granted & is as followeth vizt the foremost syde of ye Ears halfe cutt away ;

Justice George Browne appeared and sate in Co^{rt} being hindered to come sooner for want of a passage over ye Creeke ;

LASSE DALBOO P^{lt}
SWEN LOM   Def^t

Jurys names
James Sanderlins Will Boyles
John Boeyar harmen Ennis
will : orian andries peterss :
& oele raesen

The P^{lt} declares agst ye def^t for a peece of Land Lying in ye Schuylkill etc. The def^t replyes that hee has had ye first grant & survey & paid quit rent.

The P^{lt} craues a Jury wch was Granted and ye Jury Impannelled & sworne & ye : Case before them debated, they went out and returning brought in their verdict as followed vizt wee find for the deft : the Co^{rt} doe passe Judgem^t according to verdict ;

Justice Otto Ernest Coch acquaints the Court, that hee has bought and paid of ye : Indian proprieto^{rs} a certaine swampy or marshy Island called by ye Indians quistconck Lying att the upper End of Tinnach-konck Island in ye river opposit andrews Boones Creeke ; and desires ye Co^{rts} approbation. The Co^{rt} haueing well Informed themselves about ye p^{r}misses, doe allow thereof.

Upon ye Peticon of magist^r Jacobus fabritius ; ordered that ye Church wardens of ye Peticon^{rs} Church doe take care that Every one of those as haue Signed & promissed towards his maintaynance, doe pay him ye sumes promissed, upon payne of Execution agst ye : deffective ;

ANDRIES PETERSEN P^{lt}
JONAS NEALSON   Def^t

The def^t alleadging that hee was not tymely arrested ; The Case is referred til next Court ;

Upon Complaint made by ye overseers of ye highways; The Court haue and doe hereby Condemne John Champion to pay a fyne of twenty and fyve Gilders, for his not workeing upon ye highway when due warning was Given him;

Upon ye Request of william warner & william orian; ordered that ye severall people that hold Lands; of that wch ye peticon^{rs} bought of ye Indians Lying in ye Schuylkill Every one to repay to ye peticon^r proportionable to ye: quantity of Land they hold there — the whole purchaze wch ye peticon^{rs} paid being 335 gilders; and ye following p^{r}sons holding Lands wthin that Limit, vizt andries Inckoren 200 acres andries homman 200 acres Pelle Laersen (als) Put pelle 100 acres, Peter Erikson 200 acres will: warner 100 acres will: orian 100 acres John Booles & John Schoeten 400 acres Swen Lom 300 acres of Land.   Each of ye: aboves^d p^{r}sons to pay proportionable to ye quantity of Land they hold as aboves^d

Upon ye request of Peter Jocum ordered that Peter rambo Cause his marsh Land according to pattent to bee surveyed to ye End s^d Peter Jocum may know what is Left to him;

Benck Salung sworne in Co^{rt} sayeth that hendrik Colman tould him that hee heard moens Staecket say that all the Court were Rogues;

The Co^{rt} ordered that Execution should bee Granted to ye Sherrife; upon ye Co^{rts} amerciaments due according to ye List drawne out, & alreddy in ye s^d Sherrifs hands for ye Collecting of ye s^d amerciaments according to Lawe.

Upon ye severall peticons of the afternamed persons, The Co^{rt} Granted unto Each of them ye quantitys of Land hereunder Exprest, to take up they ye Peticon^{rs} seating and Improoveing ye same according to Lawe and regulacons;

Granted unto Reynier Petersen to take up	200 acres
Andries Boon	200
Will: Warner Senior	400
Rich: Tucker	100 acres
Otto Ernest Coch	400 acres
Lynall Brittall	200 acres
Jan Claassen	200 acres

Upon an Information of will: Coyles ye Constable att ye faals agst Gilbert wheeler att ye s^d faals, for selling of strong Licquors by retayle to ye Indians Contrary to ye Lawe & ye forwarning of ye s^d Constable, wch s^d Information was Lykewyse by Justice Geo: Browne auerred to bee truth ; The Co.^{rt} haue and doe hereby Condemne ye s^d Gilbert wheeler to pay as a fyne ye sume of fower pound ; for his s^d trespasse, according to ye Expresse Lawe of ye Governm^t togeather ye Costs (als) Execution.

The C^{rt} haue this day authorized and appointed William Boyles to bee surv^r & overseer of ye highwayes from the faales to Poetquessink Creek ; hee to take care that ye s^d highwayes bee made good & passable, wth bridges over all myry & dirty places ; betweene this & ye next Co.^{rt} and all ye Inhabitants Living wthin ye Compasse aboves^d to bee reddy to doe & compleat ye s^d way upon due warning given by ye s^d overseer ; the unwilling to bee fyned according to former order & practize ;

> The Co.^{rt} adjorned till ye 2^d Teus-
> day of ye month of Septemb^r next.

[Edward Armstrong, editor], *The Record of the Court at Upland, in Pennsylvania* (Pennsylvania Historical Society, *Memoirs*, VII, Philadelphia,
1860), 189–194.

———◆———

76. Records of a City Government (1700)

BY THE MAYOR, RECORDER, ALDERMEN, AND COMMON COUNCIL OF ALBANY

Very few borough or city governments existed in the colonies; this extract sets forth the activity of one of them. — Bibliography : A. J. Weise, *History of the City of Albany*, ch. x.

ATT a Common Councill held in ye Citty of Albany ye 14th of May, 1700.

It is concluded and thought requisite that ye streets within this Citty be cleared, each Inhabitant before his door, and to remove ye fyre wood thereof, and whoever shall be founde driveing a wagon or cart through ye streets, and ye drivers not walking afoot, shall forfeit for each such offence ye sum of 3s, as likewise for such as are neglecting to clean the street, and remove the wood before their doors.

It is further considered and ordered that ye Constables shall take their turns on ye sabbath day to prevent drawing of strong drink in tipling houses, and breaking the sabbath day, and whosoever shall be founde drawing of any strong liquor in said houses to any person, shall forfeit ye summe of twenty shillings for each offence.

Hendrik Oothout appointed surveyor for ye Citty and sworne.

Jacob Turke is appointed to sue the Kinderhook Justices to ye next inferior Court, fo ye arrears due to ye Citty.

May 16, 1700. — Whereas Pr. Jedon and John Pettitt and family, both French, from Sopus, appear desyring liberty to passe to Canada, and that a man or two may be allowed to carry them thither, which is permitted, and thought convenient y^t ye Persones y^t carry them thither shall enter into bonde that they shall transport noe horses or mares to Canida as ye late proclamation requires, whereupon David Ketelheyn and Elbert Harmense, who are their guides, have given bond for £100.

Itt is concluded y^t ye three Constables, each in his warde, shall goe rounde by each Inhabitant y^t have rid Stockadoes for ye Citty, and order him to show ye same, and whoever as have not ride their quota shall pay for each Stockade 18d. which is to be done in the space of twice four and twenty hours.

It is further concluded that after the Citty walls are closed, y^t ye Constables shall take care to see that no Stockadoes be broak downe and wherever they fynde or can hear of any person y^t breaks downe said Stockadoes shall forfeit for Stockadoe so broak downe ye summe of 6s. according to former custom, and then said Constable shall order Stockadoes to be sett up againe upon ye Citties costs.

May 21. — It is concluded y^t a warrant be given to ye Constables to strain all Inhabitants as have been neglecting in Riding their quota of Stockadoes for ye Citty walls, and y^t 4 men shall be employed to sett up ye Stockadoes already Ride upon ye Cittys costs.

May 24. — It is concluded by ye authority aforesaid, that a Tax of one hundred pounds be laid and assessed upon ye Inhabitants of this Citty, and y^t a warrant be issued to ye assessors of ye Citty, to make their assessment for ye same, which shall be collected and received, one half at or before ye 15th of July next ensueing, and ye other halfe at or before ye 15th of September then following ; ye assessors are to make their returns to Mr. Mayor in ye space of eight days ensueing ye 25th of this instant.

June 7. — Whereas on ye 24th of May last a warrant was directed to the assessors of this Citty, to make their assessment for £100 upon the Inhabitants therein, and to make their return in ye space of eight days to Mr. Mayor, under hand and seale, which assessment being made and produced to ye meeting, desyring approbation, but being founde not to be sealed according to order, is given over again to ye assessors and referred

P

till Harpert Jacobse, Ben. van Corlaer, assessors, come home from New York, to the sealing thereof.

David Schuyler and Jacobus Turke are appointed to inquire if there is any debts still due to Abraham Poel deceased, by Hend. Hanse and others, and make report thereof next Tuesday. . . .

[Sept. 3. —] The Churchwardens of Shinnechtady doe make application to ye Mayor, Recorder, Aldermen & Common Councill, desyreing two persones to be allowed & appoynted to goe Rounde by ye Inhabitants of ye Citty, to see if they can obtain any Contribution to make up ye Sellary due to there Minister, Do. Freman, whilst on his voyage from Amsterdam to this place, they complayning not to be capable to make out said Sellary by there own Congregation doe therefore desyre assistance.

The Commonality are unanimously of opinion that since they are censible that s^d Church wardens have not informed themselves what there Congregations will Comply to said Sellary, that they first goe and Visite there owne Congregation, and if they doe not obtain said Sellary by them, then to make there application to the Commonality at ye next Court day.

Sept. 21. — Whereas ye Church wardens of Shennechtady doe again make application that two persons may be appointed to goe Round by ye Inhabitants of this Citty to see if they can obtain any contributions for Do. freemans Sellary as there Desyre on ye 3d of this Instant doth now at large appear. Whereupon ye Commonality have concluded and doe allow and admitt two or more of s^d Church wardens of Shinnechtady to goe once Round for Contribution to use as aforesaid from ye Inhabitants of this Citty and no more in ye time of the Sessions, which will be first and second of October next Ensuing.

Albany ye 14th of October, A^o 1700. — This day being appointed by ye Charter of ye Citty for ye Aldermen in there respective Wards to make return of ye aldermen, assistants, assessors & constables for ye ensueing year, who are as follows . . .

[Nov. 15. —] It is concluded that ye following Proclamation be proclaimed.

That according to ye yearly Custome they doe hereby prohibit and forbid ye Retailing of all sorts of Strong Liquor within this Citty and County, unless by Mr Mayors Lycense, on penalty of forfeiting as a fyne upon such person or persones so offending ye summe of five pounds, according to act of assembly, as also that no such Retailers shall receive from any Souldier upon any Pretence whatsoever any of there Provisions,

Cloaths, or other accoutrements, or shall retaile to them in their house after ye ringing of ye Bell for Eight o'clock at night, upon penalty of forfeiting for each Souldier so founde as aforesaid ye summe of six shillings for ye Behooffe of such Person as shall sue for ye same.

Pursuant to an order of Councill dated ye 23^d of Sept., and another from his Excellency dated the 16th of October last, Coll. Pr. Schuyler, the Mayor, Aldermen and Commonality have hired the house of William Ketelheyn till p^mo May next, for ye summe of six pounds for two Lefts. and there wifes.   Also ye Chamber on ye south side of Elisabeth widow of Wouter Utthoft's house, with the use of her bedd and bedding to p^mo May next, for four pounds tenn shillings for one Leif^t, with ye condition that at ye present ye magistrates are to supply her with two Blankets, which at ye Expiration of ye time as afores^d are to be deducted off ye hire.

Nov. 26.— Evert Wendell sen. appears in Common Councill and makes Request verbally, that in ye time of ye late Gov. Thomas Dongan, orders were issued to demand all Patents or Ground Brieffes belonging to this Citty and County, in which time ye said Petitioner gave up his .Grond Brieffe granted to him by ye late governor Petrus Stuyvesant for a certain Lott of grounde situate lying and being on ye south side of ye Citty, on ye east side of ye hill abutting to ye north of ye Land and Orchard belonging to Isaac Casperse ; and since said Evert Wendel declares that said Ground Brieffe or any other was never returned to him.   Doth therefore humbly request of ye hon. Commonality to grant him a Release for s^d Grounde, which ye Commonality have taken into Consideration, and ·have graunted ye same, ordering a Release to be writte, which shall be signed.

It is concluded that a warrant be issued to ye fyre masters to vizite ye Chimneys and fyre places within this Citty every three weeks, beginning ye 2d of December next and so continuing during the time of three months, which fyre masters are as follows : Bastiaen Harmense, William Hogen, Warner Carstense, Guysbert Marselis, Tierk Harmense, Jonathan Broadhurst.

J[oel] Munsell, *The Annals of Albany* (Albany, 1853), IV, 112–120 *passim*.

77. Record of a Vestry Meeting (1702)

BY THE VESTRY OF ST. PAUL'S PARISH, CHOWAN PRECINCT

In the south the vestry, alongside the county court (No. 75 above), was the organ of local government, corresponding roughly to the town-meeting of New England. — Bibliography: E. Channing, *Town and County Government.*

AT a Vestry holden the 30th of June 1702 at the house of Thomas Gilliam

Present :

Col William Wilkinson	M[r] Edward Smithwick
Cap[t] Thomas Leuten	M[r] Nicholas Crisp
Cap[t] Thomas Blount	M[r] Wm Banbury
Wm Duchenfield Esq.	M[r] James Long.

Nath[l] Chevin.

In obedience to a late act of Assembly made in March last impowering the Vestry of each precinct to provide a standard for weights & measures and it being debated how the said weights and measures be procured — agreed —

That the Church Wardens shall use their utmost endeavour by the first convenience to send for weights and measure as the law directs.

And agree with some person for that purpose at as cheap a rate as possible and also one fair and large book of common Prayer, and the Book of Homilies.

Ordered that the Church Wardens shall agree with and pay the collector or collectors for collecting the precinct Levies. . . .

At a Vestry held at Thomas Gilliam's Oct. 13th 1702.

Present

The Hon[ble] Henderson Walker — President

	Church Wardens	
Col Wm Wilkison		Mr John Blount
Capt Thomas Leuten		Capt Thomas Blount
Mr Nicholas Crist.		Mr Edward Smithwick
		Mr Wm Banbury.

Whereas at the last Vestry it was ordered that there should be a standard of weights and measures sent for the use of the precinct in obedience to the act of Assembly the charge whereof with the rest of the p[r]cinct charge being as followeth. Viz[t].

	£ : sh : d
To building the Chappel to Mr John Porter	25 : 0 : 0
To Richard Curton Reader	7 : 10 : 0
To the Standard for the precinct.	12 : 10 : 0
To clearing an acre of ground, and flooring the house to. Mr Smithwick.	2 : 10 : 0
To Nathaniel Chevin acting as Clerk	1 : 10 : 0
To the Joiner for Windows. Table forms. & Benches	6 : 0 : 0
To Thomas Gilliam for trouble of his house	1 : 10 : 0
To the poor of the precinct	8 : 0 : 0
To John Tyler for Attendance	0 : 1 : 0
To Sallery for collecting at so p^r C^t———	6 : 8 : 0

The total amount. ——— 70 : 19 : 0

The list of Tythables in the precinct being taken is found to be 283 and the sum

Ordered that the church Wardens collect from each Tythable person in the precinct five shillings and Col Wm Wilkinson having undertaken the collection, and the Vestry agreeing thereto

Ordered that Col Wm Wilkinson do collect upon all and every the Tythables within this precinct (a list whereof is delivered to him under the hand of the clerk of the Vestry) five shillings p^r pole and for non payment thereof to make distress according to Law, and likewise to pay unto the several persons aforementioned the several sums due to them and allotted by this vestry, and He together with the other Church Wardens do provide and pay for the other things mentioned in the aforesaid Order, and render an account of the same to this Vestry to be holden the last tuesday in April next and finish all the collection. . . .

OCTOBER YE: 14.th 1702.

The vestry being met and having viewed the Chappel, the major part of the Vestry do declare their dislike of the ceiling of the Chappel by reason of the Boards being defaced.

Ordered that Mr Edward Smithwick and Mr Nicholas Crisp on behalf of the Vestry do choose one indifferent man that is skilled in building, and Mr John Porter shall choose another. who shall meet at the Chappel the second saturday in November to give their judgment whether the boards be fit for ceiling such a house and if these two persons chosen as aforesaid cannot agree in their opinions, then they shall choose an umpire, and what opinion he the said umpire shall give shall be a full and final determination of the matter about the ceiling and boards, and the agreement between the Church wardens and Mr John Porter shall be thence.

At a Vestry holden at the House of Mrs Sarah Gillam ye 15th Day of December 1702. . . .

Coll William Wilkinson and Capt Thomas Leuten having Served one Year in the Station of Church Wardens, and the Choice of new Church Wardens being debated :

Mr William Duckenfield and Mr Edward Smithwick are appointed Church Wardens for the ensuing year. . . .

The Chappel being this Day viewed by all the Vestry here present and are Satisfied therewith and do receive the House and Keys from Mr John Porter he promising to provide So much Lime as will Wash the Ceiling of the Chappel, and the Vestry to be at the Charge of a Workman to do the Same.

William L. Saunders, editor, *The Colonial Records of North Carolina* (Raleigh, 1886), I, 558–561 *passim*.

---

78. Proceedings of a Town-Meeting (1720/1–1721)

BY CLERK CAPTAIN RICHARD WATERMAN

Out of many records this has been chosen as including a variety of business in small compass. The elections show the number and variety of offices. — Bibliography : E. Channing, *Town and County Government ;* G. E. Howard, *Local Constitutional History.* — See also Channing and Hart, *Guide*, §§ 118, 147; *Contemporaries*, I, No. 165.

ATT a Towns Quarter meeteing held att Prouidence this 27th day of January anno Dom : 1720/21

Major William Hopkins Chosen Moderator :

Grand Jurimen Called for by the moderator Returned } William Harris
Robert Currey

Pettee jurymen Called for by the moderator
Returned } Samuel Aldrich
Roger Burllinggame
William Hopkins
Carpenter
Ebenezer Spreague

Jt is voated and ordered that | from and after ye first day of aprill next | Noo Geese shall be Lett goe vpon the Common or in the high-ways nor in the water with in this Township of Prouidence or with in the Jurisdiction there of nor vpon any other persons Land. Except those that one the Geese : on the pennilty of the forfiture of all such Geese that are so found — Past :

Jt is voated and ordered that Herndens Lane and the highway that Leads from thence to pautuckett may be fenced for the space of fiue years from hence next Comeing prouided there be sufficiant Gates sett vp and maintained in sd Lane and highway that may be Conueniant for both horse men and Cartes to pass through as well as foot men dureing all the said term

Jt is further voated and ordered that Nathan Place shall bring what deputies Bills he hath in his hands to mr James Browne that he may Jnspect into what the sum of·sd Bills amounts to and also Jndeavour to git Jnformation how big the Rate was that was Leuied vpon the Town Jn the yeare 1715 and there vpon give an account to Richard Waterman Town Clerke . . .

Jt is also voated and ordered that Each free holder with in this Town-ship of Prouidence shall from and after this day haue two pence ℙr head for euery head of a Gray Squirrill that shall be by them brought before the Towns Treasuror : and to be payed out of the Townes Treasurrey : and this order to Continue dureing the Towns pleasure
And the sd Treasuror shall be Carefull to accept of no squirrils heads but such as are killed within this Town ship

The meeteing is dissolued

Att a meeteing of the Committee Chosen to make vp the accounts with the Town Treasurer and also to audet the Townes debts this 23d day of may Anno Dom : 1720 : And to Jnspect into such accounts as shall be brought before them : And there vpon to allow of such accounts as to them shall seeme Legal : and draw a List of the same to be a Rule for the Treasurer to pay out the money by —

deputies Bills { Wee haue thought fitt to Raise Sixteene pounds to pay ye deputies } £ s d 16 – 00 – 00

Charges upon Mary Marsh	due to William Turpin To Cloatheing for Mary March	01 – 19 – 03
	And theire will be due for her keepeing ye 14th day of June next the sum of the which sum m^r Turpin saith he is Jngaged for	09 – 00 – 00

due for Sarjants wages   {   To m^r William Turpin for Sarjants wages   04 – 00 –

for other things	To 4 yards of osenbrigs for the Cripple att Nathaniel Brownes	00 – 08 – 00
	To warning the Jury and attendance in the Layeing out the highway by John Wilkinsons	00 – 12 – 00

Charges upon Richard Collins upon [ ]	due To Doctor John Jenckes for the care of Richard Collings when heis well	04 – 10 – []
	for Phissick To Bettee Saturn in the time of sickness Jn february : 1719 : 20	02 – 02 – 09

Allowed to Daniel Abbott	due to Daniel Abbott for Paying 2 Rates for William Screech	00 – 03 – 04
	& : 2 : Rates for Sam vmpotoun Jndian	00 – 02 – 06

We think fitt to Raise for Squerrils heads   {   To ye defraying the Charge of Squerrils heads   16 – 00 – 00

[ ]rges high[ ]ays   {   Wee think fitt to Raise for the defraying the Charge of the highway through Hosannah Brownes Land and the highway att or neere James Mathewsons Land   03 – 18 – 00

[ ] a Record [ ]ooke   {   due to Richard Waterman Junr for a Record Booke   00 – 14 – 00

The aboue accounts are voated and allowed att a Towne meeteing ye 30th day of may : 1720 —

Where vpon it is voated and ordered to Raise 150^£ – 00^s – 00^d

And it is further voated and ordered that the Tow[ ] Treasurer shall pay all Legal dues and duties in Geathering and such other | Lawfull | Charges that shall accrew in bring in the s^d sum of one hundred and fifty pounds in to the Towns Treasurry . . .

Att a Towne meeteing held att Prouidence this 5th day of June 1721 : Jt being the first munday in said month and the Towns Election day for Chooseing of Towne officers

Capt Richard Waterman is Chosan Town Clerk : Engaged

Robert Currie Chosen Towne Serjant :   ⎫ Engaged
Henry Eastain Chosen Constable ×   ⎬ those Crast
John Sayles Junr Chosen × Constable   ⎭ are engaged

Moses Burlinggame Chosen Constable who was dismissed for Reasonable alligations

Co^ll Joseph × Whipple   ⎫   ⎫
Mr James Browne Refused   ⎪ Chosen   ⎪ those
m^r Nicholas × Power   ⎬ Town   ⎬ Crossed are
Mr Edward Smith Refused   ⎪ Councill ⎪ Engaged
Capt Nathaniell Jenckes ×   ⎪ men   ⎪
Capt Thomas Harris ×   ⎭   ⎭

Thomas Olney w^s Chosen Town Treasuror Engaged

Mr Edward Smith   ⎫
Cap^tn Josiah Westcott ×   ⎬ Chosen Ratemakers
& m^r Joseph Brown ×   ⎭

Mr Stephen Dexter ×   ⎫
Mr John Dexter ×   ⎪
Mr Ebenezer Spreague ×   ⎪
Mr John Steere × Junr ×   ⎬ Chosen Surueyors of
Mr Nehemiah Sheldon ×   ⎪ highways
Mr Thomas Burllinggame   ⎪ those Crossed are Engaged
Mr John Bolcom   ⎪
Mr Samuell ffisk   ⎭

Mr Eliezer Arnold Engaged Mr Thomas Arnold Junr Mr William Turpin Engaged	} Chosen ouer seers for the poore
Capt James olney Mr William Whipple William Whipple Refused	} Pound Engaged keepers
M^r × James Browne Mr Richard Browne m^r × William | Hopkins | Carp^{tr} m^r Richard Sayles m^r Charles Dyer m^r × Arthur ffenner Junr m^r John Steere Junr × & m^r James Aldrich	} Chosen fence viewers those Crossed are Engaged
Mr Benjamin Tillinghast Chosen Packer & and Sealer	} Engaged
Mr Thomas Kilton m^r Daniell Angell and m^r Ebenezer × Bates	} Chosen Hog Constables Engaged

The Town Constables Chosen and Engaged for the Ciuell are

Henry Estance : —

John Sayles Junr

Samuell Gorton

Mr Nathaniell Blague Mr Thomas Kilton are Chosen hemp viewers — Engaged

Mr Jonathan Spreague Junr Js Chosen deputy to serue att the next Genr^{ll} Court of Assembly to be held att Newport Jn this Jnstant June Jn the Roome of m^r Andrew Harris

for as much as Mr James Browne hath Positiuely Refused to serue in the place of a Town Councill man : where vpon Capt James Olney is Chosen in his Roome and also m^r Edward Smith hath positiuely Refused to serue in the place and office of a Town Councill man : where vpon Mr Phillip Tillinghast is Chosen in his Roome ×

The meeteing is adjorned to Saterday next it being the 10th day of this Jnstant June att twelue a Clock in the day —

Saterday ye 10th day of June 1721 :
the meeteing is againe in being — Coll Joseph Whipple Continues
moderator

The Town Councill men Chosen to act
to the assistants and Justices for this yeare :
and Engaged are —

- Coll Joseph Whipple
- Capt Nathaniell Jenckes
- Capt Thomas Harris
- Mr Nicholas Power
- Capt James Olney
- Mr Phillip Tillinghast

John Potter Junr is Chosen Constable Jn the Roome of Moses Burllinggame

Ensign James Whipple is Chosen Pound Keeper in the Roome of
Mr William Whipple

The meeteing is adjorned to munday the 19th day of this Jnstant
June

Jn order to Engage John Potter Junr to the place of a Constable :
other ways to Chose an other in his Roome : but in Case the sd Potter
takes his ingagement before that time then this meeteing is dissolued

June ye : 19th day 1721 : the meeteing is againe in being —

Richard Waterman Chosen Moderator Coll Joseph Whipple being
absent

John Potter Junr appeared before this meeteing and made excuse of
his Enabilityes that disinabled him for serueing in the place of a Constable : and his alligations was accepted by the Justices and there vpon
the sd Potter Js dismist for this yeare Jn hopes he may be better Enabled
to performe the office by his Jndustry to acquaint himself with Larneing
against an other time
Where vpon Samuell Gorton was Chosen in to the office of a Constable and Engaged in the Roome of the said John Potter

The meeteing is dissolued :

[Record Commission], *The Early Records of the Town of Providence* (Providence, 1897), XIII, 41–55 *passim.*

79. The Dignity of a Selectman (1763–1766)

BY JOHN ADAMS

The standing executive board or committee kept up the town's business when the town-meeting was adjourned. — For Adams, see No. 24 above; on town government, see No. 78 above.

[1763] BOSTON. February. This day learned that the Caucus Club meets, at certain times, in the garret of Tom Dawes, the Adjutant of the Boston Regiment. He has a large house, and he has a movable partition in his garret which he takes down, and the whole club meets in one room. There they smoke tobacco till you cannot see from one end of the garret to the other. There they drink flip, I suppose, and there they choose a moderator, who puts questions to the vote regularly ; and selectmen, assessors, collectors, wardens, fire-wards, and representatives, are regularly chosen before they are chosen in the town. Uncle Fairfield, Story, Ruddock, Adams, Cooper, and a *rudis indigestaque moles* of others are members. They send committees to wait on the merchant's club, and to propose and join in the choice of men and measures. Captain Cunningham says, they have often solicited him to go to those caucuses ; they have assured him benefit in his business, &c. . . .

[1766] March 1. Saturday. Spent a part of last evening with Mr. Jo Cleverly. He is a tiptoe for town meeting ; he has many schemes and improvements in his head ; — namely, for separating the offices of constable and collector ; collecting taxes has laid the foundation for the ruin of many families. He is for five selectmen, and will vote for the old ones, Mr. Quincy and Major Miller. He hears they are for turning out all the old selectmen, and choosing a new set ; they for having but three, &c. The only way is to oppose schemes to schemes, and so break in upon them. Cleverly will become a great town-meeting man, and a great speaker in town meeting. *Q.* What effect will this have on the town affairs?

Brother tells me that William Veasey, Jr. tells him he has but one objection against Jonathan Bass, and that is, Bass is too forward. When a man is forward, we may conclude he has some selfish view, some self ends. Brother asked him if he and his party would carry that argument through. It holds stronger against Captain Thayer and Major Miller, than it ever did against anybody in this town, excepting Colonel Gooch and Captain Mills. But I desire the proof of Bass's forwardness. Has he been more so than Major Miller? Come, come, Mr. Veasey, says Master Jo Cleverly, don't you say too much; I an't of that mind. *Ego.* Bass is an active, capable man, but no seeker by mean begging or buying of votes.

3. Monday. My brother Peter, Mr. Etter, and Mr. Field, having a number of votes prepared for Mr. Quincy and me, set themselves to scatter them in town meeting. The town had been very silent and still, my name had never been mentioned, nor had our friends ever talked of any new selectmen at all, excepting in the south precinct; but as soon as they found there was an attempt to be made, they fell in and assisted; and, although there were six different hats with votes for as many different persons, besides a considerable number of scattering votes, I had the major vote of the assembly the first time. Mr. Quincy had more than one hundred and sixty votes. I had but one vote more than half. Some of the church people, — Mr. Jo Cleverly, his brother Ben and son, &c. and Mr. Ben Veasey, of the middle precinct, Mr. James Faxon, &c. — I found were grieved and chagrined for the loss of their dear Major Miller. Etter and my brother took a skilful method; they let a number of young fellows into the design, John Ruggles, Peter Newcomb, &c. who were very well pleased with the employment, and put about a great many votes. Many persons, I hear, acted slyly and deceitfully; this is always the case.

I own it gave me much pleasure to find I had so many friends, and that my conduct in town has been not disapproved. The choice was quite unexpected to me. I thought the project was so new and sudden that the people had not digested it, and would generally suppose the town would not like it, and so would not vote for it. But my brother's answer was, that it had been talked of last year and some years before, and that the thought was familiar to the people in general, and was more agreeable than any thing of the kind that could be proposed to many, and for these reasons his hopes were strong.

But the triumph of the party was very considerable, though not complete; for Thayer, and Miller, and the late lessees of the north commons, and many of the church people, and many others had determined to get out Deacon Penniman; but, instead of that, their favorite was dropped, and I, more obnoxious to that party than even Deacon Penniman or any other man, was chosen in his room, and Deacon Penniman was saved with more than one hundred and thirty votes, — a more reputable election than even Thayer himself had.

Mr. Jo Bass was extremely sorry for the loss of Major Miller; he would never come to another meeting. Mr. Jo Cleverly could not account for many things done at town meetings. His motion for choosing collectors was slighted; his motion for lessening his fine was thrown out; and he made no sort of figure as a speaker; so that I believe Mr. Cleverly will make no hand.

Elisha Niles says, set a knave to catch a knave. A few days before a former March meeting, he told Thayer that he had a mind to get in Deacon Penniman. Thayer asked him, who he would have with him? he answered, Captain Allen. Thayer made him no answer, but when the meeting came, was chosen himself. Mr. Thomas Faxon, of this end of the town, told my wife he never saw anybody chosen so neatly in his life, — not a word, not a whisper beforehand. Peter Newcomb gave him a vote; he had one before for Miller, and had heard nothing of me; but he thought I should have one. So he dropped that for Miller. Jo Nightingale asked my wife, "Mr. Adams will have too much business, will he not; the courts to attend, selectman, and representative at May, &c.?" Mr. John Baxter, the old gentleman, told me he was very well pleased with the choice at the north end, &c. Old Mr. John Ruggles voted for me; but says that Thayer will [be chosen] at May. If I would set up, he would vote for me, and I should go, but Mr. Quincy will not. Lieutenant Holbrook, I hear, was much in my favor, &c. Thus the town is pretty generally disputing about me, I find.

But this choice will not disconcert Thayer, at May, though it will weaken him. But, as I said before, the triumph was not complete; — Cornet Bass had the most votes the first time, and would have come in the second, but the north end people, his friends, after putting in their votes the first time, withdrew for refreshment, by which accident he lost it, to their great regret.

Mark the fruits of this election to me. Will the church people be angry, and grow hot and furious, or will they be cooler and calmer for it? Will Thayer's other precinct friends resent it and become more violent, or will they be less so? In short, I cannot answer these questions; many of them will be disheartened, I know; some will be glad.

10. Monday. Last week went to Boston, and to Weymouth, &c. I hear that Mr. Benjamin Cleverly has already bespoke Mr. John Ruggles, Jr. against May meeting, — promised him as much as he can eat and drink of the best sort, if he will vote for Captain Thayer; told him he would not have acted as he did, at March, if it had not been for Thomas

Newcomb, and that he would vote for Thayer, at May, if it was not for Thomas Newcomb. By this, the other side are alarmed; the craft, they think, is in danger; but I believe their fears are groundless, though I wish there was good reason for them.

Drank tea at Mr. Etter's. He says all the blame is laid to him, and that a certain man takes it very ill of him. By the way, I heard to-day that Major Miller and James Bracket, Jr. were heard, since March meeting, raving against Deacon Palmer, and said he was a knave, &c. *Q.* About this quarrel?

I find the late choice has brought upon me a multiplicity of new cares. The schools are one great object of my attention. It is a thing of some difficulty to find out the best, most beneficial method of expending the school money. Captain Adams says, that each parish's proportion of the school money has not been settled since my father's day. Thomas Faxon says, it would be more profitable to the children, to have a number of women's schools about than to have a fixed grammar school. *Q.* Whether he has not a desire that his wife should keep one? Jonathan Bass says the same. *Q.* His wife is a school-mistress. So that two points of examination occur; the portion between the parishes, that is, the sum which this parish ought to have; and whether a standing grammar school is preferable to a number of school-mistresses part of the year, and a grammar school part.

Another great object is the poor; persons are soliciting for the privilege of supplying the poor with wood, corn, meat, &c. The care of supplying at cash price, and in weight and measure, is something; the care of considering and deciding the pretensions of the claimants is something.

A third, and the greatest, is the assessment; here I am not so thorough; I must inquire a great while before I shall know the polls and estates, real and personal, of all the inhabitants of the town or parish. The highways, the districts to surveyors, and laying out new ways or altering old ones, are a fourth thing. Perambulations of lines are another thing. Dorchester, Milton, Stoughton, Bridgewater, Abington, Weymouth, — orders for services of many sorts to, &c.

John Adams, *Works* (edited by Charles Francis Adams, Boston, 1850), II, 144–188 *passim*.

PART IV

COLONIAL LIFE

CHAPTER XII — THE LIFE OF THE PEOPLE

80. A Lady's Travel in New England (1704)

BY MADAM SARAH KEMBLE KNIGHT

Madam Knight was the daughter of a Boston merchant, and wife of the captain of a London ship. She was for a time schoolmistress in Boston, and later settled in Connecticut. The journey described below was made to claim some property. — Bibliography: Preface to Madam Knight's *Journal*, reprinted in 1865; Tyler, *American Literature*, II, 96–98; Winsor, *Narrative and Critical History*, V, 167–169; Channing and Hart, *Guide*, § 130. — For earlier accounts of New England life, see *Contemporaries*, I, ch. xxi.

MONDAY, Octb'r. ye second, 1704. — About three o'clock afternoon, I begun my Journey from Boston to New-Haven; being about two Hundred Mile. . . .

. . . being ignorant of the way, Mad^m Billings, seing no persuasions of her good spouses or hers could prevail with me to Lodg. there that night, Very kindly went wyth me to ye Tavern, where I hoped to get my guide, And desired the Hostess to inquire of her guests whether any of them would go with mee. . . . I told her no, I would not be accessary to such extortion.

Then John shan't go, sais shee. No, indeed, shan't hee; And held forth at that rate a long time, that I began to fear I was got among the Quaking tribe, beleeving not a Limbertong'd sister among them could out do Madm. Hostes.

Upon this, to my no small surprise, son John arrose, and gravely demanded what I would give him to go with me? Give you, sais I, are you John? Yes, says he, for want of a Better; And behold! this John look't as old as my Host, and perhaps had bin a man in the last Century. Well, Mr. John, sais I, make your demands. Why, half a pss.

of eight and a dram, sais John.   I agreed, and gave him a Dram (now) in hand to bin'd the bargain.

My hostess catechis'd John for going so cheep, saying his poor wife would break her heart. . . .

When we had Ridd about an how'r, wee come into a thick swamp, wch. by Reason of a great fogg, very much startled mee, it being now very Dark.   But nothing dismay'd John : Hee had encountered a thousand and a thousand such Swamps, having a Universall Knowledge in the woods ; and readily Answered all my inquiries wch. were not a few.

In about an how'r, or something more, after we left the Swamp, we come to Billinges, where I was to Lodg.   My Guide dismounted and very Complasantly help't me down and shewd the door, signing to me wth his hand to Go in ; wch I Gladly did — But had not gone many steps into the Room, ere I was Interogated by a young Lady I understood afterwards was the Eldest daughter of the family, with these, or words to this purpose, (viz.) Law for mee — what in the world brings You here at this time a night ? — I never see a woman on the Rode so Dreadfull late, in all the days of my versall life.   Who are You?   Where are You going?   I'me scar'd out of my witts — with much more of the same Kind.   I stood aghast, Prepareing to reply, when in comes my Guide — to him Madam turn'd, Roreing out : Lawfull heart, John, is it You? — how de do !   Where in the world are you going with this woman?   Who is she? . . .

I told her shee treated me very Rudely, and I did not think it my duty to answer her unmannerly Questions.   But to get ridd of them, I told her I come there to have the post's company with me to-morrow on my Journey, &c.   Miss star'd awhile, drew a chair, bid me sitt, And then run up stairs and putts on two or three Rings, (or else I had not seen them before,) and returning, sett herself just before me, showing the way to Reding, that I might see her Ornaments, perhaps to gain the more respect. . . .

Tuesday, October ye third, about 8 in the morning, I with the Post proceeded forward without observing any thing remarkable ; And about two, afternoon, Arrived at the Post's second stage, where the western Post mett him and exchanged Letters.   Here, having called for something to eat, ye woman bro't in a Twisted thing like a cable, but something whiter ; and laying it on the bord, tugg'd for life to bring it into a capacity to spread ; wch having wth great pains accomplished, shee serv'd in a dish of Pork and Cabage, I suppose the remains of Dinner.   The

Q

sause was of a deep Purple, wch I tho't was boil'd in her dye Kettle ; the bread was Indian, and every thing on the Table service Agreeable to these. I, being hungry, gott a little down ; but my stomach was soon cloy'd. . . .

. . . the Post told mee we had neer 14 miles to Ride to the next Stage, (where we were to Lodg.) I askt him of the rest of the Rode, foreseeing wee must travail in the night. Hee told mee there was a bad River we were to Ride thro', wch was so very firce a hors could sometimes hardly stem it : But it was but narrow, and wee should soon be over. I cannot express The concern of mind this relation sett me in : no thoughts but those of the dang'ros River could entertain my Imagination, and they were as formidable as varios, still Tormenting me with blackest Ideas of my Approching fate — Sometimes seing my self drowning, otherwhiles drowned, and at the best like a holy Sister Just come out of a Spiritual Bath in dripping Garments.

Now was the Glorious Luminary, wth his swift Coursers arrived at his Stage, leaving poor me wth the rest of this part of the lower world in darkness, with which *wee* were soon Surrounded. The only Glimering we now had was from the spangled Skies, Whose Imperfect Reflections rendered every Object formidable. Each lifeless Trunk, with its shatter'd Limbs, appear'd an Armed Enymie ; and every little stump like a Ravenous devourer. Nor could I so much as discern my Guide, when at any distance, which added to the terror.

Thus, absolutely lost in Thought, and dying with the very thoughts of drowning, I come up wth the post, who I did not see till even with his Hors : he told mee he stopt for mee ; and wee Rode on Very deliberatly a few paces, when we entred a Thickett of Trees and Shrubs, and I perceived by the Hors's going, we were on the descent of a Hill, w^ch, as wee come neerer the bottom, 'twas totaly dark wth the Trees that surrounded it. But I knew by the Going of the Hors wee had entred the water, wch my Guide told mee was the hazzardos River he had told me off ; and hee, Riding up close to my Side, Bid me not fear — we should be over Imediatly. I now ralyed all the Courage I was mistriss of, Knowing that I must either Venture my fate of drowning, or be left like ye Children in the wood. So, as the Post bid me, I gave Reins to my Nagg ; and sitting as Stedy as Just before in the Cannoo, in a few minutes got safe to the other side, which hee told mee was the Narragansett country. . . .

. . . But I could get no sleep, because of the Clamor of some the of

Town tope-ers in next Room, Who were entred into a strong debate concerning ye Signifycation of the name of their Country, (viz.) *Narraganset*. One said it was named so by ye Indians, because there grew a Brier there, of a prodigious Highth and bigness, the like hardly ever known, called by the Indians Narragansett ; And quotes an Indian of so Barberous a name for his Author, that I could not write it. His Antagonist Replyed no — It was from a Spring it had its name, wch hee well knew where it was, which was extreem cold in summer, and as Hott as could be imagined in the winter, which was much resorted too by the natives, and by them called Narragansett, (Hott and Cold,) and that was the originall of their places name — with a thousand Impertinances not worth notice, wch He utter'd with such a Roreing voice and Thundering blows with the fist of wickedness on the Table, that it peirced my very head. . . . I set my Candle on a Chest by the bed side, and setting up, fell to my old way of composing my Resentments, in the following manner :

> I ask thy Aid, O Potent Rum !
> To Charm these wrangling Topers Dum.
> Thou hast their Giddy Brains possest —
> The man confounded wth the Beast —
> And I, poor I, can get no rest.
> Intoxicate them with thy fumes :
> O still their Tongues till morning comes !

And I know not but my wishes took effect ; for the dispute soon ended w^th 'tother Dram ; and so Good night !

Wednesday, Octob^r 4th. About four in the morning, we set out for Kingston (for so was the Town called) with a french Docter in our company. Hee and ye Post put on very furiously, so that I could not keep up with them, only as now and then they'd stop till they see mee. . . . But the post encourag'd mee, by saying wee should be well accommodated anon at mr. Devills, a few miles further. But I questioned whether we ought to go to the Devil to be helpt out of affliction. However, like the rest of Deluded souls that post to ye Infernal denn, Wee made all posible speed to this Devil's Habitation ; where alliting, in full assurance of good accommodation, wee were going in. But meeting his two daughters, as I suposed twins, they so neerly resembled each other, both in features and habit, and look't as old as the Divel himselfe, and quite as Ugly, We desired entertainm't, but could hardly get a word out of 'um, till with our Importunity, telling them our necesity, &c. they call'd the old Sophister, who was as sparing of his words as his daughters had bin, and no, or none, was the reply's hee made us to our demands. . . .

About seven that Evening, we come to New London Ferry : here, by reason of a very high wind, we mett with great difficulty in getting over — the Boat tos't exceedingly, and our Horses capper'd at a very surprizing Rate, and set us all in a fright. . . .

. . . between nine and ten at night waited on the Rev^d Mr. Gurdon Saltonstall, minister of the town, who kindly Invited me to Stay that night at his house, where I was very handsomely and plentifully treated and Lodg'd ; and made good the Great Character I had before heard concerning him : viz. that hee was the most affable, courteous, Genero's and best of men.

Friday, Octo^r 6th.   I got up very early, in Order to hire somebody to go with mee to New Haven, being in Great parplexity at the thoughts of proceeding alone ; which my most hospitable entertainer observing, himselfe went, and soon return'd wth a young Gentleman of the town, who he could confide in to Go with mee. . . .

. . . about two a clock afternoon we arrived at New Haven, where I was received with all Posible Respects and civility.   Here I discharged Mr. Wheeler with a reward to his satisfaction, and took some time to rest after so long and toilsome a Journey ; And Inform'd myselfe of the manners and customs of the place, and at the same time employed myselfe in the afair I went there upon.

They are Govern'd by the same Laws as wee in Boston, (or little differing,) thr'out this whole Colony of Connecticot, And much the same way of Church Government, and many of them good, Sociable people, and I hope Religious too : but a little too much Independant in their principalls, and, as I have been told, were formerly in their Zeal very Riggid in their Administrations towards such as their Lawes made Offenders, even to a harmless Kiss or Innocent merriment among Young people.   Whipping being a frequent and counted an easy Punishment, about wch as other Crimes, the Judges were absolute in their Sentances. . . .

They give the title of merchant to every trader ; who Rate their Goods according to the time and spetia they pay in : viz. Pay, mony, Pay as mony, and trusting.   *Pay* is Grain, Pork, Beef, &c. at the prices sett by the General Court that Year ; *mony* is pieces of Eight, Ryalls, or Boston or Bay shillings (as they call them,) or Good hard money, as sometimes silver coin is termed by them ; also Wampom, vizt Indian beads wch serves for change. *Pay as mony* is provisions, as afores^d, one Third cheaper then as the Assembly or Gene^l Court sets it ; and *Trust* as they and the merch^t agree for time.

Now, when the buyer comes to ask for a comodity, sometimes before the merchant answers that he has it, he sais, *is Your pay redy ?* Perhaps the Chap Reply's Yes : what do You pay in? say's the merchant. The buyer having answered, then the price is set ; as suppose he wants a sixpenny knife, in pay it is 12d — in pay as money eight pence, and hard money its own price, viz. 6d. It seems a very Intricate way of trade and what Lex Mercatoria had not thought of.

[Theodore Dwight, editor], *The Journals of Madam Knight*, etc. (New York, 1825), 9–43 *passim*.

---

81. "A Man Diligent in his Calling" (1729–1732)

BY BENJAMIN FRANKLIN (1771)

The autobiography of Franklin is not only an invaluable picture of the times, but is one of the noteworthy books in the world's literature. — For Franklin, see No. 68 above. For colonial life in general, see Lodge, *Short History of the English Colonies ;* Channing and Hart, *Guide*, §§ 133, 145.

. . . AS I could not yet begin our paper, I wrote several pieces of entertainment for Bradford's paper, under the title of the BUSY BODY, which Breintnal continu'd some months. By this means the attention of the publick was fixed on that paper, and Keimer's proposals, which we burlesqu'd and ridicul'd, were disregarded. He began his paper, however, and, after carrying it on three quarters of a year, with at most only ninety subscribers, he offer'd it to me for a trifle ; and I, having been ready some time to go on with it, took it in hand directly ; and it prov'd in a few years extremely profitable to me. . . .

Our first papers made a quite different appearance from any before in the province ; a better type, and better printed ; but some spirited remarks of my writing, on the dispute then going on between Governor Burnet and the Massachusetts Assembly, struck the principal people, occasioned the paper and the manager of it to be much talk'd of, and in a few weeks brought them all to be our subscribers.

Their example was follow'd by many, and our number went on growing continually. This was one of the first good effects of my having learnt a little to scribble ; another was, that the leading men, seeing a newspaper now in the hands of one who could also handle a pen, thought it convenient to oblige and encourage me. Bradford still printed the votes, and laws, and other publick business. He had printed an address of the House to the governor, in a coarse, blundering manner; we reprinted it elegantly and correctly, and sent one to every member. They were sensible of the difference : it strengthened the hands of our friends in the House, and they voted us their printers for the year ensuing.

Among my friends in the House I must not forget Mr. Hamilton, before mentioned, who was then returned from England, and had a seat in it. He interested himself for me strongly in that instance, as he did in many others afterward, continuing his patronage till his death. . . .

But now another difficulty came upon me which I had never the least reason to expect. Mr. Meredith's father, who was to have paid for our printing-house, according to the expectations given me, was able to advance only one hundred pounds currency, which had been paid ; and a hundred more was due to the merchant, who grew impatient, and su'd us all. We gave bail, but saw that, if the money could not be rais'd in time, the suit must soon come to a judgment and execution, and our hopeful prospects must, with us, be ruined, as the press and letters must be sold for payment, perhaps at half price.

In this distress two true friends, whose kindness I have never forgotten, nor ever shall forget while I can remember any thing, came to me separately, unknown to each other, and, without any application from me, offering each of them to advance me all the money that should be necessary to enable me to take the whole business upon myself, if that should be practicable ; but they did not like my continuing the partnership with Meredith, who, as they said, was often seen drunk in the streets, and playing at low games in alehouses, much to our discredit. These two friends were William Coleman and Robert Grace. I told them I could not propose a separation while any prospect remain'd of the Merediths' fulfilling their part of our agreement, because I thought myself under great obligations to them for what they had done, and would do if they could ; but, if they finally fail'd in their performance, and our partnership must be dissolv'd, I should then think myself at liberty to accept the assistance of my friends.

Thus the matter rested for some time, when I said to my partner, " Perhaps your father is dissatisfied at the part you have undertaken in this affair of ours, and is unwilling to advance for you and me what he would for you alone.   If that is the case, tell me, and I will resign the whole to you, and go about my business."   " No," said he, " my father has really been disappointed, and is really unable ; and I am unwilling to distress him farther.   I see this is a business I am not fit for.   I was bred a farmer, and it was a folly in me to come to town, and put myself, at thirty years of age, an apprentice to learn a new trade.   Many of our Welsh people are going to settle in North Carolina, where land is cheap. I am inclin'd to go with them, and follow my old employment.   You may find friends to assist you.   If you will take the debts of the company upon you ; return to my father the hundred pound he has advanced ; pay my little personal debts, and give me thirty pounds and a new saddle, I will relinquish the partnership, and leave the whole in your hands."   I agreed to this proposal ; it was drawn up in writing, sign'd, and seal'd immediately.   I gave him what he demanded, and he went soon after to Carolina, from whence he sent me next year two long letters, containing the best account that had been given of that country, the climate, the soil, husbandry, etc., for in those matters he was very judicious.   I printed them in the papers, and they gave great satisfaction to the publick.

As soon as he was gone, I recurr'd to my two friends ; and because I would not give an unkind preference to either, I took half of what each had offered and I wanted of one, and half of the other ; paid off the company's debts, and went on with the business in my own name, advertising that the partnership was dissolved.   I think this was in or about the year 1729.

About this time there was a cry among the people for more paper money, only fifteen thousand pounds being extant in the province, and that soon to be sunk.   The wealthy inhabitants oppos'd any addition, being against all paper currency, from an apprehension that it would depreciate, as it had done in New England, to the prejudice of all creditors. . . .

Our debates possess'd me so fully of the subject, that I wrote and printed an anonymous pamphlet on it, entitled "*The Nature and Necessity of a Paper Currency*."   It was well receiv'd by the common people in general ; but the rich men dislik'd it, for it increas'd and strengthen'd the clamor for more money, and they happening to have no writers among them that were able to answer it, their opposition slacken'd, and the point was carried by a majority in the House.   My friends there, who conceiv'd I had been of some service, thought fit to reward me by employing me in printing the money; a very profitable jobb and a great help to me. This was another advantage gain'd by my being able to write. . . .

I soon after obtain'd, thro' my friend Hamilton, the printing of the Newcastle paper money, another profitable jobb as I then thought it; small things appearing great to those in small circumstances; and these, to me, were really great advantages, as they were great encouragements. He procured for me, also, the printing of the laws and votes of that government, which continu'd in my hands as long as I follow'd the business.

I now open'd a little stationer's shop. I had in it blanks of all sorts, the correctest that ever appear'd among us, being assisted in that by my friend Breintnal. I had also paper, parchment, chapmen's books, etc. One Whitemash, a compositor I had known in London, an excellent workman, now came to me, and work'd with me constantly and diligently; and I took an apprentice, the son of Aquila Rose.

I began now gradually to pay off the debt I was under for the printing-house. In order to secure my credit and character as a tradesman, I took care not only to be in *reality* industrious and frugal, but to avoid all appearances to the contrary. I drest plainly; I was seen at no places of idle diversion. I never went out a fishing or shooting; a book, indeed, sometimes debauch'd me from my work, but that was seldom, snug, and gave no scandal; and, to show that I was not above my business, I sometimes brought home the paper I purchas'd at the stores thro' the streets on a wheelbarrow. Thus being esteem'd an industrious, thriving young man, and paying duly for what I bought, the merchants who imported stationery solicited my custom; others proposed supplying me with books, and I went on swimmingly. In the mean time, Keimer's credit and business declining daily, he was at last forc'd to sell his printing-house to satisfy his creditors. He went to Barbadoes, and there lived some years in very poor circumstances.

His apprentice, David Harry, whom I had instructed while I work'd with him, set up in his place at Philadelphia, having bought his materials. I was at first apprehensive of a powerful rival in Harry, as his friends were very able, and had a good deal of interest. I therefore propos'd a partnership to him, which he, fortunately for me, rejected with scorn. He was very proud, dress'd like a gentleman, liv'd expensively, took much diversion and pleasure abroad, ran in debt, and neglected his business; upon which, all business left him; and, finding nothing to do, he follow'd **Keimer to Barbadoes**, taking the printing-house with him.

There this apprentice employ'd his former master as a journeyman; they quarrel'd often; Harry went continually behindhand, and at length was forc'd to sell his types and return to his country work in Pensilvania. The person that bought them employ'd Keimer to use them, but in a few years he died.

There remained now no competitor with me at Philadelphia but the old one, Bradford; who was rich and easy, did a little printing now and then by straggling hands, but was not very anxious about the business. However, as he kept the post-office, it was imagined he had better opportunities of obtaining news; his paper was thought a better distributer of advertisements than mine, and therefore had many more, which was a profitable thing to him, and a disadvantage to me; for, tho' I did indeed receive and send papers by the post, yet the publick opinion was otherwise, for what I did send was by bribing the riders, who took them privately, Bradford being unkind enough to forbid it, which occasion'd some resentment on my part; and I thought so meanly of him for it, that, when I afterward came into his situation, I took care never to imitate it.

I had hitherto continu'd to board with Godfrey, who lived in part of my house with his wife and children, and had one side of the shop for his glazier's business, tho' he worked little, being always absorbed in his mathematics. Mrs. Godfrey projected a match for me with a relation's daughter, took opportunities of bringing us often together, till a serious courtship on my part ensu'd, the girl being in herself very deserving. The old folks encourag'd me by continual invitations to supper, and by leaving us together, till at length it was time to explain. Mrs. Godfrey manag'd our little treaty. I let her know that I expected as much money with their daughter as would pay off my remaining debt for the printing-house, which I believe was not then above a hundred pounds. She brought me word they had no such sum to spare; I said they might mortgage their house in the loan-office. The answer to this, after some days, was, that they did not approve the match; that, on inquiry of Bradford, they had been inform'd the printing business was not a profitable one; the types would soon be worn out, and more wanted; that S. Keimer and D. Harry had failed one after the other, and I should probably soon follow them; and, therefore, I was forbidden the house, and the daughter shut up. . . .

And now I set on foot my first project of a public nature, that for a subscription library. I drew up the proposals, got them put into form by our great scrivener, Brockden, and, by the help of my friends in the Junto, procured fifty subscribers of forty shillings each to begin with, and ten shillings a year for fifty years, the term our company was to continue. We afterwards obtain'd a charter, the company being increased to one hundred : this was the mother of all the North American subscription libraries, now so numerous. It is become a great thing itself, and continually increasing. These libraries have improved the general conversation of the Americans, made the common tradesmen and farmers as intelligent as most gentlemen from other countries, and perhaps have contributed in some degree to the stand so generally made throughout the colonies in defence of their privileges. . . .

This library afforded me the means of improvement by constant study, for which I set apart an hour or two each day, and thus repair'd in some degree the loss of the learned education my father once intended for me. Reading was the only amusement I allow'd myself. I spent no time in taverns, games, or frolicks of any kind ; and my industry in my business continu'd as indefatigable as it was necessary. I was indebted for my printing-house ; I had a young family coming on to be educated, and I had to contend with for business two printers, who were established in the place before me. My circumstances, however, grew daily easier. My original habits of frugality continuing, and my father having, among his instructions to me when a boy, frequently repeated a proverb of Solomon, "Seest thou a man diligent in his calling, he shall stand before kings, he shall not stand before mean men," I from thence considered industry as a means of obtaining wealth and distinction, which encourag'd me, tho' I did not think that I should ever literally *stand before kings*, which, however, has since happened ; for I have stood before *five*, and even had the honor of sitting down with one, the King of Denmark, to dinner.

We have an English proverb that says, *"He that would thrive, must ask his wife."* It was lucky for me that I had one as much dispos'd to industry and frugality as myself. She assisted me cheerfully in my business, folding and stitching pamphlets, tending shop, purchasing old linen rags for the paper-makers, etc., etc. We kept no idle servants, our table was plain and simple, our furniture of the cheapest. For instance, my breakfast was a long time bread and milk (no tea), and I ate it out of a twopenny earthen porringer, with a pewter spoon. But mark how luxury will enter families, and make a progress, in spite of principle : being call'd one morning to breakfast, I found it in a China bowl, with a spoon of silver ! They had been bought for me without my knowledge by my wife, and had cost her the enormous sum of three-and-twenty shillings, for which she had no other excuse or apology to make, but that she thought *her* husband deserv'd a silver spoon and China bowl as well as any of his neighbors. This was the first appearance of plate and China in our house, which afterward, in a course of years, as our wealth increas'd, augmented gradually to several hundred pounds in value.

Benjamin Franklin, *Autobiography* (edited from his manuscript by John Bigelow, Philadelphia, 1868), 177–210 *passim*.

———◆———

82. Society in Virginia (1732)

BY COLONEL WILLIAM BYRD

Byrd was a man of education and wealth, living on his Virginian estate in a style of great magnificence. His accounts of business and pleasure trips are witty and interesting. — Bibliography : Doyle, *English in America, Virginia*, 339–364; Winsor, *Narrative and Critical History*, V, 278–284; Tyler, *American Literature*, II, 270–279; Channing and Hart, *Guide*, § 99. — For earlier accounts of Virginian society, see *Contemporaries*, I, ch. x.

· · · THIS famous Town [Germanna] consists of Colo. Spotswood's enchanted Castle on one Side of the Street, and a Baker's Dozen of ruinous Tenements on the other, where so many German Familys had dwelt some Years ago ; but are now remov'd ten Miles higher, in the Fork of Rappahannock, to Land of their Own. There had also been a Chappel about a Bow-Shot from the Colonel's house, at the End of an Avenue of Cherry Trees, but some pious people had lately burnt it down, with intent to get another built nearer to their own homes. Here I arriv'd about three a'clock, and found only Mrs. Spotswood at Home, who receiv'd her Old acquaintance with many a gracious Smile. I was carry'd into a Room elegantly set off with Pier Glasses, the largest of which came soon after to an odd Misfortune. Amongst other favourite Animals that cheer'd this Lady's Solitude, a Brace of Tame Deer ran familiarly about the House, and one of them came to stare at me as a Stranger. But unluckily Spying his own Figure in the Glass, he made a spring over the Tea Table that stood under it, and shatter'd the Glass to pieces, and falling back upon the Tea Table, made a terrible Fracas among the China. This Exploit was so sudden, and accompany'd with such a Noise, that it surpriz'd me, and perfectly frighten'd Mrs. Spotswood.　But twas worth all the Damage to shew the Moderation and good humour with which she bore this disaster.　In the Evening the noble Colo. came home from his Mines, who saluted me very civilly, and Mrs. Spotswood's Sister, Miss Theky, who had been to meet him *en Cavalier*, was so kind too as to bid me welcome.　We talkt over a Legend of old Storys, supp'd about 9, and then prattl'd with the Ladys, til twas time for a Travellour to retire.　In the mean time I observ'd my old Friend to be very Uxorious, and exceedingly fond of his Children.　This was so opposite to the Maxims he us'd to preach up before he was marryed, that I cou'd not forbear rubbing up the Memory of them.　But he gave a very good-natur'd turn to his Change of Sentiments, by alleging that whoever brings a poor Gentlewoman into so solitary a place, from all her Friends and acquaintance, wou'd be ungrateful not to use her and all that belongs to her with all possible Tenderness.

We all kept Snug in our several apartments till Nine, except Miss Theky, who was the Housewife of the Family.　At that hour we met over a Pot of Coffee, which was not quite strong enough to give us the Palsy.　After Breakfast the Colo. and I left the Ladys to their Domestick Affairs, and took a turn in the Garden, which has nothing beautiful but 3 Terrace Walks that fall in Slopes one below another.　I let him understand, that besides the pleasure of paying him a Visit, I came to be instructed by so great a Master in the Mystery of Making of Iron, wherein he had led the way, and was the Tubal Cain of Virginia.　He corrected me a little there, by assuring me he was not only the first in this Country, but the first in North America, who had erected a regular Furnace.　That they ran altogether upon Bloomerys in New England & Pennsylvania, till his Example had made them attempt greater Works.　But in this last Colony, they have so few Ships to carry their Iron to Great Britain, that they must be content to make it only for their own use, and must be oblig'd to manufacture it when they have done.　That he hoped he had done the Country very great Service by setting so good an Example. . . . Our Conversation on this Subject continued till Dinner, which was both elegant and plentifull.　The afternoon was devoted to the ladys, who shew'd me one of their most beautiful Walks.　They conducted me thro' a Shady Lane to the Landing, and by the way made me drink some very fine Water that issued from a Marble Fountain, and ran incessantly. . . . Then we proceeded to the River, which is the South Branch of Rappahanock, about 50 Yards wide, and so rapid that the Ferry Boat is drawn over by a Chain, and therefore called the Rapidan. At night we drank prosperity to all the Colonel's Projects in a Bowl of Rack Punch, and then retired to our Devotions.

Having employ'd about 2 hours in Retirement, I Sally'd out at the first Summons to Breakfast, where our conversation with the Ladys, like Whip Sillabub, was very pretty, but had nothing in it. This it seems was Miss Theky's Birth day, upon which I made her my Compliments, & wish't she might live twice as long a marry'd Woman as she had liv'd a Maid. I did not presume to pry into the Secret of her Age, nor was she forward to disclose it, for this humble Reason, lest I shou'd think her Wisdom fell short of her Years. . . . We had a Michaelmas Goose for Dinner, of Miss Theky's own raising, who was now goodnatur'd enough to forget the Jeopardy of her Dog. In the afternoon we walkt in a Meadow by the River side, which winds in the form of a Horseshoe about Germanna, making it a Peninsula, containing about 400 Acres. Rappahanock forks about 14 Miles below this place, the Northern Branch being the larger, and consequently must be the River that bounds My Lord Fairfax's Grant of the Northern Neck.

The Sun rose clear this Morning, and so did I, and finisht all my little Affairs by Breakfast. It was then resolv'd to wait on the Ladys on Horseback, since the bright Sun, the fine Air, and the wholesome Exercise, all invited us to it. We forded the River a little above the Ferry, and rode 6 Miles up the Neck to a fine Level piece of Rich Land, where we found about 20 Plants of Ginseng, with the Scarlet Berrys growing on the top of the Middle Stalk. The Root of this is of wonderful Vertue in many Cases, particularly to raise the Spirits and promote Perspiration, which makes it a Specifick in Colds and Coughs. The Colo. complemented me with all we found, in return for my telling him the Vertues of it. We were all pleas'd to find so much of this King of Plants so near the Colonel's habitation, and growing too upon his own Land ; but were, however, surprized to find it upon level Ground, after we had been told it grew only upon the North Side of Stony Mountains. I carry'd home this Treasure, with as much Joy, as if every Root had been a Graft of the Tree of Life, and washt and dry'd it carefully. This Airing made us as Hungry as so many Hawks, so that between Appetite and a very good Dinner, twas difficult to eat like a Philosopher. In the Afternoon the Ladys walkt me about amongst all their little Animals, with which they amuse themselves, and furnish the Table ; the worst of it is, they are so tender-hearted, they Shed a Silent Tear every time any

of them are kill'd.   At Night the Colo. and I quitted the threadbare
Subject of Iron, and changed the Scene to Politicks.   He told me the
Ministry had receded from their demand upon New England, to raise a
standing Salary for all succeeding Governors, for fear some curious Members of the House of Commons shou'd enquire How the Money was
dispos'd of, that had been rais'd in the other American Colonys for the
Support of their Governors. . . .

William Byrd, *A Progress to the Mines, in the Year 1732,* in his *History of
the Dividing Line, between Virginia and North Carolina,* etc. (edited by
Thomas H. Wynne, Richmond, 1866), II, 59–67 *passim.*

———◆———

83. A Modern Woman (1741–1741/2)

BY ELIZA LUCAS

Bibliography as in No. 35 above.

Wappo — June 4 [1741]. . . .

AFTER a pleasant passage of about an hour we arrived safe at home
as I hope you and M.rs Pinckney did at Belmont.   but this place
appeared much less agreeable than when I left it, having lost the agreeable company & conversation of our friends — I am engaged now with
the rudiments of the Law to w.ch I am but a Stranger and what adds to
my mortification is that Doct.r Wood wants the Politeness of your Uncle
who with a graceful ease & good nature peculiar to himself is always
ready to instruct the ignorant — but this rustic seems by no means to
court my acquaintance for he often treats me with such cramp phrases
I am unable to understand him nor is he civil enough to explain them
when I desire it.   however I hope in a short time we shall be better
friends nor shall I grudge a little pains and application that will make
me useful to my poor neighbours.   We have some in this Neighbourhood
who have a little Land and a few slaves and Cattle to give their children,
that never think of making a Will till they come upon a sick bed and
find it too expensive to send to town for a Lawyer.   If you will not laugh
too immoderately at me I'll trust you with a secrett.   I have made two
Wills already.   I know I have done no harm for I conn'd my lesson
very perfect. and know how to convey by Will Estates real and personal and never forget in it's proper place him and his heirs for Ever.
nor that tis to be sign'd by 3 Witnesses in presence of one another.

but the most comfortable remembrance of all is that Doct^r Wood says
the Law makes great allowance for last Wills and Testaments presuming
the Testator could not have Council learned in the Law. but after all
what can I do if a poor creature lies a dying and the family takes it
into their head that I can serve them, I cannt refuse   but when they are
well and able to imploy a Lawyer I always shall.   A Widdow here abouts
with a pretty little fortune teazed me intolerably to draw her a marriage
settlement but it was out of my depth and I absolutely refused it — so
she got an able hand to do it — indeed she could afford it — but I could
not get off from being one of the Trustees to her settlement and an old
Gent^m the other   I shall begin to think myself an old woman before I
am a young one having such weighty affairs upon my hands . . .

Septr 20. 1741.   Wrote to my father on plantation business and Concerning a planter's importing negroes for his own use.   Col^o Pinckney
thinks not — but thinks twas proposed in the assembly and rejected —
promised to look over the act and let me know. also informed my
father of the alteration tis Soposed there will be in the value of our
money occationed by a late Act of Parliament that Extends to all America
wch is to disolve all private banks I think by the 30th of last Month or
be liable to lose their Estates and put themselves out of the King's protection.   informed him of the Tyranical Gov^{rt} at Georgia.

Octr 29. 1741   Wrote to my father acknowledging the receipt of a
p^s of rich yellow Lutstring consisting of 19 yards for myself d^o of blue
for my Mama. also for a p^s of Holland and Cambrick received from
London at the same time.   Tell him we have had a moderate and
healthy summer and preparing for the King's birth day next day.   Tell
him shall send the rice by Bullard.

Novr. 11. 1741.   Wrote to M^r. Murray to send down a boat load of
white oak staves, bacon and salted beef for the West Indies. sent up at
the same time a bar^l salt $\frac{1}{2}$ w^t salt peter. some brown sugar for the
bacon.   Vinegar and a couple bottles Wine for Mrs Murray and desire
he will send down all the butter and hogs lard.

Jany 1741-2   Wrote my father about the Exchange with Col^o Heron.
the purchasing his house at Georgia. . . .   Returned my father thanks
for a present I received from him by Capt Sutherland of twenty pistols.
and for the sweetmeats by Capt Gregory.   Shall send the preserved fruit
as they come in season   Begged the favour of him to send to England
for Dr Popashes Cantatas. Wildens Anthems. Knellers Rules for tuning.
about the Jerusalem Thorn. shall try different soils for the Lucern grass

this year. The ginger turns out but poorly. We want a supply of
Indigo Seed. Sent by this Vessel a waiter of my own Japaning my
first Essay. Sent also the Rice and beef. Sent Gov.ʳ Thomas of Philadelphia' Daughter a tea chest of my own doing also Congratulate my
father on my brother's recovery from the small pox and having a
Commission . . .

[Feb. 6] I received yesterday the favour of your advice as a
phicisian and want no arguments to convince me I should be much
ᵇetter for both my good friends Company. a much pleasanter Prescription than Doct.ʳ Meads w.ᶜʰ I have just received. To follow my inclination at this time I must endeavour to forget that I have a Sister to
instruct and a parcel of little Negroes whom I have undertaken to teach
to read . . . I am a very Dunce, for I have not acquird y.ᵉ writing short
hand yet with any degree of Swiftness but I am not always so for I
give a very good proof of the brightness of my Genius when I can distinguish well enough to Subscribe my Self with great Esteem

Sir

y.ʳ most obed.ᵗ humble Serv.ᵗ
ELIZA LUCAS.

Eliza Lucas, *Journal and Letters* (edited by Mrs. H. P. Holbrook, Wormsloe,
1850), 13–16 *passim.*

━━◆━━

84. Roisterers in Boston (1750)

BY CAPTAIN FRANCIS GOELET

For Goelet, see No. 23 above. — For life in Boston, see also *Contemporaries*, I,
ch. xxi.

SEPTEMB.ʳ 30.ᵗʰ. Being much Fatigued had no Inclination to Church.
Stayd at Home Overhaw.ᵍ my Papers &c. Dyn'd at Home with
Several Gent.ⁿ and Ladies, viz.ᵗ. Mr. Hedges, Cap.ᵗ. Stewart, and Cap.ᵗ.
Goelet, Mis.ˢ Betsey and Mis.ˢ Jenny Wendel, Miss Quincey, M.ʳ. Wen-
dell and Famely, where made my home. After Dinner took a Walk
withe Gent.ⁿ to M.ʳˢ. Grace's, Cap.ᵗ. Steward.ˢ Lodgeing where Spent the
Evening.

Octob.ʳ 1.ˢᵗ. After Breakfast went to See about the Protest, had
Ordered Satturday Night which was done. I then Gave the Cap.ᵗ.
Proper Orders what to do with the Ship, haveing First advised with
Cap.ᵗ. Wendell, who Provided a Store hous &c. to Store Our Cargoe in,

as would be Obliged to Bring Our Ship to the ways to Examine her
Leakes &c. haveing an Invitation from the Gentlemen to Dine at M[r].
Sheppard's, went Accordingly where was a Company of ab[t] 40 Gentle-
men, after haveing Dined in a very Elegant manner upon Turtle &c.
Drank about the Toasts, and Sang a Number of Songs, and where
Exceeding Merry untill 3 a Clock in the Morning, from whence Went
upon the Rake, Going Past the Commons in Our way Home, Surprised
a Comp[y] Country Young Men and Women with a Violin at A Tavern
Danceing and makeing Merry, upon Our Ent[g] the house they Young
Women Fled, we took Posession of the Room, hav[g] the Fidler and the
Young man with us with the Keg of Sugard Dram, we where very
Merry, from thence went to M[r]. Jacob Wendells where we where Obliged
to Drink Punch and Wine, and ab[t] 5 in the morn[g] made our Excit and
to Bed.

October 2[d]. Had an Invitation to day to Go to a Turtle Frolick with
a Comp[y] of Gent[n] and Ladies at M[r]. Richardsons in Cambridge, ab[t] 6
Miles from Towne. I accordingly waited on Miss Betty Wendell with
a Chaise, who was my Partner, the Companie Consisted of about 20
Couple Gent[n] and Ladies of the Best Fashion in Boston, viz. the two
Miss Phips, Lu[t] Gouern[r] Daughters, the Miss Childs, Miss Quinceys,
Miss Wendells &c. Danced Several Minuits and Country Dances, and
where very Merry about Dusk we all rode Home, and See our Partners
safe, and Spent the Evening at Cap[t]. Maglachlins &c.

October 3[d]. Went on Board my Ship in the Stream, with Several
Gent[n] my Acquaint[e], who where desirous to see the Ship, I Regald them
with some Punch Wine and Choice Cornd Mackrell, went to M[r]. Weatherheads at the Sign the Bunch Grapes in Kings street, just below the Towne
House, Being noted for the Best Punch House in Boston, and Resorted
to by most the Gent[n] Merch[ts] and Masters Vessels, and where I spent
the Evening with Several Gent[n] my Acquaintance.

October 4th. After Breakfast walkd to the South End the Towne,
relaiting some affairs the Ship, and Dined with 2 Country Esq[r] at Cap[t].
Wendells, after Dinner went downe to See the Ship how things went,
and Spent the Even[g] with some Gentlemen at Cap[t] Stewards Lodgeing.

October 5th. After Breakfast went to see how they whent on with
the Ship, And ret[d] about 12 a Clock, and to Change, from thence to
Weatherheads, with Several Gentlem[n] to drink Punch. Had an Invitation from Several Brothers to Vissett the Masters Lodge, which is kept
at Stones, in a Very Grand Manner. M[r]. Oxnard who is Provincial

R

Grand Master, Presided in the Chair, went from thence at 9 to Sup with M^r. Chue, who had a Company Gent^n to Spend the Evening with him, we had a Very Grand Supper, where Very merry and Broke up about 3 in the Morning.

October 6th. Went to the Ship, and from thence to M^r. Weatherheads, and to Change, had an Invitation to dine with Some Gentlemen at M^r. Richardson's in Cambridge, we where ab^t 15 or 16 of us in Company, all Rhode out, in Chairs. Drank Plentifully Toasted the Ladies Singing &c. ab^t Dusk the Evening returned to Boston, and Spent the Evening at Capt McGlaughlin's with some Ladies at Cards.

October 7th. Young M^r. Th° Leechmore waited of me, and Invited me to dine with him at his Father's M^r. Leachmore Surveyor General of America, which I promis'd to do. Agreeable thereto M^r. Abraham Wendell who being also Invited We Went to Geather, where very Kindly Received, and Introduced into the Company, where where Several Ladies vizt. Mis^s Leachmores, the three Miss Phips, Mis Lucie, Pegg^y and Beckie, Mis^s Brownes &c. &c. &c. after dinner were Very Merry, Past the Evening with some Friends at Capt. Stewarts Lodgeing.

October 8th. In the morning went to the Ship to see how the workmen went on and what was wanting, went to the Several Tradesmen &c. at 11 went to Weatherheads, from thence to Change, Dynd with Some Friends at Cap^ts Lodgeing, from thence went to Capt. Wendells, where they had not done Dinner Sat down with them to a Desart Sund^y. Fruit &c. and Drank Glass wine and Spent the Evening with ab^t 20 Worthy Gent^n at Weather Heads have^g Contracted a Large Acquaintance, was not at a Loss for Comp^y as long as there, which made my Detaim^t there Very agreeable.

October 9th. Went to the Ship and haveing Orderd the Needfull, from thence to Weatherhead and to Change, from thence home, where found Mes^rs John and Abra^m Wendell Waiting for me to Go and Dine with M^r. Edmund Quincey, which we did where Dynd also Miss Tenny Wendell, and Miss Betsey DeBuke, with the Family, M^rs. Quinceys and her two Daughters, after Dinner Playd Several Tunes upon the Harpsichord, and Miss Quinceys did the Like, M^r. Chief Deputy Collector, Invited me to go to the Consort of which he was a Member, I went accordingly, the Performance was as well as Could be Expected, it Consisted of One Indifrent, Small Oargon, One Base Violin, One German Flute, and Four small Violins, Spent remain^g the Even^g with Capt. Maxwill.

October 10th. After Breakfast went M[r]. Abraham Wendell to South End, to Markett, Boug[t] Several Nessasaries for the Ship, from thence to Weatherheads and to Change, went with M[r]. Wendell Agreeable to Invitation to Dine with M[r]. Bayard, where Dynd also M[r]. Bohen, A Gentlem[n] that Courted his Daughter then, and was married the Proceeding Night, after Dinner M[r]. Bayard and M[r]. Soloman Davis, Accompanied us to the Commons, to See the Militia Drawn up, from thence went to M[r]. Stones, where the Lodge was held and Parson Brockwell Presided in the Chair, and M[r]. William Coffin Merch[t] in Boston his Deputy, from thence to Cap[t]. Wendells where was a Large Comp[y] Gent[n] Drinking Toast and Singing Songs, the Comp[y] Broke up ab[t] 3 in the Morning. . . . .

October 13th. Haveing Breakfast[d], we Prepaird for a Rhide, the Chairs where Got Ready, M[r]. Ab[m] Wendell went on Horse back and Miss Bety Debuke and M[r]. M[c]Glaughlin and Spouse and Self went in Chairs, wee Passd trough Milton which is a Prety Pleasent Country Town, and arived at Scroten another Pleasant Country Town where have a Prety Prospect, Dynd at M[r]. Glovers a Publicans, its about 10 Miles from Boston, from thence, at the Request of M[r]. Edmund Quincey, halted at his Country Seat at Milton ; The Country House is a Neat Brick Building, and Finely Accomodated for Comp[y] with a Fine Hall and Large Rooms, about Ten Yards from the House is a Beautifull, Cannal, which is Supply'd by a Brook, which is well Stockt with Fine Silver Eels, we Caught a fine Parcell and Carried them Home and had them drest for Supper, the House has a Beautyfull Pleasure Garden Adjoyning it, and On the Back Part the Building is a Beautyfull Orchard with fine fruit Trees, &c. Returnd Home in the Evening &c.

October 14th. Being Sunday Dresd my Self and went wth M[r]. Abrah[m] Wendell To Parson Coopers Meeting, but he being at Rhode Island, Parson Abot Officiated for him, his Text on the Psalms (O y[e] of Little Faith), a very Good Discourse, Dynd at Cap[t]. Wendells and in the, Afternoon, went to Trinity Church, and was Introduced by M[r]. Coffin into his Piew, the Parson M[r]. Hooper Gave us an Excellent Discourse, on the follow[g] text (the Fear of the Lord is the Beginning of Wisdom). This Build is very Plain without, with Large Sash Windows, But within Verry Neat and Comodius, the Architect Modren, with a Very Neat Little Oargan Pretily Embelished, this Church hav[g] no Steeple Looks more Like a Prespetarian Meeting House.

Extracts from Capt. Francis Goelet's Journal, in *New-England Historical and Genealogical Register* (Boston, 1870), XXIV, 53-55 *passim.*

CHAPTER XIII — COMMERCE AND CURRENCY

85. Official Protection of Pirates (1698)

BY GOVERNOR THE EARL OF BELLOMONT

Bellomont was governor of New York and Massachusetts, and set himself to root out the profession of piracy. — Bibliography: Palfrey, *New England*, IV, 167–195; Channing and Hart, *Guide*, § 105.

I HAVE wrote largely of the General State of this Govern[t] in letters of this date, this is particularly to informe your Lord[ps] in relation to Pirates and the proceeding of the late Gov[r] Fletcher to encourage and protect them, which I have [been] industrious to discover in obedience to repeated orders and instruct[ns] which I have received from His Maj[ty], most strict in the matter, and I find that those Pyrates that have given the greatest disturbance in the East Indies and Red Sea, have been either fitted from New-York or Rhode Island, and mann'd from New-York. The ships commanded by Mason, Tew, Glover and Hore, had their commissions from the Gov[r] of New York. The three last from Fletcher. and although these Commissions (which are on record here) appear to be given only against the Kings enemies; yet it was known to all the inhabitants of this City that they were bound to the Indies and the Red sea, it being openly declared by the said Commanders, whereby they raised men and were quickly able to proceed, and so notoriously publick that it was generally believed that they had assurance from Coll: Fletcher, that they may returne with the spoyle to New York and be protected, as it will now plainly appear, by the protections he did give to them, at their return, and the rewards they gave him for them. It is likewise evident that Tew, Glover and Hore, had commissions granted them by Coll: Fletcher when none of them had any ship or vessell in Colonel Fletcher's Govern[t], yet they had Commissions and were permitted to raise men in New-Yorke, and the design publique of their being bound to the red sea, And Capt[n] Tew that had been before a most notorious Pirate (complained of by the East India Company) on his returne from the Indies with great riches made a visit to New York, where (although a man of most mean and infamous character) he was received and caressed by Coll : Fletcher, dined and supped often with him, and appeared publickly in his coach with him, and they exchanged presents, as gold watches ettc. with one another, all this is known to most of the City, and on this Coll : Fletcher gave him his Commission.   Mason's ship returned under the command of one Coats, about the year 1693, and the crew having shared the booty came into this Govern^t, and received incouragement, and had protections given them by Coll : Fletcher as will appear by the deposition N° 1. of one Burgesse one of the Pyrats, and by N° 2. the deposition of Edward Taylor another of the Pyrates, Your Lordships will plainly see the bargain that was made by him (in behalf of the ship's crew) with Coll : Fletcher and Mr Wm Nicoll one of His Ma$^{ty's}$ Councill and the rewards they were to have, and did receive from the said Taylor and company.   I have indeed promised on my honour to intercede with His Ma^{ty} by your Lord^{ps} for the said Burgesse and Taylors pardons ; otherwise, I should not have been able to have had their evidence and made this discovery, and therefore I must pray your Lord^{ps} favor therein, that they may have the benefit of my promise to them, which hath occasioned their criminating themselves. and I believe it much less criminal in men of their loose principles to act such things, then in a Govern^t to give them such encouragement & impunity.   And Coll : Fletcher received for his favour to that ship's crew, their ship which he sold to Coll : Heathcote for eight hundred pounds, besides what private presents report saith were made to his Lady and daughter ; and besides his reward for particular protections which, I find were commonly rated at one hundred dollars p^r man, and besides gratifications to his broaker Mr Nicoll of His Maj^{ties} Councill and other small rewards to his Clerk Daniell Honan, as doth appear by the said depositions.   I have likewise discovered that protections were publickly exposed to sale at the said rates, to Pyrats that were of other companies and I have already gain'd some originals of which I have sent the copies inclosed N° 3. by which your Lord^{ps} may see Coll : Fletchers art to get money, and how far he was from suspecting or prosecuting these Pyrats, when their guilt made them seek and buy the protection, that the lawes give all honest men, and which such had a right and claime to without purchasing Coll : Fletchers hand and seal for a further assurance, but this I submitt to your Lordships consideration. It is indeed suggested that Coll : Fletcher took bonds from these protected Pyrates that they should not depart the province without Lycence, but I am informed, several had lycence but whether they were only colourable securities from men of invisible Substances, or what the certain condition of them was, I cannot learne, for that the said bonds are not deposited any where on behalf of His Maj^{ty} nor can I find that any of the Pyrats or their bonds were ever prosecuted. Instead thereof, I find that the last mentioned protections were purchased and no bonds given for them. I also find one Coll : Bayard of His Maj^{tys} Councill was broker for Coll : Fletcher in the procuring them, and your Lord^{ps} will perceive what reward Coll : Fletcher and what Coll : Bayard had for their favour to these Pyrats, and the manner of their battering by the inclosed depositions N° 4 & N° 5. . . .

I had likewise certain information since my arrival here, that five sayle that were seen and supposed to be Pyrates, were hovering on this Coast, and one of them landed some men on the Jerseys (as the Govr of the Jerseys acquainted me) and Enquiry, who was in the Govern^t, of which, when they were informed, they went on board and departed, not daring to come under my Govern^t with the same assurances of safety they had before experienced, so that the alteration of the Govern^c is comonly reputed here to be a great loss to Coll : Fletcher on this account. On these proofs, I summoned His Maj^{ty's} Council on the 8th day of May and communicated my instructions about Pyrats, and the aforesaid evidence in relation to Coll : Fletcher and M^r .Wm Nicoll ; and the Gentlemen of the Councill then present did expresse their abhorrence of these practices and were of opinion with me that the whole evidence should have the seal of the province affixed, and be transmitted home to His Majesty, with Coll : Fletcher a prisoner. . . .

P. S. — Since my closing the foregoing I believed I had an opportunity to surprise and take a considerable number of Pyrates expected on board His Maj^{ty's} ship Richmond and gave instructions and took the best measures I could in order thereto, as your Lord^{ps} will find by the inclosed copy of my letter to the Lords of the Admiralty, with the copies of the papers refered to therein, which although it had not the success I expected, yet was all that could be done therein, and which I hope will meet with your Lord^{ps} approbation. I have just now found the records of the Commissions to the Pyrats and made discovery of the bonds the Pyrates entered into to Coll : Fletcher when he granted

them Commissions, and they appear so fraudulent that it is a manifestation that he was made acquainted with their design of Pyracy. . . .

E. B. O'Callaghan, editor, *Documents relative to the Colonial History of the State of New-York* (Albany, 1854), IV, 306–310 *passim.*

———◆———

86. A Plea for Protective Duties (1704)

ANONYMOUS

Such appeals as this below were frequent in colonial times. — Bibliography:
Weeden, *Economic and Social History of New England;* Channing and Hart,
Guide, § 133.

CONSIDERATIONS HUMBLY OFFERED, WHY NAVAL
STORES CANNOT BE BROUGHT IN GREAT QUAN-
TITY'S FROM HER MAJESTY'S PLANTA-
TIONS, UNLESS ASSISTANCE BE GIVEN
BY THE GOVERNMENT.
[19 May 1704.]

1st Planters, proprietors, or Trading people will not make it their
business to provide such Goods, nor bring them in the usual way of
Trade unless they have a prospect, they shall have sales for them at
such rates, as may afford them profit, their cost & Charges considered ;
if there be no such prospect then they will bring them only when they
can be secure of Gaine by some particular contract with the Navy
officers or other persons.

2nd This is verified by what has past in relation to Naval Stores from
the plantations, Several have offer'd to bring them upon a Contract
made, or Charter granted or other advantages, but few or none have
been brought as other Comodities to be sold at a Comon Markett Thō
it was foreseen above 50 Yeares Since ; that it would be dangerous to
depend entirely upon the Northern Crownes, for Naval Stores, and was
then taken into Consideration Now to be supplied from the Plantations,
yet few have been brought, thō in those parts there is great plenty of
Timber for building of Ships, and also to produce Pitch, Tarr & Rozin,
and a Soil capable to afford hempe.

3[ly] Upon which it may be concluded that no Methods can be effectuall, for the bringing in, of great quantity's, but such as may give

encouragement, to the Trading people, to bring them upon the same foundation, as they bring other Commodities from other parts vizt

Hopes of making proffit, by trading & dealing in them which cannot be, unless these Comodities be eased of the great burthen, which lyes on them, by the great wages paid to labouring men on the Plantations, and the high freights given to Ship Masters, for Goods brought from those parts, which being farr above the rates which are paid for the same Sorts of Goods if they come from Norway or the Baltick, deprives the traders of making proffit by these Goods from the Plantations, and gives a priority to those from the North.

4^ly The Northern Crownes are our Competitors in this Case, the advantages they have cannot be overcome, by a Charter, in which most of the proposalls that have been made do center, Corporations must have Governours, Directors, book keepers & Agents, the Charges will amount to at least ten ℔ Cent, which must be added to the Cost, and other necessary Charges, and give a Further advantage to our Competitors, by which they will be enabled to undersell our Traders in these Commodities, and yet Subsist & make profit, because they will be eased in these Several Charges & outgoings : Charters cannot remove, nor decrease the Cloggs that lye on this Trade, but rather increase them unless the Swedes & Danes and all others could be excluded from bringing those Goods into England.

Therefore

Unless these Comodities from the North can be Charged with a great Custome, and those from the Plantations be eased from all Custome : or her Majesty be graciously pleased to cause these goods to be brought freight free to the Planters or owners, or to give to them some recompense at a Certain rate ℔ Tunn for what they may bring, as may equallize the Charge of freight.

The Naval Stores from the North will always hinder their being brought from the Plantations, as Comodities in the way of Trade, which only can cause a large importation of them for the use of our Navigation in General, hinder the Exportation of our Coyne to the North and prevent the inconveniencies that may happen, by our dependance upon these Crownes.

William L. Saunders, editor, *The Colonial Records of North Carolina* (Raleigh, 1886), I, 598–599.

From all which I beg leave to conclude, that is not the names things get for the present but the real nature of them, that will be found to hold against all events & that in the instance of Paper money where it is regulated by just Laws and where the Publick have not acted contrary to them their credit is in reason better established than the credit of any private Persons or Society and that the method used to catch the common opinion of mankind by offering them their money when they please is nothing but a fashionable Bubble which People are every day sufferers by when a Banker breaks & that even the best founded Societys can not maintain their Credit when there is the Greatest need of them.   But that all Credit finally centers in the Security of ye Governm^t

I take the liberty further to observe to your Lordships on how many occasions the Government of Great Britain has found it impracticable to raise all the money wanted within the year from whence all the present debts of the nation have arisen : The same necessity lyes often upon the Plantations where frequently a sum of ready money is wanted, which it would be an intollerable Tax to raise at once, and therefore they are forced to imitate the Parliament at home, in anticipating upon remote funds.   And as there is no Bank nor East India company nor even private subscribers capable of lending the Province the money they want at least without demanding the extravagant Interest of 8 Pr Cent which is the common Interest here, but would ruin the publick to pay since this is a Case there is no possible way left to make distant funds provide ready money, when it is necessarily wanted, but making paper Bills to be sunk by such funds.   Without this Carolina would have been ruined by their Indian War   Boston could not now support theirs nor could any of the Provinces have furnished such considerable Sums to the Expeditions against Canada   Nor could at present any of the necessary repairs of this Fort be provided for, nor the arrears of the Revenue be discharged, which is done by this Act in a Tax to be levyed in 4 years nor indeed any publick Service readily and sufficiently effected

And I may add one thing more that this manner of compulsive credit does in fact keep up its value here and that it occasions much more Trade and business than would be without it and that more Specie is exported to England by reason of these Paper Bills than could be if there was no circulation but of Specie for which reason all the merchants here seem now well satisfied with it

E. B. O'Callaghan, editor, *Documents relative to the Colonial History of the State of New-York* (Albany, 1855), V, 736–738 *passim*.

89. Paper Money Forbidden (1740)

BY THE LORDS COMMISSIONERS FOR TRADE AND PLANTATIONS

This official prohibition of paper money merely put a stop to the practice; it was renewed in the Revolution (see No. 208 below). — Bibliography as in No. 88 above.

. . . WHEREAS, for preventing the many & great Inconveniences that had arisen in some of his Majesty's Colonies & Plantations in America, by passing Laws for Striking Bills of Credit, & issuing out the same, in lieu of money, the respective Governors & Commanders in chief of his Majesty's Colonies and Plantations for the time being, have been particularly instructed not to give their Assent to or pass any such laws for the future, without a Clause be inserted in such Act, declaring that the same shall not take Effect, until the said Act shall have been approved and confirm'd by his Majesty his Heirs or Successors : And whereas notwithstanding such his Majesty's Commanders to the said Governors in that behalf, Paper Bills of Credit have been created & issued in his Majesty's said Colonies & Plantations by Virtue of Acts of Assembly there, making it obligatory on all Persons to take such Bills of Credit, in payment for Debts, Dues & Demands . . . and a great Discouragement has been bro: on the Com'erce of this Kingdom by occasioning a Confusion in Dealings and a lessening of Credit in those Parts : And whereas an humble Address was presented, the last Session by the House of Commons, to his Majesry, That he would be graciously pleased to require & command the respective Governors of his Colonies & Plantations in America, punctually & effectually to observe his Maj^{tys} Royal Instructions not to give Assent to or to pass any Act, whereby Bills of Credit may be issued in lieu of money, without a Clause be inserted in such Act, declaring that the same shall be approved by his Majesty :

It is therefore his Majesty's Will & Pleasure, & you are hereby also further required & comanded under pain of his Majesty's highest displeasure and of being removed, from your Governm^t punctually & effectually to observe his Majesty's Royal Instruction not to give Assent to or pass any Act, whereby Bills of Credit may be issued in lieu of money without a Clause be inserted in such Act, declaring that the same shall not take Effect, until the said Act shall be approved by his Majesty, his Heirs or Successors.

William A. Whitehead, editor, *Documents relating to the Colonial History of the State of New Jersey* (Newark, 1882), VI, 96-98 *passim.*

CHAPTER XIV — INTELLECTUAL LIFE

90. "The History of Yale-College" (1698–1717)

BY REVEREND PRESIDENT THOMAS CLAP (1744)

Clap was president of Yale from 1739 to 1767. — Bibliography : Winsor, *Narrative and Critical History*, V, 102; W. L. Kingsley, *Yale College*, I, chs. i–vi. — For other colonial colleges, see *Contemporaries*, I, No. 137, and below, No. 95.

THE Design of founding a College in the Colony of Connecticut, was first concerted by the Ministers ; among which the Rev. Mr. *Pierpont* of *New-Haven*, Mr. *Andrew* of *Milford*, and Mr. *Russel* of *Branford,* were the most forward and active. They had sundry Meetings and Consultations, and received several Proposals or Schemes relating to the Constitution and Regulation of such a College. The first Plan was very formal and minute, drawn up by some Gentleman in Imitation of the Protestant Colleges and Universities in France, founded by their general Synods. In which it was proposed, 'That a College should be erected by a general Synod of the *consociated Churches* in the Colony of Connecticut. . . . That the Synod should agree upon a Confession of Faith to be consented to by the President, Inspectors and Tutors. That the College should be called the *School of the Church.* And that the Churches should contribute towards it's Support.' . . . in the mean Time, in the lesser Conventions of Ministers in Associations and Councils, and in private Conversation, ten of the principal Ministers in the Colony, were nominated and agreed upon by a general Consent both of the Ministers and People, to stand as Trustees or Undertakers to found, erect and govern a College, viz.

The Rev. Messrs.
James Noyes, of *Stonington.*
Israel Chauncy, of *Stratford.*
Thomas Buckingham, of *Saybrook.*
Abraham Pierson, of *Killingworth.*
Samuel Mather, of *Windsor.*
Samuel Andrew, of *Milford.*
Timothy Woodbridge, of *Hartford.*
James Pierpont, of *New-Haven.*
Noadiah Russel, of *Middletown.*
Joseph Webb, of *Fairfield.*

The Ministers so nominated, met at *New-Haven* and formed themselves into a Body or Society, to consist of eleven Ministers, including a Rector, and agreed to Found a College in the Colony of Connecticut; which they did at their next Meeting at *Branford*, in the following Manner, viz. Each Member brought a Number of Books and presented them to the Body; and laying them on the Table, said these Words, or to this Effect; *"I give these Books for the founding a College in this Colony."* Then the Trustees as a Body took Possession of them; and appointed the Rev. Mr. *Russel* of *Branford* to be the Keeper of the Library, which then consisted of about 40 Volumes in Folio. Soon after they received sundry other Donations both of Books and Money, which laid a good Foundation. This Library with the Additions, was kept at *Branford*, in a Room set apart for that Purpose near three Years, and then it was carried to *Killingworth*.

. . . After mature Consideration, they concluded that it was safe and best to have a Charter, notwithstanding any change of the Government which might possibly happen; and wrote to the Hon. Judge *Sewall*, and Mr. Secretary *Addington* of *Boston* to prepare a Draught of a Charter, to be presented to the next Assembly. . . .

The Trustees chose the Rev. Mr. Abraham Pierson, who was one of their Number, to take the Care of Instructing and Governing the Collegiate School; under the Title and Character of RECTOR. . . .

At the same Meeting, they entered upon the Consideration of the most convenient *Place* in the Colony of Connecticut, in which they might erect and fix the Collegiate School: they were not perfectly satisfied or united in it; but after a considerable Debate they fixed upon *Saybrook*, as the most convenient Place, *at Present; unless upon further Consideration they should alter their Minds:* And this Matter was debated at several Meetings afterwards.

They also desired the Rector to remove himself and Family to *Saybrook*; but till that could be effected, they ordered that the Scholars should be instructed at or near the Rector's House in *Killingworth*. As this School was some Years in forming, several young Gentlemen were preparing for it under the more private Instruction of some one of the Trustees or others: After the School became furnished with a Rector and a Tutor, eight of them were admitted, and put into different Classes, according to the proficiency they had antecedently made. So that in a Year or two some were qualified for Degrees.

The first Commencement was held at Saybrook, on Sept. 13th, 1702:

at which four young Gentlemen, who had before been graduated at the College at Cambridge, and one more, who had a private Education, received the Degrees of Master of Arts. This and several Commencements following were held privately in the House of the Rev. Mr. Buckingham, because the Trustees by a preceding Act, had forbid all publick Commencements; to avoid the Charge and other Inconveniencies attending them. . . .

The Trustees and the Colony in general were from the Beginning, not very well agreed in their Sentiments about the Place where to fix the College; and most Men's Sentiments were influenced by their Situation; and they generally chose that Place which would best accommodate themselves. Three or four Places were generally discoursed upon, viz. *Saybrook*, *Hew-Haven*, and *Hartford* or *Weathersfield*. The Scholars were also somewhat uneasy at their Situation, they thought that Saybrook was not compact enough for their Accommodation, since many of them were obliged to reside above a Mile from the Place of publick Exercises, and they were not pleased with their Instruction and Government; there being no resident Rector, and the Tutors sometimes very young. . . .

The Collegiate School being in this broken and tottering State, the People in several Parts of the Country begun to Subscribe large Sums for Building the College, to induce the Trustees to set it where it would best accommodate them. About £. 700 Sterling was subscribed for *New-Haven*; and tis said that about £. 500 Sterling was subscribed for *Saybrook*; and a considerable Sum for *Hartford* or *Weathersfield*.

The Trustees met at the Commencement at *Saybrook*, September 12, 1716, and entered upon the Consideration of the State and Place of the Collegiate School, but not being perfectly agreed they adjourned to *New-Haven*, to meet on the 17th Day of October following . . .

And Voted, 'that considering the Difficulties of continuing the Collegiate School *at Saybrook*, and that New-Haven is a very convenient Place for it, for which the most liberal Donations are given, the Trustees agree to remove the said School from *Saybrook* to *New-Haven*, and it is now settled at *New-Haven* accordingly.' . . .

The Reason assigned by the Trustees in their Votes (and other Papers) for settling the College at *New-Haven*, were these; the Difficulty of keeping it at *Saybrook*, which arose partly from the Uneasiness of the Scholars, partly from the continual Endeavours of some to carry it to *Hartford*, which they supposed to be at too great a Distance from the Sea, and would no ways accommodate the Western Colonies. That

s

they look'd upon *New-Haven* to be in itself the most convenient Place, on the Account of the commodiousness of its Situation, the agreableness of the Air and Soil, and the Cheapness of Commodities ; and that very large Donations had been made towards the Building an House there, without which they had not sufficient to defray the Charge.

The Major Part of the General Assembly, being desirous to strengthen the Hands of the Trustees in the present Difficulties, past the following Vote, in the same Session, viz. ' That under the present Circumstances of the Affairs of the Collegiate School, the Rev. Trustees be advised to proceed in that Affair ; and to finish the House they have built in *New-Haven*, for the Entertainment of the Scholars belonging to the Collegiate School.'

Thomas Clap, *The Annals or History of Yale-College* (New Haven, 1766), 2–22 *passim*.

———◆———

91. "A poetical Lamentation, occasioned by the Death of His late Majesty King George the First" (1727)

BY REVEREND MATHER BYLES

This poem illustrates at once the poetical taste of the time and the undiscriminating loyalty of the colonists. Byles was a minister in Boston; he was renowned as a wit, and, though a known Tory, was permitted to remain in that town throughout the Revolution. — Bibliography: Winsor, *Narrative and Critical History*, V, 128–130; Tyler, *American Literature*, II, 192–198.

NOW, O ye nine ! if all your pow'rs can paint
The scenes of woe which wake this loud complaint,
Breath from my muse such soft and solemn verse,
As suits to strew my matchless Sov'reign's hearse ;
And let my grief in mournful musick glide
To *Albion*'s shores, and join the gen'ral tide.

While in this talk I'd try the tenderest skill,
Beneath the subject sinks my quiv'ring quill,
Restless, my muse her awful theme surveys,
While wounded passions plead for present ease,
My grief grows wild, and strugling sorrows throng
To break in trembling accents from my tongue.

.   .   .   .

Shall unrelenting rocks forbear to bleed,
While I proclaim the great *AUGUSTUS* dead !
AUGUSTUS———— ah !———— my muse, I feel the sound
Rush thro' my soul, and all its pow'rs confound ;
Swift tow'rds my heart unusual horror climbs,
And strange convulsions seize my shudd'ring limbs ;
In my cold veins the crimson scarcely flows,
My slack'ning nerves their nat'ral aids refuse,
From aking eyes the briny sorrow breaks,
And liquid pearl, rolls down my faded cheeks,
The ling'ring remnant of my life's opprest,
And death-like damps bedew my lab'ring breast.

Had I the royal prophet's tuneful strain
When *Israel*'s breathless chiefs had ting'd the plain ;
Would but *Apollo*'s genial touch inspire
Such sounds as breathe from * * * * * warbling lyre ;
Then, might my notes in melting measures flow,
And make all nature wear the signs of woe.
Content, my muse must mourn with humbler strings,
While *GEORGE*'s death, and *Albion*'s loss she sings.

Long had the fields resign'd their smiling dress,
And herds rov'd round for food in dumb distress,
When famish'd hills, in russet robes array'd,
Seem'd to presage some dire event decreed :
While fainting nature felt such ardent fire,
As if 'twas with this fever to expire ;
Then from the King of kings, a message flies,
To call his great vicegerent to the skies :
An hasty summons snatch'd our Sov'reign's breath,
His life is set, his glory dim'd with death. ————
Let ev'ry gem which studs the *British* crown,
Look pale and wan, since *Albion*'s light is down :
No more you'll share its rays, nor mingling shed
Your trembling splendors round his sacred head.
No more the throne shall show that awful face,
Where majesty was mix'd with mildest grace :
Nor hostile realms revere their conqu'rour king,
Nor nations shroud beneath his shelt'ring wing.

That wond'rous form, which once could kingdoms sway,
Is now the grizly tyrant's helpless prey.

.   .   .   .

Come, hoary registers of ancient times,
Whose vital tide declines your wither'd Limbs ;
Babes in the dawn of life, and you whose veins,
The dancing fire of ripen'd youth contains ;
With all *Parnassus*, bring your last perfume,
With bosoms bare, and mingled mournings come,
And spread in one wide ruin round your Sov'reign's tomb.

But cease, my muse, or weep in gentler streams,
Behind this shady scene some comfort gleams ;
Lift from the dismal gloom thy aking eyes :
Refreshment springs from whence thy sorrows rise.

When at the hour of *Brunswick*'s swift discharge,
To heav'n seraphick guardians guide their charge ;
Rapid, the news thro' trembling kingdoms runs,
And all the skies are peirc'd with piteous groans ;
Then, as this light the dark'ned empire leaves,
Then, wondrous *WALES* the sinking scepter saves :
Then, with her sparkling issue, comes his QUEEN,
Like night's fair empress midst her starry train ;
With cypress crown'd, they guild th' imperial seat,
And prop, tho' weak with woe, the tott'ring state ;
While intermingling joys, and grief impress
Their different dies, in ev'ry subjects face.
Albion reviv'd, yet longs with eager eye
To see their *Sovereigns* shine in cloudless majesty.
So when in deep eclipse, the rising sun,
Streaks with a dusky light his orient throne :
With sully'd robes he mounts th' ætherial field,
And rules the day, with *Cynthia*'s sable veil'd.
Languid, and faint, his muffled front appears,
While earth and air a semblant horror wears.
'Till rapid time unfolds his fulgid face,
And spreads his golden glories quick'ning rays.

[Mather Byles], *A Collection of Poems* (no title-page), 19–24 *passim*.

92. "Some Account of the Earthquake that shook New-England" (1727)

BY REVEREND COTTON MATHER

Cotton Mather, most voluminous of colonial writers, was for many years minister at the North Church in Boston. — Bibliography : Barrett Wendell, *Cotton Mather ;* Tyler, *American Literature*, II, 73–89. See also *Contemporaries*, I, No. 148. — For other extracts on New England life, see *Contemporaries*, I, ch. xxi.

THE *Night* that followed the Twenty ninth of *October* [1727.] was a *Night* whereto NEW–ENGLAND had never in the Memory of Man, seen the like before. The *Air* never more *Calm*, the *Sky* never more *Fair* ; every thing in all imaginable Tranquillity : But about a quarter of an Hour before Eleven, there was heard in BOSTON, from one end of the Town to the other, an horrid rumbling like the Noise of many Coaches together, driving on the paved Stones with the utmost Rapidity.   But it was attended with a most awful *Trembling of the Earth*, which did heave and shake so as to Rocque the Houses, and cause here and there the falling of some smaller Things, both within Doors and without.   It cannot be imagined, but that it gave an uncommon Concern unto all the Inhabitants, and even a degree of Consternation, unto very many of them.   This *first Shock*, which was the most Violent, was followed with several others, and some Repetition of the Noise, at sundry times, pretty distant from one another.   The Number of them is not entirely agreed ; but at least Four or Five are allow'd for ; The last of which was between Five and Six of the Clock in the Morning.

How far this *Earthquake* extended thro' the Countrey, we are not yet informed ; But that it extended Scores of Miles, we have already a cer- tain Information.   And what added unto the Terrors of it, were the terrible Flames and Lights, in the Atmosphere, which accompanied it. The Vessels on the Coast were also made sensible of it, by a shivering that siezed on them.

When the greatly affected People, had a little Opportunity to look about them in the Morning, the Pastors of the *Old North-Church*, directed the *Bells* to be rung, that such of the People as could and would, might assemble immediately unto some seasonable Exercises of Religion.   The Pastors of the *New* joined with them in sending up unto Heaven, the Supplications which the solemn Occasion called for.   And the Pastors in the other part of the Town, made a speedy and hearty Appearance, and most affectionately united in a Concurrence with them. The Assembly that came together, did more than croud and fill the most capacious of our Meetinghouses; And as there was a multitude of serious Christians, who are acquainted with *Real* and *Vital* PIETY, so the whole Auditory expressed a Devotion which was truly Extraordinary.

[Cotton Mather], *The Terror of the Lord. Some Account of the Earthquake that shook New-England, in the Night, between the 29 and the 30 of October, 1727* (Boston, 1727), 1–2.

---

93. A Protest against a Wicked Newspaper (1721/2)

BY REVEREND DOCTOR INCREASE MATHER

Increase Mather was for many years minister at the Old North Church in Boston, and was also president of Harvard College. — Bibliography: Winsor, *Memorial History of Boston*, II, ch. ix, 396; Tyler, *American Literature*, II, 67–73. — See also *Contemporaries*, I, No. 135.

ADVICE to the Publick from Dr. Increase Mather. Whereas a wicked Libel called the *New England Courant,* has represented me as one among the Supporters of it; I do hereby declare, that altho' I had paid for two or three of them, I then, (before the last Courant was published) sent him word I was *extreamly offended* with it! In special, because in one of his *Vile Courants* he insinuates, that if *the Ministers of God approve of a thing, it is a Sign it is of the Devil;* which is a horrid thing to be related! And altho' in one of the *Courants* it is declared, that the London Mercury Sept. 16, 1721, affirms that Great Numbers of Persons in the City and Suburbs are under the Inoculation of the Small Pox; In his next Courant he asserts, that it was some *Busy Inoculator, that imposed on the Publick in saying so;* Whereas I myself saw and read those words in the London Mercury: And he doth frequently abuse the Ministers of Religion, and many other worthy Persons in a manner, which is intolerable. For these and such like Reasons I signified to the Printer, that I would have no more of their *Wicked Courants.* I that have known what New-England was from the Beginning, cannot but be troubled to see the Degeneracy of this Place. I can well remember when the Civil Government would have taken an effectual Course to suppress such a *Cursed Libel!* which if it be not done I am afraid that some *Awful Judgment* will come upon this Land, and the *Wrath of God will arise, and there will be no Remedy.*

I cannot but pity poor *Franklin*, who tho' but a *Young Man* it may be *Speedily* he must appear before the Judgment Seat of God, and what answer will he give for printing things so vile and abominable? And I cannot but Advise the Supporters of this Courant to consider the Consequences of being *Partakers in other Mens Sins*, and no more Coun-tenance such a Wicked *Paper.*

Boston Gazette, January 29, 1721/2; reprinted in Joseph T. Buckingham, *Specimens of Newspaper Literature* (Boston, 1850), I, 53–54.

---

94. The People's Favorite Literature (1744)

BY BENJAMIN FRANKLIN

In colonial times the almanac was a household authority, to a large extent taking the place of books, which were few and costly. Of all the almanacs Franklin's became the most noted, on account of the author's personal reputation. — Bibliography: for Franklin, see No. 68 above; as to almanacs, see James Parton, *Benjamin Franklin*, I, 227–240; Tyler, *American Literature*, II, 120–130; Channing and Hart, *Guide*, §§ 25, 32. — See also a diary kept in an almanac, No. 95 below.

Courteous Reader,

THIS is the Twelfth Year that I have in this Way laboured for the Benefit —— of Whom? —— of the Publick, if you'll be so good-natured as to believe it ; if not, e'en take the naked Truth, 'twas for the Benefit of my own dear self; not forgetting in the mean time, our gracious Consort and Du'chess the peaceful, quiet, silent Lady *Bridget.* But whether my Labours have been of any Service to the Publick or not, the Publick I must acknowledge has been of Service to me ; I have lived Comfortably by its Benevolent Encouragement; and I hope I shall always bear a grateful Sense of its continued Favour.

My Adversary *J——n J———n* has indeed made an Attempt to *out-shine* me, by pretending to penetrate *a Year deeper* into Futurity; and giving his Readers *gratis* in his Almanack for 1743 an Eclipse of the Year 1744, to be beforehand with me : His Words are, " The first Day of *April* next Year 1744, there will be a GREAT ECLIPSE of the Sun : it begins about an Hour before Sunset. It being in the Sign Aries, the House of Mars, and in the 7th, shows Heat, Difference and Animosities between Persons of the highest Rank and Quality," *&c.* I am very glad, for the Sake of these Persons of Rank and Quality, that there

Poor Richard, 1744.

AN

A l m a n a c k

For the Year of Christ

1744,

It being LEAP–YEAR,

And makes since the Creation	Years
By the Account of the Eastern *Greeks*	7252
By the Latin Church, when ☉ ent. *V*	6943
By the Computation of *W. W.*	5753
By the *Roman* Chronology	5693
By the *Jewish* Rabbies	5505

Wherein is contained

The Lunations, Eclipses, Judgment of the Weather, Spring Tides, Planets Motions & mutual Aspects, Sun and Moon's Rising and Setting, Length of Days, Time of High Water, Fairs, Courts, and observable Days.

Fitted to the Latitude of Forty Degrees, and a Meridian of Five Hours West from *London*, but may without sensible Error, serve all the adjacent Places, even from *Newfoundland* to *South-Carolina.*

By *RICHARD SAUNDERS,* Philom

PHILADELPHIA :
Printed and sold by *B. FRANKLIN.*

is *no manner of Truth* in this Prediction : They may, if they please, live in Love and Peace. And I caution his Readers (they are but few, indeed, and so the Matter's the less) not to give themselves any Trouble about observing this imaginary Great Eclipse ; for they may stare till they're blind without seeing the least Sign of it.   I might, on this Occasion, return Mr. *J———n* the Name of *Baal's false Prophet* he gave me some Years ago in his Wrath, on Account of my Predicting his Reconciliation with the *Church of Rome,* (tho' he seems now to have given up that Point) but I think such Language between old Men and Scholars unbecoming ; and I leave him to settle the Affair with the Buyers of his Almanack as well as he can, who perhaps will not take it very kindly, that he has done what in him lay (by sending them out to gaze at an invisible Eclipse on the first of *April*) to make *April Fools* of them all.   His old thread bare Excuse which he repeats Year after Year about the *Weather,* "That no Man can be infallible therein, by Reason of the many contrary Causes happening at or near the same time, and the Unconstancy of the Summer Showers and Gusts," *&c* will hardly serve him in the Affair of *Eclipses* ; and I know not where he'll get another.

I have made no Alteration in my usual Method, except adding the Rising and Setting of the Planets, and the Lunar Conjunctions.   Those who are so disposed, may thereby very readily learn to know the Planets, and distinguish them from each other.

I am, dear Reader,
Thy obliged Friend,
R. SAUNDERS.

The COUNTRY MAN.

Happy the Man whose Wish and Care
   A few paternal Acres bound,
Content to breathe his native Air,
      In his own Ground.
Whose Herds with Milk, whose Fields with Bread,
   Whose Flocks supply him with Attire,
Whose Trees in Summer yield him Shade,
      In Winter Fire.
Blest, who can unconcernedly find
   Hours, Days and Years slide soft away,

In Health of Body, Peace of Mind,
                         Quiet by Day,
Sound Sleep by Night; Study and Ease
     Together mixt; sweet Recreation;
And Innocence which most does please
                         with Meditation.
Thus let me live, unseen, unknown,
     Thus unlamented let me die,
Steal from the World, and not a Stone
                         Tell where I lie.

[Benjamin Franklin], *Poor Richard, 1744. An Almanack,* etc. (Philadelphia), 1–3.

---

95. A Year of a College Student's Life (1758)

BY NATHANIEL AMES

Ames was the son of Dr. Nathaniel Ames, publisher of almanacs. Later he also became a physician and a calculator of almanacs. The piece is characteristic of the life of the son of a well-to-do gentleman. — Bibliography: Tyler, *American Literature,* II, 122–130. — For an earlier view of Harvard College, see *Contemporaries,* I, No. 146.

CAMBRIDGE Septr. 20th 1758. They who see this in future times may know that it is the covering of an old Almanack 1758. And do not despise old times too much for remember that 2 or 3 centurys from the time of seeing this you will be counted old times folks as much as you count us to be so now, many People in these times think the Consumation very nigh much more may you think so, and do not think yourselves so much wiser than we are as to make yourselves proud for the last day is at hand in which you must give an account of what you have been about in this state of Probation & very likely you are more given to Vice than we are, and we than the last Century folks; if you have more arts than we have that you yourselves have found out impute it not to our inability that we could not find them out for if we had had only those very arts that we have now when we first came to settle in N. America very like we should have found out those very things which you have the honour to be the Inventors of.

Dinner is ready I must leave off.

January, 1758.

came home vacancy beg.
Doctr. Miller preach'd in the meeting house, went hear him.
kept school in the new room.
Mr. Havens day of prayer.
Holloway took a fine Prize La Glorie.

February.

8 Vacancy ended.
10 Went to Cambridge.
14 Mr. Epes came to College.
15 Mr. Avery came this Day to College.
17 Went to Mr. Appleton's Lecture.
21 Went to Doctr. Wigglesworth's Lecture.
22 Went to Mr. Winthrops Lecture.
23 cato brought some wood & Linnen.
27 performed all the Duties of the Day.

March.

2 Snow at night.   Class met about Logick.
3 came home in the Slay very cold.
5 went to Meting Mr. Cotton preached.
6 Town meeting.
10 Quarter day at coll.
11 Lord Loudon came to our House talked about corn.
13 Come to College, began Logick.
14 Paid Prentice ye 2 first Quarter Bills 58 : 10.
17 Paid Seward 2 first Quarter Bills and Locke ye 3 first.
18 fit with the Sophomores about Cust.
20 had another Fight with the sophomores.
22 went to Newtown Ordination.
30 read Watses Logick.

April.

1 Daniel came from home & brought some Linnen.
6 general Fast, went to meeting.
11 training day, the Governour & Col. Frasier came to Cam.
20 went a gunning after Robins with Hooper.
26 drank tea with Otis. [later note by Ames] This was father of now, 1817, H. G. Otis, a Jacobin.

MAY.

2 Training Day at Dedham.

3 Captn. Fales's Compny Met at our house, came to College.

4 the class was plac'd last Tuesday.

5 the President and Tutors met went to them.

6 Mr. Hancock went Marlborough.

8 Doctr. was bury'd.

9 no disputing in the Hall.

14 went to Meeting. Mr. Flynt preached.

17 the Court Sot in the new Town House before it was half finish'd at Camb.

20 the Court sot at Bradishes.

21 went to Meeting Mr. Prentice Preach'd.

22 went a fishing with 13 of my Class mates. sot away from Cambridge wharf at 12 o'Clock catch'd 3 cods besides dog fish skates & Sculpins ; arriv'd at Nantasket at 8 o'Clock at night. lodg'd at a Tavern, sot off in the morning between 7 & 8 o'clock, pass'd holloweys prize. arriv'd at the Castle at 2 'ck saw Mr. Gay of Dedham, dined with Mr. Bacon, did not see Captn Metcalf tho' he was on the Castle. came from the Castle to Charlestown from whence we walk'd on foot to Cambridge which we were oblidg to do, the Tide being so low we could not come up Cambridge River.

23 The Class began Gordan.

24 Hollowey took two prizes 1 a Ship the other a Snow laden with provisions, bound to Louisbourg. About this time the Regiments marched from this Province to the Lake.

26 Went to Boston, Saw my Father. Holloweys prize came in.

27 Miss Abigail Pond & Mrs. Farbank came to.

28 went to Meeting Mr. Haven preach.

29 Mr. Epes went home.

30 Gay went home.

31 bad Election rain all Day.

JUNE.

2 ye 1st Division of our Class Declaimed.

4 Mr. Minot preach'd afternoon.

5 went to Boston with Moffat & Hooper.

6 fleec'd Mr. Hancock.

8 hoisting of Palmer & Browne.

11 Mr. Jackson preach'd afternoon.

13 A 90 gun ship burnt in the Mediterranean Sea.

16 went home through Boston.

18 Mr. Haven preach'd.

20 went to Colleg with Seth.

22 Roman Father a Play.

23 Declaimed this morning left off my wigg.

25 Mr. Appleton prea.

26 Presidents Grass Mow'd.

29 went to Boston on foot saw Seth.

30 Valedictory day, I waited on the Orator.   Tom Wentworth was Orator.

JULY.

1 finished the Presidents hay.

3 Cato a Play acted at Warrens Cham.

News about Louisbourg that all except the Town itself is taken.

5 Hollowey has took another prize which the French offer'd to Ransom for 16000 pounds.   They sent out from Louisbourg in the fogs two Frigates Laden with their Riches and Women one of which we took, in which was the Governour, his Wife, & Daughter they are sent in to Hallifax.

6 Cato to perfection.

7 went to Boston with Moffat saw my father.

10 began to make arguments.

11 did not go to prayers.

12 Sirs came to receive their Quest.

13 dismis'd from reciting.

14 Cato more perfect than before.

15 Daniel came from Boston.

16 Sot in the Sophimores Seat.

18 Seniors went into the meeting house to dispute.

19 Commencement. Governours came.

20 came home with Seth.

21 Kingsby & Gay came, Ward turn'd by.

24 Gay went to Boston.

26 the City of Louisbourg surrendered to the English July 26th and now Septr 27th they are gone from Louisbourg to take Ticonderog at the Narrows & so on to Canada.

AUGUST.

11 Hedly Eaton Dana Daniel took off the Doors.
13 Quakers gen'ral meeting at Providence.
15 Hedley & Daniel went to Providence.
16 Dana run off.   Eaton paid 10 Dollars.
23 Vacancy ended did not go to Coll.
31 Went to College this Day with Daniel.

SEPTEMBER.

1 did nothing only read the Customs.
2 began Homer.
3 went to meeting Proclamation for Thanksg.
4 made Arguments.
5 Hooper came this Day.
6 read the Customs to the Freshmen.
8 Quarter Day got a horse of Bradish   home.
9 came back to College this evening.
12 Hooper shook a Freshman cu.
14 Thanksgiving din'd at Prentice.
15 Highlanders encamp'd at Boston.
16 they march'd off.
17 Colln Bradstreet with his Army took Frontenack with a vast deal of provisions a great Detriment to the French.
18 Soldiers at Water.
20 Hancock & Marsh went to ye Castle.
21 I admired Flags Box.
24 Went to meeting.   Mr. Stephens prea.
28 went to Boston went home.
29 Aunt Ellis went home.
30 went to Molly Kingsbery yesterday to get her to make my Gowne but now October 8th she hath disappointed me.

OCTOBER.

1 Mr. Balch preach.
3 Corporation Meeting Forensick Disp.
4 Whitwel here did breakfast.
6 went to Boston.   Surtout, Transports from Halifax.
9 some examined about Bulraging Monis.
12 went to Boston got my gowne.

13 sent home by Otis.

16 begin Euclid to morrow morning.

17 The President Pray'd 1st time since I came.

18 Palmer, Emerson, admonish'd.   Monis Hobs & Fuller Degraded Dunbar.

19 Dr Russell Mr. Curtis Mr Stacey drank Tea.

21 Mr. Titterton brought some Linnen, sent a Letter.

22 Mr. Jackson preach'd to Day.

23 My Father, Dean Healy came here.   Gen'ral Amherst & Col. Frasier since the surrender of Louisbourg went up to the Lake, but Gen'ral Abecrombie order'd them back so nothing this year against Canada.

24 Brooks analyz'd this evening.

25 Wore my surtout 1st time.

26 the taking of Shamburg near St. Malo and Gaspay among the Indians.

28 went to Boston on Isaac Bradish horse.

30 my Chum went to andover Ordination.

31 Daniel Oliver came here gone to Ordination with Avery.

NOVEMBER.

1 Ordination at Andover Mr. Symmes.

2 sent home by Mr. Hunting.

10 Very cold came home yesterday.

11 Soldiers returned home.

13 made two Rockets.

18 Calabogus Club begun.

19 went to Meeting Livermore Pre.

26 Fort Du Quesne taken by Gen'ral Forbes.

29 Painted Court of France.

30 Ditto.   Stay'd home a week new Maid Pitcher.

DECEMBER.

2 Returned to College with Seth.

6 got up to the Class in Euclid.

7 Hancock to Boston.

8 Quarter Day.   Skated all Day & Din'd on ye Pond.

9 went Whitfield club Hooper's chamb.

12 I responded to the Class.

14 had some cold Pig, catch'd cold.

15 Class met a new committee, I not one of them.
16 began 2d book of Euclid Left of reciting Fridays.
17 Foster preach'd forenoon Appleton after.
18 Juniors disputed forensically, we did not dispute.
19 made arguments, news of Du Quesne.
21 had a dance at Bradfords Chamber, my Chum at Boston all night.
22 Freshman began to Declaim.
23 Cato brought me some wood, very cold.
26 began 3d book of Euclid.
27 Corporation met President sick.
31 Club at my Chamber, Saturday night.

The Dedham Historical Register, 1890 (Dedham, 1890), I, No. 1, pp. 10–16.

---◆---

96. A Skit on College Examinations (1784)

BY FRANCIS HOPKINSON

Hopkinson, member of the Continental Congress, and later a judge in Pennsylvania, was one of the earliest humorous writers in America, as well as a famous contributor to the polemic literature of the Revolution. — Bibliography: Tyler, *Literary History of the Revolution*, II, 131–157. — On colleges, see Nos. 90, 95 above.

METAPHYSICS.

Prof. WHAT is a salt-box?
    Stu. It is a box made to contain salt.
Prof. How is it divided?
Stu. Into a salt-box, and a box of salt.
Prof. Very well! — shew the distinction.
Stu. A salt-box may be where there is no salt; but salt is absolutely necessary to the existence of of a box of salt.
Prof. Are not salt-boxes otherwise divided?
Stu. Yes: by a partition.
Prof. What is the use of this partition?
Stu. To separate the coarse salt from the fine.
Prof. How? — think a little.
Stu. To separate the fine salt from the coarse.
Prof. To be sure: — it is to separate the fine from the coarse: but are not salt-boxes yet otherwise distinguished?

STU. Yes : into *possible, probable* and *positive*.

PROF. Define these several kinds of salt-boxes.

STU. A *possible* salt-box is a salt-box yet unsold in the hands of the joiner.

PROF. Why so?

STU. Because it hath never yet become a salt-box *in fact*, having never had any salt in it ; and it may possibly be applied to some other use.

PROF. Very true : — for a salt-box which never had, hath not now, and perhaps never may have, any salt in it, can only be termed a *possible* salt-box.   What is a *probable* salt-box?

STU. It is a salt-box in the hand of one going to a shop to buy salt, and who hath six-pence in his pocket to pay the grocer : and a *positive* salt-box is one which hath actually and *bona fide* got salt in it.

PROF. Very good : — but is there no instance of a *positive* salt-box which hath no salt in it?

STU. I know of none.

PROF. Yes : there is one mentioned by some authors : it is where a box hath by long use been so impregnated with salt, that although all the salt hath been long since emptied out, it may yet be called a salt-box, with the same propriety that we say a salt herring, salt beef, &c. And in this sense any box that may have accidentally, or otherwise, been long steeped in brine, may be termed *positively* a salt-box, although never designed for the purpose of keeping salt.   But tell me, what other division of salt-boxes do you recollect?

STU. They are further divided into *substantive* and *pendant* : a *substantive* salt-box is that which stands by itself on the table or dresser ; and a *pendant* is that which hangs upon a nail against the wall.

PROF. What is the idea of a salt-box?

STU. It is that image which the mind conceives of a salt-box, when no salt-box is present.

PROF. What is the abstract idea of a salt-box?

STU. It is the idea of a salt-box, abstracted from the idea of a box, or of salt, or of a salt-box, or of a box of salt.

PROF. Very right : — and by these means you acquire a most perfect knowledge of a salt-box : but tell me, is the idea of a salt-box a salt idea?

STU. Not unless the ideal box hath ideal salt in it.

PROF. True : — and therefore an abstract idea cannot be either salt

T

or fresh ; round or square; long or short : for a true abstract idea must be entirely free of all adjuncts. And this shews the difference between a salt idea, and an idea of salt. — Is an aptitude to hold salt an *essential* or an *accidental* property of a salt-box?

STU. It is *essential;* but if there should be a crack in the bottom of the box, the aptitude to spill salt would be termed an *accidental* property of that salt-box.

PROF. Very well ! very well indeed ! — What is the salt called with respect to the box?

STU. It is called its contents.

PROF. And why so?

STU. Because the cook is content *quoad hoc* to to find plenty of salt in the box.

PROF. You are very right — I see you have not mispent your time : but let us now proceed to

LOGIC.

PROF. How many parts are there in a salt-box?

STU. Three. *Bottom, top,* and *sides.*

PROF. How many modes are there in salt-boxes?

STU. Four. The *formal,* the *substantial,* the *accidental,* and the *topsey-turvey.*

PRO. Define these several modes,

STU. The *formal* respects the figure or shape of the box, such as round, square, oblong, and so forth ; the *substantial* respects the work of the joiner ; and the *accidental* depends upon the string by which the box is hung against the wall.

PROF. Very well — And what are the consequences of the *accidental* mode ?

STU. If the string should break the box would fall, the salt be spilt, the salt-box broken, and the cook in a bitter passion : and this is the accidental mode with its consequences.

PROF. How do you distinguish between the top and bottom of a salt-box?

STU. The top of a box is that part which is uppermost, and the bottom that part which is lowest in all positions.

PROF. You should rather say the lowest part is the bottom, and the uppermost part is the top. — How is it then if the bottom should be the uppermost?

STU. The top would then be the lowermost; and so the bottom

would become the top, and the top would become the bottom : and this is called the *topsey-turvey* mode, which is nearly allied to the *accidental*, and frequently arises from it.

PROF. Very good — But are not salt-boxes sometimes single and sometimes double?

STU. Yes.

PROF. Well, then mention the several combinations of salt-boxes with respect to their having salt or not.

STU. They are divided into single salt-boxes having salt ; single salt-boxes having no salt ; double salt-boxes having salt ; double salt-boxes having no salt ; and single double salt-boxes having salt and no salt.

PROF. Hold ! hold ! — you are going too far.

GOV. We cannot allow further time for logic, proceed if you please to

NATURAL PHILOSOPHY.

PROF. Pray Sir, what is a salt-box?

STU. It is a combination of matter, fitted, framed, and joined by the hands of a workman in the form of a box, and adapted to the purpose of receiving, containing, and retaining salt.

PROF. Very good — What are the mechanical powers concerned in the construction of a salt-box?

STU. The ax, the saw, the plane, and the hammer. . . .

PROF. . . . Have not some philosophers considered *glue* as one of the mechanical powers?

STU. Yes ; and it is still so considered, but it is called an inverse mechanical power : because, whereas it is the property of the *direct* mechanical powers to generate motion, and separate parts ; *glue*, on the contrary, prevents motion, and keeps the parts to which it is applied fixed to each other. . . .

PROF. Is the *saw* only used in slitting timber into boards?

STU. Yes, it is also employed in cutting boards into lengths.

PROF. Not *lengths* : a thing cannot properly be said to have been cut into *lengths*.

STU. Into *shortnesses*.

PROF. Certainly — into shortnesses. Well, what are the mechanical laws of the hammer?

GOV. The time wastes fast ; pass on to another science.

Francis Hopkinson, *Miscellaneous Essays* (Philadelphia, 1792), I, 340–349 *passim*.

CHAPTER XV — RELIGIOUS LIFE

97. "The State of Religion in the Jerseys" (1700)

BY LEWIS MORRIS

For Morris, see No. 65 above.   Bibliography of religious affairs: Winsor, *Narrative and Critical History*, V, 243–245; Tyler, *American Literature*, II, 210–212; Channing and Hart, *Guide*, § 106. — For previous history of the Jerseys, see *Contemporaries*, I, ch. xxv.

THE Province of East Jersey has in it Ten Towns, (viz.) Middletown, Freehold, Amboy, Piscataway and Woodbridge, Elizabeth Town, Newark, Aqueckenonck, and Bergen, and I Judge in the whole Province there may be about Eight thousand souls.   These Towns are not like the towns in England, the houses built close together on a small spot of ground, but they include large portions of the Country of 4, 5, 8, 10, 12, 15 miles in length, and as much in breadth, and all the Settlements within such State and bounds is said to be within such a Township, but in most of those townships there is some place where a part of the Inhabitants sat down nearer together than the rest, and confined themselves to smaller portions of ground, and the town is more peculiarly designed by that Settlement.   Those towns and the whole province was peopl'd mostly from the adjacent colonies of New York and New England, and generally by Those of very narrow fortunes, and such as could not well subsist in the places they left.   And if such people could bring any religion with them, it was that of the Country they came from, and the State of them is as follows : —

BERGEN, and the out Plantations are most Dutch, and were settled from New York and the United Provinces they are pretty equally divided into Calvinist and Lutheran, they have one pretty little Church, and are a sober people, there are a few English Dissenters mixt among them.

AQUECKENONCK was peopl'd from New York also, they are Dutch mostly and generally Calvinist.

EEIZABETH TOWN & NEWARK, were peopled from New England, are generally Independents, they have a meeting house in each town for their public worship, there are some few Churchmen, Presbiterians, Anabaptists, and Quakers settled among them.

WOODBRIDGE was settled from New England and were generally Independents till about 16 years since, there was a number of Scots Presbyterians amongst them, the People are divided mostly into Presbiterians and Independents, and there is mixt amongst them Baptists, Quakers, Ranters, cum multis aliis.

PISCATAWAY was settled from New England, and is called the Anabaptist Town, from about twenty in that Town that agree in that Persuasion, the rest of the People are of all, or of no religion.

PERTH AMBOY the Capital City was settled from Europe, and we have made a shift to patch up the old ruinous house, and make a church of it, and when all the Churchmen in the Province are got together, we make up about twelve Communicants, the People of that town are a mixture of all Persuasion.

FREEHOLD was settled from Scotland (Mr. Keith began the first settlement there, and made a fine Plantation, which he afterwards Sold, and went into Pensilvania) and about the one half of it are Scotch Presbiterians, and a sober people, the other part of it was settled by People (some from New England, some from New York, and some from the forementioned towns) who are generally speaking of no religion. There is in this Town a Quaker Meeting-house, but most of the Quakers who built it are come off, with Mr. Keith, they have not fixt yet on any religion, but are most inclinable to the Church, and could Mr. Keith be persuaded to go into those Countrys, he would (with the blessing of God) not only bring to the Church the Quakers that come off with him in East & West Jersey, which are very numerous, but make many Converts in that Country.

MIDDLETOWN was settled from New York and New England, it is a large Township, there is no such thing as Church or Religion amongst them, they are p'haps the most ignorant and wicked People in the world, their meetings on Sundays is at the Public house, where they get their fill of Rum, and go to fighting & running of races which are Practices much in use that day all the Province over.

SHREWSBURY settled from New England, Rhode Island and New York, there is in it ab't thirty Quakers of both Sexes, and they have a meeting house, the rest of the People are generally of no Religion — the Youth of the whole Province are very debauch'd and very ignorant, and the Sabbath day seems there to be set apart for Rioting and Drunkenness. In a word, a general Ignorance and immorality runs through the Youth of the whole Province.

There was in the year One thousand six hundred ninety-seven some endeavors to settle a maintenance in that Country for Ministers, and the greatest part of the house of Comons there were for it, but one Richard Hartshorne a Quaker, and Andrew Broun [Bowne] an Anabaptist found means to defeat it that Session, and before the Assembly could sit again, arriv'd one Jeremiah Bass an Anabaptist Preacher with a Comission from the Proprietors of East Jersey to be their Governour, and with Instructions and Orders from them not to Consent to any act to raise a Maintenance for any Minister of what Perswasion soever, so that there is no hope of doing any thing of that kind till that Governm't is in other hands.

In West Jersey in the year 1699 there were 832 freeholders of wch there were 266 Quakers, whose number are much decreased since Mr. Keith left them. The Quakers in yt Province are ye men of the best Rank and Estates — the rest of that Province (generally speaking) are a hotch Potch of all Religions, the Quakers have several Meeting houses disperst up and down that Province and I believe none of the other perswasions have any. They have a very Debaucht Youth in that Province and very ignorant.

PENNSYLVANIA is settled by People of all languages and Religions in Europe, but the People called Quakers are the most numerous of any one perswasion, and in Philadelphia the Capital City of that Province, there is an Episcopal Church, a Quaker Meeting house, a Presbiterian Meeting house, an Anabaptist Meeting house, and I think an Independent Meeting house, and a little w'thout ye Town a Sweeds Church, the Church of England gains ground in that Country, and most of the Quakers that came off with Mr. Keith are come over to it: The Youth of that country are like those in the neighboring Provinces very Debaucht and ignorant.

I shall now suggest some measures w'ch may conduce to ye bringing over to the Church the People in those Countrys.

First That no man be sent a Governor into any of those Plantations, but a firm Churchman, and if possible none but Churchmen be in his Counsel and in the Magistracy.

2*dly* That Churchmen may have some peculiar privileges above others. This (if practicable) must be done by Act of Parliament.

3*dly* That there may be some measures fallen upon to get Ministers to preach gratis in America for some time, till there be sufficient numbers of Converts to bear the charge & I presume that may be accomplish'd this way.

Let the King, the A Bishop, ye Bishops & great Men admit no Man for so many years to any great Benefice, but such as shall oblige themselves to preach three years gratis in America, with part of the living let him maintain a Curate, & the other part let him apply to his own use. By this means we shall have the greatest & best men & in human probability such men must in a short time make a wonderful progress in the Conversion of those Countries, especially when its p'ceived the good of Souls is the only motive to this undertaking.

New Jersey Historical Society, *Proceedings*, 1849–1850 (Newark, 1850), IV, 118–121.

---

98. A Quaker's Arguments with Orthodox Ministers (1704)

BY THOMAS STORY

Story was an English Quaker who came over in 1697. He visited all the colonies, and remained some time in Pennsylvania.— Bibliography: Winsor, *Narrative and Critical History*, V, 243; Channing and Hart, *Guide*, § 215.— For earlier accounts of the Quakers, see *Contemporaries*, I, Nos. 140–142.

DURING all this Time the People were generally attentive, and seemingly pleased; but, just in the Close of the Matter, I was attacked, all of a sudden, by a jolly brisk Person, who brake into the Crowd behind me on Horseback, and, by his Garb, look'd like a Pastor of the People, (and, upon Enquiry afterwards, I found he was so) whose first Salutation was after this Manner: "Are you not ashamed thus to delude the People, imposing upon them false Glosses on the Scripture? I am a Stranger on the Road, and, drawing near this Multitude to know the Occasion of it, cannot but appear in defence of Truth against your Perversions: 'Tis true, you have a smooth Way, a gaining Countenance, and advantageous Mein; but, Sir, you look, in all this, the more like an Emissary."

THIS, being sudden, was a little surprizing at first; but, Truth being uppermost, I quickly replied, "That he rather look'd like a false Teacher of the People; and challenged him to instance any Particular wherein I had imposed upon them."

He instanced only in this, where I had said *Phebe* was a Minister of the Church; he said, "She was not a Minister, but a Servant, as appears by the Text itself in that Place; and it will not bear to be translated *Minister*, as you say."

I replied, "Servant and Minister are synonymous Terms, and the Word there used may be better translated *Minister:* And if she was a Servant, in what other respect to the Church, if not in a publick Ministry, as a Preacher? For *Theodore Beza*, in his *Latin* Translation from the *Greek*, (from which our *English* Translations are made) hath it *Minister*, and not *Servant, Ministra Ecclesiæ Cencreensis*; and, in the *Greek* Testament, it is Διαχονον; that is, *Minister*, or *Servant*." And I asked him before the People, "If he would say, upon his Reputation as a Minister, as he professed himself to be, that it might not be properly rendered *Minister*;" which he refused: and then, in Abundance of Assurance, said openly, "That I was no Quaker;" but, in a flattering Way, added, "I had more Sense than to be a Quaker; for I had an ingenious Countenance, and a Mein importing a better Education." I rejected his Flattery, and replied, "That he might have had better Education, and ought to have had more Justice, than falsely to accuse one whom he never saw before;" and put him upon his Proof in that and several other Things, in which he had overshot himself, in the Apprehension of most of the People who heard him.

And I observed to the People, who did not generally understand the Meaning of the Word *Emissary*, that as it was unduly applied by him, it imported a very high, as well as false Charge; and, as such, I return'd it upon him. Then he began to charge *Jonathan Taylor* (then in *England*) with being a Jesuit (he having been in that Country seven Years before, and instrumental to convince many in those Parts; and thereby had greatly enraged the Priests, and their envious Company, against him; which they had not forgot:) And there stood up likewise another Man, and said, The Charge was true: But I opposed them, telling the People, "I very well knew *Jonathan Taylor*; and that he was no Jesuit, nor any Thing like one in any respect;" putting the Priest in mind of what dangerous Consequence it might be to himself to charge me, or any other innocent Person, in that Manner; since, by Law, it touched the Life of the Accused, and was highly punishable in the Accuser, if not legally proved: Then he, wheeling his Horse about, said, "He could not stay any longer;" and, in the turning of his Horse, he prov'd resty, and ran back upon a Log, and his hinder Parts fell

down, (which some would have made a Judgment upon him;) but the
Priest being a brisk nimble Man, kept upon his Back, and had no Harm,
but rode hastily out of the Crowd, and went off.

THE Opposition this Priest and the others made, being for the most
part confident and notoriously false Assertions and Charges, without any
Proof, exposed him and themselves to the just Censure of the People,
and rather confirmed them in the Truth of what we had delivered, than
hurt the Cause of Truth; which we, in some Measure of the Wisdom
and Power of it, had defended against them. . . .

ANOTHER of those Opposers raised some fresh Cavils about Womens'
Preaching; which I having answered for the Sake of the Auditory, and
he raising new Cavils about Matters of small Consequence, I rebuked
him sharply as an unworthy, unruly Spirit, and neglected him.

AND having shown more Gentleness to several others, and answered
them fully, all ended, with the Day, to the Honour of Truth, and our
great Satisfaction.

THE next Day proving rainy, (as I said before) and several of us
staying there most part of the Day till the Evening, we were divinely
comforted together in the Love of GOD; in which we had many tender
Seasons together, as at other Times and Places; to the Praise of his
great Name, who is GOD worthy for ever.

THE Friends who came with me, *viz. Jacob Moral, Henry Dow* and
his Wife, *Lydia Norton, Thomas Dow,* and some others, departing, I
went, at the Request of *John Keeser,* (a young Man who had not been
long convinced) with him to the Priest of that Town, (a most imbittered
Enemy to the Way of Truth, and all that walk therein in this Dispensa-
tion) who had desired to speak with him about his dissenting from him
and the common Presbyterian Way.

AT our first Entrance into the House, this Priest look'd very surly,
haughty, and ill-natur'd, and, in an imperious Gesture, bid us sit down,
which we did; and *John Keeser* told him, "He had heard he desired
to speak with him, and was now come to know the Matter." Then he
began and said, "*John,* I have had a-mind to speak with you a long Time,
to know your Reasons for neglecting the publick Worship, and deserting me, who have Charge over you, to follow the Errors of the Quakers;
who deny Salvation by JESUS CHRIST, and follow their Light within: But
I could not meet with you, though I came to your House on purpose."

John Keeser replied, "I heard of it, and am now come to hear what
thou hast to say." Then said the Priest, "You are a perverse Fellow;

I wanted to speak with you alone, in order to reclaim you from the pernicious Errors of the Quakers, who deny Justification by CHRIST ; affirming, That to expect to be justified by the Works of CHRIST without us, is a Doctrine of Devils."

THEN said I, " Friend, if thou hast any Thing to say to the young Man, relating to any Thing he hath done or said, I am here, at his Request, to hear it ; but if thou goest on thus to reflect against, and falsely accuse that People, I am one of them, and shall oppose thee, as I do return upon thee thy false Accusations already uttered ; in which thou hast shown thy great Injustice, Unworthiness, and ill Nature : For we do not expect Salvation by any other than the LORD JESUS CHRIST and the Father ; and I challenge thee to produce any Author, approved by us, that denies the Work of the LORD JESUS CHRIST, done without us, and its Efficacy, for its proper End and Purpose, in the Redemption and Salvation of Mankind."

THEN the Priest's Wife came into the Room with an Air of Rancour, and said, " Husband, Do not talk with these Men without Witnesses ; for, when they are gone, they will tell Lies of you." Upon this I said to the Priest, " If thou hast any Authority in this House, let us be rid of this Din : " And he desired her to withdraw, which she did ; but we observed the Effects of her Resentment afterwards in the Sequel.

THEN the Priest said, " *William Penn*, in one of his Books, had called the Doctrine of Justification, by the Coming of CHRIST without, (in the Flesh) the Doctrine of Devils." I asked him, " If he had ever seen that Book ? " and he confessed he had not. Then I asked him, " How he could charge *William Penn* with such a Position ? " He replied, " He had seen it quoted out of the Book by Mr *Bugg* and Mr *Keith*." " *Francis Bugg* and *George Keith*, said I, once knew the Truth in some Degree, and made Profession of it with us ; but took Offences, first against some particular Persons, and then against the whole Body, and became Apostates, open Enemies, filled with Envy implacable ; and it is neither safe nor wise in thee to take any Thing upon Trust from them against us, or any of us, they having been, and still are notorious false Accusers, Perverters, and Misrepresenters of us, our Books, Doctrines, and Principles : But I know *William Penn*, and his Sentiments on that Subject, and have read the Passage aim'd at ; which, to the best of my Remembrance, (not having the Book here) is to this Effect ; *To teach that Men are justified before God, by the Righteousness of Christ, as wholly without us, whilst Sin is yet reigning in us, is a Doctrine of Devils.*"

Thomas Story, *Journal* (Newcastle upon Tyne, 1747), 326–330 *passim*.

99. An Evangelist in Georgia (1735/6–1737)

BY REVEREND JOHN WESLEY

Wesley was the founder of the Methodist church in England and America. His journal is one of the most valuable sources for the religious history of the time. — Bibliography : Winsor, *Narrative and Critical History*, V, 402–404; Channing and Hart, *Guide*, § 103; John Henry Overton, *John Wesley*.

SUND. Feb. 1.   We spoke with a ship of *Carolina* : and *Wedn.* 4. came within Soundings.   About Noon the Trees were visible from the Mast, and in the Afternoon from the Main Deck.   In the Evening Lesson were these Words, *A great Door and Effectual is opened.*   O let no one shut it !

Thursd. Feb. 5. Between Two and Three in the Afternoon, God brought us all safe into the *Savannah* River. We cast anchor near *Tybee*-Island, where the Groves of Pines, running along the Shore, made an agreeable Prospect, shewing, as it were the Bloom of Spring in the Depth of Winter.

Frid. 6. About eight in the Morning, we first set foot on *American* Ground. It was a small, uninhabited Island, over against *Tybee*, Mr. *Oglethorpe* led us to a rising Ground, where we all kneel'd down to give Thanks. . . .

Thursd. 19. My Brother and I took Boat, and passing by *Savannah*, went to pay our first Visit in *America* to the poor *Heathens*. But neither *Tomo Chachi* nor *Sinauky* were at home. Coming back, we waited upon Mr. *Causton*, the Chief Magistrate of *Savannah*. From him we went with Mr. *Spadgenberg* to the *Moravian* Brethren. About Eleven we returned to the Boat, and came to our Ship about Four in the Morning.

Sat. 21. *Mary Welch*, aged Eleven Days, was baptized according to the Custom or [of] the First Church, and the Rule of the Church of *England*, by Immersion. The Child was ill then, but recover'd from that Hour.

Tu. 24. . . . At our return the next day, (Mr. *Quincy* being then in the House wherein we afterwards were) Mr. *Delamotte* and I took up our Lodging with the *Germans*. We had now an Opportunity Day by Day, of observing their whole behaviour. For we were in one Room with them from Morning to Night, unless for the little Time I spent in walking. They were always employ'd, always chearful themselves, and in good Humour with one another. They had put away all Anger and

Strife and Wrath and Bitterness and Clamour and Evil-speaking. They walk'd worthy of the Vocation wherewith they were call'd, and adorn'd the Gospel of our Lord in all Things. . . .

Sund. [March] 28. A Servant of Mr. *Bradley*'s sent to desire to speak with me. Going to him, I found a young man ill, but perfectly sensible. He desired the Rest to go out, and then said, 'On *Thursday* Night, about Eleven, being in bed, but broad awake, I heard one calling aloud *" Peter ! Peter Wright !"* And looking up, the Room was as light as day, and I saw a man in very bright cloaths stand by the bed, who said, *" Prepare yourself; for your End is nigh ;"* and then immediately all was dark as before." I told him, " The Advice was good whence-soever it came." In a few days he recovered from his illness : His whole temper was changed as well as his life ; and so continued to be, till after three or four weeks he relapsed and died in peace. . . .

Sund. Apr. 4. About Four in the afternoon, I set out for *Frederica*, in a Pettianga (a sort of flat-bottom'd Barge.) The next Evening we anchor'd near *Skidoway* Island, where the water at Flood was twelve or fourteen Foot deep. I wrapt myself up from head to foot, in a large cloak, to keep off the Sand-Flies, and lay down on the Quarter Deck. Between One and Two I waked under water, being so fast asleep that I did not find where I was till my mouth was full of it. Having left my cloak, I know not how upon Deck, I swam round to the other side of the Pettiawga, where a boat was ty'd, and climed up by the rope, without any hurt, more than wetting my cloaths. Thou art the God of whom cometh Salvation : Thou art the Lord by whom we escape death. . . .

Thurs. [June] 10. We began to execute at *Frederica*, what we had before agreed to do at *Savannah*. Our Design was on *Sundays* in the Afternoon, and every Evening after Publick Service, to spend some time with the most Serious of the Communicants, in singing, reading and Conversation. This Evening we had only *Mark Hird*. But on *Sunday* Mr. *Hird*, and two more desired to be admitted. After a psalm and a little conversation, I read Mr. *Law's Christian Perfection,* and concluded with another psalm. . . .

Tuesd. 22. Observing such Coldness in Mr. ――'s behaviour, I asked him the reason of it. He answer'd, " I like nothing you do ; all your Sermons are Satires upon particular persons. Therefore I will never hear you more. And all the people are of my mind. For we won't hear ourselves abused.

" Beside, they say, they are Protestants. But as for You, they can't tell what Religion you are of. They never heard of such a religion before. They do not know what to make of it. And then, your private behaviour — All the Quarrels that have been here since you came, have been long of you. Indeed there is neither man nor woman in the Town, who minds a word you say. And so you may preach long enough; but no body will come to hear you."

He was too warm for hearing an answer. So I had nothing to do, but to thank him for his openness, and walk away. . . .

Saturd. July 31. We came to *Charles-Town*. The Church is of Brick, but plaister'd over like Stone. I believe it would contain three or four Thousand Persons. About three Hundred were present at the Morning Service the next day, (when Mr. *Garden* desired me to preach) about fifty at the Holy Communion. I was glad to see several Negroes at Church; one of whom told me, " she was there constantly; and that her old Mistress (now dead) had many times instructed her in the Christian Religion." . . .

[August 2.] At *Thunderbolt* we took Boat, and on *Friday Aug.* 13, came to *Frederica*, where I deliver'd Mr. *O.* the Letters, I had brought from *Carolina*. The next Day he set out for *Fort St. George*. From that time I had less and less Prospect of doing good at *Frederica*; many there being extremely zealous, and indefatigably diligent to prevent it: And few of the rest daring to shew themselves of another mind, for fear of their displeasure.

Sat. 28. I set apart, (out of the Few we had) a few Books towards a Library at *Frederica*. . . .

[January, 1737.] In my passage home, having procured a celebrated Book, the Works of *Nicholas Machiavel*, I set myself carefully to read and consider it. I began with a prejudice in his Favour; having been informed, he had often been misunderstood, and greatly misrepresented. I weigh'd the Sentiments that were less common; transcribed the passages wherein they were contained; compared one Passage with another, and endeavour'd to form a cool, impartial Judgment; And my cool Judgement is, That if all the other doctrines of Devils which have been committed to Writing, since Letters were in the world, were collected together in one Volume, it would fall short of this: And, that should a Prince form himself by this book, so calmly recommending Hypocrisy, Treachery, Lying, Robbery, Oppression, Adultery, Whoredom and Murder of all kinds; *Domitian* or *Nero* would be an Angel of Light, compared to that Man. . . .

Frid. March 4. I writ the Trustees for *Georgia* an account of the last year's expence from *March* 1, 1736, to *March* 1, 1737. Which, deducting extraordinary expences (such as repairing the Parsonage House, and Journeys to *Frederica*) amounted for Mr. *Delamotte* and me to 44*l*. 4*s*. 4*d*.

From the Directions I received from God this Day, touching an Affair of the greatest importance, I could not but observe (as I had done many times before) the entire mistake of those, who assert, " God will not answer your prayer, unless your Heart be wholly resign'd to his will." My Heart was not wholly resign'd to his will. Therefore, not daring to depend on my own Judgment, I cried the more earnestly to him, To supply what was wanting in me. And I know and am assured, He heard my Voice, and did send forth his Light and his Truth. . . .

Wednes. [May] 25. I was sent for by one who had been several years of the Church of *Rome* : But was now deeply convinced (as were several others) by what I had occasionally preach'd, of the grievous errors that church is in, and the great danger of continuing a member of it. Upon this occasion I could not but reflect on the many advices I had receiv'd, to beware of the increase of popery : but not one (that I remember) to beware of the increase of infidelity. That was quite surprizing when I consider'd, 1. That in every place where I have yet been, the number of Converts to popery bore no proportion to the number of the Converts to infidelity. 2. That as bad a religion as popery is, *no* religion is still worse ; a baptiz'd infidel being always found upon the trial, two-fold worse than even a bigotted Papist. 3. That as dangerous a state as a papist is in, with regard to eternity, a Deist is in a yet more dangerous state, if he be not (without repentance) an assured heir of damnation. And lastly, That as hard as it is to recover a Papist, it is still harder to recover an Infidel : I myself have known many Papists, but never one Deist re-converted. . . .

October the 7th I consulted my friends, whether God did not call me to return to *England?* The reason for which I left it had now no force : there being no possibility as yet of instructing the *Indians* : Neither had I as yet found or heard of any *Indians* on the continent of *America*, who had the least desire of being instructed. And as to *Savannah*, having never engag'd myself, either by word or letter, to stay there a day longer than I should judge convenient, nor even taken charge of the people any otherwise, than as in my passage to the heathens. I looked upon myself to be fully discharged therefrom, by the vacating of that design.   Besides, there was a probability of doing more service to that unhappy people, in *England* than I could do in *Georgia*, by representing without fear or favour to the Trustees, the real state the Colony was in.   After deeply considering these things, they were unanimous, *That I ought to go.   But not yet.*   So I laid the thoughts of it aside for the present : Being persuaded, that when the time was come, God would *make the way plain before my face.* . . .

   Friday, Dec. 2. . . .   In the Afternoon the Magistrates publish'd an Order requiring all the Officers and Centinels, to prevent my going out of the Province ; and forbidding any person to assist me so to do. Being now only a Prisoner at large, in a Place where I knew by experience, every Day would give fresh opportunity, to procure Evidence of words I never said, and actions I never did ; I saw clearly the Hour was come for leaving this Place : And as soon as Evening Prayers were over, about Eight o'Clock, the Tide then serving, I shook off the dust of my Feet, and left *Georgia*, after having preach'd the Gospel there (not as I ought, but as I was able) one Year, and nearly Nine Months.

[*An Extract of the Rev. Mr. John Wesley's Journal, from Oct. 14, 1735, to Jan. 29, 1783*], 8–52 *passim.*   (Taken from a contemporary copy, of which the title-page is missing.)

———◆———

100. A Good Man's Letter (1752)

BY GOVERNOR JONATHAN BELCHER

Belcher had been Massachusetts's agent in England, and later governor of the province.   At this time he was governor of New Jersey.   The letter is inserted as an excellent example of the formal but sincere expression of a Christian gentleman. — Bibliography: Palfrey, *New England*, IV, 517–579; Winsor, *Narrative and Critical History*, V, 166–169.

Dear Mr Whitefield & Worthy Sir

YOUR Excellently good and religious Letter of the 13th of Oct. 1750 came to my hands the May following and which I had Answered long before now But that your Sudden Motions from place to place made me quite at a loss how to get a Letter in safety to you and I now Cover this to the Care of our good Friend Mr Bradford of Phil for its better Conveyance.

   D[r] Sir how much have you disappointed great Numb[rs] of your longing Friends by not making a Stride a Cross the Ocean from Carolina hither of which we were big with Expect[n] but we must Submit believing your

great Master Steers & marks out your Paths so as shall best of all Contribute to the build^g up and Enlargement of His Kingdom of Grace here
and thereby fitting Multitudes of Souls to be His Subjects in His Kingdom of Glory thro' the endless Ages of a Happy Eternity Amen.

I thank you tho' I am quite Ashamed that any thing of mine shou'd
pass under the Correct Eye of the Excellent & pious Countess of Hunt-
ingdon who is so Bright an Ornam^t, nay I may say a Constellation in the
Church of Christ here & who will (I doubt not) hereafter Shine as the
Stars for ever & Ev^r & now thro' your kind interposition I presume to
Address Her Ladyship by the Inclos'd which I leave open for you
to read & then Clap to the Seal and deliver it and this is an honour
I shou'd not venture to do my Self but that I depend upon your Goodness to obtain Her Ladyships Pardon for the trouble of this Nature. . . .

And now, Sir, let me thank you once more for your kind & generous
Concern for the Welfare of the Infant College in this Province wch I
assure you creeps along with great difficulty — the Trustees chose
Mr Pemberton the last Fall to take a Voyage to great Britain in favour
of the College but when the thing came before his Church and Congregation they wou'd by no means be prevail'd upon to let him go.

And this Spring Mr President Burr was pitcht upon for the same purpose but his fear of the small Pox and the difficulty of finding a person
to take the Care of the College in his absence have render'd a Second
Attempt in this matter abortive however we intend at the next Meeting
of the Trustees to try if some other person can't be found for this Service
which seems to me must be the dernier resort for Encourageing and Establishing this New Seminary nor will I despair but Conclude with the
great Pharisaical D^r if it be of God it cannot be overthrown   I heartily
ask your Prayers for its prosperity.

O Sir as often as I read your ingenious & pious Letters they rejoice
my Heart and refresh my Bowels and I am particularly glad to find that
you were at good Lady Huntingdon^s with three other Clergy men that
love and preach Christ Jesus & that you can give me the pleasing Account of several Instances where the Sovereign Grace of God has taken
place in the Hearts of Persons of High Degree how pleasing is the prospect when such are posting to the Celestial Canaan with their faces
thitherward . . .   Præcepta docent Exempla cogunt.

How sweet Sir must be your Meditation when your Soul rolls inward
to Consider that you are Sincerely will^g to spend and be spent in the

Cause of your Blessed Lord & Master and may you still go on in His Strength to win many Souls to Righteousness every one of which will be a bright Gem in the glorious Crown with wch the Great God Man will wreathe your Temples in the great day of his appear^{g} Amen and Amen! . . .

William A. Whitehead, editor, *Documents relating to the Colonial History of the State of New Jersey* (Newark, 1885), VIII (i), 84–86 *passim*.

101. A Plan for American Bishops (1758)

BY ARCHBISHOP THOMAS SECKER

Secker was archbishop of Canterbury at this time. This letter is selected out of several of similar tenor. Dr. Samuel Johnson, Rector of King's (now Columbia) College, was much interested in the scheme. For its political effects, see No. 147 below. — Bibliography: Palfrey, *New England*, V, 245–255; Winsor, *Narrative and Critical History*, VI, 243–245; Channing and Hart, *Guide*, § 133.

ALL these things will contribute, directly or indirectly, to facilitate what we must ever pray and labour for, till we obtain it, the establishment of Bishops of our Church in America. This I have long had at heart : and not only said but written a great deal in favor of it to such as I hoped might be brought off from their prejudices, either wholly or in some measure. Nor, unsuccessful as the attempts have been shall I ever abandon the scheme, as long as I live. But pushing it openly at present would certainly prove both fruitless and detrimental. They alone are judges of opportunities, who know the dispositions and influences of persons and parties : which cannot always be explained to others. The design when some years ago it seemed to be in great forwardness, received a most mortifying check, by means of an unseasonable step, which a worthy and able prelate took to promote it, and of which its opposers made their advantage. The time is not yet come for retrieving the ground then lost : though I believe the King to be well disposed ; and those, whom he consults, to be, in general, either not averse, or only so through groundless fears. But in the mean while, both you and we may be seeking occasions, in friendly and seemingly accidental discourse, and with better effect as we can truly affirm, that no plan for this purpose lies now, or will be laid soon before our superiors, to shew men, that nothing was ever intended, at which Christians of any denomination have cause to be alarmed : but merely a provision

U

that those of our Communion in the Colonies might have that complete and easy exercise of every branch of their religion which others there have, and would complain bitterly if they had not; and ought therefore from the love which they profess of universal harmless liberty, not only to consent that our people should have but join to procure it for them. The powerful objection made at home against our proposal, is, that the Dissenters abroad have terrible apprehensions of being injured by it. And in proportion as their remonstrances are vehement, our endeavours will be unpromising. Therefore the principal point is to convince them, that whatever the Bishops were, from whom their ancestors fled into the New World, those of the present age are, and have always been, most sincere patrons of extensive toleration; and that we are for sending persons of our own order into America, not to claim the least jurisdiction over them, but merely to ordain Ministers for Episcopal Congregations, without the trouble, expense, and hazard of a voyage to England; a burthen, to which if they were subjected, they would think insupportable, to confirm from time to time the Youth of those congregations; a practice which rightly or wrongly we hold in high esteem; and to exercise such discipline in those congregations only, as they exercise by ordained Presbyters or lay Elders; which discipline of ours would no more hurt them, than theirs hurts us. To these Representations they will pay more regard, if we are careful not to give them unnecessary offence in any thing: but in every thing to oblige them; as far as there is room for it, without betraying the doctrines, the interests or the honour of our Church.

I conceived it would be best to lay before you, thus plainly and distinctly, my judgment concerning the due method of conducting the affairs of the Society. If in any article we differ, I beg you will communicate to me your opinion and your arguments for it, with the utmost freedom; and be assured, it will give me pleasure. Where we agree, you will have the goodness to lead others into the same way of thinking, and a suitable course of behaviour. . . . Thus let us each be doing the best we can, and leave the event to God. That his blessing may be on all who serve him in the Gospel of his Son, particularly on you and your College, our Clergy in America and their people, is the fervent prayer of

Your loving brother
(signed)   THO : CANT.

E. B. O'Callaghan, editor, *Documents relative to the Colonial History of the State of New-York* (Albany, 1856), VII, 348-349.

CHAPTER XVI — SLAVERY AND SERVITUDE

102. The First Vote against Slavery (1688)

BY THE MONTHLY MEETING OF THE GERMANTOWN QUAKERS

The agitation against slavery was at this period confined chiefly to the Quakers. The minute was sent to the Yearly Meeting at Burlington, which declined to confirm it. — Bibliography: Winsor, *Narrative and Critical History*, V, 243–245; Channing and Hart, *Guide*, § 148. — On slavery, see also *Contemporaries*, I, No. 86, and III; and Nos. 103–108 below. On the Quakers, see Nos. 98 above and 106 below.

THIS is to the monthly meeting held at Richard Worrell's :

These are the reasons why we are against the traffic of men-body, as followeth : Is there any that would be done or handled at this manner? viz., to be sold or made a slave for all the time of his life? How fearful and faint-hearted are many at sea, when they see a strange vessel, being afraid it should be a Turk, and they should be taken, and sold for slaves into Turkey. Now, what is *this* better done, than Turks do? Yea, rather it is worse for them, which say they are Christians ; for we hear that the most part of such negers are brought hither against their will and consent, and that many of them are stolen. Now, though they are black, we cannot conceive there is more liberty to have them slaves, as [than] it is to have other white ones. There is a saying, that we should do to all men like as we will be done ourselves ; making no difference of what generation, descent, or colour they are. And those who steal or rob men, and those who buy or purchase them, are they not all alike? Here is liberty of conscience, which is right and reasonable ; here ought to be likewise liberty of the body, except of evil-doers, which is another case. But to bring men hither, or to rob and sell them against their will, we stand against. In Europe, there are many oppressed for conscience-sake ; and here there are those oppressed which are of a black colour. And we who know that men must not commit adultery — some do commit adultery *in* others, separating wives from their husbands, and giving them to others : and some sell the children of these poor creatures to other men. Ah ! do consider well this thing, you who do it, if you would be done at this manner — and if it is done according to Christianity ! You surpass Holland and Germany in this thing. This makes an ill report in all those countries of

Europe, where they hear of [it,] that the Quakers do here handel men as they handel there the cattle. And for that reason some have no mind or inclination to come hither. And who shall maintain this your cause, or plead for it? Truly, we cannot do so, except you shall inform us better hereof, viz. : that Christians have liberty to practise these things. Pray, what thing in the world can be done worse towards us, than if men should rob or steal us away, and sell us for slaves to strange countries ; separating husbands from their wives and children. Being now this is not done in the manner we would be done at ; therefore, we contradict, and are against this traffic of men-body. And we who profess that it is not lawful to steal, must, likewise, avoid to purchase such things as are stolen, but rather help to stop this robbing and stealing, if possible. And such men ought to be delivered out of the hands of the robbers, and set free as in Europe. Then is Pennsylvania to have a good report, instead, it hath now a bad one, for this sake, in other countries : Especially whereas the Europeans are desirous to know in what manner *the Quakers* do rule in *their* province ; and most of them do look upon us with an envious eye. But if this is done well, what shall we say is done evil?

If once these slaves (which they say are so wicked and stubborn men,) should join themselves — fight for their freedom, and handel their masters and mistresses, as they did handel them before ; will these masters and mistresses take the sword at hand and war against these poor slaves, like, as we are able to believe, some will not refuse to do? Or, have these poor negers not as much right to fight for their freedom, as you have to keep them slaves?

Now consider well this thing, if it is good or bad. And in case you find it to be good to handel these blacks in that manner, we desire and require you hereby lovingly, that you may inform us herein, which at this time never was done, viz., that Christians have such a liberty to do so. To the end we shall be satisfied on this point, and satisfy likewise our good friends and acquaintances in our native country, to whom it is a terror, or fearful thing, that men should be handelled so in Pennsylvania.

This is from our meeting at Germantown, held yᵉ 18th of the 2d month, 1688, to be delivered to the monthly meeting at Richard Worrell's.

GARRET HENDERICH,
DERICK OP DE GRAEFF,
FRANCIS DANIEL PASTORIUS,
ABRAM OP DE GRAEFF.

At our monthly meeting, at Dublin, yᵉ 30th 2d mo., 1688, we having inspected yᵉ matter, above mentioned, and considered of it, we find it so weighty that we think it not expedient for us to meddle with it *here*, but do rather commit it to yᵉ consideration of yᵉ quarterly meeting; yᵉ tenor of it being related to yᵉ truth.

On behalf of yᵉ monthly meeting,

Jo. Hart.

The Friend, January 13, 1844; reprinted in George H. Moore, *Notes on the History of Slavery in Massachusetts* (New York, 1866), 74–77.

---

103. "The Selling of Joseph" (1700)

"BY THE HON'BLE JUDGE SEWALL IN NEW ENGLAND"

This paper was the first abolitionist tract in America. — For Sewall, see *Contemporaries*, I, No. 149, and No. 18 above.

FORASMUCH *as* LIBERTY *is in real value next unto* Life ; *None ought to part with it themselves, or deprive others of it, but upon most mature consideration.*

The Numerousness of Slaves at this Day in the Province, and the Uneasiness of them under their Slavery, hath put many upon thinking whether the Foundation of it be firmly and well laid ; so as to sustain the Vast Weight that is built upon it.   It is most certain that all Men, as they are the sons of *Adam*, are Co-heirs, and have equal Right unto Liberty, and all other outward Comforts of Life.   GOD *hath given the Earth [with all its commodities] unto the Sons of Adam, Psal.*, 115, 16. *And hath made of one Blood all Nations of Men, for to dwell on all the face of the Earth, and hath determined the Times before appointed, and the bounds of their Habitation : That they should seek the Lord.   Forasmuch then as we are the Offspring of* GOD, &c.   *Acts* 17. 26, 27, 29. Now, although the Title given by the last ADAM doth infinitely better Men's Estates, respecting GOD and themselves ; and grants them a most beneficial and inviolable Lease under the Broad Seal of Heaven, who were before only Tenants at Will ; yet through the Indulgence of GOD to our First Parents after the Fall, the outward Estate of all and every of their Children, remains the same as to one another.   So that Originally, and Naturally, there is no such thing as Slavery.   *Joseph* was rightfully no more a Slave to his Brethren, than they were to him ; and they had no more Authority to *Sell* him, than they had to *Slay* him. And if *they* had nothing to do to sell him; the *Ishmaelites* bargaining with them, and paying down Twenty pieces of Silver, could not make a Title. Neither could *Potiphar* have any better Interest in him than the *Ishmaelites* had. *Gen.* 37, 20, 27, 28. For he that shall in this case plead *Alteration of Property*, seems to have forfeited a great part of his own claim to Humanity. There is no proportion between Twenty Pieces of Silver and LIBERTY. The Commodity itself is the Claimer. If *Arabian* Gold be imported in any quantities, most are afraid to meddle with it, though they might have it at easy rates ; lest [if] it should have been wrongfully taken from the Owners, it should kindle a fire to the Consumption of their whole Estate. 'Tis pity there should be more Caution used in buying a Horse, or a little lifeless dust, than there is in purchasing Men and Women : Whereas they are the Offspring of GOD, and their Liberty is,

          .   .   .   *Auro pretiosior Omni.*

And seeing GOD hath said, *He that Stealeth a Man, and Selleth him, or if he be found in his Hand, he shall surely be put to Death.* Exod. 21, 16. This Law being of Everlasting Equity, wherein Man-Stealing is ranked among the most atrocious of Capital Crimes : What louder Cry can there be made of that Celebrated Warning.

Caveat Emptor!

And all things considered, it would conduce more to the Welfare of the Province, to have White Servants for a Term of Years, than to have Slaves for Life. Few can endure to hear of a Negro's being made free ; and indeed they can seldom use their Freedom well ; yet their continual aspiring after their forbidden Liberty, renders them Unwilling Servants. And there is such a disparity in their Conditions, Colour, and Hair, that they can never embody with us, & grow up in orderly Families, to the Peopling of the Land ; but still remain in our Body Politick as a kind of extravasat Blood. As many Negro Men as there are among us, so many empty Places are there in our Train Bands, and the places taken up of Men that might make Husbands for our Daughters. And the Sons and Daughters of *New England* would become more like *Jacob* and *Rachel*, if this Slavery were thrust quite out of Doors. Moreover it is too well known what Temptations Masters are under, to connive at the Fornication of their Slaves ; lest they should be obliged to find them

Wives, or pay their Fines. It seems to be practically pleaded that they might be lawless ; 'tis thought much of, that the Law should have satisfaction for their Thefts, and other Immoralities ; by which means, *Holiness to the Lord* is more rarely engraven upon this sort of Servitude. It is likewise most lamentable to think, how in taking Negroes out of *Africa*, and selling of them here, That which GOD has joined together, Men do boldly rend asunder; Men from their Country, Husbands from their Wives, Parents from their Children. How horrible is the Uncleanness, Mortality, if not Murder, that the Ships are guilty of that bring great Crouds of these miserable Men and Women. Methinks when we are bemoaning the barbarous Usage of our Friends and Kinsfolk in *Africa*, it might not be unreasonable to enquire whether we are not culpable in forcing the *Africans* to become Slaves amongst ourselves. And it may be a question whether all the Benefit received by *Negro* Slaves will balance the Accompt of Cash laid out upon them ; and for the Redemption of our own enslaved Friends out of *Africa*. Besides all the Persons and Estates that have perished there.

Obj. 1. *These Blackamores are of the Posterity of Cham, and therefore are under the Curse of Slavery.* Gen. 9, 25, 26, 27.

Ans. Of all Offices, one would not beg this ; viz. Uncall'd for, to be an Executioner of the Vindictive Wrath of God ; the extent and duration of which is to us uncertain. If this ever was a Commission ; How do we know but that it is long since out of Date? Many have found it to their Cost, that a Prophetical Denunciation of Judgment against a Person or People, would not warrant them to inflict that evil. If it would, *Hazael* might justify himself in all he did against his master, and the *Israelites* from 2 *Kings* 8, 10, 12.

But it is possible that by cursory reading, this Text may have been mistaken. For *Canaan* is the Person Cursed three times over, without the mentioning of *Cham*. Good Expositors suppose the Curse entailed on him, and that this Prophesie was accomplished in the Extirpation of the *Canaanites*, and in the Servitude of the *Gibeonites*. *Vide Pareum.* Whereas the Blackmores are not descended of *Canaan*, but of *Cush*. Psal. 68, 31. *Princes shall come out of Egypt* [Mizraim]. *Ethiopia* [Cush] *shall soon stretch out her hands unto God.* Under which Names, all *Africa* may be comprehended ; and their Promised Conversion ought to be prayed for. *Jer.* 13, 23. *Can the Ethiopian change his Skin ?* This shows that Black Men are the Posterity of *Cush*. Who time out of mind have been distinguished by their Colour. And for want of the true, *Ovid* assigns a fabulous cause of it.

> *Sanguine tum credunt in corpora summa vocato*
> *Æthiopum populos nigrum traxisse colorem.*
>
> Metamorph. lib. 2.

Obj. 2. *The Nigers are brought out of a Pagan Country, into places where the Gospel is preached.*

Ans. Evil must not be done, that good may come of it. The extraordinary and comprehensive Benefit accruing to the Church of God, and to *Joseph* personally, did not rectify his Brethren's Sale of him.

Obj. 3. *The Africans have Wars one with another: Our Ships bring lawful Captives taken in those wars.*

Answ. For aught is known, their Wars are much such as were between *Jacob's* Sons and their Brother *Joseph*. If they be between Town and Town; Provincial or National: Every War is upon one side Unjust. An Unlawful War can't make lawful Captives. And by receiving, we are in danger to promote, and partake in their Barbarous Cruelties. I am sure, if some Gentlemen should go down to the *Brewsters* to take the Air, and Fish: And a stronger Party from *Hull* should surprise them, and sell them for Slaves to a Ship outward bound; they would think themselves unjustly dealt with; both by Sellers and Buyers. And yet 'tis to be feared, we have no other Kind of Title to our *Nigers*. *Therefore all things whatsoever ye would that men should do to you, do you even so to them: for this is the Law and the Prophets.* Matt. 7, 12.

Obj. 4. Abraham *had Servants bought with his Money and born in his House.*

Ans. Until the Circumstances of *Abraham's* purchase be recorded, no Argument can be drawn from it. In the mean time, Charity obliges us to conclude, that He knew it was lawful and good.

It is Observable that the *Israelites* were strictly forbidden the buying or selling one another for Slaves. *Levit.* 25. 39. 46. *Jer.* 34. 8–22. And GOD gaged His Blessing in lieu of any loss they might conceit they suffered thereby, *Deut.* 15. 18. And since the partition Wall is broken down, inordinate Self-love should likewise be demolished. GOD expects that Christians should be of a more Ingenuous and benign frame of Spirit.

Christians should carry it to all the World, as the *Israelites* were to carry it one towards another.   And for Men obstinately to persist in holding their Neighbours and Brethren under the Rigor of perpetual Bondage, seems to be no proper way of gaining Assurance that God has given them Spiritual Freedom.   Our Blessed Saviour has altered the Measures of the ancient Love Song, and set it to a most Excellent New Tune, which all ought to be ambitious of Learning.   *Matt.* 5. 43. 44.   *John* 13. 34.   These *Ethiopians*, as black as they are, seeing they are the Sons and Daughters of the First *Adam*, the Brethren and Sisters of the Last ADAM, and the Offspring of GOD ; They ought to be treated with a Respect agreeable.

Servitus perfecta voluntaria, inter Christianum & Christianum, ex parte servi patientis sæpe est licita, quia est necessaria ; sed ex parte domini agentis, & procurando & exercendo, vix potest esse licita ; quia non convenit regulæ illi generali : Quæcunque volueritis ut faciant vobis homines, ita & vos facite eis.   Matt. 7. 12.

Perfecta servitus pœnæ, non potest jure locum habere, nisi ex delicto gravi quod ultimum supplicium aliquo modo meretur : quia Libertas ex naturali æstimatione proxime accedit ad vitam ipsam, & eidem a multis præferri solet.

Ames. Cas. Consc. Lib. 5. Cap. 23.   Thes. 2. 3.

[Samuel Sewall], *The Selling of Joseph A Memorial* (Boston, 1700) ; reprinted in George H. Moore, *Notes on the History of Slavery in Massachusetts* (New York, 1866), 83–87.

———◆———

104. A Slave Act Disallowed (1709)

BY THE LORDS COMMISSIONERS FOR TRADE AND PLANTATIONS

This brief document is typical of the fate of most colonial statutes taxing or otherwise restricting the slave-trade. — Bibliography : W. E. B. Du Bois, *Suppression of the Slave-Trade*, chs. ii–iv.

TO the Queens most Excell:t Maj:ty

May it Please Your Majesty.

We have considered An Act past in the General Assembly of Your Majesties Province of New Jersey in December 1704.   Entituled, *An Act for Regulating Negro, Indian & Mulato Slaves within this Province of New Jersey,* in which, tho' there are Several good & Useful

Clauses, there is one that inflicts inhumane penalties on Negroes &c not fit to be Confirmed by Your Majesty, & therefore we humbly offer that the said Act be repealed.

Which is most Humbly Submitted

DARTMOUTH
PH : MEADOWS
J PULTENEY

Whitehall
Oct.^{br} 18th 1709 }

William A. Whitehead, editor, *Documents relating to the Colonial History of the State of New Jersey* (Newark, 1881), III, 473–474.

---

105. All Sorts of Runaways (1741-1750)

BY THEIR OWNERS AND MASTERS

These extracts from contemporary newspapers show the frequency of escapes of indentured white servants and slaves, and throw some light on the brutality of the whole system. — Bibliography: Marion G. McDougall, *Fugitive Slaves*, ch. i; Channing and Hart, *Guide*, § 148.

RUN away from *Marten Ryerson*, of *Readingtown*, in the County of *Hunterdon* a Young Servant Man named *William Hains* small Stature Ruddy Complexion, big Nose, big Blew Eyes, Pock-Broken, had no Hair, Branded on the Brawn of his Thumb, of the Left Hand, had on when he Run away a white Shirt, and a Saylors Frock, a pair of Trousers, but has since got a Greek Vestment; its probable that he has chang'd his Name, for he has already pass'd by the Name of *Thomson* and *Robinson*. Whoever takes up the said Servant, and Secures him so that his said Master may have him again shall have *Five Pounds* Reward besides all Reasonable Charges paid by

Marten Ryerson.

— *The New-York Weekly Journal, June* 15. 1741.

WHereas a large Brass Wash Kettle, and a Parrot Cage were some time ago lost out of a *Brunswick* Boat, or carried to a wrong Place by Mistake, whoever can give an Account thereof to the Printer of this Paper, so that the Owner may have them again, shall have *Five Shillings* Reward with Thanks. — *The New York Weekly Journal, June* 15. 1741. . . .

Deserted from his Majesty's Service out of the American Regiment of Foot, commanded by Col. William Gooch, and lately inlisted in West-Jersey, by Lieutenant Anthony Palmer, the two following Soldiers, viz. . . .

Thomas Fury, a Labourer, Born in the North of Ireland, about 21 years of Age, 5 Foot 10 Inches high, well-set, fair complexioned, with very fair Eye Brows, grey Eyes, and much Pockfretten : Had on when he went away, a greyish homespun Coat, with brass Buttons, the lowermost but one having the Top broke off and in other Places some off. Linnen Trowsers, and a pair of new Shoes.   He worked some time since as a Labourer in Maryland and in Chester County, but lately in Trenton : Whoever secures the said Deserters so as their Officer may have them again, shall receive Three Pounds Reward for each, and all reasonable Charges : or if any one will inform the said Officer, by whom either of them are conceal'd, so that it may be prov'd, shall receive Five Pounds Sterling for each of them, paid by   Anthony Palmer.

N. B. If either of the said Deserters will return, they shall be kindly received by their Officer, and not prosecuted. — *The Pennsylvania Gazette, July* 22. 1742. . . .

THERE was lately commited to the Goal of Sussex County, upon Delaware, two Men, suspected to be Servants, viz. John Williams, a West-Countryman, aged about 32 Years, says he came into the Western Part of Virginia with one Capt. Taylor, from Bristol; He is a lusty Man, wears his own Hair, ozenbrigs Shirt, yarn Stockings, old brown Coat, very much patch'd, an old felt Hat, leather Breeches, white homespun twiled Jacket, metal Buttons of several Sorts upon all his Cloathing. And Thomas Rogers. . . . They say they came in Freemen. The Owners (if any they have) are desired to come or send for them, in one Month's Time after this Date, otherwise they will be discharged paying their Fees.   PETER HALL, Sher.

Lewistown, March 9, 1742, 3.
     — *The Pennsylvania Gazette, March* 17, 1742, 3. . . .

Run away on the 3d of August from Benjamin Thomson, of Cohansie, the two following Servants, viz.

One John Hacket, this Country-born, short and thick, aged about 28 Years : Had on an old felt Hat, two Shirts, one tow the other ozenbrigs, old patch'd Jacket, lightish colour'd Great Coat, ozenbrigs Trowsers, good Shoes, and a Pair of Shoe-Packs.

The other named Richard Lane, this Country-born. . . . Whoever secures the said Servants, so that their Master may have them again, shall have Four Pounds Reward, and reasonable Charges, paid by

Benjamin Thompson.

N. B. They took with them two Guns, one long the other short, and a middle siz'd Dog, that goes by the Name of Gunner, and when he's travelling paces. — *The Pennsylvania Gazette, Sept.* 8, 1743. . . .

Trenton, March 25, 1745.

Taken up, about 6 Months ago, as a Runaway, and now is in *Trenton* Goal, one *John Parra*, a well set Fellow, about 24 Years of Age, and pretends to know something of the Hatter's Trade. If no Person claims him before the first Day of May next, he will be sold for defraying his Charges. *By Order of the Court.*

William Brown, Under Sheriff.
— *The Pennsylvania Gazette, April* 4, 1745. . . .

Strayed or Stolen on the 15th of April past, off the Commons of this City, a black Horse, about 15 Hands high, eight Years old last Spring, a little Star in his Forehead, branded on the near Shoulder B L. Whoever brings the said Horse to the Subscriber, shall have Ten Shillings Reward, and reasonable Charges, paid by

George Miller.
— *The Pennsylvania Gazette, June* 27, 1745. . . .

RUN away, the 24th of last Month, from Bennet Bard, of Burlington, a Mulatto Spanish Slave, named George, aged about 24 Years about 5 Feet 10 Inches high, smooth-faced, well-set, and has his Hair lately cut off, speaks tolerable good English, born at the Havanna, says he was several Years with Don Blass, and is a good Shoemaker : Had on when he went away a corded Dimity Waistcoat, Ozenbrigs Shirt and Trowsers, no Stockings, old Shoes, and a new Hat. Whoever takes up and secures said Fellow, so that his Master may have him again, shall have Forty Shillings Reward, and reasonable Charges, paid by

BENNET BARD.
— *The Pennsylvania Gazette, August* 1, 1745. . . .

Philadelphia, October 6, 1745.

Broke out of Trenton Goal, on Saturday Night last, one James Johnston, a lusty, strong built Man, about six Foot high, of a fresh Complexion, and fair insinuating Speech : He is an Irishman, and his right Name is White ; he lately ran from his Bail, and entered on Board the Dreadnought, Capt. Cunningham, who upon Application caused him to be set on Shore at Newcastle, and committed to Goal there, from whence he was brought last Thursday. Whoever shall apprehend the said Johnston and secure him, shall have Five Pounds Proclamation Money as a Reward.

William Brown, Under Sheriff.
— The Pennsylvania Gazette, Nov. 7, 1745. . . .

Philadelphia, April 14. 1748.

Run away from Samuel Lippincott of Northampton in the county of Burlington, an Irish servant Maid, named Mary Muckleroy, of a middle Stature : Had on when she went away, a blue and white striped gown, of large and small stripes, cuffed with blue, a white muslin handkerchief, an old blue quilt, a new Persian black bonnet, a new pair of calf-skin shoes, a fine Holland cap, with a cambrick border, an old black short cloak lined with Bengal, blue worsted stockings, with white clocks, a very good fine shirt, and a very good white apron. She took with her a sorrel horse, about 14 hands high, shod before, and paces very well. It is supposed there is an Irishman gone with her. Whoever takes up and secures the said woman and horse, so that they may be had again, shall have Three Pounds reward, and reasonable charges paid by

Samuel Lippincott.
— The Pennsylvania Gazette, April 16, 1748. . . .

Philadelphia, June 8. 1749.

Run away from Nicholas Bearcraft of Hunterdon County, a Black Wench, named Hecatissa alias Savina, Country born, about 27 Years of Age, short Stature, gloomy down Look, often troubl'd with the Cholick, it is thought she may be gone towards Maryland. Whoever takes up and secures said Wench, so that she may be had again, shall have Twenty Shillings Reward, and reasonable Charges, paid by

Nicholas Bearcraft.
— The Pennsylvania Journal, June 8, 1749. . . .

Run away the 7th of this instant July, from Matthew Forsyth, of Chesterfield, Burlington county, an apprentice lad, named Elisha Bullingham, by trade a house-carpenter, about 16 years of age : Had on, or took with him, a half worn felt hat, old brown drugget coat, one pair leather breeches, two ozenbrigs shirts, and two pair of ozenbrigs trousers ; his hair is newly cut off, and he has his indentures with him.　Whoever takes up and secures said apprentice, so that his master may have him again, shall have *Forty Shillings* reward, and reasonable charges, paid by me　　　　　　　　　　　　MATTHEW FORSYTH

N. B. He is supposed to be going towards New-England ; wherefore all masters of vessels, or others, are forbid to carry him off at their peril.
　　　　　　　— *The Pennsylvania Gazette, July* 13, 1749. . . .

　　　　　　　　　　　Philadelphia, February 6, 1749.

　Whereas Margaret Simkins, wife of Daniel Simkins, of Stow creek, in the county of Cumberland, and province of West-Jersey, hath, and doth elope from time to time from her said husband, to his great damage ; these are to forewarn, all persons from trusting said Margaret on his account, for he will pay no debts of her contracting from the date hereof.
　　　　　　　　　　　　　　Daniel Simkins.
　　　　　　— *The Pennsylvania Gazette, Feb.* 6, 1749–50.

William Nelson, editor, *Documents relating to the Colonial History of the State of New Jersey* (Paterson, 1895), XII, 95–600 *passim*.

---

106. Exercise of a Quaker Abolitionist's Mind (1757)

BY JOHN WOOLMAN

　Woolman was a Quaker business man and preacher, who spent his life travelling throughout the American provinces preaching and agitating against slavery.　He marks the anti-slavery agitation among the Quakers.　His journal is remarkable for its simple and lucid style, as well as for its humanity. — Bibliography : Winsor, *Narrative and Critical History*, V, 243–245. — For other extracts on Quakers, see *Contemporaries*, I, Nos. 140–142, and Nos. 98, 102 above.

FEELING the exercise in relation to a visit to the Southern Provinces to increase upon me, I acquainted our Monthly Meeting therewith, and obtained their certificate.　Expecting to go alone, one of my brothers who lived in Philadelphia, having some business in North Carolina, proposed going with me part of the way ; but as he had a view of some outward affairs, to accept of him as a companion was some difficulty with me, whereupon I had conversation with him at sundry times. At length feeling easy in my mind, I had conversation with several elderly Friends of Philadelphia on the subject, and he obtaining a certificate suitable to the occasion, we set off in the fifth month, 1757. Coming to Nottingham week-day meeting, we lodged at John Churchman's, where I met with our friend, Benjamin Buffington, from New England, who was returning from a visit to the Southern Provinces. Thence we crossed the river Susquehanna, and lodged at William Cox's in Maryland.

Soon after I entered this province a deep and painful exercise came upon me, which I often had some feeling of, since my mind was drawn toward these parts, and with which I had acquainted my brother before we agreed to join as companions. As the people in this and the Southern Provinces live much on the labor of slaves, many of whom are used hardly, my concern was that I might attend with singleness of heart to the voice of the true Shepherd, and be so supported as to remain unmoved at the faces of men.

As it is common for Friends on such a visit to have entertainment free of cost, a difficulty arose in my mind with respect to saving my money by kindness received from what appeared to me to be the gain of oppression. Receiving a gift, considered as a gift, brings the receiver under obligations to the benefactor, and has a natural tendency to draw the obliged into a party with the giver. To prevent difficulties of this kind, and to preserve the minds of judges from any bias, was that Divine prohibition : " Thou shalt not receive any gift ; for a gift blindeth the wise, and perverteth the words of the righteous." (Exod. xxiii. 8.) As the disciples were sent forth without any provision for their journey, and our Lord said the workman is worthy of his meat, their labor in the gospel was considered as a reward for their entertainment, and therefore not received as a gift ; yet, in regard to my present journey, I could not see my way clear in that respect. The difference appeared thus : the entertainment the disciples met with was from them whose hearts God had opened to receive them, from a love to them and the truth they published ; but we, considered as members of the same religious society, look upon it as a piece of civility to receive each other in such visits ; and such reception, at times, is partly in regard to reputation, and not from an inward unity of heart and spirit. Conduct is more convincing than language, and where people, by their actions, manifest that the slave-trade is not so disagreeable to their principles but that it may be encouraged, there is not a sound uniting with some Friends who visit them.

The prospect of so weighty a work, and of being so distinguished from many whom I esteemed before myself, brought me very low, and such were the conflicts of my soul that I had a near sympathy with the Prophet, in the time of his weakness, when he said : " If thou deal thus with me, kill me, I pray thee, if I have found favor in thy sight." (Num. xi. 15.)   But I soon saw that this proceeded from the want of a full resignation to the Divine will.   Many were the afflictions which attended me, and in great abasement, with many tears, my cries were to the Almighty for his gracious and fatherly assistance, and after a time of deep trial I was favored to understand the state mentioned by the Psalmist more clearly than ever I had done before ; to wit : " My soul is even as a weaned child."   (Psalm cxxxi. 2.)   Being thus helped to sink down into resignation, I felt a deliverance from that tempest in which I had been sorely exercised, and in calmness of mind went forward, trusting that the Lord Jesus Christ, as I faithfully attended to him, would be a counsellor to me in all difficulties, and that by his strength I should be enabled even to leave money with the members of society where I had entertainment, when I found that omitting it would obstruct that work to which I believed he had called me.   As I copy this after my return, I may here add, that oftentimes I did so under a sense of duty.   The way in which I did it was thus : when I expected soon to leave a Friend's house where I had entertainment, if I believed that I should not keep clear from the gain of oppression without leaving money, I spoke to one of the heads of the family privately, and desired them to accept of those pieces of silver, and give them to such of their negroes as they believed would make the best use of them ; and at other times I gave them to the negroes myself, as the way looked clearest to me.   Before I came out, I had provided a large number of small pieces for this purpose and thus offering them to some who appeared to be wealthy people was a trial both to me and them.   But the fear of the Lord so covered me at times that my way was made easier than I expected ; and few, if any, manifested any resentment at the offer, and most of them, after some conversation, accepted of them.

Ninth of fifth month. — A Friend at whose house we breakfasted setting us a little on our way, I had conversation with him, in the fear of the Lord, concerning his slaves, in which my heart was tender ; I used much plainness of speech with him, and he appeared to take it kindly. We pursued our journey without appointing meetings, being pressed in my mind to be at the Yearly Meeting in Virginia. In my travelling on the road, I often felt a cry rise from the centre of my mind, thus: "O Lord, I am a stranger on the earth, hide not thy face from me." On the 11th, we crossed the rivers Patowmack and Rapahannock, and lodged at Port Royal. On the way we had the company of a colonel of the militia, who appeared to be a thoughtful man. I took occasion to remark on the difference in general betwixt a people used to labor moderately for their living, training up their children in frugality and business, and those who live on the labor of slaves; the former, in my view, being the most happy life. He concurred in the remark, and mentioned the trouble arising from the untoward, slothful disposition of the negroes, adding that one of our laborers would do as much in a day as two of their slaves. I replied, that free men, whose minds were properly on their business, found a satisfaction in improving, cultivating, and providing for their families; but negroes, laboring to support others who claim them as their property, and expecting nothing but slavery during life, had not the like inducement to be industrious.

After some further conversation I said, that men having power too often misapplied it; that though we made slaves of the negroes, and the Turks made slaves of the Christians, I believed that liberty was the natural right of all men equally. This he did not deny, but said the lives of the negroes were so wretched in their own country that many of them lived better here than there. I replied, "There is great odds in regard to us on what principle we act;" and so the conversation on that subject ended. I may here add that another person, some time afterwards, mentioned the wretchedness of the negroes, occasioned by their intestine wars, as an argument in favor of our fetching them away for slaves. To which I replied, if compassion for the Africans, on account of their domestic troubles, was the real motive of our purchasing them, that spirit of tenderness being attended to, would incite us to use them kindly, that, as strangers brought out of affliction, their lives might be happy among us. And as they are human creatures, whose souls are as precious as ours, and who may receive the same help and comfort from the Holy Scriptures as we do, we could not omit suitable endeavors to instruct them therein; but that while we manifest by our conduct that our views in purchasing them are to advance ourselves, and while our buying captives taken in war animates those parties to push

x

on the war, and increase desolation amongst them, to say they live unhappily in Africa is far from being an argument in our favor. . . .

Having travelled through Maryland, we came amongst Friends at Cedar Creek in Virginia, on the 12th ; and the next day rode, in company with several of them, a day's journey to Camp Creek. As I was riding along in the morning, my mind was deeply affected in a sense I had of the need of Divine aid to support me in the various difficulties which attended me, and in uncommon distress of mind I cried in secret to the Most High, " O Lord be merciful, I beseech thee, to thy poor afflicted creature ! " After some time, I felt inward relief, and, soon after, a Friend in company began to talk in support of the slave-trade, and said the negroes were understood to be the offspring of Cain, their blackness being the mark which God set upon him after he murdered Abel his brother ; that it was the design of Providence they should be slaves, as a condition proper to the race of so wicked a man as Cain was. Then another spake in support of what had been said. To all which I replied in substance as follows : that Noah and his family were all who survived the flood, according to Scripture ; and as Noah was of Seth's race, the family of Cain was wholly destroyed. One of them said that after the flood Ham went to the land of Nod and took a wife ; that Nod was a land far distant, inhabited by Cain's race, and that the flood did not reach it ; and as Ham was sentenced to be a servant of servants to his brethren, these two families, being thus joined, were undoubtedly fit only for slaves. I replied, the flood was a judgment upon the world for their abominations, and it was granted that Cain's stock was the most wicked, and therefore unreasonable to suppose that they were spared. As to Ham's going to the land of Nod for a wife, no time being fixed, Nod might be inhabited by some of Noah's family before Ham married a second time ; moreover the text saith " That all flesh died that moved upon the earth." (Gen. vii. 21.) I further reminded them how the prophets repeatedly declare " that the son shall not suffer for the iniquity of the father, but every one be answerable for his own sins." I was troubled to perceive the darkness of their imaginations, and in some pressure of spirit said, " The love of ease and gain are the motives in general of keeping slaves, and men are wont to take hold of weak arguments to support a cause which is unreasonable. I have no interest on either side, save only the interest which I desire to have in the truth. I believe liberty is their right, and as I see they are not only deprived of it, but treated in other respects with inhumanity in many places, I believe He who is a refuge for the oppressed will, in his own time, plead their cause, and happy will it be for such as walk in uprightness before him." And thus our conversation ended. . . .

The sense I had of the state of the churches brought a weight of distress upon me. The gold to me appeared dim, and the fine gold changed, and though this is the case too generally, yet the sense of it in these parts hath in a particular manner borne heavy upon me. It appeared to me that through the prevailing of the spirit of this world the minds of many were brought to an inward desolation, and instead of the spirit of meekness, gentleness, and heavenly wisdom, which are the necessary companions of the true sheep of Christ, a spirit of fierceness and the love of dominion too generally prevailed. . . .

The prospect of a way being open to the same degeneracy, in some parts of this newly settled land of America, in respect to our conduct towards the negroes, hath deeply bowed my mind in this journey, and though briefly to relate how these people are treated is no agreeable work, yet, after often reading over the notes I made as I travelled, I find my mind engaged to preserve them. Many of the white people in those provinces take little or no care of negro marriages; and when negroes marry after their own way, some make so little account of those marriages that with views of outward interest they often part men from their wives by selling them far asunder, which is common when estates are sold by executors at vendue. Many whose labor is heavy being followed at their business in the field by a man with a whip, hired for that purpose, have in common little else allowed but one peck of Indian corn and some salt, for one week, with a few potatoes; the potatoes they commonly raise by their labor on the first day of the week. The correction ensuing on their disobedience to overseers, or slothfulness in business, is often very severe, and sometimes desperate.

Men and women have many times scarcely clothes sufficient to hide their nakedness, and boys and girls ten and twelve years old are often quite naked amongst their master's children. Some of our Society, and some of the society called Newlights, use some endeavors to instruct those they have in reading; but in common this is not only neglected, but disapproved. These are the people by whose labor the other inhabitants are in a great measure supported, and many of them in the luxuries of life. These are the people who have made no agreement to serve us, and who have not forfeited their liberty that we know of. These are the souls for whom Christ died, and for our conduct towards them we must answer before Him who is no respecter of persons. They who know the only true God, and Jesus Christ whom he hath sent, and are thus acquainted with the merciful, benevolent, gospel spirit, will therein perceive that the indignation of God is kindled against oppression and cruelty, and in beholding the great distress of so numerous a people will find cause for mourning.

John Woolman, *Journal* (edited by John G. Whittier, Boston, 1871), 99–110 *passim.*

---

107. The Wretchedness of White Servants (1770)

BY WILLIAM EDDIS

Eddis was surveyor of customs at Annapolis. At the Revolution he remained loyal to England, fleeing from Maryland during the course of the war. — Bibliography : Channing and Hart, *Guide*, § 133. — This account may be compared with Alsop's in 1666 (*Contemporaries*, I, No. 76), and with No. 105 above.

PERSONS in a state of servitude are under four distinct denominations : negroes, who are the entire property of their respective owners : convicts, who are transported from the mother country for a limited term : indented servants, who are engaged for five years previous to their leaving England ; and free-willers, who are supposed, from their situation, to possess superior advantages. . . .

Persons convicted of felony, and in consequence transported to this continent, if they are able to pay the expence of passage, are free to pursue their fortune agreeably to their inclinations or abilities. Few, however, have means to avail themselves of this advantage. These unhappy beings are, generally, consigned to an agent, who classes them suitably to their real or supposed qualifications ; advertises them for sale, and disposes of them, for seven years, to planters, to mechanics, and to such as choose to retain them for domestic service. Those who survive the term of servitude, seldom establish their residence in this country : the stamp of infamy is too strong upon them to be easily erased : they either return to Europe, and renew their former practices ; or, if they have fortunately imbibed habits of honesty and industry, they remove to a distant situation, where they may hope to remain unknown, and be enabled to pursue with credit every possible method of becoming useful members of society. . . .

The generality of the inhabitants in this province are very little acquainted with those fallacious pretences, by which numbers are continually induced to embark for this continent. On the contrary, they too generally conceive an opinion that the difference is merely nominal between the indented servant and the convicted felon : nor will they readily believe that people, who had the least experience in life, and whose characters were unexceptionable, would abandon their friends and families, and their ancient connexions, for a servile situation, in a remote appendage to the British Empire. From this persuasion they rather consider the convict as the more profitable servant, his term being for seven, the latter only for five years ; and, I am sorry to observe, that there are but few instances wherein they experience different treatment. Negroes being a property for life, the death of slaves, in the prime of youth or strength, is a material loss to the proprietor ; they are, therefore, almost in every instance, under more comfortable circumstances than the miserable European, over whom the rigid planter exercises an inflexible severity. They are strained to the utmost to perform their allotted labour ; and, from a prepossession in many cases too justly founded, they are supposed to be receiving only the just reward which is due to repeated offences. . . .

The situation of the free-willer is, in almost every instance, more to be lamented than either that of the convict or the indented servant ; the deception which is practised on those of this description being attended with circumstances of greater duplicity and cruelty. Persons under this denomination are received under express conditions that, on their arrival in America, they are to be allowed a stipulated number of days to dispose of themselves to the greatest advantage. They are told, that their services will be eagerly solicited, in proportion to their abilities ; that their reward will be adequate to the hazard they encounter by courting fortune in a distant region ; and that the parties with whom they engage will readily advance the sum agreed on for their passage ; which, being averaged at about nine pounds sterling, they will speedily be enabled to repay, and to enjoy, in a state of liberty, a comparative situation of ease and affluence. . . .

. . . It is, therefore, an article of agreement with these deluded victims, that if they are not successful in obtaining situations, on their own terms, within a certain number of days after their arrival in the country, they are then to be sold, in order to defray the charges of passage, at the discretion of the master of the vessel, or the agent to whom he is consigned in the province.

You are also to observe, that servants imported, even under this favourable description, are rarely permitted to set their feet on shore, until they have absolutely formed their respective engagements. As soon as the ship is stationed in her birth, planters, mechanics, and others, repair on board ; the adventurers of both sexes are exposed to view, and very few are happy enough to make their own stipulations, some very extraordinary qualifications being absolutely requisite to obtain this distinction ; and even when this is obtained, the advantages are by no means equivalent to their sanguine expectations. The residue, stung with disappointment and vexation, meet with horror the moment which dooms them, under an appearance of equity, to a limited term of slavery. Character is of little importance ; their abilities not being found of a superior nature, they are sold as soon as their term of election is expired, apparel and provision being their only compensation ; till, on the expiration of five tedious laborious years, they are restored to a dearly purchased freedom.

William Eddis, *Letters from America* (London, 1792), 63–75 *passim.*

———◆———

108. "Desire of Importing Palatines" (1774)

BY GEORGE WASHINGTON

Washington was perhaps the richest and most business-like of the southern planters. The system of importing foreigners, who were not allowed to leave the vessel till some employer had paid their passage, continued till about 1820. — Bibliography of Washington, No. 195 below. — On Germans in America, see *Contemporaries*, I, No. 163.

MR. Young, hearing me express a desire of importing Palatines to settle on my lands on the Ohio, tells me, that, in discoursing of this matter in your company, you suggested an expedient, which might probably be attended with success ; and that if I inclined to adopt it, you wished to be informed before the sailing of your ship.

The desire of seating and improving my lands on the Ohio, is founded on interested as well as political views. But the intention of importing Palatines for the purpose was more the effect of sudden thought, than mature consideration, because I am totally unacquainted with the manner, as well as the expense of doing it ; and I was led into the notion principally from a report of either this or some other ship of yours being blamed, for not taking an offered freight of these Germans at forty shillings sterling. I was thus induced to think if this charge was not much accumulated by other expenses, that I could fall on no better expedient to settle my lands with industrious people, than by such an importation.

The terms upon which I have thought of importing Palatines, or people from Ireland, or Scotland, are these ; to import them at my expense, where they are unable to transport themselves, into the Potomac River, and from hence to the Ohio ; to have them, in the first case, engaged to me under indenture ; in the second, by some other contract equally valid, to become tenants upon the terms hereafter mentioned ; as without these securities, I would not encounter the expense, trouble, and hazard of such an importation.

But to make matters as easy and agreeable as possible to these emigrants, I will engage, on my part, that the indentures shall be considered in no other light, than as a security for reimbursing to me every expense I am under, with interest, in importing them, removing them to the land, and supporting them there, till they can raise a crop for their own subsistence . . . I must, for my own safety, consider them as jointly bound for this payment, till the expiration of the indented terms, otherwise I must be an inevitable loser by every death or other accident ; whilst they cannot, in the worst light, be considered as more than servants at large during the indented term. . . .

Having thus exhibited a general view of my design, I shall now be obliged to you, Sir, to inform me with as much precision as you can, what certainty there is that your ship will go to Holland ; what probability there is of her getting Palatines, if she does go ; when they may be expected in this country ; what would be the freight ; and, as near as you can judge, the whole incidental expense attending each person delivered at Alexandria ; and, moreover, whether it would be expected, that the whole of these charges, including freight, should be paid down immediately on the arrival of the ship here, as it must appear rather hard to make a certain provision for an uncertain event.

It may not be amiss further to observe, that I see no prospect of these people being restrained in the smallest degree, either in their civil or religious principles ; which I take notice of, because these are privileges, which mankind are solicitous to enjoy, and upon which emigrants must be anxious to be informed.

George Washington, *Writings* (edited by Jared Sparks, Boston, 1834), II, 383–386 *passim*.

PART V

INTERCOLONIAL, 1689–1764

===

CHAPTER XVII—THE FRENCH COLONIES

109. Foundation of Louisiana (1700–1703)

BY BÉNARD DE LA HARPE (1723)

(Translated by B. F. French, 1851)

La Harpe, supposed to be the compiler of this narrative, was a French officer of distinction who came to Louisiana in 1718; later he served under Bienville. — Bibliography: Winsor, *Narrative and Critical History*, V, 63–85; Channing and Hart, *Guide*, § 91. — On earlier French discoveries and colonies, see *Contemporaries*, I, ch. v.

. . . ON the 28th May [1700], M. d'Iberville set sail for France, and on the same day M. de Bienville took command of the fort on the Mississippi. On the 29th he dispatched M. de Saint Denis to explore the country in the Red River, and to watch the Spaniards. On the 30th May [1701], the Enflammée of twenty-six guns, commanded by M. de la Ronde, arrived at Ship Island. Among the passengers was M. Sagan, a traveller from Canada, who had presented a memoir to the minister, M. de Pontchartrain, assuring him that he had travelled all over the Mississippi, and had found mines of gold on its banks ; and that the Indians had worked them. The minister, putting faith in his statements, granted to M. Sagan some privileges, and ordered M. de Sauvolle to supply him with twenty-four pirogues and one hundred Canadians, to accompany him to the Missouri.

On the 22d August, M. de Sauvolle died at Biloxi, and M. de Bienville was left sole commander of the colony.

On the 16th September, a party of Chactas arrived at Biloxi to demand of the French some troops to assist them to fight the Chicachas. The Chactas nation contained forty villages, and over five thousand warriors. On the 25th October, twenty Mobileans arrived at Fort Biloxi. This nation was situated about one hundred and forty leagues up that river, and contained about four hundred men. On the 18th December, a shallop arrived from Pensacola with the news that MM. d'Iberville and Serigny had arrived there with the King's ships, the Renommée of fifty guns, and the Palmier of forty-four guns. This news spread joy in the garrison, as it had then been living on corn for more than three months. It had lost by sickness upwards of sixty men, leaving only one hundred and fifty persons in the colony.

M. de Bienville received orders by the shallop to evacuate Biloxi, and remove to Mobile river. On the 5th January, 1701, M. de Bienville took up his march for Mobile river, leaving but twenty men under the command of M. de Boisbriant to man the fort. At Dauphin Island, M. de Bienville had an interview with MM. de Serigny and Chateaugué, who had arrived there with a detachment of sailors and workmen, to build a magazine for the reception of the goods and provisions which had been brought from France. On the 16th M. de Bienville commenced a settlement on the Mobile river, about eighteen leagues from the sea. On the 10th M. le Sueur returned from his expedition to the Scioux, with two hundred thousand pounds weight of copper ore.

The following is an extract taken from his Journal : —

" Having arrived in the colony in December, 1699, with thirty workmen, he set out for the Tamarois in June, 1700. He stopped at the mouth of the Missouri river, and from thence proceeded to the Illinois river, where he was joined by three Canadian travellers, who brought him a letter from Father Marest, a Jesuit from the mission house of ' L'Immaculée Conception de la Sainte Vierge aux Illinois.'

" At twenty-two leagues above the Illinois, he passed a small river, which he named the Buffalo : and on going nine leagues further he met a party of Canadians descending the Mississippi, returning to the Illinois. On the 30th July, he met seventeen Scioux in seven canoes, going to avenge the death of three Scioux by the Illinois, one of whom had been burnt, and the other two killed at Tamarois, a few days before his arrival at this village. He promised the Chief of the Illinois to pacify the Scioux if they should come to make war on him. He presented to the Chief of the party some merchandise to induce him to return to his nation. He told him that the King of France did not wish them to make war, and if he would desist he should be supplied with every thing necessary. The Chief accepted the presents, and promised to obey the King. . . .

" On the 1st September, he passed the Ouisconsin river, which is about half a league wide at its mouth. On ascending this river about forty-five leagues, he found a portage of more than a mile in length, consisting in part of marshy ground, from which a little stream took its rise and flowed into the Puan bay, inhabited by a great number of Indian tribes, who trade in furs to Canada. . . .

"From the 10th to the 14th, M. de Sueur travelled seventeen leagues and a half, passed the river Raisin, and also on the same day a great river coming from the North called the Bon-Secours, on account of the great number of buffalo, deer, bears and roebucks found there. Three leagues from the banks of this river is a lead mine, and at seven leagues above, on the same side, he passed another river, in the neighborhood of which he discovered a copper mine, from which he took sixty pounds of ore in a former voyage : but to make it of any value, a peace must first be made between the Scioux and the Outagamis. At a league and a-half further to the North-West is a lake, six leagues long and more than a league in width, called Lake Pepin. . . .

" . . . On the 15th he passed a small river, and saw several canoes descending, filled with Indians. He heard them make a noise similar to that just before they are going to fall upon their enemy ; and, having placed his men behind some trees, he ordered them not to fire until the word of command was given. The chief of the party, after making some observations, advanced with the calumet, (which is a sign of peace among the Indians,) and said that, not having seen before any Frenchmen navigating the Mississippi in boats like theirs, they took them to be English, and raised the war-cry.

"M. le Sueur told them that the King of France, of whom they had heard so much in Canada, had sent him to settle in the country, and he wished all the nations who inhabited it, as well as those under his protection, to live in peace. . . .

" . . . He then entered Blue River [Minnesota], so called from some mines of blue earth which he found on its banks. At this place he met nine Scioux, who told him that this river came from the country of the Scioux of the West. He built a post here, but finding that his establishment did not please the Scioux of the East as well as the neighboring tribes, he had to tell them that his intentions were only to trade in beaver skins, although his real purpose was to explore the mines in this country, which he had discovered some years before.

"He then presented them with some powder, balls, knives and tobacco, and invited them to come to his fort, as soon as it was constructed, and he would tell them the intentions of the King his master. The Scioux of the West have, according to the accounts of those of the East, more than a thousand huts.

"They do not use canoes or cultivate the land, but wander in the prairies between the upper Mississippi and the Missouri, and live by hunting.

"All the Scioux say they have three souls, and that after death the good one goes to a warm country, the bad one to a cold country, and the third watches the body. They are very expert with their bows. Polygamy is very common among them. They are extremely jealous, and sometimes fight duels for their wives. They make their huts out of buffalo skins, sewed together, and carry them with them. Two or three families generally live together. They are great smokers. They swallow the smoke, but some time after they force it up from their stomach through their nose. . . .

"On the 1st December, they invited M. le Sueur to a great feast which they had prepared for him. They made a speech, and presented him with a slave and a sack of oats. . . ."

On the 18th March, 1702, M. d'Iberville arrived at Dauphin Island, in the frigate "Palmier," which he brought into port without any difficulty, there being twenty-one feet or more of water at the pass. On the 19th, M. de la Salle arrived with his family at For[t] Mobile, which had just been finished, and the head-quarters of the colony about to be removed there from Dauphin [Massacre] Island. On the 25th, M. de Tonty, who had been sent by M. d'Iberville on a mission to the Chactas and Chicachas, arrived at Mobile, bringing with him some of the principal Chiefs of those nations, to make a treaty of peace. By presents and entreaties M. d'Iberville made them agree to live in peace together. On the 27th, M. d'Iberville returned to Dauphin Island, and from thence he went to Pensacola. On the 13th April, M. Dugue arrived with a transport ladened with provisions. On the 31st, M. d'Iberville and de Serigny departed for France. On the 12th May, eight Alibamon Chiefs arrived at Mobile to consult with M. de Bienville whether they should continue to war with the Chicachas, Tomes, and Mobilians. He advised them to make a peace, and gave them some presents for this purpose. On the 24th June, a Spanish shallop arrived from Pensacola, on board of which was Don José de Roblas, Captain of Infantry, and a son of the nurse of Count de Montezuma, bringing a letter from Francisco Martin, Governor of Pensacola, asking to be supplied with some provisions, which M. de Bienville granted.

On the 10th August, M. de Bienville was informed that M. St. Denis and some Canadians had invaded the territory of our allies to capture slaves, which he ordered to be restored.

On the 1st October, M. Davion, missionary, and Father Limoge, a Jesuit, arrived from the Mississippi, to give notice that one of their brethren and three Frenchmen had been murdered on the Yasous river, by two young Courois, who had acted as their guides.

On the 11th November, Don Francisco Martin arrived from Pensacola, with the news that France and Spain were at war with England, and asked for a supply of arms and powder, which was given him.

On the 28th, two shallops, with two Spanish officers, arrived at the fort from St. Augustine, Florida, and brought a letter from Don Joseph de Souniga y Serda, Governor of that place, informing M. de Bienville that it was besieged by fourteen English vessels and two thousand Indians. He further requested that a small vessel might be sent to the Viceroy of Mexico, informing him of what had happened. M. de Bienville sent him one hundred muskets and five hundred pounds of powder.

Bénard de la Harpe, *Historical Journal of the Establishment of the French in Louisiana*, in B. F. French, *Historical Collections of Louisiana* (New York, 1851), Part III, 19–28 *passim*.

---

110. Danger from the French Mississippi Settlements (1718)

BY LIEUTENANT-GOVERNOR ALEXANDER SPOTSWOOD

Spotswood was an efficient governor of Virginia; his letters and state papers are of great historical value. — Bibliography: Winsor, *Narrative and Critical History*, IV, 196–202; Channing and Hart, *Guide*, § 90.

. . . HAVING of a long time endeavour'd to informe myself of ye scituation of the French to the Westward of Us, and the Advantages they Reap by an uninterrupted Communication along ye Lake, I shall here take the Liberty of communicating my thoughts to Yo'r Lord'ps, both of the dangers to w'ch his Majesty's Plantations may be exposed by this new Acquisition of our Neighbours, and how the same may be best prevented. I have often regretted that after so many Years as these Countrys have been Seated, no Attempts have been made to discover the Sources of Our Rivers, nor to Establishing Correspond-

ence w'th those Nations of Indians to ye Westw'd of Us, even after the
certain Knowledge of the Progress made by French in Surrounding us
w'th their Settlements. . . .

Having also informed myself of that extensive Communication w'ch
the French maintain by means of their water Carriage from the River
St. Lawrence to the mouth of Mississippi, I shall here set down the
route from Montreal, (a place well known and distinguished in ye ordinary Mapps,) to Maville, their Chief Town in their New Settlement
of Louisiana, according to the account given me by three Fr. Men, who
had often Travelled that way, and were taken in a late Expedition under
the Command of the Gov'r and L't-Gov'r's Sons, of Montreal, and is as
follows :

	FR. LEAGES.
From Montreal up St. Lawrence River, to Fort, Frontenac, at the Entra[n]ce of Lac Ontario, is	60
The Length of Lac Ontario, which is Navigable,	60
Up the River to the Falls of Niagara, where there is a necessity of Land Carriage,	3
From Niagara to the Lake Erie,	100
Up the River Mic., w'ch falls into Lake Erie,	60
From the River Mic. to the River Occabacke, a Land Carriage of	3
Down the River Occaback till it falls into the River Mississippi,	200
Thence down Mississippi to Maville,	360

By this Communication and the forts they have already built, the
Brittish Plantations are in a manner Surrounded by their Commerce
w'th the numerous Nations of Indians seated on both sides of the
Lakes ; they may not only Engross the whole Skin Trade, but may,
when they please, Send out such Bodys of Indians on the back of these
Plantations as may greatly distress his Maj'ty's Subjects here, And should
they multiply their Settlem'ts along these Lakes, so as to joyn their
Dominions of Canada to their new Colony of Louisiana, they might even
possess themselves of any of these Plantations they pleased. Nature,
'tis true, has formed a Barrier for us by that long Chain of Mountains
w'ch run from the back of South Carolina as far as New York, and w'ch
are only passable in some few places, but even that Natural Defence
may prove rather destructive to us, if they are not possessed by us
before they are known to them. To prevent the dangers w'ch Threaten

his Maj'ty's Dominions here from the growing power of these Neighbors, nothing seems to me of more consequence than that now while the Nations are at peace, and while the French are yet uncapable of possessing all that vast Tract w'ch lies on the back of these Plantations, we should attempt to make some Settlements on ye Lakes, and at the same time possess our selves of those passes of the great Mountains, w'ch are necessary to preserve a Communication w'th such Settlements.

As the Lake Erie lyes almost in the Center of the French Communication, and, as I observed before, not above 5 days' March from the late discovered passage of Our great Mountains, That seems the most proper for forming a Settlement on, by w'ch we shall not only share w'th the French in the Commerce and friendship of those Indians inhabiting the banks of the Lakes, but may be able to cutt off or disturb the communication between Canada and Louisiana, if a War should happen to break out. If such a Settlement were once made, I can't see how the ffrench could dispute our Right of Possession, the Law of Nations giving a Title to the first Occupant, and should they think fitt to dispossess us by force, We are nearer to Support than they to attack. . . .

. . . I . . . shall only here apply my Self to what I conceive more immediately necessary, w'ch are that of the Mississippi Settlement, and the Importance of adding St. Augustine to the British Acquisitions on this Continent. As to the first, there can be no doubt but that the French Settlement on Mississippi will, (without timely precautions,) greatly effect both the Trade and Safety of these, his Maj'ty's Plantations. Tobacco, Rice and other Commoditys, w'th w'ch the greatest part of Europe is now supplyed from these Plantations, will, no doubt, be cultivated and produced in this new French Settlement, and they w'll become our Rivals in that Trade in all fforeign Mark'ts. By this means his Maj'ty's Subjects employed here in that Manufacture will be discouraged; the British Navigation must decrease in proportion as the French advance in that Trade, and the Revenue of the Crown, of course, very much diminished. The danger w'ch threatens these, his Maj'ty's Plantations, from this new Settlement, is also very considerable, for by the Communication w'ch the French may maintain between Canada and Mississippi by the conveniency of the Lakes, they do, in a manner, surround all the British Plantations. They have it in their power, by these Lakes and the many Rivers running into them and into the Mississippi to engross all the Trade of the Indian Nations, w'ch are now supplyed from hence. They may, by possessing themselves of the

Passes of the Great Mountains, w'ch ly between Us and the Lakes, Either by themselves or their Indians, fall upon and over-run w'ch of these Provinces they think fit, And seeing, by their late Siezure of Pensacola from the Spaniards, their design seems to be to extend their Dominions Eastward from Mississippi towards South Carolina, It is certainly the British Interest to put a stop to their Advancing any further that way, w'ch, in my Opinion, w'll be best Effected by possessing our selves w'th some places on the Coast of Florida, and forming a Settlement as near as can be to cramp their's, w'ch leads me to consider the other part Yo'r Lord'ps desire to be informed in, vizt : The Importance of taking St. Augustine from the Spaniards.

St. Augustine is a small Fort on the North East part of the Coast of Florida, w'th a Village adjoyning inhabited by about 2 or 300 Spaniards. . . . This place may be of vast Consequence to Britain whenever a War shall happen with either of these Crowns, it being impossible for their Ships to pass through the Gulph without being discovered from either one side or the other, and, therefore, lyable to become prize to any of our Men of War or Privateers that may be placed on y't Station ; So that, in Case of a Rupture w'th France, the whole Trade of their Mississippi Colony may, by that means, be destroyed. But I would also humbly propose, that besides the taking of St. Augustine, the small Fort, or rather Battery of St. Mark, may be attempted. . . . From hence it is I would propose to forme a Settlement to check that of y't of Mississippi, and to extend Westward upon it, whereby we might Share w'th them at least in the Indian Trade, and keep a Balla. of those Indian Nations in our Interest, and in Case of a War, be able to annoy them from thence. Besides these two Settlements, it may not be improbable but that a good Harbour may be found among ye Islands at the Cape of Florida, w'ch might be a proper Station for Men of War or Privateers to interrupt the Spanish or French Trade from the Bay of Mexico, that Promontory lying almost in sight of the Havanna, and no other way for their Ships to return to Europe but through that Passage. This would also prove a security to our own Trade from Jamaica, w'ch, for want of places of retreat for Merchant-Men and Cruising Ships on that Coast, are often exposed to the danger of Enemy's Privateers, as well as to Storms w'ch frequently happen there. That your Lord'ps may have a Clearer Idea of the places I have now been describing, I herewith transmit a Draught of the River Mississippi and the Rivers Communicating with it and also of the Sea

Coasts along the Bay of Mexico and Gulph of Florida. . . . In it yo'r Lord'ps w'll see the many Navigable Rivers that branch out from the Mississippi towards the English Plantations, and the Situation of the several Indian Nations w'th whom both we and the French Trade. Yo'r Lord'ps w'll thereby observe that most of those Nations are more contiguous to the French Settlements than the English, and have been hitherto kept in our Interest by being more plentifully supplyed with Goods from the English than the French could afford them. I am also here to observe that the French have of late begun a traffique with the Coosta Indians, living upon a River of that name not far from the Cherokees, and it is to be feared they will soon gett footing too among the latter, the people of So. Carolina having already abandoned y't Trade . . .

The Official Letters of Alexander Spotswood (Virginia Historical Society, *Collections*, New Series, II, Richmond, 1882), II, 295–331 *passim.*

---

111. The French and the Fur Trade (1724)

BY SURVEYOR-GENERAL CADWALLADER COLDEN

Colden was surveyor-general of New York, becoming later lieutenant-governor. He is author of a valuable book on the Five Nations of Indians. In his later years he was bitterly hated by provincials on account of his enforcement of English measures. — Bibliography: Tyler, *American Literature*, II, 213–215 ; Smith, *History of New York*, Appendix, ch. iii; Channing and Hart, *Guide*, §§ 105, 133.

IT has of late been generally believed, that the Inhabitants of the Province of *New-York* are so advantageously situated, with respect to the *Indian Trade*, and enjoy so many Advantages as to Trade in general, that it is in their Power not only to rival the *French* of *Canada*, who have almost entirely engrossed the Furr-Trade of *America*, but that it is impossible for the *French* to carry on that Trade in Competition with the People of this Province. The enquiring into the Truth of this Proposition, may not only be of some Consequence, as to the Riches and Honour of the *British Nation*, (for it is well known how valuable the Furr-Trade of *America* is) but likewise as to the Safety of all the *British Colonies* in *North-America*. *New-France* (as the *French* now claim) extends from the Mouth of the River *Misissippi*, to the Mouth of the River *St. Lawrence*, by which the *French* plainly show their Intention of enclosing the *British Settlements*, and cutting us off from all Commerce with the numerous Nations of *Indians*, that are every where settled over the vast Continent of *North-America*. The *English* in *America* have too good Reason to apprehend such a Design, when they see the *French* King's Geographer publish a Map, by which he has set Bounds to the *British Empire* in *America*, and has taken in many of the *English Settlements* both in *South-Carolina* and *New-York*, within these Boundaries of *New-France*. And the good Services they intend us, with the *Indians*, but too plainly appears at this Day, by the *Indian War* now carried on against *New-England*. . . .

The Method of carrying Goods upon the Rivers of *North-America*, into all the small Branches, and other Land, from the Branches of one River to the Branches of another, was learned from the *Indians*, and is the only Method practicable through such large Forests and Deserts as the Traders pass thro', in carrying from one Nation to another, it is this; the *Indians* make a long narrow Boat, made of the Bark of the Birch-tree, the Parts of which they join very neatly. One of these Canoes that can carry a Dozen Men, can itself be easily carried upon two Men's Shoulders; so that when they have gone as far by Water as they can (which is further than is easily to be imagined, because their loaded Canoes don't sink six Inches into the Water) they unload their Canoes, and carry both Goods and Canoes upon their Shoulders over Land, into the nearest Branch of the River they intend to follow. Thus, the *French* have an easy Communication with all the Countries bordering upon the River of *St. Lawrence*, and its Branches, with all the Countries bordering upon these In-land Seas, and the Rivers which empty themselves into these Seas, and can thereby carry their Burdens of Merchandize thro' all these large Countries, which could not by any other means than Water-carriage be carried thro' so vast a Tract of Land.

This, however, but half finishes the View the *French* have, as to their Commerce in *North-America*. Many of the Branches of the River *Mississippi* come so near to the Branches of several of the Rivers which empty themselves into the great Lakes, that in several Places there is but a short Land-Carriage from the one to the other. As soon as they have got into the River *Mississippi*, they open to themselves as large a Field for Traffick in the southern Parts of *North-America*, as was before mentioned with respect to the northern Parts. If one considers the Length of this River, and its numerous Branches, he must say, *That by means of this River, and the Lakes, there is opened to his View*

Y

such a Scene of in-land Navigation as cannot be. parallel'd in any other Part of the World.

The *French* have, with much Industry, settled small Colonies, and built stockaded Forts at all the considerable Passes between the Lakes, except between *Cataracui Lake* (called by the *French Ontario*) and *Lake Erie*, one of our Five Nations of *Indians*, whom we call *Sennekas*, (and the *French Sonontouans*) having hitherto refused them leave to erect any Buildings there.

The *French* have been indefatigable in making Discoveries, and carrying on their Commerce with Nations, of whom the *English* know nothing but what they see in the *French* Maps and Books.   The Barrenness of the Soil, and the Coldness of the Climate of *Canada*, obliges the greatest number of the Inhabitants to seek their living by travelling among the *Indians*, or by trading with those that do travel. . . .

But notwithstanding all these Advantages, the *French* labour under Difficulties that no Art or Industry can remove.   The Mouth of the River of *St. Lawrence*, and more especially the Bay of *St. Lawrence*, lies so far North, and is thereby so often subject to tempestuous Weather and thick Fogs, that the Navigation there is very dangerous, and never attempted but during the Summer Months.   The Wideness of this Bay, together with the many strong Currents that run in it, the many Shelves, and sunken Rocks that are every where spread over both the Bay and River, and the want of Places for anchoring in the Bay, all increase the Danger of this Navigation ; so that a Voyage to *Canada* is justly esteem'd much more dangerous than to any other Part of *America*. . . .

After they pass *Monreal* they have a strong Stream against them till they come near the Lakes ; so that in all that, which is about one hundred and fifty Miles in Length, they force their Canoes forward with setting Poles, or drag them with Ropes along shoar ; and at five or six different Places in that way the River falls over Rocks with such Force, that they are obliged to unload their Canoes, and carry them upon their Shoulders.   They never make this Voyage from *Monreal* to *Cataracui* in less than twenty Days, and frequently, twice that Time is necessary.

Now we are come so far as the Lake, my Design leads me no further, for at this Lake all the *far Indians*, that go to *Canada*, must pass by our Traders.   And from thence the Road to the *Indian Countries* is the same from *Albany* that it is from *Monreal*.

Besides these Difficulties in the Transportation, the *French* labour under greater in the purchasing of the principal Goods proper for the *Indian*

Market ; for the most considerable and most valuable Part of their Cargo consists in *Strouds, Duffils, Blankets,* and other *Woollens,* which are bought at a much cheaper Rate in *England* than in *France.* . . .

From *Albany* the *Indian Traders* commonly carry their Goods sixteen Miles over Land, to the *Mohawks River* at *Schenechtady,* the Charge of which Carriage is *Nine Shillings New - York* Money, or *Five Shillings Sterling* each Waggon-Load. From *Schenechtady* they carry them in Canoes up the *Mohawks River,* to the Carrying-place between the *Mohawks River,* and the River which runs into the *Oneida Lake* ; which Carrying-place between is only three Miles long, except in very dry Weather, when they are obliged to carry them two Miles further. From thence they go with the Current down the *Onondaga River* to the *Cataracui Lake.* . . .

When this Country (the Province of *New - York*) came first under the Crown of *Great-Britain,* our *Five Nations* of *Indians* were mortal Enemies of the *French* at *Canada,* and were in a continual War with them, and all the *Nations* of *Indians* round the Lakes ; so that then it was not safe for the *English* to travel further than the Countries of the *Five Nations* ; nor would our *Indians* permit the *far Indians* (with whom they had constant War) to pass thro' their Countries to *Albany.* Besides, the *Five Nations* of *Indians* were at that time so numerous. (consisting of ten times the Number of fighting Men they now do) that the Trade with them alone was very considerable for so young and small a Colony. . . .

About this Time the Revolution happen'd in *Great-Britain,* which was succeeded by a War between *Great-Britain* and *France.* In *February,* 16$\frac{89}{90}$ a Party of three hundred Men, consisting of equal Numbers of *French* and *Indians,* surprized *Schenechtady* in the Night-time, when the poor People were in their Beds, in the greatest Security, where they barbarously murdered sixty-three Men, Women, and Children, in cold Blood, laid the Village in Ashes, and then retir'd, without reaping any other Advantage besides their cruel Revenge on innocent People, for the Mischief *our Indians* had done them. This rais'd a cruel War between the two Colonies, in which there was much Mischief done, and Blood shed, without any Advantage to either side. . . .

King *William*'s Peace put an End to this War ; but the Peace lasted so short a while, that the People of this Province hardly had time to re-settle their Farms on the Frontiers, which they had deserted in the Time of the War, much less to adventure trading in the *Indian Coun-*

tries, so lately the Scene of so much Cruelty. But both Colonies having now an Abhorrence of the Cruelties of the last War, agreed on a kind of Neutrality for the *Indians*, during Queen *Anne*'s War, in which Time we lost much ground with our own *Indians :* For the *French* having learn'd, by dear Experience, that it was not possible for them to conquer *our Five Indian Nations*, resolv'd to try all Means to gain their Affections, and in this Art the *French* are always more successful than in that of War ; and the *English* failing in two ill-concerted Expeditions against *Canada*, the *Indians* lost much of the Opinion they had of the *English* Power and Valour. . . .

As soon as the Peace was proclaim'd, an open Trade with *Monreal* was carried on with such Earnestness, that *Monreal* was fill'd with *Indian Goods*, and *Albany* exhausted ; by which means *Monreal* became the principal, if not the only *Indian Market*, and the *Indians* depended entirely on the *French* for what they wanted. . . .

. . . From the whole, it seems plain, that any Difficulties and Disadvantages this Province has been under, have only proceeded from the Wars, which have continued since the first settling of the Province, to the beginning of the last general Peace. But now, that not only *this Province*, but likewise our *six Nations* of *Indians* are at Peace, and in Amity, both with the *French*, and all the *Indian Nations* with whom we can have any Commerce, these Difficulties are all remov'd, and we now enjoy the most favourable Time, that at any time can be hoped for, in order to extend the *British Commerce* in *North-America*, while the *French* not only labour under the Difficulties which I have shown to be inseparable from the Situation of their Colony, but likewise under another Disadvantage, (not before taken notice of) by the Furr-Trade of *Canada* being restrain'd to one Company. . . .

Cadwallader Colden, *Papers relating to* . . . *the* . . . *Encouragement of the Indian Trade*, etc., in his *History of the Five Indian Nations of Canada* (London, 1747), second pagination, 25–40 *passim*.

---

112. The Government of Canada (1749)

BY PROFESSOR PETER KALM

(Translated by John Reinhold Forster, 1771)

Kalm was a Swedish botanist who travelled in America during the years 1748–1751. He was a painstaking and accurate observer. — Bibliography : Winsor, *Narrative and Critical History*, IV, 367–368, V, 244 ; Channing and Hart, *Guide*, § 89.

October the 5th.   THE governor-general at *Quebec* is, as I have already mentioned before, the chief commander in *Canada*. Next to him is the intendant at *Quebec*; then follows the governor of *Montreal,* and after him the governor of *Trois Rivieres*. The intendant has the greatest power next to the governor-general; he pays all the money of government, and is president of the board of finances, and of the court of justice in this country. He is, however, under the governor-general; for if he refuses to do any thing to which he seems obliged by his office, the governor-general can give him orders to do it, which he must obey. He is allowed, however, to appeal to the government in *France*. In each of the capital towns, the governor is the highest person, then the lieutenant-general, next to him a major, and after him the captains. The governor-general gives the first orders in all matters of consequence. When he comes to *Trois Rivieres* and *Montreal,* the power of the governor ceases, because he always commands where he is. The governor-general commonly goes to *Montreal* once every year, and mostly in winter; and during his absence from *Quebec,* the lieutenant-general commands there. When the governor-general dies, or goes to *France,* before a new one is come in his stead, the governor of *Montreal* goes to *Quebec* to command in the mean while, leaving the major to command at *Montreal.*

ONE or two of the king's ships are annually sent from *France* to *Canada,* carrying recruits to supply the places of those soldiers, who either died in the service, or have got leave to settle in the country, and turn farmers, or to return to *France*. Almost every year they send a hundred, or a hundred and fifty people over in this manner. With these people they likewise send over a great number of persons, who have been found guilty of smuggling in *France*. They were formerly condemned to the gallies, but at present they send them to the colonies, where they are free as soon as they arrive, and can choose what manner of life they please, but are never allowed to go out of the country, without the king's special licence. The king's ships likewise bring a great quantity of merchandizes which the king has bought, in order to be distributed among the *Indians* on certain occasions. The inhabitants of *Canada* pay very little to the king. In the year 1748, a beginning was, however, made, by laying a duty of three *per cent.* on all the *French* goods imported by the merchants of *Canada*. A regulation was likewise made at that time, that all the furs and skins exported to *France* from hence, should pay a certain duty; but what is carried to the colonies pays nothing. The merchants of all parts of *France* and its colonies, are allowed to send ships with goods to this place ; and the *Quebec* merchants are at liberty likewise to send their goods to any place in *France*, and its colonies. But the merchants at *Quebec* have but few ships, because the sailors wages are very high. The towns in *France* which chiefly trade with *Canada*, are *Rochelle* and *Bourdeaux* ; next to them are *Marseilles, Nantes, Havre de Grace, St. Malo*, and others. The king's ships which bring goods to this country, come either from *Brest* or from *Rochefort*. The merchants at *Quebec* send flour, wheat, pease, wooden utensils, *&c.* on their own bottoms, to the *French* possessions in the *West-Indies*. The walls round *Montreal* were built in 1738, at the king's expence, on condition the inhabitants should, little by little, pay off the cost to the king. The town at present pays annually 6000 *livres* for them to government, of which 2000 are given by the seminary of priests. At *Quebec* the walls have likewise been built at the king's expence, but he did not redemand the expence of the inhabitants, because they had already the duty upon goods to pay as above mentioned. The beaver trade belongs solely to the *Indian* company in *France*, and nobody is allowed to carry it on here, besides the people appointed by that company. Every other fur trade is open to every body. There are several places among the *Indians* far in the country, where the *French* have stores of their goods ; and these places they call *les postes*. The king has no other fortresses in *Canada* than *Quebec, Fort Chamblais, Fort St. Jean, Fort St. Frederic*, or *Crown-point, Montreal, Frontenac*, and *Niagara*. All other places belong to private persons. The king keeps the *Niagara* trade all to himself. Every one who intends to go to trade with the *Indians* must have a licence from the governor-general, for which he must pay a sum according as the place he is going to is more or less advantageous for trade. A merchant who sends out a boat laden with all sorts of goods, and four or five persons with it, is obliged to give five or six hundred livres for the permission ; and there are places for which they give a thousand livres. Sometimes one cannot buy the licence to go to a certain trading place, because the governor-general has granted, or intends to grant it to some acquaintince or relation of his. The money arising from the granting of licences, belongs to the governor-general ; but it is customary to give half of it to the poor : whether this is always strictly kept to or not, I shall not pretend to determine.

Peter Kalm, *Travels into North America* (London, 1771), III, 306–310.

CHAPTER XVIII — THE INDIANS

113. The Life of an Indian Trader (1735–1775)

BY JAMES ADAIR (1775)

Adair spent a great part of his life among the Indians, and his account of them is one of the best that we have. — Bibliography: Tyler, *American Literature*, I, 154–157; Channing and Hart, *Guide*, §§ 80, 104, 131. — For other extracts on the Indians, see *Contemporaries*, I, Index.

I SHALL now describe the domestic life of the Indians, and the traders among them. The Indians settle themselves in towns or villages after an easy manner; the houses are not too close to incommode one another, nor too far distant for social defence. If the nation where the English traders reside, is at war with the French, or their red confederates, which is the same, their houses are built in the middle of the town, if desired, on account of greater security. But if they are at peace with each other, both the Indians and traders chuse to settle at a very convenient distance, for the sake of their live stock, especially the latter, for the Indian youth are as destructive to the pigs and poultry, as so many young wolves or foxes. Their parents now only give them ill names for such misconduct, calling them mad; but the mischievous, and thievish, were formerly sure to be dry-scratched, which punishment hath been already described.

Most of the Indians have clean, neat, dwelling houses, white-washed within and without, either with decayed oyster-shells, coarse-chalk, or white marly clay; one or other of which, each of our Indian nations abounds with, be they ever so far distant from the sea-shore: the Indians, as well as the traders, usually decorate their summer-houses with this favourite white-wash. — The former have likewise each a corn-house, fowl-house, and a hot-house, or stove for winter: and so have the traders likewise separate store-houses for their goods, as well as to contain the proper remittances received in exchange.

The traders hot-houses are appropriated to their young-rising prolific family, and their well-pleased attendants, who are always as kindly treated as brethren ; and their various buildings, are like towers in cities, beyond the common size of those of the Indians. Before the Indians were corrupted by mercenary empirics, their good sense led them to esteem the traders among them as their second sun, warming their backs with the British fleeces, and keeping in their candle of life both by plentiful support, and continual protection and safety, from the fire-arms and ammunition which they annually brought to them. While the Indians were simple in manners, and uncorrupt in morals, the traders could not be reckoned unhappy ; for they were kindly treated, and watchfully guarded, by a society of friendly and sagacious people, and possessed all the needful things to make a reasonable life easy. Through all the Indian countries, every person lives at his own choice, not being forced in the least degree to any thing contrary to his own inclination. Before that most impolitic step of giving general licences took place, only a sufficient number of orderly reputable traders were allowed to traffic, and reside among the Indians : by which means the last were kept under proper restraint, were easy in their minds, and peaceable, on account of the plain honest lessons daily inculcated on them. But at present, most of their countries swarm with white people, who are generally the dregs and off-scourings of our colonies. The description is so exceedingly disagreeable, that I shall only observe, the greater part of them could notably distinguish themselves, among the most profligate by land or sea, no day of the week excepted, indeed the sabbath day is the worst. This is the true situation of our Indian affairs, — the unavoidable result of ignorant and wicked clergymen settled as Missionaries on the frontiers ; and of that pernicious practice of general licences, by which crowds of disorderly people infest the Indian countries, corrupt their morals, and put their civilization out of the power of common means : the worst and meanest may readily get nominal security to intitle them to a trading licence ; and ill uses are made of them with impunity.

Till of late years, the honest traders lived among the Indians in the greatest plenty. They abounded with hogs, which made very firm streaked bacon, and much preferable to that in the English settlements chiefly owing to the acorns and hiccory-nuts they feed on : but the Indians are now grown so proud and lazy, by having goods too cheap and plenty, that very few raise any. There are at least five times the number of trading houses in all the western Indian nations, since general licences, through the wisdom of our civil rulers, were first granted, than was formerly, while experience directed South-Carolina to pursue **and enforce** proper measures. Such a number of lewd, idle white savages are very hurtful to the honest part of the traders, by heightening the value of vegetables, especially in the time of light crops, to an exorbitant price ; for by inebriating the Indians with their nominally prohibited, and poisoning spirits, they purchase the necessaries of life, at four or five hundred per cent cheaper, than the orderly traders ; which is a great check to the few, who have a love to the welfare of their country, and strictly observe the laws of trade. Besides, those men decoy the intoxicated savages to defraud the old fair dealer every winter, of many thousand pounds of drest deer-skins, by the enchanting force of liquors, which, on account of their indolence and improvident disposition, interest absolutely required him to credit them for : but when at the end of their mad career, they open their distracted eyes, and bitterly inveigh against the tempting authors of their nakedness, then there is the same necessity of trusting them a-new for the next season's hunt, and likewise the same improbability, either of better success, or any sort of redress ; for family jobs must not be interrupted or retarded on any account. . . .

Buffalo flesh is nothing but beef of a coarser grain, though of a sweeter taste than the tame sort : elk-flesh has the like affinity to venison. The deer are very fat in winter, by reason of the great quantities of chesnuts, and various sorts of acorns, that cover the boundless woods. Though most of the traders who go to the remote Indian countries, have tame stock, as already described, and are very expert at fire-arms and ranging the woods a hunting ; yet every servant that each of them fits out for the winter's hunt, brings home to his master a large heap of fat barbecued briskets, rumps, and tongues of buffalo and deer, as well as plenty of bear-ribs, which are piled on large racks : these are laid up and used not for necessity, but for the sake of variety. The traders carry up also plenty of chocolate, coffee, and sugar, which enables them with their numberless quantity of fowls-eggs, fruit, &c. to have puddings, pyes, pasties, fritters, and many other articles of the like kind, in as great plenty, as in the English settlements. Several of the Indians produce sugar out of the sweet maple-tree, by making an incision, draining the juice, and boiling it to a proper consistence.

Though in most of the Indian nations, the water is good, because of their high situation, yet the traders very seldom drink any of it at home ; for the women beat in mortars their flinty corn, till all the husks are taken off, which having well sifted and fanned, they boil in large earthen pots ; then straining off the thinnest part into a pot, they mix it with cold water, till it is sufficiently liquid for drinking : and when cold, it is both pleasant and very nourishing ; and is much liked even by the genteel strangers.   The Indians always used mortars, instead of mills, and they had them, with almost every other convenience, when we first opened a trade with them — they cautiously burned a large log, to a proper level and length, placed fire a-top, and wet mortar round it, in order to give the utensil a proper form : and when the fire was extinguished, or occasion required, they chopped the inside with their stone-instruments, patiently continuing the slow process, till they finished the machine to the intended purpose.   I have the pleasure of writing this by the side of a Chikkasah female, as great a princess as ever lived among the ancient Peruvians, or Mexicans, and she bids me be sure not to mark the paper wrong, after the manner of most of the traders ; otherwise, it will spoil the making good bread, or hommony, and of course beget the ill-will of our white women.

James Adair, *The History of the American Indians* (London, 1775), 412–416 *passim*.

———◆———

114.   Small Pox and Brandy among the Indians (1749)

BY PROFESSOR PETER KALM

(TRANSLATED BY JOHN REINHOLD FORSTER, 1771)

The extract illustrates the two most destructive agents against the Indian tribes.— For Kalm, see No. 112 above.

March the 17th.   AT the first arrival of the *Swedes* in this country, and long after that time, it was filled with *Indians*.   But as the *Europeans* proceeded to cultivate the land, the *Indians* sold their land, and went further into the country.   But in reality few of the *Indians* really left the country in this manner ; most of them ended their days before, either by wars among themselves, or by the small-pox, a disease which the *Indians* were unacquainted with before their commerce with the *Europeans*, and which since that time has killed incredible numbers of them.   For though they can heal wounds and other external hurts, yet they know not how to proceed with fevers, or in general with internal diseases.   One can imagine, how ill they would succeed with the cure of the small-pox, when as soon as the pustules appeared, they leaped naked into the cold water of the rivers, lakes, or fountains, and either dived over head into it, or poured it over their body in great abundance, in order to cool the heat of the fever.   In the same manner they carry their children, when they have the small-pox, into the water and duck them.   But brandy has killed most of the *Indians*.   This liquor was likewise entirely unknown to them, before the *Europeans* came hither ; but after they had tasted it, they could never get enough of it.   A man can hardly have a greater desire of a thing, than the *Indians* have of brandy.   I have heard them say, that to die by drinking brandy, was a desirable and an honourable death ; and indeed 'tis no very uncommon thing to kill themselves by drinking this liquor to excess.

Peter Kalm, *Travels into North America* (London, 1771), II, 93–95.

———◆———

115. A Flowery Speech to the Six Nations (1753)

BY SIR WILLIAM JOHNSON

The author of this piece lived among the Indians in the Mohawk valley, as a kind of feudal chieftain and representative of the New York government. — Bibliography: Winsor, *Narrative and Critical History*, V, 583–584; W. E. Griffis, *Sir William Johnson and the Six Nations*.

HERE follows what I said to the General Convention of the Six Nations at Onondaga spoke by Hendrick the Chief of the Mohawks.

Bretheren of the Six Nations.

The great concern I am under for the loss of our three great and beloved Brothers Caghniagarota, Onughsadego and Gahusquerowana, who in their time made your Assembly compleat, makes it incumbent on me to condole their death, and as it is a great loss to us in general, I do by these three Belts of Wampum dry up your tears that we may see each other, clear your throats that we may Speak together, and wash away their blood out of our sight, and cover their bones with these Strow'd Blankets

Here gave the three Belts of Wampum and three Blanketts of Strowd.

Bretheren of the Six Nations

I am now to acquaint you that the indisposition of the present Governor and the expectation of the sudden arrival of a new one, has occasioned the interview, proposed at Albany between you and him this summer, to be deferred, upon which I am commissioned to treat with you and at the same time to assure you that the succeeding Governor will meet you as soon as he conveniently can, with presents as usual. You will then have an opportunity of laying before him whatever is amiss, which will be redressed you may depend on, without any unnecessary delay ; till then I expect all of you will live in perfect harmony with y^r Bretheren ye English. A Belt.

Bretheren of the Six Nations.

It grieves me sorely to find the road hither so grown up with weeds for want of being used, & your fire almost expiring at Onondaga, where it was agreed by the wisdom of our Ancestors that it should never be extinguished : You know it was a saying among us that when the Fire was out here, you would be no longer a people ; I am now sent by Your Brother the Governor to clear the Road & make the fire with such wood as will never burn out, and I earnestly desire you would take care to keep it up, so as to be found always the same when he shall send among you. A Belt.

Bretheren of the Six Nations.

I have now renewed the Fire, swept clean all your rooms with a new White Wing, and leave it hanging near the Fire place, that you may use it for cleaning all dust dirt &^{e} which may have been brought in by Strangers, no friends to you or us. A string of Wampum.

Bretheren of the Six Nations.

I am sorry to find on my arrival among you that the fine shady Tree which was planted by your forefathers for your ease and shelter, should be now leaning, being almost blown down by Northerly winds. I shall now endeavour to set it upright that it may flourish as formerly, while the roots spread abroad ; so that when we sitt or stand on them you will feel them shake should any storms blow, then should you be ready to secure it. A Belt.

Bretheren of the Six Nations.

Your Fire now burns clearly at the old place, the Tree of Shelter and Protection is set up & flourishes ; I must now insist upon your quenching that fire made with brambles at Swegachey, and recall those to their proper home who have deserted thither. I can not leave disswading you from going to Canada, the French are a delusive people, always endeavouring to divide you as much as they can, nor will they let slip any opportunity of making advantage of it. 'Tis formidable news we hear that the French & some Indians are making a descent upon Ohio :

is it with your consent or leave that they proceed in this extraordinary manner, endeavouring by force of arms to dispossess your own native allies as well as your bretheren the English, and establishing themselves?

A large Belt. . . .

Bretheren of the Senecas.

As you have always been looked upon as the door of the Six Nations where all news, especially from the Westward and Southward must enter and go out, we dont hear this door open as we used to do formerly, and believe it to be worn out, & think it necessary to hang on a new one of such wood as will never decay ; the noise of which when it opens should alarm all the Confederacy. I must now desire you that whatever you hear of consequence you would send it very distinctly to the Sachems of Onondaga who will send it directly to your Bretheren. I require also as you are nearest to the Western Tribes of Indians that you will endeavour all in your power to draw as many of them into our interest as possibly you can, by which means the Six Nations may continue their strength & credit.   A Belt. . . .

Bretheren of the Six Nations.

You must imagine I was much troubled when immediately after my appointment to meet you at Onondaga, to renew and put in order every thing relating to your affairs, to hear that some of your people were returned with scalp and prisoners from the Catabaws, with whom you made so solemn a peace last year in my presence, which pleased all your bretheren the English upon this Continent, the King your Father also approved of it. Now what an everlasting shame must it be to the Six Nations if this bloody affair be not immediately made up, if it be possible. I expect at least that you return the prisoners if any you have, and committ no further hostilities on that Nation.   A Belt. . . .

Bretheren of the Six Nations.

I take this opportunity to return you the three Belts of Wampum sent by you to the Governor with a request to hinder the Rum from coming among You. He was very glad to gratifie you in it, and that you had seen the ill consequences of that bewitching liquor, and hopes you will continue in that resolution always. The proclamation forbidding Rum to be sent or sold any where among you (except at Oswego) is already published.   Here returned them their Three Belts.

Bretheren of the Six Nations.

I have now only to recommend what I have said in your Brother the Governor's name to your serious consideration, and when you are prepared to return an answer, I should be glad to hear it by the Lake where I am encamped and have a small present for you, and some provision for your Children.

E. B. O'Callaghan, editor, *Documents relative to the Colonial History of the State of New-York* (Albany, 1855), VI, 810–812 *passim*.

———◆———

116. "A Concise Character of the Indians" (1767)

BY CAPTAIN JONATHAN CARVER

Carver was a British officer who formed a plan for crossing the continent to the Pacific, but was stopped in the upper Mississippi country. He was the first English writer who visited the northwestern tribes. — Bibliography: Tyler, *Literary History of the Revolution*, I, 141–150.

THE character of the Indians, like that of other uncivilized nations, is composed of a mixture of ferocity and gentleness. They are at once guided by passions and appetites, which they hold in common with the fiercest beasts that inhabit their woods, and are possessed of virtues which do honour to human nature.

In the following estimate I shall endeavour to forget on the one hand the prejudices of Europeans, who usually annex to the word Indian epithets that are disgraceful to human nature, and who view them in no other light than as savages and cannibals ; whilst with equal care I avoid any partiality towards them, as some must naturally arise from the favourable reception I met with during my stay among them.

At the same time I shall confine my remarks to the nations inhabiting only the western regions, such as the Naudowessies, the Ottagaumies, the Chipéways, the Winnebagoes, and the Saukies : for as throughout that diversity of climates the extensive continent of America is composed of, there are people of different dispositions and various characters, it would be incompatible with my present undertaking to treat of all these, and to give a general view of them as a conjunctive body.

That the Indians are of a cruel, revengeful, inexorable disposition, that they will watch whole days unmindful of the calls of nature, and make their way through pathless, and almost unbounded woods, subsisting only on the scanty produce of them, to pursue and revenge themselves of an enemy, that they hear unmoved the piercing cries of such as unhappily fall into their hands, and receive a diabolical pleasure from the tortures they inflict on their prisoners, I readily grant; but let us look on the reverse of this terrifying picture, and we shall find them temperate both in their diet and potations (it must be remembered, that I speak of those tribes who have little communication with Europeans) that they withstand, with unexampled patience, the attacks of hunger, or the inclemency of the seasons, and esteem the gratification of their appetites, but as a secondary consideration.

We shall likewise see them sociable and humane to those whom they consider as their friends, and even to their adopted enemies; and ready to partake with them of the last morsel, or to risk their lives in their defence.

In contradiction to the report of many other travellers, all of which have been tinctured with prejudice, I can assert, that notwithstanding the apparent indifference with which an Indian meets his wife and children after a long absence, an indifference proceeding rather from custom than insensibility, he is not unmindful of the claims either of connubial or parental tenderness; the little story I have introduced in the preceding chapter of the Naudowessie woman lamenting her child, and the immature death of the father, will elucidate this point, and enforce the assertion much better than the most studied arguments I can make use of.

Accustomed from their youth to innumerable hardships, they soon become superior to a sense of danger or the dread of death; and their fortitude, implanted by nature, and nurtured by example, by precept, and accident, never experiences a moment's allay.

Though slothful and inactive whilst their store of provision remains unexhausted, and their foes are at a distance, they are indefatigable and persevering in pursuit of their game, or in circumventing their enemies.

If they are artful and designing, and ready to take every advantage, if they are cool and deliberate in their councils, and cautious in the extreme either of discovering their sentiments, or of revealing a secret, they might at the same time boast of possessing qualifications of a more animated nature, of the sagacity of a hound, the penetrating sight of a lynx, the cunning of the fox, the agility of a bounding roe, and the unconquerable fierceness of the tyger.

In their public characters, as forming part of a community, they possess an attachment for that band to which they belong, unknown to the inhabitants of any other country. They combine, as if they were actuated only by one soul, against the enemies of their nation, and banish from their minds every consideration opposed to this.

They consult without unnecessary opposition, or without giving way to the excitements of envy or ambition, on the measures necessary to be pursued for the destruction of those who have drawn on themselves their displeasure. No selfish views ever influence their advice, or obstruct their consultations. Nor is it in the power of bribes or threats to diminish the love they bear their country.

The honour of their tribe, and the welfare of their nation, is the first and most predominant emotion of their hearts; and from hence proceed in a great measure all their virtues and their vices. Actuated by this, they brave every danger, endure the most exquisite torments, and expire triumphing in their fortitude, not as a personal qualification, but as a national characteristic.

From thence also flow that insatiable revenge towards those with whom they are at war, and all the consequent horrors that disgrace their name. Their uncultivated minds being incapable of judging of the propriety of an action, in opposition to their passions which are totally insensible to the controuls of reason or humanity, they know not how to keep their fury within any bounds, and consequently that courage and resolution which would otherwise do them honour, degenerates into a savage ferocity.

But this short dissertation must suffice; the limits of my work will not permit me to treat the subject more copiously, or to pursue it with a logical regularity. The observations already made by my readers on the preceding pages, will, I trust, render it unnecessary; as by them they will be enabled to form a tolerably just idea of the people I have been describing. Experience teaches, that anecdotes, and relations of particular events, however trifling they might appear, enable us to form a truer judgment of the manners and customs of a people, and are much more declaratory of their real state, than the most studied and elaborate disquisition, without these aids.

J[onathan] Carver, *Travels through the Interior Parts of North-America, in the Years 1766, 1767, and 1768* (London, 1778), 408–414.

CHAPTER XIX — INTERCOLONIAL WARS

117. The Taking of Schenectady (1690)

BY COMPTROLLER-GENERAL DE MONSEIGNAT

(TRANSLATED BY E. B. O'CALLAGHAN, 1843)

Monseignat was a Canadian official, a protégé of Madame de Maintenon, to whom this account is addressed. — Bibliography : Winsor, *Narrative and Critical History*, V, 190; Parkman, *Frontenac and New France*, ch. xi; Channing and Hart, *Guide*, § 131. — For earlier Indian wars, see *Contemporaries*, I, Nos. 39, 40, 60, 91, 127, 134.

... NEWS arrived at Quebec of the success of the first party that had gone out against the English, and which had been organized at Montreal. It might have consisted of two hundred and ten men ; to wit, of 80 Indians of the Sault and the Mountain, sixteen Algonquins, and the remainder Frenchmen. It was commanded by Lieutenants Le Moyne de Sainte Hélène and Dailleboust de Mantet, both Canadians, under whom were Sieurs le Moyne d'Iberville and Repentigny de Montesson. The best qualified of the French were Sieurs de Bonrepos and de La Brosse, reduced lieutenants (*reformés*) Sieurs Le Moyne de Biainville, Le Bert du Chesne, and la Marque de Montigny, who all served as volunteers. They took their departure from Montreal in the fore part of February. . . .

. . . they . . . experienced inconceivable difficulties . . . having been obliged to wade up to their knees in water, and to break the ice with their feet in order to find a solid footing.

They arrived within two leagues of Corlard about four o'clock in the evening, and were harangued by the Great Mohawk, the chief of the Iroquois of the Sault. He urged on all to perform their duty, and to forget their past fatigue, in the hope of taking ample revenge for the injuries they had received from the Iroquois at the solicitation of the English, and of washing them out in the blood of those traitors. This Indian was without contradiction the most considerable of his tribe, an honest man, as full of spirit, prudence and generosity as possible, and capable at the same time of the grandest undertakings. Four squaws

z

were shortly after discovered in a wigwam who gave every information necessary for the attack on the town. The fire found in their hut served to warm those who were benumbed, and they continued their march, having previously detached Giguières, a Canadian, with nine Indians, on the scout. They discovered no one, and returned to join the main body within one league of Corlard.

At eleven of the clock at night, they came within sight of the town, resolved to defer the assault until two o'clock of the morning. But the excessive cold admitted of no further delay.

The town of Corlard forms a sort of oblong with only two gates — one opposite where our party had halted; the other opening towards Orange, which is only six leagues distant. Messieurs de Sainte Hélène and de Mantet were to enter at the first which the squaws pointed out, and which, in fact, was found wide open. Messieurs d'Iberville and de Montesson took the left with another detachment, in order to make themselves masters of that leading to Orange. But they could not discover it, and returned to join the remainder of the party. A profound silence was every where observed, until the two Commanders, who separated after having entered the town for the purpose of encircling it, met at the other extremity.

The signal of attack was given Indian fashion, and the entire force rushed on simultaneously.

M. de Mantet placed himself at the head of one detachment, and reached a small fort where the garrison was under arms. The gate was burst in after a good deal of difficulty, the whole set on fire, and all who defended the place slaughtered.

The sack of the town began a moment before the attack on the fort. Few houses made any resistance. M. de Montigny discovered several which he attempted to carry sword in hand, having tried the musket in vain. He received two thrusts of a halbert (*pertuissane*) one in the body and the other in the arm. But M. de Sainte Hélène having come to his aid, effected an entrance, and put every one who defended the place to the sword. The Massacre lasted two hours. The remainder of the night was spent in placing sentinels, and in taking some rest.

The house belonging to the Minister was ordered to be saved, so as to take him alive to obtain information from him; but as it was not known, it was not spared any more than the others. He was killed in it and his papers burnt before he could be recognized.

At day break some men were sent to the dwelling of Mr. Condre who was Major of the place, and who lived at the other side of the river. He was not willing to surrender, and put himself on the defensive with his servants and some Indians; but as it was resolved not to do him any harm, in consequence of the good treatment that the French had formerly experienced at his hands, M. d'Iberville and the Great Mohawk proceeded thither alone, promised him quarter for himself, his people and his property, whereupon he laid down his arms on their assurance, entertained them in his fort, and returned with them to see the Commandants in the town.

In order to occupy the Indians, who would otherwise have taken to drink and thus rendered themselves unable for defence, the houses had already been set on fire. None were spared in the town but one belonging to Condre, and that of a widow who had six children, whither M. de Montigny had been carried when wounded. All the rest were burnt. The lives of between fifty and sixty persons, old men, women and children were spared, they having escaped the first fury of the attack; also some thirty Iroquois, in order to show them that it was the English and not they against whom the grudge was entertained. The loss on this occasion in houses, cattle and grain, amounts to more than four hundred thousand livres. There were upwards of eighty well built and well furnished houses in the town.

The return march commenced with thirty prisoners. The wounded, who were to be carried, and the plunder with which all the Indians and some Frenchmen were loaded, caused considerable inconvenience. Fifty good horses were brought away. Sixteen of them only reached Montreal. The remainder were killed on the road for food. . . .

Such, Madam, is the account of what passed at the taking of Corlard. The French lost but twenty-one men, namely four Indians and seventeen Frenchmen. Only one Indian and one Frenchman were killed at the capture of the town. The others were lost on the road.

E. B. O'Callaghan, editor, *Documents relative to the Colonial History of the State of New-York* (Albany, 1855), IX, 466–469 *passim*.

118. The Evil Deeds of the Spaniards (1702–1740)

BY COLONEL MILES BREWTON AND OTHERS (1741)

The writers were a committee of the South Carolina legislature, appointed to draw up a statement of the ways of their countrymen. They have not spared the dark tints in their picture. — Bibliography: Winsor, *Narrative and Critical History*, V, 342–343. — For earlier accounts of the Spaniards, see *Contemporaries*, I, Nos. 17–25, 46.

IN 1702, before Queen ANNE's Declaration of War was known in these Parts, the *Spaniards* formed another Design to fall upon our Settlements by Land, at the Head of *Nine Hundred Apalatchee Indians* from thence. The *Creek Indians*, in Friendship with this Province, coming at a Knowledge of it, and sensible of the Dangers approaching, acquainted our Traders, then in the Nation with it, when this Army was actually on their March coming down that Way. The Traders having thereupon encourag'd the *Creeks* to get together an Army of *Five Hundred* Men, headed the same, and went out to meet the other. . . . the *Creeks* rushing forth fell on them, killed and took the greatest Part, and entirely routed them. . . .

In the latter End of the same Year, Queen ANNE's War being commenced, Col. *Moore* then Governor of this *Province*, with Reason expected a Visit from the *Spaniards*, and it having been suggested to him, that *St. Augustine* might be easily taken, if surprized, he judged it best to give them the first Blow. Accordingly he undertook an Expedition against it with about *Five Hundred* Whites, and *Five Hundred* Indians. He himself with *Four Hundred* of the Whites proceeded in the Vessels directly to the Bar of *St. Augustine* Harbour, whilst Col. *Daniel* landing at *St. Juan's* march'd *directly* from thence with the other *Hundred* and the *Indians*, and entered the Town with them only, the same Day as the Vessels appeared in Sight. This little Army kept the Castle close besieged above *Three* Months; and repelled several Sallies with the Loss of very few Men. Yet having no *Bombs* with them, and a *Spanish* Man of War coming to its Relief from the *Havanna* with a considerable Number of Men, on Board *Four* large Transports, which landed on *Anastatia*, they were obliged to retreat: *But not without First Burning the Town.*

In 1704, Col. *Moore* was commissioned as *Lieutenant General* by Sir *Nathaniel Johnson*, who succeeded him in the Government, to make an Expedition against the *Spaniards* and *Indians* at *Apalatchee*, about *Eighty* Miles to the West of *St. Augustine,* on the same Motives that the preceding Expedition had been undertaken. . . . By this Conquest of *Apalachee* the *Province* was freed from any Danger from that Part during the whole War. And this important Service was effected without putting this Government to the *least Expense*.

In 1706, the *Spaniards* at *St. Augustine* joined the *French* from *Martinico*, in making up a Fleet of *Ten* Sail, with *Eight Hundred* Men, *Whites*, *Mustees*, and *Negroes*, and *Two Hundred Indians*, to invade this *Province*. The Ship on Board which the Chief Commander was, being separated from the Fleet, fell into *Sewee* Bay, not knowing the Place. The rest coming over *Charles-Town* Bar, anchored just within on a *Sunday*, where they remained, sending Parties ashore on *James-Island* and *Wando-Neck*, plundering and burning Houses, &c. 'till *Friday* following Capt. *Fenwicke* going from *Charles-Town*, with *One Hundred* Men, landed at *Hobkaw* in Sight of Town, upon a Party of *One Hundred* and *Thirty* Men, who had got thither and set a Ship on Fire. He attacked them, killed and wounded about *Thirty*, and took *Seventy* Prisoners. The next Day the Ship which had lost Company, still not appearing, the whole *Fleet* set Sail again.

In 1715, Peace having been some Time concluded between the *Crowns*, the *Yamasee* Indians . . . living contiguous to, and in the most intimate Manner with the Settlers in those Parts, having been ill used by some of the *Traders* amongst them, were so far disgusted, that they broke out war with this *Province*, by massacring on the *Fifteenth* Day of *April* above *Eighty* of the Inhabitants of *Granville* County. . . . headed by *Spaniards*, they cut off several of the Settlers, and carried off their *Slaves*. The *Slaves* themselves at length, taking Advantage of those Things, deserted of their own Accord to St. *Augustine*, and upon being demanded back by *this Government* they were not returned, but such Rates paid for those that could not be concealed as that Government was pleased to set upon them. The Evil encreasing, altho' Col. *Barnwell* who was sent from hence to St. *Augustine*, immediately after the Conclusion of Queen *Anne's* Peace, had in Behalf of *this Government* then entered into a stipulation with *that*, mutually to return any Slaves that should for the future desert either Government; Col. *Hall* was sent to St. *Augustine* in 1725, with whom *that* Government confirmed the said Stipulation. Notwithstanding which, the very year following:

In 1727, Peace between the *Crowns* continuing, fresh Depradations were committed on *this Province* from *Augustine*, both by Land and Water; which created the Expense of *Two* Expeditions to prevent the

Progress of them. . . . At the same Time a Party of *Yamasee* Indians, headed by *Spaniards* from St. *Augustine*, having murdered our *Out-Scouts*, made an Incursion into our Settlements. . . .

In the latter End of 1737, *still Peace subsisting*, great Preparations were made to invade openly *this Province* and *Georgia*. For that Purpose a great Body of Men arrived at St. *Augustine*, in Galleys from the *Havana*; which put *this Province* to a very large Expense to provide against. But happily they were countermanded just as they were ready to set off.

In 1738, *altho' Peace subsisted*, and Governor *Johnson* after his Arrival here had, in 1733, renewed the before mentioned Stipulation, another Method was taken by the *Spaniards* to answer their Ends. Hitherto the Government of St. *Augustine* had not dared to acknowledge, much less to justify, the little Villainies and Violences offered to our Properties : But now an Edict of his Catholic Majesty himself, bearing Date in *November* 1733, was published by Beat of Drum round the Town of St. *Augustine* (where many *Negroes* belonging to *English* Vessels that carried thither Supplies of Provisions, &c., had the Opportunity of hearing it) promising Liberty and Protection to *all Slaves* that should desert thither from any of the *English* Colonies, but more especially from this. And, lest that should not prove sufficient of itself, *secret* Measures were taken to make it known to our *Slaves* in *general*. In Consequence of which Numbers of *Slaves* did, from Time to Time, by Land and Water desert to St. *Augustine*; And, the better to facilitate their Escape, carried off their Master's *Horses*, *Boats*, *&c.* some of them first commiting Murder ; and were accordingly received and declared free. Our present *Lieutenant Governor*, by Deputies sent from hence on that Occasion to *Seignor Don Manuel de Montiano*, the present Governor of St. *Augustine*, set forth the Manner in which *those* Slaves had escaped : and redemanded them pursuant to the *Stipulation* between the *Two* Governments, and to the *Peace subsisting* between the *Crowns*. Notwithstanding which, tho' *that* Governor acknowledged *those Slaves* to be there, yet producing the King of *Spain's* said *Edict* he declared that *he could not deliver them up, without a positive Order for that purpose from* the King, *and that he should continue to receive all others that should resort thither, it having been an article of Complaint against his Predecessor, that he had not put the said Edict in force sooner*. The Success of those Deputies being too well known at their Return, Conspiracies were form'd and Attempts made by more *Slaves to* desert to St. *Augustine :* But . . . by great Vigilance, they were prevented from succeeding. However,

In *September* 1739, our *Slaves* made an Insurrection at *Stono*, in the Heart of our Settlements not *Twenty* Miles from *Charles-Town;* in which they massacred Twenty-Three Whites, after the most cruel and barbarous Manner to be conceiv'd; and having got Arms and Ammunition out of a Store, they bent their Course to the Southward, burning all the Houses on the Road. But they marched so slow, in full Confidence of their own Strength from their first Success, that they gave Time to a Party of our *Militia* to come up with them. The Number was in a Manner equal on both sides; and an Engagement ensued, such as may be supposed in such a Case. But by the Blessing of God the *Negroes* were defeated, the greatest Part being killed on the Spot or taken; and those that then escaped were so closely pursued, and hunted Day after Day, that in the End all but *Two* or *Three* were killed or taken and executed. That the *Negroes* would not have made this Insurrection had they not depended on St. *Augustine* for a Place of Reception afterwards, was very certain; and that the *Spaniards* had a Hand in prompting them to this particular Action, there was but little room to doubt. . . .

On this Occasion every Breast was filled with Concern. Evil brought home to us, within our very Doors, awaken'd the Attention of the most Unthinking. Every one that had any Relation any Tie of Nature; every one that had a Life to lose, were in the most sensible Manner shocked at such Danger daily hanging over their Heads. With Regret we bewailed our peculiar Case, that we could not enjoy the Benefits of Peace like the rest of Mankind; and that our own Industry should be the Means of taking from us all the Sweets of Life, and of rendering us liable to the Loss of our Lives and Fortunes. With Indignation we looked at St. *Augustine* (like another *Sallee!*) That Den of Thieves and Ruffians! Receptacle of Debtors, Servants and Slaves! Bane of Industry and Society! And revolved in our Minds all the Injuries *this Province* had received from thence, ever since its first Settlement: That they had, from first to last, in Times of *profoundest Peace*, both publickly and privately, by *Themselves, Indians* and *Negroes,* in every Shape molested us, not without some Instances of *uncommon* Cruelty. And what aggravated the same was, that *this Government* (on the contrary) had never been wanting in its good Offices with our *Indians* in their Behalf: And even during Queen *Ann's* War had exercised so much Humanity towards them that, in order to prevent those *Indians* from *scalping* them, according to their Custom; when they should take any of them Prisoners, a Law was passed to give them *Five Pounds* Proclamation Money for every one they should bring in alive; and accordingly a great Number of the *Spaniards*, by that Means, were brought in alive, and the Reward paid for them.

B. R. Carroll, compiler, *Historical Collections of South Carolina* (New York, 1836), II, 351–359 *passim*.

---

119. A Ballad of Pigwacket (1725)

ANONYMOUS

This lively poem is a reasonably accurate account of one of the skirmishes in which the frontier wars abounded. The fight occurred May 8, 1725. — Bibliography: Thomas Symmes, *Historical Memoirs of the Late Fight at Piggwackett* (Boston, 1725). — For other colonial verse, see *Contemporaries*, I, Nos. 82, 138, and below, Nos. 159, 164, 171, 182.

1. OF worthy Captain LOVEWELL, I purpose now to sing,
    How valiantly he served his country and his King;
    He and his valiant soldiers, did range the woods full wide,
    And hardships they endured to quell the Indian's pride.

2. 'Twas nigh unto Pigwacket, on the eighth day of May,
    They spied a rebel Indian soon after break of day;
    He on a bank was walking, upon a neck of land,
    Which leads into a pond as we're made to understand.

3. Our men resolv'd to have him, and travell'd two miles round,
    Until they met the Indian, who boldly stood his ground;
    Then speaks up Captain LOVEWELL, "take you good heed," says he,
    "This rogue is to decoy us, I very plainly see.

4. "The Indians lie in ambush, in some place nigh at hand,
    In order to surround us upon this neck of land;
    Therefore we'll march in order, and each man leave his pack,
    That we may briskly fight them when they make their attack."

5. They came unto this Indian, who did them thus defy,
    As soon as they came nigh him, two guns he did let fly,
    Which wounded Captain LOVEWELL, and likewise one man more,
    But when this rogue was running, they laid him in his gore.

6. Then having scalp'd the Indian, they went back to the spot,
   Where they had laid their packs down, but there they found them
      not,
   For the Indians having spy'd them, when they them down did lay,
   Did seize them for their plunder, and carry them away.

7. These rebels lay in ambush, this very place hard by,
   So that an English soldier did one of them espy,
   And cried out, " here's an Indian," with that they started out,
   As fiercely as old lions, and hideously did shout.

8. With that our valiant English, all gave a loud huzza,
   To shew the rebel Indians they fear'd them not a straw :
   So now the fight began, and as fiercely as could be,
   The Indians ran up to them, but soon were forced to flee.

9. Then spake up Captain LOVEWELL, when first the fight began
   " Fight on my valiant heroes ! you see they fall like rain."
   For as we are inform'd, the Indians were so thick,
   A man could scarcly fire a gun and not some of them hit.

10. Then did the rebels try their best our soldiers to surround,
    But they could not accomplish it, because there was a pond,
    To which our men retreated and covered all the rear,
    The rogues were forc'd to flee them, altho' they skulked for fear.

11. Two logs there were behind them that close together lay,
    Without being discovered, they could not get away ;
    Therefore our valiant English, they travell'd in a row,
    And at a handsome distance as they were wont to go.

12. 'Twas ten o'clock in the morning, when first the fight begun,
    And fiercely did continue until the setting sun ;
    Excepting that the Indians some hours before 'twas night,
    Drew off into the bushes and ceas'd a while to fight,

13. But soon again returned, in fierce and furious mood,
    Shouting as in the morning, but yet not half so loud;
    For as we are informed, so thick and fast they fell,
    Scarce twenty of their number, at night did get home well.

14. And that our valiant English, till midnight there did stay,
    To see whether the rebels would have another fray ;
    But they no more returning, they made off towards their home,
    And brought away their wounded as far as they could come.

15. Of all our valiant English, there were but thirty-four,
    And of the rebel Indians, there were about forescore.
    And sixteen of our English did safely home return,
    The rest were kill'd and wounded, for which we all must mourn.

16. Our worthy Captain LOVEWELL among them there did die,
    They killed Lieut. ROBBINS, and wounded good young FRYE,
    Who was our English Chaplain ; he many Indians slew,
    And some of them he scalp'd when bullets round him flew.

17. Young FULLAM too I'll mention, because he fought so well,
    Endeavouring to save a man, a sacrifice he fell ;
    But yet our valiant Englishmen in fight were ne'er dismay'd,
    But still they kept their motion, and WYMAN's Captain made,

18. Who shot the old chief PAUGUS, which did the foe defeat,
    Then set his men in order, and brought off the retreat ;
    And braving many dangers and hardships in the way,
    They safe arriv'd at Dunstable, the thirteenth day of May.

J. Farmer and J. B. Moore, editors, *Collections, Historical and Miscellaneous*
(Concord, 1824), III, 64–66.

———◆———

120. The Louisburg Expedition (1745)

BY CAPTAIN SAMUEL CURWEN

Curwen was a Salem man, who later took the wrong turn in the Revolution, and
became a loyalist refugee in England; see No. 169 below. — Bibliography : on Curwen, see Tyler, *Literary History of the Revolution*, I, 367–368; on the Louisburg
expedition, Winsor, *Narrative and Critical History*, V, 434–452; Channing and
Hart, *Guide*, § 131.

*B*OSTON, *March* 23, 1745. The General is embarking, and we shall
sail this afternoon. — Commodore Warren is coming to our assistance, which with the blessing of God will be of great advantage. — There
will go down in the first embarkation at least twenty-five hundred soldiers.

Sheepscot, March 27.   We have in our mess Mr. Walter, our chaplain, who is a very pleasant companion. — I dined to-day on board of Capt. Grant, who to-morrow with Capt. King will breakfast with me. — Our troops were landed at Chapeaurouge on the 29th March.

Canso, April 17.   Wrote home for provisions and stores to be sent in case the goods I expect shall arrive safe from England. — We are almost reduced to pork and pease.

Our men-of-war and privateers are stationed all round the Island to prevent vessels going in or coming out.   This evening another prize arrived, taken by Capt. Donahue, in the Swan of Marblehead, who behaved very bravely.   The prize had captured the packet sent from Boston to Canso to notify us that Commodore Warren was coming to our assistance, which heightens our spirits.

Canso, April 22.   Capt. Durell is come in this afternoon to our assistance ; as yet we have no news of Commodore Warren ; hope it will not be long before he arrives with an account of the French men-of-war expected.   Our last transport arrived this afternoon ; we had almost given her up.

I believe our campaign will be short, and expect the place will surrender without bloodshed.

Last night our chaplain and doctor went with two companies to attack St. Peter's, and we are momently looking for their return.   I long to be once within the walls of Louisburg.   This is the strangest country I ever knew ; not two fair days together.

Canso, April 27.   The Connecticut fleet arrived, and Col. Lathrop handed me my letter.   The scheme of attacking Louisburg is altered every day.

Commodore Warren has arrived.   I trust the expedition will prove successful, and that our friends will remember we are going against our common enemy.   May 1st, a small party went to the harbour and burned a small quantity of wine, brandy, and naval stores.

Camp before Louisburg, May 6.   We have got possession of the Grand Battery ; the French departed from it three days ago ; they spiked all the guns, but we have got seven of them clear, and five of them are continually playing upon the town.   Our soldiers are all in good heart, and I doubt not in a few days we shall have the town. We have taken a great number of prisoners.

Commodore Warren this day came ashore to visit the General ; he and all our officers have a good understanding among themselves.

Yesterday a gun at the Grand Battery split and wounded five of our men. They now and then throw a bomb, but do no damage.

This morning came in Col. Moulton with his detachment from St. Peter's, which they have demolished with the loss of but one man. Providence has signally smiled, and I doubt not the campaign will be crowned with success. I am willing to undergo any thing for the good of our cause.

Camp before Louisburg, May 12, 1745. Commodore Warren has had two hundred marines and sailors ashore for three days past in order to attack the Island battery, but something or other has always prevented its accomplishment, so the Commodore has ordered them all aboard and gone on board himself not a little dissatisfied.

Camp before Louisburg, May 26. Commodore Warren has taken the Vigilante, a 64 gun ship from France, coming with ammunition for this garrison. She was manned with five hundred men, had five hundred barrels gunpowder on board : she lost thirty men before she struck. The command of her is given to Captain Douglass, who before had the Mermaid, and Capt. Montague is to have the Mermaid. This has given new life to all our officers and soldiers.

Capt. Gayton is safely arrived at last, which affords great joy, for we almost despaired of him, being out so long after all the transports had arrived that left under his convoy.

Capt. Fletcher has had the misfortune to lose ten men by the Indians; seven killed, and three taken prisoners. They went ashore ten miles above where we lay to get wood, and keeping no guard, were beset by the Indians and cut off.

Camp before Louisburg, June 2*d*. We have made an attempt upon the Island battery, and failed. Abbot, a townsman of mine, was wounded in the leg, and I fear he will lose his life. — An hundred men are missing, and we are in hopes they are taken, as two boats laden with men were seen going into the town after the attack, when the French gave three hurrahs. Young Gray is dead, and three of Capt. Grant's men are missing, all of Salem. Our scouts have had an engagement with a number of French and Indians which we routed ; killed thirty and wounded forty ; we lost but six killed ; among them is the brave Capt. Dimmock, of Barnstable, and twenty wounded, some very dangerously. Our men got under the very walls before the French fired a gun.

Louisburg, June 17*th*, 1745. The Governor, aware of our preparations for a general assault, thought it best to capitulate, and has just surrendered the city to our arms.

Louisburg, July 25th, 1745. An East India ship, worth at least £200,000 sterling, came off the harbour, and fired a gun for a pilot. The Commodore sent out two sixty gun ships, which came up with, and took her in three hours ; we had the pleasure from the walls to see her strike to them. Two others, sent out three weeks before her, bound hither, are hourly expected to heave in sight. Col. Graham goes to-morrow in a sloop as a flag of truce for Canada, with about thirty French prisoners ; he is the only Englishman that goes in her.

I am going on board Capt. Lovett to St. Peter's, with a number of my soldiers, to guard the wood-vessels going there : our affairs will soon be settled, and I shall, to my great joy, return home.

Samuel Curwen, *Journal and Letters* (edited by George Atkinson Ward, New York, etc., 1842), 12–14.

———◆———

121. A Spanish Privateer in the Delaware (1748)

FROM THE NEWSPAPERS

Philadelphia, June 2. SUNDAY Evening arrived a Number of Mariners, that had been Prisoners on board the Clinton, who inform'd that the Richa, Capt. Burk, bound from Philadelphia to London with a very valuable Cargo, was taken by the said Privateer on the 16th past, about 25 Leagues from the Capes ; that on the 17th she took a Sloop bound from Providence to Philadelphia, George Smith, Master, laden with Sugar and Indigo ; that on the 21st she took a Hermaphrodite Vessel, Capt. Hinsley, bound from Virginia to Bristol ; that on the 25th she came to an Anchor in Hoar kill Road, and they used all their endeavours to get a Pilot to carry her up into the River, but in vain ; and a Sloop standing in for the Road, she weigh'd and gave chase to her, but the Sloop stood out again and got clear ; during the Chase they saw a large Brigt, which stood toward them, and proved to be another French Privateer, commanded by Capt. Berneau, with 180 Men, 14 carriage Guns and 30 Swivels, in 33 Days from Cape Francois, during which Time they had taken 6 Prizes. Standing in again for the Shore, they saw two Sloops lying at Anchor in Townsend's Inlet, about 16 Miles Northward of Cape May ; and manning out their two Boats, they sent them in to take them, which was done accordingly.

A Boat belonging to one of these Sloops was given to about 27 Prisoners to carry them to the Jersey Shore. While they were on board the Clinton, they learnt that she had been out from Cape Francois between 8 and 9 weeks, and had taken eleven Prizes, five of which they had [brought] out of Ocricot, in North Carolina; and that there were then fourteen Sail of Privateers cruizing between Sandy-Hook and South Carolina.

Yesterday arrived here Capt. Thomas Blake, late of the Schooner Martha, bound from Georgia for this Place, laden with white Sugar, &c. taken by the Sloop La Fortune, Capt. Ramong, from the Havannah, of 10 Carriage Guns, Consort to the St. Michael, and bound into Delaware to join her; this Privateer came up on the Jersey Side of the Bay, and miss'd her Consort, who went down the other Channel: She landed her Prisoners at Cohansy, and returned to the Capes. While the Prisoners were on board they learnt, that 4 Sail more of Spanish Privateers, were fitting out for this Coast. This Sloop had taken Capt. Edwards, in a Sloop from St. Kitts, bound hither with West India Goods. At the same Time Capt. Thompson, who had been bound from Virginia to Scotland, was taken off the Coast; and Capt. Roberts, who had been taken in a Ship bound from Jamaica to London, by a French Privateer, after an Engagement of 4 Hours, in which the Enemy lost 12 Men, and Capt. Roberts one. — *The Boston Weekly News Letter, June 23,* 1748. *No.* 2410.

New-York, June 6.
Wednesday last arrived here the Privateer Brig Castor, Capt. Arnold, of this Port from a Cruize of about 11 Months, but without any great Success; which we hear is chiefly owing to her being a heavy Sailer.

This Morning hove in Sight, from a Cruize of about 5 Weeks, the Privateer Snow Royal Catherine of this Port, Capt. John Burges, Commander, with three Prizes; two of which we hear are Sugar Ships, and the other a French or Spanish Privateer Brig with upward of 100 Men on board; which they took lying at Sandy Hook, as they were coming in, on Friday last: But further Particulars must be deferred till our next. . . . — *The Boston Weekly Post-Boy, June 20,* 1748. *No.* 709.

Philadelphia, June 9. Since our last arrived two French Flags of Truce from Hispaniola, one of which is taken by a Boat and Hands with a Commission from the Government of the Jerseys, and carried to Burlington for Condemnation. She had before been plundered of her most valuable Goods by a Providence Privateer. The other is seiz'd by the Collector of his Majesty's Customs of this Port. 'Tis said there is another in this River, and that more are expected. There is Advice by these Flags, that a very large French Fleet lies at Cape Francois, waiting for Convoy to return Home; that they were in great Want of Provisions, and under continual Apprehensions of being attack'd by Admiral Knowles.

The Enemies Privateers have left our River at present. — *The Boston Evening Post, June* 20, 1748. *No.* 671. . . .

New-York, *June* 20. By an Express which came Yesterday Afternoon from Philadelphia to his Excellency our Governour, we hear, That on Friday the 17th Mr. Jenkins arrived there in a Sloop, and made his Affidavit before the President and Council, that he had been taken Wednesday the 15th on his passage from Boston bound to Philadelphia, about 5 Miles from Cape May, by a Spanish Privateer Sloop commanded by Don Joseph Hantenoau, mounted with 6 Carriage Guns and about 10 Swivels, having on board about 40 Men, who plunder'd his Vessel of every Thing valuable, and then gave him his Vessel again, with which he arrived in Philadelphia. This Privateer that took him was then in Company with six others, viz. 2 Ships, 2 Brigs, and 2 Sloops. This we suppose to be Don Pedro's Fleet from the Havannah.

Boston. Last Night several Vessels arrived here from Philadelphia, who came out with above 30 others, bound to other Ports, and convoy'd out of Delaware River by the Love Man of War, with her Tender the Privateer Snow above-mention'd which she had mann'd and brought with her from Virginia. — These Vessels left Cape May last Thursday, and we are inform'd, That 4 Days before they sail'd, the said Man of War took another Spanish Privateer Sloop of 8 Carriage Guns and a Number of Swivels, within Sight of the people on Shore. This is the Privateer that took Capt. Jenkins, mention'd in the above Paragraph under New York. — *The Boston Weekly News-Letter, June* 30, 1748. *No.* 2411.

William Nelson, editor, *Documents relating to the Colonial History of the State of New Jersey* (Paterson, 1895), XII, 452-461 *passim.*

CHAPTER XX — THE FRENCH AND INDIAN WAR

122. The Question of Colonial Independence (1748)

BY PROFESSOR PETER KALM

(TRANSLATED BY JOHN REINHOLD FORSTER, 1770)

This is one of many contemporary suggestions that there was danger of independence. — On Kalm, see No. 112 above. Bibliography of independence: Frothingham, *Rise of the Republic*, 145–157; George Bancroft, *United States* (10 vol. ed.), IV, ch. i; Lecky, *England in the Eighteenth Century*, III, ch. xii; Winsor, *Narrative and Critical History*, VI, ch. iii.

. . . IT is to be observed that each *English* colony in *North America* is independent of the other, and that each has its proper laws and coin, and may be looked upon in several lights, as a state by itself. From hence it happens, that in time of war, things go on very slowly and irregularly here : for not only the sense of one province is sometimes directly opposite to that of another ; but frequently the views of the governor, and those of the assembly of the same province, are quite different : so that it is easy to see, that, while the people are quarrelling about the best and cheapest manner of carrying on the war, an enemy has it in his power to take one place after another. It has commonly happened that whilst some provinces have been suffering from their enemies, the neighbouring ones were quiet and inactive, and as if it did not in the least concern them. They have frequently taken up two or three years in considering whether they should give assistance to an oppressed sister colony, and sometimes they have expresly declared themselves against it. There are instances of provinces who were not only neuter in these circumstances, but who even carried on a great trade with the power which at that very time was attacking and laying waste some other provinces.

THE *French* in *Canada*, who are but an inconsiderable body, in comparison with the *English* in *America*, have by this position of affairs been able to obtain great Advantages in times of war; for if we judge from the number and power of the *English*, it would seem very easy for them to get the better of the *French* in *America*.

It is however of great advantage to the crown of *England*, that the *North American* colonies are near a country, under the government of the *French*, like *Canada*. There is reason to believe that the king never was earnest in his attempts to expel the *French* from their possessions there; though it might have been done with little difficulty. For the *English* colonies in this part of the world have encreased so much in their number of inhabitants, and in their riches, that they almost vie with *Old England*. Now in order to keep up the authority and trade of their mother country, and to answer several other purposes, they are forbid to establish new manufactures, which would turn to the disadvantage of the *British* commerce : they are not allowed to dig for any gold or silver, unless they send them to *England* immediately : they have not the liberty of trading to any parts that do not belong to the *British* dominions, excepting some settled places, and foreign traders are not allowed to send their ships to them. These and some other restrictions, occasion the inhabitants of the *English* colonies to grow less tender for their mother country. This coldness is kept up by the many foreigners such as *Germans, Dutch* and *French* settled here, and living among the *English*, who commonly have no particular attachment to *Old England*; add to this likewise that many people can never be contented with their possessions, though they be ever so great, and will always be desirous of getting more, and of enjoying the pleasure which arises from changing; and their over great liberty, and their luxury often lead them to licentiousness.

I have been told by *Englishmen*, and not only by such as were born in *America*, but even by such as came from *Europe*, that the *English* colonies in *North-America*, in the space of thirty or fifty years, would be able to form a state by themselves, entirely independent on [of] *Old England*. But as the whole country which lies along the sea shore, is unguarded, and on the land side is harassed by the *French*, in times of war these dangerous neighbours are sufficient to prevent the connection of the colonies with their mother country from being quite broken off. The *English* government has therefore sufficient reason to consider the *French* in *North-America*, as the best means of keeping the colonies in their due submission. . . .

Peter Kalm, *Travels into North America* (Warrington, 1770), I, 262–265.

2 A

123. The French Title to the Beautiful River (1752)

FROM ROYAL MINISTERIAL MINUTES

(Translated by E. B. O'Callaghan, 1843)

The Ohio, or "la Belle Rivière," was the tributary of the Mississippi having branches nearest to the English settlements, and thus became the centre of the conflict for the possessions of the West. — Bibliography of the French and Indian War: Winsor, *Narrative and Critical History*, V, ch. viii, notes; Parkman, *Conspiracy of Pontiac*, ch. v; Channing and Hart, *Guide*, § 132.

IT appears from a letter of the Marquis de la Jonquière, that the efforts the English are making, and the expenses they incur, to gain over the Indians, are not without success among several Nations.

Information has been received last year of the progress they had already made among the Indians in the environs of the River Ohio, where they have undertaken, since the peace, to form some establishments.

The Marquis de la Jonquière had rendered an account of a plan he had prepared both to drive the English from that river and to chastise the Indians who allowed themselves to be gained over. . . . But all the consequent operations reduce themselves to the seizure of some English traders with their goods, and to the murder of two Indians of the Miamis Nation.

The seizure of the English traders whose effects have been confiscated and even plundered by our Indians, cannot but produce a good effect, by disgusting the other traders of that Nation. . . .

The English may pretend that we are bound by the Treaty of Utrecht to permit the Indians to trade with them. But it is certain that nothing can oblige us to suffer this trade on our territory.

Accordingly in all the alliances or quasi treaties or propositions we have had with the Far Indians, we have never obliged them expressly to renounce going to the English to trade ; we have merely exhorted them to that effect, and never did we oppose that treaty by force.

The River Ohio, otherwise called the Beautiful river, and its tributaries belong indisputably to France, by virtue of its discovery by Sieur de la Salle ; of the trading posts the French have had there since, and of possession which is so much the more unquestionable as it constitutes the most frequent communication from Canada to Louisiana. It is only within a few years that the English have undertaken to trade there ; and now they pretend to exclude us from it.

They have not, up to the present time, however, maintained that these rivers belong to them ; they pretend only that the Iroquois are masters of them and being the Sovereigns of these Indians, that they can exercise their rights. But 'tis certain that these Indians have none, and that, besides, the pretended sovereignty of the English over them is a chimera.

Meanwhile 'tis of the greatest importance to arrest the progress of the pretensions, and expeditions of the English in that quarter. Should they succeed there, they would cut off the communication between the two Colonies of Canada and Louisiana, and would be in a position to trouble them, and to ruin both the one and the other, independent of the advantages they would at once experience in their trade to the prejudice of ours.

Any complaints that may be presented to the Court of England against the English Governors would be altogether futile. On the one hand it would be very difficult to obtain proofs of the most serious facts ; and on the other, no matter what proofs may be produced, that Court would find means to elude all satisfaction, especially as long as the boundaries are not settled.

It is necessary then to act on the spot, and the question to be determined is, what means are the most proper. . . .

Therefore, without undertaking, as the Marquis de la Jonquière appears to have proposed, to drive from the River Ohio the Indians who are looked upon as rebels or suspected, and without wishing even to destroy the liberty of their trade, it is thought best to adhere to two principal points.

1st To make every possible effort to drive the English from our territory, and to prevent them coming there to trade.

2^d To give the Indians to understand at the same time that no harm is intended them, that they will have liberty to go as much as they please to the English to trade, but will not be allowed to receive these on our territory.

There is reason to believe that by this course of conduct ; by providing our posts with plenty of goods and preventing our traders dictating to the Indians, our trade will soon recover the superiority over that of the English in those parts ; for 'tis certain the Indians do not like to go into their towns, nor forts. . . .

However that be, 'tis considered proper to direct Mr Duquesne to lay down henceforward in Canada a different system from that always followed hitherto in regard to wars among the Indians. With a view to occupy and weaken them, the principle has been to excite and foment these sorts of wars. That was of advantage in the infancy of the settlement of Canada. But in the condition to which these Nations are now reduced, and in their present dispositions generally, it is in every respect more useful that the French perform between them the part of protectors and pacificators. They will, thereby, entertain more consideration and attachment for us ; the Colony will be more tranquil in consequence, and we shall save considerable expense. Cases, however, may occur in which it will be proper to excite war against certain Nations attached to the English ; but even such cases call for two observations ; one, to endeavor, first, to gain over these same Nations by reconciling them with ours ; and the other, to be as sure as possible that our Indians will not suffer too much from these wars.

E. B. O'Callaghan, editor, *Documents relative to the Colonial History of the State of New-York* (Albany, 1858), X, 242–244 *passim.*

———◆———

124. Royal Orders to Resist the French (1753)

BY SECRETARY THE EARL OF HOLDERNESSE

Holdernesse was secretary of state for the northern department, and hence mouthpiece of the decision of the ministry. — Bibliography: Stanhope, *William Pitt ;* Winsor, *Narrative and Critical History,* V, 452.

HIS Majesty having received Information of the March of a considerable number of Indians not in alliance with the King, supported by some regular European Troops, intending as it is apprehended, to commit some hostilities on parts of his Majesty's dominions in America, I have the King's commands to send you this intelligence, and to direct you to use your utmost diligence, to learn, how far the same may be well grounded, and to put you upon your guard, that you may, at all events, be in a condition to resist any hostile attempts that may be made upon any parts of His Majesty's Dominions within your Government ; and to direct you in the King's Name, that in case the subjects of any Foreign Prince or State, should presume to make any incroachment on the limits of His Maj$^{ty's}$ dominions, or to erect Forts on His Majesty's Land, or comit any other act of hostility, you are immediately, to represent the injustice of such proceeding, and to require them forthwith to desist from any such unlawful undertaking ;

but if notwithstanding your requisition, they should still persist, you are then to draw forth the armed Force of the Province, and to use your best endeavours, to repell force by force. But as it is His Majesty's determination not to be the agressor, I have the King's commands, most strictly to enjoin you, not to make use of the armed force under your direction, excepting within the undoubted limits of his Majesty's dominions.

And whereas it may be greatly conducive to His Majesty's service, that all his Provinces in America should be aiding and assisting each other, in case of any invasion, I have it particularly in charge from his Majesty, to acquaint you, that it is his Royal will and pleasure, that you should keep up an exact correspondence with all His Majesty's Governors on the Continent; and in case you shall be informed by any of them, of any hostile attempts, you are immediately to assemble the general assembly within your Government, and lay before them, the necessity of a mutual assistance, and engage them to grant such supplies as the exigency of affairs may require. — I have wrote by this conveyance to all his Majesty's Gov^{rs} to the same purpose.

E. B. O'Callaghan, editor, *Documents relative to the Colonial History of the State of New-York* (Albany, 1855), VI, 794–795.

———◆———

125. The Albany Plan of Union (1754)

BY CHIEF JUSTICE STEPHEN HOPKINS (1755)

Hopkins was one of the first to see the need of unity of action among the colonies. He was governor of Rhode Island at intervals from 1755 to about 1770, and later became a member of the Continental Congress. The plan submitted at Albany failed of acceptance by either the colonies or the mother country. — Bibliography: Rider, *Rhode Island Historical Tracts*, No. 9, ix–xx; Winsor, *Narrative and Critical History*, VI, 65–66; Channing and Hart, *Guide*, § 132.

THUS having seen Abstracts of the Authorities given the Commissioners who were at Albany, and of those Letters from the Crown, which occasioned such Authorities to be given; together with the State of the British and French Colonies in America, and the proposed Plan of Union, formed in Consequence of the whole: From an impartial View thereof, let every Man judge, Whether it was not the Intent of all the Colonies who sent Commissioners, that they should form some General Scheme or Plan, for the Safety and Defence of the English Colonies, and the Indians in their Alliance? Look into the Commission from Governor Greene; and after full Powers are given to do every Thing relative to the Indians in Alliance with us, What mean these following Words? "And also, what else may be necessary to prohibit the French, and their Allies the Indians, from encroaching on the Lands within the Dominions of His Majesty. And in general, as far as the Abilities of this Government will permit, to act in Conjunction with the said Commissioners, in every Thing necessary for the Good of His Majesty's Subjects in these Parts. And to answer as far as we can, the Designs of His Majesty's Instructions to this Colony, communicated to us by the Earl of Holdernesse." Surely such Words as these, have some Meaning; and if the Commissioners were so unhappy as quite to mistake their Meaning, let those penetrating Wits who think so, shew to the World, how they are to be understood. But if those Authorities were too extensive, let them be blamed who gave such Authorities, and not those who executed them in the most sparing Manner possible. And will any Man believe, such exact Likeness in Substance, should be in the Authorities given by every Government to to their Commissioners, without having any Conference together about it, if the Directions from the Crown had not pointed it out to them in so plain a Manner, that they all understood them alike? And is it not as plain, from the Letters since received from the Secretaries of State, that they all understood them in the Sense the King intended them?

Altho' all this were allowed, yet some may say, If you had Powers given you to enter into some such General Scheme, you ought not to have consented to one so hurtful and destructive of our Liberties as this is! Whether the Plan formed at Albany, be a good one, or a bad one, I shall not undertake to determin; yet let it be considered, that the Rhode-Island Commissioners were but two of the whole Number, and therefore were far from being able to govern or form Things as they might think best; neither did they ever pretend they could not be mistaken; and Errors of Judgment will always be forgiven by Men of Candor.

And now let us examin what the Commissioners did relating to this Plan, and we shall find, they did no more than form it, and agree to lay it before the General Assemblies of the Colonies from whence they came, for their Consideration. They did not, as is falsly asserted, order it to be sent home. They did not establish it as an Act or Ordinance of the Board of Commissioners, as they all might have done, by the

Authorities given them.   They did not leave it in the Power of any one
to obtain a Copy of it, and send it Home ; but strictly forbid theii
Secretary to give any Copy, except to the Colonies.   Nor did they ever
agree to any Thing more, than to carry it to their respective Governments, and lay it before their Constituents.   And agreeable to the
Resolve of the Board of Commissioners, those from Rhode-Island, did
lay this Plan, with all other their Proceedings at Albany, before the
General Assembly, at their Session in August last, for their Consideration.   Was this criminal !   Was this betraying their Trust !   Or was
there any Thing more in this, than their Duty !   Even Envy and Ignorance joined together, cannot say there was !   And those who have been
bold enough to assert, That any Thing more relating to this Plan of
Union, was done, suffered to be done, or connived at, by the Commissioners, are hereby publicly called upon, to prove their Assertions, or
confess their Falshood.

Once more, let us hold up this so much talked of Plan of Union, and
view it in another Light :   And here, to do my Adversaries all the Justice they can possibly desire, I will, for Argument-sake, confess it to be
as bad as they represent it to be.   Viewing it in this Light, it must be
found contrary to, and subversive of our happy Constitution, and all
those valuable Privileges we enjoy under it.   This destructive Plan was
laid before the General Assembly, for their Consideration, in the Month
of August last :   This gave an Opportunity to those Patriots belonging
to the Council, who now say so much against this Plan, to have exerted
themselves in Defence of our Liberties, so much in Danger, and prevented the Dismal Effects so much feared.   Well ! What have these
Champions for Liberty, done in this Matter?   Have they not let it lie
before the Assembly between six and seven Months, without taking it
once under Consideration?   Or, Have they ever rejected it? or so
much as once in all this Time, moved to have one Word wrote Home,
to prevent its taking Place?   Was it bad, as they say 'tis, then certainly
'twas their Duty to have done all in their Power to prevent its taking
Effect.   All Men must confess, the Plan was either good or bad ; if
'twas good, Why do they blame it? if 'twas bad, Why have they done
Nothing about it? . . .

What could the Commissioners for Rhode-Island have done more?
or what could they have done less than they did, relative to this Plan?
It was not in their Power to procure a better ; and whether it was good
or bad, it was equally their Duty to lay it before the Assembly who sent

them: They did so, and did no more; and every Member of both
Houses of Assembly can bear Witness, I have never used the least
Endeavour to induce them to accede to it.   If it is bad, as some are
pleas'd to represent it, Must not every Man say, They who have suffered
it to lie thus long, are the very Men who have betrayed their Trust, and
the Interest of the Colony?

Real want of Merit occasions these Men's Endeavour to rise upon the
Ruin of their Neighbour's Reputation.   But can the Faults of my Neighbour, make me fit for an Office?   And can the valuable Privileges of
this Colony be safe in those Hands, where every Thing else seems to be
neglected, but what will serve their private Purposes?   As I am a
Candidate for an Office, I sincerely desire all Men may put their Country's Interest in the first Place, and give their Votes only where they
think 'tis most safe; and assure themselves, such a Conduct will perfectly please the Colony's, and their Friend,

STEPHEN HOPKINS.

Stephen Hopkins, *A True Representation of the Plan formed at Albany, in
1754, for Uniting all the British Northern Colonies (Rhode Island Historical Tracts*, No. 9, Providence, 1880), 40–46 *passim*.

126. Deportation of the Acadians (1755)

BY COLONEL JOHN WINSLOW

Winslow was a Massachusetts officer, to whom was assigned the painful duty of
removing the resident French population of Nova Scotia at the beginning of the
war.   The question of the necessity of this removal has been much disputed; Parkman thinks it was inevitable. — Bibliography: Winsor, *Narrative and Critical History*, V, 452; Parkman, *Montcalm and Wolfe*, I, 234; Channing and Hart, *Guide*,
§ 131.

August 30th.   LAST Evening Capt. Murray Arived and Brought
with him the afore resights Commissions & In-
structions & Letters and with whome I Consulted Methods for removing
the whole Inhabitants of the Villages of Grand Pre, Mines, Rivers Cannard, Habbertong and Gaspereau, and agreed that it would be Most
Convenient to Sight all the Male Inhabitants of sd Villages to assemble
at the Church in this Place on the 5th of September next to hear the
King's Orders, and that at the Same time Capt. Murray to Collect the
Inhabitants of Piziquid, and Villages adjatent to Forte Edward for

the Same Purpose, and wrote Colo Lawrance this Day our Determination, and after Capt. Murray's Departure Convened the Captains, vizt, Adams, Hobbs & Osgood togather and after Taking an Oath of Secressy from them Lade before them my Instructions & Papers and also of the Proposd agreement made between Capt. Murray and my Self, of which they unanimously approved. . . .

1755 Augt 31. Sunday. Dispatched Leivt Crooker in the Large whale Boat with the Halifax Letters together with mine to Colo Monckton in the afternoon Took a Touer with Doctr Whitworth & Mr. Gay & 50 men Two Third parts round Grand Pre. Finde abundance of wheat &c on the Ground. returned in the Evening. . . .

September 1st, 1755. Detached Lievt Buckley with the Party ordered yesterday for Piziquid having before agreed with Captain Murray an officer & So many Men as we have No People acquainted with the Countrey the Party I am to Receive to Serve us as Pilotes, and in the Evening Lievt Mercer and his party arived who I incampt by them Selves on the West Side of the Church, an Took the officer to my Quarters.

2nd. Sett out Early in the Morning in a whale Boat for Fort Edward having with me Doctr Whitworth and adjutant Kennedy to Consult with Capt. Murray in this Crittical Conjuncter. Confirmed our Proposd Plan and Determined three of the Clock in the afternoon to be the time. Made out a Citation to the Inhabitants to Convene them, vizt. : those in my Districk att the Church in Grand Pre, those of Capt. Murray at Forte Edward at Piziquid. Got it put into French by Mr. Beauchamp, a Merchant. . . .

Septr. 3rd. This Morning Capt Adams and Party returned from their March to the River Cannard &c and reported it was a Fine Country and Full of Inhabitants, a Butifull Church & abundance of ye Goods of the world. Provisions of all Kinds in great Plenty.

Capt Hobbs ordered with one Sub 2 Serjants 2 Corporals and 50 Private men to Visset the Village Melanson on the River Gaspereau, and Capt Osgood with the Like Number of officers and men to Reconuiter the Country In the Front or to the Southward of our Incampment. Both of which Party's returned in the Evening and Gave Each accoumts that it was a Fine Countrey.

This Day had a Consultation with the Captains the Result of which was that I Should Give out my Citation to the Inhabitants tomorrow Morning. . . .

1755, *September the 4th.* This Morning Sent for Docter Rodion and Delivd him a Citation to the Inhabitants with a Strict Charge to See it Executed. which he Promist Should be Faithfully Done.

A Fine Day and the Inhabitants Very Busy about their Harvest, &c.

September 5th. This Morning had returns of the Horns of the Several Companys and ordered Such as had them to Deliver up what Cartherages they had to Compleat those who had No Horns which near about Did it & then Ddd out to those who had Hornes Powder at half a Pound Each to the amount of Half a Barrell and Twelve Balls to Each half Pound of Powder. ordered the whole Camp to Lye upon their arms this Day.

Att Three in the afternoon The French Inhabitants appeard agreable to their Citation at the Church in Grand Pre amounting To 418 of Their Best Men upon which I ordered a Table to be Sett in the Center of the Church and being attended with those of my officers who were off Gaurd   Delivered them by Interpretors the King's orders In the Following woords :

GENTLEMEN,

I have Received from his Excellency Govenor Lawrance. The Kings Commission which I have in my hand and by whose orders you are Convened togather to Manifest to you his Majesty's Final resolution to the French Inhabitants of this his Province of Nova Scotia. who for almost half a Centry have had more Indulgence Granted them, then any of his Subjects in any part of his Dominions. what use you have made of them. you your Self Best Know.

The Part of Duty I am now upon is what thoh Necessary is Very Disagreable to my natural make & Temper as I Know it Must be Grevious to you who are of the Same Specia.

But it is not my Buisness to annimedvert, but to obey Such orders as I receive and therefore without Hessitation Shall Deliver you his Majesty's orders and Instructions vizt.

That your Lands & Tennements, Cattle of all Kinds and Live Stock of all Sortes are Forfitted to the Crown with all other your Effects Saving your money and Household Goods and you your Selves to be removed from this his Province.

Thus it is Preremtorily his Majesty's orders That the whole French Inhabitants of these Districts, be removed, and I am Throh his Majesty's Goodness Directed to allow you Liberty to Carry of your money and Household Goods as Many as you Can without Discomemoading the

Vessels you Go in.   I Shall do Every thing in my Power that all Those
Goods be Secured to you and that you are Not Molested in Carrying
of them of and also that whole Familys Shall go in the Same Vessel.   and
make this remove which I am Sensable must give you a great Deal of
Trouble as Easey as his Majesty's Service will admit and hope that in
what Ever part of the world you may Fall you may be Faithfull Subjects,
a Peasable & happy People.

I Must also Inform you That it is his Majesty's Pleasure that you
remain in Security under the Inspection & Direction of the Troops that
I have the Honr. to Command.   and then Declared them the Kings
Prisoners. . . .

After Delivering These Things I returned to my Quarters and they
the French Inhabitants Soon Moved by their Elders that it was a Great
Greif to them, that they had Incurd his Majty's Displeasure and that
they were Fearfull that the Suprise of their Detention here would Quite
over Come their Familys whome they had No Means to apprise of these
their Maloncolly Circumstances and Prayd that parte of them might be
returned as Hostages for the appearance of the rest and the Biger number admitted to Go home to their Families, and that as some of their
Men were absent they would be obliged to Bring them in.   I Informed
them I would Consider of their Motion, and reporte.

And Immediatly Convened my officers, to advise, who with Me all
agreed that it would be well that they them Selves Should Chuse Twenty
of their Number for whome they would be answerable vizt Ten of the
Inhabitants of Grand Pre & Village & other Ten of the River Cannard
and Habitant   nd they to acquaint the Families of their Districts how
Maters where and to assure them that the women & children Should be
in Safety in their absence in their Habitations and that it was Exspected
the Party Indulged Should take Care to Bring in an Exact Account
of their absent Bretheren & their Circumstances on the Morrow. . . .

Septr 5th.   The French People not having any Provissions with them
and Pleading Hunger Begd for Bread on which I Ddd them   and
ordered that for the Future they be Supplyd from their respective
Familys.   Thus Ended the Memerable fifth of September, a Day of
Great Fatigue & Troble. . . .

1755 *Septr 7.*   Proved a Very Buissy Day, advice arived from Every
Quarter which I Answered as well as I Could in the Foregoing Letters.
the French remd in Quiate.   We mounted Gaurd with half our Party
Capt Adams & Osgood Doing Duty by Turns.   Capt Hobbs Sick.   we

all Lay on our Arms Since Detaining the French hear. Kept a Good
Look Out & I not wanting in Turning out at all Times when I waked So
that I was on Both watches. . . .

Septr 10. The French this Morning Discovered Some Uncommon
Motions among them Selves which I did Not Like. Called my officers
togather and Communicated to them what I had observed, and after
Debating Matters it was Determined Neme Contra Dissent, that it
would be best to Divide the Prisoners, and that as there was Five
Transporte Idle which Came from Boston, it would be for ye Good of
his Majestys Service and that it Tended to the Better Security of the
whole, That Fifty men of the French Inhabitants be Embarkd on Board
Each of the five Vessels, taking First all their young men, and that Capt
Adams in the Warren be Desierd and Directed as he was a Vessel
of Force & in his Majestys Service to Take the Transportes under his
Directions and when the Prisoners were Embarked to Give Such Orders
to the Masters of the Transportes as would be best for his Majesty's
Service, and also Determind that Six Non Commission officers or Private men be put on Board Each Transporte as a Gaurd and that Capt
Adams and the Masters be Immediately Ordered to Get things in readiness for that Service after which I Sent for Father Landrey Their Principal Speaker who Talks English and Told him the Time was Come for
part of the Inhabitants to Embarke and that the Number Concluded
for this Day was 250 and that we Should begin with the young men and
Desierd he would Inform his bretherin of it. he was greatly Surprised.
I Told him it must be Done and that I Shoud order the whole Prisoners
to be Drawn up Six Deep, their young men on the Left, and as the
Tide in a Very Little time Favoured my Design Could not Give them
above an Houer to Prepare for going on Board, and ordered our whole
Party to be under Arms and Post them Selves between the Two Gates &
the Church in the rear of my Quarters, which was obeyed, and agreable
to my Directions The whole of the French Inhabitants where Drawn
togather In one Body their young men as Directed on the Left. I then
orderd Capt Adams with a Lievt 80 Non Commission officers and Private Men to Draw of from the main Body to Gaurd the young men of
the French amounting to 141 Men to the Transports and order ye
Prisoners to March. they all answered they would No go without their
Fathers. I Told them that was a word I did not understand for that
the Kings Command was to me absolute & Should be absolutely obeyed
& That I Did not Love to use Harsh Means but that the time Did not

admit of Parlies or Delays and Then ordered the whole Troops to Fix their Bayonets and advance Towards the French, and Bid the 4 right hand Files of the Prisoners Consisting of 24 men wch I told of my Self to Divied from the rest, one of whome I Took hold on (who oposed the Marching) and bid March. he obeyed & the rest followed. thoh Slowly, and went of Praying, Singing & Crying being Met by the women & Children all the way (which is 1½ mile) with Great Lamentations upon their Knees praying &c.

I then ordered the remaining French to Chuse out 109 of Their marryed men to follow their young People (the Ice being Broke) they readily Complyed and Drew up in a Body as said the number who upon Capt Adams return I ordered of under a Gaurd Commanded by Capt Osgood one Subaltern 80 non Commission officers and Private men. who marched of them, but when he Came to put them on board the Vessels Found them but 89 Instead of 109. So that the Number Embarqued was but 230 and Thus Ended this Troblesome Jobb, which was Scheen of Sorrow. After this Capt Adams with the Transports Fell Down from Gaspereau and anchored in the Mouth of that river and Piziquid. . . .

Journal of Colonel John Winslow, in Nova Scotia Historical Society, *Report and Collections*, 1882–1883 (Halifax, 1883), III, 87–110 *passim*.

————◆————

127. A French Account of Braddock's Defeat (1755)

ANONYMOUS

(TRANSLATED BY E. B. O'CALLAGHAN, 1843)

This brief account from the victor's side, found in the archives at Paris, shows how nearly the fortunes of war had gone the other way. — Bibliography: Winsor, *Narrative and Critical History*, V, 577–579; Parkman, *Montcalm and Wolfe*, I, ch. vii; Channing and Hart, *Guide*, § 132.

M. DE Contrecœur, Captain of Infantry, Commandant of Fort Duquesne, on the Ohio, having been informed that the English were taking up arms in Virginia for the purpose of coming to attack him, was advised, shortly afterwards, that they were on the march. He dispatched scouts, who reported to him faithfully their progress. On the 17th instant he was advised that their army, consisting of 3000 regulars from Old England, were within six leagues of this fort. That officer employed the next day in making his arrangements ; and on the ninth detached M. de Beaujeu, seconded by Messrs Dumas and de Lignery, all three Captains, together with four Lieutenants, 6 Ensigns, 20 Cadets, 100 Soldiers, 100 Canadians and 600 Indians, with orders to lie in ambush at a favorable spot, which he had reconnoitred the previous evening. The detachment, before it could reach its place of destination, found itself in presence of the enemy within three leagues of that fort. Mr de Beaujeu, finding his ambush had failed, decided on an attack. This he made with so much vigor as to astonish the enemy, who were waiting for us in the best possible order ; but their artillery, loaded with grape (*à cartouche*), having opened its fire, our men gave way in turn. The Indians, also, frightened by the report of the cannon rather than by any damage it could inflict, began to yield, when M. de Beaujeu was killed. M. Dumas began to encourage his detachment. He ordered the officers in command of the Indians to spread themselves along the wings so as to take the enemy in flank, whilst he, M. de Lignery and the other officers who led the French, were attacking them in front. This order was executed so promptly that the enemy, who were already shouting their " Long live the King," thought now only of defending themselves. The fight was obstinate on both sides and success long doubtful ; but the enemy at last gave way. Efforts were made, in vain, to introduce some sort of order in their retreat. The whoop of the Indians, which echoed through the forest, struck terror into the hearts of the entire enemy. The rout was complete. We remained in possession of the field with six brass twelves and sixes, four howitz-carriages of 50, 11 small royal grenade mortars, all their ammunition, and, generally, their entire baggage. Some deserters, who have come in since, have told us that we had been engaged with only 2000 men, the remainder of the army being four leagues further off. These same deserters have informed us that the enemy were retreating to Virginia, and some scouts, sent as far as the height of land, have confirmed this by reporting that the thousand men who were not engaged, had been equally panic-stricken and abandoned both provisions and ammunition on the way. On this intelligence, a detachment was dispatched after them, which destroyed and burnt everything that could be found. The enemy have left more than 1000 men on the field of battle. They have lost a great portion of the artillery and ammunition, provisions, as also their General, whose name was Mr Braddock, and almost all their officers.

We have had 3 officers killed ; 2 officers and 2 cadets wounded.   Such a victory, so entirely unexpected, seeing the inequality of the forces, is the fruit of Mr Dumas' experience, and of the activity and valor of the officers under his command.

E. B. O'Callaghan, editor, *Documents relative to the Colonial History of the State of New-York* (Albany, 1858), X, 303–304.

———◆———

128.   "The Empire is no more" (1757)

BY SECRETARY WILLIAM PITT

The coming forward of Pitt (later Lord Chatham) as head of the administration was the turning-point in the war, and made possible the brilliant campaigns in America.   This piece brings out the fact that the American conflict led to the general European " Seven Years' War," which lasted till 1763.   It is addressed to the British ambassador in Spain, and shows the apprehensions of England's most courageous statesman. — Bibliography : Lecky, *England*, II, ch. viii; Mahon, *England*, ch. xxxiv.

Whitehall, August 23, 1757. . . .

IT is judged the most compendious and sure method of opening and conveying to your excellency with due clearness and precision, the scope and end of the measure in question, to refer you to the minute itself, *in extenso*, unanimously approved by all his Majesty's servants consulted in his most secret affairs, and containing the sum and substance, as well as the grounds, of the King's royal intention in this violent and dangerous crisis, which minute is conceived in the following words, viz. —

" Their lordships, having taken into consideration the formidable progress of the arms of France, and the danger to Great Britain and her allies resulting from a total subversion of the system of Europe, and more especially from the most pernicious extension of the influence of France, by the fatal admission of French garrisons into Ostend and Nieuport, their lordships are most humbly of opinion, that nothing can so effectually tend, in the present unhappy circumstances, to the restoration of Europe in general, and in particular to the successful prosecution of the present just and necessary war, until a peace can be made on safe and honourable terms, as a more intimate union with the crown of Spain.   In this necessary view their lordships most humbly submit their opinion to your Majesty's great wisdom — that overtures of a negociation should be set on foot with that court, in order to engage Spain, if possible, to join their arms to those of your Majesty, for the obtaining a just and honourable peace, and mainly for recovering and restoring to the crown of England the most important island of Minorca, with all the ports and fortresses of the same, as well as for re-establishing some solid system in Europe ; and inasmuch as it shall be found necessary for the attaining these great and essential ends, to treat with the crown of Spain, as an effectual condition thereunto, concerning an exchange of Gibraltar for the island of Minorca, with the ports and fortresses thereof, their lordships are most humbly of an unanimous opinion, that the court of Spain should without loss of time be sounded with respect to their dis-positions thereupon ; and if the same shall be found favourable, that the said negociation should be carried forward and ripened for execution, with all possible dispatch and secrecy. Their lordships are farther of opinion, that satisfaction should be given to Spain on the complaints touching the establishment made by the subjects of England on the Mosquito shore, and in the bay of Honduras, since the treaty concluded at Aix la Chapelle, in October, 1748, in order that all establishments so made be evacuated.''

. . . it is impossible for me to pass in silence that affecting and calamitous part of the subversions of Europe, namely, the French con-quests and desolations in Lower Saxony, which afford the afflicting spec-tacle of his Majesty's ancient patrimonial dominions, transmitted down with glory in his most illustrious house through a long series of centuries, now lying a prey to France ; and still farther, the fatality of his Majesty's army of observation, now retiring under the orders of his Royal High-ness to Stade, exposed to the most alarming uncertainties, whether even the royal magnanimity of his Majesty, seconded by the valour and ability of his Royal Highness, can find means to surmount the cruel necessity of receiving the law of the conqueror.

As it would be needless to lead your excellency farther on in this gloomy track of mortifying reflections, I will only observe, before I pass to the execution of the plan now opened, that the day is come when the very inadequate benefits of the treaty of Utrecht, the indelible reproach of the last generation, are become the necessary, but almost unattainable wish of the present, when the empire is no more, the ports of the Neth-erlands betrayed, the Dutch Barrier treaty an empty sound, Minorca, and with it, the Mediterranean lost, and America itself precarious.

From this state of things, calamitous as it is, your excellency has a fresh proof that nothing can ever shake his Majesty's firmness, or abate one moment his royal concern for the glory of his crown, and the rights of his kingdoms ; nor can any events withdraw the necessary attention of his Majesty's consummate wisdom from the proper interests of Europe, or divert his generous cares from endeavouring to prevent the final overthrow of all Europe, and independency amongst the powers of the continent. In this salutary view it is that the King has, in his great prudence, come to a resolution of ordering the dispositions of the court of Madrid, in this alarming conjuncture, to be sounded ; and, as the same shall be found favourable, a negociation to be, without loss of time, opened on the grounds and to the ends contained in the minute above recited. . . .

William Pitt, Earl of Chatham, *Correspondence* (edited by W. S. Taylor and J. H. Pringle, London, 1840), I, 247–251 *passim*.

———◆———

129. The Fall of Quebec (1759)

BY CAPTAIN JOHN KNOX

Knox was an officer in the English navy, a trustworthy eye-witness of the events which he describes. This is the best of several contemporary narratives. — Bibliography : Winsor, *Narrative and Critical History*, V, 603–606; Lecky, *England*, II, 494–496; Parkman, *Montcalm and Wolfe*, II, chs. xxv, xxviii; Channing and Hart, *Guide*, § 132.

. . . GREAT preparations are making, throughout the fleet and army, to surprise the enemy, and compel them to decide the fate of Quebec by a battle : all the long-boats below the town are to be filled with seamen, marines, and such detachments as can be spared from Points Levi and Orleans, in order to make a feint off Beauport and the Point de Lest, and endeavour to engross the attention of the Sieur de Montcalm, while the army are to force a descent on this side of the town. The Officer of our regiment, who commanded the escort yesterday on the reconnoitring party, being asked, in the General's hearing, after the health of one of the gentlemen who was reported to be ill, replied, — 'he was in a very low indifferent state ; ' which the other lamented, saying, 'he has but a puny, delicate constitution.' — This struck his Excellency, it being his own case, who interrupted, 'Don't tell me of constitution, that Officer has good spirits, and good spirits will carry a man through every thing.' . . .

The Brigadiers Monckton and Murray, with the troops under their command, reimbarked this day, from the parish of St. Nicholas, and returned to their ships. This evening all the boats of the fleet below the town were filled with marines, &c. &c. covered by frigates and

2 B

sloops of war, worked up, and lay half-channel over, opposite to Beauport, as if intending to land in the morning, and thereby fix the enemy's
whole attention to that quarter; the ships attending them are to edge
over, at break of day, as near as possible without grounding, and cannonade the French intrenchments. At nine o'clock this night, our
army in high spirits, the first division of them put into the flat-bottomed
boats, and, in a short time after, the whole squadron moved up the
river with the tide of flood, and, about an hour before day-light next
morning, we fell down with the ebb. Weather favourable, a star-light
night.

Thursday, September 13, 1759.

Before day-break this morning we made a descent upon the north
shore, about half a quarter of a mile to the eastward of Sillery; and
the light troops were fortunately, by the rapidity of the current, carried
lower down, between us and Cape Diamond; we had, in this debarka-
tion, thirty flat-bottomed boats, containing about sixteen hundred men.
This was a great surprise on the enemy, who, from the natural strength
of the place, did not suspect, and consequently were not prepared
against, so bold an attempt. The chain of centries, which they had
posted along the summit of the heights, galled us a little, and picked off
several men, and some Officers, before our light infantry got up to dis-
lodge them. This grand enterprise was conducted, and executed with
great good order and discretion; as fast as we landed, the boats put off
for reinforcements, and the troops formed with much regularity: the
General, with Brigadiers Monckton and Murray, were a-shore with the
first division. We lost no time here, but clambered up one of the steep-
est precipices that can be conceived, being almost a perpendicular, and
of an incredible height. As soon as we gained the summit, all was quiet,
and not a shot was heard, owing to the excellent conduct of the light
infantry under Colonel Howe; it was by this time clear day-light.
Here we formed again, the river and the south country in our rear, our
right extending to the town, our left to Sillery, and halted a few minutes.
The General then detached the light troops to our left to route the
enemy from their battery, and to disable their guns, except they could
be rendered serviceable to the party who were to remain there; and
this service was soon performed. We then faced to the right, and
marched towards the town by files, till we came to the plains of Abraham; an even piece of ground which Mr. Wolfe had made choice of,
while we stood forming upon the hill. Weather showery: about six

o'clock the enemy first made their appearance upon the heights, between us and the town; whereupon we halted, and wheeled to the right, thereby forming the line of battle. . . . The enemy had now likewise formed the line of battle, and got some cannon to play on us, with round and canister-shot; but what galled us most was a body of Indians and other marksmen they had concealed in the corn opposite to the front of our right wing, and a coppice that stood opposite to our center, inclining towards our left; but the Colonel Hale, by Brigadier Monckton's orders, advanced some platoons, alternately, from the forty-seventh regiment, which, after a few rounds, obliged these sculkers to retire: we were now ordered to lie down, and remained some time in this position. About eight o'clock we had two pieces of short brass six-pounders playing on the enemy, which threw them into some confusion, and obliged them to alter their disposition, and Montcalm formed them into three large columns; about nine the two armies moved a little nearer each other. The light cavalry made a faint attempt upon our parties at the battery of Sillery, but were soon beat off, and Monsieur de Bougainville, with his troops from Cape Rouge, came down to attack the flank of our second line, hoping to penetrate there; but, by a masterly disposition of Brigadier Townshend, they were forced to desist, and the third battalion of Royal Americans was then detached to the first ground we had formed on after we gained the heights, to preserve the communication with the beach and our boats. About ten o'clock the enemy began to advance briskly in three columns, with loud shouts and recovered arms, two of them inclining to the left of our army, and the third towards our right, firing obliquely at the two extremities of our line, from the distance of one hundred and thirty —, until they came within forty yards; which our troops withstood with the greatest intrepidity and firmness, still reserving their fire, and paying the strictest obedience to their Officers: this uncommon steadiness, together with the havoc which the grape-shot from our field-pieces made among them, threw them into some disorder, and was most critically maintained by a well-timed, regular, and heavy discharge of our small arms, such as they could no longer oppose; hereupon they gave way, and fled with precipitation, so that, by the time the cloud of smoke was vanished, our men were again loaded, and, profiting by the advantage we had over them, pursued them almost to the gates of the town, and the bridge over the little river, redoubling our fire with great eagerness, making many Officers and men prisoners. The weather cleared up, with a comfortably warm sun-shine : the Highlanders chaced them vigorously towards Charles's river, and the fifty-eighth to the suburb close to John's gate, until they were checked by the cannon from the two hulks; at the same time a gun, which the town had brought to bear upon us with grape-shot, galled the progress of the regiments to the right, who were likewise pursuing with equal ardour, while Colonel Hunt Walsh, by a very judicious movement, wheeled the battalions of Bragg and Kennedy to the left, and flanked the coppice where a body of the enemy made a stand, as if willing to renew the action ; but a few platoons from these corps completed our victory. Then it was that Brigadier Townshend came up, called off the pursuers, ordered the whole line to dress, and recover their former ground. Our joy at this success is inexpressibly damped by the loss we sustained of one of the greatest heroes which this or any other age can boast of, — GENERAL JAMES WOLFE, who received his mortal wound, as he was exerting himself at the head of the grenadiers of Louisbourg. . . .

. . . The Sieur de Montcalm died late last night ; when his wound was dressed, and he settled in bed, the Surgeons who attended him were desired to acquaint him ingenuously with their sentiments of him, and, being answered that his wound was mortal, he calmly replied, ' he was glad of it : ' his Excellency then demanded, — ' whether he could survive it long, and how long ? ' He was told, ' about a dozen hours, perhaps more, peradventure less.' ' So much the better,' rejoined this eminent warrior ; ' I am happy I shall not live to see the surrender of Quebec.' . . .

After our late worthy General, of renowned memory, was carried off wounded, to the rear of the front line, he desired those who were about him to lay him down ; being asked if he would have a Surgeon? he replied, ' it is needless ; it is all over with me.' One of them then cried out, ' they run, see how they run.' ' Who runs !' demanded our hero, with great earnestness, like a person roused from sleep? The Officer answered, ' The enemy, Sir ; Egad they give way every-where.' Thereupon the General rejoined. ' *Go one of you, my lads, to Colonel Burton* — ; *tell him to march Webb's regiment with all speed down to Charles's river, to cut off the retreat of the fugitives from the bridge.*' Then, turning on his side, he added, ' *Now, God be praised, I will die in peace :* ' and thus expired.

Captain John Knox, *An Historical Journal of the Campaigns in North-America* [1757–1760], (London, 1769), II, 65–79 *passim.*

PART VI

CAUSES OF THE REVOLUTION

═══════════

CHAPTER XXI — NEW CONDITIONS OF ENG-LISH CONTROL

130. The Character of George Third (1758)

BY JAMES, EARL OF WALDEGRAVE

Waldegrave was at one time tutor of the young prince. — Bibliography: Donne, *Correspondence of George III;* Mahon, *England,* VI, 100, and Appendix; Lecky, *England,* III, 10–14.

THE Prince of Wales is entering into his 21st year, and it would be unfair to decide upon his character in the early stages of life, when there is so much time for improvement.

His parts, though not excellent, will be found very tolerable, if ever they are properly exercised.

He is strictly honest, but wants that frank and open behaviour which makes honesty appear amiable.

When he had a very scanty allowance, it was one of his favorite maxims that men should be just before they are generous: his income is now very considerably augmented, but his generosity has not increased in equal proportion.

His religion is free from all hypocrisy, but is not of the most charitable sort; he has rather too much attention to the sins of his neighbour.

He has spirit, but not of the active kind; and does not want resolution, but it is mixed with too much obstinacy.

He has great command of his passions, and will seldom do wrong, except when he mistakes wrong for right; but as often as this shall happen, it will be difficult to undeceive him, because he is uncommonly indolent, and has strong prejudices.

His want of application and aversion to business would be far less dangerous, was he eager in the pursuit of pleasure; for the transition

373

from pleasure to business is both shorter and easier than from a state of total inaction.

He has a kind of unhappiness in his temper, which, if it be not conquered before it has taken too deep a root, will be a source of frequent anxiety. Whenever he is displeased, his anger does not break out with heat and violence ; but he becomes sullen and silent, and retires to his closet ; not to compose his mind by study or contemplation, but merely to indulge the melancholy enjoyment of his own ill humor. Even when the fit is ended, unfavorable symptoms very frequently return, which indicate that on certain occasions his Royal Highness has too correct a memory.

Though I have mentioned his good and bad qualities, without flattery, and without aggravation, allowances should still be made, on account of his youth, and his bad education : for though the Bishop of Peterborough, now Bishop of Salisbury, the preceptor ; Mr. Stone, the sub-governor ; and Mr. Scott, the sub-preceptor, were men of sense, men of learning, and worthy, good men, they had but little weight and influence. The mother and the nursery always prevailed.

During the course of the last year, there has, indeed, been some alteration ; the authority of the nursery has gradually declined, and the Earl of Bute, by the assistance of the mother, has now the intire confidence. But whether this change will be greatly to his Royal Highness's advantage, is a nice question, which cannot hitherto be determined with any certainty.

James [2d] Earl Waldegrave, *Memoirs from 1754 to 1758* (edited by H. R. V. Fox, London, 1821), 8–16.

---

131. Argument on Writs of Assistance (1761)

BY JAMES OTIS

(REPORTED BY JOHN ADAMS)

Otis was a Boston lawyer whose powers of debate and fervid oratory made him the most prominent of the Americans in the first phase of the Revolution. This argument was a public assertion of the right of the colonists to be free from a means of executing the acts of trade. — Bibliography : Tyler, *Literary History of the Revolution*, I, 36–52; William Tudor, *Life of Otis;* Winsor, *Narrative and Critical History*, VI, 68–70; Channing and Hart, *Guide*, §134. — On the acts of trade, see *Contemporaries*, I, No. 54, and above, Nos. 45, 55, 87.

I WAS desired by one of the Court to look into the books, and consider the question now before them concerning writs of assistance. I have accordingly considered it, and now appear, not only in obedience to your order, but likewise in behalf of the inhabitants of this town, who have presented another petition, and out of regard to the liberties of the subject. And I take this opportunity to declare, that whether under a fee or not (for in such a cause as this I despise a fee) I will to my dying day oppose with all the powers and faculties God has given me, all such instruments of slavery on the one hand, and villany on the other, as this writ of assistance is.

It appears to me the worst instrument of arbitrary power, the most destructive of English liberty and the fundamental principles of law, that ever was found in an English law-book. I must, therefore, beg your Honors' patience and attention to the whole range of an argument, that may perhaps appear uncommon in many things, as well as to points of learning that are more remote and unusual; that the whole tendency of my design may the more easily be perceived, the conclusions better discerned, and the force of them be better felt. I shall not think much of my pains in this cause, as I engaged in it from principle. I was solicited to argue this cause as Advocate-General; and because I would not, I have been charged with desertion from my office. To this charge I can give a very sufficient answer. I renounced that office, and I argue this cause, from the same principle; and I argue it with the greater pleasure, as it is in favor of British liberty, at a time when we hear the greatest monarch upon earth declaring from his throne that he glories in the name of Briton, and that the privileges of his people are dearer to him than the most valuable prerogatives of his crown; and as it is in opposition to a kind of power, the exercise of which, in former periods of English history, cost one King of England his head, and another his throne. I have taken more pains in this cause, than I ever will take again, although my engaging in this and another popular cause has raised much resentment. But I think I can sincerely declare, that I cheerfully submit myself to every odious name for conscience' sake; and from my soul I despise all those, whose guilt, malice, or folly has made them my foes. Let the consequences be what they will, I am determined to proceed. The only principles of public conduct, that are worthy of a gentleman or a man, are to sacrifice estate, ease, health, and applause, and even life, to the sacred calls of his country. These manly sentiments, in private life, make the good citizen; in public life, the patriot and the hero. I do not say, that when brought to the test, I shall be invincible. I pray God I may never be brought to the melancholy trial; but if ever I should, it will be then known how far I can reduce to practice principles, which I know to be founded in truth. In the mean time I will proceed to the subject of this writ.

In the first place, may it please your Honors, I will admit that writs of one kind may be legal; that is, special writs, directed to special officers, and to search certain houses, &c. specially set forth in the writ, may be granted by the Court of Exchequer at home, upon oath made before the Lord Treasurer by the person who asks it, that he suspects such goods to be concealed in those very places he desires to search. The act of 14 Charles II. which Mr. Gridley mentions, proves this. And in this light the writ appears like a warrant from a Justice of the Peace to search for stolen goods. Your Honors will find in the old books concerning the office of a Justice of the Peace, precedents of general warrants to search suspected houses. But in more modern books you will find only special warrants to search such and such houses specially named, in which the complainant has before sworn that he suspects his goods are concealed; and you will find it adjudged that special warrants only are legal. In the same manner I rely on it, that the writ prayed for in this petition, being general, is illegal. It is a power, that places the liberty of every man in the hands of every petty officer. I say I admit that special writs of assistance, to search special places, may be granted to certain persons on oath; but I deny that the writ now prayed for can be granted, for I beg leave to make some observations on the writ itself, before I proceed to other acts of Parliament. In the first place, the writ is universal, being directed ' to all and singular Justices, Sheriffs, Constables, and all other officers and subjects;' so, that, in short, it is directed to every subject in the King's dominions. Every one with this writ may be a tyrant; if this commission be legal, a tyrant in a legal manner also may control, imprison, or murder any one within the realm. In the next place, it is perpetual; there is no return. A man is accountable to no person for his doings. Every man may reign secure in his petty tyranny, and spread terror and desolation around him. In the third place, a person with this writ, in the daytime, may enter all houses, shops, &c. at will, and command all to assist him. Fourthly, by this writ not only deputies, &c., but even their menial servants, are allowed to lord it over us. Now one of the most essential branches of English liberty is the freedom of one's house. A man's house is his castle ; and whilst he is quiet, he is as well guarded as a prince in his castle. This writ, if it should be declared legal, would totally annihilate this privilege. Custom-house officers may enter our houses, when they please ; we are commanded to permit their entry. Their menial servants may enter, may break locks, bars, and every thing in their way ; and whether they break through malice or revenge, no man, no court, can inquire. Bare suspicion without oath is suffi- cient. This wanton exercise of this power is not a chimerical suggestion of a heated brain. I will mention some facts. Mr. Pew had one of these writs, and when Mr. Ware succeeded him, he endorsed this writ over to Mr. Ware ; so that these writs are negotiable from one officer to another ; and so your Honors have no opportunity of judging the persons to whom this vast power is delegated. Another instance is this : Mr. Justice Walley had called this same Mr. Ware before him, by a constable, to answer for a breach of Sabbath-day acts, or that of profane swearing. As soon as he had finished, Mr. Ware asked him if he had done. He replied, Yes. Well then, said Mr. Ware, I will show you a little of my power. I command you to permit me to search your house for un- customed goods. And went on to search his house from the garret to the cellar ; and then served the constable in the same manner. But to show another absurdity in this writ ; if it should be established, I insist upon it, every person by the 14 Charles II. has this power as well as custom-house officers. The words are, ' It shall be lawful for any person or persons authorized,' &c. What a scene does this open ! Every man, prompted by revenge, ill humor, or wantonness, to inspect the inside of his neighbor's house, may get a writ of assistance. Others will ask it from self-defence ; one arbitrary exertion will provoke another, until society be involved in tumult and in blood.

Again, these writs are not returned. Writs in their nature are tempo- rary things. When the purposes for which they are issued are answered, they exist no more ; but these live forever ; no one can be called to account. Thus reason and the constitution are both against this writ. Let us see what authority there is for it. Not more than one instance can be found of it in all our law-books ; and that was in the zenith of arbitrary power, namely, in the reign of Charles II., when star-chamber powers were pushed to extremity by some ignorant clerk of the ex- chequer. But had this writ been in any book whatever, it would have been illegal. All precedents are under the control of the principles of law. Lord Talbot says it is better to observe these than any precedents, though in the House of Lords, the last resort of the subject. No Acts of Parliament can establish such a writ; though it should be made in the very words of the petition, it would be void. An act against the constitution is void. (vid. Viner.) But these prove no more than what I before observed, that special writs may be granted *on oath and probable suspicion*. The act of 7 & 8 William III. that the officers of the plantations shall have the same powers, &c. is confined to this sense; that an officer should show probable ground; should take his oath of it; should do this before a magistrate; and that such magistrate, if he think proper, should issue a special warrant to a constable to search the places. That of 6 Anne can prove no more.

John Adams, *Works* (edited by Charles Francis Adams, Boston, 1850), II, Appendix, 523–525.

———◆———

132. Opposition to Arbitrary Power (1763)

BY JOHN WILKES

These extracts are taken from the famous No. 45 of *The North Briton*, published by Wilkes, then a member of Parliament. Wilkes was clever but profligate, and his paper was scurrilous; yet he stood for liberty of the subject and for parliamentary reform in England at the time when the treatment of the American colonies was under discussion. — Bibliography: Fitzgerald, *Life of Wilkes;* May, *Constitutional History of England*, II, chs. ix–x, III, ch. xi; Lecky, *England*, III, 68–82, and ch. xi.

THE *Preliminary Articles of Peace* were such as have drawn the contempt of mankind on our wretched negociators. All our most valuable conquests were agreed to be restored, and the *East-India company* would have been infallibly ruined by a single article of this fallacious and baneful negociation. No hireling of the minister has been hardy enough to dispute this; yet the minister himself has made our sovereign declare, *the satisfaction which he felt at the approaching re-establishment of peace upon conditions so honourable to his crown, and so beneficial to his people*. As to the *entire approbation* of parliament, which is so vainly boasted of, the world knows how that was obtained. The large debt on the *Civil List*, already above half a year in arrear, shews pretty clear the transactions of the winter. It is, however, remarkable, that the minister's speech dwells on the *entire approbation* given by parliament to the *Preliminary Articles*, which I will venture to say, he must by this time be ashamed of; for he has been brought to confess the total want of that knowledge, accuracy and precision, by which such immense advantages, both of trade and territory, were sacrificed to our inveterate enemies. These gross blunders, are, indeed, in some measure set right by the *Definitive Treaty*; yet the most important articles, relative to *cession, commerce*, and the FISHERY, remain as they were, with respect to the *French*. The proud and feeble *Spaniard* too does not RENOUNCE, but only DESISTS *from all pretensions, which he may have formed, to the right of fishing* — where? Only *about the island of* NEW-FOUNDLAND — till a favourable opportunity arises of *insisting* on it, *there, as well as elsewhere*.

The minister cannot forbear, even in the *King's Speech*, insulting us with a dull repetition of the word *œconomy*. I did not expect so soon to hear that word again, after it had been so lately exploded, and more than once by a most numerous audience, *hissed* off the stage of our *English* theatres. It is held in derision by the *voice of the people*, and every tongue loudly proclaims the universal contempt, in which these empty professions are held by *this* nation. Let the public be informed of a single instance of *œconomy*, except indeed in the houshold. . . . Lord *Ligonier* is now no longer at the head of the army; but lord *Bute* in effect is; I mean that every preferment given by the crown will be found still to be obtained by *his* enormous influence, and to be bestowed only on the creatures of the *Scottish* faction. The nation is still in the same deplorable state, while *he* governs, and can make the tools of *his* power pursue the same odious measures. Such a retreat, as he intends, can only mean the personal indemnity, which, I hope, guilt will never find from an injured nation. The negociations of the late inglorious *peace* and the *excise*, will haunt him wherever he goes, and the terrors of the just resentment which he must be sure to meet from a brave and insulted people, and which must finally crush him, will be for ever before his eyes.

In vain will such a minister, or the foul dregs of his power, the tools of corruption and despotism, preach up in *the speech that spirit of concord, and that obedience to the laws, which is essential to good order*. They have sent the *spirit of discord* through the land, and I will prophecy, that it will never be extinguished, but by the extinction of their power. Is the *spirit of concord* to go hand in hand with the PEACE and EXCISE, through this nation? Is it to be expected between an insolent EXCISEMAN, and *a peer, gentleman, freeholder, or farmer*, whose private houses are now made liable to be entered and searched at pleasure? *Gloucestershire, Herefordshire,* and in general all the *cyder* counties, are not surely the *several counties* which are alluded to in the *speech.* The *spirit of concord* hath not gone forth among them, but the *spirit of liberty* has, and a noble opposition has been given to the wicked instruments of oppression. A nation as sensible as the *English,* will see that a *spirit of concord* when they are oppressed, means a tame submission to injury, and that a *spirit of liberty* ought then to arise, and I am sure ever will, in proportion to the weight of the grievance they feel. *Every* legal *attempt of a contrary tendency* to the *spirit of concord* will be deemed a justifiable resistance, warranted by the *spirit of the English constitution.*

A despotic minister will always endeavour to dazzle his prince with high-flown ideas of the *prerogative* and *honour* of the *crown,* which the minister will make a parade of *firmly maintaining.* I wish as much as any man in the kingdom to see *the honour of the crown* maintained in a manner truly becoming *Royalty.* . . .

The *Stuart* line has ever been intoxicated with the slavish doctrines of the *absolute, independent, unlimited* power of the crown. Some of that line were so weakly advised, as to endeavour to reduce them into practice : but the *English* nation was too spirited to suffer the least encroachment on the antient liberties of this kingdom. The *King of England* is only the first magistrate of this country ; but is invested by the law with the whole executive power. He is, however, responsible to his people for the due execution of the royal functions, in the choice of ministers, &c. equal with the meanest of his subjects in his particular duty. The personal character of our present amiable sovereign makes us easy and happy that so great a power is lodged in such hands ; but the *favourite* has given too just cause for him to escape the general odium. The *prerogative* of the crown is to exert the constitutional powers entrusted to it in a way not of blind favour and partiality, but of wisdom and judgment. This is the spirit of our constitution. The people too have their *prerogative,* and I hope the fine words of DRYDEN will be engraven on our hearts :

Freedom *is the English Subject's* Prerogative.

John Wilkes, Charles Churchill, and others, editors, *The North Briton, from No. I to No. XLVI inclusive* (London, 1769), No. XLV, [156 *a-b*] *passim.*

133. Grenville's Scheme of Taxation (1763–1764)

BY COMMISSIONER BENJAMIN FRANKLIN (1778)

Grenville was at this time the English prime minister. — Bibliography on his scheme: Winsor, *Narrative and Critical History*, VI, 62–68; Channing and Hart, *Guide*, § 134. — For Franklin, see No. 68 above.

PASSY, 12 March, 1778.

DEAR SIR : — In the pamphlets you were so kind as to lend me there is one important fact misstated, apparently from the writers not having been furnished with good information. It is the transaction between Mr. Grenville and the colonies, wherein he understands that Mr. Grenville demanded of them a specific sum, that they refused to grant any thing, and that it was on their refusal only that he made the motion for the *Stamp Act*. No one of the particulars was true. The fact was this :

Some time in the winter of 1763–4 Mr. Grenville called togethei the agents of the several colonies, and told them that he purposed to draw a revenue from America ; and to that end his intention was to levy a stamp duty on the colonies by act of Parliament in the ensuing session, of which he thought it fit that they should be immediately acquainted, that they might have time to consider ; and if any other duty equally productive would be more agreeable to them, they might let him know it. The agents were therefore directed to write this to their respective Assemblies, and communicate to him the answers they should receive : the agents wrote accordingly.

I was a member in the Assembly of Pennsylvania when this notification came to hand. The observations there made upon it were, that the ancient, established, and regular method of drawing aid from the colonies was this : The occasion was always first considered by their sovereign in his Privy Council, by whose sage advice he directed his Secretary of State to write circular-letters to the several governors, who were directed to lay them before their Assemblies. In those letters the occasion was explained to their satisfaction, with gracious expressions of his Majesty's confidence in their known duty and affection, on which he relied that they would grant such sums as should be suitable to their abilities, loyalty, and zeal for his service ; that the colonies had always granted liberally on such requisitions, and so liberally during the late war, that the king, sensible they had granted much more than their proportion, had recommended it to Parliament five years successively to make them some compensation, and the Parliament accordingly returned them £200,000 a year, to be divided among them ; that the proposition of taxing them, in Parliament, was therefore both cruel and unjust; that, by the constitution of the colonies, their business was with the king in matters of aid ; they had nothing to do with any financier, nor he with them ; nor were the agents the proper channels through which requisitions should be made ; it was therefore improper for them to enter into any stipulation, or make any proposition to Mr. Grenville about laying taxes on their constituents by Parliament, which had really no right at all to tax them, especially as the notice he had sent them did not appear to be by the king's order, and perhaps was without his knowledge, as the king, when he would obtain any thing from them, always accompanied his requisition with good words, but this gentleman, instead of a decent demand, sent them a menace, that they should certainly be taxed, and only left them the choice of the manner. But all this notwithstanding, they were so far from refusing to grant money that they resolved to the following purpose : " That they always had, so they always should think it their duty to grant aid to the crown, according to their abilities, whenever required of them in the usual constitutional manner." I went soon after to England, and took with me an authentic copy of this resolution, which I presented to Mr. Grenville before he brought in the Stamp Act. I asserted in the House of Commons (Mr. Grenville being present) that I had done so, and he did not deny it. Other colonies made similar resolutions, and had Mr. Grenville, instead of that act, applied to the king in council for such requisitional letters to be circulated by the Secretary of State, I am sure he would have obtained more money from the colonies by their voluntary grants than he himself expected from his stamps. But he chose compulsion rather than persuasion, and would not receive from their good-will what he thought he could obtain without it. And thus the golden bridge which the ingenious author thinks the Americans unwisely and unbecomingly refused to hold out to the minister and Parliament, was actually held out to them, but they refused to walk over it.

This is the true history of that transaction ; and as it is probable there may be another edition of that excellent pamphlet, I wish this may be communicated to the candid author, who, I doubt not, will correct that error. . . .

Benjamin Franklin, *Complete Works* (edited by John Bigelow, New York, etc., 1888), VI, 142-145.

CHAPTER XXII — THE WEST

134. "The Adventures of Col. Daniel Boon"
(1769–1775)

BY JOHN FILSON (1784)

. This narrative purports to be autobiographical, but was put into its literary form by John Filson, an emigrant from Pennsylvania just after the Revolutionary War. Filson was a school-teacher, surveyor, and historian. — Bibliography: Winsor, *Narrative and Critical History*, VI, 708; Roosevelt, *Winning of the West*, I, ch. vi.

IT was on the first of May, in the year 1769, that I resigned my domestic happiness for a time, and left my family and peaceable habitation on the Yadkin River, in North-Carolina, to wander through the wilderness of America, in quest of the country of Kentucke, in company with John Finley, John Stewart, Joseph Holden, James Monay, and William Cool. We proceeded successfully, and after a long and fatiguing journey through a mountainous wilderness, in a westward direction, on the seventh day of June following, we found ourselves on Red-River, where John Finley had for merly been trading with the Indians, and, from the top of an eminence, saw with pleasure the beautiful level of Kentucke. . . . In this forest, the habitation of beasts of every kind natural to America, we practised hunting with great success until the twenty-second day of December following.

This day John Stewart and I had a pleasing ramble, but fortune changed the scene in the close of it. . . . In the decline of the day, near Kentucke river, as we ascended the brow of a small hill, a number of Indians rushed out of a thick cane-brake upon us, and made us prisoners. The time of our sorrow was now arrived, and the scene fully opened. The Indians plundered us of what we had, and kept us in confinement seven days, treating us with common savage usage. During this time we discovered no uneasiness or desire to escape, which made them less suspicious of us; but in the dead of night, as we lay in a thick cane-brake by a large fire, when sleep had locked up their senses, my situation not disposing me for rest, I touched my companion and gently awoke him. We improved this favourable opportunity, and departed, leaving them to take their rest, and speedily directed our course towards our old camp, but found it plundered, and the company dispersed and gone home. About this time my brother, Squire Boon, with another adventurer, who came to explore the country shortly after us, was wandering through the forest, determined to find me, if possible, and accidentally found our camp. . . .

. . . We were then in a dangerous, helpless situation, exposed daily to perils and death amongst savages and wild beasts, not a white man in the country but ourselves. . . .

We continued not in a state of indolence, but hunted every day, and prepared a little cottage to defend us from the Winter storms. We remained there undisturbed during the Winter; and on the first day of May, 1770, my brother returned home to the settlement by himself, for a new recruit of horses and ammunition, leaving me by myself, without bread, salt or sugar, without company of my fellow creatures, or even a horse or dog. I confess I never before was under greater necessity of exercising philosophy and fortitude. . . .

Thus, through an uninterrupted scene of sylvan pleasures, I spent the time until the 27th day of July following, when my brother, to my great felicity, met me, according to appointment, at our old camp. Shortly after, we left this place, not thinking it safe to stay there longer, and proceeded to Cumberland river, reconnoitring that part of the country until March, 1771, and giving names to the different waters.

Soon after, I returned home to my family with a determination to bring them as soon as possible to live in Kentucke, which I esteemed a second paradise, at the risk of my life and fortune.

I returned safe to my old habitation, and found my family in happy circumstances. I sold my farm on the Yadkin, and what goods we could not carry with us; and on the twenty-fifth day of September, 1773, bade a farewel to our friends, and proceeded on our journey to Kentucke, in company with five families more, and forty men that joined us in Powel's Valley, which is one hundred and fifty miles from the now settled parts of Kentucke. This promising beginning was soon overcast with a cloud of adversity; for upon the tenth day of October, the rear of our company was attacked by a number of Indians, who killed six, and wounded one man. Of these my eldest son was one that fell in the action. Though we defended ourselves, and repulsed the enemy, yet this unhappy affair scattered our cattle, brought us into extreme difficulty, and so discouraged the whole company, that we retreated forty miles, to the settlement on Clench river. . . .

I remained with my family on Clench until the sixth of June, 1774, when I and one Michael Stoner were solicited by Governor Dunmore, of Virginia, to go to the Falls of the Ohio, to conduct into the settlement a number of surveyors that had been sent thither by him some months before ; this country having about this time drawn the attention of many adventurers. We immediately complied with the Governor's request, and conducted in the surveyors, compleating a tour of eight hundred miles, through many difficulties, in sixty-two days.

Soon after I returned home, I . . . was solicited by a number of North-Carolina gentlemen, that were about purchasing the lands lying on the S. side of Kentucke River, from the Cherokee Indians, to attend their treaty at Wataga, in March, 1775, to negotiate with them, and, mention the boundaries of the purchase. This I accepted, and at the request of the same gentlemen, undertook to mark out a road in the best passage from the settlement through the wilderness to Kentucke . . . .

I soon began this work, having collected a number of enterprising men, well armed. We proceeded with all possible expedition until we came within fifteen miles of where Boonsborough now stands, and where we were fired upon by a party of Indians that killed two, and wounded two of our number ; yet, although surprised and taken at a disadvantage, we stood our ground. This was on the twentieth of March, 1775. Three days after, we were fired upon again, and had two men killed, and three wounded. Afterwards we proceeded on to Kentucke river without opposition ; and on the first day of April began to erect the fort of Boonsborough, at a salt lick, about sixty yards from the river, on the S. side.

On the fourth day, the Indians killed one of our men. — We were busily employed in building this fort, until the fourteenth day of June following, without any farther opposition from the Indians ; and having finished the works, I returned to my family, on Clench.

In a short time, I proceeded to remove my family from Clench to this garrison ; where we arrived safe without any other difficulties than such as are common to this passage, my wife and daughter being the first white women that ever stood on the banks of Kentucke river.

John Filson, *The Discovery, Settlement and present State of Kentucke,* etc. (Wilmington, 1784), Appendix, 50–60 *passim.*

2 C

135. Cold Water on an Ohio Colony (1770)

BY GOVERNOR THE EARL OF DUNMORE

Dunmore was an unpopular governor, and at the Revolution was driven out of his colony. — On the proposition to establish a new " back colony," see Winsor, *Narrative and Critical History*, V, 570–574; Franklin, *Works* (Sparks's ed.), V, 1–82.

I HAVE made it my business to enquire and find out the opinion of the people here, on the scheme in agitation of establishing a Colony on the Ohio ; I find, all who have any knowledge of such affairs concurr in condemning the project ; they alledge among a variety of reasons, that a Colony, at such an immense distance from the settled parts of America and from the Ocean, can neither benefit either those settled parts or the mother Country ; that they must become immediately a lost people to both, & all communication of a commercial nature with them, be a vain attempt, from the difficulty and expence attending the Transport of commodities to them, which would so enhance the price thereof, as to make it utterly impossible for them to purchase such commodities, for they could not raise a produce of any kind, that would answer so difficult and expensive transport back ; such Colony must therefore be their own Manufacturers ; and the great expence of maintaining Troops there for their protection be a dead weight on Govern^t, without the hopes of reaping any advantage hereafter. The scheme alarms extremely all the settled parts of America, the people of property being justly apprehensive of consequences that must inevitably ensue ; that such a Colony will only become a drain to them (now but thinly peopled) of an infinite number of the lower Class of inhabitants, who, the desire of novelty alone will induce to change their situation ; and the withdrawing of those Inhabitants will reduce the value of Lands in the provinces even to nothing, and make it impossible for the Patentees to pay the Quit Rents ; by which, it is evident, His Maj^{ty's} interest must be very much prejudiced. Add to this the great probability, I may venture to say . . . certainty, that the attempting a settlement on the Ohio, will draw on, an Indian war ; it being well known, how ill affected the Ohio Indians have always been to our interest, and their jealousy of such a settlement, so near them, must be easily foreseen ; therefore, as such a war would affect, at least, the nearest provinces, as well as the new Colony. Your Lord^p must expect those provinces, will not fail to make heavy complaints of the inattention of Govern^t to their interest. I cannot therefore, but think it my duty to recommend to your Lord^p, not to suffer this scheme to have effect, at least, until your Lord[p] shall have, from the most substantial and clear proofs, be [en] made thoroughly sensible of its utility.

E. B. O'Callaghan, editor, *Documents relative to the Colonial History of the State of New-York* (Albany, 1857), VIII, 253.

———◆———

136. The Settlement of the Western Country (1772-1774)

BY REVEREND JOSEPH DODDRIDGE (1824)

Doddridge grew up in the pioneer settlements which he describes. He was an itinerant Methodist preacher, becoming later an Episcopalian minister and physician. — Bibliography: Roosevelt, *Winning of the West*, I-II; Winsor, *Narrative and Critical History*, V, 580–584.

THE Settlements on this side of the mountains commenced along the Monongahela, and between that river and the Laurel Ridge, in the year 1772. In the succeeding year they reached the Ohio river. The greater number of the first settlers came from the upper parts of the then colonies of Maryland, and Virginia. Braddock's trail, as it was called, was the rout by which the greater number of them crossed the mountains. A less number of them came by the way of Bedford and Fort Ligonier, the military road from Pennsylvania to Pittsburgh. They effected their removals on horses furnished with pack-saddles. This was the more easily done, as but few of these early adventurers into the wilderness were encumbered with much baggage.

Land was the object which invited the greater number of these people to cross the mountain, for as the saying then was, " It was to be had here for taking up ; " that is, building a cabin and raising a crop of grain, however small, of any kind, entitled the occupant to four hundred acres of land, and a preemption right to one thousand acres more adjoining, to be secured by a land office warrant. This right was to take effect if there happened to be so much vacant land or any part thereof, adjoining the tract secured by the settlement right.

At an early period, the government of Virginia appointed three commissioners to give certificates of settlement rights. These certificates together with the surveyor's plat were sent to the land office of the state, where they laid six months, to await any caveat which might be offered. If none was offered the patent then issued.

There was at an early period of our settlements an inferior kind of land title denominated a "tomahawk right," which was made by deadening a few trees near the head of a spring, and marking the bark of some one, or more of them with the initials of the name of the person who made the improvement. I remember having seen a number of those "tomahawk rights," when a boy. For a long time many of them bore the names of those who made them. I have no knowledge of the efficacy of the tomahawk improvement, or whether it conferred any right whatever, unless followed by an actual settlement. These rights however were often bought and sold. Those who wished to make settlements on their favorite tracts of land, bought up the tomahawk improvements, rather than enter into quarrels with those who had made them. Other improvers of the land with a view to actual settlement, and who happened to be stout veteran fellows, took a very different course from that of purchasing the "tomahawk rigths [rights]." When annoyed by the claimants under those rights, they deliberately cut a few good hiccories, and gave them what was called in those days "a laced jacket," that is a sound whipping.

Some of the early settlers took the precaution to come over the mountains in the spring, leaving their families behind to raise a crop of corn, and then return and bring them out in the fall. This I should think was the better way. Others, especially those whose families were small, brought them with them in the spring. My father took the latter course. His family was but small and he brought them all with him. The indian meal which he brought over the mountain was expended six weeks too soon, so that for that length of time we had to live without bread. The lean venison and the breast of the wild turkies, we were taught to call bread. The flesh of the bear was denominated meat. This artifice did not succeed very well, after living in this way for some time we became sickly, the stomach seemed to be always empty, and tormented with a sense of hunger. I remember how narrowly the children watched the growth of the potatoe tops, pumpkin and squash vines, hoping from day to day, to get something to answer in the place of bread. How delicious was the taste of the young potatoes when we got them! What a jubilee when we were permitted to pull the young corn for roasting ears. Still more so when it had acquired sufficient hardness to be made into johnny cakes by the aid of a tin grater. We then became healthy, vigorous and contented with our situation, poor as it was.

My father with a small number of his neighbours made their settlements in the spring of 1773. Tho' they were in a poor and destitute situation, they nevertheless lived in peace ; but their tranquility was not of long continuance. Those most attrocious murders of the peaceable inoffensive Indians at Captina and Yellow creek, brought on the war of Lord Dunmore in the spring of the year 1774. Our little settlement then broke up. The women and children were removed to Morris' fort in Sandy creek glade some distance to the east of Uniontown. The Fort consisted of an assemblage on [of] small hovels, situated on the margin of a large and noxious marsh, the effluvia of which gave the most of the women and children the fever and ague. The men were compelled by necessity to return home, and risk the tomahawk and scalping knife of the Indians, in raising corn to keep their families from starvation, the succeeding winter. Those sufferings, dangers, and losses were the tribute we had to pay to that thirst for blood, which actuated those veteran murderers who brought the war upon us ! The memory of the sufferers in this war as well as that of their descendants still looks back upon them with regret, and abhorrence, and the page of history will consign their names to posterity, with the full weight of infamy they deserve. . . .

. . . our early land laws . . . allowed four hundred acres, and no more, to a settlement right. Many of our first settlers seemed to regard this amount of the surface of the earth, as the allotment of divine providence for one family, and believed that any attempt to get more would be sinful. Most of them, therefore contented themselves with that amount ; although they might have evaded the law, which allowed but one settlement right to any one individual, by taking out the title papers in the names of others, to be afterwards transferred to them, as if by purchase. Some few indeed pursued this practice ; but it was held in de[te]station.

My father, like many others, believed, that having secured his legal allotment, the rest of the country belonged of right, to those who choose to settle in it. There was a piece of vacant land adjoining his tract amounting to about two hundred acres. To this tract of land he had the preemption right, and accordingly secured it by warrant ; but his conscience would not permit him to retain it in his family, he therefore gave it to an apprentice lad whom he had raised in his house. This lad sold it to an uncle of mine for a cow and calf, and a wool hat.

Owing to the equal distribution of real property directed by our land laws, and the sterling integrity of our forefathers, in their observance of them, we have no districts of "sold land" as it is called, that is large tracts of land in the hands of individuals, or companies who neither sell nor improve them, as is the case in Lower Canada, and the north-western part of Pennsylvania. These unsettled tracts make huge blanks in the population of the country where they exist.

The division lines between those whose lands adjoined, were generally made in an amicable manner, before any survey of them was made, by the parties concerned. In doing this they were guided mainly by the tops of ridges and water courses, but particularly the former. Hence the greater number of farms in the western parts of Pennsylvania and Virginia bear a striking resemblance to an amphitheatre. The buildings occupy a low situation and the tops of the surrounding hills are the boundaries of the tract to which the family mansion belongs.

Our forefathers were fond of farms of this description, because, as they said, they are attended with this convenience "that every thing comes to the house down hill." In the hilly parts of the state of Ohio, the land having been laid off in an arbitrary manner, by straight parellel lines, without regard to hill or dale, the farms present a different aspect from those on the east side of the river opposite. There the buildings as frequently occupy the tops of the hills, as any other situation.

Our people had become so accustomed to the mode of "getting land for taking it up," that for a long time it was generally believed, that the land on the west side of the Ohio would ultimately be disposed of in that way. Hence almost the whole tract of country between the Ohio and Muskingum was parcelled out in tomahawk improvements; but these latter improvers did not content themselves with a single four hundred acre tract a piece. Many of them owned a great number of tracts of the best land, and thus, in imagination, were as "Wealthy as a South sea dream." Many of the land jobbers of this class did not content themselves with marking the trees, at the usual height, with the initials of their names; but climbed up the large beech trees, and cut the letters in their bark, from twenty to forty feet from the ground. To enable them to identify those trees, at a future period, they made marks on other trees around them as references.

Most of the early settlers considered their land as of little value, from an apprehension that after a few years cultivation it would lose its fertility, at least for a long time. I have often heard them say that such a field would bear so many crops and another so many, more or less than that. The ground of this belief concerning the short lived fertility of the land in this country, was the poverty of a great proportion of the land in the lower parts of Maryland and Virginia, which after producing a few crops, became unfit for use and was thrown out into commons.

In their unfavorable opinion of the nature of the soil of our country, our forefathers were utterly mistaken. The native weeds were scarcely destroyed, before the white clover, and different kinds of grass made their appearance. — These soon covered the ground, so as to afford pasture for the cattle, by the time the wood range was eaten out, as well as protect the soil from being washed away by drenching rains, so often injurious in hilly countries. . . .

The furniture for the table, for several years after the settlement of this country, consisted of a few pewter dishes, plates, and spoons ; but mostly of wooden bowls, trenchers and noggins. If these last were scarce, gourds and hard shelled squashes made up the deficiency.

The iron pots, knives, and forks were brought from the east side of the mountains along with the salt, and iron on pack horses.

These articles of furniture, corresponded very well with the articles of diet, on which they were employed. " Hog and hominy " were proverbial for the dish of which they were the component parts. Jonny cake and pone were at the outset of the settlements of the country, the only forms of bread in use for breakfast and dinner. At supper, milk and mush were the standard dish. When milk was not plenty, which was often the case, owing to the scarcity of cattle, or the want of proper pasture for them, the substantial dish of hominy had to supply the place of them ; mush was frequently eaten with sweetened water, molasses, bears oil, or the gravey of fried meat. . . .

The introduction of delft ware was considered by many of the backwoods people as a culpable innovation. It was too easily broken, and the plates of that ware dulled their scalping and clasp knives ; tea ware was too small for *men* ; they might do for women and children. Tea and coffee were only slops, which in the adage of the day " did not stick by the ribs." The idea was that they were designed only for people of quality, who do not labor, or the sick. A genuine backwoodsman would have thought himself disgraced by showing a fondness for those slops. Indeed, many of them have to this day, very little respect for them.

Jos[eph] Doddridge, *Notes, on the Settlement and Indian Wars, of the Western Parts of Virginia & Pennsylvania* (Wellsburgh, Virginia, 1824), 99–112 *passim*.

137. How the Frontiers were Settled (1780)

BY FRANÇOIS JEAN, MARQUIS DE CHASTELLUX (1786)

(TRANSLATED BY GEORGE GREIVE, 1787)

Chastellux was one of the French officers who served in America under Rochambeau; and his travels, made during the years 1780–1782, give us the impressions of
an intelligent and sympathetic foreign observer.— Bibliography: Roosevelt, *Winning
of the West*, II; Channing and Hart, *Guide*, § 150.

WHILE I was meditating on the great process of Nature, which
employs fifty thousand years in rendering the earth habitable, a
new spectacle, well calculated as a contrast to those which I had been
contemplating, fixed my attention, and excited my curiosity : this was
the work of a single man, who in the space of a year had cut down
several arpents of wood, and had built himself a house in the middle of
a pretty extensive territory he had already cleared. I saw, for the first
time, what I have since observed a hundred times ; for, in fact, whatever mountains I have climbed, whatever forests I have traversed,
whatever bye-paths I have followed, I have never travelled three miles
without meeting with a new settlement, either beginning to take form,
or already in cultivation. The following is the manner of proceeding in
these improvements, or new settlements. Any man who is able to procure a capital of five or six hundred livres of our money, or about twenty-
five pounds sterling, and who has strength and inclination to work, may
go into the woods and purchase a portion of one hundred and fifty or
two hundred acres of land, which seldom costs him more than a dollar or
four shillings and six-pence an acre, a small part of which only he pays
in ready money. There he conducts a cow, some pigs, or a full sow,
and two indifferent horses which do not cost him more than four guineas
each. To these precautions he adds that of having a provision of flour
and cyder. Provided with this first capital, he begins by felling all the
smaller trees, and some strong branches of the large ones : these he
makes use of as fences to the first field he wishes to clear ; he next
boldly attacks those immense oaks, or pines, which one would take for
the ancient lords of the territory he is usurping ; he strips them of their
bark, or lays them open all round with his axe. These trees mortally
wounded, are the next spring robbed of their honors ; their leaves no
longer spring, their branches fall, and their trunk becomes a hideous
skeleton. This trunk still seems to brave the efforts of the new colonist ; but where there are the smallest chinks or crevices, it is sur-

rounded by fire, and the flames consume what the iron was unable to destroy. But it is enough for the small trees to be felled, and the great ones to lose their sap. This object compleated, the ground is cleared ; the air and the sun begin to operate upon that earth which is wholly formed of rotten vegetables, and teems with the latent principles of production. The grass grows rapidly ; there is pasturage for the cattle the very first year ; after which they are left to increase, or fresh ones are brought, and they are employed in tilling a piece of ground which yields the enormous increase of twenty or thirty fold. The next year the same course is repeated ; when, at the end of two years, the planter has wherewithal to subsist, and even to send some articles to market : at the end of four or five years, he completes the payment of his land, and finds himself a comfortable planter. Then his dwelling, which at first was no better than a large hut formed by a square of the trunks of trees, placed one upon another, with the intervals filled by mud, changes into a handsome wooden house, where he contrives more convenient, and certainly much cleaner apartments than those in the greatest part of our small towns. This is the work of three weeks or a month. His first habitation, that of eight and forty hours. I shall be asked, perhaps, how one man, or one family can be so quickly lodged? I answer, that in America a man is never alone, never an isolated being. The neighbours, for they are every where to be found, make it a point of hospitality to aid the new farmer. A cask of cyder drank in common, and with gaiety, or a gallon of rum, are the only recompence for these services. Such are the means by which North America, which one hundred years ago was nothing but a vast forest, is peopled with three millions of inhabitants ; and such is the immense, and certain benefit of agriculture, that notwithstanding the war, it not only maintains itself where-ever it has been established, but it extends to places which seems the least favourable to its introduction. Four years ago one might have travelled ten miles in the woods I traversed, without seeing a single habitation.

Marquis [François Jean] de Chastellux, *Travels in North-America, in the Years 1780, 1781, and 1782* (London, 1787), I, 44–48.

CHAPTER XXIII — THE STAMP ACT CONTROVERSY

138. A Colonist's Defence of Taxation (1765)

BY MARTIN HOWARD

Howard was an eminent Rhode Island lawyer and politician, and had been a delegate from Rhode Island to the Albany Congress. For the publication of this tract and similar ones, under the name of "A Gentleman of Halifax," Howard's house at Newport was wrecked; in 1778 he fled to England. — Bibliography : Tyler, *Literary History of the Revolution*, I, 70–80; Winsor, *Narrative and Critical History*, VI, 68–71.

. . . DEPEND upon it, my Friend, a people like the *English*, arrived to the highest pitch of glory and power, the envy and admiration of surrounding slaves, who hold the balance of *Europe* in their hands, and rival in arts and arms every period of ancient or modern story ; a nation who, for the defence and safety of *America* only, staked their all in the late war ; this people, I say, justly conscious of their dignity, will not patiently be dictated to by those whom they have ever considered as dependant upon them.   Happy will it be for the colonies, yea happy for the honourable author, if his pamphlet should meet with nothing more than contempt and neglect ; for should it catch the attention of men in power, measures may be taken to stifle in the birth " *the low murmurs of submissive fear,*" and crush in embryo "*the mingled rage,*" which now so prettily adorns the head of his honour's pamphlet.

However disguised, polished or softened the expression of this pamphlet may seem, yet every one must see, that its professed design is sufficiently prominent throughout, namely, to prove, *that the colonies have rights independant of, and not controulable by, the authority of parliament.* It is upon this dangerous and indiscreet position I shall communicate to you my real sentiments. . . .

The several *New-England* charters ascertain, define and limit the respective rights and privileges of each colony, and I cannot conceive how it has come to pass that the colonies now claim any other or greater rights than are therein expressly granted to them. I fancy when we speak, or think of the rights of free-born *Englishmen,* we confound those rights which are personal, with those which are political : There is a distinction between these, which ought always to be kept in view.

Our personal rights, comprehending those of life, liberty and estate, are secured to us by the common law, which is every subject's birthright, whether born in *Great-Britain,* on the ocean, or in the colonies ; and it is in this sense we are said to enjoy all the rights and privileges of *Englishmen.* The political rights of the colonies, or the powers of government communicated to them, are more limited, and their nature, quality and extent depend altogether upon the patent or charter which first created and instituted them. As individuals, the colonists participate of every blessing the *English* constitution can give them : As corporations created by the crown, they are confined within the primitive views of their institution. Whether therefore their indulgence is scanty or liberal, can be no cause of complaint ; for when they accepted of their charters, they tacitly submitted to the terms and conditions of them.

The colonies have no rights independant of their charters, they can claim no greater than those give them, by those the parliamentary jurisdiction over them is not taken away, neither could any grant of the king abridge that jurisdiction, because it is founded upon common law, as I shall presently shew, and was prior to any charter or grant to the colonies : Every *Englishman,* therefore, is subject to this jurisdiction, and it follows him wherever he goes. It is of the essence of government, that there should be a supreme head, and it would be a solecism in politicks to talk of members independant of it. . . .

I am aware that the foregoing reasoning will be opposed by the maxim, " That no *Englishman* can be taxed but by his own consent, or by representatives."

It is this dry maxim, taken in a literal sense, and ill understood, that, like the song of *Lillibullero,* has made all the mischief in the colonies : And upon this, the partizans of the colonies rights chiefly rest their cause. I don't despair, however, of convincing you, that this maxim affords but little support to their argument, when rightly examined and explained.

It is the opinion of the house of commons, and may be considered as a law of parliament, that they are the representatives of every *British* subject, wheresoever he be. In this view of the matter then, the aforegoing maxim is fully vindicated in practice, and the whole benefit of it, in substance and effect, extended and applied to the *colonies.* Indeed the maxim must be considered in this latitude, for in a literal sense or construction it ever was, and ever will be, impracticable. Let me ask, is the isle of *Man, Jersey,* or *Guernsey,* represented? What is the value or amount of each man's representation in the kingdom of *Scotland,* which contains near two millions of people, and yet not more than three thousand have votes in the election of members of parliament? But to shew still further, that, in fact and reality, this right of representation is not of that consequence it is generally thought to be, let us take into the argument the moneyed interest of *Britain,* which, though immensely great, has no share in this representation ; a worthless freeholder of forty shillings *per annum* can vote for a member of parliament, whereas a merchant, tho' worth one hundred thousand pounds sterling, if it consist only in personal effects, has no vote at all : But yet let no one suppose that the interest of the latter is not equally the object of parliamentary attention with the former. . . .

The jurisdiction of parliament being established, it will follow, that this jurisdiction cannot be apportioned ; it is transcendant and entire, and may levy internal taxes as well as regulate trade ; there is no essential difference in the rights : A stamp duty is confessedly the most reasonable and equitable that can be devised, yet very far am I from desiring to see it established among us, but I fear the shaft is sped, and it is now too late to prevent the blow. . . .

Enlarging the power of the court of admiralty, is much complain'd of by the honourable author. I shall open my mind to you freely on this head.

It is notorious, that smuggling, which an eminent writer calls a crime against the law of nature, had well nigh become established in some of the colonies. Acts of parliament had been uniformly dispensed with by those whose duty it was to execute them ; corruption, raised upon the ruins of duty and virtue, had almost grown into a system ; courts of admiralty, confined within small territorial jurisdictions, became subject to mercantile influence ; and the king's revenue shamefully sacrificed to the venality and perfidiousness of courts and officers. — If, my friend, customs are due to the crown ; if illicit commerce is to be put an end to, as ruinous to the welfare of the nation : — If, by reason of the interested views of traders, and the connivance of courts and custom-house officers, these ends could not be compassed or obtained in the common and ordinary way ; tell me, what could the government do, but to apply a remedy desperate as the disease : There is, I own, a severity in the method of prosecution, in the new established court of admiralty, under

Doctor *SPRY*, here ; but it is a severity we have brought upon ourselves. When every mild expedient, to stop the atrocious and infamous practice of smuggling, has been try'd in vain, the government is justifiable in making laws against it, even like those of *Draco*, which were written in blood. . . .

Believe me, my Friend, it gives me great pain to see so much ingratitude in the colonies to the mother country, whose arms and money so lately rescued them from a *French* government. I have been told, that some have gone so far as to say, that they would, as things are, prefer such a government to an *English* one. — Heaven knows I have but little malice in my heart, yet, for a moment, I ardently wish that these spurious, unworthy sons of *Britain* could feel the iron rod of a *Spanish* inquisitor, or a *French* farmer of the revenue ; it would indeed be a punishment suited to their ingratitude. . . .

. . . I am very sure the loyalty of the colonies has ever been irreproachable ; but from the pride of some, and the ignorance of others, the cry against mother country has spread from colony to colony ; and it is to be feared, that prejudices and resentments are kindled among them which it will be difficult ever, thoroughly, to sooth or extinguish. It may become necessary for the supreme legislature of the nation to frame some code, and therein adjust the rights of the colonies, with precision and certainty, otherwise *Great-Britain* will always be teazed with new claims about liberty and privileges.

A Letter from a Gentleman at Halifax, to his Friend in Rhode-Island, containing Remarks upon a Pamphlet, entitled, The Rights of Colonies Examined (Newport, 1765), 5–22 *passim.*

———◆———

139. The Hutchinson Riot (1765)

BY JOSIAH QUINCY, JR.

Quincy was a young Boston lawyer when the troubles with England became manifest. He was sent to England to state the wrongs of America to sympathetic statesmen ; and had an interview with Lord North. — Bibliography : Winsor, *Narrative and Critical History*, VI, 72–73 ; Tyler, *Literary History of the Revolution*, I, 271–273 ; Hosmer, *Thomas Hutchinson ;* Channing and Hart, *Guide*, § 134.

AUG. 27, 1765. — There cannot, perhaps, be found in the records of time a more flagrant instance to what a pitch of infatuation an incensed populace may arise than the last night afforded. The destructions, demolitions, and ruins caused by the rage of the Colonies in general — perhaps too justly inflamed — at that singular and ever-memorable statute called the Stamp Act, will make the present year one of the most remarkable eras in the annals of North America. And that peculiar inflammation, which fired the breasts of the people of New England in particular, will always distinguish them as the warmest lovers of liberty ; though undoubtedly, in the fury of revenge against those who they thought had disclaimed the name of sons, for that of enslavers and oppressive tax-masters of their native country, they committed acts totally unjustifiable.

The populace of Boston, about a week since, had given a very notable instance of their detestation of the above unconstitutional Act, and had sufficiently shown in what light they viewed the man who would under-take to be the stamp distributor. But, not content with this, the last night they again assembled in King's Street ; where, after having kindled a fire, they proceeded, in two separate bodies, to attack the houses of two gentlemen of distinction, who, it had been suggested, were acces-sories to the present burthens ; and did great damage in destroying their houses, furniture, &c., and irreparable damage in destroying their papers. Both parties, who before had acted separately, then unitedly proceeded to the Chief-Justice's house, who, not expecting them, was unattended by his friends, who might have assisted, or proved his inno-cence. In this situation, all his family, it is said, abandoned the house, but himself and his eldest daughter, whom he repeatedly begged to depart ; but as he found all ineffectual, and her resolution fixed to stay and share his fate, with a tumult of passions only to be imagined, he took her in his arms, and carried her to a place of safety, just before the incensed mob arrived. This filial affection saved, it is more than prob-able, his life. Thus unexpected, and nothing removed from the house, an ample field offered to satiate, if possible, this rage-intoxicated rabble. They beset the house on all sides, and soon destroyed every thing of value : —

" Furor arma ministrat." — *Virgil.*

The destruction was really amazing ; for it was equal to the fury of the onset. But what above all is to be lamented is the loss of some of the most valuable records of the country, and other ancient papers ; for, as his Honor was continuing his history, the oldest and most important writings and records of the Province, which he had selected with great care, pains, and expense, were in his possession. This is a loss greatly to be deplored, as it is absolutely irretrievable.

The distress a man must feel on such an occasion can only be conceived by those who the next day saw his Honor the Chief-Justice come into court, with a look big with the greatest anxiety, clothed in a manner which would have excited compassion from the hardest heart, though his dress had not been strikingly contrasted by the other judges and bar, who appeared in their robes. Such a man in such a station, thus habited, with tears starting from his eyes, and a countenance which strongly told the inward anguish of his soul, — what must an audience have felt, whose compassion had before been moved by what they knew he had suffered, when they heard him pronounce the following words in a manner which the agitations of his mind dictated?

AUGUST TERM, 3 George III. in B. R., &c. — Present: The Hon. Thomas Hutchinson, Esq., Chief-Justice; John Cushing, Peter Oliver, Esqs., Justices.

The Chief-Justice, addressing the whole court, said, —

" GENTLEMEN, —There not being a quorum of the court without me, I am obliged to appear. Some apology is necessary for my dress: indeed, I had no other. Destitute of every thing, — no other shirt; no other garment but what I have on; and not one in my whole family in a better situation than myself. The distress of a whole family around me, young and tender infants hanging about me, are infinitely more insupportable than what I feel for myself, though I am obliged to borrow part of *this* clothing.

" Sensible that I am innocent, that all the charges against me are false, I can't help feeling: and though I am not obliged to give an answer to all the questions that may be put me by every lawless person, yet I call God to witness, — and I would not, for a thousand worlds, call my Maker to witness to falsehood, — I say, I call my Maker to witness, that I never, in New England or Old, in Great Britain or America, neither directly nor indirectly, was aiding, assisting, or supporting — in the least promoting or encouraging — what is commonly called the Stamp-Act; but, on the contrary, did all in my power, and strove as much as in me lay, to prevent it. This is not declared through timidity; for I have nothing to fear. They can only take away my life, which is of but little value when deprived of all its comforts, all that was dear to me, and nothing surrounding me but the most piercing distress.

" I hope the eyes of the people will be opened, that they will see how easy it is for some designing, wicked man to spread false reports, to raise suspicions and jealousies in the minds of the populace, and enrage them against the innocent; but, if guilty, this is not the way to proceed. The laws of our country are open to punish those who have offended. This destroying all peace and order of the community, — all will feel its effects; and I hope all will see how easily the people may be deluded, inflamed, and carried away with madness against an innocent man.

" I pray God give us better hearts ! "

The court was then adjourned, on account of the riotous disorders of the preceding night, and universal confusion of the town, to the 15th of October following.

Learn wisdom from the present times! O ye sons of Ambition! beware lest a thirst of power prompt you to enslave your country! O ye sons of Avarice! beware lest the thirst for gold excite you to enslave your native country! O ye sons of Popularity! beware lest a thirst for applause move you groundlessly to inflame the minds of the people! For the end of slavery is misery to the world, your country, fellow-citizens, and children; the end of popular rage, destruction, desolation, and ruin.

Who, that sees the fury and instability of the populace, but would seek protection under the arm of power? Who, that beholds the tyranny and oppression of arbitrary power, but would lose his life in defence of his liberty? Who, that marks the riotous tumult, confusion, and uproar of a democratic, the slavery and distress of a despotic, state, — the infinite miseries attendant on both, — but would fly for refuge from the mad rage of the one, and oppressive power of the other, to that best asylum, that glorious medium, the British Constitution? Happy people who enjoy this blessed constitution! Happy, thrice happy people, if ye preserve it inviolate! May ye never lose it through a licentious abuse of your invaluable rights and blood-purchased liberties! May ye never forfeit it by a tame and infamous submission to the yoke of slavery and lawless despotism!

> "Remember, O my friends! the laws, the rights,
> The generous plan of power delivered down,
> From age to age, by your renowned forefathers,
> So dearly bought, the price of so much blood:
> Oh! let it never perish in your hands,
> But piously transmit it to your children.
> Do thou, great Liberty! inspire our souls,
> And make our lives in thy possession happy,
> Or our death glorious in thy just defence."

From the diary of Josiah Quincy, Jr., in Massachusetts Historical Society *Proceedings*, 1858–1860 (Boston, 1860), 47–51.

140. A Spirited Remonstrance (1765)

BY THE TOWN-MEETING OF CAMBRIDGE

This piece is selected as a spirited example of the protests made against the Stamp Act by all sorts of public bodies and public meetings. — Bibliography: Winsor, *Narrative and Critical History*, VI, 29–33; Frothingham, *Rise of the Republic*, 183–184; Channing and Hart, *Guide*, § 134.

AT a Legal meeting of the freehold^{rs} & other Inhabitants of the Town of Cambridge this 14 day of October 1765.

The Hon^{bl} William Brattle Esqr Chosen Moderat^r

Voted (that with all humility) It is the opinion of the Town that the Inhabitants of this Province have a Legal Claim to all the natural Inherent Constitutional Rights of Englishmen notwithstanding their distance from Great Brittain ; That the Stamp Act is an Infraction upon these Rights ; one Instance out of many in our Opinion is this : The Distributor of Stamps will have a Soveranity over Every thing, but the lives of the People, since it is in his Power to Summon Every one he pleases to Qebeck, Montreal, or New found land, to answer for the pretended or Real Breaches of this Act, and when the faithfull Subject arrives there ; By whom is he to be Tryed, not by his Peers (the Birth Right of Every English man) No but by the Iudge of Admiralty without a Iury, and it is possible without Law.

Under these Circumstances the Stamp Master may unrighteously get more than His Majesty will upon a Ballance by the Stamps. for who would not Rather pay the fine then be thus harrassed, thus Tryed ; Why are not His Majest^{es} Subjects in Great Brittain Treated in this manner, Why must we in America who have in Every Instance discovered as much Loyalty for His Majesty & Obedience to His Laws as any of His Brittish Subjects (and whose Exertion in some of the Provinces during the Last Warr have been Greater ; be thus Discriminated ; at this time Especially whilst we are under an almost unsupportable load of Debt the Consequence of this Exertion ; We believe it may be Truly said that no one in Great Brittain pays so great a Tax as some do in this Province in proportion to their Estates ; let this Act but take place, Liberty will be no more, Trade will Languish & dye ; Our Medium will be Sent into His Majest^{es} Exchequer, And Poverty come upon us as an Armed man ; The Town therefore hereby Advise & Direct their Representatives by no means whatsoever to do any one thing that may Aid said Act in its opperation ; But that in Conjunction with the friends

2 D

of Liberty they use their utmost Endeavours, that the same might be Repealed; That this Vote be Recorded in the Town Book that the Children yet unborn may see the desire their Ancestors had for their freedom & happiness . . . .

From the manuscript records in the Cambridge City Hall.

———◆———

141. "Declarations of the Rights and Grievances of the Colonists" (1765)

BY THE STAMP ACT CONGRESS

This is the most significant action of the Stamp Act Congress, called to protest against taxation. — Bibliography as in No. 140 above.

SATURDAY, Oct. 19th, 1765, A.M. — The congress met according to adjournment, and resumed, &c. as yesterday; and upon mature deliberation, agreed to the following declarations of the rights and grievances of the colonists in America, which were ordered to be inserted:

The members of this Congress, sincerely devoted, with the warmest sentiments of affection and duty to his majesty's person and government, inviolably attached to the present happy establishment of the protestant succession, and with minds deeply impressed by a sense of the present and impending misfortunes of the British colonies on this continent, having considered as maturely as time would permit, the circumstances of the said colonies, esteem it our indispensable duty to make the following declarations, of our humble opinion respecting the most essential rights and liberties of the colonists, and of the grievances under which they labor, by reason of several late acts of parliament.

1st. That his majesty's subjects in these colonies owe the same allegiance to the crown of Great Britain, that is owing from his subjects born within the realm, and all due subordination to that august body, the parliament of Great Britain.

2d. That his majesty's liege subjects in these colonies are entitled to all the inherent rights and privileges of his natural born subjects within the kingdom of Great Britain.

3d. That it is inseparably essential to the freedom of a people, and the undoubted rights of Englishmen, that no taxes should be imposed on them, but with their own consent, given personally, or by their representatives

4th. That the people of these colonies are not, and from their local circumstances, cannot be, represented in the house of commons in Great Britain.

5th. That the only representatives of the people of these colonies, are persons chosen therein, by themselves ; and that no taxes ever have been, or can be constitutionally imposed on them, but by their respective legislatures.

6th. That all supplies of the crown, being free gifts of the people, it is unreasonable and inconsistent with the principles and spirit of the British constitution, for the people of Great Britain to grant to his majesty, the property of the colonists.

7th. That trial by jury is the inherent and invaluable right of every British subject in these colonies.

8th. That the late act of parliament, entitled, An act for granting and applying certain stamp duties, and other duties in the British colonies and plantations in America, &c. by imposing taxes on the inhabitants of these colonies, and the said act, and several other acts, by extending the jurisdiction of the courts of admiralty beyond its ancient limits, have a manifest tendency to subvert the rights and liberties of the colonists.

9th. That the duties imposed by several late acts of parliament, from the peculiar circumstances of these colonies, will be extremely burthensome and grievous, and from the scarcity of specie, the payment of them absolutely impracticable.

10th. That as the profits of the trade of these colonies ultimately centre in Great Britain, to pay for the manufactures which they are obliged to take from thence, they eventually contribute very largely to all supplies granted there to the crown.

11th. That the restrictions imposed by several late acts of parliament on the trade of these colonies will render them unable to purchase the manufactures of Great Britain.

12th. That the increase, prosperity and happiness of these colonies depend on the full and free enjoyment of their rights and liberties, and an intercourse with Great Britain, mutually affectionate and advantageous.

13th. That it is the right of the British subjects in these colonies to petition the king or either house of parliament.

Lastly, That it is the indispensable duty of these colonies to the best of sovereigns, to the mother country, and to themselves, to endeavor, by a loyal and dutiful address to his majesty, and humble application to both houses of parliament, to procure the repeal of the act for granting and applying certain stamp duties, of all clauses of any other acts of parliament, whereby the jurisdiction of the admiralty is extended as aforesaid, and of the other late acts for the restriction of the American commerce.

H[ezekiah] Niles, editor, *The Weekly Register*, July 25, 1812 (Baltimore), II, 340-341.

---

142. An Englishman's Protest against Taxation (1766)

BY WILLIAM PITT, LATER EARL OF CHATHAM

For Pitt, see No. 128 above. His speech represents the strong opposition to putting a pressure on the colonies, and shows how far the whole question involved the relative rights of the crown and Parliament in England. — Bibliography: Mahon, *England*, V, 129-140; Winsor, *Narrative and Critical History*, VI, 74.

GENTLEMEN, Sir (to the Speaker), I have been charged with giving birth to sedition in America. They have spoken their sentiments with freedom against this unhappy act, and that freedom has become their crime. Sorry I am to hear the liberty of speech in this House imputed as a crime. But the imputation shall not discourage me. It is a liberty I mean to exercise. No gentleman ought to be afraid to exercise it. It is a liberty by which the gentleman who calumniates it might have profited. He ought to have desisted from his project. The gentleman tells us, America is obstinate; America is almost in open rebellion. I rejoice that America has resisted. Three millions of people so dead to all the feelings of liberty, as voluntarily to submit to be slaves, would have been fit instruments to make slaves of the rest. I come not here armed at all points, with law cases and acts of Parliament, with the statute-book doubled down in dog's-ears, to defend the cause of liberty: if I had, I myself would have cited the two cases of Chester and Durham. I would have cited them, to have shewn that, even under former arbitrary reigns, Parliaments were ashamed of taxing a people without their consent, and allowed them representatives. . . . The gentleman tells us of many who are taxed, and are not represented. — The India Company, merchants, stock-holders, manufacturers. Surely many of these are represented in other capacities, as owners of land, or as freemen of boroughs. It is a misfortune that more are not equally represented. But they are all inhabitants, and as such, are they not virtually represented? Many have it in their option to be actually represented. They have connections with those that elect, and they have influence over them. . . .

. . . The gentleman boasts of his bounties to America! Are not these bounties intended finally for the benefit of this kingdom? If they are not, he has misapplied the national treasures. I am no courtier of America — I stand up for this kingdom. I maintain, that the Parliament has a right to bind, to restrain America. Our legislative power over the colonies is sovereign and supreme. When it ceases to be sovereign and supreme, I would advise every gentleman to sell his lands, if he can, and embark for that country. When two countries are connected together, like England and her colonies, without being incorporated, the one must necessarily govern; the greater must rule the less; but so rule it, as not to contradict the fundamental principles that are common to both.

If the gentleman does not understand the difference between external and internal taxes, I cannot help it; but there is a plain distinction between taxes levied for the purposes of raising a revenue, and duties imposed for the regulation of trade, for the accommodation of the subject; although, in the consequences, some revenue might incidentally arise from the latter.

The gentleman asks, when were the colonies emancipated? But I desire to know, when they were made slaves? But I dwell not upon words. When I had the honour of serving his Majesty, I availed myself of the means of information, which I derived from my office : I speak, therefore from knowledge. My materials were good, I was at pains to collect, to digest, to consider them ; and I will be bold to affirm, that the profits to Great Britain from the trade of the colonies, through all its branches, is two millions a year. This is the fund that carried you triumphantly through the last war. The estates that were rented at two thousand pounds a year, threescore years ago, are at three thousand pounds at present. Those estates sold then from fifteen to eighteen years purchase ; the same may now be sold for thirty. You owe this to America. This is the price America pays for her protection. And shall a miserable financier come with a boast, that he can bring a pepper-corn into the Exchequer, to the loss of millions to the nation ! I dare not say, how much higher these profits may be augmented. Omitting the immense increase of people by natural population, in the northern colonies, and the emigration from every part of Europe, I am convinced the commercial system of America may be altered to advantage. You have prohibited where you ought to have encouraged, and encouraged where you ought to have prohibited. . . .

A great deal has been said without doors, of the power, of the strength of America. It is a topic that ought to be cautiously meddled with. In a good cause, on a sound bottom, the force of this country can crush America to atoms. I know the valour of your troops. I know the skill of your officers. There is not a company of foot that has served in America, out of which you may not pick a man of sufficient knowledge and experience to make a governor of a colony there. But on this ground, on the Stamp Act, when so many here will think it a crying injustice, I am one who will lift up my hands against it.

In such a cause, your success would be hazardous. America, if she fell, would fall like the strong man. She would embrace the pillars of the state, and pull down the constitution along with her. Is this your boasted peace ? Not to sheath the sword in its scabbard, but to sheath it in the bowels of your countrymen ? Will you quarrel with yourselves ; now the whole House of Bourbon is united against you ? . . . The Americans have not acted in all things with prudence and temper. The Americans have ·been wronged. They have been driven to madness by injustice. Will you punish them for the madness you have occasioned.? Rather let prudence and temper come first from this side. I will undertake for America, that she will follow the example. There are two lines in a ballad of *Prior*'s, of a man's behaviour to his wife, so applicable to you, and your colonies, that I cannot help repeating them :

> *Be to her faults a little blind :*
> *Be to her virtues very kind.*

Upon the whole, I will beg leave to tell the House what is really my opinion. It is, that the Stamp Act be *repealed absolutely, totally*, and *immediately.* That the reason for the repeal be assigned, because it was founded on an erroneous principle. At the same time, let the sovereign authority of this country over the colonies be asserted in as strong terms as can be devised, and be made to extend to every point of legislation whatsoever. That we may bind their *trade*, confine their *manufactures*, and exercise every *power* whatsoever, except that of taking their money out of their pockets without their consent.

[John Almon, compiler], *Anecdotes of the Life of the Right Hon. William Pitt, Earl of Chatham* (London, 1797), I, 494–503 *passim*.

---

143. The State of the Colonies (1766)

BY BENJAMIN FRANKLIN AND A COMMITTEE OF THE HOUSE OF COMMONS

For Franklin, see No. 68 above. The examination was conducted in great part by the friends of the colonies, and the answers were prepared beforehand. — Bibliography: McMaster, *Benjamin Franklin;* Winsor, *Narrative and Critical History*, VI, 74.

Q. WHAT is your Name, and Place of abode?
A. Franklin, of Philadelphia.

Q. Do the Americans pay any considerable taxes among themselves?
A. Certainly many, and very heavy taxes.

Q. What are the present taxes in Pennsylvania, laid by the laws of the Colony?
A. There are taxes on all estates real and personal, a poll-tax, a tax on all offices, professions, trades and businesses, according to their profits ; an excise upon all wine, rum and other spirits ; and a duty of ten pounds per head on all negroes imported, with some other duties. . . .

Q. Are not the Colonies, from their circumstances, very able to pay the stamp-duty?
A. In my opinion, there is not gold and silver enough in the Colonies to pay the stamp duty for one year.

Q. Don't you know that the money arising from the stamps was all to be laid out in America?
A. I know it is appropriated by the act to the American service ; but it will be spent in the conquered Colonies, where the soldiers are, not in the Colonies that pay it.

Q. Is there not a ballance of trade due from the Colonies where the troops are posted, that will bring back the money to the old Colonies.
A. I think not. I believe very little would come back. I know of no trade likely to bring it back. I think it would come from the Colonies where it was spent directly to England ; for I have always observed,

that in every Colony the more plenty the means of remittance to England the more goods are sent for, and the more trade with England carried on. . . .

Q. How many white men do you suppose there are in North America?

A. About 300,000 from sixteen to sixty years of age.

Q. What may be the amount of one year's imports into Pennsylvania from Britain?

A. I have been informed that our merchants compute the imports from Britain to be above 500,000 Pounds.

Q. What may be the amount of the produce of your province exported to Britain?

A. It must be small, as we produce little that is wanted in Britain. I suppose it cannot exceed 40,000 Pounds.

Q. How then do you pay the ballance?

A. The ballance is paid by our produce carried to the West-Indies, and sold in our own islands, or to the French, Spanian[r]ds, Danes and Dutch ; by the same carried to other colonies in North-America, as to New-England, Nova-Scotia, Newfoundland, Carolina and Georgia ; by the same carried to different parts of Europe, as Spain, Portugal and Italy : In all which places we receive either money, bills of exchange, or commodities that suit for remittance to Britain ; which, together with all the profits on the industry of our merchants and mariners, arising in those circuitous voyages, and the freights made by their ships, center finally in Britain, to discharge the ballance, and pay for British manufactures continually used in the province, or sold to foreigners by our traders.

Q. Have you heard of any difficulties lately laid on the Spanish trade?

A. Yes, I have heard that it has been greatly obstructed by some new regulations, and by the English men of war and cutters stationed all along the coast of America.

Q. Do you think it right America should be protected by this country, and pay no part of the expence.

A. That is not the case. The colonies raised, cloathed and paid, during the last war, near 25,000 men, and spent many millions.

Q. Were you not reimbursed by parliament?

A. We were reimbursed what, in your opinion, we had advanced beyond our proportion, or beyond what might be reasonably expected from us ; and it was a very small part of what we spent. Pennsylvania, in particular, disbursed about 500,000 pounds, and the reimbursements, in the whole, did not exceed 60,000 pounds. . . .

Q. Do not you think the people of America would submit to pay the stamp duty, if it was moderated?

A. No, never, unless compelled by force of arms. . . .

Q. What was the temper of America towards Great Britain before the year 1763?

A. The best in the world. They submitted willingly to the government of the Crown, and paid, in all their courts, obedience to acts of parliament. Numerous as the people are in the several old provinces, they cost you nothing in forts, citadels, garrisons or armies, to keep them in subjection. They were governed by this country at the expence only of a little pen, ink and paper. They were led by a thread. They had not only a respect, but an affection, for Great Britain, for its laws, its customs and manners, and even a fondness for its fashions, that greatly increased the commerce. Natives of Britain were always treated with particular regard; to be an Old England-man, was, of itself, a character of some respect, and gave a kind of rank among us.

Q. And what is their temper now?

A. O, very much altered.

Q. Did you ever hear the authority of parliament to make laws for America questioned till lately?

A. The authority of parliament was allowed to be valid in all laws, except such as should lay internal taxes. It was never disputed in laying duties to regulate commerce. . . .

Q. In what light did the people of America use to consider the parliament of Great Britain?

A. They considered the parliament as the great bulwark & security of their liberties and privileges, and always spoke of it with the utmost respect and veneration: arbitrary ministers, they thought, might possibly, at times, attempt to oppress them, but they relied on it, that the parliament, on application, would always give redress. They remembered, with gratitude, a strong instance of this, when a bill was brought into parliament, with a clause to make royal instructions laws in the colonies, which the house of commons would not pass, and it was thrown out.

Q. And have they not still the same respect for parliament?

A. No; it is greatly lessened.

Q. To what cause is that owing?

A. To a concurrence of causes; the restraints lately laid on their trade, by which the bringing of foreign gold and silver into the colonies was prevented; the prohibition of making paper money among themselves; and then demanding a new and heavy tax by stamps; taking away at the same time, trials by juries, and refusing to receive & hear their humble petitions.

Q. Don't you think they would submit to the stamp-act, if it was modified, the obnoxious parts taken out, and the duties reduced to some particulars, of small moment?

A. No; they will never submit to it. . . .

Q. Was it an opinion in America before 1763, that the parliament had no right to lay taxes and duties there?

A. I never heard any objection to the right of laying duties to regulate commerce; but a right to lay internal taxes was never supposed to be in parliament, as we are not represented there. . . .

Q. Would the repeal of the stamp-act be any discouragement of your manufactures? Will the people that have begun the manufacture decline it?

A. Yes, I think they will; especially, if, at the same time, the trade is opened again, so that remittances can be easily made. I have known several instances that make it probable. In the war before last, tobacco being low, and making little remittance, the people of Virginia went generally into family manufactures. Afterwards, when tobacco bore a better price, they returned to the use of British manufactures. So fulling mills were very much disused in the last war in Pennsylvania, because bills were then plenty, and remittance could easily be made to Britain for English cloth and other goods.

Q. If the stamp-act should be repealed, would it induce the assemblies of America to acknowledge the rights of parliament to tax them, and would they erase their resolutions?   A. No, never.

Q. Is there no means of obliging them to erase those resolutions?

A. None that I know of; they will never do it unless compelled by force of arms.

Q. Is there no power on earth that can force them to erase them?

A. No power, how great soever, can force men to change their opinions. . . .

Q. Would it be most for the interest of Great-Britain, to employ the hands of Virginia in tobacco, or in manufactures?

A. In tobacco to be sure.

Q. What used to be the pride of the Americans?

A. To indulge in the fashions and manufactures of G. Britain.

Q. What is now their pride?

A. To wear their old cloaths over again, till they can make new ones.

Withdrew.

[*The Examination of Doctor Benjamin Franklin . . . relating to the Repeal of the Stamp-Act, &c.*],(no title-page, Philadelphia, 1766), 1–23 *passim.*

---

144. The Repeal of the Stamp Act (1766)

BY SECRETARY HENRY SEYMOUR CONWAY

Conway was one of the two secretaries of state, and his letter is an official state-ment to the governors. — Bibliography: Winsor, *Narrative and Critical History*, VI, 74; Channing and Hart, *Guide*, § 134.

HEREWITH I have the pleasure of transmitting to you copies of two Acts of Parliament just passed. The first for securing the dependency of the Colonies on the Mother Country; the second for the repeal of the Act of [the] last session, granting certain stamp duties in America; and I expect shortly to send you a third, for the Indemnity of such persons, as have incurred the penalties imposed by the Act just repealed, as such a Bill is now depending, and has made a considerable progress in the house of Commons.

The moderation, the forbearance, the unexampled lenity and tender-ness of Parliament towards the Colonies, which are so signally displayed in those Acts, cannot but dispose the province, committed to your care, to that return of chearful obedience to the Laws and Legislative author-ity of Great Britain and to those sentiments of respectful gratitude to the Mother Country, which are the natural, and, I trust, will be the cer-tain effects of so much grace and condescention, so remarkably mani-fested on the part of his Maj[ty] and of the Parliament; and the future happiness and prosperity of the Colonies will very much depend on the testimonies, they shall now give of these dispositions.

For, as a dutiful and affectionate return to such peculiar proofs of indulgence and affection, may, now at this great crisis, be a means of fixing the mutual interests and inclinations of G. Britain and her Colonies on the most firm and solid foundations, so it can not, but appear visible that the least coldness or unthankfulness, the least murmuring or dissatisfaction on any ground whatever, of former heat, or too much prevailing prejudice, may fatally endanger that Union, and give the most severe and affecting blow to the future interests of both Countries.

You will think it scarce possible, I imagine, that the paternal care of His Maj^ty for his Colonies, or the lenity or indulgence of the Parliament should go further than I have already mentioned : yet, so full of true magnanimity are the sentiments of both, and so free from the smallest colour of passion or prejudice, that they seem disposed not only to forgive, but to forget those most unjustifiable marks of an undutiful disposition too frequent in the late transactions of the Colonies, and which, for the honor of those Colonies, it were to be wished, had been more discountenanced & discouraged by those, who had knowledge to conduct themselves otherwise.

A Revision of the late American Trade Laws is going to be the immediate object of Parliament ; nor will the late transactions there, however provoking, prevent, I dare say, the full operation of that, kind and indulgent disposition prevailing both in His Maj^ty and his Parl^nt to give to the Trade and interests of America every relief which the true State of their circumstances demands or admits. — Nothing will tend more effectually to every conciliating purpose, & there is nothing therefore I have it in command more earnestly to require of you, than that you should exert yourself in recommending it strongly to the Assembly, that full and ample compensation be made to those, who, from the Madness of the people, have suffered for their deference to Acts of the British Legislature ; and you will be particularly attentive, that such persons be effectually secured from any further insults ; and that as far as in you lies, you will take care, by your example & influence, that they may be treated with that respect to their persons, and that justice in regard to all their pretensions, which their merit and their sufferings undoubtedly claim. The Resolutions of the house of Commons, which, by His Maj^ty's Commands I transmit to you, to be laid before the Assembly, will shew you the sense of that house on those points ; and I am persuaded it will, as it certainly ought, be, the glory of that Assembly to adopt and imitate those sentiments of the British Parliament, founded on the clearest principles of humanity and justice. . . .

E. B. O'Callaghan, editor, *Documents relative to the Colonial History of the State of New-York* (Albany, 1856), VII, 823-824.

CHAPTER XXIV — THE REVENUE CONTROVERSY

145. Townshend's Revenue Scheme (1767)

BY HORACE WALPOLE, EARL OF ORFORD

Walpole, the son of the prime minister under George I and George II, knew everybody and has left entertaining memoirs, the details of which, however, cannot be accepted without question.— Bibliography: Frothingham, *Rise of the Republic*, ch. vi; Bancroft, *United States* (10 vol. ed.), VI, chs. xxv–xxx; Channing and Hart, *Guide*, § 135.

ON the 13th of May came on at last the great American questions. Charles Townshend had already hinted, when he opened the budget, at new taxes which he proposed to lay on the Colonies. He now opened them; and very inadequate indeed did they prove, even in calculation, to the loss of a shilling in the pound on land, part of which deficiency they were intended to supply. Being so inconsiderable, and estimated by himself as likely to produce but from 35,000*l.* to 40,000*l.* a-year, the House too lightly adopted his plan before it had been well weighed, and the fatal consequences of which did not break out till six years after. A concurrent cause weighed with many, and added weight to the arguments of more, for inflicting a kind of punishment on the refractory Colonies, some of which had stubbornly refused to comply with the late Act enjoining them to make provision for the army, with other parliamentary injunctions. Massachusetts Bay had, as I have said, taken upon themselves to execute the Act in their own names, and on their own sole authority. This deed Townshend said the Privy Council had advised his Majesty to annul. That Colony contained a set of men disposed to inflame all the rest. He stated fully, clearly, and with both authority and moderation, these several topics; and concluded, he said, that many would think he proposed too little, others too much. The Mutiny Bill had been opposed almost everywhere; but Pennsylvania, and some few Colonies, had executed all our orders. He wished he could name any more instances. New Jersey had avoided the Act by appointing commissioners, with injunctions to act *according to the* *custom of the provinces.*   New York was so opulent that he thought they ought to be kept in dependence.   General Gage, accordingly, was sending troops thither.   Yet did the New Yorkists commend themselves and boast that they could not remember the time when they had refused aid to Britain.   They had resolved, that if they should grant the present demand, it *might* exceed their abilities.   This was an extraordinary excuse.   More contemptuously still, they promised aid on the requisition of the Crown, but said nothing of Parliament.   Were these, he asked, the descendants of those men who had fled from prerogative to America?   Yet even this gracious compliance they held themselves at liberty to refuse, if not in proportions to the other provinces : if unreasonable — nay, if inconvenient.   They would insist, too, on his Majesty's repaying what they should furnish to his troops, when he should think proper.   He would not read, he said, the letters to their Governor, Sir Henry More, as too inflammatory.   To comply, they alleged, would be very serious ; yet desired Sir Henry to represent their obedience favourably.   The Massachusets termed our acts *our* ordinances, and asserted their own rights of taxation.   Many they had discountenanced and frightened from their assembly.   Governor Bernard, he believed, was a little heated against them ; yet the facts which he charged on them were true.   In general, it did not become Parliament to engage in controversy with its Colonies, but by one act to assert its sovereignty.   He warned the House to beware lest the provinces engaged in a common cause.   Our right of taxation was indubitable ; yet himself had been for repealing the Stamp Act to prevent mischief.   Should their disobedience return, the authority of Parliament had been weakened, and unless supported with spirit and dignity, must be destroyed.   The salaries of governors and judges in that part of the world must be made independent of their assemblies; but he advised the House to confine their resolutions to the offending provinces.   Pennsylvania was an answer to New York.   New Jersey had limited the sum, but had not said it would not comply.   He thought it would be prudent to inflict censure on New York alone ; that some burthen ought to be lightened at home, and imposed on America.   He had hinted at taxes ; he would name some, though not as Chancellor of the Exchequer.   They were duties on wine, oil, and fruits from Spain and Portugal as they come back ; on china ; and to take off the drawback on glass, paper, lead, and colours.   A commissioner of the customs, too, would be necessary in America. Parliament ought to exercise its authority ; but not contrary to the constitution of the provinces. He then moved a resolution that New York had disobeyed the Act, and that, till they should comply, the Governor should be restrained from passing *any* act of their Assembly. This, he owned, some had said would be confounding the innocent and the guilty, and would dissolve their Assembly. On the contrary, others had advised to block up harbours and quarter soldiers, but himself could bear to hear of nothing military. Some were for a local tax ; but that would be to accept penalty in lieu of obedience.

This speech, so consonant to the character of a man of business, and so unlike the wanton sallies of the man of parts and pleasure, was (however modified) but too well calculated to inflame the passions of a legislature whose authority was called in question, and who are naturally not prone to weigh the effusions of men entitled to as much freedom as themselves, while in an apparent situation of dependence. . . .

Horace Walpole, *Memoirs of the Reign of King George the Third* (edited by Sir Denis Le Marchant, London, 1845), III, 28–32.

———◆———

146. Complaint against the Acts of Trade (1767)

BY AGENT DENNIS DE BERDT

De Berdt was London agent for Massachusetts, previous to the selection of Franklin for that position. This piece illustrates the most serious grievance which led to the Revolution, the exploitation of American trade for the benefit of the British. — Bibliography : Winsor, *Narrative and Critical History*, VI, 63–64; Channing and Hart, *Guide*, § 135.

TO the Right hon'ble Lord Shelburne, one of his Majesty's Principal Secretaries of State, the Memorial of Dennis De Berdt, Agent for the House of Representatives of Massachusetts Bay,
Humbly Showeth,

That the said Colony duly observes and are thankful for, the great tenderness and concern the present and late Ministry have discovered for the Interest of that Colony and the Ample testimony they have given of their readiness to relieve them of every Burden relating to their Commercial Interest, induces them to make the following Representations of the Embarrassments which at present attend their Trade.

Your Mem'ist humbly begs leave to represent to your Lordships several things contained in his Instructions ; the Restrictions of the Trade to the Sugar Islands and the heavy duty Imposed on Foreign Sugars will destroy our Navigation and Fishery and will prevent any but the finest sorts being Imported into America, and thereby give the french the advantage of Manufacturing them.

The deeming all sugars imported from the Continent french prevents a valuable return to G. B. for her Manufactures.

The great care of the officers in America in Loading Vessels there makes it needless for those vessels to call and unload at G. B. occasions so large an expence, as entirely to destroy that Trade.

The multiplicity of Bonds occasions an expense equal to the first cost of the Lumber and some of them are twelve months before they are cancelled.

Another Grievance is the unlimited power of the officer to carry the vessel he seizes into what Port he pleases in the Continent, and after miscarrying in a tedious process is liable to no cost.

Your Memorialist's Constituents further observe that in those Ports where a regular Custom House is settled the Naval Officer may be removed.

Another difficulty is on their Trade to Spain and Portugal by the Ships from thence being obliged to stop in England, by which fruit and other perishable comodities are liable to be spoiled, by the length of the voyage.

But the grand matter of Complaint is the Restraint laid on their Fishery, no American being suffered to take Cod in the Straits of Belisle, or on Labrador shore, and thereby rendering our new watery acquisitions entirely useless, and the Restraint itself be attended with a very large expence, and instead of endeavoring to make the most of that extensive Fishery, it is become a scene of Violence between the Europeans and Americans — the interruption of the Fishery is weakening our Naval Power and depriving the Americans of the most valuable source for taking of and paying for the Manufactures of G. B.

Your Memorialist takes the liberty to lay before your Lordship a few Sentiments relating to the Fishery, that inexhaustable fund of Riches and power to G. B. this valuable Treasure may be viewed in a two fold light, as a Nursery for Seamen and as occasioning a Consumption and affording means to pay for our Manufactures.

The Fishery carried on from G. B. to America may produce a Number of Seamen for the speedy manning a fleet, the N. E. fishery in the Straits of Belisle is absolutely necessary for furnishing Sailors either for the recruit of the cruize or acting offencively in America, as its remarkably evident they did when the forces of America without any assistance from Home took the Strong Fortifications of Cape Breton, and therefore they are as really necessary as the European Supplies.

The other view of the Fishery is its being a source of Riches, nay, an inexhaustable source, exceeding the Mines of Mexico and Peru, to lay any restraint upon it in this view, is diminishing the National Treasures, stinting the growth of the Colonies and the greatest disadvantage to the Manufacturers of G. B. Restraints that are laid upon it are of that nature that your Memorialist apprehends they will not be fully removed, but by an Act of Parliament to explain that of William 3rd. and give free Liberty to all the British subjects to Improve the Fishery to the utmost, which greatly strengthens our Naval Power.

Your Memorialist's Constituents, have such an Opinion of the Justice and Wisdom of the present Administration that they doubt not it will appear reasonable to them and that as soon as these grievances are made known they will be redressed. . . .

To put any difficulties on the American Trade, will inevitably diminish our exports to that Country, from their inability to pay the Merchants for the Manufactures imported by them, which inability will be the same whether the people in America resolve to take goods or not.

The Governor and Judges being independent of the people which must render the course of Justice precarious, will be a further discouragement to Trade, and will raise fresh in the minds of the Americans the evils that attended such a measure when their forefathers left their native Country.

When the Merchants dare no longer venture their substance on such uncertainties, the Americans will be under the necessity of using their own Manufactures, tho' contrary to their present taste and inclination, to prevent them pursuing this only resource and remedy, must be the most manifest Injustice and as absurd as to make a Law to oblige them to go naked.

[Seventy-Six Society], *Papers relating to Public Events in Massachusetts preceding the American Revolution* (Philadelphia, 1856), 44–47 *passim*.

2 E

147. Fears of Episcopacy (1767)

BY REVEREND CHARLES CHAUNCY

Chauncy was pastor of the First Church in Boston from 1727 to 1787, and, with Jonathan Mayhew, was a champion against any form of Episcopalian establishment. The fear here expressed was one of the main causes of the uneasiness of New Englanders at the outbreak of the Revolution. — Bibliography: Tyler, *American Literature*, II, 199–203; Winsor, *Narrative and Critical History*, VI, 70–71; Channing and Hart, *Guide*, § 133.

HIS Lordship now comes to the last and greatest inconvenience, "the want of Bishops in our Colonies." "This," says he, pag. 22. "Besides other disadvantages attending it, appears, in particular, to be the fundamental cause of the want of native Ministers. The one removed; the other, it seems, would cease of course. For can it be imagined, could orders be had on the same terms there as elsewhere, that a number of the natives sufficient for the service of the Church, would not offer themselves in those, as they do, in all other parts of Christendom."

The want of "native ministers," if this is really the case, is not, I believe, owing to any of the causes his Lordship has mentioned, not excepting that of there being "no Bishops in the Colonies." If I may speak here with the same freedom that I think, I would say, there is, in one respect, an obvious difference between our people, and those who profess themselves Church-men. The former generally send their sons to one or other of our Colleges with a view to their being educated for the ministry; this is rarely done by the latter. Should any ask the reason of this; — it must be plainly said, our Churches are numerous for a new Country, many of them large, and well capable of providing for their ministers; and, by a swift increase of inhabitants and new-settlements, they are daily growing both in number and ability to support their Clergy. There is herefrom the prospect of a tolerable provision for our sons, if educated to serve in the ministry. Whereas, there are very few Episcopal churches that "stand upon their own legs"; — and by far the greater part of the other are small in number, weak in ability, and insufficient to maintain their own ministry, unless assisted by the Society at home. It is this that discourages the Church-people from bringing up their sons for Clergymen. They chuse rather to provide for them some other way. And as to proselytes from us, the temptation ordinarily is so small, that few are overcome by it until they have found there was little or no prospect of their being employed to greater advantage.   No one need now be at a loss to assign the true cause of the " want of native ministers."

But if Bishops should be sent to the Colonies, the people would generally turn Church-men ; — the Ecclesiastical state of things would soon be inverted ; — Episcoparians would quickly exceed the other denominations of Christians, as much as they now exceed them.

This, without all doubt, is the grand point aimed at ; and there may be some, both at home and here, who really think all this would speedily come into event.   But those who are best acquainted with the genius, temper and principles of the Colonists, at least in those parts where they are most numerous, have not the least motion of fear excited in them from the prospect of any such .effect of the mission of Bishops. They are rather concerned, least it should be the occasion of hurtful consequences both to them and us.   Such consequences would certainly be the effect, if these Bishops should make use of their SUPERIORITY, as most probably they would, sooner or later, to influence our great men here, and much greater ones at home, to project, and endeavour to carry into execution, measures to force the growth of the Church.   It may be relied on, our people would not be easy, if rest[r]ained in the exercise of that " liberty wherewith Christ has made them free ; " yea, they would hazard every thing dear to them, their estates, their very lives, rather than suffer their necks to be put under that yoke of bondage, which was so sadly galling to their fathers, and occasioned their retreat into this distant land, that they might enjoy the freedom of men and christians. . . .

But they have "no Bishops." Very true ; and they have no just reason for complaint upon this head.   For, let it be considered,

Throughout an extent of territory more than 500 miles in length, comprehending seven Provinces, the four New-England ones, and those of New-York, the Jersies, and Pensylvania ; I say, throughout these largely extended Provinces, so well inhabited that they contain more than a million of souls, there are not, by the best information I can get, more than eight or nine Episcopal churches that support themselves. All the rest, to the amount of about sixty, more or less, chiefly made up of converts from the other denominations of Christians, are so far upheld in their existence by the Society at home, at the expence of not less than some thousands sterling per annum, that, should this be withdrawn, they would soon sink away for want of needed assistance.   Instead now of being contented with the receipt of so much pious charity, they think it hard, and complain of it as a most lamentable thing, that as many thousands sterling more are not annually laid out for the maintainance of Bishops among them. Is this reasonable? Would Church-men themselves think it so in regard of other denominations of christians besides themselves? Should any of these denominations, in like circumstances, make the like complaints, insisting that they were not suffered " fully to enjoy their religion," none, it may be, would treat their complaints with more contempt, than those who are themselves so loud in making them. And yet, I know not, in regard of real merit, but other denominations would have as good a right to complain, as those who profess themselves members of the Church of England. For they are the descendants from ancestors, who subdued & cultivated this rude wilderness, amidst a thousand difficulties & hazards, so as to make it the pleasant fruitful land we now behold it; hereby adding to the extent, strength and glory of the British Crown: Nor has that sacred Majesty who wears it more loyal subjects, even in England itself: And as they are far more numerous than the Episcoparians, they are in proportion more able, and I am sure they would be as willing, to exert themselves, if called to it, at the peril of their lives, in defence of his Person and Dominions.

Charles Chauncy, *A Letter to a Friend, containing Remarks on certain Passages in a Sermon preached by . . . John Lord Bishop of Landaff* (Boston, 1767), 44–50 *passim*

---

148. Troops and Sons of Liberty in Boston (1768)

BY CHIEF JUSTICE THOMAS HUTCHINSON

These private letters, written by Hutchinson (later governor of Massachusetts) to a friend in England, fell into Franklin's hands and were by him in 1773 sent to leaders of the patriot party in Boston, by whom they were published as evidence of an attempt by a royal official to undermine their liberties. — Bibliography: Frothingham, *Rise of the Republic*, 183–184; Winsor, *Narrative and Critical History*, VI, 72, and *Memorial History of Boston*, III, 11–26; Channing and Hart, *Guide*, § 135.

Boston, 4th October 1768.

. . . IT is not strange that measures should be immediately taken to reduce the colonies to their former state of government and order, but that the national funds should be effected by it is to me a little mysterious and surprizing. Principles of government absurd enough, spread thro' all the colonies ; but I cannot think that in any colony, people of any consideration have ever been so mad as to think of a revolt.   Many of the common people have been in a frenzy, and talk'd of dying in defence of their liberties, and have spoke and printed what is highly criminal, and too many of rank above the vulgar, and some *in public posts* have countenanced and encouraged them until they increased so much in their numbers and in their opinion of their importance as to submit to government no further than they thought proper.   The legislative powers have been influenced by them, and the executive powers intirely lost their force.   There has been continual danger of mobs and insurrections, but they would have spent all their force within ourselves, the officers of the Crown and some of the few friends who dared to stand by them possibly might have been knock'd in the head, and some such fatal event would probably have brought the people to their senses. . . .

Whilst we were in this state, news came of two regiments being ordered from Halifax, and soon after two more from Ireland.   The minds of people were more and more agitated, broad hints were given that the troops should never land, a barrel of tar was placed upon the beacon, in the night to be fired to bring in the country when the troops appeared, and all the authority of the government was not strong enough to remove it.   The town of Boston met and passed a number of weak but very criminal votes ; and as the governor declined calling an assembly they sent circular letters to all the towns and districts to send a person each that there might be a general consultation at so extraordinary a crisis. They met and spent a week, made themselves ridiculous, and then dissolv'd themselves, after a message or two to the governor which he refused to receive ; a petition to the King which I dare say *their agent* will never be allow'd to present, and a result which they have published ill-natured and impotent.

In this confusion the troops from Halifax arrived.   I never was much afraid of the people's taking arms, but I was apprehensive of violence from the mob, it being their last chance before the troops could land. As the prospect of revenge became more certain their courage abated in proportion.   Two regiments are landed, but a new grievance is now rais'd.   The troops are by act of parliament to be quartered no where else but in the barracks until they are full.   There are barracks enough at the castle to hold both regiments.   It is therefore against the act to bring any of them into town. . . .   I hear the commander in chief has provided barracks or quarters, but a doubt still remains with some of the council, whether they are to furnish the articles required, unless the men are in the province barracks, and they are to determine upon it to day.

The government has been so long in the hands of the populace that it must come out of them by degrees, at least it will be a work of time to bring the people back to just notions of the nature of government. . . .

Boston, 20th January 1769.

. . . What marks of resentment the parliament will show, whether they will be upon the province in general or particular persons, is extremely uncertain, but that they will be placed somewhere is most certain, and I add, because *I think it ought to be so,* that those who have been most steady in preserving the constitution and opposing the licenciousness of such as call themselves sons of liberty will certainly meet with favor and encouragement.

This is most certainly a crisis. I really wish that there may not have been the least degree of severity beyond what is absolutely necessary to maintain, I think I may say to you the *dependance* which a colony ought to have upon the parent state ; but if no measures shall have been taken to secure this dependance, or nothing more than some declaratory acts or resolves, *it is all over with us.* The friends of government will be utterly disheartned, and the friends of anarchy will be afraid of nothing, be it ever so extravagant.

. . . I never think of the measures necessary for the peace and good order of the colonies without pain. There must be an abridgment of what are called English liberties. I relieve myself by considering that in a remove from the state of nature to the most perfect state of government there must be a great restraint of natural liberty. I doubt whether it is possible to project a system of government in which a colony 3000 miles distant from the parent state shall enjoy all the liberty of the parent state. I am certain I have never yet seen the projection. I wish the good of the colony when I wish to see some further restraint of liberty rather than the connexion with the parent state should be broken ; for I am sure such a breach must prove the ruin of the colony. Pardon me this excursion, it really proceeds from the state of mind into which our perplexed affairs often throws me. . . .

Boston, 20th October, 1769.

. . . So much has been said upon the repeal of the duties laid by the last act, that it will render it very difficult to keep people's minds quiet if that should be refused them. They deserve punishment you will say, but laying or continuing taxes upon all cannot be thought equal, seeing many will be punished who are not offenders. *Penalties of another kind seem better adapted.* . . .

I must beg the favor of you to keep secret every thing I write, until we are in a more settled state, for the party here either by their *agent* or by some of their emissaries in London, have sent them every report or rumor of the contents of letters wrote from hence. I hope we shall see better times both here and in England.

Copy of Letters sent to Great-Britain, by his Excellency Thomas Hutchinson, etc. (Boston, 1773), 9–18 *passim.*

---

149. The Pennsylvania Farmer's Remedy (1768)

BY JOHN DICKINSON

Dickinson was a Pennsylvania lawyer. His pamphlets published previous to the outbreak of the Revolution exercised remarkable influence; but he was opposed to independence, and took no part in the Revolution after 1776. — Bibliography: Tyler, *Literary History of the Revolution,* I, 235–240, II, 21–34; Winsor, *Narrative and Critical History,* VI, 82–83; Channing and Hart, *Guide,* § 134.

I HOPE, my dear countrymen, that you will in every colony be upon your guard against those who may at any time endeavour to stir you up, under pretences of patriotism, to any measures disrespectful to our sovereign and our mother country. Hot, rash, disorderly proceedings, injure the reputation of a people as to wisdom, valour and virtue, without procuring them the least benefit. I pray God, that he may be pleased to inspire you and your posterity to the latest ages with that spirit, of which I have an idea, but find a difficulty to express; to express in the best manner I can, I mean a spirit that shall so guide you, that it will be impossible to determine, whether an *American*'s character is most distinguishable for his loyalty to his sovereign, his duty to his mother country, his love of freedom, or his affection for his native soil.

Every government, at some time or other, falls into wrong measures; these may proceed from mistake or passion. — But every such measure does not dissolve the obligation between the governors and the governed; the mistake may be corrected; the passion may pass over.

It is the duty of the governed, to endeavour to rectify the mistake, and appease the passion. They have not at first any other right, than to represent their grievances, and to pray for redress, unless an emergence is so pressing, as not to allow time for receiving an answer to their applications which rarely happens. If their applications are disregarded, then that kind of opposition becomes justifiable, which can be made without breaking the laws, or disturbing the public peace. This consists in the prevention of the oppressors reaping advantage from their oppressions, and not in their punishment. For experience may teach them what reason did not ; and harsh methods, cannot be proper, till milder ones have failed.

If at length it become undoubted, that an inveterate resolution is formed to annihilate the liberties of the governed, the English history affords frequent examples of resistance by force. What particular circumstances will in any future case justify such resistance, can never be ascertained till they happen. Perhaps it may be allowable to say, generally, that it never can be justifiable, until the people are FULLY CONVINCED, that any further submission will be destructive to their happiness.

When the appeal is made to the sword, highly probable it is, that the punishment will exceed the offence ; and the calamities attending on war out weigh those preceding it. These considerations of justice and prudence, will always have great influence with good and wise men.

To these reflections on this subject, it remains to be added, and ought for ever to be remembred ; that resistance in the case of colonies against their mother country, is extremely different from the resistance of a people against their prince. A nation may change their King or race of Kings, and retain[ing] their antient form of government, be gainers by changing. Thus Great-Britain, under the illustrious house of Brunswick, a house that seems to flourish for the happiness of mankind, has found a felicity, unknown in the reigns of the Stuarts. But if once we are separated from our mother country, what new form of government shall we accept, or when shall we find another Britain to supply our loss ? Torn from the body to which we are united by religion, liberty, laws, affections, relations, language, and commerce, we must bleed at every vein.

In truth, the prosperity of these provinces is founded in their dependance on Great-Britain ; and when she returns to " her old good humour, and old good nature," as Lord Clerendon expresses it, I hope they will always esteem it their duty and interest, as it most certainly will be, to promote her welfare by all the means in their power.

We cannot act with too much caution in our disputes. Anger produces anger ; and differences that might be accommodated by kind and respectful behaviour, may by imprudence be changed to an incurable rage.

In quarrels between countries, as well as in those between individuals, when they have risen to a certain heighth, the first cause of dissention is no longer remembred, the minds of the parties being wholly engaged in recollecting and resenting the mutual expressions of their dislike. When feuds have reached that fatal point, all considerations of reason and equity vanish ; and a blind fury governs, or rather confounds all things. A people no longer regards their interest, but the gratification of their wrath. The sway of the Cleon's, and Clodius's, the designing and detestable flatter[er]s of the prevailing passion, becomes confirmed.

Wise and good men in vain oppose the storm, and may think themselves fortunate, if, endeavouring to preserve their ungrateful fellow citizens, they do not ruin themselves. Their prudence will be called baseness; their moderation, guilt ; and if their virtue does not lead them to destruction, as that of many other great and excellent persons has done, they may survive, to receive from their expiring country, the mournful glory of her acknowledgment, that their councils, if regarded, would have saved her.

The constitutional modes of obtaining relief, are those which I would wish to see pursued on the present occasion, that is, by petitioning of our assemblies, or, where they are not permitted to meet, of the people to the powers that can afford us relief.

We have an excellent prince, in whose good dispositions towards us we may confide. We have a generous, sensible, and humane nation, to whom we may apply. They may be deceived : they may, by artful men, be provoked to anger against us ; but I cannot yet believe they will be cruel or unjust ; or that their anger will be implacable. Let us behave like dutiful children, who have received unmerited blows from a beloved parent. Let us complain to our parents; but let our complaints speak at the same time, the language of affliction and veneration.

If, however, it shall happen by an unfortunate course of affairs, that our applications to his Majesty and the parliament for the redress, prove ineffectual, let us then take another step, by witholding from Great-Britain, all the advantages she has been used to receive from us. Then let us try, if our ingenuity, industry, and frugality, will not give weight to our remonstrances. Let us all be united with one spirit in one cause. Let us invent ; let us work ; let us save ; let us at the same time, keep up our claims, and unceasingly repeat our complaints; but above all, let us implore the protection of that infinite good and gracious Being, " by whom kings reign and princes decree justice."

" *Nil desperandum.*"
Nothing is to be despaired of.   A FARMER.

[John Dickinson], *Letters from a Farmer in Pennsylvania, to the Inhabitants of the British Colonies* (Boston, 1768), 30–35.

———◆———

150. Riot of the North Carolina Regulators (1770)

BY JUDGE RICHARD HENDERSON

Henderson was an associate justice of the province of North Carolina, holding a Superior Court where the riot described below occurred.   This is a typical example of the many local disturbances of the period throughout the colonies. — Bibliography : Moore, *North Carolina*, I, ch. vii; Winsor, *Narrative and Critical History*, VI, 80–82.

WITH the deepest concern for my Country I have lately been witness to a scene which not only threatened the peace and well being of this Province for the future, but was in itself the most horrid and audacious insult to Government, perpetrated with such circumstances of cruelty and madness as (I believe) scarcely has been equaled at any time.   However flattering your Excellency's prospects may have been with respect to the people called Regulators, their late conduct too sufficiently evince that a wise, mild and benevolent administration comes very far short of bringing them to a sense of their duty. They are abandoned to every principle of virtue and desperately engaged not only in the most shocking barbarities but a total subversion of the Constitution.

On Monday last being the second day of Hillsborough Superior Court, early in the morning the Town was filled with a great number of these people shouting, hallooing & making a considerable tumult in the streets. At about 11 o'clock the Court was opened, and immediately the House filled as close as one man could stand by another, some with clubs others with whips and switches, few or none without some weapon. When the House had become so crowded that no more could well get in, one of them (whose name I think is called Fields) came forward and told me he had something to say before I proceeded to business. The accounts I had previously received together with the manner and appearance of these men and the abruptness of their address rendered

my situation extremely uneasy.   Upon my informing Fields that he
might speak on he proceeded to let me know that he spoke for the
whole Body of the People called Regulators.   That they understood that
I would not try their causes, and their determination was to have them
tryed, for they had come down to see justice done and justice they w^d
have, and if I would proceed to try those causes it might prevent much
mischief.   They also charged the Court with injustice at the preceding
term and objected to the Jurors appointed by the Inferior Court and
said they would have them altered and others appointed in their room,
with many other things too tedious to mention here.   Thus I found
myself under a necessity of attempting to soften and turn away the fury
of this mad people, in the best manner in my power, and as much as
could well be, pacifie their rage and at the same time preserve the little
remaining dignity of the Court.   The consequence of which was that
after spending upwards of half an hour in this disagreeable situation the
mob cried out " Retire, retire, and let the Court go on."   Upon which
most of the regulators went out and seemed to be in consultation in a
party by themselves.

The little hopes of peace derived from this piece of behaviour were
very transient, for in a few minutes Mr Williams an Attorney of that
Court was coming in and had advanced near the door when they fell on
him in a most furious manner with Clubs and sticks of enormous size
and it was with great difficulty he saved his life by taking shelter in a
neighbouring Store House.   Mr Fanning was next the object of their
fury, him they seized and took with a degree of violence not to be
described from off the bench where he had retired for protection and
assistance and with hideous shouts of barbarian cruelty dragged him by
the heels out of doors, while others engaged in dealing out blows with
such violence that I made no doubt his life would instantly become a
sacrifice to their rage and madness.   However Mr Fanning by a manly
exertion miraculously broke holt and fortunately jumped into a door
that saved him from immediate dissolution.   During the uproar several
of them told me with oaths of great bitterness that my turn should be
next.   I will not deny that in this frightful affair my thoughts were much
engaged on my own protection, but it was not long before James Hunter
and some other of their Chieftains came and told me not to be uneasy
for that no man should hurt me on proviso I would set and hold Court
to the end of the term.

I took advantage of this proposal and made no scruple at promising what was not in my intention to perform for the Terms they would admit me to hold Court on were that no Lawyer, the King's Attorney excepted, should be admitted into Court, and that they would stay and see justice impartially done.

It would be impertinent to trouble your Exc^y with many circumstances that occurred in this barbarous riot, Messrs. Thomas Hart, Alexander Martin, Michael Holt, John Litterell (Clerk of the Crown) and many others were severely whipped. Col. Gray, Major Lloyd, Mr Francis Nash, John Cooke, Tyree Harris and sundry other persons timorously made their escape or would have shared the same fate. In about four or five hours their rage seemed to subside a little and they permitted me to adjourn Court and conducted me with great parade to my lodgings. Col^o Fanning whom they had made a prisoner of was in the evening permitted to return to his own House on his word of honour to surrender himself next day. At about ten o'clock that evening, I took an opportunity of making my escape by a back way, and left poor Col. Fanning and the little Borough in a wretched situation. . . .

The number of Insurgents that appeared when the Riot first began was, I think, about one hundred and fifty, tho' they constantly increased for two days and kept a number with fire arms at about a mile distance from Town ready to fall on whenever they were called for. This amount is contradicted by some and believed by others; certain it is that a large number of men constantly lay near the Town, whether they had arms or not is not yet sufficiently determined.

As the burden of conducting Hillsborough Superior Court fell on my shoulders alone, the Task was extremely hard and critical. I made every effort in my power consistent with my Office and the Duty the Publick is entitled to claim to preserve peace and good order, but as all attempts of that kind were ineffectual, thought it more advisable to break up Court than sit and be made a mock Judge for the sport & entertainment of those abandoned wretches. . . .

P. S. My Express has this instant arrived from Hillsborough with the following accounts, Colonel Fanning is alive and well as could be expected. The Insurgents left the Town on Wednesday night having done very little mischief after spoiling Mr Fanning's House except breaking the windows of most of the Houses in Town, among which Mr Edward's did not escape. . . .

William L. Saunders, editor, *The Colonial Records of North Carolina* (Raleigh, 1890), VIII, 241–244 *passim*.

151. An Eye-Witness of the Boston Massacre (1770)

BY JOHN TUDOR

Tudor was a Boston merchant who was an eye-witness of the stirring events in that city from 1732 to 1793. The soldiers who fired on this occasion were indicted for murder, defended by John Adams, and acquitted. — Bibliography: Winsor, *Narrative and Critical History*, VI, 85–88, and *Memorial History of Boston*, III, 31–40; Channing and Hart, *Guide*, § 135.

ON Monday Evening the 5th current, a few Minutes after 9 O'Clock a most horrid murder was committed in King Street before the Customhouse Door by 8 or 9 Soldiers under the Command of Cap[t] Tho[s] Preston drawn of from the Main Guard on the South side of the Townhouse.

This unhappy affair began by Some Boys & young fellows throwing Snow Balls at the sentry placed at the Customhouse Door. On which 8 or 9 Solders Came to his assistance. Soon after a Number of people colected, when the Cap[t] commanded the Soldiers to fire, which they did and 3 Men were Kil'd on the Spot & several Mortaly Wounded, one of which died next morning. The Cap[t] soon drew off his Soldiers up to the Main Guard, or the Consequencis mite have been terable, for on the Guns fiering the people were alarm'[d] & set the Bells a Ringing as if for Fire, which drew Multitudes to the place of action. Lev[t] Governor Hutchinson, who was commander in Chefe, was sent for & Came to the Council Chamber, w[h]ere som of the Magistrates attended. The Governor desired the Multitude about 10 O'Clock to sepperat & go home peaceable & he would do all in his power that Justice shold be don &c. The 29 Rigiment being then under Arms on the south side of the Townhouse, but the people insisted that the Soldiers should be ordered to their Barracks 1st before they would sepperat, Which being don the people sepperated aboute 1 O'Clock. — Cap[t] Preston was taken up by a warrent given to the high Sherif by Justice Dania & Tudor and came under Examination about 2 O'clock & we sent him to Goal soon after 3, having Evidence sufficient, to committ him, on his ordering the soldiers to fire: So aboute 4 O'clock the Town became quiet. The next forenoon the 8 Soldiers that fired on the inhabitants was allso sent to Goal. Tuesday A. M. the inhabitants mett at Faneuil Hall & after som pertinant speches, chose a Committee of 15 Gentlem[n] to waite on the Lev[t]. Governor in Council to request the immediate removeal of the Troops. The message was in these Words. That it is the unanimous opinion of this Meeting, that the inhabitants & soldiery can no longer live together in safety ; that nothing can Ratonaly be expected to restore the peace of the Town & prevent Blood & Carnage, but the removal of the Troops : and that we most fervently pray his Honor that his power & influance may be exerted for their instant removal.   His Honor's Reply was.   Gentlmen I am extreemly sorry for the unhappy difference & especially of the last Evening & Signifieng that it was not in his power to remove the Troops &c &c.

The Above Reply was not satisfactory to the Inhabitants, as but one Rigiment should be removed to the Castle Barracks.   In the afternoon the Town Adjourned to Dr Sewill's Meetinghouse, for Fanieul Hall was not larg enough to hold the people, their being at least 3,000, som supos'd near 4,000, when they chose a Committee to waite on the Lev^t. Governor to let him & the Council Know that nothing less will satisfy the people, then a total & immediate removal of the Troops oute of the Town. — His Honor laid before the Council the Vote of the Town. The Council thereon expressed themselves to be unanimously of opinion that it was absolutely Necessary for his Majesty service, the good order of the Town &c that the Troops Should be immeditly removed oute of the Town. — His Honor communicated this advice of the Council to Col Dalrymple & desir'd he would order the Troops down to Castle William.   After the Col. had seen the Vote of the Council He gave his Word & honor to the Town's Committe that both the Rigiments should be remov'd without delay.   The Com^{te} return'd to the Town Meeting & Mr Hancock, chairman of the Com^{te} Read their Report as above, which was Received with a shoute & clap of hands, which made the Meeting-house Ring : So the Meeting was dessolved and a great number of Gen-tlemen appear'd to Watch the Center of the Town & the prison, which continued for 11 Nights and all was quiet again, as the Soldiers was all moved of to the Castle.

(Thursday) Agreeable to a general request of the Inhabitants, were follow'd to the Grave (for they were all Buried in one) in succession the 4 Bodies of Mess^s Saml Gray Saml Maverick James Caldwell & Crispus Attucks, the unhappy Victims who fell in the Bloody Massacre. On this sorrowfull Occasion most of the shops & stores in Town were shut, all the Bells were order'd to toll a solom peal in Boston, Charles-ton, Cambridge & Roxbery.   The several Hearses forming a junction in King Street, the Theatre of that inhuman Tradgedy, proceeded from thence thro' the main street, lengthened by an immence Concourse of people, So numerous as to be obliged to follow in Ranks of 4 & 6 abreast and brought up by a long Train of Carriages. The sorrow Visible in the Countenances, together with the peculiar solemnity, Surpass description, it was suppos'd that the Spectators & those that follow'd the corps amounted to 15000, som supposed 20,000. Note Capt Preston was tried for his Life on the affare of the above Octob^r 24 1770. The Trial lasted 5 Days, but the Jury brought him in not Guilty.

William Tudor, editor, *Deacon Tudor's Diary* (Boston, 1896), 30–34.

---

152. The Boston Tea-Party (1773)

BY JOHN ANDREWS

Andrews was for five years a selectman of Boston. The letters from which these extracts are taken were written to a relative, describing scenes most of which the writer had witnessed. The destruction of the tea was an act of violence, but no other means of preventing the sale of taxed tea could be found. — Bibliography: Winsor, *Narrative and Critical History*, VI, 91–92, and *Memorial History of Boston*, III, 44–51; Channing and Hart, *Guide*, § 135.

NOVEMBER 29th [1773]. Hall and Bruce arriv'd Saturday evening with each an hundred and odd chests of the detested Tea. What will be done with it, can't say : but I tremble for ye consequences should ye consignees still persist in their obstinacy and not consent to reship it. They have softened down so far as to offer it to the care of Council or the town, till such times as they hear from their friends in England, but am perswaded, from the present dispositions of ye people, that no other alternative will do, than to have it immediately sent back to London again. . . . Y^e bells are ringing for a general muster, and a third vessel is now arriv'd in Nantasket road. Handbills are stuck up, calling upon Friends ! Citizens ! and Countrymen !

December 1st. Having just return'd from Fire Club, and am now, in company with the two Miss Masons and Mr. Williams of your place, at Sam. Eliot's, who has been dining with him at Col^o. Hancock's, and acquaints me that Mr. Palfrey sets off Express for New York and Philadelphia at five o'clock tomorrow morning, to communicate ye transactions of this town respecting the tea. . . . I acquainted you that Bruce and Hall had arrived, which was a mistake, as only Hall has arriv'd ; which has caus'd ye most spirited and firm conduct to be observ'd that

ever was known : the regularity and particulars of which proceedings
Mr. Palfrey will be able to tell you. The consignees have all taken
their residence at the Castle, as they still persist in their refusal to take
the tea back. Its not only y.ᵉ town, but the country are unanimous
against the landing it, and at the Monday and Tuesday Meetings, they
attended to the number of some hundreds from all the neighboring
towns within a dozen miles : — 'twould puzzle any person to purchase a
pair of p——ls in town, as they are all bought up, with a full determination to repell force by force.

December 18*th*. However precarious our situation may be, yet *such*
is the present calm composure of the people that a stranger would
hardly think that ten thousand pounds sterling of the East India
Company's *tea* was destroy'd the night, or rather evening before last,
yet its a serious truth ; and if your's, together with y.ᵉ other Southern
provinces, should rest satisfied with *their* quota being stor'd, poor
Boston will feel the whole weight of ministerial vengeance. However,
its the opinion of most people that we stand an equal chance now,
whether troops are sent in consequence of it or not ; whereas, had it
been stor'd, we should inevitably have had 'em, to enforce the sale of
it. — The affair was transacted with the greatest regularity and despatch.
Mr. Rotch finding he exposed himself not only to the loss of his ship
but for yᵉ value of the tea in case he sent her back with it, *without a
clearance from the custom house,* as y.ᵉ Admiral kept a ship in readiness
to make a seizure of it whenever it should sail under *those circumstances;* therefore declin'd complying with his former promises, and
absolutely declar'd his vessel should not carry it, without a *proper* clearance could be procur'd or he to be indemnified for the value of her : —
when a general muster was assembled, from this and all yᵉ neighbouring
towns, to the number of five or six thousand, at 10 o'clock Thursday
morning in the Old South Meeting house, where they pass'd a *unanimous*
vote that the *Tea* should go out of the *harbour* that afternoon, and sent
a committee with Mr. Rotch to y.ᵉ Custom house to *demand* a clearance,
which the collector told 'em was not in his power to give, without the
duties being first paid. They then sent Mr. Rotch to Milton, to ask a
pass from y.ᵉ Governor, who sent for answer, that " consistent with the
rules of government and his duty to the King he could not grant one
without they produc'd a previous clearance from the office." — By the
time he return'd with this message the candles were light in [the] house,
and upon reading it, such prodigious shouts were made, that induc'd

me, while drinking tea at home, to go out and know the cause of it.
The house was so crouded I could get no farther than yᵉ porch, when I
found the moderator was just declaring the meeting to be *dissolv'd*,
which caused another general shout, out doors and in, and three cheers.
What with that, and the consequent noise of breaking up the meeting,
you'd thought that the inhabitants of the infernal regions had broke
loose.   For my part, I went contentedly home and finish'd my tea, but
was soon inform'd what was going forward : but still not crediting it
without ocular demonstration, I went and was *satisfied*.   They muster'd,
I'm told, upon Fort Hill, to the number of about two hundred, and proceeded, two by two, to Griffin's wharf, where Hall, Bruce, and Coffin
lay, each with 114 chests of the *ill fated* article on board ; the two former
with *only* that article, but yᵉ latter arriv'd at yᵉ wharf only yᵉ day before,
was freighted with a large quantity of other goods, which they took the
greatest care not to injure in the least, and before *nine* o'clock in
yᵉ evening, every chest from on board the three vessels was knock'd to
pieces and flung over yᵉ sides.   They say the actors were *Indians* from
Narragansett.   Whether they were or not, to a transient observer they
appear'd as *such*, being cloath'd in Blankets with the heads muffled, and
copper color'd countenances, being each arm'd with a hatchet or axe,
and pair pistols, nor was their *dialect* different from what I conceive
these geniusses to *speak*, as their jargon was unintelligible to all but
themselves.   Not the least insult was offer'd to any person, save one
Captain Conner, a letter of horses in this place, not many years since
remov'd from *dear Ireland*, who had ript up the lining of his coat and
waistcoat under the arms, and watching his opportunity had nearly fill'd
'em with tea, but being detected, was handled pretty roughly.   They
not only stripp'd him of his cloaths, but gave him a coat of mud, with
a severe bruising into the bargain ; and nothing but their utter aversion
to make *any* disturbance prevented his being tar'd and feather'd.

Should not have troubled you with this, by this Post, hadn't I thought
you would be glad of a more particular account of so *important a
transaction*, than you could have obtain'd by common report ; and if it
affords my brother but a *temporary* amusement, I shall be more than
repaid for the trouble of writing it.

Letters of John Andrews, Esq., of Boston. 1772–1776; edited by Winthrop
   Sargent, in Massachusetts Historical Society, *Proceedings*, 1864–1865,
   (Boston, 1866), 324–326.

CHAPTER XXV — THE ISSUE OF COERCION

153. The First Continental Congress (1774)

BY DELEGATE JOHN ADAMS

For John Adams, see No. 24 above. For the First Continental Congress, see Froth-ingham, *Rise of the Republic*, ch. ix ; Winsor, *Narrative and Critical History*, **VI**, 99–104 ; Channing and Hart, *Guide*, § 137.

[Sept.] 5. Monday. AT ten the delegates all met at the City Tavern, and walked to the Carpenters' Hall, where they took a view of the room, and of the chamber where is an excellent library ; there is also a long entry where gentlemen may walk, and a convenient chamber opposite to the library. The general cry was, that this was a good room, and the question was put, whether we were satisfied with this room? and it passed in the affirmative. A very few were for the negative, and they were chiefly from Pennsylvania and New York. Then Mr. Lynch arose, and said there was a gentleman present who had presided with great dignity over a very respectable society, greatly to the advantage of America, and he therefore proposed that the Honorable Peyton Randolph, Esquire, one of the delegates from Virginia, and the late Speaker of their House of Burgesses, should be appointed Chairman, and he doubted not it would be unanimous.

The question was put, and he was unanimously chosen.

Mr. Randolph then took the chair, and the commissions of the delegates were all produced and read.

Then Mr. Lynch proposed that Mr. Charles Thomson, a gentleman of family, fortune, and character in this city, should be appointed Secretary, which was accordingly done without opposition, though Mr. Duane and Mr. Jay discovered at first an inclination to seek further.

Mr. Duane then moved that a committee should be appointed to prepare regulations for this Congress. Several gentlemen objected.

I then arose and asked leave of the President to request of the gentleman from New York an explanation, and that he would point out some particular regulations which he had in his mind. He mentioned particularly the method of voting, whether it should be by Colonies, or by the poll, or by interests.

Mr. Henry then arose, and said this was the first General Congress which had ever happened; that no former Congress could be a precedent; that we should have occasion for more general congresses, and therefore that a precedent ought to be established now; that it would be great injustice if a little Colony should have the same weight in the councils of America as a great one, and therefore he was for a committee.

Major Sullivan observed that a little Colony had its all at stake as well as a great one. . . .

Mr. Henry. Government is dissolved. Fleets and armies and the present state of things show that government is dissolved. Where are your landmarks, your boundaries of Colonies? We are in a state of nature, sir. I did propose that a scale should be laid down; that part of North America which was once Massachusetts Bay, and that part which was once Virginia, ought to be considered as having a weight. Will not people complain? Ten thousand Virginians have not outweighed one thousand others.

I will submit, however; I am determined to submit, if I am overruled.

A worthy gentleman (ego) near me seemed to admit the necessity of obtaining a more adequate representation.

I hope future ages will quote our proceedings with applause. It is one of the great duties of the democratical part of the constitution to keep itself pure. It is known in my Province that some other Colonies are not so numerous or rich as they are. I am for giving all the satisfaction in my power.

The distinctions between Virginians, Pennsylvanians, New Yorkers, and New Englanders, are no more. I am not a Virginian, but an American.

Slaves are to be thrown out of the question, and if the freemen can be represented according to their numbers, I am satisfied.

Mr. Lynch. I differ in one point from the gentleman from Virginia, that is, in thinking that numbers only ought to determine the weight of Colonies. I think that property ought to be considered, and that it ought to be a compound of numbers and property that should determine the weight of the Colonies.

I think it cannot be now settled.

Mr. Rutledge. We have no legal authority; and obedience to our determinations will only follow the reasonableness, the apparent utility and necessity of the measures we adopt. We have no coercive or legislative authority. Our constituents are bound only in honor to observe our determinations.

Governor Ward. There are a great number of counties, in Virginia, very unequal in point of wealth and numbers, yet each has a right to send two members.

Mr. Lee. But one reason, which prevails with me, and that is, that we are not at this time provided with proper materials. [I] am afraid we are not.

Mr. Gadsden. I can't see any way of voting, but by Colonies.

Colonel Bland. I agree with the gentleman (ego) who spoke near me, that we are not at present provided with materials to ascertain the importance of each Colony. The question is, whether the rights and liberties of America shall be contended for, or given up to arbitrary powers.

Mr. Pendleton. If the committee should find themselves unable to ascertain the weight of the Colonies, by their numbers and property, they will report this, and this will lay the foundation for the Congress to take some other steps to procure evidence of numbers and property at some future time.

Mr. Henry. I agree that authentic accounts cannot be had, if by authenticity is meant attestations of officers of the Crown.

I go upon the supposition that government is at an end. All distinctions are thrown down. All America is thrown into one mass. We must aim at the minutiæ of rectitude.

Mr. Jay. Could I suppose that we came to frame an American constitution, instead of endeavoring to correct the faults in an old one — I can't yet think that all government is at an end. The measure of arbitrary power is not full, and I think it must run over, before we undertake to frame a new constitution.

To the virtue, spirit, and abilities of Virginia, we owe much. I should always, therefore, from inclination as well as justice, be for giving Virginia its full weight.

I am not clear that we ought not to be bound by a majority, though ever so small, but I only mentioned it as a matter of danger, worthy of consideration. . . .

7. Wednesday. Went to Congress again, heard Mr. Duché read

prayers; the collect for the day, the 7th of the month, was most admirably adapted, though this was accidental, or rather providential. A prayer which he gave us of his own composition was as pertinent, as affectionate, as sublime, as devout, as I ever heard offered up to Heaven. He filled every bosom present. . . .

10. Saturday. Attended my duty upon the sub-committee. Dined at home. Dr. Morgan, Dr. Cox, Mr. Spence, and several other gentlemen, Major Sullivan and Colonel Folsom, dined with us upon salt fish. Rambled in the evening with Jo Reed, and fell into Mr. Sprout's meeting, where we heard Mr. Spence preach. Mr. Reed returned with Mr. Adams and me to our lodgings, and a very sociable, agreeable, and communicative evening we had. He says we never were guilty of a more masterly stroke of policy, than in moving that Mr. Duché might read prayers; it has had a very good effect, &c. He says the sentiments of people here are growing more and more favorable every day.

11. Sunday. There is such a quick and constant succession of new scenes, characters, persons, and events, turning up before me, that I can't keep any regular account. . . .

12. Monday. . . . dined with Mr. Dickinson at his seat at Fair Hill. . . . Mr. Dickinson has a fine seat, a beautiful prospect of the city, the river, and the country, fine gardens, and a very grand library. . . . Mr. Dickinson is a very modest man, and very ingenious as well as agreeable; he has an excellent heart, and the cause of his country lies near it. He is full and clear for allowing to Parliament the regulation of trade, upon principles of necessity, and the mutual interest of both countries.

13. Tuesday. Attended my duty all day on the sub-committee Agreed on a report.

14. Wednesday. Visited Mr. Gadsden, Mr. Deane, Colonel Dyer, &c. at their lodgings. Gadsden is violent against allowing to Parliament any power of regulating trade, or allowing that they have any thing to do with us. "Power of regulating trade," he says, "is power of ruining us; as bad as acknowledging them a supreme legislative in all cases whatsoever; a right of regulating trade is a right of legislation, and a right of legislation in one case is a right in all; this I deny." Attended the Congress and committee all the forenoon; dined with Dr. Cox. . . . A mighty feast again; nothing less than the very best of Claret, Madeira, and Burgundy; melons, fine beyond description, and pears and peaches as excellent. This day Mr. Chase introduced to us

a Mr. Carroll, of Annapolis, a very sensible gentleman, a Roman Catholic, and of the first fortune in America. His income is ten thousand pounds sterling a year now, will be fourteen in two or three years, they say; besides, his father has a vast estate which will be his after his father. . . .

17. Saturday. This was one of the happiest days of my life. In Congress we had generous, noble sentiments, and manly eloquence. This day convinced me that America will support the Massachusetts or perish with her. . . .

28. Wednesday. Dined with Mr. R. Penn; a magnificent house, and a most splendid feast, and a very large company. Mr. Dickinson and General Lee were there, and Mr. Moylan, besides a great number of the delegates. Spent the evening at home, with Colonel Lee, Colonel Washington, and Dr. Shippen, who came in to consult with us. . . .

[Oct.] 10. Monday. The deliberations of the Congress are spun out to an immeasurable length. There is so much wit, sense, learning, acuteness, subtlety, eloquence, &c. among fifty gentlemen, each of whom has been habituated to lead and guide in his own Province, that an immensity of time is spent unnecessarily. Johnson of Maryland has a clear and a cool head, an extensive knowledge of trade as well as law. He is a deliberating man, but not a shining orator; his passions and imagination don't appear enough for an orator; his reason and penetration appear, but not his rhetoric. Galloway, Duane, and Johnson are sensible and learned, but cold speakers. Lee, Henry, and Hooper, are the orators; Paca is a deliberator too; Chase speaks warmly; Mifflin is a sprightly and spirited speaker; John Rutledge don't exceed in learning or oratory, though he is a rapid speaker; young Edward Rutledge is young and zealous, a little unsteady and injudicious, but very unnatural and affected as a speaker; Dyer and Sherman speak often and long, but very heavily and clumsily. . . .

20. Thursday. Dined with the whole Congress, at the City Tavern, at the invitation of the House of Representatives of the Province of Pennsylvania. The whole House dined with us, making near one hundred guests in the whole; a most elegant entertainment. A sentiment was given: "May the sword of the parent never be stained with the blood of her children." Two or three broad-brims over against me at table; one of them said, this is not a toast, but a prayer; come, let us join in it. And they took their glasses accordingly. . . .

24. Monday. In Congress, nibbling and quibbling as usual. There

is no greater mortification than to sit with half a dozen wits, deliberating upon a petition, address, or memorial.   These great wits, these subtle critics, these refined geniuses, these learned lawyers, these wise states-men, are so fond of showing their parts and powers, as to make their consultations very tedious.   Young Ned Rutledge is a perfect Bob-o-Lincoln, — a swallow, a sparrow, a peacock ; excessively vain, exces-sively weak, and excessively variable and unsteady ; jejune, inane, and puerile.   Mr. Dickinson is very modest, delicate, and timid.   Spent the evening at home.   Colonel Dyer, Judge Sherman, and Colonel Floyd came in, and spent the evening with Mr. Adams and me.   Mr. Mifflin and General Lee came in.   Lee's head is running upon his new plan of a battalion. . . .

26. Wednesday.   Dined at home.   This day the Congress finished. Spent the evening together at the City Tavern ; all the Congress, and several gentlemen of the town. . . .

28. Friday.   Took our departure, in a very great rain, from the happy, the peaceful, the elegant, the hospitable, and polite city of Philadelphia.   It is not very likely that I shall ever see this part of the world again, but I shall ever retain a most grateful, pleasing sense of the many civilities I have received in it, and shall think myself happy to have an opportunity of returning them.

John Adams, *Works* (edited by Charles Francis Adams, Boston, 1850), II, 365–402 *passim*.

---

154. Enforcement of the Association (1774)

BY GOVERNOR THE EARL OF DUNMORE

For Dunmore, see above, No. 135.

THE Associations first in part entered into, recommended by the people of this Colony, and adopted by what is called the Con-tinental Congress, are now enforcing throughout this country with the greatest rigour.   A Committee has been chosen in every County, whose business it is to carry the Association of the Congress into execution, which Committee assumes an authority to inspect the books, invoices, and all other secrets of the trade and correspondence of Merchants ; to watch the conduct of every inhabitant, without distinction, and to send for all such as come under their suspicion into their presence ; to interrogate them respecting all matters which, at their pleasure, they think fit objects of their inquiry ; and to stigmatize, as they term it, such as they find transgressing what they are now hardy enough to call the Laws of the Congress, which stigmatizing is no other than inviting the vengeance of an outrageous and lawless mob to be exercised upon the unhappy victims. Every County, besides, is now arming a Company of men, whom they call an Independent Company, for the avowed purpose of protecting their Committees, and to be employed against Government, if occasion require. The Committee of one County has proceeded so far as to swear the men of their Independent Company, to execute all orders which shall be given them from the Committee of their County.

As to the power of Government, which your Lordship, in your letter of *November* 11, directs should be exerted to counteract the dangerous measures pursuing here, I can assure your Lordship that it is entirely disregarded, if not wholly overturned. There is not a Justice of the Peace in *Virginia* that acts, except as a Committee-man. The abolishing the Courts of Justice was the first step taken, in which the men of fortune and pre-eminence joined equally with the lowest and meanest. The General Court of Judicature of the Colony is much in the same predicament ; for though there are at least a majority of his Majesty's Council, who, with myself, are the Judges of that Court, that would steadily perform their duty, yet the Lawyers have absolutely refused to attend, nor indeed would the people allow them to attend, or evidences to appear. The reason commonly assigned for this proceeding, is the want of a Fee Bill, which expired at the last session of Assembly ; and it is a popular argument here, that no power but the Legislature can establish Fees ; and the Fee Bill not having been renewed, it is attributed to the dissolution. But the true cause of so many persons joining in so opprobrious a measure, was to engage their *English* creditors, who are numerous, to join in the clamours of this country ; and not a few to avoid paying the debts in which many of the principal people here are much involved.

With regard to the encouraging of those, as your Lordship likewise exhorts me, who appeared, in principle, averse to these proceedings, I hope your Lordship will do me the justice to believe I have left no means in my power unessayed to draw all the assistance possible from them to his Majesty's Government ; but I presume your Lordship will not think it very extraordinary, that my persuasions should have been unavailing, against the terrours, which, on the other hand, are held out by the Committee.

Independent Companies, &c., so universally supported, who have set themselves up superiour to all other authority, under the auspices of their Congress, the Laws of which they talk of in a style of respect, and treat with marks of reverence, which they never bestowed on their legal Government, or the Laws proceeding from it.   I can assure your Lordship, that I have discovered no instance where the interposition of Government, in the feeble state to which it is reduced, could serve any other purpose than to suffer the disgrace of a disappointment, and thereby afford matter of great exultation to its enemies, and increase their influence over the minds of the people.

But, my Lord, every step which has been taken by these infatuated people, must inevitably defeat its own purpose.   Their Non-Importation, Non-Exportation, &c., cannot fail in a short time to produce a scarcity, which will ruin thousands of families.   The people, indeed, of fortune, may supply themselves and their negroes for two or three years, but the middling and poorer sort, who live from hand to mouth, have not the means of doing so ; and the produce of their lands will not purchase those necessaries, (without which themselves and negroes must starve,) of the Merchants who may have goods to dispose of ; because the Merchants are prevented from turning such produce to any account.   As to manufacturing for themselves, the people of *Virginia* are very far from being naturally industrious ; and it is not by taking away the principal, if not the only encouragement to industry, that it can be excited ; nor is it in times of anarchy and confusion, that the foundation of such improvements can be laid.   The lower class of people, too, will discover that they have been duped by the richer sort, who, for their part, elude the whole effects of the Association by which their poor neighbours perish.   What, then, is to deter those from taking the shortest mode of supplying themselves ? and unrestrained as they are by laws, from taking whatever they want wherever they can find it ?

The arbitrary proceedings of these Committees, likewise, cannot fail of producing quarrels and dissensions, which will raise partisans of Government ; and I am firmly persuaded that the Colony, even by their own acts and deeds, must be brought to see the necessity of depending on its mother country, and of embracing its authority.

Peter Force, compiler, *American Archives*, Fourth Series (Washington, 1837), I, 1061–1063.

155. The Necessity of Self-Defence (1775)

BY THE SECOND CONTINENTAL CONGRESS

This is one of the most celebrated state papers of the time, and is a fervid statement of the grievances of the colonists. — Bibliography: Winsor, *Narrative and Critical History*, VI, 108; Frothingham, *Rise of the Republic*, ch. x; Channing and Hart, *Guide*, §§ 136, 137.

A DECLARATION *by the* REPRESENTATIVES *of the United Colonies of North-America, now met in Congress at Philadelphia, setting forth the Causes and Necessity of their taking up Arms. . . .*

Our Forefathers, Inhabitants of the Island of *Great-Britain*, left their Native Land, to seek on these Shores a Residence for civil and religious Freedom. At the Expence of their Blood, at the Hazard of their Fortunes, without the least Charge to the Country from which they removed, by unceasing Labour and an unconquerable Spirit, they effected Settlements in the distant and inhospitable Wilds of *America*, then filled with numerous and warlike Nations of Barbarians. — Societies or Governments, vested with perfect Legislatures, were formed under Charters from the Crown, and an harmonious Intercourse was established between the Colonies and the Kingdom from which they derived their Origin. The mutual Benefits of this Union became in a short Time so extraordinary, as to excite Astonishment. It is universally confessed, that the amazing Increase of the Wealth, Strength, and Navigation of the Realm, arose from this Source ; and the Minister, who so wisely and successfully directed the Measures of *Great-Britain* in the late War, publicly declared, that these Colonies enabled her to triumph over her Enemies. — Towards the Conclusion of that War, it pleased our Sovereign to make a Change in his Counsels. — From that fatal Moment, the Affairs of the *British* Empire began to fall into Confusion, and gradually sliding from the Summit of glorious Prosperity to which they had been advanced by the Virtues and Abilities of one Man, are at length distracted by the Convulsions, that now shake it to its deepest Foundations. — The new Ministry finding the brave Foes of *Britain*, though frequently defeated, yet still contending, took up the unfortunate Idea of granting them a hasty Peace, and of then subduing her faithful Friends.

These devoted Colonies were judged to be in such a State, as to present Victories without Bloodshed, and all the easy Emoluments of statuteable Plunder. — The uninterrupted Tenor of their peaceable and respectful Behaviour from the Beginning of Colonization, their dutiful, zealous, and useful Services during the War, though so recently and amply acknowledged in the most honourable Manner by his Majesty, by the late King, and by Parliament, could not save them from the meditated Innovations. — Parliament was influenced to adopt the pernicious Project, and assuming a new Power over them, have in the Course of eleven Years given such decisive Specimens of the Spirit and Consequences attending this Power, as to leave no Doubt concerning the Effects of Acquiescence under it. They have undertaken to give and grant our Money without our Consent, though we have ever exercised an exclusive Right to dispose of our own Property; Statutes have been passed for extending the Jurisdiction of Courts of Admiralty and Vice-Admiralty beyond their ancient Limits; for depriving us of the accustomed and inestimable Privilege of Trial by Jury in Cases affecting both Life and Property; for suspending the Legislature of one of the Colonies; for interdicting all Commerce to the Capital of another; and for altering fundamentally the Form of Government established by Charter, and secured by Acts of its own Legislature solemnly confirmed by the Crown; for exempting the " Murderers " of Colonists from legal Trial, and in Effect, from Punishment; for erecting in a neighbouring Province, acquired by the joint Arms of *Great-Britain* and *America,* a Despotism dangerous to our very Existence; and for quartering Soldiers upon the Colonists in Time of profound Peace. It has also been resolved in Parliament, that Colonists charged with committing certain Offences, shall be transported to *England* to be tried.

But why should we enumerate our Injuries in detail? By one Statute it is declared, that Parliament can "of right make Laws to bind us *in all Cases whatsoever.*" What is to defend us against so enormous, so unlimited a Power? Not a single Man of those who assume it, is chosen by us; or is subject to our Controul or Influence; but on the Contrary, they are all of them exempt from the Operation of such Laws, and an *American* Revenue, if not diverted from the ostensible Purposes for which it is raised, would actually lighten their own Burdens in Proportion, as they increase ours. We saw the Misery to which such Despotism would reduce us. We for ten Years incessantly and ineffectually besieged the Throne as Supplicants; we reasoned, we remonstrated with Parliament in the most mild and decent Language.

Administration sensible that we should regard these oppressive Measures as Freemen ought to do, sent over Fleets and Armies to enforce them. The Indignation of the *Americans* was roused, it is true; but it was the Indignation of a virtuous, loyal, and affectionate People. A Congress of Delegates from the United Colonies was assembled at *Philadelphia*, on the *fifth* Day of last *September*. We resolved again to offer an humble and dutiful Petition to the King, and also addressed our Fellow Subjects of *Great-Britain*. We have pursued every temperate, every respectful Measure ; we have even proceeded to break off our commercial Intercourse with our Fellow Subjects, as the last peaceable Admonition, that our Attachment to no Nation upon Earth should supplant our Attachment to Liberty. — This, we flattered ourselves, was the ultimate Step of the Controversy : But subsequent Events have shewn, how vain was this Hope of finding Moderation in our Enemies. . . .

. . . In brief, a part of these Colonies now feel, and all of them are sure of feeling, as far as the Vengeance of Administration can inflict them, the complicated Calamities of Fire, Sword, and Famine. We are reduced to the alternative of chusing an unconditional Submission to the tyranny of irritated Ministers, or resistance by Force. — The latter is our choice. — We have counted the cost of this contest, and find nothing so dreadful as voluntary Slavery. — Honour, Justice, and Humanity, forbid us tamely to surrender that Freedom which we received from our gallant Ancestors, and which our innocent Posterity have a right to receive from us. We cannot endure the infamy and guilt of resigning succeeding Generations to that wretchedness which inevitably awaits them, if we basely entail hereditary Bondage upon them.

Our cause is just. Our union is perfect. Our internal Resources are great, and, if necessary, foreign Assistance is undoubtedly attainable. — We gratefully acknowledge, as signal Instances of the Divine Favour towards us, that his Providence would not permit us to be called into this severe Controversy, until we were grown up to our present strength, had been previon[u]sly exercised in warlike Operation, and possessed of the means of defending ourselves. With hearts fortified with these animating Reflections, we most solemnly, before God and the World, DECLARE, that, exerting the utmost Energy of those Powers, which our beneficent Creator hath graciously bestowed upon us, the Arms we have been compelled by our Enemies to assume, we will, in defiance of every Hazard, with unabating Firmness and Perseverence, employ for the preservation of our Liberties ; being with one Mind resolved to die Freemen rather than to live Slaves.

. . . We have not raised Armies with ambitious Designs of separating from *Great-Britain*, and establishing Independent States. We fight not for Glory or for Conquest. We exhibit to Mankind the remarkable Spectacle of a People attacked by unprovoked Enemies, without any imputation or even suspicion of Offence. *They* boast of their Privileges and Civilization, and yet proffer no milder Conditions than Servitude or Death.

In our own native Land, in defence of the Freedom that is our Birth-right, and which we ever enjoyed till the late Violation of it — for the protection of our Property, acquired solely by the honest Industry of our fore-fathers and ourselves, against Violence actually offered, we have taken up Arms. We shall lay them down when Hostilities shall cease on the part of the Aggressors, and all danger of their being renewed shall be removed, and not before.

Journals of Congress, Sept. 5, 1774–Jan. 1, 1776 (Philadelphia, 1777), I, 143–148 *passim*.

---

156. A Diatribe on the American Arguments (1775)

BY DOCTOR SAMUEL JOHNSON

This piece, by the most eminent man of letters then living in the English-speaking world, is a reply to the declaration in No. 155, and an example of the fierce logic of the ultra-Tory party in England. — Bibliography of Johnson: Winsor, *Narrative and Critical History*, VI, 109; G. Birbeck Hill, *Boswell's Johnson*, II, 312–317.

THE Congress of Philadelphia, an assembly convened by its own authority, has promulgated a declaration, in compliance with which the communication between Britain and the greatest part of North America is now suspended. They ceased to admit the importation of English goods in December 1774, and determine to permit the exportation of their own no longer than to November 1775.

THIS might seem enough, but they have done more. They have declared, that they shall treat all as enemies who do not concur with them in disaffection and perveresness [perverseness], and that they will trade with none that shall trade with Britain. . . .

THESE hostile declarations they profess themselves ready to maintain by force. They have armed the militia of their provinces and seized the publick stores of ammunition. They are therefore no longer sub-jects, since they refuse the laws of their Sovereign, and in defence of that refusal are making open preparations for war. . . .

. . . They have tried to infect the people of England with the contagion of disloyalty. Their credit is happily not such as gives them influence proportionate to their malice. When they talk of their pretended immunities *guarrantied by the plighted faith of Government, and the most solemn compacts with English Sovereigns*, we think ourselves at liberty to inquire when the faith was plighted and the compact made; and when we can only find that King James and King Charles the First promised the settlers in Massachuset's Bay, now famous by the appellation of Bostonians, exemption from taxes for seven years, we infer with Mr. Mauduit, that by this *solemn compact*, they were, after the expiration of the stipulated term, liable to taxation.

WHEN they apply to our compassion, by telling us, that they are to be carried from their own country to be tried for certain offences, we are not so ready to pity them, as to advise them not to offend. While they are innocent they are safe.

WHEN they tell of laws made expressly for their punishment, we answer, that tumults and sedition were always punishable, and that the new law prescribes only the mode of execution.

WHEN it is said that the whole town of Boston is distressed for a misdemeanour of a few, we wonder at their shamelessness; for we know that the town of Boston, and all the associated provinces, are now in rebellion to defend or justify the criminals.

IF frauds in the imposts of Boston are tried by commission without a jury, they are tried here in the same mode; and why should the Bostonians expect from us more tenderness for them than for ourselves?

IF they are condemned unheard, it is because there is no need of a trial. The crime is manifest and notorious. All trial is the investigation of something doubtful. An Italian philosopher observes, that no man desires to hear what he has already seen.

IF their assemblies have been suddenly dissolved, what was the reason? Their deliberations were indecent, and their intentions seditious. The power of dissolution is granted and reserved for such times of turbulence. Their best friends have been lately soliciting the King to dissolve his Parliament, to do what they so loudly complain of suffering.

THAT the same vengeance involves the innocent and guilty is an evil to be lamented, but human caution cannot prevent it, nor human power always redress it. To bring misery on those who have not deserved it, is part of the aggregated guilt of rebellion.

THAT governours have been sometimes given them only that a great man might get ease from importunity, and that they have had judges not always of the deepest learning, or the purest integrity, we have no great reason to doubt, because such misfortunes happen to ourselves. Whoever is governed will sometimes be governed ill, even when he is most concerned in his own government.

THAT improper officers or magistrates are sent, is the crime or folly of those that sent them. When incapacity is discovered, it ought to be removed; if corruption is detected, it ought to be punished. No government could subsist for a day, if single errors could justify defection.

ONE of their complaints is not such as can claim much commiseration from the softest bosom. They tell us, that we have changed our conduct, and that a tax is now laid by Parliament on those which were never taxed by Parliament before. To this we think it may be easily answered, that the longer they have been spared, the better they can pay.

IT is certainly not much their interest to represent innovation as criminal or invidious; for they have introduced into the history of mankind a new mode of disaffection, and have given, I believe, the first example of a proscription published by a Colony against the Mother-country.

To what is urged of new powers granted to the Courts of Admiralty, or the extension of authority conferred on the judges, it may be answered in a few words, that they have themselves made such regulations necessary; that they are established for the prevention of greater evils; at the same time, it must be observed, that these powers have not been extended since the rebellion in America. . . .

IT were a curious, but an idle speculation to inquire, what effect these dictators of sedition expect from the dispersion of their letter among us. If they believe their own complaints of hardship, and really dread the danger which they describe, they will naturally hope to communicate their own perceptions to their fellow-subjects. But probably in America, as in other places, the chiefs are incendiaries, that hope to rob in the tumults of a conflagration, and toss brands among a rabble passively combustible. Those who wrote the Address, though they have shown no great extent or profundity of mind, are yet probably wiser than to believe it: but they have been taught by some master of mischief, how to put in motion the engine of political electricity; to attract by the sounds of Liberty and Property, to repel by those of Popery and Slavery; and to give the great stroke by the name of Boston.

WHEN subordinate communities oppose the decrees of the general legislature with defiance thus audacious, and malignity thus acrimonious, nothing remains but to conquer or to yield; to allow their claim of independence, or to reduce them by force to submission and allegiance. . . .

WHILE these different opinions are agitated, it seems to be determined by the Legislature, that force shall be tried. Men of the pen have seldom any great skill in conquering kingdoms, but they have strong inclination to give advice. I cannot forbear to wish, that this commotion may end without bloodshed, and that the rebels may be subdued by terrour rather than by violence; and therefore recommend such a force as may take away, not only the power, but the hope of resistance, and by conquering without a battle, save many from the sword.

IF their obstinacy continues without actual hostilities, it may perhaps be mollified by turning out the soldiers to free quarters, forbidding any personal cruelty or hurt. It has been proposed, that the slaves should be set free, an act which surely the lovers of liberty cannot but commend. If they are furnished with fire arms for defence, and utensils for husbandry, and settled in some simple form of government within the country, they may be more grateful and honest than their masters.

FAR be it from any Englishman to thirst for the blood of his fellow-subjects. Those who most deserve our resentment are unhappily at less distance. The Americans, when the Stamp Act was first proposed, undoubtedly disliked it, as every nation dislikes an impost; but they had no thought of resisting it, till they were encouraged and incited by European intelligence from men whom they thought their friends, but who were friends only to themselves.

ON the original contrivers of mischief let an insulted nation pour out its vengeance. With whatever design they have inflamed this pernicious contest, they are themselves equally detestable. If they wish success to the Colonies, they are traitors to this country; if they wish their defeat, they are traitors at once to America and England. To them and them only must be imputed the interruption of commerce, and the miseries of war, the sorrow of those that shall be ruined, and the blood of those that shall fall.

[Samuel Johnson], *Taxation no Tyranny; an Answer to the Resolutions and Address of the American Congress* (London, 1775), 55–87 *passim*.

157. The Tyranny of King George Third (1776)

BY CHIEF JUSTICE WILLIAM HENRY DRAYTON

Drayton was one of the most ardent patriots, and, as in this instance, often made his charges to the grand jury statements of the American grievances. His arraignment of the king marks a change from the first theory, that "wicked ministers" alone were responsible for bad measures. — Bibliography: Winsor, *Narrative and Critical History*, VI, 119; Tyler, *Literary History of the Revolution*, I, 491–493.

SOUTH-CAROLINA.

A T an adjournment of the court of general sessions of the peace, oyer and terminer, assize and general goal delivery, held at Charlestown, *for the district of* Charlestown, *on Tuesday the 23d day of April,* 1776. *before the Hon.* William Henry Drayton, *Esq*; *Chief Justice, and his associates justices of the colony of* South Carolina. . . .

With joyful acclamations, our ancestors by act of assembly passed on the 18th day of August 1721, recognized the British monarch : the virtues of the *second* George are still revered among us — he, was the father of his people : and it was with extacy we saw his grandson George the Third mount the throne possessed of the hearts of his subjects.

But alas ! Almost with the commencement of his reign, his subjects felt causes to complain of government. The reign advanced — the grievances became more numerous and intolerable — the complaints more general and loud — the whole empire resounded with the cries of injured subjects ! At length, grievances being unredressed and ever increasing ; all patience being borne down ; all hope destroyed ; all confidence in royal government blasted ! — Behold ! the empire is rent from pole to pole ! perhaps to continue asunder for ever !

The catalogue of our oppressions, continental and local, is enormous. Of such oppressions, I will mention only some of the most weighty.

Under colour of law, the [king] and parliament of Great Britain have made the most arbitrary attempts to enslave America.

By claiming a right to bind the colonies, in all cases whatsoever.

By laying duties at their mere will and pleasure, upon all the colonies.

By suspending the legislature of New-York.

By rendering the American charters of no validity, having annulled the most material parts of the charter of the Massachusetts Bay.

By divesting multitudes of the colonists of their property, without legal accusation or trial.

2 G

By depriving whole colonies of the bounty of providence on their own proper coasts; in order to coerce them by famine.

By restricting the trade and commerce of America.

By sending to, and continuing in America, in time of peace, an armed force without, and against the consent of the people.

By granting impunity to a soldiery instigated to murder the Americans.

By declaring, that the people of Massachusetts Bay are liable for offences, or pretended offences done in that colony, to be sent to, and tried for the same in England, or in any colony, where they cannot have the benefit of a jury of the vicinage.

By establishing in Quebec the Roman Catholic religion, and an arbitrary government; instead of the Protestant religion and a free government. . . .

Thus forced to take up arms in our own defence, America yet again most dutifully petitioned the king that he would ' be pleased to direct some mode, by which the united applications of his faithful colonists to the throne, in presence of their common councils, might be improved into a happy and permanent reconciliation; and that in the mean time, measures might be taken for preventing the further destruction of the lives of his majesty's subjects : ' — But, it was in vain ! . . .

In this enlightened age, humanity must be particularly shocked at a recital of such violences ; and it is scarce to be believed, that the British tyranny could entertain an idea of proceeding against America, by a train of more dishonourable machinations. But nothing less than absolute proof has convinced us, that in the carrying on the conspiracy against the rights of humanity, the tyranny is capable of attempting to perpetrate whatever is infamous. . . .

. . . Oh Almighty director of the universe ! What confidence can be put in a government ruling by such engines, and upon such principles of unnatural destruction ! A government, that on the 21st day of December last, made a law, *ex post facto*, to justify what had been done, not only without law, but in its nature unjust ! a law to make prize of all vessels trading in, to, or from the United Colonies ; a law to make slaves of the crews of such vessels, and to compel them to bear arms against their conscience, their fathers, their bleeding country ! The world, so old as it is, heretofore had never heard of so attrocious a procedure. It has no parallel in the registers of tyranny. . . .

. . . our liberties and safety cannot be depended upon, if the King of Great Britain should be allowed to hold our forts and cannon ; or to have authority over a single regiment in America, or a single ship of war in our ports ; for if he holds our forts, he may turn them against us, as he did Boston against her proprietors.   If he acquires our cannon, he will effectually disarm the colony ; if he has a command of troops among us, even if we raise and pay them, shackles are fixed upon us — witness Ireland and her national army.   The most express act of parliament cannot give us security ; for acts of parliament are as easily repealed as made.   Royal proclamations are not to be depended upon — witness the disappointments of the inhabitants of Quebec and St. Augustine. Even a change of ministry will not avail us ; because, notwithstanding the rapid succession of ministers, for which the British court has been famous during the present reign, yet the same ruinous policy ever continued to prevail against America.   In short, I think it my duty to declare, in the awful seat of justice, and before Almighty God, that in my opinion, the Americans can have no safety but by the divine favour, their own virtue, and their being so prudent, as not to leave it in the power of the British rulers to injure them.   Indeed, the ruinous and deadly injuries received on our side ; and the jealousies entertained, and which, in the nature of things, must daily encrease against us on the other ; demonstrate to a mind in the least given to reflection, upon the rise and fall of empires, that true reconcilement never can exist between Great Britain and America, the latter being in subjection to the former. The Almighty created America to be independent of Britain — Let us beware of the impiety of being backward to act as instruments in the Almighty hand, now extended to accomplish his purpose ; and by the completion of which alone, America, in the nature of human affairs, can be secure against the craft and insidious designs of her enemies, who think her prosperity and power already by far too great.   In a word, our piety and political safety are so blended, that to refuse our labours in this divine work, is to refuse to be a great, a free, a pious, and a happy people !

[John Almon, compiler], *The Remembrancer*, 1776 (London, 1776), Part II, 320–330 *passim*.

---

158. An Obstinate Guelph (1777–1778)

BY KING GEORGE THIRD

One of the most serious reasons for the Revolution was the unflinching determination of the king to assert his authority both over the colonies and against Parliament.

These extracts are from his intimate correspondence with Lord North, his prime minister. — For the character of George III, see No. 130 above. — Bibliography: Winsor, *Narrative and Critical History*, VII, 166; May, *Constitutional History of England*, I, ch. i.

Queen's House, Feb. 24th, 1777. 50 min. pt. 5 p. m.

LORD NORTH, — I am sorry to find your cold is encreased, and I strongly recommend ABSTINENCE and WATER as the ablest and safest physicians.

The accounts from America are most comfortable. The surprize and want of spirit of the Hessian officers as well as soldiers at Trenton is not much to their credit, and will undoubtedly rather elate the rebels, who till then were in a state of the greatest despondency. I wish Sir W. Howe had placed none but British troops in the outposts; but I am certain by a letter I have seen from Lord Cornwallis that the rebells will soon have sufficient reason to fall into the former dejection.

Lord George Germaine will to-morrow propose Gen. Clinton for Canada, and Burgoyne to join Howe. I thoroughly approve of this; he wants [Carleton?] to be recalled, but I have thrown cold water on that, and Ld. Suffolk and Ld. Gower will oppose it at your meeting. . . .

[May 31, 1777.] LORD NORTH, — I am much pleased at finding you have concluded the Committee on the African business, by referring the abuses mentioned in the Report of the Board of Trade to the next Sessions of Parliament. I have as yet not heard from Lord Weymouth concerning the debate on the House of Lords, and consequently am much pleased with your attention in sending unto me a copy of Lord Chatham's highly unseasonable motion, which can have no other use but to convey some fresh fuel if attended to by the rebels. Like most of the other productions of that extraordinary brain, it contains nothing but specious words and malevolence, for no one that reads it, if unacquainted with the conduct of the mother country and its colonies, [but] must suppose the Americans poor mild persons, who after unheard-of and repeated grievances had no choise but slavery or the sword; whilst the truth is, that the too great lenity of this country encreased their pride and encouraged them to rebel. But, thank God! the nation does not see the unhappy contest through his mirour; if his sentiments were adopted, I should not esteem my situation in this country as a very dignified one, for the islands would soon cast off all obedience. . . .

[Dec. 21, 1777.] LORD NORTH with great propriety terms the enclosed letter a singular one; I cannot help adding the epithets of offensive, and calculated alone to encrease animossity. But Franklin is too deep to draw it up solely from malevolence ; it occurs to me therefore that if he could obtain any answer it would be tacitly acknowledging hi..n and his collegues in the capacity they assume, and consequently admitting the right of the rebel colonies to make such appointment, and to be united states ; and perhaps, if he does not succeed in this object, publishing something in Europe that may carry the air of our having acted with cruelty, which I am certain no officer, either military or civil, in my service would be guilty of. They certainly could not make much distinction among rebels, but if they have erred I should rather think it has been in too much civility towards them. . . .

[Jan. 13, 1778.] . . . It also appears from these letters that Franklin and Deane either have no power of treating, or that they are not enclined to furnish any lights how an accommodation can be effected ; for whilst nothing short of independency will be accepted, I do not think there is a man either bold or mad enough to presume to treat for the mother country on such a basis. Perhaps the time may come when it will be wise to abandon all North America but Canada, Nova Scotia, and the Floridas, but then the generality of the nation must see it first in that light, but to treat with Independence can never be possible. . . .

What I have now to propose is, that without loss of time the mode of conducting the American war be deliberated upon, that Lord Amherst be examined at the Cabinet on the subject ; he is clear that after the disaster of Burgoyne not ess than an additional army to what is there at present of 40,000 men can carry on with any effect an offensive land war ; that a sea war is the only wise plan ; that the preventing the arrival of military stores, cloathing, and the other articles necessary from Europe, must distress them, and make them come into what Britain may decently consent to ; that at this hour they will laugh at any proposition. . . .

What is still more material to be settled is the plan on which Administration is to repell the different attacks of Opposition when Parliament meets, as to the calling for papers, the proposing enquiries, &c. This must be digested by you, and I hope is already so nearly ready that you may open the whole to the Cabinet when next it meets, and have a minute taken, that, when the debate [comes on] in both Houses on the state of the nation, from want of previous concert the conduct may not be opposite.

W. Bodham Donne, editor, *The Correspondence of King George the Third with Lord North* (London, 1867), II, 55–119 *passim*.

PART VII

CONDITIONS OF THE REVOLUTION

CHAPTER XXVI — THE PATRIOTS

159. "Liberty Tree" (1775)

BY THOMAS PAINE

Paine was the son of a staymaker in England, and emigrated to America in the midst of the political excitement of 1774. His various pamphlets had a wide and powerful influence. — Bibliography: Tyler, *Literary History of the Revolution*, I, 452–471. — For the Liberty Tree, see Winsor, *Memorial History of Boston*, III, 159.

IN a chariot of light from the regions of day,
    The Goddess of Liberty came ;
Ten thousand celestials directed the way,
    And hither conducted the dame.
A fair budding branch from the gardens above,
    Where millions with millions agree,
She brought in her hand, as a pledge of her love,
    And the plant she named, *Liberty Tree.*

II.

The celestial exotic struck deep in the ground,
    Like a native it flourish'd and bore.
The fame of its fruit drew the nations around,
    To seek out this peaceable shore.
Unmindful of names or distinctions they came,
    For freemen like brothers agree,
With one spirit endued, they one friendship pursued,
    And their temple was *Liberty tree.*

III.

Beneath this fair tree, like the patriarchs of old,
    Their bread in contentment they eat,
Unvex'd with the troubles of silver and gold,
    The cares of the grand and the great.
With timber and tar they Old England supply'd,
    And supported her power on the sea ;
Her battles they fought, without getting a groat,
    For the honour of *Liberty tree.*

IV.

But hear, O ye swains, ('tis a tale most profane,)
    How all the tyrannical powers,
King, Commons, and Lords, are uniting amain,
    To cut down this guardian of ours ;
From the east to the west, blow the trumpet to arms,
    Thro' the land let the sound of it flee,
Let the far and the near, — all unite with a cheer,
    In defence of our *Liberty tree.*

ATLANTICUS.

Thomas Paine, editor, *The Pennsylvania Magazine,* July, 1775 (Philadelphia, 1775), I, 328–329.

———◆———

160. A Troublous Year in a Country Village (1776)

BY REVEREND STEPHEN WILLIAMS

Williams was the first minister at Longmeadow, Massachusetts. His diary gives a picture of the life of a small village in the tumultuous Revolutionary times. — Bibliography of civil life during the Revolution : Winsor, *Narrative and Critical History,* VI, ch. i, and bibliographical notes.

JANUARY 1, 1776 — Grant us help in this day of trouble ; a very remarkable year past ; the most that I ever saw — unnatural war, great sickness, and remarkable drought. 100 years ago we were in a struggle with the Indians, who rose up in rebellion and designed the ruin of the country, but God preserved us. In the year past the leaders of our nation have sent troops to subdue and bring us under in this country, to submit to their arbitrary and tyrannical measures. Much blood has been shed — towns destroyed. I do humbly pray that God would humble and reform us, and heal our backslidings, and yet regard us in our low estate, and relieve us in this calamity, and grant that real religion may yet revive and flourish, and that we may know God and turn to Him and accept the punishment of our sins, and answer the ends of it.

5 — By post we have the king's speech to Parliament and observe that he seems resolutely set to bring the Americans under. O Lord, be pleased to restrain the wrath of man and cause it to praise thee. — 12 — Report that the great mortar and some cannon are brought through the woods from Ticonderoga. What the design is I do not know. The Lord mercifully regard and help ; otherwise all these schemes and pains and labors and expenses will be to no purpose.

March 28 — This day our military company was called together and chose their officers. I prayed with them at the meeting house.

April 9 — I hear of tumults and disorderly practices, stupidity, hardness of heart, atheism, and unbelief prevail. The British ministry breathe out cruelty against the colonies still. Things look darker and darker. 21 — Sabbath, and a quiet Sabbath. No alarm or tumult, praised be God.

May 1. — A report of 20,000 troops at Halifax from England, not yet confirmed.

July 24. — A number of people gathered together, some dressed like Indians with blankets, and manifested uneasiness with those that trade in rum, molasses, sugar, etc. I understand that a number went to Merchant Colton's and have again taken away his goods. I don't see the justice or equity of it. Many don't approve of it, but have not resolution enough to interpose and endeavour redress. I am fearful of special troubles in this place, not only on account of Samuel Colton's goods, but also because several of our people are going into service in Connecticut, and so our quota will be deficient, and possibly men may be drafted.

August 11. — This day I read publickly, being required thereto by the Provincial Council, the Declaration of the Continental Congress for Independency. 21. — Joseph Bumstead (a trusty man servant of the family) and grandson Stephen set out for Roxbury to join the army.

14 — Sabbath. This day a number of soldiers came from town on their march to the southward and breakfasted eastward of Dea. Ely's. Not so much interruption as we feared. The men behaved with moderation. They are under the conduct of Gen. Lee, who is gone down the other side.

16 — Report, probably true, that our forces at Quebec have met with a great rebuff. Gen. Montgomery killed, Col. Arnold wounded, 70 men killed, 300 taken.

Sept. 4 — Awful work ; our troops driven from Long Island ; reports more affecting and distressing ; thousands destroyed, especially Connecticut people. 6 — A gentleman of intelligence came from New York and gave me a more favorable account. 12 — Report of regulars and Indians coming down the Mohawk river towards Albany ; likely to divide our forces and distress us on every side. Report that the General Court has voted that every fifth man of our militia be ready at a minute's warning. 14 — In the evening an order came to have the militia ready at a minute's warning. Sabbath disturbed.

Oct. 1 — Several persons inimical to American liberty brought to town some confined in the jail ; others carried to Worcester, brought from the Westward, near Hudson river.

Nov. 16 — This day a number of men called tories were escorted by a party of armed men and came to Dea. Ely's and breakfasted, from Long Island, who have showed themselves unfriendly to the liberties of America. Lord grant moderation and kindness. 25 — Dark weather, dark things, stupidity, and obstinacy ; disregard of the business of the house of God.

30 — Military Co. called together at a minute's warning to go wherever called. *People don't appear forward.*

December 4 — Our soldiers begin to return that enlisted for a stated time, and people seem engaged to get money, and I fear by oppression and unjust measure. 6 — Reported a large fleet appears before New London. People are in a fright and the Connecticut militia flocking down to New London.

31 — The last day of the year. It has been one of the most remarkable in the history of America. The people, by their Congress, have declared Independency, and the king's troops and fleets are come against us. Battles have been fought ; forts and towns taken ; much blood shed ; many taken captive and wounded ; many sick, and many have died in our army. Sickness has everywhere prevailed ; deaths have been many ; a day of darkness indeed.

[R. S. Storrs and others, editors], *Proceedings at the Centennial Celebration of the Incorporation of the Town of Longmeadow* ([Hartford], 1884), 210–212 *passim*.

161. Reign of King Mob (1775)

BY "PLAIN ENGLISH"

This piece sums up the view of the loyalists as to the process by which the Revolution was brought about. Such violence undoubtedly checked the opposition to the movement. — Bibliography as in No. 166 below.

YOUR assuming the government of Massachusetts Bay, makes it unnecessary for me to make any apology for addressing you in this public manner, further, than by acquainting you that it is to represent to you the distresses of some of those people, who, from a sense of their duty to the king, and a reverence for his laws, have behaved quietly and peaceably ; and for which reason they have been deprived of their liberty, abused in their persons, and suffered such barbarous cruelties, insults, and indignities, besides the loss of their property, by the hands of lawless mobs and riots, as would have been disgraceful even for savages to have committed. The courts of justice being shut up in most parts of the province, and the justices of those courts compelled by armed force, headed by some who are members of your Congress, to refrain from doing their duties, at present it is rendered impracticable for those sufferers to obtain redress, unless it be by your interposition, or the aid of military force, which will be applied for in case this application fails. A particular enumeration of all the instances referred to, is apprehended unnecessary, as many of your members are personally knowing to them, and for the information of any of you who may pretend ignorance of them, the following instances are here mentioned. In August last, a mob in Berkshire forced the justices of the court of Common Pleas from their seats, and shut up the court-house. They also drove David Ingersoll from his house, and damaged the same, and he was obliged to leave his estate ; after which his enclosures were laid waste. At Taunton, Daniel Leonard was driven from his house, and bullets fired into it by the mob, and he obliged to take refuge in Boston, for the supposed crime of obeying his Majesty's requisition as one of his council for this province. Colonel Gilbert, of Freetown, a firm friend to government, in August last being at Dartmouth, was attacked at midnight by a mob of about an hundred, but by his bravery, with the assistance of the family where he lodged, they were beaten off. The same night Brigadier Ruggles was also attacked by another party, who were routed after having painted and cut the hair off of one of his horse's mane and tail. Afterwards he had his arms taken from his

dwelling-house in Hardwick, all of which are not yet returned.   He had
at another time a very valuable English horse, which was kept as a
stallion, poisoned, his family disturbed, and himself obliged to take
refuge in Boston, after having been insulted in his own house, and twice
on his way, by a mob. The chief justice of the province in Middleborough, was threatened to be stopped on the highway in going to
Boston court, but his firmness and known resolution, supporting government in this as well as many other instances, intimidated the mob
from laying hands on him ; he was also threatened with opposition in
going into court, but the terror of the troops prevented. The whole
bench were hissed by a mob as they came out of court. In September,
Mr. Sewall, his Majesty's Attorney-General for Massachusetts Bay, was
obliged to repair to Boston for refuge. His house at Cambridge was
attacked by a mob, and his windows were broken, but the mob was beaten
off by the gallant behavior and bravery of some young gentlemen of his
family. About the same time the Lieutenant-Governor Oliver, president
of his Majesty's council, was attacked at Cambridge, by a mob of about
four thousand, and was compelled to resign his seat at the board, since
which, upon further threats, he has been obliged to leave his estate, and
take refuge with his family in Boston. At Worcester, a mob of about
five thousand collected, prevented the court of Common Pleas from
sitting, (about one thousand of them had fire-arms,) and all drawn up
in two files, compelled the judges, sheriffs, and gentlemen of the bar,
to pass them with cap in hand, and read their disavowal of holding
courts under the new acts of parliament, not less than thirty times in
their procession. Daniel Oliver, Esq., of Hardwick, was disarmed by
a mob, and has been obliged to take refuge in Boston, to the total loss
of his business. Colonel Phips, the very reputable and highly esteemed
sheriff of the county of Middlesex, by a large mob was obliged to promise not to serve any processes of courts, and to retire to Boston for protection from further insults. Colonel Saltonstall, the very humane
sheriff of the county of Essex, has been obliged to take refuge in Boston,
to screen himself from the violence of the mob. The court of Common
Pleas was forbidden to sit at Taunton, by a large mob, with a justice
acting as one of their committee. At Middleborough, Peter Oliver,
Esq., was obliged to sign a paper, not to execute his office, under the
new acts. . . .
   The Plymouth protesters, addressers, and military officers, were compelled by a mob of two thousand, collected from Plymouth and Barn-

stable counties, to recant and resign their military commissions. Thomas Foster, Esq., an ancient gentleman, was obliged to run into the woods, and had like to have been lost, and the mob, although the justices, with Mr. Foster, were sitting in the town, ransacked his house, and damaged his furniture. He was obnoxious as a friend to government, and for that reason they endeavored to deprive him of his business, and to prevent even his taking the acknowledgment of a deed. Richard Clark, Esq., a consignee of the tea, was obliged to retire from Salem to Boston, as an asylum; and his son Isaac went to Plymouth to collect debts, but in the night was assaulted by a mob and obliged to get out of town at midnight. Jesse Dunbar, of Halifax, in Plymouth county, bought some fat cattle of Mr. Thomas the counsellor, and drove them to Plymouth for sale; one of the oxen being skinned and hung up, the committee came to him, and finding he bought it of Mr. Thomas, they put the ox into a cart, and fixing Dunbar in his belly, carted him four miles, and there made him pay a dollar, after taking three more cattle and a horse from him. The Plymouth mob delivered him to the Kingston mob, which carted him four miles further, and forced from him another dollar, then delivered him to the Duxborough mob, who abused him by throwing the tripe in his face, and endeavoring to cover him with it to the endangering his life. They then threw dirt at him, and after other abuses carried him to said Thomas's house, and made him pay another sum of money, and he not taking the beef, they flung it in the road and quitted him. Daniel Dunbar, of Halifax, an ensign of militia there, had his colors demanded by the mob, some of the selectmen being the chief actors. He refused; they broke into his house, took him out, forced him upon a rail, and after keeping him for two or three hours in such abuses, he was forced to give his colors up to save his life. A constable of Hardwick, for refusing to pay his collections, directly contrary to the oath of his office, was bound and confined six and thirty hours, and threatened with being sent to Simsbury mines. His wife being dangerously ill, he was released after signing a something which one of the mob had prepared for him. The mob committee of the county of York, ordered that no one should hire any of Sir William Pepperell's estates, buy no wood of him, or pay any debts due to him. In February, at Plymouth, a number of ladies attempted to divert themselves at their assembly room, but the mob collected, (the committee having met previous thereto,) and flung stones which broke the shutters and windows, and endangered their lives. They were forced to get out of the hall, and were pelted and abused to their own homes. After this the ladies diverted themselves by riding out, but were followed by a mob, pelted and abused, with the most indecent Billingsgate language. These things happened at the time when some of the people of Plymouth, in conjunction with the committee men from other towns in that county, aided and assisted by four dissenting clergymen, were presenting to General Gage, by their memorial, the peaceable state they were in before the arrival of a party of soldiers at Marshfield, in that county.

The Honorable Israel Williams, Esq., one who was appointed of his Majesty's new council, but had declined the office through infirmity of body, was taken from his house by the mob in the night, carried several miles, put into a room with a fire, the chimney at the top, the doors of the room closed, and kept there for many hours in the smoke, till his life was in danger ; then he was carried home, after being forced to sign what they ordered, and a guard placed over him to prevent his leaving the house.

To recount the suffering of all from mobs, rioters, and trespassers, would take more time and paper than can be spared for that purpose. It is hoped the foregoing will be sufficient to put you upon the use of proper means and measures for giving relief to all that have been injured by such unlawful and wicked practices.

Rivington's Gazette, March 9, 1775 ; reprinted in Frank Moore, *Diary of the American Revolution* (New York, etc., 1860), I, 37–42 *passim*.

---

162. A Soldier's Love-Letter (1777)

BY COLONEL ALEXANDER SCAMMELL

Scammell was an excellent officer, a favorite of Washington, and at one time adjutant-general of the American army. He served through the war, but was killed at the siege of Yorktown. The original letter has been preserved by a descendant of Nabby Bishop. — Bibliography : Winsor, *Narrative and Critical History*, VI, Index.

My Dearest Naby.   June 8th 1777.

AFTER a very severe march one hundred miles of the way on foot, through the woods in an excessive miry Road, wet, rainy weather accompanied with Snow and Hail, I arrived the 20th of May at Ticon-

Turn over.

deroga. Am now stationed at what is called the French Lines, where the british army last year met with such a fatal defeat, and lost so many men — and if they make an attempt upon us in the same place I nothing doubt we shall be able by the smiles of superintendant Providence to give them as fatal an overthrow— Our men are well supplied, and I am of opinion will behave well— The blood of our murder'd countrymen cry for Vengence on those british Villains and I hope we shall be the just Instruments of revenge. Tho I should much rather be able to retire to enjoy the sweets of Liberty and domestick happiness, but more especially the pleasing Charms of your dear Company. But so long as my Country demands my utmost Exertions, I must devote myself entirely to it's Service — Tho accustomed to the Service, I am now enter'd upon a new scene, I have an agreable and worthy sett of Officers — But my men are undisciplin'd, they are expos'd to severe Duty, many of them sick — and but poorly coverd. They look up to me as a common Father — and you may well Judge of my disagreable Sensations, when I am unable to afford them, or procure wherewithal to make them comfortable— However I shall endeavor to do all that I can for them, and if possible make them pay me ready and implicit Obedience, through Love and Affection, rather than through Fear and Dread— We at present have a very agreable, & healthy Situation — In good Spirits, and have good provisions — And hope early next Fall or Winter to do myself the pleasure of waiting upon you at Mistic unless you should forbid it.

The tender moments which we have spent together still, and ever will, remain fresh in my memory — You are ever present in my enraptur'd heart — & a mutual return of Affection from you, I find more and more necessary to my Happiness — cherish the Love my dearest Nabby, which you have so generously professed for me — Altho I am far distant from you, still remember that I am your constant, and most affectionate admirerer — I should have wrote you sooner, but being orderd upon the disagreable Command of sitting as president of a Genl.-Court martial to try men for their Lives, many of which have justly forfeited them — and to try several Villains who have attempted to spread the small Pox — I assure you that it is a most trying Birth, and has worried my mind more than any command I was ever upon — But hope I shall ever be able to discharge my Duty in such a manner as never to be subject to any disagreable Reflections — I have been upon

Turn over.

said Court steady since my arrival and this is the first opportunity I had of writing to you — I hope therefore that you will not impute any neglect to me But ever consider me unalterably thine — My Lovely Girl, write every Opportunity to

Y<u>s</u>

Alexd Scammell

Write to me every Opportunity.

Miss Naby Bishop.

PS — I long for the time when through you I can send my dutiful Regards to your Hon<u>d</u> Parents by the tender Name of Father & Mother — June 23<u>d</u> 1777.

I congratulate you upon the Cause of your Fear being remov'd as Burgoyne is going to attack Ticonderoga & not Boston.   I hope we shall be able to keep him off.

To
Miss Abigail Bishop
at
Mistick.

From the MS. in the possession of Mrs. Mary Putnam Hart of Cambridge.

* * *

163. Regulation of Prices (1777)

BY BENJAMIN HUNTINGTON

Huntington was a member of Congress and governor of Connecticut. The family letters, of which this is one, are an entertaining source of knowledge as to the daily life of the period. — On the regulation of prices, see Winsor, *Narrative and Critical History*, VII, 15, 69; Channing and Hart, *Guide*, § 133; ch. xxxiii below.

M<u>RS</u> HUNTINGTON   HARTFORD *May 29th 1777*

I TAKE this Opportunity to Convey a Line which have more Leisure to Write than I had to Answer yours by John Stockwell

It is with Concern that I hear of any Difficulty you Meet with in your (*Widowhood*) but hope you will not Suffer among a Civil People Especially when you are able to Pay for all the Favours & Supplies you want — we Read that " the full fed Soul Loatheth the Honey Comb, when we are put to Distress for an Article for the Support of Life we know better how to prize it I wish to be more Thankfull for every Enjoyment than I have been, & hope to see a Greater Scarsity of Money than we have at Present. That the Worshipers of Mammon may be Put to Difficulty to Come at the Shrine of their Idol whose Worship must be Supported and will be kept up at the Expence of all that is Good & Praiseworthy — That God has but one Perfection and that is the Idea of Infinite Increase or Augmentation and when the Materials of Increase are Plenty his Size must Grow to an amazing Bulk his Worshipers are hearty Sincear & True for they Give their Hearts and Souls to him and his Service is their Most Perfect Freedom a Freedom that Differs not from Slavery — The Assembly Yesterday had a Most Serious Debate upon the Question whether they would Repeal the Act for Regulating Prizes [prices] This Debate was brought on by Gentlemen in Trade and Seconded by Farmers who have No Avertion to Money nor to the Ways of Gitting of it Seriousness Brooded on their Countenances they Declared that articles of Life & for the Army would always be Scarse untill the Poor Farmer and the Honest Importer Could be Encouraged to their Several Emplo[y]ments of Raising, Importing &c and that the Prices stated by Law were in many Instances low & Disheartening and Would bring on a Scarsity, these Men were such as I am sure Wished well to their Country, but the God of this World had blinded their Eyes I Never Saw More Seriousness appear on hearing a Most Authodox Hopkintonian Sermon than was in the House & on full Debate & Consideration the Question was Put whether The House would give Liberty to a Certain Great Patriot to bring in a Bill for the Repeal of the Law against Monopolies & Oppression, there were but about ten or Twelve Hands up for the Repeal, to the Great Mortification of the Mammonites who will yet be seen to worship on Every high Hill and under every Green Tree

It is now under Consideration whether an Act Shall be Passed to make it more Dangerous to Violate the Law against Oppression, That no man shall, after his Covinction [conviction] for a Breach of that Law be Capable of Holding any office Civil or Military nor to Recover a Debt or Receive a Deed of Land and that None shall hold an Office untill he has taken a Solomn Oath that he has not Violated that Law Directly nor Indirectly after the 10th Day of June Next which Act I hope will Pass and that Justice & Virtue May in our Day Triumph over Iniquity — I have a New appointment on the Commit of Safety for the year Ensuing but am very Sorry to See Gen¹ Huntington left out he is a Useful Man in that Busi-

ness & has Rendered good Service to his Country but it is in Vain to
Expect a Reward for any Good Deed in this World if the Reward is to
Come from the Hands of Designing Men — There were about Eighty
Prisoners brought into this Town yesterday taken from Long Island by
a Party who went over & brought them off the [Point] agreeable M^r
Joseph Chew is one of those Captives.   Capt Benj Throop was one of
the Captains in the Expedition & Little Joseph Lothrop of Norwich was
in the Party, they Came up with the feelings and appeara[n]ce of Victors
no Doubt they had Sensations of the Similar Kind that were had by
Alexander the Great — I am at a Loss when I Shall Come home as I
Cannot Conceive of the Assembly Rising this Week If you have spent
your Money you must Try my Credit a few Days among Friends — My
Love to the Children & Compliments to Capt Abel & other Friends and
Good Wishes to Enemies, that they may become Friends — There is
one Stone to be Executed here this Morning between the Hours of 8 &
10 for Conspiracy against his Country — May God be Merciful to him
— I am afraid he will Suffer too Much for his Crime, but am not his
Judge if his own Account of his Case is True his Case is hard — I know
not the Truth of what he says and Indeed Suspect it much — I am &c

BENJ HUNTINGTON

M^{RS} HUNTINGTON

W. D. McCrackan, editor, *The Huntington Letters* (New York, 1897), 34-40.

---

164. "Columbia, Columbia to Glory Arise" (1777)

BY REVEREND TIMOTHY DWIGHT

Dwight was a graduate and tutor at Yale, later president of Yale.   This song was
written while he was acting as chaplain to the American army, in the campaign
against Burgoyne. — Bibliography: Tyler, *Literary History of the Revolution*, II,
173-174.

COLUMBIA, Columbia, to glory arise,
    The queen of the world, and the child of the skies !
Thy genius commands thee ; with rapture behold,
While ages on ages thy splendors unfold.
Thy reign is the last, and the noblest of time,
Most fruitful thy soil, most inviting thy clime ;
Let the crimes of the east ne'er encrimson thy name,
Be freedom, and science, and virtue thy fame.

To conquest and slaughter let Europe aspire;
Whelm nations in blood, and wrap cities in fire;
Thy heroes the rights of mankind shall defend,
And triumph pursue them, and glory attend.
A world is thy realm: for a world be thy laws,
Enlarged as thine empire, and just as thy cause;
On freedom's broad basis, that empire shall rise,
Extend with the main, and dissolve with the skies.

Fair Science her gates to thy sons shall unbar,
And the east see thy morn hide the beams of her star.
New bards, and new sages, unrivall'd shall soar
To fame unextinguish'd, when time is no more;
To thee, the last refuge of virtue designed,
Shall fly from all nations the best of mankind;
Here, grateful to heaven, with transport shall bring
Their incense, more fragrant than odors of spring.

Nor less shall thy fair ones to glory ascend,
And genius and beauty in harmony blend;
The graces of form shall awake pure desire,
And the charms of the soul ever cherish the fire;
Their sweetness unmingled, their manners refined,
And virtue's bright image, instamp'd on the mind,
With peace, and soft rapture, shall teach life to glow,
And light up a smile in the aspect of woe.

Thy fleets to all regions thy power shall display,
The nations admire, and the ocean obey;
Each shore to thy glory its tribute unfold,
And the east and the south yield their spices and gold.
As the day-spring unbounded, thy splendor shall flow,
And earth's little kingdoms before thee shall bow:
While the ensigns of union, in triumph unfurl'd,
Hush the tumult of war, and give peace to the world.

Thus, as down a lone valley, with cedars o'erspread,
From war's dread confusion I pensively stray'd —
The gloom from the face of fair heaven retired;
The winds ceased to murmur; the thunders expired;

　　　Perfumes, as of Eden, flow'd sweetly along,
　　　And a voice, as of angels, enchantingly sung :
　　　" Columbia, Columbia, to glory arise,
　　　The queen of the world and the child of the skies."

Samuel Kettell, *Specimens of American Poetry* (Boston, 1829), I, 246-247.

---

165. Woman's Work for the Soldiers (1780)

BY MRS. ESTHER REED AND GENERAL GEORGE WASHINGTON

Mrs. Reed was the wife of Joseph Reed, for whom see No. 61 above. The letter shows the interest and spirit of self-sacrifice of the time. — Bibliography : W. B. Reed, *Life and Correspondence of Joseph Reed*, II, 253-255, and *Life of Esther Reed*. — For Washington, see No. 195 below.

Sir,
　　　　　　　　　　　　　　　　　　　Philadelphia, July 4th, 1780.

THE subscription set on foot by the ladies of this City for the use of the soldiery, is so far completed as to induce me to transmit to your Excellency an account of the money I have received, and which, although it has answered our expectations, it does not equal our wishes, but I am persuaded will be received as a proof of our zeal for the great cause of America and our esteem and gratitude for those who so bravely defend it.

The amount of the subscription is 200,580 dollars, and £625 6s. 8d. in specie, which makes in the whole in paper money 300,634 dollars.

The ladies are anxious for the soldiers to receive the benefit of it, and wait your directions how it can best be disposed of. We expect some considerable additions from the country and have also wrote to the other States in hopes the ladies there will adopt similar plans, to render it more general and beneficial.

With the utmost pleasure I offer any farther attention and care in my power to complete the execution of the design, and shall be happy to accomplish it agreeable to the intention of the donors and your wishes on the subject.

The ladies of my family join me in their respectful compliments and sincerest prayer for your health, safety, and success.

　　　　　I have the honour to be,
　　　　　　　With the highest respect,
　　　　　　　　　Your obedient humble servant,

　　　　　　　　　　　　　　　　　　　　　E. Reed.

SIR,   Banks of Schuylkill, July 31st, 1780.

Ever since I received your Excellency's favour of the 20th of this month, I have been endeavouring to procure the linen for the use of the soldiers, and it was not till Saturday last I have been able to meet with any fit for the purpose, it being unavoidably delayed so long. I have been informed of some circumstances, which I beg leave to mention, and from which perhaps the necessity for shirts may have ceased; one is the supply of 2000 sent from this State to their line, and the other, that a considerable number is arrived in the French fleet, for the use of the army in general. Together with these, an idea prevails among the ladies, that the soldiers will not be so much gratified, by bestowing an article to which they are entitled from the public, as in some other method which will convey more fully the idea of a reward for past services, and an incitement to future duty. Those who are of this opinion propose the whole of the money to be changed into hard dollars, and giving each soldier two, to be entirely at his own disposal. This method I hint only, but would not, by any means wish to adopt it, or any other, without your full approbation. If it should meet with your concurrence, the State of Pennsylvania will take the linen I have purchased, and, as far as respects their own line, will make up any deficiency of shirts to them, which they suppose will not be many after the fresh supplies are received. If, after all, the necessity for shirts, which, though it may cease, as to the Pennsylvania Troops, may still continue to other parts of the army, the ladies will immediately make up the linen we have, which I think can soon be effected, and forward them to camp, and procure more as soon as possible, having kept in hand the hard money I have received, until I receive your reply.

The circumstances I have mentioned will, I hope, appear a sufficient motive for the ladies postponing the execution of the plan your Excellency proposed; I will not, therefore, take up your time in apologizing for the delay.

I have to acknowledge the receipt of a letter from your Excellency of the 20th, to which I would reply, that if the scheme to give the soldiers hard money, should be thought proper, of course, the putting the money I have, into the Bank, could not be done, and I find, on inquiry, that considerable advantage may be had, by laying out hard money either in linen or any other article. . . .

E. REED.

                    Head-Quarters, Orange Town, August 10th, 1780.
MADAM,

I have the honour to thank you for your favour of the 31st ult. It was not my intention to divert the benevolent donation of the ladies from the channel they wished it to flow in. I gave my opinion in consequence of their request, but I shall be equally ready to subscribe to theirs, and will execute their commands in the manner most agreeable to themselves. At the same time I have my apprehensions (from the peculiar circumstances of our army) that a taste of hard money may be productive of much discontent, as we have none but depreciated paper for their pay.

A few provident soldiers will probably avail themselves of the advantages which may result from the generous bounty of two hard dollars in specie, but it is equally probable that it will be the means of bringing punishment on a number of others whose propensity to drinking, overcoming all other considerations, too frequently leads them into irregularities and disorder which must be corrected.

A shirt would render the condition of the soldiery much more comfortable than it is at present, and no prospect of public supplies (in any degree adequate to our wants) are yet opened to my view. The provision made or making for the troops of Pennsylvania, and the late importation from France, is small, in comparison of our aggregate call, and affords a melancholy prospect of continued sufferings.

                    I have the honour to be,
                Madam, with the most perfect respect,
                    Your most obedient servant,
                        GEORGE WASHINGTON.

                    Banks of Schuylkill, August 10th, 1780.
SIR,

I had the honour of receiving yours of the 10th instant, to which I would reply, that the ladies had not the most distant wish that their donation should be bestowed in any manner, that did not perfectly accord with your opinion. I shall, therefore, without delay, put the plan in execution, and I am in hopes our expedition will prove, at once, our industry, our earnest desires to promote the comfort of the soldiery, and our cheerfulness to comply with your request. . . .

                                        E. REED.

William B. Reed, *Life and Correspondence of Joseph Reed* (Philadelphia, 1847), II, 262–266 *passim*.

CHAPTER XXVII — THE LOYALISTS

166. A Tory's Recantation (1775)

BY R. H. AND A COMMITTEE OF CORRESPONDENCE

This piece shows some of the processes applied to the refractory to make them adhere to the measures of the majority, and discloses one of the functions of the committees of correspondence. — Bibliography of the loyalists: Tyler, *Literary History of the Revolution*, I, chs. xiii–xvii, xxii; L. Sabine, *Biographical Sketches of Loyalists*, Introduction; Winsor, *Narrative and Critical History*, VII, 185–214; Channing and Hart, *Guide*, § 141.

I ACKNOWLEDGE to have wrote a piece, and did not sign it, since said to be an extract of a letter from Kent county, on Delaware, published in Humphreys' Ledger, No. 3. It was not dated from any place, and is some altered from the original. I folded it up and directed the same to J. F. and Sons. I had no intention to have it published; and further, I let them know the author thought best it should not be published; nor did I think they would. — I am sincerely sorry I ever wrote it, as also for its being published, and hope I shall be excused for this, my first breach in this way, and I intend it shall be the last.

R. H.

To the committee of correspondence for Kent county, on Delaware. May 2d, 1775.

SIR. — The president of the committee of correspondence, by and with the advice of such other of the members of that committee as he was able to collect and consult, this day laid before the committee of inspection for this county, your letter wherein you confess yourself to be the author of the Kentish letter (commonly so called) published in 3d No. of Humphreys' Ledger.

The committee took the same into consideration, and have unanimously resolved that it is unsatisfactory, and you are requested to attend the committee at their next meeting on Tuesday the 9th inst. at French Battell's, in Dover, and render such satisfaction to the committee, as

will enable them to clear the good people of this county from the aspertions of that letter, and justify them in the eyes of the public.
Signed by order of the committee.
To R. H.

GENTLEMEN. — With sorrow and contrition for my weakness and folly, I confess myself the author of the letter, from which an extract was published in the 3d No. of Humphreys' Ledger, said to be from Kent county, on Delaware; but at the same time to declare it was published without my consent, and not without some alterations.

I am now convinced that the political sentiments therein contained, were founded on the grossest error; more especially that malignant insinuation, that " if the king's standard were now erected, nine out of ten would repair to it," could not have been suggested, but from the deepest infatuation. True indeed it is, the people of this county have ever shewn a zealous attachment to his majesty's person and government, and whenever he raised his standard in a just cause, were ready to flock to it : but let the severe account I now render to an injured people, witness to the world, that none are more ready to oppose tyranny or to be first in the cause of liberty, than the inhabitants of Kent county.

Conscious that I can render no satisfaction adequate to the injury I have done my country, I can only beg the forgiveness of my countrymen, upon those principles of humanity, which may induce them to consider the frailty of human nature — and I do profess and promise, that I will never again oppose those laudable measures, necessarily adopted by my countrymen, for the preservation of American freedom : but will co-operate with them to the utmost of my abilities, in their virtuous struggle for liberty (so far as is consistent with my religious principles.)   R. H.

Resolved unanimously, that the committee do think the above recantation fully satisfactory.   THO'S. NIXON, Jr. Clerk.
May 9th, 1775.

GENTLEMEN. — Whatever the public opinion may be of what I have heretofore said respecting the contest between Great Britain and the colonies, I do solemnly assure you that I have never had any thing in view but a reconciliation between them, upon the full establishment of all the constitutional rights and privileges of America. Which rights and privileges I am determined to defend with my life and property against all invasions whatsoever. This you will please to make known to my brethren in this county.

I am, gentlemen, with great respect, your humble servant, R. S. [H]

To the committee of observation for Kent county, on Delaware.

H[ezekiah] Niles, *Principles and Acts of the Revolution in America* (Baltimore, 1822), 260–261.

---

167. The Arrest of a Loyalist Parson (1776)

BY REVEREND JONATHAN ODELL

Odell was a New Jersey man, of old New England stock, and was rector of Burlington. He escaped to New York, became chaplain of a loyalist regiment, and wrote many satirical poems against the Revolution. — Bibliography: Tyler, *Literary History of the Revolution*, II, ch. xxix. — See No. 166 above.

YOU may possibly have heard that I attempted to send a Letter to you above a twelve month since, and that my Letter being intercepted embarassed me not a little with Committees and Conventions, who were willing to find offence where none was intended. I told them and have had several occasions of telling them since, a very honest truth, that I did not mean to *dissemble* my sentiments concerning the measures of Congress, but that I had made it a Rule to myself from the beginning of our troubles, not to interfere directly or indirectly in Public Affairs, and tho' I neither could nor would make any sacrifice of my principles or duty, either as a Loyal Subject or a Minister of the Church of England, yet my political conduct should be inoffensive, if they would allow a passive conduct to be so, and in short that I presumed it reasonable in me to expect I should be indulged in the unmolested enjoyment of my private sentiments so long as I did not attempt to influence the sentiments or conduct of other men, and that private sentiments ought not to be made matter of public notice, much less of public censure. I concluded such a tenor of conduct *in our situation* was not only *necessary* but at the same time becoming the characters of Clergymen and especially of Missionaries and therefore would be approved of by the Society. But this specific system did not screen me in particular from much jealousy and misrepresentation.

A Parole was demanded of me, limiting me to within 8 miles of Burlington & binding me to forbear all political correspondence on the subject of the public dispute, not to furnish any provisions nor to give any intelligence to the Kings Troops. After giving this Parole I remain'd unmolested at home till about the middle of last Month, when a Body of Hessians under the command of Count Donop came to Burlington intending to take Post with us for the Winter. Some of my Neighbours thought it advisable to meet the Commandant on his approach to the Town and to request him to spare the Inhabitants from Insult and their property from pillage, they requested me to go with them & assist in this charitable Address as an Interpreter. I did so and had the pleasure to find that I had a pretty good prospect of being of real service to my peaceable Neighbours. But five Gondolas lying in the River began to cannonade the Town in order to prevent the Troops taking Quarter with us. Many Houses were damaged but nobody hurt. The Hessian Commandant however having with him no heavy Cannon thought proper to retire that Night to Bordentown intending to return with Artillery sufficient to make good his quarters. In the mean time tho' I believe every candid man will wonder why we should be punished for having been left defenceless and for having solicited safety from the Kings Troops in our defenceless condition, even supposing us to have assented to those measures which had brought the Troops into the country & even to our Doors ; yet true it is, that as soon as it was known on board of the Gondolas that the Troops had left us, the Town was cruelly insulted and from day to day kept in Alarm by those River Tyrants. Mr Lawrence, young Mr Hawlings & myself were in particular pursued by two captains & a number of armed men. We made our escapes & were under the necessity of taking refuge among the King's Troops, and as the design of taking Post at Burlington was soon after given up, I have been obliged to leave my wife & 3 children (the youngest not five weeks old) and to ramble as a Refugee God knows when to return.

In this situation I take the liberty to request that you will communicate the contents of this Letter to the Society ; perhaps I ought rather to have written to the Secretary, but my little narrative seemed to require a stile of more minute freedom than one can well use, unless to an intimate acquaintance and I hope the Society will admit of this apology. I suppose it can hardly be necessary to tell you what I presume you will take for granted that I among most of my Brethren thought it my duty to shut up my Church and discontinue my attendance on the Public Worship from the fatal day of the Declaration of Independency.

Public news I need not give you as you will receive better intelligence from others.　I shall **only** mention that if the Kings Troops on their arrival at Trenton had crossed the River Delaware (which notwithstanding the want of Boats was most undoubtedly practicable) they would certainly have taken possession of Philadelphia without any opposition. You will oblige me by informing the Society that I lost almost all the Fence round the Point Lot last Winter by the Soldiers quartered in the Barracks at Burlington, who made Fuel of the Rails and it has cost me £36 to renew the Fence, which after all will probably be again destroy'd this Winter.　Two years Rent of the Glebe Land near Prince Town amounting to £60 I expect to lose and indeed there is no prospect of my getting any Rent from that quarter nor any Salary from my Parishioners in future, until this unnatural War is happily terminated, and when that will be God only knows, though I hope it may be nearer than many are apt to imagine.

George Morgan Hills, *History of the Church in Burlington* (Trenton, 1876), 314–316.

---

168. Vengeance on the Tories! (1779)

BY "A WHIG"

The fierce hatred between patriots and tories is shown in this extract, which voices the sentiments of most of the patriots. — Bibliography as in No. 166 above.

JUNE 1. — Among the many errors America has been guilty of during her contest with Great Britain, few have been greater, or attended with more fatal consequences to these States, than her lenity to the Tories.　At first it might have been right, or perhaps political; but is it not surprising that, after repeated proofs of the same evils resulting therefrom, it should still be continued?　We are all crying out against the depreciation of our money, and entering into measures to restore it to its value; while the Tories, who are one principal cause of the depreciation, are taken no notice of, but suffered to live quietly among us. We can no longer be silent on this subject, and see the independence of the country, after standing every shock from without, endangered by internal enemies.　Rouse, America! your danger is great — great from a quarter where you least expect it.　The Tories, the Tories will yet be the ruin of you!　'Tis high time they were separated from among you. They are now busy engaged in undermining your liberties.　They have a thousand ways of doing it, and they make use of them all. Who were the occasion of this war? The Tories! Who persuaded the tyrant of Britain to prosecute it in a manner before unknown to civilized nations, and shocking even to barbarians? The Tories! Who prevailed on the savages of the wilderness to join the standard of the enemy? The Tories! Who have assisted the Indians in taking the scalp from the aged matron, the blooming fair one, the helpless infant, and the dying hero? The Tories! Who advised and who assisted in burning your towns, ravaging your country, and violating the chastity of your women? The Tories! Who are the occasion that thousands of you now mourn the loss of your dearest connections? The Tories! Who have always counteracted the endeavors of Congress to secure the liberties of this country? The Tories! Who refused their money when as good as specie, though stamped with the image of his most sacred Majesty? The Tories! Who continue to refuse it? The Tories! Who do all in their power to depreciate it? The Tories! Who propagate lies among us to discourage the Whigs? The Tories! Who corrupt the minds of the good people of these States by every species of insidious counsel? The Tories! Who hold a traitorous correspondence with the enemy? The Tories! Who daily sends them intelligence? The Tories! Who take the oaths of allegiance to the States one day, and break them the next? The Tories! Who prevent your battalions from being filled? The Tories! Who dissuade men from entering the army? The Tories! Who persuade those who have enlisted to desert? The Tories! Who harbor those who do desert? The Tories! In short, who wish to see us conquered, to see us slaves, to see us hewers of wood and drawers of water? The Tories!

And is it possible that we should suffer men, who have been guilty of all these and a thousand other calamities which this country has experienced, to live among us! To live among us, did I say? Nay, do they not move in our Assemblies? Do they not insult us with their impudence? Do they not hold traitorous assemblies of their own? Do they not walk the streets at noon day, and taste the air of liberty? In short, do they not enjoy every privilege of the brave soldier who has spilt his blood, or the honest patriot who has sacrificed his all in our righteous cause? Yes — to our eternal shame be it spoken — they do. Those very men who wish to entail slavery on our country, are caressed and harbored among us. Posterity will not believe it; if they do, they will curse the memory of their forefathers for their shameful lenity.

Can we ever expect any grateful return for our humanity, if it deserves that name? Believe not a spark of that or any other virtue is to be found in the Tory's breast; for what principle can that wretch have who would sell his soul to subject his country to the will of the greatest tyrant the world at present produces? 'Tis time to rid ourselves of these bosom vipers. An immediate separation is necessary. I dread to think of the evils every moment is big with, while a single Tory remains among us. May we not soon expect to hear of plots, assassinations, and every species of wickedness their malice and rancor can suggest? for what can restrain those who have already imbrued their hands in their country's blood? Did not that villain Matthews, when permitted to live among us at New York, plot the assassination of General Washington? He did; he was detected, and had he received his deserts, he would now have been in gibbets, instead of torturing our unfortunate friends, prisoners in New York, with every species of barbarity. Can we hear this, and still harbor a Tory among us? For my own part, whenever I meet one in the street, or at the coffee house, my blood boils within me. Their guilt is equalled only by their impudence. They strut, and seem to bid defiance to every one. In every place, and in every company, they spread their damnable doctrines, and then laugh at the pusillanimity of those who let them go unpunished. I flatter myself, however, with the hopes of soon seeing a period to their reign, and a total end to their existence in America. Awake, Americans, to a sense of your danger. No time to be lost. Instantly banish every Tory from among you. Let America be sacred alone to freemen.

Drive far from you every baneful wretch who wishes to see you fettered with the chains of tyranny. Send them where they may enjoy their beloved slavery to perfection — send them to the island of Britain; there let them drink the cup of slavery and eat the bread of bitterness all the days of their existence — there let them drag out a painful life, despised and accursed by those very men whose cause they have had the wickedness to espouse. Never let them return to this happy land — never let them taste the sweets of that independence which they strove to prevent. Banishment, perpetual banishment, should be their lot.

Pennsylvania Packet, August 5, 1779; reprinted in Frank Moore, *Diary of the American Revolution* (New York, etc., 1860). II, 166–168.

169. The Lot of the Refugee (1775–1779)

BY JUDGE SAMUEL CURWEN

Curwen was a man of education and social position, a resident of Salem, Massachusetts. He was Judge of Admiralty at the beginning of the war, but became a refugee and lived in England till the war terminated. Other refugees who left journals or letters are Van Schaack and Hutchinson. — Bibliography as in No. 120 above.

*L*ONDON, *July* 4 [1775]. Arrived at the New England coffee-house, Threadneedle-street, at 7 o'clock P.M. — July 5. Met my townsman and friend Benjamin Pickman, which rejoiced me ; we walked to Westminster Hall, — in Chancery saw Sir Thomas Sewell, master of the rolls, sitting with his hat on, — at Common Pleas saw Judge Black-stone and Sergeant Glynn ; and the King's Bench, Lord Mansfield and Mr. Sergeant Wedderburne. Lord Mansfield's manner is like the late Judge Dudley's of Massachusetts. His peering eyes denote a penetration and comprehension peculiarly his own. Mr. Wedderburne spoke, but at no great length.

July 9, 1775. Went to old Jewry meeting-house, where I met Gov. Hutchinson, his son and daughter, — a cordial reception and invitation to visit him. Mr. Isaac Smith and Mr. Deberdt sat in the pew next me. . . .

Dec. 31. . . . May the afflictions I have suffered the past year, in an unhappy banishment from my family, friends and country, be the means of increasing my reliance on, and submission to the all-disposing hand of the wise and righteous Governor of the universe.

January 1, 1776. May the events of the following year, however unfavorable to the pride of my heart, be productive of more moral improvement than the last. . . .

April 1, A. M. At Gov. Hutchinson's ; he was alone, reading a new pamphlet entitled "*An Inquiry whether Great Britain or America is most in fault.*" I accepted an invitation to return to dinner : taking leave for the present, I departed, walking through the palace and park to Mr. Bliss's lodgings, where I met Judge Sewall, Mr. Oxnard and Mr. Smith ; returned to the governor's, with whom only young Oliver and myself dined. From thence, in passing through Leicester-square, I called in at Mr. Copley's to see Mr. Clarke and the family, who kindly pressed my staying to tea ; and in the mean time amused myself by seeing his performances in painting. He was then at work on a family piece containing himself, Mr. Clarke, his wife and four children, of all of whom I observed a very striking likeness. At tea was present

Mr. West, a Philadelphian, a most masterly hand in historic painting; author of the well-known and applauded piece, now in print, called "*West's Death of Wolfe*," and taken from his painting. He is now at work on a piece called the "*Death of Stephen*," for the king, and for which he is to have one thousand pounds. Mr. West is the king's history-painter, and was kind enough to put me into a way of obtaining a sight of the queen's palace, which he tells me contains, except Houghton Hall, the finest collection of capital paintings of any house in England. Returned with Mr. Clarke, who was going to see his son Jonathan, sick. . . .

May 7. Attempted to get into Drury Lane theatre, to see Mr. Garrick in the character of Archer, but the crowd so great, that after suffering thumps, squeezes, and almost suffocation for two hours, I was obliged to retire without effecting it. Went to Mr. Silsbee's lodgings to tea. . . .

[*June* 6.] London, my favorite place of abode, is, as the peasant said, "*a sad lickpenny*," and truly one cannot breathe the vital air without great expense. The numerous applications to the treasury by Americans whose pretensions are so much beyond mine, exclude the most distant hope of relief for me, should inadvertence or more unjustifiable principles of conduct reduce me to the necessity of asking a favor, which I am determined at all events to defer to the longest period, if it please the great Disposer of events to prolong my uneasy abode in this country of aliens for many days yet to come. . . .

[*June* 10.] I find my finances so visibly lessening, that I wish I could remove from this expensive country, (being heartily tired of it,) and old as I am, would gladly enter into a business connection anywhere consistently with decency and integrity, which I would fain preserve. The use of the property I left behind me I fear I shall never be the better for; little did I expect from affluence to be reduced to such rigid economy as prudence now exacts. To beg is a meanness I wish never to be reduced to, and to starve is stupid; one comfort, as I am fast declining into the vale of life, my miseries cannot probably be of long continuance. . . .

[*Oct.* 31.] By a letter from Mr. Danforth I was informed some of my countrymen were about to apply to the administration for relief. — As my residence has been much longer than the most, and the suddenness of my departure from home rendering it morally impossible for me to become possessed of much money, and my pretensions, for aught I know, being as good as any and better than many, I presume I shall not be the only exile left in a forlorn condition if any provision be made ; and if never made, forlorn I shall truly be, my finances every day very sensibly lessening. Had I received Mr. Deberdt's letter in time I should have returned to London, but it was otherwise ; and if my presence now can be dispensed with, it will be more agreeable, as I live pleasantly enough among a few acquaintances, at the rate of twenty guineas a year, in a state of rigid economy that I never before was reduced to the necessity of putting in practice. . . .

[*Dec.* 31.] My little bark is in imminent hazard of being stranded unless the wind shifts quickly, or some friendly boat appears for its relief. In plain English, my purse is nearly empty ; — which circumstance has of late frequently reminded me of an emblematical device in the beginning of Fuller's History of the Holy Wars, wherein on the right is a purse distended with gold and standing upright, on the left the same turned upside down, in a lank condition, emptied wholly of its contents, with these words under the former, "*we went out full*," and under the latter, "*we returned empty*." I do not know but I am departed from my country, family and friends, on as foolish and fantastic grounds as the misguided devotees of that time did to rescue the Holy Land from infidels, though on opposite principles, I confess ; they to fight, I to avoid fighting. I now begin to tremble lest the same fate awaits me that befell them. I dislike the motives of the chief agents in America, and their whole system from its first small beginnings to its full monstrous growth of independency ; and I trust from a very just motive, *love of my country ;* which this place I am convinced has no tendency to promote the welfare of. But what of that? It is my duty, and sure the state is not to reward the loyalty of every subject ; the court in this case would have more than enough to do to satisfy the demands of all claimants.

I cannot foresee what I may hereafter do, but easily that I must suffer hunger and nakedness in the comfortless mansions of the wretched. These ideas I have not been accustomed to associate. . . .

Exeter, March 7 [1777]. I received a letter from London informing me of my wife's health and welfare in November last, and that she had been obliged to pay ten pounds sterling to find a man for the American army in my stead. . . .

March 10. Walked out to Judge Sewall's, he having the day before engaged to accompany me to the Treasury, where after a compliment I received information of a hundred pounds down, and a hundred per annum during the troubles in America, which I esteem as a providential provision procured by the friendship of my respected friend Judge Sewall. I received an order on the bank ; accompanied by him and Mr. Thomas Danforth, I took a note at the cashier's office for seventy pounds payable to myself on demand, and thirty pounds in cash, departing very joyous and I hope grateful to that Being who has, by friends, been pleased in the midst of gloomy prospects to set my feet on firm ground and establish my goings : may I wisely improve this gracious indulgence. . . .

Dec. 31. The lenity shown to General Burgoyne and his army is allowed on all hands to do more honor to America, than the laurels, reaped by the Howes, can bring to this distracted country. God knows what is for the best, but I fear our perpetual banishment from America is written in the book of fate ; nothing but the hopes of once more revisiting my native soil, enjoying my old friends within my own little domain, has hitherto supported my drooping courage ; but that prop taken away leaves me in a condition too distressing to think of ; however, amidst the increasing evils of old age I have this consolation, that, mortifying as my lot is, severe as my sufferings may be, their continuance cannot be lasting. . . .

Exeter, Sept. 6 [1779]. Am informed that I am suspected to be an American spy, disaffected to government ; this was reported by one Calhier, a violent hater of the inhabitants of the American continent and of all its friends and well-wishers : his malice I despise, and his power to injure me with government I defy. Exeter has become the seat of scandal, pride, inhospitality, foppery ; an awkward imitation of London manners, to their folly, prevails.

Samuel Curwen, *Journal and Letters* (edited by George Atkinson Ward, New York, etc., 1842), 30–221 *passim.*

CHAPTER XXVIII—THE AMERICAN FORCES

170. The Recruiting Service (1776)

BY CAPTAIN ALEXANDER GRAYDON (1811)

Graydon served in the continental army, was made a prisoner, and later was released on parole. Most of his life was spent in Pennsylvania. His work has the faults of reminiscence, but undoubtedly gives us the spirit of his experiences. — Bibliography of Graydon: Duyckinck, *Cyclopædia of American Literature*, I, 352–353. — On the American troops, Winsor, *Narrative and Critical History*, VIII, 482; Greene, *Historical View*.

THE object now was to raise my company, and as the streets of the city had been pretty well swept by the preceding and contemporary levies, it was necessary to have recourse to the country. My recruiting party was therefore sent out in various directions; and each of my officers as well as myself, exerted himself in the business. Among the many unpleasant peculiarities of the American service, it was not the least that the drudgery, which in old military establishments belongs to serjeants and corporals, here devolved on the commissioned officers; and that the whole business of recruiting, drilling, &c. required their unremitted personal attention. This was more emphatically the case in recruiting; since the common opinion was, that the men and the officers were never to be separated, and hence, to see the persons who were to command them, and above all, the captain, was deemed of vast importance by those inclining to enlist: for this reason I found it necessary, in common with my brother officers, to put my feelings most cruelly to the rack; and in an excursion I once made to Frankford, they were tried to the utmost. A number of fellows at the tavern, at which my party rendezvoused, indicated a desire to enlist, but although they drank freely of our liquor, they still held off. I soon perceived that the object was to amuse themselves at our expense, and that if there might be one or two among them really disposed to engage, the others would prevent them. One fellow in particular, who had made the greatest shew of taking the bounty, presuming on the weakness of our party, consisting only of a drummer, corporal, my second lieutenant and myself, began to grow insolent, and manifested an intention to begin a quarrel, in the issue of which, he no doubt calculated on giving us a drubbing. The disgrace of such a circumsts[a]nce, presented itself to my mind in colors the most dismal, and I resolved, that if a scuffle should be unavoidable, it should, at least, be as serious as the hangers which my lieutenant and myself carried by our sides, could make it. Our endeavor, however, was to guard against a contest ; but the moderation we testified, was attributed to fear. At length the arrogance of the principal ruffian, rose to such a height, that he squared himself for battle and advanced towards me in an attitude of defiance. I put him by, with an admonition to be quiet, though with a secret determination, that, if he repeated the insult, to begin the war, whatever might be the consequence. The occasion was soon presented ; when taking excellent aim, I struck him with the utmost force between the eyes and sent him staggering to the other end of the room. Then instantly drawing our hangers, and receiving the manful co-operation of the corporal and drummer, we were fortunate enough to put a stop to any further hostilities. It was some time before the fellow I had struck, recovered from the blow, but when he did, he was quite an altered man. He was as submissive as could be wished, begging my pardon for what he had done, and although he would not enlist, he hired himself to me for a few weeks as a fifer, in which capacity he had acted in the militia ; and during the time he was in this employ, he bore about the effects of his insolence, in a pair of black eyes. This incident would be little worthy of relating, did it not serve in some degree to correct the error of those who seem to conceive the year 1776 to have been a season of almost universal patriotic enthusiasm. It was far from prevalent in my opinion, among the lower ranks of the people, at least in Pennsylvania. At all times, indeed, licentious, levelling principles are much to the general taste, and were of course popular with us ; but the true merits of the contest, were little understood or regarded. The opposition to the claims of Britain originated with the better sort : it was truly aristocratic in its commencement ; and as the oppression to be apprehended, had not been felt, no grounds existed for general enthusiasm. The cause of liberty it is true, was fashionable, and there were great preparations to fight for it ; but a zeal proportioned to the magnitude of the question, was only to be looked for in the minds of those sagacious politicians, who inferred effects from causes, and who, as Mr. Burke expresses it, " snuffed the approach of tyranny in every tainted breeze."

Certain it was, at least, that recruiting went on but heavily. Some officers had been more successful than others, but none of the companies were complete : mine perhaps contained about half its complement of men, and these had been obtained by dint of great exertion. In this situation, captain Lenox of Shee's regiment also, suggested the trying our luck on the Eastern shore of Maryland, particularly at Chester, situated on the river of that name. It having been a place of some trade, it was supposed there might be seamen or *long shore* men there, out of employ. . . . Mr. Heath . . . helped us . . . to a recruit, a fellow, he said, who would do to stop a bullet as well as a better man, and as he was a truly worthless dog, he held, that the neighborhood would be much indebted to us for taking him away. . . .

. . . With such unfavorable prospects in Maryland, it would have been folly to have proceeded further : we therefore, set off on our way home the next morning. . . . Returning by Warwick, we sent forward our solitary recruit, for whom we tossed up ; and in winning, I was, in fact, but a very small gainer, since his merits had been set at their full value by Mr. Heath ; and he was never fit for any thing better than the inglorious post of camp colour man.

After this unsuccessful jaunt I bent my course to the Four-lane ends, Newtown, and Corryell's ferry ; thence passing into Jersey, I proceeded to the Hickory tavern, to Pittstown, Baptisttown, Flemmingtown, and other towns, whose names I do not remember. As captain Stewart (the late general Walter Stewart) of our regiment, had recently reapt this field, I was only a gleaner : In the whole of my tour, therefore, I picked up but three or four men : and could most sincerely have said,

> That the recruiting trade, with all its train,
> Of endless care, fatigue, and endless pain,

I could most gladly have renounced, even without the very preferable alternative of captain Plume. My number of privates might now have amounted to about forty, but these were soon augmented by the noble addition of one and twenty stout native Americans, brought by lieutenants Edwards and Forrest from Egg Harbour.

[Alexander Graydon], *Memoirs of a Life, chiefly passed in Pennsylvania* (Harrisburg, 1811), 117–122 *passim*.

171. A Brave Man's Death (1776)

ANONYMOUS

Nathan Hale was a graduate of Yale, and was teaching school when the war broke out. At the earnest request of Washington he agreed to act as a spy, and was captured and hung. The heroic episode made a great impression in favor of the patriots. — Bibliography: Tyler, *Literary History of the Revolution*, II, 183–186; Winsor, *Narrative and Critical History*, VI, 333–334; Benson J. Lossing, *The Two Spies*, 3–34.

THE breezes went steadily thro' the tall pines,
　　A saying "oh! hu-ush!" a saying "oh! hu-ush!"
As stilly stole by a bold legion of horse,
　　For Hale in the bush, for Hale in the bush.

"Keep still!" said the thrush as she nestled her young,
　　In a nest by the road; in a nest by the road.
"For the tyrants are near, and with them appear,
　　What bodes us no good, what bodes us no good."

The brave captain heard it, and thought of his home,
　　In a cot by the brook; in a cot by the brook.
With mother and sister and memories dear,
　　He so gaily forsook; he so gaily forsook.

Cooling shades of the night were coming apace,
　　The tattoo had beat; the tattoo had beat.
The noble one sprang from his dark lurking place,
　　To make his retreat; to make his retreat.

He warily trod on the dry rustling leaves,
　　As he pass'd thro' the wood; as he pass'd thro' the wood;
And silently gain'd his rude launch on the shore,
　　As she play'd with the flood; as she play'd with the flood.

The guards of the camp, on that dark, dreary night,
　　Had a murderous will; had a murderous will.
They took him and bore him afar from the shore,
　　To a hut on the hill; to a hut on the hill.

No mother was there, nor a friend who could cheer,
　　In that little stone cell; in that little stone cell.
But he trusted in love, from his father above.
　　In his heart, all was well; in his heart, all was well

An ominous owl with his solemn base voice,
    Sat moaning hard by ; sat moaning hard by.
"The tyrant's proud minions most gladly rejoice,
    For he must soon die ; for he must soon die."

The brave fellow told them, no thing he restrain'd,
    The cruel gen'ral ; the cruel gen'ral.
His errand from camp, of the ends to be gain'd,
    And said that was all ; and said that was all.

They took him and bound him and bore him away,
    Down the hill's grassy side ; down the hill's grassy side.
'Twas there the base hirelings, in royal array,
    His cause did deride ; his cause did deride.

Five minutes were given, short moments, no more,
    For him to repent ; for him to repent ;
He pray'd for his mother, he ask'd not another,
    To Heaven he went ; to Heaven he went.

The faith of a martyr, the tragedy shew'd,
    As he trod the last stage ; as he trod the last stage.
And Britons will shudder at gallant Hale's blood,
    As his words do presage, as his words do presage.

"Thou pale king of terrors, thou life's gloomy foe,
    Go frighten the slave, go frighten the slave ;
Tell tyrants, to you, their allegiance they owe.
    No fears for the brave ; no fears for the brave."

Frank Moore, *Songs and Ballads of the American Revolution* (New York, 1856), 131–133.

———◆———

172. Arrival of a French Volunteer (1777)

BY GENERAL MARIE PAUL JOSEPH, MARQUIS DE LAFAYETTE

(TRANSLATED BY JARED SPARKS, 1834)

Lafayette was the most distinguished of the many French officers in the American service, and had great influence later in securing the French alliance. — Bibliography : Winsor, *Narrative and Critical History*, VI, 547; Charlemagne Tower, Jr., *Lafayette in the American Revolution*.

Charleston, 19 June, 1777.

MY last letter to you, my dear love, has informed you, that I arrived safely in this country, after having suffered a little from sea-sickness during the first weeks of the voyage ; that I was then, the morning after I landed, at the house of a very kind officer; that I had been nearly two months on the passage, and that I wished to set off immediately. It spoke of every thing most interesting to my heart; of my sorrow at parting from you, and of our dear children; and it said, besides, that I was in excellent health. I give you this abstract of it, because the English may possibly amuse themselves by seizing it on its way. I have such confidence in my lucky star, however, that I hope it will reach you. This same star has befriended me, to the astonishment of every body here. Trust to it yourself, and be assured that it ought to calm all your fears. I landed after having sailed several days along a coast, which swarmed with hostile vessels. When I arrived, every body said that my vessel must inevitably be taken, since two British frigates blockaded the harbour. I even went so far as to send orders to the captain, both by land and sea, to put the men on shore and set fire to the ship, if not yet too late. By a most wonderful good fortune, a gale obliged the frigates to stand out to sea for a short time. My vessel came in at noon-day, without meeting friend or foe.

At Charleston I have met General Howe, an American officer now in the service. The Governor of the State is expected this evening from the country. All with whom I wished to become acquainted here, have shown me the greatest politeness and attention. I feel entirely satisfied with my reception, although I have not thought it best to go into any detail respecting my arrangements and plans. I wish first to see Congress. I hope to set out for Philadelphia in two days. Our route is more than two hundred and fifty leagues by land. We shall divide ourselves into small parties. I have already purchased horses and light carriages for the journey. Some French and American vessels are here, and are to sail together to-morrow morning, taking advantage of a moment when the frigates are out of sight. They are armed, and have promised me to defend themselves stoutly against the small privateers, which they will certainly meet. I shall distribute my letters among the different ships.

I will now tell you about the country and its inhabitants. They are as agreeable as my enthusiasm had painted them. Simplicity of manners, kindness, love of country and of liberty, and a delightful equality every where prevail. The wealthiest man and the poorest are on a level; and, although there are some large fortunes, I challenge any one to discover the slightest difference between the manners of these two classes respectively towards each other. I first saw the country life at

the house of Major Huger.   I am now in the city, where every thing
is very much after the English fashion, except that there is more simplicity, equality, cordiality, and courtesy here than in England.   The
city of Charleston is one of the handsomest and best built, and its inhabitants among the most agreeable, that I have ever seen.   The American women are very pretty, simple in their manners, and exhibit a
neatness, which is every where cultivated even more studiously than in
England.   What most charms me is, that all the citizens are brethren.
In America, there are no poor, nor even what we call peasantry.   Each
individual has his own honest property, and the same rights as the
most wealthy landed proprietor.   The inns are very different from those
of Europe ; the host and hostess sit at table with you, and do the
honors of a comfortable meal ; and, on going away, you pay your bill
without higgling.   When one does not wish to go to an inn, there are
country-houses where the title of a good American is a sufficient passport to all those civilities paid in Europe to one's friend.

As to my own reception, it has been most agreeable in every quarter ;
and to have come with me secures the most flattering welcome.   I
have just passed five hours at a grand dinner, given in honor of me by
an individual of this city.   Generals Howe and Moultrie, and several
officers of my suite, were present.   We drank healths and tried to talk
English.   I begin to speak it a little.   To-morrow I shall go with these
gentlemen to call on the Governor of the State, and make arrangements
for my departure.   The next day the commanding officers here will
show me the city and its environs, and then I shall set out for the army.

Considering the pleasant life I lead in this country, my sympathy
with the people, which makes me feel as much at ease in their society
as if I had known them for twenty years, the similarity between their
mode of thinking and my own, and my love of liberty and of glory, one
might suppose that I am very happy.   But you are not with me ; my
friends are not with me ; and there is no happiness for me far from you
and them.   I ask you, if you still love me ; but I put the same question
much oftener to myself, and my heart always responds, Yes.   I am
impatient beyond measure to hear from you.   I hope to find letters at
Philadelphia.   My only fear is, that the privateer, which is to bring
them, may be captured on her passage.   Although I suppose I have
drawn upon me the special displeasure of the English, by taking the
liberty to depart in spite of them, and by landing in their very face, yet
I confess they will not be in arrears with me, should they capture this

vessel, my cherished hope, on which I so fondly depend for letters from you. Write frequent and long letters. You do not know the full extent of the joy with which I shall receive them. Embrace Henrietta tenderly. May I say embrace tenderly our *children ?* The father of these poor children is a rover, but a good and honest man at heart ; a good father, who loves his family dearly, and a good husband, who loves his wife with all his heart.

Remember me to your friends and my own, to the dear society, once the society of the court, but which by the lapse of time has become the society of the *Wooden Sword.* We republicans think it all the better. I must leave off for want of paper and time ; and if I do not repeat to you ten thousand times that I love you, it is not from any want of feeling, but from modesty ; since I have the presumption to hope, that I have already convinced you of it. The night is far advanced, and the heat dreadful. I am devoured by insects ; so, you see, the best countries have their disadvantages. Adieu.

LAFAYETTE.

George Washington, *Writings* (edited by Jared Sparks, Boston, 1834), V, Appendix, 451–453.

---

173. " Battalions of Negroes " (1779)

BY COLONEL ALEXANDER HAMILTON

Hamilton was a young West Indian, at the outbreak of the war a student at King's (Columbia) College. He came forward at once as an effective pamphleteer, entered the army, and attracted Washington's favorable notice. Later he was member of the Congress of the Confederation, and Secretary of the Treasury (see *Contemporaries,* III).— Bibliography : Ford, *Bibliotheca Hamiltoniana ;* Winsor, *Narrative and Critical History,* VII, 325–326; Channing and Hart, *Guide,* §152.

DEAR SIR, Head-quarters, March 14th, 1779.

COLONEL Laurens, who will have the honour of delivering you this letter, is on his way to South Carolina, on a project which I think, in the present situation of affairs there, is a very good one, and deserves every kind of support and encouragement. This is to raise two, three, or four battalions of negroes, with the assistance of the government of that State, by contributions from the owners, in proportion to the number they possess. If you should think proper to enter upon the subject with him, he will give you a detail of his plan. He wishes to have it recommended by Congress to the State ; and, as an inducement, that they would engage to take those battalions into continental pay.

It appears to me that an expedient of this kind, in the present state of southern affairs, is the most rational that can be adopted, and promises very important advantages. Indeed, I hardly see how a sufficient force can be collected in that quarter without it; and the enemy's operations there are growing infinitely serious and formidable. I have not the least doubt that the negroes will make very excellent soldiers with proper management; and I will venture to pronounce that they cannot be put into better hands than those of Mr. Laurens. He has all the zeal, intelligence, enterprise, and every other qualification necessary to succeed in such an undertaking. It is a maxim with some great military judges, that with sensible officers, soldiers can hardly be too stupid; and, on this principle, it is thought that the Russians would make the best troops in the world, if they were under other officers than their own. The King of Prussia is among the number who maintain this doctrine, and has a very emphatical saying on the occasion, which I do not exactly recollect. I mention this, because I hear it frequently objected to the scheme of imbodying negroes, that they are too stupid to make soldiers. This is so far from appearing to me a valid objection, that I think their want of cultivation (for their natural faculties are probably as good as ours), joined to that habit of subordination, which they acquire from a life of servitude, will make them sooner become soldiers than our white inhabitants. Let officers be men of sense and sentiment, and the nearer the soldiers approach to machines, perhaps the better.

I foresee that this project will have to combat much opposition from prejudice and self-interest. The contempt we have been taught to entertain for the blacks, makes us fancy many things that are founded neither in reason nor experience; and an unwillingness to part with property of so valuable a kind, will furnish a thousand arguments to show the impracticability, or pernicious tendency, of a scheme which requires such a sacrifice. But it should be considered, that if we do not make use of them in this way, the enemy probably will; and that the best way to counteract the temptations they will hold out, will be to offer them ourselves. An essential part of the plan is to give them their freedom with their muskets. This will secure their fidelity, animate their courage, and, I believe, will have a good influence upon those who remain, by opening a door to their emancipation. This circumstance, I confess, has no small weight in inducing me to wish the success of the project; for the dictates of humanity and true policy equally interest me in favour of this unfortunate class of men.

With the truest respect and esteem,

I am, sir your most obedient servant,

ALEX. HAMILTON.

William Jay, *The Life of John Jay: with Selections from his Correspondence,* etc. (New York, 1833), II, 31–32.

———◆———

174. The Inconveniences of Militia (1780)

BY GENERAL GEORGE WASHINGTON

Upon the character and service of the various classes of American soldiers no testimony is so good as that of the commander-in-chief. Yet out of these irregular levies came the armies which defeated Howe, Burgoyne, Clinton, and Cornwallis. — Bibliography as in No. 195 below.

. . . IT is the true policy of America not to content herself with temporary expedients, but to endeavor, if possible, to give consistency and solidity to her measures. An essential step to this will be immediately to devise a plan, and put it in execution, for providing men in time to replace those who will leave us at the end of the year, for subsisting and making a reasonable allowance to the officers and soldiers. The plan for this purpose ought to be of general operation, and such as will execute itself. Experience has shown, that a peremptory draft will be the only effectual one. If a draft for the war or three years can be effected, it ought to be made on every account. A shorter period than a year is inadmissible. To one, who has been witness to the evils brought upon us by short enlistments, the system appears to have been pernicious beyond description, and a crowd of motives present themselves to dictate a change. It may easily be shown, that all the misfortunes we have met with in the military line are to be attributed to this cause.

Had we formed a permanent army in the beginning, which, by the continuance of the same men in service, had been capable of discipline, we never should have had to retreat with a handful of men across the Delaware in '76, trembling for the fate of America, which nothing but the infatuation of the enemy could have saved; we should not have remained all the succeeding winter at their mercy, with sometimes scarcely a sufficient body of men to mount the ordinary guards, liable at every moment to be dissipated, if they had only thought proper to march against us : we should not have been under the necessity of fighting at Brandywine, with an unequal number of raw troops, and afterwards of seeing Philadelphia fall a prey to a victorious army ; we should not have been at Valley Forge with less than half the force of the enemy, destitute of every thing, in a situation neither to resist nor to retire ; we should not have seen New York left with a handful of men, yet an overmatch for the main army of these States, while the principal part of their force was detached for the reduction of two of them ; we should not have found ourselves this spring so weak, as to be insulted by five thousand men, unable to protect our baggage and Magazines, their security depending on a good countenance, and a want of enterprise in the enemy ; we should not have been the greatest part of the war inferior to the enemy, indebted for our safety to their inactivity, enduring frequently the mortification of seeing inviting opportunities to ruin them pass unimproved for want of a force, which the country was completely able to afford ; to see the Country ravaged, our towns burnt, the inhabitants plundered, abused, murdered with impunity from the same cause.

Nor have the ill effects been confined to the military line. A great part of the embarrassments in the civil departments flow from the same source. The derangement of our finances is essentially to be ascribed to it. The expenses of the war, and the Paper emissions, have been greatly multiplied by it. We have had, a great part of the time, two sets of men to feed and pay, the discharged men going home and the Levies coming in. This was more remarkable in '75 and '76. The difficulty and cost of engaging men have increased at every successive attempt, till among the present levies we find there are some, who have received a hundred and fifty dollars in specie for five months' service, while our officers are reduced to the disagreeable necessity of performing the duties of drill sergeants to them, and with this mortifying reflection annexed to the business, that, by the time they have taught those men the rudiments of a soldier's duty, their term of service will have expired, and the work is to recommence with an entire new set. The consumption of Provision, arms, accoutrements, stores of every kind, has been doubled in spite of every precaution I could use, not only from the cause just mentioned, but from the carelessness and licentiousness incident to militia and irregular Troops. Our discipline also has been much injured, if not ruined, by such frequent changes. The frequent calls upon the militia have interrupted the cultivation of the Land, and of course have lessened the quantity of its produce, occasioned a scarcity, and enhanced the prices. In an army so unstable as ours, order and economy have been impracticable. No person, who has been a close observer of the progress of our affairs, can doubt that our currency has depreciated without comparison more rapidly from the system of short enlistments, than it would have done otherwise.

There is every reason to believe, the War has been protracted on this account. Our opposition being less, made the successes of the enemy greater. The fluctuation of the army kept alive their hopes, and at every period of the dissolution of a considerable part of it, they have flattered themselves with some decisive advantages. Had we kept a permanent army on foot, the enemy could have had nothing to hope for, and would in all probability have listened to terms long since.

If the army is left in its present situation, it must continue an encouragement to the efforts of the enemy ; if it is put upon a respectable one, it must have a contrary effect, and nothing, I believe, will tend more to give us peace the ensuing winter. It will be an interesting winter. Many circumstances will contribute to a negotiation. An army on foot not only for another campaign, but for several campaigns, would determine the enemy to pacific measures, and enable us to insist upon favorable terms in forcible language ; an army insignificant in numbers, dissatisfied, crumbling into pieces, would be the strongest temptation they could have to try the experiment a little longer. It is an old maxim, that the surest way to make a good peace is to be well prepared for war.

I am inclined to hope a draft for the war, or for three years, would succeed. Many incentives of immediate interest may be held up to the people to induce them to submit to it. They must begin to consider the repeated bounties they are obliged to pay as a burthen, and be willing to get rid of it by sacrificing a little more once for all. Indeed it is probable, the bounties may not be much greater in that case than they have been. The people of the States near the Seat of War ought to enter into such a plan with alacrity, as it would ease them in a variety of respects ; among others, by obviating the frequent calls upon the Militia.

George Washington, *Writings* (edited by Worthington Chauncey Ford, New York, etc., 1890), VIII, 393–397.

175. Military Punishments (1780)

BY SURGEON JAMES THACHER

Thacher was a medical student who joined the army in 1775 and served in the medical service until 1783. His interesting journal was modified and polished when published forty years later, and hence does not give quite his contemporary views. — Bibliography: Tyler, *Literary History of the Revolution*, II, 416–418.

[January 1, 1780.] AS if to make up the full measure of grief and embarrassment to the Commander in Chief, repeated complaints have been made to him that some of the soldiers are in the practice of pilfering and plundering the inhabitants of their poultry, sheep, pigs, and even their cattle, from their farms. This marauding practice has often been prohibited in general orders, under the severest penalties, and some exemplary punishments have been inflicted. General Washington possesses an inflexible firmness of purpose, and is determined that discipline and subordination in camp shall be rigidly enforced and maintained. The whole army has been sufficiently warned, and cautioned against robbing the inhabitants on any pretence whatever, and no soldier is subjected to punishment without a fair trial, and conviction by a court martial. Death has been inflicted in a few instances of an atrocious nature, but in general, the punishment consists in a public whipping, and the number of stripes is proportioned to the degree of offence. The law of Moses prescribes forty stripes save one, but this number has often been exceeded in our camp. In aggravated cases, and with old offenders, the culprit is sentenced to receive one hundred lashes, or more. It is always the duty of the drummers and fifers to inflict the chastisement, and the drum major must attend and see that the duty is faithfully performed. The culprit being securely tied to a tree, or post, receives on his naked back the number of lashes assigned him, by a whip formed of several small knotted cords, which sometimes cut through the skin at every stroke. However strange it may appear, a soldier will often receive the severest stripes without uttering a groan, or once shrinking form [from] the lash, even while the blood flows freely from his lacerated wounds. This must be ascribed to stubbornness or pride. They have however, adopted a method which they say mitigates the anguish in some measure, it is by putting between the teeth a leaden bullet, on which they chew while under the lash, till it is made quite flat and jagged. In some instances of incorrigible villains, it is adju[d]ged by the court that the culprit receive his punishment at several different times, a certain number of stripes repeated at intervals of two or three days, in which case the wounds are in a state of inflammation, and the skin rendered more sensibly tender; and the terror of the punishment is greatly aggravated. Another mode of punishment is that of running the *gantlet*, this is done by a company of soldiers standing in two lines, each one furnished with a switch, and the criminal is made to run between them and receive the scourge from their hands on his naked back; but the delinquent runs so rapidly, and the soldiers are so apt to favor a comrade, that it often happens in this way that the punishment is very trivial; but on some occasions, a soldier is ordered to hold a bayonet at his breast to impede his steps. If a noncommissioned officer is sentenced to corporeal punishment, he is always degraded to the soldier's rank. The practice of corporeal punishment in an army has become a subject of animadversion, and both the policy and propriety of the measure have been called in question. It may be observed that the object of punishment is to exhibit examples, to deter others from committing crimes; that corporeal punishment may be made sufficiently severe as a commutation for the punishment of death in ordinary cases; it is more humane, and by saving the life of a soldier, we prevent the loss of his services to the public. In justification of the practice, it is alleged also, that in the British army it has long been established in their military code, and it is not uncommon to sentence a criminal to receive a thousand lashes, and that they aggravate its horrors in the most cruel manner, by repeating the stripes from day to day, before the wounds are healed; and instances are not wanting of its having been attended with fatal consequences. On the other hand, it is objected, that corporeal punishment is disreputable to an army, it will never reclaim the unprincipled villain, and it has a tendency to repress the spirit of ambition and enterprize in the young soldier; and the individual thus ignominiously treated, can never, in case of promotion for meritorious services, be received with complacency as a companion for other officers. These objections will apply to most other modes of punishment, and it remains to be decided, which is the most eligible for the purpose of maintaining that subordination so indispensable in all armies.

James Thacher, *A Military Journal during the American Revolutionary War, from 1775 to 1783* (Boston, 1823), 222–224.

176. At Washington's Headquarters (1780)

BY FRANÇOIS JEAN, MARQUIS DE CHASTELLUX (1786)

(TRANSLATED BY GEORGE GREIVE, 1787)

For Chastellux, see above, No. 137. — This is perhaps the best account of the camp-life of Washington.

. . . AT length, after riding two miles along the right flank of the army, and after passing thick woods on the right, I found myself in a small plain, where I saw a handsome farm ; a small camp which seemed to cover it, a large tent extended in the court, and several waggons round it, convinced me that, this was his *Excellency*'s quarter ; for it is thus Mr. Washington is called in the army, and throughout America. M. de la Fayette was in conversation with a tall man, five foot nine inches high, (about five foot ten inches and a half English) of a noble and mild countenance. It was the General himself. I was soon off horseback, and near him. The compliments were short ; the sentiments with which I was animated, and the good wishes he testified for me were not equivocal. He conducted me to his house, where I found the company still at table, although the dinner had been long over. He presented me to the Generals Knox, Waine, Howe, &c. and to his *family*, then composed of Colonels Hamilton and Tilgman, his Secretaries and his Aides de Camp, and of Major Gibbs, commander of his guards ; for in England and America, the Aides de Camp, Adjutants and other officers attached to the General, form what is called his *family*. A fresh dinner was prepared for me, and mine ; and the present was prolonged to keep me company. A few glasses of claret and madeira accelerated the acquaintances I had to make, and I soon felt myself at my ease near the greatest and the best of men. The goodness and benevolence which characterize him, are evident from every thing about him ; but the confidence he gives birth to, never occasions improper familiarity ; for the sentiment he inspires has the same origin in every individual, a profound esteem for his virtues, and a high opinion of his talents. About nine o'clock the general officers withdrew to their quarters, which were all at a considerable distance ; but as the General wished me to stay in his own house, I remained some time with him, after which he conducted me to the chamber prepared for my Aides de Camp and me. This chamber occupied the fourth part of his lodgings ; he apologized to me for the little room he had in his disposal, but always with a noble politeness, which was neither complimentary nor troublesome.

At nine the next morning they informed me that his Excellency was come down into the parlour. This room served at once as audience chamber, and dining-room. I immediately went to wait on him, and found breakfast prepared. . . .

Whilst we were at breakfast, horses were brought, and General Washington gave orders for the army to get under arms at the head of the camp. The weather was very bad, and it had already began raining; we waited half an hour; but the General seeing that it was more likely to increase than to diminish, determined to get on horseback. Two horses were brought him, which were a present from the State of Virginia; he mounted one himself, and gave me the other. Mr. Lynch and Mr. de Montesquieu, had each of them, also, a very handsome blood horse, such as we could not find at Newport for any money. We repaired to the artillery camp, where *General Knox* received us: the artillery was numerous, and the gunners, in very fine order, were formed in parade, in the foreign manner, that is, each gunner at his battery, and ready to fire. The General was so good as to apologize to me for the cannon not firing to salute me; he said, that having put all the troops on the other side of the river in motion, and apprized them that he might himself march along the right bank, he was afraid of giving the alarm, and of deceiving the detachments that were out. We gained, at length, the right of the army, where we saw the Pensylvania line; it was composed of two brigades, each forming three battalions, without reckoning the light infantry, which were detached with the Marquis de la Fayette. General Waine, who commanded it, was on horseback, as well as the Brigadiers and Colonels. They were all well mounted: the officers also had a very military air; they were well ranged, and saluted very gracefully. Each brigade had a band of music; the march they were then playing was the *Huron*. I knew that this line, though in want of many things, was the best cloathed in the army; so that his Excellency asking me whether I would proceed, and see the whole army, or go by the shortest road to the camp of the *Marquis*, I accepted the latter proposal. The troops ought to thank me for it, for the rain was falling with redoubled force; they were dismissed, therefore, and we arrived heartily wet at the Marquis de la Fayette's quarters, where I warmed myself with great pleasure, partaking, from time to time, of a large bowl of grog, which is stationary on his table, and is presented to every officer who enters. . . .

The rain spared us no more at the camp of the Marquis, than at that of the main army ; so that our review being finished, I saw with pleasure General Washington set off in a gallop to regain his quarters. We reached them as soon as the badness of the roads would permit us. At our return we found a good dinner ready, and about twenty guests, among whom were Generals Howe and Sinclair. The repast was in the English fashion, consisting of eight or ten large dishes of butcher's meat, and poultry, with vegetables of several sorts, followed by a second course of pastry, comprized under the two denominations of pies and puddings. After this the cloth was taken off, and apples and a great quantity of nuts were served, which General Washington usually continues eating for two hours, *toasting* and conversing all the time. These nuts are small and dry, and have so hard a shell, (hickory nuts) that they can only be broken by the hammer ; they are served half open, and the company are never done picking and eating them. The conversation was calm and agreeable ; his Excellency was pleased to enter with me into the particulars of some of the principal operations of the war, but always with a modesty and conciseness, which proved that it was from pure complaisance he mentioned it. . . .

Marquis [François Jean] de Chastellux, *Travels in North-America, in the Years 1780, 1781, and 1782* (London, 1787), I, 112–125 *passim*.

———◆———

177. Life on a Privateer (1780)

BY DOCTOR SOLOMON DROWNE

Drowne, a surgeon in the Revolutionary army, made this one cruise as surgeon on the privateer Hope. These extracts give us a picture of the most attractive and most profitable mode of warfare. The American cruisers and privateers made about seven hundred captures of British vessels during the war.—Bibliography of naval warfare: Winsor, *Narrative and Critical History*, VI, 591–592; Maclay, *United States Navy*, I, pt. i; Channing and Hart, *Guide*, § 140.

TUESDAY, Oct. 3 [1780]. Sailed from Providence on board the Sloop HOPE, mounting seven guns. Wind at N. E. drizzly, dirty weather. Outsailed Mr. John Brown in his famous boat. Put about for Capt. Munro, and take Mr. Brown and Capt. S—— Smith on board, who dine with us. Some time after noon Capt. Munro comes on board, and a few glasses of good wishes founded on Hope having circled, Col. Nightingale, &c. depart, and we proceed on our course. . . .

11th. Whilst at Dinner, a Sail cried. Immediately give chase, and

2 K

discover another. One, a sloop which bears down upon us; the other a brig. Make every preparation for an engagement; but, on approaching and hailing the Sloop, she proved to be the Randolph, Capt. Fosdick from New London, — mounting 18 four pounders, [140 tons.] The Brig, with only two guns, her prize from England, taken at 8 o'clock this morning. — Capt. Fosdick says her Cargo amounted to £20,000 Sterling. What good and ill fortune were consequent on that capture! — Hard for those poor fellows, their tedious Voyage being just accomplished, thus to have their brightening prospect clouded in a moment. If Virtue is the doing good to others, privateering cannot be justified upon the principles of Virtue; — though I know it is not repugnant to THE LAWS OF NATIONS, but rather deemed policy amongst warring powers thus to distress each other, regardless of the suffering individual. But however agreeable to, and supportable by the rights of war; yet, when individuals come thus to despoil individuals of their property, 'tis hard: — the cruelty then appears, however, political.

12th. Early this morning two sail in sight, a Ship and Brig. Chase them chief of the day to no purpose. We conclude they sail well, and may be bound to Philadelphia. — Lat. 39° 6'. Soundings 19 fathoms. Lost sight of the Randolph by the chase.

13th. A foggy morning and Scotch mist. Clears away pleasant. Lat. 39° 31'. This Afternoon a Sloop discovered under the lee bow standing before the wind: All hands upon deck preparing for the chase: — but little wind so the oars are to be plied. I must go and see how we come on. — Night obliges us to give over the pursuit.

14th. A sail seen from Mast-head; proves a Ship. We chase. Catch a Herring-Hog, which makes us a fine Breakfast, and dinner for the whole crew. Another sail heaves in sight. Upon a nearer approach the Ship appears to be of the line. Several in sight. Towards evening signal guns heard. We take them to be men of War, standing in, N. W. by W. Longitude by reckoning 73° 30". Lat. 39° 34." 26 fathoms. A pleasant moon-light Evening. Spend it in walking the Quarter Deck.

15th. A pleasant day. See a Sail to windward; as she rather approaches us we lie a hull for her. I think it is more agreeable waiting for them, than rowing after them. Get a fishing line under way: catch a Hake and a few Dog-fish. It being Sunday, try the efficacy of a clean shirt, in order to be something like folks ashore. Give chase, as the vessel comes down rather slow. On approaching discover her to be a *Snow*. She hauls her wind and stands from us; — sails very heavy, and Capt. Munro is sanguine in the belief we shall make a prize of her. Get everything in readiness to board her. There seems something awful in the preparation for an attack, and the immediate prospect of an action. She hauls up her courses and hoists English Colours. I take my station in the Cabin; where, remain not long before I hear the Huzza on deck in consequence of her striking. Send our boat for the Captain & his papers. She sailed from Kingston, Jamaica, upwards of 40 days since, in a fleet, and was bound to New York: Capt. William Small, Commander. She has ten men on board and four excellent four pounders. Her Cargo consists of 149 Puncheons, 23 Hogsheads, 3 Quarter Casks and 9 Barrels of Rum, and 20 Hogsheads Muscovado Sugar. Send two prize Masters and ten men on board, get the prisoners on board our Vessel, and taking the prize in tow, stand towards Egg Harbour. We hardly know what to do with the prize: the wind shifting a little we stand to the eastward.

16th Keep an eastern course, to try to get her into our harbour if possible. Now we are terribly apprehensive of seeing a sail.—About sunset a sail seen from mast-head, which excites no small anxiety. Cast off the Snow's hawser, &c.—however night coming on and seeing no more of said sail, pursue our course. Sound, 42 fathoms of water. . . .

19th. The Snow in sight this morning; run along side and take her in tow again. . . . Lat. 40.° 30." At this rate the West Indies will bring us up sooner than Martha's Vineyard or Nantucket. 49 fathoms. Have our Pistols hung up in the Cabin, to be in readiness for the prisoners, should they take it into their heads to rise upon the watch in the night. . . .

22nd. Sunday. Very foggy. What wind there is, ahead.—Weigh Anchor, and out oars.—A fair gentle breeze springs from the South. Pass through Bristol Ferry way with hard tugging about the middle of the afternoon: come to Anchor in the Bay, but where rendered uncertain by the fog having come up again. . . .

23rd. Early, after breakfast, we set off again in the boat, with the Compass, being still surrounded with an excessive fog.   Run ashore to the Eastward of Nayat Point, and mistake it for Connimicut: however, arrive at Providence about 11 o'clock, it having cleared off very pleasant. Thus ends our short, but tedious cruise. —— At sunset the Sloop and Snow arrive, firing 13 cannon each. ——

Solomon Drowne, *Journal of a Cruise in the Fall of 1780 in the Private-Sloop of War, Hope* (Analectic press, New York, 1872), 3–18 *passim.*

CHAPTER XXIX — THE BRITISH FORCES

178. "Appeal to the Hessians sold by their Princes" (1776)

BY HONORÉ GABRIEL RIQUETTI, COUNT DE MIRABEAU

(TRANSLATED BY GEORGE N. HENNING, 1897)

This spirited protest, by the French pamphleteer and later statesman of the French Revolution, reflects the opinion of thinking men in Europe on the English purchase of mercenary troops. — Bibliography of the Hessian question: Winsor, *Narrative and Critical History*, VII, 75-76; Lowell, *Hessians in the Revolution;* Channing and Hart, *Guide*, § 138.

> Quis furor iste novus? quò nunc, quo tenditis? —
> Heu! miseri cives! non hostem, inimica que castra;
> — Vestras spes uritis.
>
> VIRG.

BRAVE Germans, what a brand of shame you allow to be marked on your noble brows! What! can it be at the end of the eighteenth century that the nations of central Europe are the mercenary satellites of an odious despotism! What! those valorous Germans, who so fiercely defended their liberty against the conquerors of the world and braved the Roman armies, now, like the base Africans, are sold and hasten to shed their blood in the cause of tyrants! They suffer the SLAVE-TRADE to be carried on amongst them, their cities to be depopulated, their fields to be ravaged, so as to help overbearing rulers to lay waste another hemisphere. — Will you share much longer in the stupid blindness of your masters? — You, honorable soldiers, faithful and formidable maintainers of their power, of that power which was trusted to them only to protect their subjects, — you are bartered away! — Ah! for what an employment, just gods! — Huddled together like flocks of sheep in the ships of foreigners, you cross the seas; you hasten through reefs and storms, to attack a people who have done you no harm, who are defending the most just of causes, who are setting you the noblest of examples. — Ah! why do you not imitate that brave people, instead of striving to destroy them! They are breaking their fetters; they are fighting to maintain their natural rights and to guarantee their liberty;

they are stretching out their arms to you ; they are your brothers ; they are doubly so : nature made them such, and social ties have strengthened these sacred claims ; more than half of this people is composed of your fellow-countrymen, of your friends, of your relatives. They have fled from tyranny to the uttermost parts of the world, and tyranny has pursued them even there ; oppressors, equally avaricious and ungrateful, have forged fetters for them, and the worthy Americans have welded these fetters into swords to drive back their oppressors. — The New World then is going to count you in the number of the monsters hungering for gold and blood, who have ravaged it ! — Germans, you whose most marked characteristic has always been fairness, do you not shudder at such a reproach ? —

To these motives, of a nature to touch men, must one join the motives of an interest affecting equally slaves and free citizens ?

Do you know what nation you are going to attack ? Do you realize the power of the fanaticism of liberty ? It is the only fanaticism which is not odious, it is the only one which is worthy ; but it is also the most powerful of all. — You do not know it, O blind peoples, you who think yourselves free, while grovelling under the most hateful of all despotisms, the despotism which forces men to commit crimes ! You do not know it, you whom the whim or the cupidity of a despot may arm against men who deserve well of all mankind, since they are defending its cause, and preparing a refuge for it ! — O mercenary warriors, O satellites of tyrants, O enervate Europeans, you are going to fight men stronger, more industrious, more courageous, more active than you can be : they are inspired by a strong interest, you are led on by vile lucre ; they are defending their property, and are fighting for their hearths ; you are leaving yours, and are not fighting for yourselves. It is in the bosom of their country, in their native clime, aided by all the resources of home, that they are making war against hordes which the Ocean spewed forth, after having prepared their defeat : the most powerful and the most sacred motives urge on their valor, and summon victory in their train. Chiefs who scorn you while making use of you, will oppose in vain their harangues to the irresistible eloquence of liberty, of need, of necessity. In short, and to say all in one word, the cause of the Americans is just : heaven and earth condemn the one which you do not blush to uphold. —

O Germans, who can have infused in you this thirst of combat, this barbarous frenzy, this odious devotion to tyranny ? — No, I will not compare you to those fanatical Spaniards, who destroyed for the sake of destroying, who bathed in blood, when nature, utterly drained, forced their insatiable cupidity to give way to a more atrocious passion; nobler sentiments, more excusable errors lead you astray. That faithfulness to your chiefs, which distinguished the Germans your ancestors, that habit of obeying, without stopping to reflect that there are duties more sacred than obedience and taking precedence of all oaths, that credulity which makes men yield to the influence of a small number of madmen or of the ambitious, those are your wrongs; but they will be crimes, if you do not check yourselves on the brink of the abyss. — Already those of your fellow-countrymen who have preceded you recognize their blindness; they are deserting, and the acts of kindness from those people whom they were recently slaughtering, and who treat them like brothers, now that they no longer see in their hands the executioner's sword, aggravate their remorse and double their repentance.

Profit by their example, O soldiers; think of your honor, think of your rights. — Have you not indeed some rights as well as your chiefs? — Yes, undoubtedly: it can not be repeated too often, men take precedence of princes, who, for the most part, are not worthy of such a name; leave to infamous courtiers, to impious blasphemers, the task of vaunting the royal prerogative, and its unbounded rights; but do not forget that *all* men were not made for *one* man; that there is an authority superior to all authorities; that he who orders a crime must not be obeyed, and that thus your conscience is the first of your chiefs. —

Question that conscience; it will tell you that your blood should flow only for your fatherland, that it is atrocious to receive money to go to slaughter, several thousand leagues away, men who have no other relations with you than those which ought to win them your good will.

She pretends to be carrying on a just war, this mother-country which is straining every nerve to destroy her children! She claims her rights, and will discuss them only with the thunderbolt of battle! But even if these rights were real, have you examined them? Is it for you to judge this dispute? Is it for you to pronounce the sentence? Is it for you to carry it out? — Ah, after all, what matter these idle claims, so problematical and so contested? Man, in every country of the world, has the right to be happy. That is the first of laws, that is the first of claims: the founders of colonies do not go forth to make uncultivated lands fertile, to augment the glory and power of the mother-country, in order to be oppressed by her. — Are they oppressed? then they have the right to shake off the yoke, because the YOKE is not made for man.

But who has told you that the English had signed the decree of out-lawry launched against the Americans? — Brave Germans, you have been deceived; do not degrade by such a suspicion a nation which has produced great men and fine laws, which long nourished in her bosom the sacred fire of liberty, and which deserves, from these claims, con-sideration and respect. — Alas! in the British Isles, as in the rest of the world, a small number of ambitious men stir up the people, and produce public calamities. The critical moment has arrived: England, unhappy nation, is at war with her brothers only because despotism, for several years, has been waging there a successful contest against liberty. Do not believe therefore that you are defending the cause of the English; you are fighting to increase the authority of a few ministers whom they abhor and scorn.

Do you wish to know the true motives which put arms in your hands?

Vain luxury, despicable expenditures have ruined the finances of the princes who govern you; their extortions have utterly drained their resources; they have too often deceived the confidence of their neigh-bors to be able to have recourse to them again. They would therefore have to give up that excessive luxury, those every-recurring whims, which are their most important occupation; they can not make up their minds to it, they will not do so. England, drained of men and money, is purchasing at great expense money and men; your princes seize eagerly this temporary and ruinous resource; they levy soldiers, they sell them, they deliver them: that is the employment of your arms; that is for what you are destined. Your blood will be the price of corruption and the plaything of ambition. This money which has just been acquired by trafficking in your lives, will pay shameful debts or help to contract new ones. An avaricious usurer, a vile courtesan, a base actor, are going to receive these guineas given in exchange for your existence.

O blind spendthrifts, who gamble with men's lives, and waste the fruits of their toil, of their sweat, of their substance, a tardy repentance, heart-rending remorse, will be your executioners, but will not relieve those nations which you trample upon; you will regret your husband-men and their crops, your soldiers, your subjects; you will weep over the misfortunes which you will have wrought with your own hands, and which will involve you together with all your people. A formidable neighbor smiles at your blindness, and is preparing to take advantage of it; he is already forging the fetters with which he plans to load you;

you will groan under the weight of your chains, even should they be of gold, and your conscience, then more just than your heart was easy to touch, will be the avenging fury of the woes which you will have brought about.

And you, nations betrayed, harassed, sold, blush at your error; let your eyes be unsealed; leave this ground sullied by despotism; cross the seas, hasten to America; but embrace there your brothers; defend this noble people against the haughty rapacity of their persecutors; share their happiness; double their strength; assist them with your industry; make their riches your own, by increasing them. Such is the object of society; such is the duty of man, whom nature made to love his fellowmen, and not to slaughter them; learn from the Americans the art of being free, of being happy, of turning social institutions to the profit of each of the individuals who compose society; forget, in the honorable refuge which they offer to suffering humanity, the frenzy of which you were the accomplices and the victims; learn to know true greatness, true glory, true felicity; let the nations of Europe envy you and bless the moderation of the inhabitants of the New World, who will disdain to come and punish them for their crimes, and to conquer depopulated lands which are trampled on by cruel tyrants, and watered by the tears of downtrodden slaves.

[Honoré Gabriel Riquetti, Comte de Mirabeau], *Avis aux Hessois, et autres Peuples de l'Allemagne* (*Œuvres*, Paris, 1822, VII, 1–8); translated for this work by George N. Henning.

———◆———

179. Army Life (1776–1777)

BY CAPTAIN GEORG PAUSCH

(TRANSLATED BY WILLIAM L. STONE, 1886)

Pausch was in command of some Hanau artillerymen, hired as mercenaries by the English. His observations show the state of feeling between the English and German contingents, and the trials of the camp. — Bibliography: Winsor, *Narrative and Critical History*, VI, 360.

[September 8, 1776.] THE Regiments are gradually drawing nearer together; and some of them are advancing closer to St. Johns. Those of the boats which are completed and were on the river have mostly been transported toward Lake Champlain, which Lake is still in possession of both parties. We have two frigates on the

Lake; and from all appearances, there will be a demonstration against it without waiting for the arrival of the two thousand Brunswick troops, which left at the same time as I did, and are destined to act with us. The Rebels are said to be strongly entrenched on the other side [end] of the Lake among the mountains, and from 600 to 1000 Savages are said to form the attacking force of the right wing. We are all on foot; and I am sorry to say that I, also, am in the same fix. We cannot get a two wheeled calash — for which, too, we have to pay one shilling an hour — without trouble and asking permission of one or another general. We even have to pay out of our own pocket, the above price per hour for the small carts of the peasants on which to transport the Company's baggage, clothing and other necessary articles. This expense I hope his Majesty, the King, will most graciously consent to make up to our Company; for we cannot, as yet, tell whether our means, including the money for our rations, will, or will not be sufficient.

For these several reasons, I cannot take into consideration those things which belong and are essential to, position; nor, can I form an idea, until God leads me there on foot, where we shall all meet together for action. This state of affairs will certainly make campaigns — such as no man, since the existence of Hessian troops, has ever witnessed in this world! According to an old history by a certain Italian King and Campaigner, the Hessian troops had, generally, one ass for the baggage of two officers; but I am very much afraid — and the English prophesy the same thing — that in a short time, each officer will have to gird a saddle on his own back and carry his own baggage! . . .

[November 8.]   Indeed, I have been, from the start, the most miserable and unfortunate of all the commanders of the German Companies. Each of my men who was sent to the Hospital was not only afflicted with dysentery, but, as the hospital doctors told me, talked day and night of fathers, mothers, brothers, sisters, cousins, and aunts — besides, also, talking over and repeating all kinds of German village deviltry — calling now this one, and now that one by his baptismal name until they had to stop for actual want of breath! For this disease there is, as is well known, but one remedy in the world, viz: dear peace, and a speedy return; and with this hope I comfort my sick daily. With those still alive and well, I am perfectly satisfied; for they find plenty of solace in the Canadian girls and women. For this reason, and in their companionship they are happy and contented. . . .

April [1777].   All the officers have to add money of their own, or else live poorly. A bombadier, for example, has to pay for a pair of boots 20 florins; for a pair of leather pants 20 florins; for a coat, five times as much as in Hanau; and everything else in the same proportion. Why, a bottle of the poorest red wine costs, in our money, 36 kreutzers, and a bottle of Madeira 1 piastre! . . .

Regarding the charges against head-smith Brads concerning discipline, service and insubordination, the Brigadier General will send in his reports and protocols. I wish to gracious that I had never seen such a " cuss;" also, I hope never to see another one like him. I fervently hope that he will sit in chains in a London jail — for this is all he is good for in this world. There is no more despicable beast in this world than he. He respects neither God nor his Superiors. This is the second time that he has been confined in jail. . . .

[May 15.] For the last three weeks I have drilled every morning from 6 to 8 o'clock, after the lately introduced fashion — with only one Company. In the afternoon, two of my cannon are served by the English, and two by men from my Company when [ball] cartridges are used. I, for one, never am present but send my officers instead — for the reason, that only an English captain is sent there, and only an English officer commands them on these occasions.

The National pride and arrogant conduct of these people allow them to command *my* men, while I am not permitted to command *theirs!*

I lately requested Gen. Phillips that he would furnish me powder for my own drill. This request he at once granted. This was at one o'clock. At three o'clock, it was countermanded through the influence either of the Major or some one else. Jealousy was the cause of my not being allowed to drill separately any longer; and I was thus forced to drill at 4 o'clock in the afternoon, according to their orders and by their drums, which my men do not understand at all, and who, if I left them to drill alone, would be totally demoralized. In fact, the Devil of Jealousy has been aroused because the English see that my men drill quicker and more promptly, and because, also, the spectators do us the justice publicly to acknowledge this to be the case. Hence, instead of the former friendship between us, there is now enmity. They imitate our Artillery in different things, as, for example, in the matter of our wipers — of which they are having some made for their 3 and 6 pound cannon. Every day, to my disgust, I have to practice the [lately] introduced quick-step, which we do not have, nor do they have it in Prussia — nay not in the world, except in the chase, with fast horses and good dogs ! This is a splendid exercise for the men in winter; but in the summer, when the weather is warm, it is detrimental to the health of the men. It has no good result except to make the spectators laugh — for by this manœuvre no closed ranks could be kept in an attack upon the enemy. In case, therefore, of a retreat we would not only fare badly, but would be exposed to the well deserved censures of the European and American press. . . .

Maj. Williamson got it into his head that he could order me to forbid my men going out in the evening with their sabres. But I told him that I would not dare receive such an order from any one except my Gracious Prince, and therefore I could not obey him : further : that should I meet any one of my men either during the day or at the time for retiring at 9 o'clock, going to his quarters without his sabre, I should have him flogged the next morning. I further said, that it was a standing order at our Capital, where four or five battalions were collected at a time, that no soldier in uniform should be without his side-arms.

Since then, I have never been asked to do this ; and in fact, it would fare ill with my men were such an order enforced — since were they to depend on boxing for protection, some would return to Germany cross-eyed and some blind ! . . .

[May 17.] Respecting that miserable rascal and head-smith, Brads . . . I gave it as my opinion that the fellow had already been somewhat punished ; and as I did not wish to belittle the General, the wretch had better be released from further punishment, and allowed to continue at his work.

In time of war, I find sentences of this kind out of place, as long, that is, as the offence is not a criminal one. Prompt punishment — such as running the gauntlet, whipping, or confining in fetters for a time — is the best that can be done on these occasions, as by these light punishments, the service does not suffer.

19th. Brought to a close, the 19th of May, 1777, in the Winter-quarters at Montreal. It looks, now, as if we were on the point of starting ; and, perhaps, we will really do so before the end of the month.

Captain [Georg] Pausch, *Journal* (translated by William L. Stone, Albany, 1886), 69–121 *passim*.

180. An Investigation of British Military Prisons (1778)

BY COMMISSARY-GENERAL ELIAS BOUDINOT (ABOUT 1800)

Boudinot was sent by New Jersey to the Continental Congress, and later became president of that body. At the time of this episode he was in charge of British prisoners and exchanges. The cruelties of the British prison-ships in New York, and the corresponding cruelties suffered by the loyalists in the Connecticut copper-mine prison at Simsbury, are typical of an age when ordinary criminals were treated with much the same barbarity, both in England and in America. — Bibliography: Jane J. Boudinot, *Life of Elias Boudinot;* Winsor, *Narrative and Critical History*, VII, 87–88.

THE Complaints of the very cruel Treatment our Prisoners met with, in the Enemy's Lines rose to such a Height that in the Fall of this Year 1777 the General wrote to Gen[l] Howe (or Clinton) repeating their Complaints and proposing to send an Officer into New York to examine into the Truth of them — This was agreed to and a regular Passport returned accordingly — The General ordered me on this Service — I accordingly went over on the third of February, 1778 in my own sloop — . . . We arrived at the Wharf of New York a little before Sundown, when I sent the Sergeant to the Commandant of the City (who was General Robertson whom I had formerly known,) to inform him of my Arrival and request to land — . . . The General with great Politeness assured me that tho' Lodgings were prepared, yet I might go where I pleased, on consideration of my breakfasting with him in the Morning — This I promised to do & retired — Taking it for granted that I was to be put under the expected Restrictions in the Morning, I waited on the General at Breakfast . . . The General answered me, that he knew We had heard strange Stories within our Lines of their Conduct to our Prisoners — That he had rejoiced that Gen[l] Washington had taken the Measure of sending me in to examine for ourselves, for that he was sure that we should find them a parcel of damned Lies — That he had ordered every Place that I should choose to visit to be freely opened to me, and that as I was a Gentleman, all that he expected was, that I should behave as such ; and that I might use my own Pleasure & go where I pleased — I confess I was surprised at this generous Conduct ; and immediately replied, that I could not accept this gentlemanly Offer — That I had come on a fair and open Business — . . . That therefore I should not see a Prisoner or have any Communication with one, but in the Presence of a British Officer, who I hoped he would oblige me by appointing to attend me — The General expressed himself well pleased with the Proposal, and appointed one accordingly, observing again, that he was sure I should find the Reports we had heard totally false — Accordingly I went to the Provost with the Officer where we found near 30 officers from Colonels downwards in close confinement in the Gaol in New York — After some Conversation with Coll Ethan Allen I told him my Errand on which he was very free in his abuse of the British on account of the cruel treatment he had rec^d during months close confinement — We then proceeded upstairs to the room of their confinement — I had the Officers drawn up in a Ring, and informed them of my Mission — . . . On this after some little Hesitation from a Dread of their Keeper the Provost Marshal, one of them began & informed us — that they had been confined on the most frivolous Pretences, some for having been the Oppressors of the Friends of Government, for taking Refugees & Property while Officers under Command and in Obedience to Orders, for being out of their bounds of Parole, tho' weeks after their Return — Some confined in the Dungeon for a Night to await the Leisure of General to examine them & forgot for Months — for being Committee Men, &c. &c. — That they had received the most cruel Treatment from the Provost Marshal, being locked up in the Dungeon on the most trifling Pretence, such as asking for more Water for Drink on a hotter Day than usual — For sitting up a little longer in the Evening than the Orders allowed — For writing a Letter to the General making their Complaints of ill-usage & throwing out of the Windows — That some of them were kept 10, 12 & 14 weeks in the Dungeon on these trifling Pretences — A Capt. Vandyke had been confined 18 Months for being concerned in setting Fire to the City, when on my calling for the Provost Books it appeared that he had been made Prisoner & closely confined by the Provost 4 Days before the Fire happened — A Major Paine had been confined 11 months for killing a Capt. Campbell in the Engagement when he was taken Prisoner, when on Examination it appeared that the Captain had been killed in another part of the Action — The Charge was that Major Paine when taken had no Commission, tho' acknowledged by us as a Major — Capt Flabwen was confined for breaking a soldier's thigh with the butt of his gun after he was shot down when the British surgeon on Examination acknowledged that the Thigh was broken by a Ball &c. &c. — Most of the Cases examined into turned out either wholly false or too trifling to be regarded — It also appeared by the Declaration of some of the Gent^l that their Water would be sometimes, as the Caprice of the Provost Marshall led him, brought up to them in the Tubs they used in their Rooms, when the Weather was so hot that they must drink or perish — On hearing a number of these Instances of Cruelty — I asked who was the Author of them — They answered the Provost Keeper — I desired the Officer to call him up that we might have him Face to Face — He accordingly came in and on being informed of what had passed was asked if the Complaints were true — He with great Insolence answered that every Word was true — on which the British Officer abusing him very much asked him how he dared treat Gent¹ in that cruel Manner — He insolently putting his Hands to his side swore that he was as absolute there as Gen¹ Howe was at the Head of his Army — I observed to the Officer that now there could be no Dispute about Facts as the Fellow had acknowledged every Word to be true — I stated all the Facts and Substance & waited again on Genl Robertson, who hoped I was quite satisfied of the falsity of the Reports I had heard — I then stated to him the Facts, and assured him that they turned out worse than anything we had heard — On his hesitating as to the truth of this assertion, I observed to him the Propriety of having an Officer with me to whom I now appealed for the Truth of the Facts — He being present confirmed them — On which the Gen¹ expressed great Dissatisfaction & promised that the Author of them should be punished — . . . after this I visited two Hospitals of our sick Prisoners and the Sugar House ; in the two first were 211 Prisoners & in the last about 190 — They acknowledged that for about two Months past they fared pretty well, being allowed 2 lbs of good Beef and a Proportion of Flour or Bread pr Week by Mr. Lewis Pintard my Agent, over and above the Allowance recd from the British, which was professed to be ⅔ Allowance — but before they had suffered much from the small Allowance they had recᵈ & that their Bread was very bad, being musty Biscuit, but that the British Soldiers made the same Complaint as to the Bread — From every Account I recᵈ I found that their Treatment had been greatly changed for the better, within a few Months past, except at the Provost — They all agreed that previous to the Capture of Genl Burgoyne, and for sometime after, their Treatment had been cruel beyond Measure — That the Prisoners in the French Church amounting on an Average to 3 & 400 could not all lay down at once — That from the 15th of Octʳ to the 1st of Janʸ they never recᵈ a single stick of Wood, and that for the most Part they eat their Pork raw — When the Pews & Door & Window facings failed them for fuel — But as to my own personal Knowledge, I found

Gen[l] Robertson very ready to agree to every Measure for alleviating the
Miseries of War and very candidly acknowledging many Faults committed by the inferior Officers, and even the Mistakes of the General himself, by hearkening to the Representations of those around him — . . .

J[ane] J. Boudinot, editor, *The Life, Public Services, Addresses, and Letters
of Elias Boudinot, LL.D.* (Boston, etc., 1896), I, 89–98 *passim.*

———◆———

181. A Loyalist Corps (1777)

BY LIEUTENANT-COLONEL JOHN GRAVES SIMCOE (1787)

Simcoe was commander of a British battalion serving in America, and was later
made governor of Upper Canada. He was one of the most hated loyalists. — Bibliography, Winsor, *Narrative and Critical History*, VII, 196–197. — For the loyalists
in general, see ch. xxvii above.

ON the 15th of October, 1777, Sir William Howe was pleased to
appoint Captain Simcoe of the Grenadiers, with the Provincial
rank of Major, to the command of the Queen's Rangers; the next day
he joined that regiment, which was encamped with the army in the
vicinity of German-Town.

On the 19th the army marched to Philadelphia, the Queen's Rangers
formed the rear guard of the left column, and, in the encampment, their
post was on the right of the line, in front of the village of Kensington;
the army extending from the Delaware to the Schuylkill.

On the 20th the regiment was augmented with nearly an hundred
men, who had been enlisted by Captain Smyth during the various
marches from the landing of the army in the Chesapeak to this period.

This was a very seasonable recruit to the regiment; it had suffered
materially in the action at Brandywine, and was too much reduced in
numbers to be of any efficient service; but if the loss of a great number
of gallant officers and soldiers had been severely felt, the impression
which that action had left upon their minds was of the highest advantage
to the regiment; officers and soldiers became known to each other;
they had been engaged in a more serious manner, and with greater disadvantages than they were likely again to meet with in the common chance
of war; and having extricated themselves most gallantly from such a situation, they felt themselves invincible.   This spirit vibrated among them
at the time Major Simcoe joined them; and it was obvious, that he had
nothing to do but to cherish and preserve it.   Sir William Howe, in con-

sequence of their behaviour at Brandywine, had promised that all promotions should go in the regiment, and accordingly they now took place.

The Queen's Rangers had been originally raised in Connecticut, and the vicinity of New-York, by Colonel Rogers, for the duties which their name implies, and which were detailed in his commission ; at one period they mustered above four hundred men, all Americans, and all Loyalists. Hardships and neglect had much reduced their numbers, when the command of them was given to Colonel French, and afterwards to Major Weymess, to whom Major Simcoe succeeded ; their officers also had undergone a material change ; many gentlemen of the southern colonies who had joined Lord Dunmore, and distinguished themselves under his orders, were appointed to supersede those who were not thought competent to the commissions they had hitherto borne ; to these were added some volunteers from the army, the whole consisting of young men, active, full of love of the service, emulous to distinguish themselves in it, and looking forward to obtain, through their actions, the honor of being enrolled with the British army.

The Provincial corps, now forming, were raised on the supposed influence which their officers had among their loyal countrymen, and were understood to be native American Loyalists ; added to an equal chance among these, a greater resource was opened to the Queen's Rangers, in the exclusive privilege of enlisting old country-men (as Europeans were termed in America), and deserters from the rebel army ; so that could the officers to whom the Commander in Chief delegated the inspection of the Provincial corps have executed their orders, the Queen's Rangers, however dangerously and incessantly employed, would never have been in want of recruits ; at the same time, the original Loyalists, and those of this description, who were from time to time enlisted, forming the gross of the corps, were the source from whence it derived its value and its discipline ; they were men who had already been exiled for their attachment to the British government, and who now acted upon the firmest principles in its defence ; on the contrary, the people they had to oppose, however characterised by the enemies of Great Britain, had never been considered by them as engaged in an honourable cause, or fighting for the freedom of their country ; they estimated them not by their words, but by an intimate observance of their actions, and to civil desecration, experience had taught them to add military contempt. . . .

. . . A light corps, augmented as that of the Queen's Rangers was, and employed on the duties of an outpost, had no opportunity of being instructed in the general discipline of the army, nor indeed was it very necessary : the most important duties, those of vigilance, activity, and patience of fatigue, were best learnt in the field ; a few motions of the manual exercise were thought sufficient ; they were carefully instructed in those of firing, but above all, attention was paid to inculcate the use of the bayonet, and a total reliance on that weapon. The divisions being fully officered, and weak in numbers, was of the greatest utility, and in many trying situations was the preservation of the corps ; two files in the centre, and two on each flank, were directed to be composed of trained soldiers, without regard to their size or appearance. It was explained, that no rotation, except in ordinary duties, should take place among light troops, but that those officers would be selected for any service who appeared to be most capable of executing it : it was also enforced by example, that no service was to be measured by the numbers employed on it, but by its own importance, and that five men, in critical situations or employment, was a more honourable command than an hundred on common duties. Serjeants guards were in a manner abolished, a circumstance to which in a great measure may be attributed, that no centinel or guard of the Queen's Rangers was ever surprised ; the vigilance of a gentleman and an officer being transcendantly superior to that of any non-commissioned officer whatsoever. . . . It was observed, that regularity in messing, and cleanliness in every respect, conduced to the health of the soldier ; and from the numbers that each regiment brought into the field, superior officers would in general form the best estimate of the attention of a corps to its interior œconomy ; and to enforce the performance of these duties in the strongest manner, it was declared in public orders, " that to such only when in the field, the commanding officer would entrust the duties of it, who should execute with spirit what belongs to the interior œconomy of the regiment when in quarters." . . .

Lieutenant-Colonel [John Graves] Simcoe, *A Journal of the Operations of the Queen's Rangers, from the End of the Year* 1777, *to the Conclusion of the late American War* (Exeter, [1787]), 1-5 *passim.*

2 L

182. "The Lords of the Main " (1780)

BY JOSEPH STANSBURY

Stansbury was the ablest and most effective of the loyalist verse writers.   He came
to Philadelphia in 1767, and remained till 1778, when he went with the British to New
York.   The piece suggests the confidence of the British in their navy. — Bibliography :
Tyler, *Literary History of the Revolution*, II, 80–96. — For other extracts on the navy,
see No. 177 above and Nos. 194, 204 below.

WHEN Faction, in league with the treacherous Gaul,
  Began to look big and paraded in state ;
A meeting was held at *Credulity Hall*,
  And Echo proclaim'd their Ally *good and great !*
    By sea and by land
    Such wonders are plann'd ;
No less than the bold British Lion to chain !
    Well hove ! says *Jack Lanyard,*
    French, Congo and Spaniard,
Have at you — remember we're Lords of the Main !
  Lords of the Main — aye, Lords of the Main ;
The Tars of Old England are Lords of the Main.

Though party-contention a while may perplex,
  And lenity hold us in doubtful suspense ;
If perfidy rouse, or ingratitude vex
  In defiance of Hell we'll chastise the offence.
    When danger alarms,
    'Tis then that in arms
United we rush on the foe with disdain :
    And when the storm rages
    It only presages
Fresh triumphs to Britons, as Lords of the Main.
  Lords of the Main — ay, Lords of the Main —
Let *Thunder* proclaim it, we're Lords of the Main.

Then Britons, *strike home* — make sure of your blow :
  The chase is in view ; never mind a lee-shore.
With vengeance o'ertake the confederate foe :
  'Tis now we may rival our heroes of yore !
    Brave *Anson* and *Drake,*
    Hawke, Russell and *Blake,*

With ardour like your's we defy France and Spain' !
  Combining with *Treason*
  They're deaf to all reason :
Once more let them *feel* we are Lords of the Main.
  Lords of the Main — ay, Lords of the Main —
The first-born of Neptune are Lords of the Main.

Nor are we alone in the noble career ;
  The *Soldier* partakes of the generous flame :
To glory he marches, to glory we steer ;
  Between us we share the rich harvest of fame.
    Recorded on high,
    Their names never die,
Of heroes by sea and by land what a train !
  To the *King*, then, God bless him !
  The *World* shall confess him
' The Lord of those men who are Lords of the Main.'
  Lords of the Main — ay, Lords of the Main —
The Tars of Old England are Lords of the Main.

LIBERTY.

[Joseph Stansbury], *The Lords of the Main*, published in Rivington's *Royal Gazette*, Feb. 16, 1780 ; reprinted in *The Loyal Verses of Joseph Stansbury and Doctor Jonathan Odell* (edited by Winthrop Sargent, Albany, 1860), 61–62.

---

183. The Experiences of a British Spy (1780)

BY MAJOR JOHN ANDRÉ

The André episode is one of the most painful in the whole war. André, a British officer of high character and standing, was persuaded to meet Benedict Arnold in disguise. Washington justly held him to be a spy, and he suffered the penalty of death. — Bibliography : Winsor, *Narrative and Critical History*, VI, 447–468 ; Isaac N. Arnold, *Life of Benedict Arnold ;* Channing and Hart, *Guide*, § 138.

A. MAJOR ANDRÉ TO GENERAL WASHINGTON

Salem, 24 September, 1780.

SIR,

WHAT I have as yet said concerning myself was in the justifiable attempt to be extricated ; I am too little accustomed to duplicity to have succeeded.

I beg your Excellency will be persuaded, that no alteration in the temper of my mind, or apprehension for my safety, induces me to take the step of addressing you, but that it is to rescue myself from an imputation of having assumed a mean character for treacherous purposes or self-interest ; a conduct incompatible with the principles that actuate me, as well as with my condition in life.

It is to vindicate my fame that I speak, and not to solicit security.

The person in your possession is Major John André, adjutant-general to the British army.

The influence of one commander in the army of his adversary is an advantage taken in war.   A correspondence for this purpose I held ; as confidential (in the present instance) with his Excellency Sir Henry Clinton.

To favor it, I agreed to meet upon ground not within the posts of either army, a person who was to give me intelligence ; I came up in the Vulture man of war for this effect, and was fetched by a boat from the ship to the beach.   Being there, I was told that the approach of day would prevent my return, and that I must be concealed until the next night. I was in my regimentals, and had fairly risked my person.

Against my stipulation, my intention, and without my knowledge beforehand, I was conducted within one of your posts.   Your Excellency may conceive my sensation on this occasion, and will imagine how much more must I have been affected by a refusal to reconduct me back the next night as I had been brought.   Thus become a prisoner, I had to concert my escape.   I quitted my uniform, and was passed another way in the night, without the American posts, to neutral ground, and informed I was beyond all armed parties and left to press for New York.   I was taken at Tarrytown by some volunteers.

Thus, as I have had the honor to relate, was I betrayed (being adjutant-general of the British army) into the vile condition of an enemy in disguise within your posts.

Having avowed myself a British officer, I have nothing to reveal but what relates to myself, which is true on the honor of an officer and a gentleman.

The request I have to make to your Excellency, and I am conscious I address myself well, is, that in any rigor policy may dictate, a decency of conduct towards me may mark, that though unfortunate I am branded with nothing dishonorable, as no motive could be mine but the service of my King, and as I was involuntarily an impostor.

Another request is, that I may be permitted to write an open letter to Sir Henry Clinton, and another to a friend for clothes and linen.

I take the liberty to mention the condition of some gentlemen at Charleston, who, being either on parole or under protection, were engaged in a conspiracy against us. Though their situation is not similar, they are objects who may be set in exchange for me, or are persons whom the treatment I receive might affect.

It is no less, Sir, in a confidence of the generosity of your mind, than on account of your superior station, that I have chosen to importune you with this letter. I have the honor to be, with great respect, Sir, your Excellency's most obedient humble servant,

JOHN ANDRÉ, *Adjutant-general.*

B. PAPER DRAWN UP BY MAJOR ANDRÉ

ON the 20th of September, I left New York to get on board the Vulture, in order (as I thought) to meet General Arnold there in the night. No boat, however, came off, and I waited on board until the night of the 21st. During the day, a flag of truce was sent from the Vulture to complain of the violation of a military rule in the instance of a boat having been decoyed on shore by a flag, and fired upon. The letter was addressed to General Arnold, signed by Captain Sutherland, but written in my hand and countersigned 'J. Anderson, secretary.' Its intent was to indicate my presence on board the Vulture. In the night of the 21st a boat with Mr. [Smith] and two hands came on board, in order to fetch Mr. Anderson on shore, and, if too late to bring me back, to lodge me until the next night in a place of safety. I went into the boat, landed, and spoke with Arnold. I got on horseback with him to proceed to [Smith's] house, and in the way passed a guard I did not expect to see, having Sir Henry Clinton's directions not to go within an enemy's post, or to quit my own dress.

In the morning A. quitted me, having himself made me put the papers I bore between my stockings and feet. Whilst he did it, he expressed a wish in case of any accident befalling me, that they should be destroyed, which I said, of course would be the case, as when I went into the boat I should have them tied about with a string and a stone. Before we parted, some mention had been made of my crossing the river, and going by another route; but, I objected much against it, and thought it was settled that in the way I came I was also to return.

Mr. [Smith] to my great mortification persisted in his determination of carrying me by the other route ; and, at the decline of the sun, I set out on horseback, passed King's Ferry, and came to Crompond, where a party of militia stopped us and advised we should remain. In the morning I came with [Smith] as far as within two miles and a half of Pine's Bridge, where he said he must part with me, as the Cow-boys infested the road thence forward. I was now near thirty miles from Kingsbridge, and left to the chance of passing that space undiscovered. I got to the neighbourhood of Tarrytown, which was far beyond the points described as dangerous, when I was taken by three volunteers, who, not satisfied with my pass, rifled me, and, finding papers, made me a prisoner.

I have omitted mentioning, that, when I found myself within an enemy's posts, I changed my dress.

C. MAJOR ANDRÉ TO GENERAL WASHINGTON

TAPPAN, 1 October, 1780. — Sir ; Buoyed above the terror of death, by the consciousness of a life devoted to honorable pursuits, and stained with no action that can give me remorse, I trust that the request I make to your Excellency at this serious period, and which is to soften my last moments, will not be rejected.

Sympathy towards a soldier will surely induce your Excellency and a military tribunal to adapt the mode of my death to the feelings of a man of honor.

Let me hope, Sir, that if aught in my character impresses you with esteem towards me, if aught in my misfortunes marks me as the victim of policy and not of resentment, I shall experience the operation of these feelings in your breast, by being informed that I am not to die on a gibbet.

I have the honor to be your Excellency's most obedient and most humble servant,

JOHN ANDRÉ,
Adj. Gen. to the British Army.

George Washington, *Writings* (edited by Jared Sparks, Boston, 1835), VII, Appendix, 531–543 *passim.*

PART VIII

PROGRESS OF THE REVOLUTION

CHAPTER XXX — UNION AND INDEPEND-ENCE

184. Proceedings of a Revolutionary Convention (1775)

BY CLERK GABRIEL DU VALL

The first step in the Revolution was to overthrow the existing colonial govern-ments. In some colonies, as Maryland, the governors refused to call assemblies, and the control of colonial matters was taken over by an irregular and revolutionary body elected by the patriots. The proceedings printed below are typical of those in county, town, and provincial assemblies throughout the country. — Bibliography: Frothing-ham, *Rise of the Republic*, ch. xii; Curtis, *History of the Constitution*, I, ch. iii; Chan-ning and Hart, *Guide*, § 137. — Compare with assembly proceedings, ch. ix above.

AT a Meeting of the Delegates appointed by the Several Counties of the Province of Maryland, at Annapolis, on Wednesday the 26th of July 1775 . . .

Friday July 28. . . .

The petition of Patrick Graham of Charles County, Taylor, praying a " Remission of the Sentence of the Committee of Charles County, and that he might be restored to the privileges of a Citizen " being read and considered, It is thereupon Resolved, that the said Patrick Graham be allowed to exercise his former Trade of a Taylor, and that he also be permitted to buy provisions and other necessaries for the use of his family ; And that the said Patrick Graham be allowed and permitted to collect, and receive all just Debts due to him ; and that all persons be permitted to employ the said Patrick Graham as a Taylor, and to sell him provisions and other necessaries for his Family. But that the said

Patrick Graham be not allowed to carry on any Traffick or merchandize, until it be otherwise resolved by this, or some future Convention. . . .

Monday, 31 July 1775 . . .

On Motion, Resolved, That the value of £5900, common money be borrowed on the credit of this Convention to be laid out in the purchase of 48 Tons of Lead, one hundred pounds value in Gun-Flints, two Tons of Cannon powder, and the residue of the said sum in Musquetry powder, for the use of this Province, to be repaid out of the first notes of Credit to be issued by this Convention. . . .

Wednesday 2ᵈ August. . . .

On Motion Resolved, That a Committee of seven members of this Convention be appointed to consider of a proper mode to be adopted to prevent the Inhabitants of this Province being harrassed with suits at law, and for laying such restriction on the proceedings of the Courts of Law as may be necessary and expedient in the present circumstances of this Province. . . .

Thursday 3ᵈ August . . .

Colᵒ Richard Lloyd and Dʳ Richard Brooke have leave of absence.

On motion Resolved, That an alteration be made in the Resolve of December Convention, relative to the killing of Lamb.

Resolved, that the resolution of this Province " that no person ought to kill Lamb, dropt before the first day of May yearly, or other Sheep, after the first day of January then next, under four years of age " be repealed so far as relates to killing of Lamb ; but it is earnestly recommended that the Continental Resolve respecting the killing of Sheep be most strictly observed. . . .

Friday 4th August . . .

Resolved, That if any persons will lend and advance to the Public any sums of money not exceeding in the whole four thousand pounds common money, and will pay the same into the hands of Messʳˢ Purviance, Smith & Stewart, to be by them laid out in the purchase and importation of Gunpowder and good substantial musquets, Bayonets, and accoutrements for Soldiers for the use of this Province, the Lenders shall be repaid their money out of the Bills of Credit to be issued, or if Bills of Exchange shall be lent, then the same shall be repaid in the same manner as the other loans of Bills of Exchange to this Convention. . . .

On reading and considering the Petition of Richard Henderson of Bladensburgh, setting forth his apprehensions, that some people of the neighbourhood of that place, if not advised to the contrary by this Convention may do violence to his person or property . . . this Convention strongly impressed with an idea of the confusion and disorder which must inevitably ensue, and the disunion which must necessarily follow, from the people at large being collected and inflicting punishments before a cool and temperate investigation of the case ; and consequently the injury which may be thereby done to the common cause of Liberty, confide, that the Virtue of the people, and their attachment to the liberties of America, will guard them against a commission of the Excess apprehended. . . .

Monday 7ᵗʰ August . . .

The memorial of James Christie Junᵣ of Baltimore Town was read ; and upon reading the Letter of the said James Christie therein referred to, dated the 22ᵈ of February 1775, to Gabriel Christie, Lieutenant Colonel of the 60th Regiment in which the said Christie represented the inhabitants of that Town, as concerned in measures, in his opinion, treasonable and rebellious ; and that a number of Soldiers would keep them very quiet; the same was considered by this Convention and thereupon it is Resolved, that the said James Christie, by the said Letter hath manifested a spirit & principle altogether inimical to the Rights and Liberties of America ; that the said James Christie by insinuating the necessity of introducing a Military Force into this Province, has manifested an inveterate enmity to the Liberties of this Province in particular, and of British America in general.

Therefore Resolved, that the said James Christie is, and ought to be considered as an enemy to America, and that no person trade, deal or barter with him hereafter unless for necessaries and provisions, or for the sale or purchase of any part of his real or personal Estate, of which he may at this time be seised or possessed.

Resolved that the said James Christie be Expelled and banished this Province for ever, and that he depart this Province before the first Day of September next.

Resolved, That no punishment be inflicted on the said James Christie other than what is now directed by this Convention.

Resolved, That the said James Christie deposit in the Hands of this

Convention, or into the hands of such person or persons as they shall appoint, the sum of five hundred pounds sterling, to be expended occasionally towards his proportion of all Charges and Expenses incurred, or to be incurred, for the defence of America, during the present contest with Great Britain; the overplus, if any, after a Reconciliation shall happily be effected, to be returned to the said James Christie. . . .

Friday 11th August. . . .

On reading and considering the memorial of Messrs Lux and Ridley, of Baltimore Town, merchants, relative to the Brig Nancy, Capt. Sims; Resolved, that the prayer of the said memorial be granted, on proof of the allegations therein being made to the Committee of observation for Baltimore County, who are hereby empowered to examine and take the said proof, and if the said Vessel shall not be reladen and depart before 10th day of September next, then oath to be made before her departure, by the Captain and Mate, that no commodities, goods, wares or merchandise, is or shall be laden on board for Exportation, other than such as shall have been laden on Board, as part of her Cargo, before the said 10th day of September, and shall have been relanded. . . .

Monday 14th. Augt

Ordered, That the Rules and Regulations established by the Continental Congress for the government of the Continental Army, be published with the proceedings of this Convention. . . .

Resolved unanimously, That the following Association be signed by the Members of this Convention, and by all other the Freemen of this Province.

Association of the Freemen of Maryland 26th July 1775.

The long premeditated, and now avowed Design of the British Government, to raise a Revenue from the property of the Colonists without their consent, on the gift, grant and disposition of the Commons of Great Britain, the arbitrary and vindictive statutes passed under colour of punishing a Riot, to subdue by Military force, and by Famine, the Massachusetts Bay; the unlimited power assumed by Parliament to alter the Charter of that Province, and the Constitution of all the Colonies, thereby destroying the essential securities of the Lives, Liberties and properties of the Colonists; the Commencement of hostilities by the Ministerial Forces, and the cruel prosecution of the War against the

people of the Massachusetts Bay, followed by General Gage's proclamation, declaring almost the whole of the Inhabitants of the United Colonies, by name, or description, Rebels and Traitors, are sufficient causes
to arm a free people in defence of their Liberty, and to justify resistance,
no longer dictated by prudence merely, but by necessity, and leave no
alternative but base submission or manly opposition to uncontroulable
Tyranny.   The Congress chose the latter, and for the express purpose
of securing & defending the United Colonies and preserving them in
Safety, against all attempts to carry the above mentioned Acts into
Execution by Force of Arms, Resolved, that the said Colonies be immediately put into a State of Defence, and now supports at the joint expense, an army to restrain the further violence and repel the future
attacks of a disappointed and exasperated Enemy. — We therefore,
Inhabitants of the Province of Maryland, firmly persuaded that it is
necessary and justifiable to repel Force by Force, do approve of the
opposition by arms to the British Troops employed to enforce obedience
to the late acts and statutes of the British Parliament, for raising a
Revenue in America, and altering and changing the Charter and Constitution of the Massachusetts Bay, and for destroying the essential
securities for the Lives, Liberties and properties of the Subjects in the
United Colonies.

And We do unite and associate, as one Band & firmly and solemnly
engage and pledge ourselves to each other and to America, that we will,
to the utmost of our power, promote and support the present opposition
carrying on as well by Arms, as by the Continental Association restraining our Commerce. —

And as in these times of Public danger, and until a Reconcilliation
with Great Britain on Constitutional Principles is effected (an event, we
most ardently wish may soon take place) the energy of Government
may be greatly impaired, so that even Zeal unrestrained may be productive of Anarchy & confusion ; We do in like manner unite, associate
and solemnly engage, in maintenance of good order, and the public
peace, to support the civil power in the due execution of the Laws, so
far as may be consistent with the present plan of opposition, and to
defend with our utmost power all persons from every species of outrage
to themselves or their property, and to prevent any punishment, from
being inflicted on any offenders, other than such, as shall be adjudged
by the Civil Magistrate, the Continental Congress, our Convention,
Council of Safety, or Committees of observation.

That the Committees of Observation, in every County, as soon as conveniently may be, appoint persons in each Parish, or Hundred, to offer or carry the said Association to all Freemen resident within their County, (the Household of His Excellency the Governor excepted) and require their subscription to the same, which Associations, when subscribed shall be returned by the Committees to the Convention. And in case any Freeman within their County, shall not subscribe upon application, or within ten days thereafter, his name shall be returned by the said Committee to the next Convention, to the end that the Convention may take order therein. . . .

Resolved, That the Honorable Matthew Tilghman Esqr and Thomas Johnson Junr Robert Goldsborough, William Paca, Samuel Chase, Thomas Stone and John Hall Esq^{rs} or any three or more of them, be Deputies to represent this Province in Continental Congress, and that they or any three or more of them, have full and ample power to consent and agree to all measures, which such Congress shall deem necessary and effectual to obtain a redress of American grievances ; and further we do authorise our said Deputies to represent and act for this Province, in any Continental Congress which may be held before the 25th day of March next.

Ordered that the Treasurer of the Western Shore pay to Thomas Johnson Junr Samuel Chase, William Paca, John Hall and Thomas Stone Esquires, or either of them, the sum of five hundred pounds common money, and that the Treasurer of the Eastern Shore pay to the Honorable Matthew Tilghman and Robert Goldsborough Esquires, or either of them, the sum of two hundred pounds, common money, to defray the expenses of their Deputation, to the next Continental Congress. . . .

Resolved, That there be a Convention of Delegates of this Province at Annapolis on the third Tuesday of March next, or on such day before that time, as shall be appointed by the Council of Safety. . . .

Ordered, that John Hall, Charles Carroll of Carrollton, William Paca and Matthias Hammond Esq^{rs} be a Committee to revise the proceedings of this Convention, and publish such of them as they may think proper, and convey a number securely made up to each County, as soon as may be.

So ends this Convention.

Test,   G. DuVall, Clk.

Journal of the Maryland Convention, July 26— August 14, 1775, in *Archives of Maryland* (edited by William Hand Browne, Baltimore, 1892), XI, 3–35 *passim*.

185. The Activities of the Continental Congress (1775)

BY DELEGATE RICHARD SMITH

Smith had been for years clerk of the New Jersey House of Representatives, and was a delegate from New Jersey to the first and second Continental Congresses. — Bibliography of Congress: Winsor, *Narrative and Critical History*, VI, 107–109; Frothingham, *Rise of the Republic*, ch. ix; Curtis, *History of the Constitution*, I, ch. ii; Channing and Hart, *Guide*, § 137. — Compare with earlier Congresses, Nos. 125, 141, 153 above.

TUESDAY, 12 September 1775. I attended at Congress for the first Time since the Adjournment. Mʳ Hancock having a Touch of the Gout there was no President in the Chair. The Colonies of New Hampshire and N Carolina absent as also sundry Members from other Colonies. Dʳ Franklin read several Letters recieved today by Capᵗ Falkner from London and informed the Members that he had some Bales of Household Goods on Board of Falkner, desiring the Congress's Leave to land them. no Objection to it only Willing and John Rutledge thought it irregular to do Business without a President and it was referred. Mʳ Gadsden and others moved for an Adjornment to 10 Tomorrow, which was complyed with. 3 of the Georgia Delegates were present with Mʳ Peyton Randolph and the new Delegates from Virginia, their Credentials not yet delivered, and little Business hitherto done this session.

Wednesday 13ᵗʰ. Mʳ President (Hancock) in the Chair. The Credentials of the Georgia, Virginia and Maryland Delegates were read and accepted without any Objection. the Marylanders were the same as at the last Session. An Order was made that the Pennsᵃ Delegates shall send off to Gen. Washington under a proper Guard, the remainder of his Money amounting in the whole to 700,000 Dollars, and they were at the same Time to send the Cloathing for Two Regiments lately seized at Philadᵃ. Duane and Rob. R. Livingston came today from the Indian Treaty at Albany. another Treaty is about to be held at Pittsburg. Dʳ Franklins Goods allowed to be landed. a great Number of Letters and Papers were read, some from Gen. Washington giving a particular State of his Army they want Powder and Money — some from Gen. Schuyler stating his Situation; others from Col. Lewis Morris and Jaˢ Wilson Dated at Fort Pitt recommending an Expedition agᵗ Detroit to be conducted by Col. Arthur Sᵗ Clair — others from Gov. Trumbull and sundry more.

Thursday 14 Sept. . . . The Georgia Delegates laid the Proceedings of their Provincial Convention before us cont'g a Petition to the King, another to certain Resolves and other Matters, and motioned for Leave to sell the Cargoes of Two Ships which were shipped without Knowledge of their Agreement of Non Importⁿ, and motioned also for Exportation of certain Articles under certain Limitations. these Motions were opposed by Chase and J. Adams and supported by Nelson, Houstoun and Dr. Zubley, the latter out of Humor with Chase. the Consideration of it was put off till Tomorrow. the proposed Expedition to Detroit canvassed and disagreed to and various other Matters.

Friday 15 Sept. . . . the Affair of the Two Cargoes at Georgia referred from Yesterday, was largely agitated and in the End a Resolution drawn by Jay took place importing that the cargoes should be sold and the Proffits if any put into the Hands of the Georgia Convention or Com^{ee}. of Safety to be applied in Defence of the Province. an incidental Matter took up some Time viz, Whether M^r. Nelson should vote for Virginia he being the only Delegate present and whether any lesser Number than the Quorum shall represent any Colony. Mr. Nelson waved his Question, and the other went off without a Determination (since that Time no Colony votes without the Quorum present as limited by their Colony, some authorize 3. some 2 some one Delegate to give a Vote). Two of the Georgia Delegates are possessed of Homespun Suits of Cloaths, an Adornment few other Members can boast of, besides my Bro^r Crane and myself.

Saturday 16 Sep. the greater Part of the Time lost in considering Whether One Officer in our Army may be allowed to hold Two Commissions it was postponed . . . .

Monday 18. Motion to appoint a Com^{ee}. to procure 500 Ton of Gunpowder from abroad, together with 10,000 Stand of Arms 20,000 Gun Locks &c with power to draw on the Continental Treasury for the Amount, was carried by Vote, the Payment in Produce was opposed and the further Consideration postponed. Com^{ee} on the Accounts asked Direction how to settle them and the Matter left unsettled Motion by E. Rutledge to enlarge Col. Fenton a Prisoner in Connect^t. from New Hampshire, opposed by Langdon and deferred. . . .

Tuesday 19 Sept. . . . agreed to banish John Fenton to England at his own Request after considerable Debate. Dr Franklin the PostMaster General desired the Delegates of New Jersey to nominate Deputy PostMasters throughout that Colony which we did accordingly.

Wednesday 20. An Expedition is on Foot against the Kings Forces in Canada via Kennebec under Col. Arnold from Washingtons Camp at Cambridge. . . . Gen. Wooster with a considerable Detachment or dered to join Schuyler. this Morning a Letter in French was delivered to the President directed for Gen. Washington said to be from the Governor of Hispaniola. Whether the Letter shall be opened and whether by a select Com^ee or by the President, were made Questions. the general Opinion seemed to be that the President should open it and the Secretary (Charles Thomson) translate it and if of a public Nature that it should be laid before Congress but it was dropt. . . .

Thursday 21 Sept. On a Question Whether Col. Armstrong or Col. Fry shall be Brig. Gen. in the Room of Pomeroy retired, the Colonies were divided 6 against 6 — North Car^a being absent, consequently there was no Appointment. . . .

Friday 22. — Andrew MacNair Doorkeeper's Acco^t ordered to be paid. . . . Major Rogers ordered to be discharged if Nothing appears ag^t Him but being a Half Pay Officer, he was arrested by the Com^ee of Safety of Pennsylvania. a committee of 7 appointed by Ballot to con sider the State of Trade in America. — Wm Shads Acco^t as Messenger ordered to be paid.

Saturday 23 Sept. a Letter from Thos Mifflin Quarter Master to the Army directed to Wm Barrell Merch^t was read, desiring Him to forward Cloathing for the Army, the Congress took that Subject into Considera tion and appointed by Ballot a Com^ee of 5 to supply the Two Armies with Cloathing to the Amount of £5000 sterl'g, and allowed each Quarter Master 5 ℔ Cent for selling out to the Soldiers.

Monday 25. A Com^ee of 3 named to draw an Answer to Gen Wash ingtons Letters. . . . De Hart moved to restrict all Conventions and Assemblies from issuing any more Paper Money and to recall what they have done without Permission from hence, he was not seconded. On reading Wilson and Morris's Letters and other Papers Willing moved that the Congress would interfere in settling a temporary Line between Virginia and Pennsylvania, a Letter was read from the Delegates of those Two Colonies to the Inhabitants recomm'g Peace &c. several Orders of the King in Council Dated in June last relative to this Line were read.

Tuesday 26 Sept. Com^ee brought in a Letter to Gen Washington, in the Course of it E Rutledge moved that the Gen. shall discharge all the Negroes as well Slaves as Freemen in his Army. he (Rutledge) was

strongly supported by many of the Southern Delegates but so powerfully opposed that he lost the Point. the Question of the Lines between
Penn? and Virginia agitated but Nothing determined. the Letters between Washington and Gage ordered to be published, then the Journal
was read in Order for Publication and some Parts of it ordered not to
be printed as improper for Public Inspection particularly all that was
there about fortifying the Passes on Hudsons River and the Directions
to the New Yorkers to arm themselves &c.

Wednesday 27. . . . the Journal continued to be read and various
Parts ordered not to be published, as the Instructions to Gen Wash? the
Directions to the German Ministers &c. A Petition was read from Mess⁣ʳˢ.
Purviance of Baltimore praying Leave to ship off a Cargo of Wheat which
the late Storm prevented, refused and ordered to lie on the Table.

Thursday 28 Sept? No Congress. the Members dined by Invitation
on Board of the RowGallies which sailed down to the Chevaux de Frize
near Mud Island and up to Point no Point. I amused myself all the
Morning in M. du Simitiere's curious Museum.

Friday 29. Letters from Gen. Washington with a Return of his
Army, about 19,000 effective Men who are to be disbanded in Dec? by
the Terms of Inlistment, he prays Directions how to keep or raise an
Army. Expenses run very high, great Want of Powder and Money.
Chief Part of the Morn'g was spent on a Motion to send a Com⁣ᵉᵉ of the
Congress to the Army to take proper Measures for the Winter Cam-
paign, it passed in the Affirmative. some Powder said to be just arrived
in Delaware our Com⁣ᵉᵉ were desired to purchase it. above 80 of our
Men have deserted to Gen. Gage in the Course of this Campaign accord'g
to Gen. Wash⁣ⁿˢ Dispatches.

Saturday 30 Sept? A Com⁣ᵉᵉ of 3, viz Harrison, Franklin and Lynch
was appointed by Ballot to proceed to the Camp at Cambridge. . . .

[Wednesday, December 13.] . . . the Order for this day was to consider of giving Gen Washington Directions to storm Boston but various
other Matters intervening it was put off till Tomorrow. M⁣ᶜKean informed the Congress that many Persons in Penns?, Maryland and Jersey
sell Tea and drink Tea upon a Report that Congress had granted Leave
so to do and he doubted Whether the Committees had Power to restrain them, a Day was fixed for considering the Matter (in April 1776
the Congress gave Leave to sell and use what Tea was in the Country,
forbidding any further Importation of it) — M. Crane went home, Livingston and myself remain, Kinsey and De Hart have lately resigned. . . .

Friday Dec. 15. . . . Motion by Wilson that all Officers below a Major in the Continental Troops now raising in Penns^a shall be appointed by the several Committees of Correspondence and Observation was at length rejected and the Mode of Appointment there and in the Lower Counties settled. . . . Robert Morris moved that a Com^{ee} be nominated to consider of Ways and Means to bring in Gold and Silver and keep it in the Country, it is reported that Half Joes have already risen to £3–2–6, it was debated and postponed till Tomorrow. Col. Lee moved that George Mead & Co. of Philad^a may export from that City to Virginia 6000 Bushels of Salt and carry abroad Produce to the Amount from thence, opposed by Jay, Lewis and others and supported by Nelson, Wyth, Rob. Morris &c. it passed in the Affirmative 7 Colonies to 4   Com^{ee} on Public Acco^{ts} reported a Number of Accounts which were allowed and ordered to be paid (the mode of Payment is the President signs an Order to the joint Treasurers Hillegas and Clymer and then they pay the Money) several other Motions and Matters, for these Memoirs only contain what I could readily recollect.

Saturday 16 Dec. . . . A Com^{ee} of 3 prepared a Speech to be delivered by the President to Capt White Eyes a chief of the Delaware Indians said to reside on the Muskingham, who was then introduced into the Congress accompanied by One of his Councellors and an Interpreter. the Chief was dressed in a good Suit of Blue Cloth with a Laced Hat and his Counsellor was wrapped in a Blanket, Capt White Eyes shook all the Members heartily by the Hand, beginning with the President and used the same Ceremony at his Departure, he stayed about an Hour, Our President delivered the Speech and the Chief answered by his Interpreter that he was well pleased to hear such a good Speech and meet his Brethren in the Grand Council Fire, that he would faithfully report to his Friends the kind Disposition of the Congress and proposed to stay in Town all Winter — he wanted a Clergyman, Schoolmaster and Blacksmith established among his People and said they inclined to embrace Christianity and a more civilized Way of Life. A Copy of the Congress's Speech was given to him when he withdrew, his Councellor said Nothing. . . .

Monday Dec. 18. . . . An Express arrived from Montreal with Letters from Gen. Montgomery, Col. Arnold and others. Eleven Vessels are taken near Montreal by our people who have also seized Brig. Prescot who had caused all the Powder to be thrown overboard, but the Ships contain plenty of Provision. Ethan Allen is sent to England in

2 M

Irons.   Col. James Livingston is about to raise a Regiment of Canadians
in our pay for One Year.   Arnold is near Quebec but has not Men
enough to surround it and his Powder so damaged, that he has only
5 Rounds apiece.   Montgomerys Soldiers very disobedient and many
of them come Home without Leave.   Frauds discovered in some of his
Officers.   Gen. Wash.ⁿ in great Want of Powder and most of the Con-
nect! Troops have left his Army.   Accounts of a Skirmish in Virginia
and great Preparations in England for an Invasion of Us in the Spring.
We sat from 10 oCloc till the Dusk of the Evening.

Diary of Richard Smith in the Continental Congress, in *American Historical
Review* (New York, etc., 1896), I, 289–296 *passim*.

---

186. A Call for Independence (1776)

BY THOMAS PAINE

For Paine, see No. 159 above. — Bibliography of independence : Winsor, *Narrative and Critical History*, VI, 255–262; Frothingham, *Rise of the Republic*, chs. v,
vi, xi; Lecky, *England*, iii, 412–459; Channing and Hart, *Guide*, § 137. — For earlier
suggestions of independence, see above, Nos. 122, 148, 153.

LEAVING the moral part to private reflection, I shall chiefly
confine my farther remarks to the following heads :
First, That it is the interest of America to be seperated from Britain.
Secondly, Which is the easiest and most practicable plan, reconciliation or independance? with some occasional remarks.
In support of the first, I could, if I judged it proper, produce the
opinion of some of the ablest and most experienced men on this continent ; and whose sentiments, on that head, are not yet publicly known.
It is in reality a self-evident position : For no nation, in a state of foreign dependance, limited in its commerce, and cramped and fettered in
its legislative powers, can ever arrive at any material eminence.   America doth not yet know what opulence is ; and although the progress
which she hath made, stands unparalleled in the history of other nations,
it is but childhood, compared with what she would be capable of arriving at, had she, as she ought to have, the legislative powers in her own
hands.   England is, at this time, proudly coveting what would do her
no good, were she to accomplish it ; and the continent hesitating on a
matter, which will be her final ruin if neglected.   It is the commerce,
and not the conquest of America, by which England is to be benefited,

and that would in a great measure continue, were the countries as independant of each other as France and Spain ; because in many articles,
neither can go to a better market.   But it is the independance of this
country on Britain or any other, which is now the main and only object
worthy of contention, and which, like all other truths discovered by
necessity, will appear clearer and stronger every day.

First.   Because it will come to that one time or other.

Secondly.   Because the longer it is delayed, the harder it will be to
accomplish.

I have frequently amused myself both in public and private companies,
with silently remarking the specious errors of those who speak without
reflecting.   And among the many which I have heard, the following
seems the most general, viz. that had this rupture happened forty or
fifty years hence, instead of *now*, the Continent would have been more
able to have shaken off the dependance.   To which I reply, that our
military ability *at this time*, arises from the experience gained in the late
war, and which in forty or fifty years time, would have been totally
extinct. . . .

Should affairs be patched up with Britain, and she to remain the governing and sovereign power of America, (which as matters are now
circumstanced, is giving up the point entirely) we shall deprive ourselves of the very means of sinking the debt we have, or may contract.
The value of the back lands, which some of the provinces are clandes-
tinely deprived of, by the unjust extension of the limits of Canada, valued
only at five pounds sterling per hundred acres, amount to upwards of
twenty five millions, Pennsylvania currency ; and the quit-rents at one
penny sterling per acre, to two millions yearly. . . .

I proceed now to the second head, viz.   Which is the easiest and
most practicable plan, *Reconciliation or Independance* ; with some occasional remarks.

He who takes nature for his guide, is not easily beaten out of his
argument, and on that ground, I answer *generally, That* Independance
being a single simple line, *contained within ourselves ; and reconciliation,
a matter exceedingly perplexed and complicated, and in which, a treacherous capricious court is to interfere, gives the answer without a doubt.*

The present state of America is truly alarming to every man who is
capable of reflection.   Without law, without government, without any
other mode of power than what is founded on, and granted by courtesy.
Held together by an unexampled concurrence of sentiment, which, is

nevertheless subject to change, and which, every secret enemy is en-deavouring to dissolve. Our present condition, is, Legislation without law ; wisdom without a plan ; a constitution without a name ; and, what is strangely astonishing, perfect Independance, contending for depend-ance. The instance is without a precedent ; the case never existed before ; and who can tell what may be the event? The property of no man is secure in the present unbraced system of things. The mind of the multitude is left at random, and seeing no fixed object before them, they pursue such as fancy or opinion starts. Nothing is criminal ; there is no such thing as treason ; wherefore, every one thinks himself at liberty to act as he pleases. The Tories would not have dared to assem-ble offensively, had they known that their lives, by that act, were forfeited to the laws of the state. A line of distinction should be drawn, between English soldiers taken in battle, and inhabitants of America taken in arms. The first are prisoners, but the latter traitors. The one forfeits his liberty, the other his head. . . .

Put us, say some, upon the footing we were on in sixty-three. . . . To be on the footing of sixty-three, it is not sufficient, that the laws only be put on the same state, but that our circumstances, likewise be put on the same state ; our burnt and destroyed towns repaired or built up, our private losses made good, our public debts (contracted for de-fence) discharged ; otherwise we shall be millions worse than we were at that enviable period. Such a request, had it been complied with a year ago, would have won the heart and soul of the Continent, but now it is too late. " The Rubicon is passed."

Besides, the taking up arms, merely to enforce the repeal of a pecun-iary law, seems as unwarrantable by the divine law, and as repugnant to human feelings, as the taking up arms to enforce the obedience thereto. The object, on either side, doth not justify the means ; for the lives of men are too valuable, to be cast away on such trifles, It is the violence which is done and threatened to our persons ; the destruction of our property by an armed force ; the invasion of our country by fire and sword, which conscientiously qualifies the use of arms : And the instant, in which such a mode of defence became necessary, all subjection to Britain ought to have ceased ; and the independancy of America, should have been considered, as dating its æra from, and published by, *the first musket that was fired against her.* This line is a line of consistency ; neither drawn by caprice, nor extended by ambition ; but produced by a chain of events, of which the colonies were not the authors.

I shall conclude these remarks, with the following timely and well intended hint. We ought to reflect, that there are three different ways, by which an independancy may hereafter be effected; and that *one* of those *three*, will one day or other, be the fate of America, viz. By the legal voice of the people in Congress; by a military power; or by a mob: It may not always happen that our soldiers are citizens, and the multitude a body of reasonable men; vertue, as I have already remarked, is not hereditary, neither is it perpetual. Should an independancy be brought about by the first of those means, we have every opportunity and every encouragement before us, to form the noblest purest constitution on the face of the earth. We have it in our power to begin the world over again. A situation, similar to the present, hath not happened since the days of Noah until now. The birth day of a new world is at hand, and a race of men, perhaps as numerous as all Europe contains, are to receive their portion of freedom from the event of a few months. The reflection is awful and in this point of view, how trifling, how ridiculous, do the little paltry cavillings, of a few weak or interested men appear, when weighed against the business of a world. . . .

In short, Independance is the only BOND that can tye and keep us together. We shall then see our object, and our ears will be legally shut against the schemes of an intriguing, as well as a cruel enemy. We shall then too be on a proper footing to treat with Britain; for there is reason to conclude, that the pride of that court will be less hurt by treating with the American states for terms of peace, than with those she denominates " rebellious subjects," for terms of accommodation. It is our delaying it that encourages her to hope for conquest, and our backwardness tends only to prolong the war. As we have, without any good effect therefrom, withheld our trade to obtain a redress of our grievances, let us now try the alternative, by *independantly* redressing them ourselves, and then offering to open the trade. The mercantile and reasonable part in England will be still with us; because, peace with trade, is preferable to war without it. And if this offer is not accepted, other courts may be applied to. On these grounds I rest the matter. And as no offer hath yet been made to refute the doctrine contained in the former editions of this pamphlet, it is a negative proof, that either the doctrine cannot be refuted, or, that the party in favour of it are too numerous to be opposed. *Wherefore*, instead of gazing at each other with suspicious or doubtful curiosity, let each of us hold out to his neighbour the hearty hand of friendship, and unite in drawing a line, which, like an act of oblivion, shall bury in forgetfulness every former dissention. Let the names of Whig and Tory be extinct; and let none other be heard among us, than those of *a good citizen, an open and resolute friend, and a virtuous supporter of the rights of mankind and of the free and inde-pendant states of America.*

[Thomas Paine], *Appendix to Common Sense*; appended to *Common Sense: addressed to the Inhabitants of America. . . . Written by an Englishman* (Philadelphia, 1776), 66–71 *passim.*

◆

187. Difficulties in Framing a State Constitution (1776)

BY CHAIRMAN MESHECH WEARE, SECRETARY E. THOMPSON, AND OTHERS

New Hampshire was the first colony to draw up a constitution. This piece illus-trates the foundation of the system of formal state constitutions. — Bibliography: Win-sor, *Narrative and Critical History*, VI, 268–274; Channing and Hart, *Guide*, § 143. — Compare with earlier colonial governments, Part III above.

In Congress, at Exeter, January 5, 1776.

WE, the Members of the Congress of the Colony of *New-Hampshire*, chosen and appointed by the free suffrages of the people of said Colony, and authorized and empowered by them to meet together, and use such means, and pursue such measures, as we should judge best for the publick good; and, in particular, to establish some form of Gov-ernment, provided that measure should be recommended by the Conti-nental Congress; and a recommendation to that purpose having been transmitted to us, from the said Congress, have taken into our seri-ous consideration the unhappy circumstances into which this Colony is involved, by means of many grievous and oppressive acts of the *British* Parliament, depriving us of our native and constitutional rights and privileges; to enforce obedience to which acts, a powerful fleet and army have been sent into this country by the Ministry of *Great Britain*, who have exercised a wanton and cruel abuse of their power, in destroying the lives and properties of the Colonists, in many places with fire and sword, taking the ships and lading from many of the honest and industrious inhabitants of this Colony employed in com-merce, agreeable to the laws and customs a long time used here.

The sudden and abrupt departure of his Excellency *John Wentworth*, Esq., our late Governour, and several of the Council, leaving us destitute of Legislation ; and no Executive Courts being open to punish criminal offenders, whereby the lives and properties of the honest people of this Colony, are liable to the machinations and evil designs of wicked men :

Therefore, for the preservation of peace and good order, and for the security of the lives and properties of the inhabitants of this Colony, we conceive ourselves reduced to the necessity of establishing a form of Government, to continue during the present unhappy and unnatural contest with *Great Britain;* protesting and declaring that we never sought to throw off our dependance - upon *Great Britain*, but felt ourselves happy under her protection, while we could enjoy our constitutional rights and privileges, and that we shall rejoice if such a reconciliation between us and our parent state, can be effected as shall be approved by the Continental Congress, in whose prudence and wisdom we confide.

Accordingly, pursuant to the trust reposed in us, we do

Resolve, That this Congress assume the name, power, and authority of a House of Representatives or Assembly, for the Colony of *New-Hampshire.* And that said House then proceed to choose twelve persons, being reputable freeholders and inhabitants within this Colony, in the following manner, viz : Five in the County of *Rockingham ;* two in the County of *Strafford;* two in the County of *Hillsborough ;* two in the County of *Cheshire;* and one in the County of *Grafton*, to be a distinct and separate branch of the Legislature, by the name of a Council for this Colony, to continue as such until the third *Wednesday* in *December* next ; any seven of whom to be a quorum to do business.

That such Council appoint their President ; and in his absence, that the senior Counsellor preside.

That a Secretary be appointed by both Branches, who may be a Counsellor, or otherwise, as they shall choose.

That no act or resolve be valid, and put into execution, unless agreed to and passed by both branches of the Legislature.

That all publick officers for the said Colony, and each County, for the current year, be appointed by the Council and Assembly, except the several Clerks of the Executive Courts, who shall be appointed by the Justices of the respective Courts.

That all Bills, Resolves, or Votes for raising, levying, and collecting Money, originate in the House of Representatives.

That at any sessions of the Council and Assembly, neither Branch shall adjourn for any longer time than from *Saturday* till the next *Monday*, without consent of the other.

And it is further Resolved, That if the present unhappy dispute with *Great Britain* should continue longer than this present year, and the Continental Congress give no instructions or directions to the contrary, the Council be chosen by the people of each respective County, in such manner as the Council and House of Representatives shall order.

That General and Field-Officers of the Militia, on any vacancy, be appointed by the two Houses, and all inferior Officers be chosen by the respective Companies.

That all Officers of the Army be appointed by the two Houses, except they should direct otherwise, in case of any emergency.

That all Civil Officers for the Colony, and for each County, be appointed, and the time of their continuance in office be determined by the two Houses, except Clerks of Courts, and County Treasurers, and Recorders of Deeds.

That a Treasurer, and a Recorder of Deeds, for each County, be annually chosen by the people of each County respectively ; the votes for such officers to be returned to the respective Courts of General Sessions of the Peace in the County, there to be ascertained as the Council and Assembly shall hereafter direct.

That Precepts, in the name of the Council and Assembly, signed by the President of the Council, and the Speaker of the House of Representatives, shall issue, annually, at or before the first day of *November*, for the choice of a Council and House of Representatives, to be returned by the third *Wednesday* in *December*, then next ensuing, in such manner as the Council and Assembly shall hereafter prescribe.

A true copy. Attest :

              E. THOMPSON, *Secretary.*

We, the subscribers, chosen by the people of several Towns in the Colony of *New-Hampshire,* to represent them in the Congress of said Colony, held at *Exeter,* on the 21st day of *December,* 1775. beg leave to enter and dissent to, and protest against the present plan of taking up Government, for the following reasons :

First. That the vote of the Continental Congress countenancing the same, was obtained by the unwearied importunity (both within doors and without) of our Delegates there, as appears by their letter.

Second. That the said vote does not appear to have been unanimous; but, we have reason to think, far otherway.

Third. Because the Colonies of *New-York* and *Virginia*, which are in similar circumstances with us, are much larger and more opulent, and we presume much wiser, to whom we would wish to pay all due deference, have not attempted any thing of the kind, nor, as we can learn, ever desired it.

Fourth. Because we have no ground on which to pretend to make a Council, as our neighbours of the *Massachusetts*, who act by charter, never vacated on any legal trial.

Fifth. Because it appears assuming for so small and inconsiderable a Colony to take the lead in a matter of so great importance.

Sixth. Because our constituents never expected us to make a new form of Government, but only to set the Judicial and Executive wheels in motion.

Seventh. Because the Congress, as such, could have done what was necessary, and their power could not be enlarged by any act of their own.

Eighth. Because the expense of the Colony is greatly augmented thereby.

Ninth. Because it appears to us to be absolutely setting up an independency on the mother country.

[12 signatures.]

Peter Force, *American Archives*, Fourth Series (Washington, 1843), IV, 998–1000.

---

188. Drafting of the Declaration of Independence (1776)

BY DELEGATE THOMAS JEFFERSON

Jefferson, then thirty-three years of age, was a delegate from Virginia to the Continental Congress, later governor of Virginia, member of the Congress of the Confederation, ambassador to France, secretary of state, vice-president, and president. — Bibliography of Jefferson: Winsor, *Narrative and Critical History*, VII, 303–307; H. B. Tompkins, *Bibliotheca Jeffersoniana;* Henry Adams, *United States*, I–III; Channing and Hart, *Guide*, § 167. — See above, No. 186.

IN Congress, Friday June 7. 1776. The delegates from Virginia moved in obedience to instructions from their constituents that the Congress should declare that these United colonies are & of right ought

to be free & independent states, that they are absolved from all allegiance to the British crown, and that all political connection between
them & the state of Great Britain is & ought to be, totally dissolved;
that measures should be immediately taken for procuring the assistance
of foreign powers, and a Confederation be formed to bind the colonies
more closely together. . . .

It appearing in the course of these debates that the colonies of
N. York, New Jersey, Pennsylvania, Delaware, Maryland, and South
Carolina were not yet matured for falling from the parent stem, but that
they were fast advancing to that state, it was thought most prudent to
wait a while for them, and to postpone the final decision to July 1. but
that this might occasion as little delay as possible a committee was
appointed to prepare a declaration of independence. The commee
were J. Adams, Dr. Franklin, Roger Sherman, Robert R. Livingston &
myself. Committees were also appointed at the same time to prepare
a plan of confederation for the colonies, and to state the terms proper
to be proposed for foreign alliance. The committee for drawing the
declaration of Independence desired me to do it. It was accordingly
done, and being approved by them, I reported it to the house on Friday
the 28th of June when it was read and ordered to lie on the table. On
Monday, the 1st of July the house resolved itself into a commee of the
whole & resumed the consideration of the original motion made by the
delegates of Virginia, which being again debated through the day, was
carried in the affirmative by the votes of N. Hampshire, Connecticut,
Massachusetts, Rhode Island, N. Jersey, Maryland, Virginia, N. Carolina,
& Georgia. S. Carolina and Pennsylvania voted against it. Delaware
having but two members present, they were divided. The delegates
for New York declared they were for it themselves & were assured their
constituents were for it, but that their instructions having been drawn
near a twelvemonth before, when reconciliation was still the general
object, they were enjoined by them to do nothing which should impede
that object. They therefore thought themselves not justifiable in voting
on either side, and asked leave to withdraw from the question, which
was given them. The commee rose & reported their resolution to the
house. Mr. Edward Rutledge of S. Carolina then requested the determination might be put off to the next day, as he believed his colleagues,
tho' they disapproved of the resolution, would then join in it for the
sake of unanimity. The ultimate question whether the house would
agree to the resolution of the committee was accordingly postponed to

the next day, when it was again moved and S. Carolina concurred in voting for it.   In the meantime a third member had come post from the Delaware counties and turned the vote of that colony in favour of the resolution.   Members of a different sentiment attending that morning from Pennsylvania also, their vote was changed, so that the whole 12 colonies who were authorized to vote at all, gave their voices for it; and within a few days, the convention of N. York approved of it and thus supplied the void occasioned by the withdrawing of her delegates from the vote.

Congress proceeded the same day to consider the declaration of Independance which had been reported & lain on the table the Friday preceding, and on Monday referred to a commee of the whole. / The pusillanimous idea that we had friends in England worth keeping terms with, still haunted the minds of many.   For this reason those passages which conveyed censures on the people of England were struck out, lest they should give them offence.   The clause too, reprobating the enslaving the inhabitants of Africa, was struck out in complaisance to South Carolina and Georgia, who had never attempted to restrain the importation of slaves, and who on the contrary still wished to continue it.   Our northern brethren also I believe felt a little tender under those censures; for tho' their people have very few slaves themselves yet they had been pretty considerable carriers of them to others. / The debates having taken up the greater parts of the 2d 3d & 4th days of July were, in the evening of the last, closed the declaration was reported by the commee, agreed to by the house and signed by every member present except Mr. Dickinson. . /. . the sentiments of men are known not only by what they receive, but what they reject also. . . .

Thomas Jefferson, *Writings* (edited by Paul Leicester Ford, New York, etc., 1892), I, 18–29 *passim*.

———◆———

189. Difficulties in Framing Articles of Confederation (1776)

REPORTED BY DELEGATE JOHN ADAMS

It was the intention of Congress to frame Articles of Confederation at the same time as the Declaration of Independence; but the difficulties which are illustrated in this piece delayed the completion of the draft till November, 1777; and the quarrel over the Virginia land claim (No. 205 below) prevented ratification till March 1, 1781

(No. 209 below). — Bibliography : Winsor, *Narrative and Critical History*, VI, 274; Frothingham, *Rise of the Republic*, ch. xi; Channing and Hart, *Guide*, § 142. — Compare earlier forms of federation, *Contemporaries*, I, Nos. 129, 131, and No. 125 above.

[July 30, 1776.] *CHASE*. Moves that the word "white," should be inserted in the eleventh Article. The negroes are wealth. Numbers are not a certain rule of wealth. It is the best rule we can lay down. Negroes a species of property, personal estate. If negroes are taken into the computation of numbers to ascertain wealth, they ought to be, in settling the representation. The Massachusetts fisheries, and navigation, ought to be taken into consideration. The young and old negroes are a burthen to their owners. The eastern Colonies have a great advantage in trade. This will give them a superiority. We shall be governed by our interests, and ought to be. If I am satisfied in the rule of levying and appropriating money, I am willing the small Colonies should have a vote.

Wilson. If the war continues two years, each soul will have forty dollars to pay of the public debt. It will be the greatest encouragement to continue slave-keeping, and to increase it, that can be, to exempt them from the numbers which are to vote and pay. Slaves are taxables in the Southern Colonies. It will be partial and unequal. Some Colonies have as many black as white ; these will not pay more than half what they ought. Slaves prevent freemen from cultivating a country. It is attended with many inconveniences.

Lynch. If it is debated, whether their slaves are their property, there is an end of the confederation. Our slaves being our property, why should they be taxed more than the land, sheep, cattle, horses, &c. ?

Freemen cannot be got to work in our Colonies ; it is not in the ability or inclination of freemen to do the work that the negroes do. Carolina has taxed their negroes ; so have other Colonies their lands.

Dr. Franklin. Slaves rather weaken than strengthen the State, and there is therefore some difference between them and sheep ; sheep will never make any insurrections.

Rutledge. I shall be happy to get rid of the idea of slavery. The slaves do not signify property ; the old and young cannot work. The property of some Colonies is to be taxed, in others, not. The Eastern Colonies will become the carriers for the Southern ; they will obtain wealth for which they will not be taxed.

August 1. *Hooper*. North Carolina is a striking exception to the general rule that was laid down yesterday, that the riches of a country are in proportion to the numbers of inhabitants. A gentleman of three or four hundred negroes don't raise more corn than feeds them. A laborer can't be hired for less than twenty-four pounds a year in Massachusetts Bay. The net profit of a negro is not more than five or six pounds per annum. I wish to see the day that slaves are not necessary. Whites and negroes cannot work together. Negroes are goods and chattels, are property. A negro works under the impulse of fear, has no care of his master's interest.

Article 17. *Dr. Franklin* moves that votes should be in proportion to numbers. *Mr. Middleton* moves that the vote should be according to what they pay.

Sherman thinks we ought not to vote according to numbers. We are representatives of States, not individuals. States of Holland. The consent of every one is necessary. Three Colonies would govern the whole, but would not have a majority of strength to carry those votes into execution. The vote should be taken two ways ; call the Colonies, and call the individuals, and have a majority of both.

Dr. Rush. Abbé Raynal has attributed the ruin of the United Provinces to three causes. The principal one is, that the consent of every State is necessary ; the other, that the members are obliged to consult their constituents upon all occasions. We lose an equal representation ; we represent the people. It will tend to keep up colonial distinctions. We are now a new nation. Our trade, language, customs, manners, don't differ more than they do in Great Britain. The more a man aims at serving America, the more he serves his Colony. It will promote factions in Congress and in the States ; it will prevent the growth of freedom in America ; we shall be loth to admit new Colonies into the confederation. If we vote by numbers, liberty will be always safe. Massachusetts is contiguous to two small Colonies, Rhode Island and New Hampshire ; Pennsylvania is near New Jersey and Delaware ; Virginia is between Maryland and North Carolina. We have been too free with the word independence ; we are dependent on each other, not totally independent States. Montesquieu pronounces the confederation of Lycia, the best that ever was made ; the cities had different weights in the scale. China is not larger than one of our Colonies ; how populous ! It is said that the small Colonies deposit their all ; this is deceiving us with a word. I would not have it understood that I am pleading the cause of Pennsylvania ; when I entered that door, I considered myself a citizen of America.

Dr. Witherspoon.   Representation in England is unequal.   Must I have three votes in a county, because I have three times as much money as my neighbor?   Congress are to determine the limits of Colonies.

G. Hopkins.   A momentous question ; many difficulties on each side ; four larger, five lesser, four stand indifferent.   Virginia, Massachusetts, Pennsylvania, Maryland, make more than half the people.

Connecticut, New York, two Carolinas, not concerned at all.   The disinterested coolness of these Colonies ought to determine.   I can easily feel the reasoning of the larger Colonies ; pleasing theories always gave way to the prejudices, passions, and interests of mankind.   The Germanic Confederation.   The King of Prussia has an equal vote.   The Helvetic confederacy.   It can't be expected that nine Colonies will give way to be governed by four.   The safety of the whole depends upon the distinctions of Colonies.

Dr. Franklin.   I hear many ingenious arguments to persuade us that an unequal representation is a very good thing.   If we had been born and bred under an unequal representation, we might bear it ; but to set out with an unequal representation, is unreasonable.   It is said the great Colonies will swallow up the less.   Scotland said the same thing at the union.

Dr. Witherspoon rises to explain a few circumstances relating to Scotland ; that was an incorporating union, not a federal ; the nobility and gentry resort to England.

In determining all questions, each State shall have a weight, in proportion to what it contributes to the public expenses of the United States.

August 2.   "Limiting the bounds of States, which by charter, &c. extend to the South Sea."

Sherman thinks the bounds ought to be settled.   A majority of States have no claim to the South Sea.   Moves this amendment to be substituted in place of this clause, and also instead of the fifteenth article ; — "No lands to be separated from any State, which are already settled, or become private property."

Chase denies that any Colony has a right to go to the South Sea.

Harrison.   How came Maryland by its land, but by its charter?   By its charter, Virginia owns to the South Sea.   Gentlemen shall not pare away the Colony of Virginia.   Rhode Island has more generosity than to wish the Massachusetts pared away.   Delaware does not wish to pare away Pennsylvania.

Huntington. Admit there is danger from Virginia, does it follow that Congress has a right to limit her bounds? The consequence is, not to enter into confederation. But as to the question of right, we all unite against mutilating charters. I can't agree to the principle. We are a spectacle to all Europe. I am not so much alarmed at the danger from Virginia as some are; my fears are not alarmed; they have acted as noble a part as any. I doubt not the wisdom of Virginia will limit themselves. A man's right does not cease to be a right, because it is large; the question of right must be determined by the principles of the common law.

Stone. This argument is taken up upon very wrong ground. It is considered as if we were voting away the territory of particular Colonies, and gentlemen work themselves up into warmth upon that supposition. Suppose Virginia should. The small Colonies have a right to happiness and security; they would have no safety if the great Colonies were not limited. We shall grant lands, in small quantities, without rent or tribute or purchase-money. It is said that Virginia is attacked on every side. Is it meant that Virginia shall sell the lands for their own emolument? All the Colonies have defended these lands against the King of Britain, and at the expense of all. Does Virginia intend to establish quit rents? I don't mean that the United States shall sell them, to get money by them.

Jefferson. I protest against the right of Congress to decide upon the right of Virginia. Virginia has released all claims to the land settled by Maryland, &c.

John Adams, *Works* (edited by Charles Francis Adams, Boston, 1850), II, 496–502.

———◆———

190. Falling-off of the Character of Congress (1778)

BY COLONEL ALEXANDER HAMILTON

For Hamilton, see above, No. 173. — Bibliography of Congress: Curtis, *History of the Constitution*, I, 125–131; Channing and Hart, *Guide*, §§ 136, 142.

[February 13, 1778.] THERE is a matter, which often obtrudes itself upon my mind, and which requires the attention of every person of sense and influence among us; I mean a degeneracy of representation in the great council of America.   It is a melancholy truth, Sir, the effects of which we daily see and feel, that there is not so much wisdom in a certain body as there ought to be, and as the success of our affairs absolutely demands.   Many members of it are no doubt men, in every respect, fit for the trust ; but this cannot be said of it as a body.   Folly, caprice, a want of foresight, comprehension, and dignity, characterize the general tenor of their actions. Of this, I dare say, you are sensible, though you have not perhaps so many opportunities of knowing it as I have.   Their conduct, with respect to the army especially, is feeble, indecisive, and improvident ; insomuch that we are reduced to a more terrible situation than you can conceive. False and contracted views of economy have prevented them, though repeatedly urged to it, from making that provision for officers, which was requisite to interest them in the service.   This has produced such carelessness and indifference to the service, as is subversive of every officer-like quality   They have disgusted the army by repeated instances of the most whimsical favoritism in their promotions ; and by an absurd prodigality of rank to foreigners, and to the meanest staff of the army.   They have not been able to summon resolution enough to withstand the impudent importunity and vain boasting of foreign pretenders ; but have manifested such a ductility and inconstancy in their proceedings, as will warrant the charge of suffering themselves to be bullied by every petty adventurer, who comes armed with ostentatious pretensions of military merit and experience.   Would you believe it, Sir ? it is become almost proverbial in the mouths of the French officers and other foreigners, that they have nothing more to do, to obtain whatever they please, than to assume a high tone, and assert their own merit with confidence and perseverance.   These things wound my feelings as a republican more than I can express, and in some degree make me contemptible in my own eyes.

America once had a representation, that would do honor to any age or nation.   The present falling off is very alarming and dangerous. What is the cause ? and How is it to be remedied ? are questions that the welfare of these States requires should be well attended to.   The great men, who composed our first council, — are they dead, have they deserted the cause, or what has become of them ?   Very few are dead, and still fewer have deserted the cause ; they are all, except the few who still remain in Congress, either in the field or in the civil offices of their respective States ; far the greater part are engaged in the latter.

The only remedy then is to take them out of these employments, and return them to the place where their presence is infinitely more important.

Each State, in order to promote its own internal government and prosperity, has selected its best members to fill the offices within itself, and conduct its own affairs. Men have been fonder of the emoluments and conveniences of being employed at home ; and local attachment, falsely operating, has made them more provident for the particular interests of the States to which they belonged, than for the common interests of the confederacy. This is a most pernicious mistake, and must be corrected. However important it is to give form and efficiency to your interior constitutions and police ; it is infinitely more important to have a wise general council ; otherwise a failure of the measures of the Union will overturn all your labors for the advancement of your particular good, and ruin the common cause. You should not beggar the councils of the United States to enrich the administration of the several members. Realize to yourself the consequences of having a Congress despised at home and abroad. How can the common force be exerted, if the power of collecting it be put in weak, foolish, and unsteady hands? How can we hope for success in our European negotiations, if the nations of Europe have no confidence in the wisdom and vigor of the great Continental government? This is the object on which their eyes are fixed ; hence it is, America will derive its importance or insignificance in their estimation.

You and I had some conversation, when I had the pleasure of seeing you last, with respect to the existence of a certain faction. Since I saw you, I have discovered such convincing traits of the monster, that I cannot doubt its reality in the most extensive sense. I dare say you have seen and heard enough to settle the matter in your own mind. I believe it unmasked its batteries too soon, and begins to hide its head ; but, as I imagine it will only change the storm to a sap, all the true and sensible friends to their country, and of course to a certain great man, ought to be upon the watch, to counterplot the secret machinations of his enemies.

George Washington, *Writings* (edited by Jared Sparks, Boston, 1834), V, Appendix, 508–509.

2 N

CHAPTER XXXI—FIRST STAGE OF THE WAR, 1775–1778

191. Conflicting Accounts of Lexington and Concord (1775)

FROM THE SALEM GAZETTE AND THE LONDON GAZETTE

These two simultaneous accounts show the difficulty of establishing historical truth even by contemporaneous evidence. This battle was the turning-point between the period of protests and the period of resistance. — Bibliography: Winsor, *Narrative and Critical History*, VI, 174–184, and *Memorial History of Boston*, III, 67–103; Channing and Hart, *Guide*, § 136. — For earlier colonial wars, see *Contemporaries*, I, *passim*, and chs. xviii, xix above.

A. THE AMERICAN STATEMENT

Salem, April 25, 1775.

LAST *Wednesday* the 19th of *April*, the Troops of His *Britannick* Majesty commenced hostilities upon the people of this Province, attended with circumstances of cruelty, not less brutal than what our venerable ancestors received from the vilest Savages of the wilderness. The particulars relative to this interesting event, by which we are involved in all the horrours of a civil war, we have endeavoured to collect as well as the present confused state of affairs will admit.

On *Tuesday* evening a detachment from the Army, consisting, it is said, of eight or nine hundred men, commanded by Lieutenant Colonel *Smith*, embarked at the bottom of the Common in *Boston*, on board a number of boats, and landed at *Phipps's* farm, a little way up *Charles* River, from whence they proceeded with silence and expedition on their way to *Concord*, about eighteen miles from *Boston*. The people were soon alarmed, and began to assemble in several Towns, before daylight, in order to watch the motion of the Troops. At *Lexington*, six miles below *Concord*, a company of Militia, of about one hundred men, mustered near the Meeting-House; the Troops came in sight of them just before sunrise; and running within a few rods of them, the Commanding Officer accosted the Militia in words to this effect: "Disperse, you rebels — damn you, throw down your arms and disperse;" upon which the Troops huzzaed, and immediately one or two officers discharged

546

their pistols, which were instantaneously followed by the firing of four or five of the soldiers, and then there seemed to be a general discharge from the whole body : eight of our men were killed, and nine wounded. In a few minutes after this action the enemy renewed their march for *Concord;* at which place they destroyed several Carriages, Carriage Wheels, and about twenty barrels of Flour, all belonging to the Province. Here about one hundred and fifty men going towards a bridge, of which the enemy were in possession, the latter fired and killed two of our men, who then returned the fire, and obliged the enemy to retreat back to *Lexington,* where they met Lord *Percy,* with a large reinforcement, with two pieces of cannon. The enemy now having a body of about eighteen hundred men, made a halt, picked up many of their dead, and took care of their wounded. At *Menotomy,* a few of our men attacked a party of twelve of the enemy, (carrying stores and provisions to the Troops,) killed one of them, wounded several, made the rest prisoners, and took possession of all their arms, stores, provisions, &c., without any loss on our side. The enemy having halted one or two hours at *Lexington,* found it necessary to make a second retreat, carrying with them many of their dead and wounded, who they put into chaises and on horses that they found standing in the road. They continued their retreat from *Lexington* to *Charlestown* with great precipitation ; and notwithstanding their field-pieces, our people continued the pursuit, firing at them till they got to *Charlestown Neck,* (which they reached a little after sunset,) over which the enemy passed, proceeded up *Bunker's* Hill, and soon afterwards went into the Town, under the protection of the *Somerset* Man-of-War of sixty-four guns.

In *Lexington* the enemy set fire to Deacon *Joseph Loring's* house and barn, Mrs. *Mullikin's* house and shop, and Mr. *Joshua Bond's* house and shop, which were all consumed. They also set fire to several other houses, but our people extinguished the flames. They pillaged almost every house they passed by, breaking and destroying doors, windows, glasses, &c., and carrying off clothing and other valuable effects. It appeared to be their design to burn and destroy all before them ; and nothing but our vigorous pursuit prevented their infernal purposes from being put in execution. But the savage barbarity exercised upon the bodies of our unfortunate brethren who fell, is almost incredible : not contented with shooting down the unarmed, aged, and infirm, they disregarded the cries of the wounded, killing them without mercy, and mangling their bodies in the most shocking manner.

We have the pleasure to say, that, notwithstanding the highest provocations given by the enemy, not one instance of cruelty, that we have heard of, was committed by our victorious Militia; but, listening to the merciful dictates of the Christian religion, they "breathed higher sentiments of humanity."

The consternation of the people of *Charlestown*, when our enemies were entering the Town, is inexpressible; the Troops however behaved tolerably civil, and the people have since nearly all left the Town.

The following is a List of the Provincials who were killed and wounded:
    [49 killed; 34 wounded; 5 missing.] . . .

Mr. *James Howard* and one of the Regulars discharged their pieces at the same instant, and each killed the other. . . .

The publick most sincerely sympathize with the friends and relations of our deceased brethren, who gloriously sacrificed their lives in fighting for the liberties of their Country. By their noble and intrepid conduct, in helping to defeat the forces of an ungrateful tyrant, they have endeared their memories to the present generation, who will transmit their names to posterity with the highest honour.

B. THE BRITISH STATEMENT

Whitehall, June 10, 1775.

LIEUTENANT *Nunn*, of the Navy, arrived this morning at Lord *Dartmouth's*, and brought letters from General *Gage*, Lord *Percy*, and Lieutenant-Colonel *Smith*, containing the following particulars of what passed on the nineteenth of *April* last between a detachment of the King's Troops in the Province of *Massachusetts-Bay*, and several parties of rebel Provincials, viz:

General *Gage* having received intelligence of a quantity of military stores being collected at *Concord*, for the avowed purpose of supplying a body of troops to act in opposition to His Majesty's Government, detached, on the eighteenth of *April* at night, the Grenadiers of his Army, and the Light-Infantry, under the command of Lieutenant-Colonel *Smith*, of the Tenth Regiment, and Major *Pitcairn*, of the Marines, with orders to destroy the said stores; and the next morning eight Companies of the Fourth, the same number of the Twenty-Third and Forty-Ninth, and some Marines, marched under the command of Lord *Percy*, to support the other detachment.

Lieutenant-Colonel *Smith* finding, after he had advanced some miles on his march, that the country had been alarmed by the firing of guns and ringing of bells, despatched six Companies of Light-Infantry, in order to secure two bridges on different roads beyond *Concord*, who, upon their arrival at *Lexington*, found a body of the country people under arms, on a green close to the road ; and upon the King's Troops marching up to them, in order to inquire the reason of their being so assembled, they went off in great confusion, and several guns were fired upon the King's Troops from behind a stone wall, and also from the meeting-house and other houses, by which one man was wounded, and Major *Pitcairn's* horse shot in two places. In consequence of this attack by the rebels, the troops returned the fire and killed several of them. After which the detachment marched on to *Concord* without any thing further happening, where they effected the purpose for which they were sent, having knocked off the trunnions of three pieces of iron ordnance, burnt some new gun carriages and a great number of carriage-wheels, and thrown into the river a considerable quantity of flour, gunpowder, musket-balls, and other articles. Whilst this service was performing, great numbers of the rebels assembled in many parts, and a considerable body of them attacked the Light-Infantry, posted at one of the bridges, on which an action ensued, and some few were killed and wounded.

On the return of the Troops from *Concord*, they were very much annoyed, and had several men killed and wounded by the rebels firing from behind walls, ditches, trees, and other ambushes ; but the brigade, under the command of Lord *Percy*, having joined them at *Lexington* with two pieces of cannon, the rebels were for a while dispersed ; but as soon as the troops resumed their march, they began to fire upon them from behind stone walls and houses, and kept up in that manner a scattering fire during the whole of their march of fifteen miles, by which means several were killed and wounded ; and such was the cruelty and barbarity of the rebels, that they scalped and cut off the ears of some of the wounded men who fell into their hands.

It is not known what numbers of the rebels were killed and wounded, but it is supposed that their loss was considerable.

General *Gage* says that too much praise cannot be given to Lord *Percy* for his remarkable activity during the whole day ; and that Lieutenant-Colonel *Smith* and Major *Pitcairn* did every thing that men could do, as did all the officers in general, and that the men behaved with their usual intrepidity.

Return of the Commission, Non-commission Officers, and Rank and File, killed, wounded, prisoners, and missing, on the 19*th of April,* 1775. . . .

Total : One Lieutenant-Colonel killed ; two Lieutenant-Colonels wounded ; two Captains wounded ; nine Lieutenants wounded ; one Lieutenant missing ; two Ensigns wounded ; one Sergeant killed, four wounded, two missing ; one Drummer killed, one wounded ; sixty-two rank and file killed, one hundred and fifty-seven wounded, and twenty-four missing.

N. B. Lieutenant *Isaac Potter* reported to be wounded and taken prisoner.

Salem Gazette, April 25, 1775 ; reprinted in Peter Force, *American Archives,* Fourth Series (Washington, 1839), II, 391–393 *passim.*
Official bulletin, *London Gazette,* June 10, 1775 ; reprinted *Ibid.*, 945–946 *passim.*

———◆———

192. A Woman at the Front (1775-1776)

BY MRS. ABIGAIL ADAMS

Mrs. Adams was one of the most famous women of the Revolutionary time. These letters, directed to her husband, John Adams, then in Congress, illustrate one of the most valuable kinds of sources, private letters written by well-informed persons but not intended for publication. — Bibliography of Mrs. Adams : Memoir, in *Letters of Mrs. Adams.* — Bibliography of the siege and capture of Boston : Winsor, *Narrative and Critical History,* VI, 152–158, and *Memorial History of Boston,* III, 67–118 ; Frothingham, *Siege of Boston ;* Channing and Hart, *Guide,* § 136.

Sunday, 18 June, 1775. . . .

THE day, — perhaps, the decisive day, — is come, on which the fate of America depends. My bursting heart must find vent at my pen. I have just heard, that our dear friend, Dr. Warren, is no more, but fell gloriously fighting for his country ; saying, better to die honorably in the field, than ignominiously hang upon the gallows. Great is our loss. He has distinguished himself in every engagement, by his courage and fortitude, by animating the soldiers, and leading them on by his own example. A particular account of these dreadful, but I hope glorious days will be transmitted you, no doubt, in the exactest manner.

" The race is not to the swift, nor the battle to the strong ; but the God of Israel is he, that giveth strength and power unto his people. Trust in him at all times, ye people, pour out your hearts before him ;

God is a refuge for us." Charlestown is laid in ashes. The battle began upon our intrenchments upon Bunker's Hill, Saturday morning about three o'clock, and has not ceased yet, and it is now three o'clock Sabbath afternoon.

It is expected they will come out over the Neck to-night, and a dreadful battle must ensue. Almighty God, cover the heads of our countrymen, and be a shield to our dear friends! How many have fallen, we know not. The constant roar of the cannon is so distressing, that we cannot eat, drink, or sleep. May we be supported and sustained in the dreadful conflict. I shall tarry here till it is thought unsafe by my friends, and then I have secured myself a retreat at your brother's, who has kindly offered me part of his house. I cannot compose myself to write any further at present. I will add more as I hear further. . . .

. . . 16 July, 1775. . . .

The appointment of the generals Washington and Lee gives universal satisfaction. The people have the highest opinion of Lee's abilities, but you know the continuation of the popular breath depends much upon favorable events. I had the pleasure of seeing both the generals and their aids-de-camp soon after their arrival, and of being personally made known to them. They very politely express their regard for you. . . .

I was struck with General Washington. You had prepared me to entertain a favorable opinion of him, but I thought the half was not told me. Dignity with ease and complacency, the gentleman and soldier, look agreeably blended in him. Modesty marks every line and feature of his face. . . .

. . . As to intelligence from Boston, it is but very seldom we are able to collect any thing that may be relied on ; and to report the vague, flying rumors, would be endless. I heard yesterday, by one Mr. Roulstone, a goldsmith, who got out in a fishing schooner, that their distress increased upon them fast. Their beef is all spent ; their malt and cider all gone. All the fresh provisions they can procure, they are obliged to give to the sick and wounded. Thirteen of our men who were in jail, and were wounded at the battle of Charlestown, were dead. No man dared now to be seen talking to his friend in the street. They were obliged to be within, every evening, at ten o'clock, according to martial law ; nor could any inhabitant walk any street in town after that time, without a pass from Gage. He has ordered all the molasses to be distilled up into rum for the soldiers; taken away all licenses, and given out others, obliging to a forfeiture of ten pounds, if any rum is sold without written orders from the general. . . .

As to the situation of the camps, our men are in general healthy, much more so at Roxbury than at Cambridge, and the camp is in vastly better order. General Thomas has the character of an excellent officer. His merit has certainly been overlooked, as modest merit generally is. I hear General Washington is much pleased with his conduct.

Every article here in the West India way is very scarce and dear. In six weeks we shall not be able to purchase any article of the kind. I wish you would let Bass get me one pound of pepper, and two yards of black calamanco for shoes. I cannot wear leather, if I go barefoot. Bass may make a fine profit if he lays in a stock for himself. You can hardly imagine how much we want many common small articles, which are not manufactured amongst ourselves; but we will have them in time; not one pin to be purchased for love or money. I wish you could convey me a thousand by any friend travelling this way. It is very provoking to have such a plenty so near us, but, Tantalus-like, not be able to touch. I should have been glad to have laid in a small stock of the West India articles, but I cannot get one copper; no person thinks of paying any thing, and I do not choose to run in debt.

We have not yet been much distressed for grain. Every thing at present looks blooming. O that peace would once more extend her olive branch . . . .

. . . 12 November, 1775.

The intelligence you will receive before this reaches you, will, I should think, make a plain path, though a dangerous one, for you. I could not join to-day, in the petitions of our worthy pastor, for a reconciliation between our no longer parent state, but tyrant state, and these colonies. Let us separate; they are unworthy to be our brethren. Let us renounce them; and, instead of supplications as formerly, for their prosperity and happiness, let us beseech the Almighty to blast their counsels, and bring to nought all their devices. . . .

Saturday Evening, 2 March, 1776. . . .

. . . I heartily wish every Tory was extirpated from America; they are continually, by secret means, undermining and injuring our cause.

I am charmed with the sentiments of "Common Sense," and wonder how an honest heart, one who wishes the welfare of his country and the happiness of posterity, can hesitate one moment at adopting them. I want to know how these sentiments are received in Congress. I dare say there would be no difficulty in procuring a vote and instructions from all the Assemblies in New England for Independency. I most sincerely wish, that now, in the lucky moment, it might be done.

I have been kept in a continual state of anxiety and expectation, ever since you left me. It has been said "to-morrow" and "to-morrow" for this month, but when the dreadful to-morrow will be, I know not. But hark! The house this instant shakes with the roar of cannon. I have been to the door and find it is a cannonade from our army. Orders, I find, are come for all the remaining militia to repair to the lines Monday night by twelve o'clock. No sleep for me to-night. And if I cannot, who have no guilt upon my soul with regard to this cause, how shall the miserable wretches, who have been the procurers of this dreadful scene, and those who are to be the actors, lie down with the load of guilt upon their souls?

Sunday Evening, 3 March.

I went to bed after twelve, but got no rest; the cannon continued firing, and my heart beat pace with them all night. We have had a pretty quiet day, but what to-morrow will bring forth, God only knows.

Monday Evening.

Tolerably quiet. To-day the militia have all mustered, with three days' provision, and are all marched by three o'clock this afternoon, though their notice was no longer ago than eight o'clock, Saturday. And now we have scarcely a man, but our regular guards, either in Weymouth, Hingham, Braintree, or Milton, and the militia from the more remote towns are called in as seacoast guards. Can you form to yourself an idea of our sensations?

I have just returned from Penn's Hill, where I have been sitting to hear the amazing roar of cannon, and from whence I could see every shell which was thrown. The sound, I think, is one of the grandest in nature, and is of the true species of the sublime. 'Tis now an incessant roar; but O! the fatal ideas, which are connected with the sound! How many of our dear countrymen must fall!

Tuesday Morning.

I went to bed about twelve, and rose again a little after one. I could no more sleep, than if I had been in the engagement; the rattling of the windows, the jar of the house, the continual roar of twenty-four pounders, and the bursting of shells, give us such ideas, and realize a scene to us of which we could form scarcely any conception. About six, this morning, there was quiet. I rejoiced in a few hours' calm. I hear we got possession of Dorchester hill last night; four thousand men upon it to-day; lost but one man. The ships are all drawn round the town. To-night we shall realize a more terrible scene still. I sometimes think I cannot stand it. I wish myself with you, out of hearing, as I cannot assist them. I hope to give you joy of Boston, even if it is in ruins, before I send this away. I am too much agitated to write as I ought, and languid for want of rest.

Charles Francis Adams, editor, *Letters of Mrs. Adams* (Boston, 1840), I, 39-90 *passim*.

---

193. Abandonment of New York (1776)

BY GENERAL GEORGE CLINTON

Clinton was a New York man, later vice-president of the United States. — Bibliography of the Long Island and New York campaign: Winsor, *Narrative and Critical History*, VI, 315-317; James Grant Wilson, *Memorial History of New York*, II, 515-517; Channing and Hart, *Guide*, § 138.

King's Bridge, September 18, 1776. . . .

ABOUT the middle of last week it was determined, for many reasons, to evacuate the City of *New-York;* and accordingly, orders were given for removing the ordnance, military, and other stores from thence, which, by *Sunday* morning was nearly effected. On *Saturday*, four of the enemy's large ships passed by the city up the *North River*, and anchored near *Grenage*, and about as many up the *East River*, which anchored in *Turtle Bay;* and from the movements of the enemy on *Long-Island* and the small Islands in the *East River*, we had great reason to apprehend they intended to make a landing, and attack our lines somewhere near the city. Our army for some days had been moving upwards this way, and encamping on the heights, southwest of Colonel *Morris's*, where we intended to form lines, and make our grand stand. On *Sunday* morning the enemy landed a very considerable body of troops, principally consisting of their Light Infantry and Grenadiers, near *Turtle Bay*, under cover of a very heavy cannonade from their shipping. Our lines were but thinly manned, as they were then intended only to secure a retreat to the rear of our army, and unfortunately by such troops as were so little disposed to stand in the way of grape-shot that the main body of them almost instantly retreated, nay, fled, without a possibility of rallying them, though General *Washington* himself, (who rid to the spot on hearing the cannonade) with some other General Officers, exerted themselves to effect it.

The enemy, on landing, immediately formed a line across the Island. Most of our people were luckily north of it, and joined the army. The few that were in the city crossed the river, chiefly to *Paulus-Hook*, so that our loss in men, artillery, or stores, is very inconsiderable ; I don't believe it exceeds one hundred men, and I fancy most of them, from their conduct, staid out of choice. Before evening, the enemy landed the main body of their army, took possession of the city, and marched up the Island, and encamped on the heights extending from *McGown's* and the *Black-Horse* to the *North River*.

On *Monday* morning, about ten o'clock, a party of the enemy, consisting of *Highlanders, Hessians*, the Light Infantry, Grenadiers, and *English* troops, (number uncertain,) attacked our advanced party, commanded by Colonel *Knowlton*, at *Martje Davit's Fly*. They were opposed with spirit, and soon made to retreat to a clear field, southwest of that about two hundred paces, where they lodged themselves behind a fence covered with bushes. Our people attacked them in front, and caused them to retreat a second time, leaving five dead on the spot. We pursued them to a buckwheat field on the top of a high hill, distant about four hundred paces, where they received a considerable reinforcement, with several field-pieces, and there made a stand. A very brisk action ensued at this place, which continued about two hours. Our people at length worsted them a third time, caused them to fall back into an orchard, from thence across a hollow, and up another hill not far distant from their own lines. A large column of the enemy's army being at this time discovered to be in motion, and the ground we then occupied being rather disadvantageous, a retreat likewise, without bringing on a general action, (which we did not think prudent to risk,) rather insecure, our party was therefore ordered in, and the enemy was well contented to hold the last ground we drove them to.

We lost, on this occasion, Colonel *Knowlton*, a brave officer, and sixteen privates, killed. Major *Leitch*, from *Virginia*, and about eight or ten subaltern officers and privates wounded. The loss of the enemy is uncertain. They carried their dead and wounded off, in and soon after the action; but we have good evidence of their having upwards of sixty killed, and violent presumption of one hundred. The action, in the whole, lasted about four hours.

I consider our success in this small affair, at this time, almost equal to a victory. It has animated our troops, gave them new spirits, and erased every bad impression the retreat from *Long-Island*, &c., had left on their minds. They find they are able, with inferiour numbers, to drive their enemy, and think of nothing now but conquest.

Since the above affair, nothing material has happened. The enemy keep close to their lines. Our advance parties continue at their former station. We are daily throwing up works to prevent the enemy's advancing. Great attention is paid to *Fort Washington*, the posts opposite to it on the *Jersey* shore, and the obstructions in the river, which, I have reason to believe, are already effectual, so as to prevent their shipping passing; however, it is intended still to add to them, as it is of the utmost consequence to keep the enemy below us.

Peter Force, *American Archives*, Fifth Series (Washington, 1851), II, 383–384 *passim*.

———◆———

194. The Foundation of the Navy (1776)

BY ROBERT MORRIS

Morris was a Philadelphia merchant and banker, considered the richest colonist of his time. He was a member of Congress; from 1781 to 1784 superintendent of finance; later senator from Pennsylvania. This piece is from a letter written to the commissioners in France. — Bibliography of the navy: Winsor, *Narrative and Critical History*, VI, 589; Maclay, *United States Navy*, I, pt. i, chs. iii–vi; Channing and Hart, *Guide*, §§ 139, 140. — See Nos. 177 above and 204 below.

[Philadelphia, December 21, 1776.]

YOU will doubtless be surprised that we have not made better progress with our Navy, because you are unacquainted with the many difficulties and causes of delay that have encountered us. The want of sea-coal for our anchor-smiths has been a great bar to our progress, the disappointment in our first attempts to cast cannon has been another, but above all, we have been hindered by the constant calling out of our Militia, in a manner that did not admit of the necessary tradesmen being exempted. You will wonder at this; it would be a long story to unfold the reasons, therefore suffice that it is so. Doctor *Franklin* can inform you of many particulars respecting the Flying-Camp; therefore, I shall give you the present state of our Navy, according to the best of my knowledge at this time.

The frigate in *New-Hampshire* is a very fine ship, completed in every particular, except the want of cannon, which was to have been cast in *Rhode-Island,* but the spirit of privateering has prevailed so eminently there, that they have sacrificed every other pursuit to it, both publick and private, as I am informed ; and we have ordered the guns cast in *Connecticut* for that frigate to be sent to *Portsmouth.* As soon as they arrive, the *Raleigh* will be manned, and sail on a cruise.

At *Boston* they have also two fine frigates. The *Boston,* of twenty-four guns, I expect is at sea before this time, commanded by Captain *McNeil,* a very clever officer. The other is nearly ready, commanded by Captain *Manly.*

In *Rhode-Island* were built the two worst frigates, as I have been informed by those that have seen the whole. These two are completely fitted, and were partly manned when we last heard from them ; so that I hope they are now at sea.

In *Connecticut,* the frigate is said to be a fine ship ; but she cannot get to sea this winter for want of cordage and other stores.

In *New-York,* two very fine frigates are blocked up by the enemy, and hauled into *Esopus Creek* for safety.

At this place, we have four very fine ships. One of them, the *Randolph,* Captain *Biddle,* of twenty-six twelve-pounders, will, I hope, go to sea in company with this letter ; another, the *Delaware,* Captain *Alexander,* is getting ready, and I hope will get out this winter. The other two want guns, anchors, and men.

At *Baltimore,* is a fine frigate, now only waiting for an anchor and men.

Besides these, we have in service, the *Alfred, Columbus,* and *Reprisal,* ships from sixteen to twenty-four guns, the brigantines *Cabot, Camden, Andrew Doria,* and *Lexington,* of twelve to sixteen guns ; the sloops *Providence, Hornet, Fly, Independence, Sachem ;* and schooners *Wasp, Musquito,* and *Georgia Packet,* all in actual service ; and they have had great success in taking valuable prizes, as indeed have numbers of privateers from all parts of *America.* We have besides, two very fine row-galleys, built here, of ninety feet keel, but they are not yet rigged ; and it has lately been determined by Congress to build some line-of-battle ships, and at all events to push forward and pay the utmost attention to an *American* Navy.

The greatest encouragement is given to seamen, which ought to be made known throughout *Europe*. Their pay in our Navy is eight dollars per month, with the best chance for prize money that men ever had, and liberty of discharges after every cruise, if they choose it. In the merchant service they now get from thirty to forty dollars per month; and this leads me to the state of our commerce.

In the Eastern States they are so intent on privateering that they mind little else. However, there is some exportation of produce from thence, and as to imports, they are the best supplied of any part of *America*, having been surprisingly successful in captures. *New-York* being in the hands of the enemy, we have nothing to say to it; and the produce of *New-Jersey* will be totally consumed by their army and ours. In this State, (*Pennsylvania*,) we had last season the worst crop of wheat ever known, both as to quantity and quality. This being our staple commodity, and stores prohibited, our merchants have been led to purchase much tobacco in *Maryland* and *Virginia*, and their ships are employed in the export of this article, with some flour, boards, bees-wax, &c. We have a good many imports, but as fast as goods arrive, they are bought up for the Army, or for the use of neighbouring States, and therefore continue to bear high prices.

The value of ships has risen in the same enormous proportion with every thing else, and ships that were deemed worth £1,000 twelve months ago, now sell for £3,000, or upwards. Every article belonging to them is also excessively dear, and hard to be got, and the insolence and difficulty of seamen is beyond bearing. In *Maryland, Virginia, South-Carolina*, and *Georgia*, they have plenty of valuable produce on hand, but no ships to carry it away, and constant cruisers all along the coast make it very dangerous to send ships from one port to another; so that look which way you will, you find us surrounded with difficulties — in the land service, in the sea service, and in our commerce.

Agriculture and mechanicks have their impediments, by the enlisting of soldiers, and frequent calls on the Militia. In short, nothing but the most arduous exertions, and virtuous conduct in the leaders, seconded by a spirited behaviour in the Army, and a patient endurance of hard-ships by the people in general, can long support the contest; therefore the Court of *France* should strike at once, as they will reap an imme-diate harvest. They may sell their manufactures for any price they please to ask; they will get in payment tobacco, rice, indigo, deer-skins, furs, wheat, flour, iron, beeswax, lumber, fish, oil, whalebone, pot and pearl ashes, and various other articles, and, if they please, here is an ample field to employ their shipping, and raise seamen for their Navy.

Peter Force, *American Archives*, Fifth Series (Washington, 1853), III, 1335–1336.

---

195. "The Game is pretty near up" (1776)

BY GENERAL GEORGE WASHINGTON

These letters, written to Washington's brother and the president of Congress, December 18 and 20, 1776, afford an inside view of the discouragements of the winter of 1776–77. Nothing but Washington's own indomitable resolution prevented the collapse of the Revolution. — For Washington, see Winsor, *Narrative and Critical History*, VII, 299–301; Lodge, *George Washington.* — Bibliography of the period: Winsor, *Narrative and Critical History*, VI, 403–447; Carrington, *Battles of the Revolution*, 247–297; Channing and Hart, *Guide*, § 138.

A. TO AUGUSTINE WASHINGTON

OWING to the number of letters I write, the recollection of any particular one is destroyed, but I think my last to you was by Colonel Woodford, from Hackinsac. Since that time, and a little before, our affairs have taken an adverse turn, but not more than was to be expected from the unfortunate measures, which had been adopted for the establishment of our army. The Retreat of the Enemy from the White Plains led me to think, that they would turn their thoughts to the Jerseys, if no farther, and induced me to cross the North River with some of the Troops, in order if possible to oppose them. I expected to have met at least five thousand men of the Flying Camp and militia; instead of which I found less than one half of that number, and no disposition in the Inhabitants to afford the least aid. This being perfectly well known to the Enemy, they threw over a large body of Troops, which pushed us from place to place, till we were obliged to cross the Delaware with less than three thousand men fit for duty, owing to the dissolution of our force by short Enlistments; the Enemy's numbers, from the best accounts, exceeding ten or twelve thousand men. . . .

. . . We are in a very disaffected part of the Province; and, between you and me, I think our affairs are in a very bad situation; not so much from the apprehension of General Howe's army, as from the defection of New York, Jerseys, and Pennsylvania. . . .

I have no doubt but General Howe will still make an attempt upon

Philadelphia this winter.   I see nothing to oppose him a fortnight hence, as the time of all the troops, except those of Virginia reduced (almost to nothing,) and Smallwood's Regiment of Maryland, equally as bad, will expire in less than that time.   In a word, my dear Sir, if every nerve is not strained to recruit the new army with all possible expedition, I think the game is pretty near up, owing, in a great measure, to the insidious arts of the Enemy, and disaffection of the colonies before mentioned, but principally to the accursed policy of short enlistments, and placing too great a dependence on the militia, the evil consequences of which were foretold fifteen months ago, with a spirit almost Prophetic.   Before this reaches you, you will no doubt have heard of the captivity of Géneral Lee.   This is an additional misfortune, and the more vexatious, as it was by his own folly and Imprudence, (and without a view to answer any good,) he was taken, going three miles out of his own camp, and within twenty of the enemy to lodge, a rascally Tory rid in the night to give notice of it to the enemy, who sent a party of light-Horse that seized and carried him, with every mark of triumph and indignity.

You can form no idea of the perplexity of my situation.   No man, I believe, ever had a greater choice of difficulties, and less means to extricate himself from them.   However, under a full persuasion of the justice of our cause, I cannot entertain an Idea, that it will finally sink, tho' it may remain for some time under a cloud. . . .

B. TO THE PRESIDENT OF CONGRESS

. . .   THE present exigency of our affairs will not admit of delay, either in council or the field ; for well convinced I am, that, if the enemy go into quarters at all, it will be for a short season.   But I rather think the design of General Howe is to possess himself of Philadelphia this winter, if possible ; and in truth I do not see what is to prevent him, as ten days more will put an end to the existence of our army.   That one great point is to keep us as much harassed as possible, with a view to injure the recruiting service and hinder a collection of stores and other necessaries for the next campaign, I am as clear in, as I am of my existence.   If, therefore, we have to provide in the short interval and make these great and arduous preparations, every matter that in its nature is self-evident is to be referred to Congress, at the distance of a hundred and thirty or forty miles, so much time must necessary elapse, as to defeat the end in view.

It may be said, that this is an application for powers that are too dangerous to be entrusted. I can only add, that desperate diseases require desperate remedies; and I with truth declare, that I have no lust after power, but I wish with as much fervency as any man upon this wide-extended continent for an opportunity of turning the sword into the ploughshare. But my feelings, as an officer and a man, have been such as to force me to say, that no person ever had a greater choice of difficulties to contend with than I have. It is needless to add, that short enlistments, and a mistaken dependence upon militia, have been the origin of all our misfortunes, and the great accumulation of our debt. We find, Sir, that the enemy are daily gathering strength from the disaffected. This strength, like a snow-ball by rolling, will increase, unless some means can be devised to check effectually the progress of the enemy's arms. Militia may possibly do it for a little while; but in a little while, also, and the militia of those States, which have been frequently called upon, will not turn out at all; or, if they do, it will be with so much reluctance and sloth, as to amount to the same thing. Instance New Jersey! Witness Pennsylvania! Could any thing but the river Delaware have saved Philadelphia? Can any thing (the exigency of the case indeed may justify it) be more destructive to the recruiting service, than giving ten dollars' bounty for six weeks' service of the militia, who come in, you cannot tell how, go, you cannot tell when, and act, you cannot tell where, consume your provisions, exhaust your stores, and leave you at last at a critical moment?

These, Sir, are the men I am to depend upon, ten days hence; this is the basis, on which your cause will and must for ever depend, till you get a large standing army sufficient of itself to oppose the enemy. I therefore beg leave to give it as my humble opinion, that eighty-eight battalions are by no means equal to the opposition you are to make, and that a moment's time is not to be lost in raising a greater number, not less, in my opinion and the opinion of my officers, than a hundred and ten. It may be urged that it will be found difficult enough to complete the first number. This may be true, and yet the officers of a hundred and ten battalions will recruit many more men, than those of eighty-eight. In my judgment this is not a time to stand upon expense; our funds are not the only object of consideration. The State of New York have added one battalion (I wish they had made it two) to their quota. If any good officers will offer to raise men upon Continental pay and establishment in this quarter, I shall encourage them to do so, and

2 O

regiment them when they have done it.   If Congress disapprove of this proceeding, they will please to signify it, as I mean it for the best.   It may be thought that I am going a good deal out of the line of my duty, to adopt these measures, or to advise thus freely.   A character to lose, an estate to forfeit, the inestimable blessing of liberty at stake, and a life devoted, must be my excuse.

George Washington, *Writings* (edited by Worthington Chauncey Ford, New York, etc., 1890), V, 109–116 *passim.*

---

196. "The Battle of the Kegs" (1777)

BY FRANCIS HOPKINSON

This cheerful satire illustrates the occupation of Philadelphia by the British in 1777.   The note at the end of the piece is by Hopkinson (see No. 96 above). — Bibliography: Winsor, *Narrative and Critical History*, VI, 404–405; Channing and Hart, *Guide*, § 138.

GALLANTS attend and hear a friend,
　　Trill forth harmonious ditty,
Strange things I'll tell which late befel
　　In Philadelphia city.

'Twas early day, as poets say,
　　Just when the sun was rising,
A soldier stood on a log of wood,
　　And saw a thing surprising.

As in amaze he stood to gaze,
　　The truth can't be denied, sir,
He spied a score of kegs or more
　　Come floating down the tide, sir.

A sailor too in jerkin blue,
　　This strange appearance viewing,
First damn'd his eyes, in great surprise,
　　Then said some mischief's brewing.

These kegs, I'm told, the rebels bold,
　　Pack'd up like pickling herring ;
And they're come down t' attack the town,
　　In this new way of ferrying.

The soldier flew, the sailor too,
    And scar'd almost to death, sir,
Wore out their shoes, to spread the news,
    And ran till out of breath, sir.

Now up and down throughout the town,
    Most frantic scenes were acted ;
And some ran here, and others there,
    Like men almost distracted.

Some fire cry'd, which some denied,
    But said the earth had quaked ;
And girls and boys, with hideous noise,
    Ran thro' the streets half naked.

Sir William he, snug as a flea,
    Lay all this time a snoring,
Nor dream'd of harm as he lay warm,
    In bed with Mrs. L——g.

Now in a fright, he starts upright,
    Awak'd by such a clatter ;
He rubs both eyes, and boldly cries,
    For God's sake, what's the matter?

At his bed-side he then espy'd,
    Sir Erskine at command, sir,
Upon one foot, he had one boot,
    And th' other in his hand, sir.

" Arise, arise, sir Erskine cries,
    The rebels — more's the pity,
Without a boat are all afloat,
    And rang'd before the city.

" The motly crew, in vessels new,
    With Satan for their guide, sir.
Pack'd up in bags, or wooden kegs,
    Come driving down the tide, sir.

"Therefore prepare for bloody war,
    These kegs must all be routed,
Or surely we despised shall be,
    And British courage doubted."

The royal band, now ready stand
    All rang'd in dread array, sir,
With stomach stout to see it out,
    And make a bloody day, sir.

The cannons roar from shore to shore.
    The small arms make a rattle ;
Since wars began I'm sure no man
    E'er saw so strange a battle.

The rebel dales, the rebel vales,
    With rebel trees surrounded ;
The distant wood, the hills and floods,
    With rebel echos sounded.

The fish below swam to and fro,
    Attack'd from ev'ry quarter ;
Why sure, thought they, the devil's to pay,
    'Mongst folks above the water.

The kegs, 'tis said, tho' strongly made,
    Of rebel staves and hoops, sir,
Could not oppose their powerful foes,
    The conqu'ring British troops, sir.

From morn to night these men of might
    Display'd amazing courage ;
And when the sun was fairly down,
    Retir'd to sup their porrage.

An hundred men with each a pen,
    Or more upon my word, sir.
It is most true would be too few,
    . Their valour to record, sir.

> Such feats did they perform that day,
>   Against these wick'd kegs, sir,
> That years to come, if they get home,
>   They'll make their boasts and brags, sir.

N. B. This ballad was occasioned by a real incident. Certain machines, in the form of kegs, charg'd with gun powder, were sent down the river to annoy the British shipping then at Philadelphia. The danger of these machines being discovered, the British manned the wharfs and shipping, and discharged their small arms and cannons at every thing they saw floating in the river during the ebb tide.

Francis Hopkinson, *Miscellaneous Essays and Occasional Writings* (Philadelphia, 1792), III, *Poems*, 169–173.

---◆---

197. The Surrender of Burgoyne (1777)

BY FREDERIKA CHARLOTTE LOUISE, BARONESS VON RIEDESEL

(Translated by Jules Wallenstein, 1827)

This spirited lady was the wife of General Riedesel, who commanded part of the German troops in Burgoyne's army. After the surrender, both husband and wife were prisoners in Cambridge and in Virginia. This is one of the best accounts that we have of the conditions of the British army. — Bibliography of Madame Riedesel: Winsor, *Narrative and Critical History*, VII, 75. — Bibliography of Burgoyne's campaign: Winsor, *Narrative and Critical History*, VI, 348–366; William L. Stone, *Campaign of Burgoyne;* Channing and Hart, *Guide*, § 138.

WE were halted at six o'clock in the morning [October 9, 1777], to our general amazement. General Burgoyne ordered the artillery to be drawn up in a line, and to have it counted. This gave much dissatisfaction, as a few marches more would have ensured our safety. My husband was exhausted by fatigue, and took a seat in the calash, where my maids made room for him ; and he slept for three hours upon my shoulder. In the mean time, captain Willoe brought me his pocket-book, containing bank-notes, and captain Geismar, a beautiful watch, a ring, and a well-provided purse, requesting me to keep them, which I promised to do to the last. At length we recommenced our march ; but scarcely an hour had elapsed, before the army was again halted, because the enemy was in sight. They were but two hundred in number, who came to reconnoitre, and who might easily have been taken, had not general Burgoyne lost all his presence of mind. The rain fell in torrents. . . . On the 9th, it rained terribly the whole day ; nevertheless we kept ourselves ready to march. The savages had lost their courage, and they walked off in all d.rections. The least untoward event made them dispirited, especially when there was no opportunity for plunder. My chamber-maid exclaimed the whole day against her fate, and seemed mad with despair. I begged her to be quiet, unless she wished to be taken for a savage. Upon this she became still more extravagant, and asked me, " If I should be sorry for it ? " — " Surely," replied I. — She then tore her cap from her head, and let her hair fall upon her face. " You take it quite easily," said she, " for you have your husband ; but we have nothing but the prospect of being killed, or of losing the little we possess." . . .

We reached Saratoga about dark, which was but half an hour's march from the place where we had spent the day. I was quite wet, and was obliged to remain in that condition, for want of a place to change my apparel. I seated myself near the fire, and undressed the children, and we then laid ourselves upon some straw. — I asked general Phillips, who came to see how I was, why we did not continue our retreat, my husband having pledged himself to cover the movement, and to bring off the army in safety. " My poor lady," said he, " you astonish me. Though quite wet, you have so much courage as to wish to go farther in this weather. What a pity it is that you are not our commanding general ! He complains of fatigue, and has determined upon spending the night here, and giving us a supper." It is very true, that general Burgoyne liked to make himself easy, and that he spent half his nights in singing and drinking, and diverting himself . . . I refreshed myself at 7 o'clock, the next morning, (the 10th of October,) with a cup of tea, and we all expected that we should soon continue our march. . . . About 2 o'clock, we heard again a report of muskets and cannon, and there was much alarm and bustle among our troops. My husband sent me word, that I should immediately retire into a house which was not far off. I got into my calash with my children, and when we were near the house, I saw, on the opposite bank of the Hudson, five or six men, who aimed at us with their guns. Without knowing what I did, I threw my children into the back part of the vehicle, and laid myself upon them. At the same moment the fellow fired, and broke the arm of a poor English soldier, who stood behind us, and who being already wounded, sought a shelter. Soon after our arrival, a terrible cannonade began, and the fire was principally directed against the house, where we had hoped to find a refuge, probably because the enemy inferred, from the great number of people who went towards it, that this was the head-quarters of the generals, while, in reality, none were there except women and crippled soldiers. We were at last obliged to descend into the cellar, where I laid myself in a corner near the door. My children put their heads upon my knees. An abominable smell, the cries of the children, and my own anguish of mind, did not permit me to close my eyes, during the whole night. On the next morning, the cannonade begun anew, but in a different direction. . . . Eleven cannon-balls passed through the house, and made a tremendous noise. A poor soldier, who was about to have a leg amputated, lost the other by one of these balls. All his comrades ran away at that moment, and when they returned, they found him in one corner of the room, in the agonies of death. I was myself in the deepest distress, not so much on account of my own dangers, as of those to which my husband was exposed, who, however, frequently sent me messages, inquiring after my health. . . .

The want of water continuing to distress us, we could not but be extremely glad to find a soldier's wife so spirited as to fetch some from the river, an occupation from which the boldest might have shrunk, as the Americans shot every one who approached it. They told us after-wards that they spared her on account of her sex. . . .

On the 17th of October, the capitulation was carried into effect. The generals waited upon the American general Gates, and the troops surrendered themselves prisoners of war and laid down their arms. The time had now come for the good woman who had risked her life to supply us with water, to receive the reward of her services. Each of us threw a handful of money into her apron; and she thus received more than twenty guineas. At such a moment at least, if at no other, the heart easily overflows with gratitude.

At last, my husband's groom brought me a message to join him with the children. I once more seated myself in my dear calash, and, while riding through the American camp, was gratified to observe that no body looked at us with disrespect, but, on the contrary, greeted us, and seemed touched at the sight of a captive mother with three children. I must candidly confess that I did not present myself, though so situated, with much courage to the enemy, for the thing was entirely new to me. When I drew near the tents, a good looking man advanced towards me, and helped the children from the calash, and kissed and caressed them :

he then offered me his arm, and tears trembled in his eyes. " You tremble," said he ; " do not be alarmed, I pray you." " Sir," cried I, " a countenance so expressive of benevolence, and the kindness which you have evinced towards my children, are sufficient to dispel all apprehension." He then ushered me into the tent of general Gates . . . .

. . . The gentleman who had received me with so much kindness, came and said to me, " You may find it embarrassing to be the only lady in such a large company of gentlemen ; will you come with your children to my tent, and partake of a frugal dinner, offered with the best will ? " " By the kindness you show to me," returned I, " you induce me to believe that you have a wife and children." He informed me that he was general Schuyler. He regaled me with smoked tongues, which were excellent, with beefsteaks, potatoes, fresh butter, and bread. Never did a dinner give me so much pleasure as this. I was easy, after many months of anxiety, and I read the same happy change in the countenances of those around me. . . .

Madame de Riedesel, *Letters and Memoirs relating to the War of American Independence,* etc. (New York, 1827), 173-189 *passim.*

---

198. Life at Valley Forge (1777–1778)

BY DOCTOR ALBIGENCE WALDO

Doctor Waldo was a surgeon from Connecticut. This is perhaps the best account of the heroism of the darkest period in American affairs, before the French alliance (No. 199 below) assured money, ships, and troops in aid of the Revolution. — Bibliography : Winsor, *Narrative and Critical History,* VI, 436-438 ; Channing and Hart, *Guide,* § 138.

DEC. 12th [1777]. — A Bridge of Waggons made across the Schuylkill last Night consisting of 36 waggons, with a bridge of Rails between each. Some Skirmishing over the River. Militia and draggoons brought into Camp several Prisoners. Sun Set. — We are order'd to march over the River — It snows — I'm Sick — eat nothing — No Whiskey — No Baggage — Lord — Lord — Lord. The Army were 'till Sun Rise crossing the River — some at the Waggon Bridge, & some at the Raft Bridge below. Cold & Uncomfortable.

Dec. 13th. — The Army march'd three miles from the West side the River and encamp'd near a place call'd the Gulph and not an improper name neither — For this Gulph seems well adapted by its situation to keep us from the pleasure & enjoyments of this World, or being conversant with any body in it — It is an excellent place to raise the Ideas of a Philosopher beyond the glutted thoughts and Reflexions of an Epicurian. His Reflexions will be as different from the Common Reflexions of Mankind as if he were unconnected with the world, and only conversant with material beings. It cannot be that our Superiors are about to hold consul[t]ation with Spirits infinitely beneath their Order — by bringing us into these utmost regions of the Terraqueous Sphere. No — it is, upon consideration, for many good purposes since we are to Winter here — 1st There is plenty of Wood & Water. 2dly There are but few families for the soldiery to Steal from — tho' far be it from a Soldier to Steal — 4^{ly} There are warm sides of Hills to erect huts on. 5^{ly} They will be heavenly Minded like Jonah when in the belly of a great Fish. 6^{ly}. They will not become home Sick as is sometimes the Case when Men live in the Open World — since the reflections which must naturally arise from their present habitation, will lead them to the more noble thoughts of employing their leizure hours in filling their knapsacks with such materials as may be necessary on the Jorney to another Home.

Dec. 14*th.* — Prisoners & Deserters are continually coming in. The Army who have been surprisingly healthy hitherto — now begin to grow sickly from the continued fatigues they have suffered this Campaign. Yet they still show spirit of Alacrity & Contentment not to be expected from so young Troops. I am Sick — discontented — and out of humour. Poor food — hard lodging — Cold Weather — fatigue — Nasty Cloaths — nasty Cookery — Vomit half my time — smoak'd out of my senses — the Devil's in't — I can't Endure it — Why are we sent here to starve and freeze — What sweet Felicities have I left at home ; — A charming Wife — pretty Children — Good Beds — good food — good Cookery — all agreeable — all harmonious. Here, all Confusion — smoke Cold — hunger & filthyness — A pox on my bad luck. Here comes a bowl of beef soup — full of burnt leaves and dirt, sickish enough to make a hector spue, — away with it Boys — I'll live like the Chameleon upon Air. Poh ! Poh ! crys Patience within me — you talk like a fool. Your being sick Covers your mind with a Melanchollic Gloom, which makes every thing about you appear gloomy. See the poor Soldier, when in health — with what chearfullness he meets his foes and encounters every hardship — if barefoot — he labours thro' the Mud & Cold with a Song in his mouth extolling War & Washington — if his food be bad — he eats it notwithstanding with seeming content — blesses God for a good Stomach — and Whis[t]les it into digestion. But harkee Patience — a moment — There comes a Soldier — His bare feet are seen thro' his worn out Shoes — his legs nearly naked from the tatter'd remains of an only pair of stockings — his Breeches not sufficient to cover his Nakedness — his Shirt hanging in Strings — his hair dishevell'd — his face meagre — his whole appearance pictures a person forsaken & discouraged. He comes, and crys with an air of wretchedness & dispair — I am Sick — my feet lame — my legs are sore — my body cover'd with this tormenting Itch — my Cloaths are worn out — my Constitution is broken — my former Activity is exhausted by fatigue — hunger & Cold — I fail fast I shall soon be no more ! and all the reward I shall get will be — " Poor Will is dead." . . .

Dec. 18*th.* — Universal Thanksgiving — a Roasted Pig at Night. God be thanked for my health which I have pretty well recovered. How much better should I feel, were I assured my family were in health — But the same good Being who graciously preserves me — is able to preserve them — & bring me to the ardently wish'd for enjoyment of them again.

☞ Rank & Precedence make a good deal of disturbance & confusion in the American Army. The Army are poorly supplied with Provision, occationed it is said by the Neglect of the Commissary of Purchases. Much talk among Officers about discharges. Money has become of too little consequence. . . .

Dec. 21*st.* — Preparations made for hutts. Provision Scarce. Mr. Ellis went homeward — sent a Letter to my Wife. Heartily wish myself at home — my Skin & eyes are almost spoil'd with continual smoke.

A general cry thro' the Camp this Evening among the Soldiers — " No Meat ! — No Meat ! " — the Distant vales Echo'd back the melancholly sound — " No Meat ! No Meat ! " Immitating the noise of Crows & Owls, also, made a part of the confused Musick.

What have you for our Dinners Boys? " Nothing but Fire Cake & Water, Sir." At night — " Gentlemen the Supper is ready." What is your Supper, Lads? " Fire Cake & Water, Sir."

Dec. 22*d.* — Lay excessive Cold & uncomfortable last Night — my eyes are started out from their Orbits like a Rabbit's eyes, occation'd by a great Cold — and Smoke.

What have you got for Breakfast, Lads? " Fire Cake & Water, Sir." The Lord send that our Commissary of Purchases may live on, Fire Cake & Water . . . .

Our Division are under Marching Orders this morning. I am ashamed to say it, but I am tempted to steal Fowls if I could find them — or even a whole Hog — for I feel as if I could eat one. But the Impoverish'd Country about us, affords but little matter to employ a Thief — or keep a Clever Fellow in good humour — But why do I talk of hunger & hard usage, when so many in the World have not even fire Cake & Water to eat. . . .

23*d*. — The Party that went out last evening not Return'd to Day. This evening an excellent Player on the Violin in that soft kind of Musick, which is so finely adapted to stirr up the tender Passions, while he was playing in the next Tent to mine, these kind of soft Airs — it immediately called up in remembrance all the endearing expressions — the Tender Sentiments — the sympathetic friendship that has given so much satisfaction and sensible pleasure to me from the first time I gained the heart & affections of the tenderest of the Fair. . . .

Dec. 24*th*. — Party of the 22ᵈ returned. Hutts go on Slowly — Cold & Smoke make us fret. But mankind are always fretting, even if they have more than their proportion of the Blessings of Life. We are never Easy — allways repining at the Providence of an Allwise & Benevolent Being — Blaming Our Country — or faulting our Friends. But I don't know of any thing that vexes a man's Soul more than hot smoke continually blowing into his Eyes — & when he attempts to avoid it, is met by a cold and piercing Wind. . . .

Dec. 25*th*, *Christmas*. — We are still in Tents — when we ought to be in huts — the poor Sick, suffer much in Tents this cold Weather — But we now treat them differently from what they used to be at home, under the inspection of Old Women & Doct. Bolus Linctus. We give them Mutton & Grogg — and a Capital Medicine once in a While — to start the Disease from its foundation at once. We avoid — Piddling Pills, Powders, Bolus's Linctus's — Cordials — and all such insignificant matters whose powers are Only render'd important by causing the Patient to vomit up his money instead of his disease. But very few of the sick Men Die.

Dec. 26*th*. — Party of the 22ᵈ not Return'd. The Enemy have been some Days the west Schuylkill from Opposite the City to Derby — There intentions not yet known. The City is at present pretty Clear of them — Why don't his Excellency rush in & retake the City, in which he will doubtless find much Plunder? — Because he knows better than to leave his Post and be catch'd like a . . . fool cooped up in the City. He has always acted wisely hitherto — His conduct when closely scrutinised is uncensurable. Were his Inferior Generals as skillfull as himself — we should have the grandest Choir of Officers ever God made. . . .

Dec. 28th. — Yesterday upwards of fifty Officers in Gen! Green's Division resigned their Commissions — Six or Seven of our Regiment are doing the like to-day. All this is occation'd by Officers Families being so much neglected at home on account of Provisions. Their Wages will not by considerable, purchase a few trifling Comfortables here in Camp, & maintain their families at home, while such extravagant prices are demanded for the common necessaries of Life — What then have they to purchase Cloaths and other necessaries with? It is a Melancholly reflection that what is of the most universal importance, is most universally neglected — I mean keeping up the Credit of Money.

The present Circumstances of the Soldier is better by far than the Officer — for the family of the Soldier is provided for at the public expence if the Articles they want are above the common price — but the Officer's family, are obliged not only to beg in the most humble manner for the necessaries of Life — but also to pay for them afterwards at the most exhorbitant rates — and even in this manner, many of them who depend entirely on their Money, cannot procure half the material comforts that are wanted in a family — this produces continual letters of complaint from home. . . .

Dec. 31st. — Ajutant Selden learn'd me how to Darn Stockings — to make them look like knit work — first work the Thread in a parallel manner, then catch these over & over as above. . . .

1778. *January 1st.* — *New Year.* I am alive. I am well.

Hutts go on briskly, and our Camp begins to appear like a spacious City. . . .

Bought an embroidered Jacket.

How much we affect to appear of consequence by a superfluous Dress, — and yet Custom — (that law which none may fight against) has rendered this absolutely necessary & commendable. An Officer frequently fails of being duly noticed, merely from the want of a genteel Dress . . . .

Sunday, Jan. 4th. — Properly accouter'd I went to work at Masonry — None of my Mess were to dictate me — and before Night (being found with Mortar & Stone) I almost compleated a genteel Chimney to my Magnificent Hutt — however, as we had short allowance of food & no Grogg — my back ached before Night.

I was call'd to relieve a Soldier tho't to be dying — he expir'd before

I reach'd the Hutt. He was an Indian — an excellent Soldier — and
an obedient good natur'd fellow. . . .

8th. — Unexpectedly got a Furlow. Set out for home. The very
worst of Riding — Mud & Mire.

We had gone thro' Inoculation before this furlow.

Lodged at — Porters	£0	12	0
Breakfasted at Weaver Jany 9th· just by Bartholomews	0	5	
Grogg	0	4	
Hyelyars Tavern 3½ from Caryls, dined	0	5	10
Shocking riding !			
Lodged at a private house three miles this side Delaware in Jersey & Breakfasted	0	6	0
Treat Serj. Palmer with Baggage	0	5	2
Mattersons Tavern 13 m De War	0	4	0
Mattersons	£0	2	0
Conarts Tavern 10 M.	0	5	0
Sharps or McCurdys, 4 M. .	0	13	0
Capt. Porter's Cross Road 2 M. from McCurdy's Lodged — 5 Dol. 1 Sixth	£1	11	0
Breakfasted at the pretty Cottagers Jany 11th	0	5	6
1 M. from Porters — Horses	0	0	
Lodging &c.	0	11	0
Bullions Tavern (Vealtown)	0	5	0
Morristown Din'd	0	5	0
Poquonnack 10 M. from N. Y. at Jennings Tavern & a narrow Bed — Lodg'd here. Landlady wth Teethache — Children keep a squalling	0	19	
Roomë's or Romer's Tavern — Good Tavern — 11 Mile from Jennings	0	20	0
For 2 boles Grog & Phyal of Rum Vaulk's house —	0	10	0
Honey & Bread & Oats	0	12	
Good Old squeaking Widow Ann Hopper, 26 M. from Jenning's, fine Living, for Horse, Supp'r, Lodg'd, Break'^d	£0	12	0
Satyr Tavern — Lodged & Supped	0	9	6
Judge Coe's, 9 M. from King's Ferry Dinner, Oats	0	6	0
	8	**19**	**6**

CHAPTER XXXII — FRENCH ALLIANCE, 1778–1779

199. A Treaty with France (1778)

BY COMMISSIONER BENJAMIN FRANKLIN

This letter, addressed to Thomas Cushing, is a brief announcement of the conclusion of negotiations that began with the sending of Silas Deane to France in 1775. The treaties continued in force till the war with France in 1798. — For Franklin, see Nos. 68, 81 above. — Bibliography of the treaties: Winsor, *Narrative and Critical History*, VII, ch. i; Wharton, *Diplomatic Correspondence*, II, 490, 568–578; Channing and Hart, *Guide*, § 139. — For later French relations, see chs. xxxiv, xxxv below.

Passy, 21 February, 1778.

. . . I RECEIVED your favor by Mr. Austin, with your most agreeable congratulations on the success of the American arms in the Northern Department. In return, give me leave to congratulate you on the success of our negotiations here, in the completion of the two treaties with his most Christian Majesty: the one of amity and commerce, on the plan of that proposed by Congress, with some good additions; the other of alliance for mutual defence, in which the most Christian king agrees to make a common cause with the United States, if England attempts to obstruct the commerce of his subjects with them; and guarantees to the United States their liberty, sovereignty, and independence, absolute and unlimited, with all the possessions they now have, or may have, at the conclusion of the war; and the States in return guarantee to him his possessions in the West Indies. The great principle in both treaties is a perfect equality and reciprocity; no advantage to be demanded by France, or privileges in commerce, which the States may not grant to any and every other nation.

In short, the king has treated with us generously and magnanimously; taken no advantage of our present difficulties, to exact terms which we would not willingly grant, when established in prosperity and power. I may add that he has acted wisely, in wishing the friendship contracted by these treaties may be durable, which probably might not be if a contrary conduct had taken place.

574

Several of the American ships, with stores for the Congress, are now about sailing under the convoy of a French squadron. England is in great consternation, and the minister, on the 17th instant confessing that all his measures had been wrong and that peace was necessary, proposed two bills for quieting America; but they are full of artifice and deceit, and will, I am confident, be treated accordingly by our country.

I think you must have much satisfaction in so valuable a son, whom I wish safe back to you, and am, with great esteem, etc.,

B. FRANKLIN.

P. S. — The treaties were signed by the plenipotentiaries on both sides February 6th, but are still for some reasons kept secret, though soon to be published. It is understood that Spain will soon accede to the same. The treaties are forwarded to Congress by this conveyance.

Benjamin Franklin, *Complete Works* (edited by John Bigelow, New York, etc., 1888), VI, 131–134.

———◆———

200. A Dashing Young Officer in the Field (1778)

BY COLONEL JOHN TRUMBULL (1841)

Trumbull, the son of the governor of Connecticut, became an artist, and painted some of the pictures now in the Capitol at Washington. — Bibliography of the Rhode Island campaigns: Winsor, *Narrative and Critical History*, VI, 592–603; Channing and Hart, *Guide*, § 138. — On the army, see ch. xxviii above.

IN the year 1778, a plan was formed for the recovery of Rhode Island from the hands of the British, by the coöperation of a French fleet of twelve sail of the line, commanded by the Count D'Estaing, and a body of American troops, commanded by General Sullivan. The fleet arrived off New York early in July, and in August sailed for Rhode Island. I seized this occasion to gratify my slumbering love of military life, and offered my services to General Sullivan, as a volunteer aid-du-camp. My offer was accepted, and I attended him during the enter-prise.

The French fleet, which had passed Newport, and lay at anchor above the town, were drawn off from their well selected station by a clever manœuvre of Lord Howe, the very day after the American army had landed on the island. The two fleets came to a partial action off the capes of the Chesapeake, in which they were separated by a severe gale of wind; the French, more damaged by the tempest than by the enemy, put into Boston to refit, and General Sullivan was left to pursue the enterprise with the army alone. The enemy shut themselves up in Newport, while he advanced to the town in admirable order, and the place was invested in form.

It soon became evident that the attempt was vain, so long as the enemy could receive supplies and reinforcements by water, unmolested ; so soon as it was ascertained that the French fleet would not resume its station, the enterprise was abandoned — on the night between the 28th and 29th of August, the army was withdrawn, and reoccupied their former position on Butts' Hill, near Howland's ferry, at the north end of the island.

Soon after daybreak the next morning, the rear-guard, commanded by that excellent officer, Col. Wigglesworth, was attacked on Quaker, otherwise called Windmill Hill ; and Gen. Sullivan, wishing to avoid a serious action on that ground, sent me with orders to the commanding officer to withdraw the guard. In performing this duty, I had to mount the hill by a broad smooth road, more than a mile in length from the foot to the summit, where was the scene of the conflict, which, though an easy ascent, was yet too steep for a trot or a gallop. It was necessary to ride at a leisurely pace, for I saw before me a hard day's work for my horse, and was unwilling to fatigue him.

Nothing can be more trying to the nerves, than to advance thus deliberately and alone into danger. At first, I saw a round shot or two drop near me and pass bounding on. Presently I met poor Col. Tousard, who had just lost one arm, blown off by the discharge of a field piece, for the possession of which there was an ardent struggle. He was led off by a small party. Soon after, I saw Capt. Walker, of H. Jackson's regiment, who had received a musket ball through his body, mounted behind a person on horseback. He bid me a melancholy farewell, and died before night. Next, grape shot began to sprinkle around me, and soon after musket balls fell in my path like hailstones. This was not to be borne, — I spurred on my horse to the summit of the hill, and found myself in the midst of the melée. " Don't say a word, Trumbull," cried the gallant commander, " I know your errand, but don't speak ; we will beat them in a moment." " Col. Wigglesworth, do you see those troops crossing obliquely from the west road towards your rear ? " " Yes, they are Americans, coming to our support." " No, sir, those are Germans ; mark, their dress is blue and *yellow*, not buff ; they are moving to fall into your rear, and intercept your retreat. Retire instantly — don't lose a moment, or you will be cut off." The gallant man obeyed reluctantly, and withdrew the guard in fine style, slowly but safely.

As I rode back to the main body on Butts' Hill, I fell in with a party of soldiers bearing a wounded officer on a litter, whom I found to be my friend, H. Sherburne, brother of Mrs. John Langdon of Portsmouth, New Hampshire, a fellow volunteer. They were carrying him to the surgeons in the rear, to have his leg amputated. He had just been wounded by a random ball while sitting at breakfast. This was a source of lasting mortification, as he told me afterwards, — " If this had happened to me in the field, in active duty, the loss of a leg might be borne, but to be condemned through all future life to say I lost my leg under the breakfast table, is too bad." Mr. Rufus King was acting that day as a volunteer aid-du-camp to General Glover, whose quarters were in a house at the foot and east of Quaker Hill, distant from the contested position of the rear-guard a long mile. The general and the officers who composed his family were seated at breakfast, their horses standing saddled at the door. The firing on the height of the hill became heavy and incessant, when the general directed Mr. King to mount and see what and where the firing was. He quitted the table, poor Sherburne took his chair, and was hardly seated, when a spent cannon ball from the scene of action bounded in at the open window, fell upon the floor, rolled to its destination, the ancle of Sherburne, and crushed all the bones of his foot. Surely there is a providence which controls the events of human life, and which withdrew Mr. King from this misfortune.

Soon after this, as I was carrying an important order, the wind, which had risen with the sun, blew off my hat. It was not a time to dismount for a hat. I therefore tied a white handkerchief round my head, and as I did not recover my hat until evening, I formed, the rest of the day, the most conspicuous mark that ever was seen on the field — mounted on a superb bay horse, in a summer dress of nankeen — with this headdress, duty led me to every point where danger was to be found, and I escaped without the slightest injury. It becomes me to say with the Psalmist, " I thank thee, Oh thou Most High, for thou hast covered my head in the day of battle ! " For never was aid-du-camp exposed to more danger than I was during that entire day, from daylight to dusk.

The day was passed in skirmishing, and towards evening a body of

2 P

the enemy (Germans) had pushed our right wing, and advanced so far as to endanger themselves. I was ordered to take Gen. Lovell's brigade of Massachusetts militia, and aid in repulsing them . . . . I therefore moved on until the front division of the column was within ten yards of the wall, and then gave the word of command as if on parade, " Column, halt — leading division, ground your arms — step forward, comrades, and level this fence, it stands in our way—quick, quick ! " The order was obeyed with precision; the fence was leveled in an instant, and we resumed our forward march without having a man hurt. From that moment the firing from the wood ceased, and we could find no enemy ; they had been already engaged with, and overmatched by other troops, before we approached, and when they saw our cool manœuvre, they probably mistook us for veterans coming to the rescue, and prudently withdrew.

Still I hoped to be able to strike an important blow, and requested General Lovell to incline his march to the right, (by which means his movement would be screened from the view of the enemy by the form of the ground,) to move slowly and carefully, and to keep the men together in their actual order. I rode forward to reconnoitre and ascertain the position of the enemy. As I rose the crest of the hill, I saw the German troops, who had just been repulsed, in evident disorder, endeavoring to re-form their line, but fatigued, disconcerted and vacillating. I thought it a glorious moment, and hurried back to my brave column with the intention of leading it (under cover of the ground) into the rear of the enemy's flank. Judge of my vexation, when I found my men, not in slow motion and good order, as I had directed, but halted behind another strong fence, dispersed, without the shadow of order, their arms grounded, or leaning against the fence, exulting in their good conduct and success in having made the enemy run. I was cruelly disappointed ; but as the success of the blow which I had meditated depended entirely upon rapidity of movement, and much time must be wasted before we could recover our original order and be prepared to move, I gave up my projected attack, and returned to make my report to my general.

John Trumbull, *Autobiography, Reminiscences and Letters* [1756-1841], (New York, etc., 1841), 51-56 *passim*.

201. The Conquest of the Illinois Country (1779)

BY COLONEL GEORGE ROGERS CLARK

Clark was sent out by the state of Virginia in command of an expedition to seize the British posts north of the Ohio, and Virginia therefore claimed his conquests. Clark left several accounts of his movements ; the manuscript of this piece was captured by the British, and is in the Canadian archives. — Bibliography: Winsor, *Narrative and Critical History*, VI, 716–742 ; Roosevelt, *Winning of the West*, II, 31–33; Hinsdale, *Old Northwest*, II, 293–294; *Clark's Campaign in the Illinois* (Ohio Valley Historical Series, No. 3); Channing and Hart, *Guide*, § 144. — For previous accounts of the West, see above, ch. xxii. See also No. 205 below.

WHAT preceeds this part of Col^n Clarke's journal is only an account of his setting out and his march till the 23rd Feby. Sett off very early, waded better than three miles on a stretch, our people prodigious, yet they keep up a good heart in hopes of a speedy sight of our enemys. At last about two o'clock we came in sight of this long sought town and enemy, all quiet, the spirits of my men seemed to revive we marched up under cover of a wood called the Warriours Island where we lay concealed untill sunset, several of the inhabitants were out a shooting by which was assur'd they had no intelligence of us yet. I sent out two men to bring in one who came and I sent him to town to inform the inhabitants I was near them ordering all those attached to the King of England to enter the Fort and defend it, those who desired to be friends to keep in their houses. I order'd the march in the first division Capt. Williams, Capt. Worthington's Company and the Cascaskia Volunteers, in the 2nd commanded by Capt. Bowman his own Company and the Cohos Volunteers. At sun down I put the divisions in motion to march in the greatest order and regularity and observe the orders of their officers — above all to be silent — the 5 men we took in the canoes were our guides ; we entered the town on the upper part leaving detached Lt. Bayley and 15 riflemen to attack the Fort and keep up a fire to harrass them untill we took possession of the town and they were to remain on that duty till relieved by another party, the two divisions marched into the town and took possession of the main street, put guards &c without the least molestation I continued all night sending parties out to annoy the enemy and caused a trench to be thrown up across the main street about 200 yds from the Fort Gate . . . .

24th As soon as daylight appeared the enemy perceived our work and began a very smart fire of small arms at it, but could not bring their cannon to bear on them, about 8 o'clock I sent a flag of truce with a letter desiring Lt. Gov. Hamilton in order to save the impending storm that hung over his head immediately to surrender up the Garrison, Fort, Stores &.ᶜ &.ᶜ and at his peril not to destroy any one article now in the said Garrison — or to hurt any house &.ᶜ belonging to the Inhabitants for if he did by Heaven, he might expect no mercy — his answer was Gov. H. begs leave to acquaint Col. C. that he and his Garrison were not disposed to be awed into any action unworthy of British subjects — I then ordered out parties to attack the Fort and the firing began very smartly on both sides one of my men thro' a bravery known but to Americans walking carlesly up the main street was slightly wounded over the left eye but no ways dangerous — About 12 o'clock the firing from the Fort suspended a Flag coming out I order'd my people to stop firing till further orders. I soon perceived it was Capt. Helm who after salutations inform'd me that the purport of his commission was, that Lt. Gov. Hamilton was willing to surrender up the Fort and Garrison provided Col. Clarke would grant him honourable terms and that he beg'd Col. Clarke to come into the Fort to confer with him, first I desired Capt. Helm not to give any intelligence of G. H's strength &ᵉ being on his Parole, second my answer to Gov. H was that I should not agree to any other terms than that Lt Gov. H should immediately surrender at discretion and allowed him half an hour to consider thereof — as to entering the Fort my offʳˢ and men would not allow of it, for it was with difficulty I restrained them from storming the Garrison — I dismissed Capt. Helm, with my answer, at the time allowed Capt. Helm came back with Lieut. Gov. H's second proposals which were — Lt Govʳ Hamilton proposes to Col. Clarke a truce for three days, during which time there shall no defensive works be carried on in the Garrison provided Col. Clarke shall observe the like cessation on his part — he further proposes that whatever may pass between them two and any person mutually agreed upon to be present shall remain secret untill matters be finally determined. As he wishes that whatever the result of this conference may be — the Honor and credit of each may be considered — so he wishes he may confer with Col. Clarke as soon as may be — as Col. Clarke makes a difficulty of coming into the Fort Lt Gov. H will speak to him before the Gate

24 Febʸ 1779 (signed) H. H.

This moment received intelligence that a party of Indians were coming up from the falls with Prisʳˢ or Scalps, which party was sent out by G. Hamilton for that purpose, my people were so enraged they immedi-

ately intercepted the party which consisted of 8 Indians and a french
man of the Garrison. they killed three on the spot and brought 4 in
who were tomahawked in the street oposite the Fort Gate and thrown
into the river — the frenchman we shewd mercy as his aged father had
behaved so well in my party — I relieved the two poor Pris^{rs} who were
French hunters on the Ohio, after which C^t Helm carried my answer
thus — Col. Clarks comp^{ts} to G. H. and begs leave to inform him that
Col. Clarke will not agree to any other terms than of G. H. surrendering
himself and Garrison prisoners at discretion — if G. H. desires a conference with Col. Clarke, he will meet him at the church with Capt. Helm.

24 Feb^{ry} 1779 (signed) G. R. CLARK.

I imediately repaired there to confer with G. Hamilton where I met
with him and Capt Helm.

Gov. Hamilton then begd I would consider the situation of both
parties that he was willing to surrender the Garrison but was in hopes
that Col. Clark would let him do it with Honour — I answered him I
have been informed that he had 800 men — I have not that number
but I came to fight that number. G. H. then replied who could give
you this false information I am Sir (replied I) well acquainted with
your strength and force and am able to take your Fort, therefore I will
give no other terms but to submit yourself and Garrison to my discretion
and mercy — he reply'd Sir my men are brave and willing to stand by
me to the last, if I can't surrender upon Honble terms I'll fight it out to
the last — Answered, Sir this will give my men infinite satisfaction and
pleasure for it is their desire, he left me and went a few pays aloof,
I told Capt Helm Sir you are a prisoner on your parole, I desire you to
reconduct G. H. into the Fort and there remain till I retake you. Lt
Gov. Hamilton then returned saying, Col. Clarke why will you force me
to dishonour myself when you cannot acquire more honor by it — I told
him could I look on you as a Gentleman I would do to the utmost of
my power, but on you Sir who have embrued your hands in the blood
of our women and children, Honor, my country, everything calls on me
alloud for Vengeance. G. H. I know my character has been stained
but not deservedly for I have allwaise endeavour'd to instill Humanity
as much as in my power to the Indians whom the orders of my superi-
ours obliged me to employ. C. C. Sir I speak no more on this subject
my blood glows within my veins to think on the crueltys your Indian
parties have committed, therefore repair to your Fort and prepare for

battle on which I turned off and the Gov and C^t Helm towards the Fort — when Capt Helm says Gentlemen don't be warm, strive to save many lives which may be usefull to their country which will unavoidably fall in case you don't agree on which we again conferd — G Hamilton said, is there nothing to be done but fighting — Yes, Sir, I will send you such articles as I think proper to allow, if you accept them, well — I will allow you half an hour to consider on them on which C^t Helm came with me to take them to G. H. — having assembled my officers I sent the following articles vizt

1st Lt. Gov. Hamilton engages to deliver up to Col. Clark Fort Sackville as it is at present with all the stores, ammunition, provisions, &c^e

2nd. The Garrison will deliver themselves up Pris^{rs} of War to march out with their arms accoutrements, Knapsacks &c

3. The Garrison to be delivered up tomorrow morning at 10 o'clock.

4th. Three days to be allowed to the Garrison to settle their accounts with the traders of this place and inhabitants.

5. The officers of the Garrison to be allowed their necessary baggage &c.   (signed) Post Vincent 24$\underset{\cdot}{\text{th}}$ Feby 1779   G. R. CLARK.

Within the limitted time Capt. Helm returned with the articles signed thus, vizt

Agreed to for the following reasons, remoteness from succours, the state and quantity of Provisions &c^e the unanimity of officers and men on its expediency, the Honb^{le} terms allow^d and lastly the confidence in a generous Enemy.   (signed) H. HAMILTON Lt Gov & Superintend^t

Journal of Colonel Clark, in *American Historical Review* (New York, etc., 1896), I, 91–94 *passim*.

---

202. A Foreign Officer well Received (1778–1779)

BY GENERAL FREDERICK WILLIAM, BARON VON STEUBEN

(TRANSLATED BY W. L. STONE, 1891)

Steuben was a German officer who had won distinction in the Seven Years' War and was invited to America to systematize the drill and tactics of the army. His great services were well rewarded by Congress, and he spent the rest of his life in America. — Bibliography: Winsor, *Narrative and Critical History*, VI, 515; Friedrich Kapp, *Life of Steuben;* Channing and Hart, *Guide*, §§ 138, 139. — For other accounts of the army, see ch. xxviii and No. 200 above.

[July 4, 1779.]

UPON my arrival at the army I was . . . received with more marks
of distinction than I had expected. General Washington came
some miles to meet me and accompanied me to my quarters, where I
found an officer and 25 men on guard. On my remonstrating against
this on the ground that I was simply to be regarded as a volunteer, he
replied in the most courteous manner that the entire army took pleasure
in protecting such volunteers. He presented Major-General Lord Stir-
ling and several other generals to me, and also Lieutenant-Colonel
Fernans and Major Walker, whom Congress had designated as my
adjutant-generals. On the same day my name was given to the army
as the password, and on the following day the army turned out, General
Washington accompanying me to review it. In a word, if Prince Ferdi-
nand of Brunswick or the first field-marshal of Europe had arrived in
my place he could not have been received with more marks of distinction
than I was.

My services as a volunteer lasted no longer than five weeks, during
which I drilled the army and made various dispositions in it which met
with such approbation that I received my commission as a major-general
on the 26th of April. This was also accompanied at the same time with
another commission of inspector-general of all the armies of the United
States. My salary was now fixed at 16,400 French livres ; while, in
addition, my table and all of my official staff were maintained free of
cost by a commissary of our own, and furnished with everything needful. Moreover, 22 horses for myself and equipage, 1 captain of horse,
2 lieutenants, and 40 dragoons to act as a body-guard were assigned to
me by Congress. Furthermore, my adjutants and officers received the
requisite number of horses and servants commensurate with their rank.
I have 2 adjutant-generals, 2 inspection-adjutants, and 2 secretaries
whose salaries are paid by Congress. . . .

Flattering as these decided marks of distinction have been, it only,
my friend, makes me the more desirous to merit them. As far as my
mental faculties and bodily vigor will allow, I shall unremittingly devote
them to fulfilling the demands of a nation which has honored me with
such great confidence. No difficulties, no troubles, no danger, shall,
nor can they, prevent my success. My department is extensive, and
one eighth of the world seem to think that my talents may be of service
to them. Thank God that up to the present they have been ; and cheerfully will I die for a nation that has so highly honored me with its confi-

dence. Up to the present time all of my undertakings have progressed
successfully, and I can say that the trust reposed in me by the army
increases daily. I commanded the left wing in the first engagement of
the battle of Monmouth last year, and was so fortunate as to turn the
day in our favor ; and in all the smaller engagements, both of the last and
present campaigns, I have been lucky enough to have all the soldiers
anxious to be under my command. Last winter I completed the " Infantry
and Cavalry Tactics," which were at once printed and promulgated.

Congress testified its thanks to me, both by a letter of acknowledgment, which was published in all the newspapers, and by a present of
two saddle-horses and 4000 thalers (a thaler is 5 livre and 10 sous) ; and
not only my adjutants, but even my secretaries, received gratuities. . . .

I am at present on a tour of inspection for the purpose not only of
reviewing all the regiments, but of introducing the system laid down in
my tactics. Indeed, my friend, I have been fortunate in everything I
have here undertaken. I am now fifth in rank as general ; and if my
career be not ended by a fever or by half an ounce of lead, the possibili-
ties are vast enough to satisfy the most ambitious. Two or three years
of toil, and then, my friend, you must promise to visit me in Paris ; and
there we will discuss the question whether we are to dine together in
Europe or in America. Oh ! my dearest F——, why have I wasted
my years in such a manner ! Two years of work — if one is not afraid
of toil and danger — can make a man successful. Experience has convinced me of this ; nor can I forgive myself for my past indolence.

What a beautiful, what a happy country this is ! Without kings, without prelates, without blood-sucking farmer-generals, and without idle
barons ! Here everybody is prosperous. Poverty is an unknown evil.
Indeed, I should become too prolix were I to give you an account of
the prosperity and happiness of these people. The account of them
by Abbé Reynal is not entirely accurate, but it is the best. Read it
and judge for yourself. . . .

. . . I must candidly admit to you that six foreign officers cause more
trouble to me here than two hundred American ones ; and indeed most
of the foreigners have so utterly lost their credit, that it is daily becoming more difficult to employ foreign officers. A large number of German
barons and French marquises have already sailed away ; and I am always
nervous and apprehensive when a baron or a marquis announces himself.
While here we are in a republic ; and Mr. Baron does not count a farthing
more than Mister Jacob or Mister Peter. Indeed, German and French

noses can hardly accustom themselves to such a state of things! Our general of artillery [Knox], for instance, was a bookbinder in Boston. He is a worthy man, thoroughly understands his trade, and fills his present position with much credit.

Baron von Kalbe and myself are now the only foreign generals in the United States service; and Kalbe, who has an income of over 30,000 livres in France, will resign at the end of this campaign.

Finally, my friend, I will only state to you my prospects and then close my letter. I will finish the war here, or it will finish me. Without doubt England, at the utmost, can continue the game but two years longer. It will then be my care to put the army and the militia in the thirteen provinces on a uniform and solid footing ; and this having been accomplished, I shall render an account to Congress as to what we owe each other. My ability to keep up my appointments on 16,400 livres is assured to me for life. Congress has promised me, not gifts, but a landed estate either in New Jersey or Pennsylvania, two of the best provinces. A considerable pension from France, after the (successful) termination of the war, was pledged to me by the French Court before my departure for America ; besides which, I can depend upon receiving a substantial gratuity especially from the thirteen provinces. To acquire all this requires on my part only three years, at the farthest, of life, health, steadfastness of purpose and courage. The first two conditions do not depend upon me : the last two are within my power and control. And then, my friend, when these have been fulfilled ! *Then* shall I see you in Europe ; and *then* we can talk the matter over, and decide whether you shall in future dine with me in Paris or Philadelphia !

Believe me, my friend, this globe of ours is not so large as we imagine it ! An ant does not deserve its food if it is too lazy to seek it at the other side of its hill ; and I have already wasted fourteen years of my life. Now, is Canada my hunting-lodge ; Georgia my country-seat ; and this strip of land the eighth of the world. At each of these extreme ends an order signed by me will be executed. This is somewhat flattering to an ambitious man ; and you can, therefore, recognize your friend !

When you write to me, my best of friends, address your letters . . .

"To His Excellence, the honorable Baron of Steuben, Inspector-General and Major-General of the Armies of the United States in North America."

William L. Stone, translator, *Letters of Brunswick and Hessian Officers during the American Revolution* (Albany, 1891), 244–255 *passim*.

203. A Warning against Conciliation (1778)

BY GOVERNOR PATRICK HENRY

No account of the Revolution would be complete without some quotation from Patrick Henry, the southern counterpart of Samuel Adams, member of Congress, governor, and leader of the patriots. Unfortunately there is no text preserved of a single one of his glowing speeches. The extract below, from a letter to Richard Henry Lee, shows his spirit: the issue was a plan of conciliation proposed by Great Britain after the French alliance. — Bibliography: William Wirt Henry, *Patrick Henry;* Moses Coit Tyler, *Patrick Henry;* Winsor, *Narrative and Critical History,* VI, 107. — Bibliography of the plan of conciliation: Wharton, *Diplomatic Correspondence,* I, ch. iii; Channing and Hart, *Guide,* § 139.

WILLIAMSBURG June 18th, 1778.

. . . BOTH your last letters came to hand to-day. I felt for you, on seeing the order in which the balloting placed the delegates in Congress. It is an effect of that rancorous malice, that has so long followed you, through that arduous path of duty which you have invariably travelled, since America resolved to resist her oppressors. Is it any pleasure to you, to remark, that at the same era in which these men figure against you, public spirit seems to have taken its flight from Virginia? It is too much the case; for the quota of our troops is not half made up, and no chance seems to remain for completing it. The Assembly voted three hundred and fifty horse, and two thousand men, to be forthwith raised, and to join the grand army. Great bounties are offered, but I fear, the only effect will be, to expose our State to contempt, for I believe no soldiers will enlist, especially in the infantry. Can you credit it; no effort was made for supporting, or restoring public credit! I pressed it warmly on some, but in vain. This is the reason we get no soldiers. We shall issue fifty or sixty thousand dollars in cash, to equip the cavalry, and their time is to expire at Christmas. I believe they will not be in the field before that time. Let not Congress rely on Virginia for soldiers. I tell you my opinion, they will not be got here until a different spirit prevails. I look at the past condition of America, as at a dreadful precipice, from which we have escaped, by means of the generous French, to whom I will be everlastingly bound by the most heartfelt gratitude. But I must mistake matters, if some of those men who traduce you, do not prefer the offers of Britain. You will have a different game to play now with the commissioners. How comes Governor Johnstone there? I do not see how it comports with his past life. Surely Congress will never recede from our French friends.

Salvation to America depends upon our holding fast our attachment to them. I shall date our ruin from the moment that it is exchanged for anything Great Britain can say or do. She can never be cordial with us. Baffled, defeated, disgraced by her colonies, she will ever meditate revenge. We can find no safety but in her ruin, or at least in her extreme humiliation, which has not happened, and cannot happen until she is deluged with blood, or thoroughly purged by a revolution, which shall wipe from existence the present king with his connexions, and the present system, with those who aid and abet it. For God's sake, my dear sir, quit not the councils of your country, until you see us forever disjoined from Great Britain. *The old leaven still works. The flesh pots of Egypt are still savoury to degenerate palates.* Again, we are undone if the French alliance is not religiously observed. Excuse my freedom. I know your love to our country, and this is my motive. May heaven give you health and prosperity.

William Wirt Henry, *Patrick Henry: Life, Correspondence and Speeches* (New York, 1891), I, 564-565.

---

204. A Desperate Sea-Fight (1779)

BY CAPTAIN JOHN PAUL JONES

The capture of the Serapis was the most striking naval victory of the war. Jones was born in Scotland, but had served as a brilliant officer in the American navy from its organization in 1775 (see No. 194 above). — Bibliography: Winsor, *Narrative and Critical History*, VI, 568-591; Mackenzie, *Life of Paul Jones;* Maclay, *United States Navy*, I, 114-136.

ON the morning of that day, the 23d [September, 1779], the brig from Holland not being in sight, we chased a brigantine that appeared laying to, to windward. About noon, we saw and chased a large ship that appeared coming round Flamborough Head, from the northward, and at the same time I manned and armed one of the pilot boats to send in pursuit of the brigantine, which now appeared to be the vessel that I had forced ashore. Soon after this, a fleet of forty-one sail appeared off Flamborough Head, bearing N. N. E. This induced me to abandon the single ship which had then anchored in Burlington Bay; I also called back the pilot boat, and hoisted a signal for a general chase. When the fleet discovered us bearing down, all the merchant ships crowded sail towards the shore. The two ships of war that protected the fleet at the same time steered from the land, and made the disposition for battle.　In approaching the enemy, I crowded every possible sail, and made the signal for the line of battle, to which the Alliance showed no attention.　Earnest as I was for the action, I could not reach the commodore's ship until seven in the evening, being then within pistol shot, when he hailed the Bon Homme Richard.　We answered him by firing a whole broadside.

The battle being thus begun, was continued with unremitting fury. Every method was practised on both sides to gain an advantage, and rake each other; and I must confess that the enemy's ship, being much more manageable than the Bon Homme Richard, gained thereby several times an advantageous situation, in spite of my best endeavours to prevent it.　As I had to deal with an enemy of greatly superior force, I was under the necessity of closing with him, to prevent the advantage which he had over me in point of manœuvre.　It was my intention to lay the Bon Homme Richard athwart the enemy's bow; but as that operation required great dexterity in the management of both sails and helm, and some of our braces being shot away, it did not exactly succeed to my wish.　The enemy's bowsprit, however, came over the Bon Homme Richard's poop by the mizen-mast, and I made both ships fast together in that situation, which, by the action of the wind on the enemy's sails, forced her stern close to the Bon Homme Richard's bow, so that the ships lay square alongside of each other, the yards being all entangled, and the cannon of each ship touching the opponent's.　When this position took place, it was eight o'clock, previous to which the Bon Homme Richard had received sundry eighteen-pound shots below the water, and leaked very much.　My battery of twelve-pounders, on which I had placed my chief dependence, being commanded by Lieutenant Dale and Colonel Weibert, and manned principally with American seamen and French volunteers, was entirely silenced and abandoned.　As to the six old eighteen-pounders that formed the battery of the lower gun-deck, they did no service whatever, except firing eight shot in all. Two out of three of them burst at the first fire, and killed almost all the men who were stationed to manage them.　Before this time, too, Colonel de Chamillard, who commanded a party of twenty soldiers on the poop, had abandoned that station after having lost some of his men. I had now only two pieces of cannon, (nine-pounders,) on the quarter-deck, that were not silenced, and not one of the heavier cannon was fired during the rest of the action.　The purser, M. Mease, who commanded the guns on the quarter-deck, being dangerously wounded in the head, I was obliged to fill his place, and with great difficulty rallied a few men, and shifted over one of the lee quarter-deck guns, so that we afterwards played three pieces of nine-pounders upon the enemy. The tops alone seconded the fire of this little battery, and held out bravely during the whole of the action, especially the main-top, where Lieutenant Stack commanded.   I directed the fire of one of the three cannon against the main-mast, with double-headed shot, while the other two were exceedingly well served with grape and canister shot, to silence the enemy's musketry and clear her decks, which was at last effected. The enemy were, as I have since understood, on the instant of calling for quarter, when the cowardice or treachery of three of my under-officers induced them to call to the enemy.   The English commodore asked me if I demanded quarter, and I having answered him in the most determined negative, they renewed the battle with double fury. They were unable to stand the deck ; but the fire of their cannon, especially the lower battery, which was entirely formed of ten-pounders, was incessant ; both ships were set on fire in various places, and the scene was dreadful beyond the reach of language.   To account for the timidity of my three under-officers, I mean, the gunner, the carpenter, and the master-at-arms, I must observe, that the two first were slightly wounded, and, as the ship had received various shot under water, and one of the pumps being shot away, the carpenter expressed his fears that she would sink, and the other two concluded that she was sinking, which occasioned the gunner to run aft on the poop, without my knowledge, to strike the colours.   Fortunately for me, a cannon ball had done that before, by carrying away the ensign-staff ; he was therefore reduced to the necessity of sinking, as he supposed, or of calling for quarter, and he preferred the latter.

All this time the Bon Homme Richard had sustained the action alone, and the enemy, though much superior in force, would have been very glad to have got clear, as appears by their own acknowledgments, and by their having let go an anchor the instant that I laid them on board, by which means they would have escaped, had I not made them well fast to the Bon Homme Richard. . . .

. . . My situation was really deplorable ; the Bon Homme Richard received various shot under water from the Alliance ; the leak gained on the pumps, and the fire increased much on board both ships.   Some officers persuaded me to strike, of whose courage and good sense I entertain a high opinion. My treacherous master-at-arms let loose all my prisoners without my knowledge, and my prospects became gloomy indeed. I would not, however, give up the point. The enemy's mainmast began to shake, their firing decreased fast, ours rather increased, and the British colours were struck at half an hour past ten o'clock.

This prize proved to be the British ship of war the Serapis, a new ship of forty-four guns, built on the most approved construction, with two complete batteries, one of them of eighteen-pounders, and commanded by the brave Commodore Richard Pearson. I had yet two enemies to encounter, far more formidable than the Britons, I mean, fire and water. The Serapis was attacked only by the first, but the Bon Homme Richard was assailed by both; there was five feet water in the hold, and though it was moderate from the explosion of so much gunpowder, yet the three pumps that remained could with difficulty only keep the water from gaining. The fire broke out in various parts of the ship, in spite of all the water that could be thrown in to quench it, and at length broke out as low as the powder magazine, and within a few inches of the powder. In that dilemma, I took out the powder upon deck, ready to be thrown overboard at the last extremity, and it was ten o'clock the next day, the 24th, before the fire was entirely extinguished. With respect to the situation of the Bon Homme Richard, the rudder was cut entirely off, the stern frame and transoms were almost entirely cut away, and the timbers by the lower deck, especially from the mainmast towards the stern, being greatly decayed with age, were mangled beyond my power of description, and a person must have been an eye witness to form a just idea of the tremendous scene of carnage, wreck, and ruin, which every where appeared. Humanity cannot but recoil from the prospect of such finished horror, and lament that war should be capable of producing such fatal consequences. . . .

. . . The wind augmented in the night, and the next day, the 25th, so that it was impossible to prevent the good old ship from sinking. They did not abandon her till after nine o'clock; the water was then up to the lower deck, and a little after ten I saw, with inexpressible grief, the last glimpse of *the Bon Homme Richard*. No lives were lost with the ship, but it was impossible to save the stores of any sort whatever. I lost even the best part of my clothes, books, and papers; and several of my officers lost all their clothes and effects.

[Robert Charles Sands, editor], *Life and Correspondence of John Paul Jones* (New York, 1830), 180–188 *passim*.

CHAPTER XXXIII — CRISIS IN DOMESTIC AFFAIRS, 1779–1782

205. The Confederation Incomplete (1779)

BY THE ASSEMBLY OF MARYLAND

This remonstrance, drawn up December 15, 1778, was presented to Congress by the Maryland delegates on May 21, 1779; and the state continued to stand out till January 30, 1781. The issue was upon the lands acquired by the Rogers Clark expedition (No. 201 above), and resulted in the cession of the disputed territory by Virginia to the United States, a step which prepared the way for a national public domain. — Bibliography : Winsor, *Narrative and Critical History*, VI, 527; Curtis, *History of the Constitution*, I, 131–141; Roosevelt, *Winning of the West*, III; Hinsdale, *Old Northwest*, II, 213–214 (with maps); Channing and Hart, *Guide*, §§ 142, 150. — See No. 209 below.

. . . WE think it our duty to instruct as followeth on the subject of the confederation, a subject in which, unfortunately, a supposed difference of interest has produced an almost equal division of sentiments among the several states composing the union. We say a supposed difference of interests ; for if local attachments and prejudices, and the avarice and ambition of individuals, would give way to the dictates of a sound policy, founded on the principles of justice (and no other policy but what is founded on those immutable principles deserves to be called sound) we flatter ourselves, this apparent diversity of interests would soon vanish, and all the states would confederate on terms mutually advantageous to all ; for they would then perceive that no other confederation than one so formed can be lasting. Although the pressure of immediate calamities, the dread of their continuance from the appearance of disunion, and some other peculiar circumstances, may have induced some states to accede to the present confederation, contrary to their own interests and judgments, it requires no great share of foresight to predict, that when those causes cease to operate, the states which have thus acceded to the confederation will consider it as no longer binding, and will eagerly embrace the first occasion of asserting their just rights, and securing their independence. Is it possible that those states who are ambitiously grasping at territories, to which in our judgment they have not the least shadow of exclusive right, will use with greater moderation the increase of wealth and power derived from those territories, when acquired, than what they have displayed in their endeavours to acquire them? We think not. We are convinced the same spirit which hath prompted them to insist on a claim so extravagant, so repugnant to every principle of justice, so incompatible with the general welfare of all the states, will urge them on to add oppression to injustice. If they should not be incited by a superiority of wealth and strength to oppress by open force their less wealthy and less powerful neighbours; yet depopulation and consequently the impoverishment of those states will necessarily follow, which, by an unfair construction of the confederation, may be stripped of a common interest, and the common benefits derivable from the western country. Suppose, for instance, Virginia indisputably possessed of the extensive and fertile country to which she has set up a claim, what would be the probable consequences to Maryland of such an undisturbed and undisputed possession? They cannot escape the least discerning.

Virginia, by selling on the most moderate terms a small proportion of the lands in question, would draw into her treasury vast sums of money; and in proportion to the sums arising from such sales, would be enabled to lessen her taxes. Lands comparatively cheap, and taxes comparatively low, with the lands and taxes of an adjacent state, would quickly drain the state thus disadvantageously circumstanced of its most useful inhabitants; its wealth and its consequence in the scale of the confederated states would sink of course. A claim so injurious to more than one half, if not to the whole of the United States, ought to be supported by the clearest evidence of the right. Yet what evidences of that right have been produced? What arguments alleged in support either of the evidence or the right? None that we have heard of deserving a serious refutation.

It has been said, that some of the delegates of a neighbouring state have declared their opinion of the impracticability of governing the extensive dominion claimed by that state. Hence also the necessity was admitted of dividing its territory, and erecting a new state under the auspicies and direction of the elder, from whom no doubt it would receive its form of government, to whom it would be bound by some alliance or confederacy, and by whose councils it would be influenced. Such a measure, if ever attempted, would certainly be opposed by the other states as inconsistent with the letter and spirit of the proposed confederation.   Should it take place by establishing a sub confederacy, imperium in imperio, the state possessed of this extensive dominion must then either submit to all the inconveniences of an overgrown and unwieldly government, or suffer the authority of Congress to interpose at a future time, and to lop off a part of its territory to be erected into a new and free state, and admitted into a confederation on such conditions as shall be settled by nine states.   If it is necessary for the happiness and tranquillity of a state thus overgrown, that Congress should hereafter interfere and divide its territory, why is the claim to that territory now made, and so pertinaciously insisted on?   We can suggest to ourselves but two motives ; either the declaration of relinquishing at some future period a proportion of the country now contended for, was made to lull suspicion asleep, and to cover the designs of a secret ambition, or, if the thought was seriously entertained, the lands are now claimed to reap an immediate profit from the sale.   We are convinced, policy and justice require, that a country unsettled at the commencement of this war, claimed by the British crown, and ceded to it by the treaty of Paris, if wrested from the common enemy by the blood and treasure of the thirteen states, should be considered as a common property, subject to be parcelled out by Congress into free, convenient and independent governments, in such manner and at such times as the wisdom of that assembly shall hereafter direct.

Thus convinced, we should betray the trust reposed in us by our constituents, were we to authorize you to ratify on their behalf the confederation, unless it be farther explained.   We have coolly and dispassionately considered the subject ; we have weighed probable inconveniences and hardships against the sacrifice of just and essential rights ; and do instruct you not to agree to the confederation, unless an article or articles be added thereto in conformity with our declaration.   Should we succeed in obtaining such article or articles, then you are hereby fully empowered to accede to the confederation. . . .

We have spoken with freedom, as becomes free men ; and we sincerely wish that these our representations may make such an impression on that assembly as to induce them to make such addition to the articles of confederation as may bring about a permanent union.

Secret Journals of the Acts and Proceedings of Congress (Boston, 1821), I, 434–438 *passim*.

2 Q

206. Revolutionary Finance (1781)

BY GENERAL GEORGE WASHINGTON

This letter was sent to John Laurens, as a basis of information for his mission abroad. — For Washington, see No. 195 above. — Bibliography of Revolutionary finance : Winsor, *Narrative and Critical History*, VII, 81; W. G. Sumner, *Financier [Morris] and Finances of the American Revolution;* Bolles, *Financial History of the United States*, I, 1–332; Channing and Hart, *Guide*, §151.

NEW WINDSOR, 15 January, 1781. . . .

IN compliance with your request I shall commit to writing the result of our conferences on the present state of American affairs, in which I have given you my ideas with that freedom and explicitness, which the objects of your commission, my entire confidence in you, and the exigency demand. To me it appears evident :

1st. That, considering the diffused population of these States, the consequent difficulty of drawing together its resources, the composition and temper of *a part* of the inhabitants, the want of a sufficient stock of national wealth as a foundation for revenue, and the almost total extinction of commerce, the efforts we have been compelled to make for carrying on the war have exceeded the natural abilities of this country, and by degrees brought it to a crisis, which renders immediate and efficacious succors from abroad indispensable to its safety.

2dly. That, notwithstanding, from the confusion always attendant on a revolution, from our having had governments to frame and every species of civil and military institutions to create, from that inexperience in affairs necessarily incident to a nation in its commencement, some errors may have been committed in the administration of our finances, to which a part of our embarrassments are to be attributed ; yet they are principally to be ascribed to an essential defect of means, to the want of a sufficient stock of wealth, as mentioned in the first article, which, continuing to operate, will make it impossible by any merely interior exertions to extricate ourselves from those embarrassments, restore public credit, and furnish the funds requisite for the support of the war.

3dly. That experience has demonstrated the impracticability long to maintain a paper credit without funds for its redemption. The depreciation of our currency was in the main a necessary effect of the want of those funds ; and its restoration is impossible for the same reason, to which the general diffidence that has taken place among the people is an additional and, in the present state of things, an insuperable obstacle.

4thly. That the mode, which for want of money has been substituted for supplying the army, by assessing a proportion of the productions of the earth, has hitherto been found ineffectual, has frequently exposed the army to the most calamitous distress, and, from its novelty and incompatibility with ancient habits, is regarded by the people as burthensome and oppressive, has excited serious discontents, and in some places alarming symptoms of opposition. This mode has, besides, many particular inconveniences, which contribute to make it inadequate to our wants, and ineligible but as an auxiliary.

5thly. That, from the best estimates of the annual expense of the war and the annual revenues which these States are capable of affording, there is a large balance to be supplied by public credit. The resource of domestic loans is inconsiderable, because there are properly speaking few moneyed men, and the few there are can employ their money more profitably otherwise ; added to which, the instability of the currency and the deficiency of funds have impaired the public credit.

6thly. That the patience of the army, from an almost uninterrupted series of complicated distress, is now nearly exhausted, and their discontents matured to an extremity, which has recently had very disagreeable consequences, and which demonstrates the absolute necessity of speedy relief, a relief not within the compass of our means. You are too well acquainted with all their sufferings for want of clothing, for want of provisions, for want of pay.

7thly. That, the people being dissatisfied with the mode of supporting the war, there is cause to apprehend, that evils actually felt in the prosecution may weaken those sentiments which began it, founded, not on immediate sufferings, but on a speculative apprehension of future sufferings from the loss of their liberties. There is danger, that a commercial and free people, little accustomed to heavy burthens, pressed by impositions of a new and odious kind, may not make a proper allowance for the necessity of the conjuncture, and may imagine they have only exchanged one tyranny for another.

8thly. That, from all the foregoing considerations result, 1st, absolute necessity of an immediate, ample, and efficacious succor in money, large enough to be a foundation for substantial arrangements of finance, to revive public credit, and give vigor to future operations ; 2dly, the vast importance of a decided effort of the allied arms on this continent, the ensuing campaign, to effectuate once for all the great objects of the alliance, the liberty and independence of these States. Without the first we may make a feeble and expiring effort the next campaign, in all probability the period to our opposition. With it, we should be in a condition to continue the war, as long as the obstinacy of the enemy might require. The former is essential to the latter; both combined would bring the contest to a glorious issue, crown the obligations, which America already feels to the magnanimity and generosity of her ally, and perpetuate the union by all the ties of gratitude and affection, as well as mutual advantage, which alone can render it solid and indissoluble.

9thly. That, next to a loan of money, a constant naval superiority on these coasts is the object most interesting. This would instantly reduce the enemy to a difficult defensive, and, by removing all prospect of extending their acquisitions, would take away the motives for prosecuting the war. Indeed, it is not to be conceived how they could subsist a large force in this country, if we had the command of the seas, to interrupt the regular transmission of supplies from Europe. This superiority, (with an aid in money,) would enable us to convert the war into a vigorous offensive. I say nothing of the advantages to the trade of both nations, nor how infinitely it would facilitate our supplies. With respect to us, it seems to be one of *two* deciding points; and it appears, too, to be the interest of our allies, abstracted from the immediate benefits to this country, to transfer the naval war to America. The number of ports friendly to them, hostile to the British, the materials for repairing their disabled ships, the extensive supplies towards the subsistence of their fleet, are circumstances which would give them a palpable advantage in the contest of these seas.

10thly. That an additional succor in troops would be extremely desirable. Besides a reinforcement of numbers, the excellence of French troops, that perfect discipline and order in the corps already sent, which have so happily tended to improve the respect and confidence of the people for our allies, the conciliating disposition and the zeal for the service, which distinguish every rank, sure indications of lasting harmony, — all these considerations evince the immense utility of an accession of force to the corps now here. Correspondent with these motives, the enclosed minutes of a conference between their Excellencies the Count de Rochambeau, the Chevalier de Ternay, and myself will inform you, that an augmentation to fifteen thousand men was judged expedient for the next campaign; and it has been signified to me, that an application has been made to the court of France to this effect.   But if the sending so large a succor in troops should necessarily diminish the pecuniary aid, which our allies may be disposed to grant, it were preferable to diminish the aid in men ; for the same sum of money, which would transport from France and maintain here a body of troops with all the necessary apparatus, being put into our hands to be employed by us, would serve to give activity to a larger force within ourselves, and its influence would pervade the whole administration.

11thly. That no nation will have it more in its power to repay what it borrows than this.   Our debts are hitherto small.   The vast and valuable tracts of unlocated lands, the variety and fertility of climates and soils, the advantages of every kind which we possess for commerce, insure to this country a rapid advancement in population and prosperity, and a certainty, its independence being established, of redeeming in a short term of years the comparatively inconsiderable debts it may have occasion to contract.

That, notwithstanding the difficulties under which we labor, and the inquietudes prevailing among the people, there is still a fund of inclination and resource in the country, equal to great and continued exertions, provided we have it in our power to stop the progress of disgust, by changing the present system, and adopting another more consonant with the spirit of the nation, and more capable of activity and energy in public measures ; of which a powerful succor of money must be the basis.   The people are discontented ; but it is with the feeble and oppressive mode of conducting the war, not with the war itself.   They are not unwilling to contribute to its support, but they are unwilling to do it in a way that renders private property precarious ; a necessary consequence of the fluctuation of the national currency, and of the inability of government to perform its engagements oftentimes coercively made.   A large majority are still firmly attached to the independence of these States, abhor a reunion with Great Britain, and are affectionate to the alliance with France ; but this disposition cannot supply the place of means customary and essential in war, nor can we rely on its duration amidst the perplexities, oppressions, and misfortunes, that attend the want of them.

George Washington, *Writings* (edited by Worthington Chauncey Ford, New York, etc., 1891), IX, 102–10⌒

207. The State of the National Debt (1781)

BY DUANE, SHARPE, AND WOLCOTT

This is a report made by a committee to Congress on April 18, 1781. It shows the bonded debt, French advances, certificates to contractors, outstanding claims, and the remnant of the paper money. The debt as here shown was honorably paid after 1789. The piece also illustrates the character of the records of Congress. — Bibliography as in Nos. 155, 185, 206 above.

THE committee, consisting of Mr. Duane, Mr. Sharpe, and Mr. Wolcott, appointed to estimate and state the amount of the debts due from the United States, with the necessary estimates for the current year, as near as can be done, in order that the same may be laid before the respective legislatures, report,

That they have attended to this business; but from the unsettled condition of the publick accounts they can only give a general view of the publick debts.

By returns made to the board of treasury up to the 10th February, 1781, it appears that from the opening of the loan offices to the first day of March, 1778, there has been borrowed, the

	Dollars.	Int. payable in bills on France.	An. Interest.
sum of - - - -	7,313,306		438,798$\frac{31}{90}$
From last February, 1778, to dates of last returns, 53,245,130, valued at - -	4,962,172	-	297,730$\frac{29}{90}$
Amount of the bills of exchange drawn on commissioners and ministers at the court of France, for payment of three years interest, - -	1,316,394		
Do. drawn on ministers at that and other courts for supplies, and to answer pressing emergencies on account of deficiency in the publick treasury, -	2,165,578		
Supplies by them purchased and sent over, for which			

	Dollars.	An. Interest.

payment has not been made, and of which no exact returns have yet been obtained, together with expenses of commissioners and ministers abroad, estimated at -   1,518,028   6,000,000   360,000

                            18,275,478

Deduct for depreciation on money borrowed from 1st Sept. 1777, to 1st March, 1778 -   -   -   •   883,914

Principal sum specie   17,391,564 An. Interest 1,096,528⅔

Due to the army for pay and subsistence, up to the last of December, 1780, estimated   -   •   1,000,000

                            18,391,564

Due to the civil officers of government   -   -   98,927

Besides the above, there are large debts contracted by the quartermaster and commissary, for part of which they have settled with the persons who have furnished the supplies, and given them certificates, bearing interest, viz :

The late quartermaster has returned debts settled -   20,758,850

Unsettled, (excluding those contracted in North Carolina, South Carolina and Georgia) estimated at   -   -   -   7,149,870

	Dollars.
The present quartermaster has not made returns; but as it is well known that he has not been supplied with money, whatever exertions have been made or supplies furnished in that department must have been on credit. It is to be presumed that the debts by him contracted up to 1st Jan. 1781, amount in specie to - - - -	500,000
The commissary of purchases has made returns of debts due in his department amounting to 11,388,903	
To this is to be added what yet remains of the old currency unredeemed, suppose - 160,000,000	
To which may be added for navy debts, &c., for debts due in the departments of the board, of the commissary general of military stores and the clothier general, estimated at - - 10,702,377	
Total in continental at 75 for 1 230,000,000 is 3,066,666⅔	
To which added the new money issued in lieu of the old which is called in and destroyed - - - 2,000,000	
Total debts in specie 24,057,157⅔	

208. Not worth a Continental (1781)

BY WILLIAM PYNCHON

Pynchon was a Salem gentleman, a conspicuous member of the Essex bar, and not disposed to favor the Revolution.   His diary gives an interesting picture of social and business life during the war. — Bibliography of Pynchon: Introduction to the *Diary*. — Bibliography of paper money: Henry Phillips, *Paper Currency;* Winsor, *Narrative and Critical History*, VII, 13–15; Channing and Hart, *Guide*, §§ 142, 151.

[May, 1781] 18. *FRIDAY*. Cloudy. The continental currency, old emission, passeth no more here.

19. *Saturday*. Some take the old emission on pretence of patriotism. . . .

24. *Thursday*. Fair and cool. Exchange between old emission and silver is at 150 for one ; at Boston at 120 to 140 for one. The jurymen in the Maritime Court here yesterday refused to give in any more verdicts to the Court without an assurance that they shall be paid in new emission. So ! so ! so ! members of Congress, whither is your credit going ? Down hill surely ; but they will bring it up with a heavy tax.

26. *Saturday*. Cloudy, but less cold than yesterday. It is said that Morris, the financier, hath reported to Congress in favour of hard-money currency.

27. *Sunday*. Clear, and wind S. and moderate. Soh ! soh ! The register, Pickering, says he is not at liberty to record Mr. Robie's mortgage deeds of his house and land, which he made for securing his creditors in England. Johnson comes in and says that Gibraltar is relieved by the English fleet. What ailed ye Powers and ye Fleets of the House of Bourbon that ye have been so often driven back by the English, — that all your attempts against Gibraltar have hitherto failed ?

28. *Monday*. Fine, clear, and warm day. Exchange is now at 3 for one between hard money and new emission, and at . . . . for one between hard money and old emission.

29. *Tuesday*. A fine, warm day ; So. W. wind. Trade in Boston in great confusion, almost stagnated ; the credit of the new emission sunk 30 per ct. upon failure of the old in its credit ; all growl ; some rave and stamp ; others curse and swear, some at Congress, some at the General Court, some at Whiggs, others at Tories, — all at the French. The moderate Whiggs express their joy that Gibraltar is relieved and the siege raised ; they who trouble the waters first have seldom the benefit of fishing.

30. *Wednesday.* Election Day ; very dark and cloudy ; wind S. W. No public dinner, no parade; the most miserable procession ever seen. . . .

June 2. Saturday. Cloudy and moderate. The marketmen refuse bills of the old emission for provisions ; the jurymen refused it at the Maritime Court, here in open Court; the Judge declined to take it : and yet this is our established currency, established by law ! O Congress ! O legislators ! O money-makers all ! what ails ye ? This day Sheriff Chandler took Carlton on a warrant from the Inferior Court against him for a riot in breaking windows, etc., at the rejoicings at the taking of Burgoyne ; he was carried to the town house, and a justice was sent for to bail him, but he departed, and left justice, sheriff, and all in the lurch ; threats were given out at the jail that if he was to be committed the jail would not stand long. Mark the end ! . . .

9. *Saturday.* A fine, pleasant day. We have a letter from Jno. at Cambridge ; his chum ill, and he unwell. Mr. Goodale and [Mr.] Ward from the G. Court. The Court had written to the Congress respecting the currency, and can do nothing about it before they have an answer. A few weeks ago, who even held paper money not to be as good as silver were called Tories, enemies to the country. . . .

July 1. Sunday. A fine, warm day. Mr. Winthrop and Stewart and co. here. The General Court sit all this day, as we hear, upon matters of great importance, and relating to congress at Vienna, proceedings as to peace, etc. Last evening Mr. Ford was buried in the churchyard. Mr. Barnard prayed at his house and attended at the funeral; the bearers were all dissenters, as I remember. . . .

8. *Sunday.* Very hot last night ; slept all hands with windows open, my honoured self on the floor. Mr. Higginson from Boston says that the bills of the new emission are to pass in payment of taxes at $1\frac{7}{8}$ paper for one silver dollar, or 11s. 3d. paper for six shillings in silver, and that the old emission passeth no more, not even for payment of taxes. . . .

16. *Monday.* Town meeting to raise more men, about ninety in all. Rumour that Gen'l Lee of Virginia is gone over to the Regulars. Church meeting adjourned to September 17th. . . .

20. *Friday.* We return to Salem with Mrs. Mason, and find neighbour Satchel greatly disturbed about his new chaise, which he lent me, Foster not having procured him one to ride with in my absence ; neither money nor concessions appease his piratical ire. From purse-pride, good Lord, deliver me, — and my prayer is answered.

21. *Saturday*. Fair day. A wine prize to Grand Turk comes in; paper money, new emission, goes fast down hill. . . .

24. *Tuesday*. A fine day. The market people will not take any paper money for provisions. . . .

31. *Tuesday*. Cloudy morning. I return by half past eight o'clock from Malden, and breakfast at Salem. Continental bills, whither is your credit flown? And where the credit of your makers and creators? " Oh ! " says Dr. C., " they have answered well the purposes of their creation : they have *supported the army* for some years, and it is time for them to rest, being of no more service." O pious doctor, rare Dr. C. ! when fraud and deceit can no longer prevail, let them be laid aside as useless. . . .

[August] 9. *Thursday*. A fine, cool morning; very warm at noon. Dine at the Fort on turtle, — about four persons ; Professor Williams, Mr. Barnard, Mr. Hopkins, and Dr. Whitaker, the latter by far the strongest man; he seized Esquire Blaney and took him up on his shoulders and laid him flat on his back in a masterly manner, to the entertainment of his parishioners. " Aye," says T. Mason, " the doctor is fit for anything ; he would have made as stout a sailor as any in the town of Salem ; he is a smart man, and fit for any business ; he made as good an agent for the privateers as ever was." At about five o'clock we sit down to dinner.

10. *Friday*. A fine, cool morning. I returned to Mr. Oliver the dollar which I borrowed of him at the Fort.

12. *Sunday*. Fair and warm. Mrs. Orne and her maid Landor come.

13. *Monday*. Fair and cool. News that Mrs. Fairfield's son died in the prison ship at New York. Three more privateers are taken and carried to Halifax. Mrs. Cabot makes her will ; in it gives Titus, her negro, £40 and his freedom in case he shall continue in her service henceforth till her death. Titus cares not, as he gets money apace, being one of the agents for some of the privateersmen, and wears cloth shoes, ruffled shirts, silk breeches and stockings, and dances minuets at Commencement ; it is said he has made more profits as agent than Mr. Ansil Alcock or Dr. Whitaker by their agencies. A plentiful rain last night.

William Pynchon, *Diary* (edited by Fitch Edward Oliver, Boston, etc., 1890), 95–103 *passim*.

209. The Federal Arch Completed (1781)

FROM THE PENNSYLVANIA PACKET

This brief newspaper item sets forth the completion of the Articles of Confederation by the signature of Maryland on March 1, 1781. — For the formation of the Articles, see above, Nos. 189, 205.

MARCH 1 [1781]. — This day will be memorable in the annals of America to the last posterity, for the final ratification in Congress, of the articles of confederation and perpetual union between the States.

This great event, which will confound our enemies, fortify us against their arts of seduction, and frustrate their plans of division, was announced to the public at twelve o'clock, under the discharge of the artillery on the land and the cannon of the shipping in the Delaware. The bells were rung, and every manifestation of joy shown on this occasion. The Ariel frigate, commanded by the gallant Paul Jones, fired a *feu de joie*, and was beautifully decorated with a variety of streamers in the day, and ornamented with a brilliant appearance of lights in the night.

At two o'clock in the afternoon his Excellency the president of Congress received the congratulations of the legislative and executive bodies of Pennsylvania, of the civil and military officers, and many of the principal citizens, who partook of a collation provided on this happy occasion. The evening was ushered in by an elegant exhibition of fireworks.

Thus has the union, began by necessity, been indissolubly cemented. Thus America, (like a well-constructed arch, whose parts harmonizing and mutually supporting each other, are the more closely united the greater the pressure upon them,) is growing up in war into greatness and consequence among the nations. But Britain's boasted wealth and grandeur are crumbling to pieces, never to be again united. Her empire of the ocean is dividing among her insulted neighbors; and if she persists in her present self-destroying system, there will be a time when scarcely a monument of her former glory will remain. The fragments of her empire, and its history, will then be of little other use to mankind, but like a landmark to warn against the shoals and rocks on which her political navigators had shipwrecked that infatuated nation.

Pennsylvania Packet, March 3, 1781; reprinted in Frank Moore, *Diary of the American Revolution* (New York, etc., 1860), II, 390-391.

210. The Bank of North America (1782)

BY SUPERINTENDENT ROBERT MORRIS

This piece is a circular sent out by the head of the treasury to the governors of the states. The bank was one of Morris's favorite devices for strengthening the credit of the United States. — For Morris, see No. 194 above. — Bibliography of the bank : Winsor, *Narrative and Critical History*, VII, 81; W. G. Sumner, *Financier and Finances;* Channing and Hart, *Guide*, § 142.

Office of Finance, January 8th, 1782. . . .

I HAVE the honor to transmit herewith an ordinance passed by the United States in Congress assembled the 31st day of December, 1781, incorporating the subscribers of the Bank of North America, together with sundry resolutions recommending to the several States to pass such laws as they may judge necessary for giving the said ordinance its full operation. The resolutions of the 26th of May last speak so clearly to the points necessary to be established by those laws, that I need not enlarge on them. Should anything more be found necessary upon experience, the President and Directors will no doubt make suitable applications to Congress, or to the States respectively, as the case may require.

It affords me great satisfaction to inform you that this Bank commenced its operations yesterday, and I am confident that with proper management, it will answer the most sanguine expectations of those who befriend the institution. It will facilitate the management of the finances of the United States. The several States may, when their respective necessities require, and the abilities of the bank will permit, derive occasional advantages and accommodations from it. It will afford to the individuals of all the States a medium for their intercourse with each other, and for the payment of taxes more convenient than the precious metals, and equally safe. It will have a tendency to increase both the internal and external commerce of North America, and undoubtedly will be infinitely useful to all the traders of every State in the Union, provided, as I have already said, it is conducted on principles of equity, justice, prudence, and economy. The present directors bear characters, which cannot fail to inspire confidence, and as the corporation is amenable to the laws, power can neither sanctify any improper conduct, nor protect the guilty. . . .

Jared Sparks, editor, *The Diplomatic Correspondence of the American Revolution* (Boston, 1830), XII, 76–77.

CHAPTER XXXIV — THE END OF THE WAR,

1780–1781

211. A Review of the War (1780–1781)

BY JAMES MADISON

Madison was at this time a young Virginian, recently graduated from Princeton College; later he became member of Congress, secretary of state, and president. — Bibliography of Madison: Rives, *James Madison;* Winsor, *Narrative and Critical History*, VII, 315; Foster, *Presidential Administrations*, 12–15. — Bibliography of the southern campaigns: Winsor, *Narrative and Critical History*, VI, 519–555; G. W. Greene, *Nathanael Greene;* Channing and Hart, *Guide*, § 140.

PHILADELPHIA, July 7, 1781. . . .

THE insuperable difficulties which opposed a general conquest of America seemed as early as the year 1779 to have been felt by the enemy, and to have led them into the scheme of directing their operations and views against the Southern States only. Clinton accordingly removed with the principal part of his force from New York to South Carolina, and laid siege to Charleston, which, after an honorable resistance, was compelled to surrender to a superiority of force. Our loss in men, besides the inhabitants of the town, was not less than two thousand. Clinton returned to New York. Cornwallis was left with about five thousand troops to pursue his conquests. General Gates was appointed to the command of the Southern department, in place of Lincoln, who commanded in Charleston at the time of its capitulation. He met Cornwallis on the 16th of August, 1780, near Camden, in the upper part of South Carolina and on the border of North Carolina. A general action ensued, in which the American troops were defeated with considerable loss, though not without making the enemy pay a good price for their victory. Cornwallis continued his progress into North Carolina, but afterwards retreated to Camden. The defeat of Gates was followed by so general a clamor against him, that it was judged expedient to recall him. Greene was sent to succeed in the command. About the time of his arrival at the army, Cornwallis, having been reinforced from New York, resumed his enterprise into North Carolina. A detachment of his best troops was totally defeated by Morgan with an inferior number, and consisting of a major part of militia detached from Greene's army. Five hundred were made prisoners, between two and three hundred killed and wounded, and about the like number escaped. This disaster, instead of checking the ardor of Cornwallis, afforded a new incentive to a rapid advance, in the hope of recovering his prisoners. The vigilance and activity, however, of Morgan, secured them. Cornwallis continued his pursuit as far as the Dan river, which divides North Carolina from Virginia. Greene, whose inferior force obliged him to recede this far before the enemy, received such succors of militia on his entering Virginia that the chase was reversed. Cornwallis, in his turn, retreated precipitately. Greene overtook him on his way to Wilmington, and attacked him. Although the ground was lost on our side, the British army was so much weakened by the loss of five or six hundred of their best troops, that their retreat towards Wilmington suffered little interruption. Greene pursued as long as any chance of reaching his prey remained, and then, leaving Cornwallis on his left, took an oblique direction towards Camden, which, with all the other posts in South Carolina except Charleston and Ninety-Six, have, in consequence, fallen again into our possession. His army lay before the latter when we last heard from him. It contained seven or eight hundred men and large quantities of stores. It is nearly two hundred miles from Charleston, and, without some untoward accident, cannot fail of being taken. Greene has detachments all over South Carolina, some of them within a little distance of Charleston; and the resentments of the people against their late insolent masters ensure him all the aids they can give in re-establishing the American Government there. Great progress is also making in the redemption of Georgia.

As soon as Cornwallis had refreshed his troops at Wilmington, abandoning his Southern conquests to their fate, he pushed forward into Virginia. The parricide Arnold had a detachment at Portsmouth when he lay on the Dan; Philips had reinforced him so powerfully from New York, that the junction of the two armies at Petersburg could not be prevented. The whole force amounted to about six thousand men. The force under the Marquis De La Fayette, who commanded in Virginia, being greatly inferior, did not oppose them, but retreated into Orange and Culpeper in order to meet General Wayne, who was on his way from Pennsylvania to join him. Cornwallis advanced northward as far as Chesterfield, in the county of Caroline, having parties at the same time at Page's warehouse and other places in its vicinity. A party of horse, commanded by Tarleton, was sent with all the secrecy and celerity possible to surprise and take the General Assembly and Executive who had retreated from Richmond to Charlottesville. The vigilance of a young gentleman who discovered the design and rode express to Charlottesville prevented a complete surprise. As it was, several Delegates were caught, and the rest were within an hour of sharing the same fate. Among the captives was Colonel Lyon of Hanover. Mr. Kinlock, a member of Congress from South Carolina, was also caught at Mr. John Walker's, whose daughter he had married some time before. Governor Jefferson had a very narrow escape. The members of the Government rendezvoused at Stanton, where they soon made a House. Mr. Jefferson's year having expired, he declined a re-election, and General Nelson has taken his place. Tarleton's party retreated with as much celerity as it had advanced. On the junction of Wayne with the Marquis and the arrival of militia, the latter faced about and advanced rapidly on Cornwallis, who retreated to Richmond, and thence precipitately to Williamsburg, where he lay on the 27th ultimo. The Marquis pursued, and was at the same time within twenty miles of that place. One of his advanced parties had had a successful skirmish within six miles of Williamsburg. Bellini has, I understand, abided patiently in the college the dangers and inconveniences of such a situation. I do not hear that the consequences have condemned the experiment. Such is the present state of the war in the Southern Department. In the Northern, the operations have been for a considerable time in a manner suspended. At present, a vigorous siege of New York by General Washington's army, aided by five or six thousand French troops under Count De Rochambeau, is in contemplation, and will soon commence. As the English have the command of the water, the result of such an enterprise must be very uncertain. It is supposed, however, that it will certainly oblige the enemy to withdraw their force from the Southern States, which may be a more convenient mode of relieving them than by marching the troops from New York at this season of the year to the southward. On the whole, the probable conclusion of this campaign is, at this juncture, very flattering, the enemy being on the defensive in every quarter. . . .

The great advantage the enemy have over us lies in the superiority of their navy, which enables them continually to shift the war into defenceless places, and to weary out our troops by long marches. The squadron sent by our ally to our support did not arrive till a reinforcement on the part of the enemy had counteracted their views. They have been almost constantly blocked up at Rhode Island by the British fleet. The effects of a hurricane in the last spring on the latter gave a temporary advantage to the former, but circumstances delayed the improvement of it till the critical season was past. Mr. Destouches, who commanded the French fleet, nevertheless hazarded an expedition into Chesapeake bay. The object of it was to co-operate with the Marquis de la Fayette in an attack against Arnold, who lay at Portsmouth with about fifteen hundred British troops. Had he got into the bay, and taken a favorable station, the event would certainly have been adequate to our hopes. Unfortunately, the British fleet, which followed the French immediately from Rhode Island, reached the capes of Virginia first. On the arrival of the latter, a regular and fair combat took place. It lasted for several hours, and ended rather in favor of our allies. As the enemy, however, were nearest the capes, and one of the French ships had lost her rudder, and was otherwise much damaged, the commander thought it best to relinquish his object, and return to his former station. The damage sustained by the enemy, according to their own representation, exceeded that of the French ; and as their number of ships and weight of metal were both superior, it does great honor to the gallantry and good conduct of Mr. Destouches. Congress, and indeed the public at large, were so sensible of this, that their particular thanks were given him on the occasion.

James Madison, *Letters and Other Writings* (Philadelphia, 1865), I, 44–49 *passim*.

---

212. Affairs in the South (1780–1781)

BY GENERAL NATHANAEL GREENE

After the defeat of Gates at Camden in 1780, Greene, a Rhode Island man, was put in command. This letter, written to President Reed, illustrates the difficulties of regular campaigns in the south, and also brings out the frightful border warfare. — Bibliography of Greene : G. W. Greene, *Nathanael Greene.* — Bibliography of southern affairs as in No. 211 above.

Camp on the Pedee, January 9th, 1781. . . .

I INTENDED to have written you before, but I have been so employed since I left Philadelphia, that I have been obliged to deny myself the pleasure of writing to my friends, to attend to the more immediate duties of my department. On my journey I visited the

2 R

Maryland and Virginia Assemblies, and laid before them the state of this army, and urged the necessity of an immediate support. They both promised to do everything in their power, but such was their poverty, even in their Capitals, that they could not furnish forage for my horses. I have also written to the States of Delaware and North Carolina, neither of which have taken any measures yet for giving effectual aid to this army. I left General Gist in Maryland, and Baron Steuben in Virginia, to forward the recruits and supplies. Measures are taking in Virginia which promise us some aid, though very trifling to what they ought to give, and what our state requires. All the way through the country, as I passed, I found the people engaged in matters of interest and in pursuit of pleasure, almost regardless of their danger. Public credit totally lost, and every man excusing himself from giving the least aid to Government, from an apprehension that they would get no return for any advances. This afforded but a dull prospect, nor has it mended since my arrival.

I overtook the army at Charlotte, to which place General Gates had advanced. The appearance of the troops was wretched beyond description, and their distress, on account of provisions, was little less than their suffering for want of clothing and other necessaries. General Gates had lost the confidence of the officers, and the troops all their discipline, and so addicted to plundering, that they were a terror to the inhabitants. The General and I met upon very good terms, and parted so. The old gentleman was in great distress, having but just heard of the death of his son before my arrival.

The battle of Camden is spoken of very differently here to what it is to the Northward, and as for a regular retreat, there was none; every man got off the ground in the best manner he could. This is the account Colonel Williams gives, who was one of the last on the field. Indeed, the whole business was a short fight and then a perfect flight, and the greatest loss happened after the troops broke, and attempted to make their escape. From all I can learn, if General Gates had stopped at Charlotte, little more disgrace would have fallen to his share than is common to the unfortunate. Generals Gates and Smallwood were not upon good terms; the former suspected the latter of having an intention to supplant him. Some think General Gates's suspicions were groundless, and had no other foundation but the General's own imagination. Others are of opinion that they were well founded, and that my appointment was a great disappointment as well as mortification to Smallwood. How the matter was I know not. The General (Smallwood) is gone to the Northward, having declared, for reasons, that he could not think of submitting to the command of Baron Steuben, and that if justice was done him and the State, his commission would be dated at least two years earlier than his appointment. I expostulated with him upon the impossibility of the thing, let his private merit be ever so great, but it was all to no purpose. He was fixed in the principle, and determined upon the measure. He has many enemies in the Maryland line, but upon the whole I think him a sensible man and a good officer.

The wants of this army are so numerous and various, that the shortest way of telling you is to inform you that we have nothing, as General Du Portail can inform you from his own observation. The great departments of the army had nobody at the head of them, fit to provide in a country like this for a sergeant's party. I have got Colonel Carrington to accept of the Quartermaster-General's department, and am in hopes of getting a good man at the head of the Commissaries, without which I foresee we must starve. I am endeavouring to bring everything into order, and perfect our arrangements as much as possible, but it is all an up-hill business.

The loss of our army in Charleston, and the defeat of General Gates has been the cause of keeping such vast shoals of militia on foot, who, like the locusts of Egypt, have eaten up everything, and the expense has been so enormous, that it has ruined the currency of the State. It is my opinion there is no one thing upon the Continent that wants regulating so much, as the right which the States exercise of keeping what militia on foot they please at the Continental expense. I am persuaded North Carolina has militia enough to swallow up all the revenues of America, especially under their imperfect arrangements, where every man draws and wastes as much as he pleases. The country is so extensive and the powers of Government so weak, that everybody does as he pleases. The inhabitants are much divided in their political sentiments, and the Whigs and Tories pursue each other with little less than savage fury. The back-country people are bold and daring in their make, but the people upon the sea-shore are sickly and but indifferent militia. The ruin of the State is inevitable if there are such large bodies of militia kept on foot. No army can subsist in the country long if the ravages continue. Indeed, unless this army is better supported than I see any prospect of, the Country is lost beyond redemption, for it is impossible for the people to struggle much longer under their present difficulties. There appears a foolish pride in the representation of things from this quarter ; the strength and resources of the Country are far overrated, and those who are engaged in this business, to indulge their pride, will sacrifice their Country. The inhabitants are beginning to move off in great bodies, and unless a firmer barrier can be formed, this quarter will be all depopulated. We are living upon charity, and subsist by daily collections. Indian meal and beef is our common diet, and not a drop of spirits have we had with us since I came to the army. An army naked and subsisted in this manner, and not more than one-third equal to the enemy in numbers, will make but a poor fight, especially as one has been accustomed to victory and the other to flight. It is difficult to give spirits to troops that have nothing to animate them.

I have been obliged to take an entire new position with the army. General Morgan is upon Broad River with a little flying army, and Colonel Washington since his arrival there has defeated a party of Tories, the particulars of which I beg leave to refer you to the President of Congress for. This Camp I mean as a Camp of repose, for the purpose of repairing our wagons, recruiting our horses, and disciplining the troops.

Colonel Lee has just arrived, and his corps is in good order, and I am told Colonel Greene from Virginia is at hand.

General Lesly with his detachment has arrived at Camden, and we have reports that another is coming.

William B. Reed, *Life and Correspondence of Joseph Reed* (Philadelphia, 1847), II, 344–346.

———◆———

213. Exploits of De Grasse in the West Indies (1781)

ANONYMOUS

(ANONYMOUS TRANSLATION)

This account, written by an officer who made the cruise described, relates to the one period in the war between France and England when the English lost control of the West Indian waters. The capture of Cornwallis (No. 214) was thus made possible. — Bibliography: Winsor, *Narrative and Critical History*, VI, 499–502; Channing and Hart, *Guide*, § 140.

THE thirteen United States of North America had declared themselves sovereign and independent in 1776. So far were they from being so in 1781, that those in the south were on the point of being

compelled to acknowledge their former master, which would have rendered the liberty of the others very uncertain.   Nevertheless, England,
at the close of 1782, declared them all free.

The relation of these successes forms part of the campaign of the
Count de Grasse.   In this view it is offered entire to the public, as the
check which the arms of France sustained on the 12th of April, 1782,
did not embolden England to continue her non-recognition of the
sovereignty of the United States ; the advantages obtained in 1781,
must, therefore, have established it beyond peradventure.

The events of 1780, and of the first months of 1781, had not even
prepared those of the rest of that year and of the early months of the
next.   In 1780, the fleet of the two powers had fought no less than
three times, without obtaining any decisive advantage.   The empire of
the West India waters remained unsettled, and no enterprise was undertaken on either side before wintering. . . .

' Such was the situation of the belligerent parties in America, when
the Count de Grasse was appointed to command the king's naval forces
in that part of the world. . . . the Count de Grasse, who had reached
Paris, February 1st, left the 18th, and arrived at Brest on the 26th.

There a considerable squadron was preparing, which was to escort a
convoy of one hundred and fifty sail, with a reinforcement of troops . . .
and the fleet and convoy set sail, March 22d, with a favorable wind, in
spite of the equinox.

We doubled the cape on the 27th ; and then, to keep the convoy
always together, and to prevent the sailing of the slow craft from retard-
ing that of the rest, the admiral had them towed by his ships, taking
one himself.

Thanks to this precaution, in thirty-six days the fleet and the whole
convoy (an unheard of thing till then for so many vessels), came at
day-break, on the 28th of April, in sight of the land of Martinique.

. . . at 11, an English frigate was perceived making signals, and at
2 o'clock twenty-two hostile sails were signalled towards *Diamond Rock*.
. . .   17 vessels of the line and five frigates had, for the last fifty days,
blockaded the roadstead of Fort Royal and the four French vessels
anchored there ; the latter had orders, during the course of the night,
to hoist sail the next morning and attack the head or rear of the English
squadron, as soon as they saw the French fleet.

On the 29th, in the morning, the fleet, covering the convoy, steered
for Fort Royal ; at 8 o'clock the English squadron was signalled, and

at noon the French fleet was on the beam of the English flagship. The English began a very distant fire, to which the French paid no attention till the English bullets went far beyond them. The convoy had lain to the windward of Diamond Rock, and when the action began it continued its route to its destination, without the loss of a single vessel from its leaving Brest.

The English fleet, while fighting, crowded sail; the admiral sent orders by the frigates for each French vessel to engage the English vessel opposite, and for the surplus with the four vessels from the road-stead of Fort Royal, as a light squadron to turn the English line and get it between two fires. This order was not executed. Of the English fleet only three vessels of the rear guard were ever engaged, because the French van which served as rear guard, instead of bearing down, according to all the signals, kept the wind constantly with light sails, while, on the contrary, the rear guard became van, bore down on the enemy and engaged them vigorously. Thus the English fleet could always bear away in order; and at six o'clock there were only thirteen out of the twenty-four French vessels in pursuit of the seventeen English; these covered the retreat of the *Russell*, 74, which then ran before the wind to St. Eustatius, where it arrived with seven feet of water in the hold, and much cut up; the *Centaur*, the *Torbay*, the *Intrépide*, were not less so. . . .

The naval and military commanders lost no time in their operations; it seems that they wished to undertake nothing the execution of which was not certain, before the 1st of July, since they decided to attack the isle of Tobago, the only one that interrupted the communication of the French Windward Isles with the Spanish mainland. This communication, established from isle to isle, secured fresh provisions, not abundant on the islands, and deprived the hostile cruisers of all refuge in those ports. . . .

The enemy were still at St. Christopher's; but on the 22d news came that they had sailed and were manœuvring to windward. The French fleet again set sail on the 25th, to go and cover the attack on Tobago. The French had landed there on the 24th, and the artillery of the vessels had soon silenced the batteries which defended the anchorage; the fleet came in sight of the island on the 30th; it perceived six hostile vessels with a convoy, destined, doubtless, to carry in supplies; but they renounced their project by a prompt flight. On the 31st the fleet landed the Marquis de Bouillé, with a corps of troops, at Courland Bay, and on the 1st of June, the Marquis du Chilleau, with other troops, at Man of War's Bay. . . .

On arriving at the cape, the admiral found the frigate *Concorde*, from North America. The news spread that the dispatches of the naval and military commanders, and those of the envoy of France, at Philadelphia, joined in assuring him that, without a prompt relief of vessels, men, money and ammunition, Virginia would fall again under the English yoke ; and that the French army had pay only to the 20th of August. These fears and these wants were set forth without fixed projects to remedy them ; they left the admiral a choice only between an attack on New York by sea and by land, or to transfer the theatre of war to Virginia by a sudden occupation of Chesapeake Bay with sufficient naval forces. For either plan, nothing less was asked than a reinforcement of 6000 men, 1,200,000 livres in specie, munitions in proportion, and all in the course of August ; without all this relief, the most disastrous events were menaced. The admiral's reply was expected by the same frigate. . . .

On the 30th of August Cape Henry was discovered N. W. $\frac{1}{4}$ W. Chesapeake Bay was reconnoitred, and the fleet anchored behind Cape Henry on the 31st. Thus, on the day named, Lord Cornwallis could no longer hope to return to New York, or derive any aid from there.

Journal of an Officer in the Naval Army in America, in 1781 and 1782 (Amsterdam, 1783) ; reprinted in *The Operations of the French Fleet under the Count De Grasse in 1781-2* (Bradford Club Series, No. 3, New York, 1864), 137–153 *passim.*

---

214. The Capitulation of Yorktown (1781)

BY LIEUTENANT-GENERAL CHARLES, MARQUIS CORNWALLIS

Out of the many journals and letters by participants in the Virginia campaign, this letter, addressed to Sir Henry Clinton, has been chosen, as the official statement of the defeated general. — Bibliography of Cornwallis : Winsor, *Narrative and Critical History*, VI, 474. — Bibliography of the campaign : Winsor, *Narrative and Critical History*, VI, 547–551 ; Channing and Hart, *Guide*, § 140.

Yorktown, Virginia, Oct. 20, 1781. . . .

I HAVE the mortification to inform your Excellency that I have been forced to give up the posts of York and Gloucester, and to surrender the troops under my command, by capitulation, on the 19th instant, as prisoners of war to the combined forces of America and France.

I never saw this post in a very favourable light, but when I found I was to be attacked in it in so unprepared a state, by so powerful an army and artillery, nothing but the hopes of relief would have induced me to attempt its defence, for I would either have endeavoured to escape to New York by rapid marches from the Gloucester side, immediately on the arrival of General Washington's troops at Williamsburg, or I would, notwithstanding the disparity of numbers, have attacked them in the open field, where it might have been just possible that fortune would have favoured the gallantry of the handful of troops under my command, but being assured by your Excellency's letters that every possible means would be tried by the navy and army to relieve us, I could not think myself at liberty to venture upon either of those desperate attempts ; therefore, after remaining for two days in a strong position in front of this place in hopes of being attacked, upon observing that the enemy were taking measures which could not fail of turning my left flank in a short time, and receiving on the second evening your letter of the 24th of September, informing me that the relief would sail about the 5th of October, I withdrew within the works on the night of the 29th of September, hoping by the labour and firmness of the soldiers to protract the defence until you could arrive. Everything was to be expected from the spirit of the troops, but every disadvantage attended their labour, as the works were to be continued under the enemy's fire, and our stock of intrenching tools, which did not much exceed 400 when we began to work in the latter end of August, was now much diminished.

The enemy broke ground on the night of the 30th, and constructed on that night, and the two following days and nights, two redoubts, which, with some works that had belonged to our outward position, occupied a gorge between two creeks or ravines, which come from the river on each side of the town. On the night of the 6th of October they made their first parallel, extending from its right on the river, to a deep ravine on the left, nearly opposite to the centre of this place, and embracing our whole left at a distance of 600 yards. Having perfected this parallel, their batteries opened on the evening of the 9th against our left, and other batteries fired at the same time against a redoubt advanced over the creek upon our right, and defended by about 120 men of the 23rd Regiment and marines, who maintained that post with uncommon gallantry. The fire continued incessant from heavy cannon, and from mortars and howitzers throwing shells from 8 to 16 inches, until all our guns on the left were silenced, our work much damaged, and our loss of men considerable. On the night of the 11th they began their second parallel, about 300 yards nearer to us. The troops being much weakened by sickness, as well as by the fire of the besiegers, and observing that tne enemy had not only secured their flanks, but proceeded in every respect with the utmost regularity and caution, I could not venture so large sorties as to hope from them any considerable effect, but otherwise, I did everything in my power to interrupt this work by opening new embrasures for guns and keeping up a constant fire from all the howitzers and small mortars that we could man. On the evening of the 14th they assaulted and carried two redoubts that had been advanced about 300 yards for the purpose of delaying their approaches, and covering our left flank, and during the night included them in their second parallel, on which they continued to work with the utmost exertion. Being perfectly sensible that our works could not stand many hours after the opening of the batteries of that parallel, we not only continued a constant fire with all our mortars and every gun that could be brought to bear upon it, but a little before daybreak on the morning of the 16th, I ordered a sortie of about 350 men, under the direction of Lieut.-Colonel Abercrombie, to attack two batteries which appeared to be in the greatest forwardness, and to spike the guns. A detachment of Guards with the 80th company of Grenadiers, under the command of Lieut.-Colonel Lake, attacked the one, and one of light infantry, under the command of Major Armstrong, attacked the other, and both succeeded in forcing the redoubts that covered them, spiking 11 guns, and killing or wounding about 100 of the French troops, who had the guard of that part of the trenches, and with little loss on our side. This action, though extremely honourable to the officers and soldiers who executed it, proved of little public advantage, for the cannon having been spiked in a hurry, were soon rendered fit for service again, and before dark the whole parallel and batteries appeared to be nearly complete. At this time we knew that there was no part of the whole front attacked on which we could show a single gun, and our shells were nearly expended. I, therefore, had only to choose between preparing to surrender next day, or endeavouring to get off with the greatest part of the troops, and I determined to attempt the latter. . . . In this situation, with my little force divided, the enemy's batteries opened at daybreak. The passage between this place and **Gloucester** was much exposed, but the boats **having now returned, they** were ordered to bring back the troops that had passed during the night, and they joined us in the forenoon without much loss. Our works, in the mean time, were going to ruin, and not having been able to strengthen them by an abattis, nor in any other manner but by a slight fraizing, which the enemy's artillery were demolishing wherever they fired, my opinion entirely coincided with that of the engineer and principal officers of the army, that they were in many places assailable in the forenoon, and that by the continuance of the same fire for a few hours longer, they would be in such a state as to render it desperate, with our numbers, to attempt to maintain them. We at that time could not fire a single gun; only one 8-inch and little more than 100 Cohorn shells remained. A diversion by the French ships of war that lay at the mouth of York River was to be expected. Our numbers had been diminished by the enemy's fire, but particularly by sickness, and the strength and spirits of those in the works were much exhausted, by the fatigue of constant watching and unremitting duty. Under all these circumstances, I thought it would have been wanton and inhuman to the last degree to sacrifice the lives of this small body of gallant soldiers, who had ever behaved with so much fidelity and courage, by exposing them to an assault which, from the numbers and precautions of the enemy, could not fail to succeed. I therefore proposed to capitulate; and I have the honour to enclose to your Excellency the copy of the correspondence between General Washington and me on that subject, and the terms of capitulation agreed upon. I sincerely lament that better could not be obtained, but I have neglected nothing in my power to alleviate the misfortune and distress of both officers and soldiers. The men are well clothed and provided with necessaries, and I trust will be regularly supplied by the means of the officers that are permitted to remain with them. The treatment, in general, that we have received from the enemy since our surrender has been perfectly good and proper, but the kindness and attention that has been shown to us by the French officers in particular — their delicate sensibility of our situation — their generous and pressing offer of money, both public and private, to any amount — has really gone beyond what I can possibly describe, and will, I hope, make an impression on the breast of every British officer, whenever the fortune of war should put any of them into our power.

Charles, First Marquis Cornwallis, *Correspondence* (edited by Charles Ross, London, 1859), I, Appendix, 510–512 *passim*.

CHAPTER XXXV — PEACE

215. "The Sudden Change of Sentiments" (1781–1782)

BY KING GEORGE THIRD

Throughout the war there was a vigorous opposition in Parliament which protested against the justice and expediency of the contest; and after France and Spain both declared war on England, in 1778 and 1779, this opposition strengthened. The defeat of Cornwallis was practically the end of hostilities; and the wrath of the king is shown in this correspondence. — For George III, see No. 130 above. — Bibliography of the treaties of 1782 and 1783: Winsor, *Narrative and Critical History*, VII, 165–174; Wharton, *Diplomatic Correspondence*, I, ch. xxi, V, 228–276; Channing and Hart, *Guide*, § 141.

Windsor, June 13th, 1781.
25 min. pt. 7 a.m.

IT is difficult to express which appears more strongly, the manly fortitude of the great majority last night in rejecting the hacknied question of a Committee for considering the American war, or the impudence of the minority in again bringing it forward ; for whoever the most ardently wishes for peace must feel that every repetition of this question in Parliament only makes the rebels and the Bourbon family more desirous of continuing the war, from the hopes of tiring out this country. We have it not at this hour in our power to make peace ; it is by steadiness and exertions that we are to get into a situation to effect it ; and with the assistance of Divine Providence I am confident we shall soon find our enemies forced to look for that blessing. Among our many misfortunes I feel one satisfaction — that we have but one line to follow ; therefore, at least, diffidence and perplexity cannot attend us ; and we have the greatest objects to make us zealous in our pursuit, for we are contending for our whole consequence, whether we are to rank among the great Powers of Europe, or be reduced to one of the least considerable. He that is not stimulated by this consideration does not deserve to be a member of this community. . . .

[Dec. 15, 1781.] THE account of the very great majority on the first motion on the Army Estimates last night gives me much pleasure, and shews the country gentlemen begin to see that, though internal continental opperations in North America are not advisable, the prosecution of the war can alone preserve us from a most ignominious peace, which, when once concluded, would certainly occasion much greater internal uneasiness than any difficulties at present to be contended with. . . .

[Feb. 26, 1782.] . . . Undoubtedly the House of Commons seem to be wild at present, and to be running on to ruin, that no man can answer for the event of any question. I certainly till drove to the wall [will] do what I can to save the empire, and, if I do not succeed, I will at least have the self-approbation of having done my duty, and of not letting myself be a tool in the destruction of the honour of the country. . . .

[March 17, 1782.] I AM sorry to find by Ld. North's note that the majority this morning did not exceed nine; it looks as if the House of Commons is going lengths that could not have been expected. I am resolved not to throw myself into the hands of Opposition at all events, and shall certainly, if things go as they seem to lead, know what my conscience as well as honour dictates as the only way left for me. . . .

[March 19, 1782.] . . . After having yesterday in the most solemn manner assured you that my sentiments of honour will not permit me to send for any of the leaders of Opposition and personally treat with them, I could not but be hurt at your letter of last night. Every man must be the sole judge of his feelings; therefore whatever you or any man can say on that subject has no avail with me. . . .

[March 27, 1782.] . . . At last the fatal day has come which the misfortunes of the times and the sudden change of sentiments of the House of Commons have drove me to of changing the Ministry, and a more general removal of other persons than I believe ever was known before. I have to the last fought for individuals, but the number I have saved, except my Bedchamber, is incredibly few. You would hardly believe that even the Duke of Montagu was strongly run at, but I declared that I would sooner let confusion follow than part with the governor of my sons and so unexceptionable a man: at last I have succeeded so that he and Ld. Ashburnham remain. The effusion of my sorrows has made me say more than I had intended, but I ever did and ever shall look on you as a friend, as well as a faithful servant. . . .

W. Bodham Donne, editor, *The Correspondence of King George the Third with Lord North* (London, 1867), II, 376-420 *passim*.

216. A Protest against the Breach of the Instructions of Congress (1782)

BY CHARLES GRAVIER, COUNT DE VERGENNES

(ANONYMOUS TRANSLATION)

Vergennes was French Minister of Foreign Affairs; and Congress had instructed the envoys to make no terms to which he did not agree. This piece is his protest at the breach of these instructions by the envoys, who were nevertheless justified by Congress. — Bibliography : Wharton, *Diplomatic Correspondence*, I, 349–364.

VERSAILLES, 19 December, 1782. . . .

YOU will surely be gratified, as well as myself, with the very extensive advantages which our allies, the Americans, are to receive from the peace ; but you certainly will not be less surprised than I have been at the conduct of the commissioners. According to the instructions of Congress, they ought to have done nothing without our participation. I have informed you that the king did not seek to influence the negotiation any further than his offices might be necessary to his friends. The American commissioners will not say that I have interfered, and much less that I have wearied them with my curiosity. They have cautiously kept themselves at a distance from me. Mr. Adams, one of them, coming from Holland, where he had been received and served by our ambassador, had been in Paris nearly three weeks, without imagining that he owed me any mark of attention, and probably I should not have seen him till this time if I had not caused him to be reminded of it. Whenever I have had occasion to see any one of them, and inquire of them briefly respecting the progress of the negotiation, they have constantly clothed their speech in generalities, giving me to understand that it did not go forward, and that they had no confidence in the sincerity of the British ministry.

Judge of my surprise when, on the 30th of November, Dr. Franklin informed me that the articles were signed. The reservation retained on our account does not save the infraction of the promise, which we have mutually made, not to sign except conjointly. I owe Dr. Franklin the justice to state, however, that on the next day he sent me a copy of the articles. He will hardly complain that I received them without demonstrations of sensibility. It was not till some days after that, when this minister had come to see me, I allowed myself to make him perceive that his proceeding in this abrupt signature of the articles had little in it which could be agreeable to the king. He appeared sensible of it, and excused, in the best manner he could, himself and his colleagues. Our conversation was amicable.

Dr. Franklin spoke to me of his desire to send these articles to the Congress, and said that for this purpose he and his colleagues had agreed to an exchange of passports with the English minister for the safety of the vessels which should be sent. I observed to him that this form appeared to me dangerous; that, the articles being only provisional and dependent on the fate of our negotiation, which was then very uncertain, I feared this appearance of an intelligence with England, in connection with the signature of the articles, might make the people of America think a peace was consummated, and embarrass Congress, of whose fidelity I had no suspicion. I added many other reasons, the force of which Dr. Franklin, and Mr. Laurens who accompanied him, seemed to acknowledge. They spared nothing to convince me of the confidence which we ought to have in the fidelity of the United States, and they left me with the assurance that they should conform to my wishes.

You may imagine my astonishment, therefore, when, on the evening of the 15th, I received from Dr. Franklin the letter, a copy of which is herewith enclosed. The tone of this letter seemed to me so singular, that I thought it my duty to write the answer, which I likewise send to you. I am ignorant of the effect which this answer may have produced. I have not since heard from the American commissioners. The courier has not come for my despatches, and I know not whether he has in reality been sent off. It would be singular, after the intimation which I have given them, if they should not have the curiosity to acquaint themselves with the state of our negotiation, that they may communicate the intelligence to Congress. This negotiation is not yet so far advanced in regard to ourselves as that of the United States; not that the king, if he had shown as little delicacy in his proceedings as the American commissioners, might not have signed articles with England long before them. There is no essential difficulty at present between France and England; but the king has been resolved that all his allies should be satisfied, being determined to continue the war, whatever advantage may be offered to him, if England is disposed to wrong any one of them.

We have now only to attend to the interests of Spain and Holland. I have reason to hope that the former will be soon arranged. The fundamental points are established, and little remains but to settle the forms. I think the United States will do well to make an arrangement with Spain. They will be neighbors. As to Holland, I fear her affairs will cause embarrassments and delays. The disposition of the British ministry towards that republic appears to be any thing but favorable.

Such is the present state of things. I trust it will soon be better; but, whatever may be the result, I think it proper that the most influential members of Congress should be informed of the very irregular conduct of their commissioners in regard to us. You may speak of it not in the tone of complaint. I accuse no person ; I blame no one, not even Dr. Franklin. He has yielded too easy to the bias of his colleagues, who do not pretend to recognize the rules of courtesy in regard to us. All their attentions have been taken up by the English whom they have met in Paris. If we may judge of the future from what has passed here under our eyes, we shall be but poorly paid for all that we have done for the United States, and for securing to them a national existence.

I will add nothing in respect to the demand for money, which has been made upon us. You may well judge if conduct like this encourages us to make demonstrations of our liberality. . . .

Benjamin Franklin, *Complete Works* (edited by John Bigelow, New York, etc., 1888), VIII, 231–234 *passim*.

---

217. Explanation of the Peace of 1782 (1782)

BY ADAMS, FRANKLIN, JAY, AND LAURENS

This is the official statement to Livingston, then Superintendent of Foreign Affairs, of the conditions of the preliminary treaty. The treaty described in this piece was made definitive September 3, 1783, and thus ended the war. — Bibliography as in No. 215 above.

Paris, 14 December, 1782.

. . . WE have the honor to congratulate congress on the signature of the preliminaries of a peace between the Crown of Great Britain and the United States of America, to be inserted in a definitive treaty so soon as the terms between the Crowns of France and Great Britain shall be agreed on. A copy of the articles is here inclosed, and we cannot but flatter ourselves that they will appear to congress, as they do to all of us, to be consistent with the honor and interest of the United States, and we are persuaded congress would be more fully of that opinion, if they were apprised of all the circumstances and reasons which have influenced the negotiation. Although it is impossible for us to go into that detail, we think it necessary, nevertheless, to make a few remarks on such of the articles as appear most to require elucidation.

Remarks on Article 2d, relative to Boundaries.

The Court of Great Britain insisted on retaining all the territories comprehended within the Province of Quebec, by the act of parliament respecting it. They contended that Nova Scotia should extend to the River Kennebec; and they claimed not only all the lands in the western country and on the Mississippi, which were not expressly included in our charters and governments, but also such lands within them as remained ungranted by the King of Great Britain. It would be endless to enumerate all the discussions and arguments on the subject.

We knew this Court and Spain to be against our claims to the western country, and having no reason to think that lines more favorable could ever have been obtained, we finally agreed to those described in this article; indeed, they appear to leave us little to complain of, and not much to desire. Congress will observe, that although our northern line is in a certain part below the latitude of forty-five, yet in others it extends above it, divides the Lake Superior, and gives us access to its western and southern waters, from which a line in that latitude would have excluded us.

Remarks on Article 4th, respecting Creditors.

We had been informed that some of the States had confiscated British debts; but although each State has a right to bind its own citizens, yet, in our opinion, it appertains solely to congress, in whom exclusively are vested the rights of making war and peace, to pass acts against the subjects of a power with which the confederacy may be at war. It therefore only remained for us to consider, whether this article is founded in justice and good policy.

In our opinion, no acts of government could dissolve the obligations of good faith resulting from lawful contracts between individuals of the two countries, prior to the war. We knew that some of the British creditors were making common cause with the refugees and other adversaries of our independence; besides, sacrificing private justice to reasons of state and political convenience, is always an odious measure; and the purity of our reputation in this respect, in all foreign commercial countries, is of infinitely more importance to us than all the sums in question. It may also be remarked, that American and British creditors are placed on an equal footing.

Remarks on Articles 5th and 6th, respecting Refugees.

These articles were among the first discussed and the last agreed to.

And had not the conclusion of this business at the time of its date been particularly important to the British administration, the respect, which both in London and Versailles, is supposed to be due to the honor, dignity, and interest of royalty, would probably have forever prevented our bringing this article so near to the views of congress and the sovereign rights of the States as it now stands.   When it is considered that it was utterly impossible to render this article perfectly consistent, both with American and British ideas of honor, we presume that the middle line adopted by this article, is as little unfavorable to the former as any that could in reason be expected.

As to the separate article, we beg leave to observe, that it was our policy to render the navigation of the River Mississippi so important to Britain as that their views might correspond with ours on that subject. Their possessing the country on the river north of the line from the Lake of the Woods affords a foundation for their claiming such navigation.   And as the importance of West Florida to Britain was for the same reason rather to be strengthened than otherwise, we thought it advisable to allow them the extent contained in the separate article, especially as before the war it had been annexed by Britain to West Florida, and would operate as an additional inducement to their joining with us in agreeing that the navigation of the river should forever remain open to both.   The map used in the course of our negotiations was Mitchell's.

As we had reason to imagine that the articles respecting the boundaries, the refugees, and fisheries, did not correspond with the policy of this Court, we did not communicate the preliminaries to the minister until after they were signed ; (and not even then the *separate article*). We hope that these considerations will excuse our having so far deviated from the spirit of our instructions.   The Count de Vergennes, on perusing the articles appeared surprised, (but not displeased), at their being so favorable to us.

We beg leave to add our advice, that copies be sent us of the accounts directed to be taken by the different States, of the unnecessary devastations and sufferings sustained by them from the enemy in the course of the war.   Should they arrive before the signature of the definitive treaty, they might possibly answer very good purposes.

John Adams, *Works* (edited by Charles Francis Adams, Boston, 1853), VIII, 18–20.

2 s

218. Foundation of the Society of the Cincinnati (1783)

BY GENERAL WILLIAM HEATH (1798)

Heath was a Massachusetts officer, brave and distinguished. His memoirs were put into form later in life. — Bibliography of Heath: Winsor, *Narrative and Critical History*, VI, 127–128. — Bibliography of the Cincinnati: Winsor, *Narrative and Critical History*, VI, 746.

A LITTLE before this time [June, 1783], the officers of the army beginning to realize that the dissolution of the army was drawing nigh, and wishing to perpetuate that friendship which numerous hardships, sufferings, and common dangers had inspired in their breasts, — resolved to form themselves into a Society, by the name of the *Cincinnati*. Several meetings were had for the purpose, and an Institution was digested and completed ; and although our General presided at one of the meetings, and cheerfully, at the request of his brother officers, transmitted copies of the Institution, covered by a letter, to the officer commanding the southern army, and to the senior officers of the respective State lines, from Pennsylvania to Georgia — yet he had serious objections to the Institution, as it stood, and refused for some time to sign it. He wished, as much as any one in the army, to perpetuate the happy friendship cemented in the breasts of the officers by an eight years common danger and sufferings ; but he thought this would be best done, by simply forming a Society, to meet annually in their respective States, for the purpose of a social hour, and to brighten the chain of friendship, with a fund for the relief of the unfortunate of their brethren ; but he was opposed to any idea of any thing that had any resemblance of an order, or any insignia or badge of distinction, *asserting* that it would only serve to mark them in an unfavourable light with their fellow-citizens : but the prevailing opinion of the officers was otherwise. Our General was finally induced to sign the Institution, from the following consideration — (but not until all the officers were appointed, and he nearly ready to leave the army) conversing with an officer of rank, who was of the same opinion with him, they parted in the resolution not to sign the Institution ; but the next morning, the officer called upon him, and observed, that one consideration, not before mentioned, had occurred to him, viz. that it might happen in the days of their posterity, in case they did not sign, that the descendant of one who was a member might happen to fall in company with the descendant of one who was not ;

that the latter, on observing the badge, might inquire what it was, and what its intention? upon its being answered, that it was the insignia of a Society, of which his ancestor, who served in the American army, during the revolution, was a member — the other might reply, my ancestor too served during that war, but I never heard any thing of such a badge in our family; to which it might probably be answered, it is likely your ancestor was guilty of some misconduct, which deprived him of it. Upon this, our General broke out — " I see it, I see it, and spurn the idea;" which led him to sign the general Institution: and he subscribed to the State fund, 166 dollars, being one month's pay, as was stipulated in the Institution. He however never met with the Society, although no one has cherished a warmer affection for every member of the army. After the revolution in France, finding that the insignias of distinctions were doing away, it led him *anew* to review the distinction which the *badge* of the Society to which he belonged, if not in fact, yet in appearance seemed to exhibit, and brought to mind all his former objections, which induced him to write to the Secretary-General to erase his name from the Institution; but that his subscription to the fund should remain, so long as it was applied to the purpose for which it was given — the relief of the unfortunate.

Major-General [William] Heath, *Memoirs. . . . Written by himself* (Boston, 1798), 380–382.

219. The Closing Scene (1783)

BY DOCTOR WILLIAM GORDON

Gordon was an Englishman, from 1772 till after the Revolution a minister in Roxbury, Massachusetts. He made careful researches while the Revolution was going on, but afterwards pruned his manuscript to suit the British public. — Bibliography: Tyler, *Literary History of the Revolution*, II, 423–428; Winsor, *Narrative and Critical History*, VI, 518.

GENERAL Washington, after delivering in his accounts, hastened to Annapolis, where he arrived on the evening of the 19th of December. The next day he informed congress of his arrival in that city, with the intention of asking leave to resign the commission he had the honor of holding in their service, and desired to know their pleasure in what manner it would be most proper to offer his resignation — whether in writing or at an audience. , They resolved that it should be at a public audience, the following Tuesday at twelve o'clock. The general had been so reserved with regard to the time of his intended resignation, that congress had not the least apprehension of its being either so soon or so sudden.

When the day was arrived, and the hour approached for fixing the patriotic character of the AMERICAN CHIEF, the gallery was filled with a beautiful group of elegant ladies, and some graced the floor of congress. On this were likewise the governor, council and legislature of Maryland, several general officers, the consul general of France, and the respectable citizens of Annapolis. Congress were seated and covered, as representatives of the sovereignty of the Union, the spectators were uncovered and standing. The general was introduced to a chair by the secretary, who, after a decent interval, ordered silence. A short pause ensued, when the honorable Thomas Mifflin, the president, informed the general, that "the United States in congress assembled were prepared to receive his communications:" on which he rose with great dignity, and delivered this address —— "Mr. President, The great events on which my resignation depended having at length taken place, I have now the honor of offering my sincere congratulations to Congress, and of presenting myself before them, to surrender into their hands the trust committed to me, and to claim the indulgence of retiring from the service of my country.

"Happy in the confirmation of our independence and sovereignty, and pleased with the opportunity afforded the United States, of becoming a respectable nation, I resign with satisfaction the appointment I accepted with diffidence — a diffidence in my abilities to accomplish so arduous a task; which however was superseded by a confidence in the rectitude of our cause, the support of the supreme power of the union, and the patronage of Heaven.

"The successful termination of the war has verified the most sanguine expectations; and my gratitude for the interposition of Providence, and the assistance I have received from my countrymen, increases with every review of the momentous contest.

"While I repeat my obligations to the army in general, I should do injustice to my own feelings not to acknowledge, in this place, the peculiar services and distinguished merits of the gentlemen who have been attached to my person during the war. It was impossible the choice of confidential officers to compose my family should have been more fortunate. Permit me, sir, to recommend in particular, those who have continued in the service to the present moment, as worthy of the favorable notice and patronage of Congress.

" I consider it as an indispensable duty to close this last act of my official life by commending the interests of our dearest country to the protection of Almighty God, and those who have the superintendence of them to his holy keeping.

" Having now finished the work assigned me, I retire from the great theatre of action, and bidding an affectionate farewel to this august body, under whose orders I have so long acted, I here offer my commission, and take my leave of all the employments of public life."

The general was so powerfully impressed, with the great and interesting scenes that crowded in upon his imagination while speaking, that he would have been scarce able to have uttered more than the closing period. He advanced and delivered to the president his commission, with a copy of his address. Having resumed his place, he received in a standing posture the . . . answer of congress ; which the president delivered with elegance ; but not without such a sensibility as changed, and spread a degree of paleness over, his countenance. . . .

William Gordon, *The History of the Rise, Progress, and Establishment, of the Independence of the United States of America* (London, 1788), IV, 386–389.

---

220. " The Advantages and Disadvantages of the Revolution " (1783)

BY DOCTOR DAVID RAMSAY

Ramsay was a South Carolinian, and at one time a prisoner of the British in Charleston. His book is the most judicial contemporary history, and his analysis of the results of the Revolution is that of a shrewd, well-informed, and patriotic man. — Bibliography : Winsor, *Narrative and Critical History*, VI, 507–508. — Bibliography of the effects of the Revolution : Winsor, *Narrative and Critical History*, VI, 743–746 ; Lecky, *England*, IV, 247–256.

THE American revolution, on the one hand, brought forth great vices ; but on the other hand, it called forth many virtues, and gave occasion for the display of abilities which, but for that event, would have been lost to the world. When the war began, the Americans were a mass of husbandmen, merchants, mechanics and fishermen ; but the necessities of the country gave a spring to the active powers of the inhabitants, and set them on thinking, speaking and acting, in a line far beyond that to which they had been accustomed. The difference between nations is not so much owing to nature, as to education and circumstances. While the Americans were guided by the leading strings of the mother country, they had no scope nor encouragement for exertion. All the departments of government were established and executed for them, but not by them. In the years 1775 and 1776 the country, being suddenly thrown into a situation that needed the abilities of all its sons, these generally took their places, each according to the bent of his inclination. As they severally pursued their objects with ardor, a vast expansion of the human mind speedily followed. This displayed itself in a variety of ways. It was found that the talents for great stations did not differ in kind, but only in degree, from those which were necessary for the proper discharge of the ordinary business of civil society. . . .

. . . It seemed as if the war not only required, but created talents. Men whose minds were warmed with the love of liberty, and whose abilities were improved by daily exercise, and sharpened with a laudable ambition to serve their distressed country, spoke, wrote, and acted, with an energy far surpassing all expectations which could be reasonably founded on their previous acquirements.

The Americans knew but little of one another, previous to the revolution. Trade and business had brought the inhabitants of their seaports acquainted with each other, but the bulk of the people in the interior country were unacquainted with their fellow citizens. A continental army, and Congress composed of men from all the States, by freely mixing together, were assimilated into one mass. Individuals of both, mingling with the citizens, disseminated principles of union among them. Local prejudices abated. By frequent collision asperities were worn off, and a foundation was laid for the establishment of a nation, out of discordant materials. Intermarriages between men and women of different States were much more common than before the war, and became an additional cement to the union. Unreasonable jealouses had existed between the inhabitants of the eastern and of the southern States; but on becoming better acquainted with each other, these in a great measure subsided. A wiser policy prevailed. Men of liberal minds led the way in discouraging local distinctions, and the great body of the people, as soon as reason got the better of prejudice, found that their best interests would be most effectually promoted by such practices and sentiments as were favourable to union. Religious bigotry had broken in upon the peace of various sects, before the American war.

This was kept up by partial establishments, and by a dread that the church of England through the power of the mother country, would be made to triumph over all other denominations. These apprehensions were done away by the revolution. . . . The world will soon see the result of an experiment in politics, and and be able to determine whether the happiness of society is increased by religious establishments, or diminished by the want of them.

Though schools and colleges were generally shut up during the war, yet many of the arts and sciences were promoted by it. The Geography of the United States before the revolution was but little known ; but the marches of armies, and the operations of war, gave birth to many geographical enquiries and discoveries, which otherwise would not have been made. . . . The necessities of the States led to the study of Tactics, Fortification, Gunnery, and a variety of other arts connected with war, and diffused a knowledge of them among a peaceable people, who would otherwise have had no inducement to study them. . . .

The science of government, has been more generally diffused among the Americans by means of the revolution. The policy of Great Britain, in throwing them out of her protection, induced a necessity of establishing independent constitutions. This led to reading and reasoning on the subject. The many errors that were at first committed by unexperienced statesmen, have been a practical comment on the folly of unbalanced constitutions, and injudicious laws. . . .

When Great Britain first began her encroachments on the colonies, there were few natives of America who had distinguished themselves as speakers or writers, but the controversy between the two countries multiplied their number. . . .

In establishing American independence, the pen and the press had merit equal to that of the sword. As the war was the people's war, and was carried on without funds, the exertions of the army would have been insufficient to effect the revolution, unless the great body of the people had been prepared for it, and also kept in a constant disposition to oppose Great Britain. To rouse and unite the inhabitants, and to persuade them to patience for several years, under present sufferings, with the hope of obtaining remote advantages for their posterity, was a work of difficulty : This was effected in a great measure by the tongues and pens of the well informed citizens, and on it depended the success of military operations. . . .

. . . Such have been some of the beneficial effects, which have resulted from that expansion of the human mind, which has been produced by the revolution, but these have not been without alloy.

To overset an established government unhinges many of those principles, which bind individuals to each other. A long time, and much prudence, will be necessary to reproduce a spirit of union and that reverence for government, without which society is a rope of sand. The right of the people to resist their rulers, when invading their liberties, forms the corner stone of the American republics. This principle, though just in itself, is not favourable to the tranquillity of present establishments. The maxims and measures, which in the years 1774 and 1775 were successfully inculcated and adopted by American patriots, for oversetting the established government, will answer a similar purpose when recurrence is had to them by factious demagogues, for disturbing the freest governments that were ever devised.

War never fails to injure the morals of the people engaged in it. The American war, in particular, had an unhappy influence of this kind. Being begun without funds or regular establishments, it could not be carried on without violating private rights ; and in its progress, it involved a necessity for breaking solemn promises, and plighted public faith. The failure of national justice, which was in some degree unavoidable, increased the difficulties of performing private engagements, and weakened that sensibility to the obligations of public and private honor, which is a security for the punctual performance of contracts. . . .

It is now your turn to figure on the face of the earth, and in the annals of the world. You possess a country which in less than a century will probably contain fifty millions of inhabitants. You have, with a great expence of blood and treasure, rescued yourselves and your posterity from the domination of Europe. Perfect the good work you have begun, by forming such arrangements and institutions as bid fair for ensuring to the present and future generations the blessings for which you have successfully contended.

May the Almighty Ruler of the Universe, who has raised you to Independence, and given you a place among the nations of the earth, make the American Revolution an Era in the history of the world, remarkable for the progressive increase of human happiness ! —

David Ramsay, *The History of the American Revolution* (Philadelphia, 1789), II, 315–356 *passim.*

INDEX

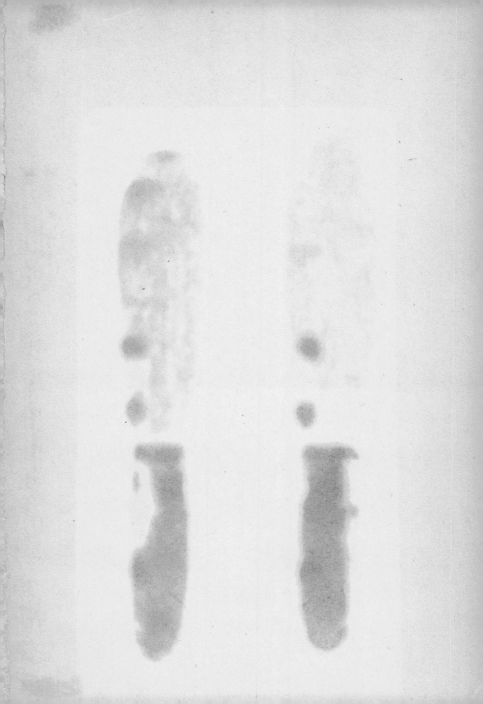

DATE DUE